SpringerWienNewYork

Tort and Insurance Law
Vol. 14

Edited by the
European Centre of Tort
and Insurance Law

together with the

Research Unit for European Tort Law
of the Austrian Academy of Sciences

Michael Faure
Ton Hartlief (eds.)

Financial Compensation for Victims of Catastrophes
A Comparative Legal Approach

With Contributions by

Tola Amodu, Suzanne A. Bratis
Michel Cannarsa, Filippo A. Chiaves
Isabelle C. Durant, Michael Faure
Ton Hartlief, Dagmar Hinghofer-Szalkay
Michael Huber, Bernhard A. Koch
Fabien Lafay, Ulrich Magnus
Alberto Monti, Olivier Moréteau
Siv Nyquist, Erik Persson
Robert L. Rabin, Roger Van den Bergh

SpringerWienNewYork

European Centre of Tort and Insurance Law
Landesgerichtsstraße 11
1080 Vienna, Austria
Tel.: +43 1 40127 1688
Fax: +43 1 40127 1685
E-Mail: ectil@ectil.org

Austrian Academy of Sciences
Research Unit for European Tort Law
Landesgerichtsstraße 11
1080 Vienna, Austria
Tel.: +43 1 40127 1687
Fax: +43 1 40127 1685
E-Mail: etl@oeaw.ac.at

Printed in Germany

Springer-Verlag Wien New York is part of
Springer Science + Business Media
springeronline.com

Typesetting: Composition & Design Services, Minsk, Belarus
Printing and binding: Strauss GmbH, 69509 Mörlenbach, Germany

Printed on acid-free and chlorine-free bleached paper
SPIN: 11382768

CIP data applied for

ISSN 1616-8623
ISBN-10 3-211-24481-6 SpringerWienNewYork
ISBN-13 978-3-211-24481-4 SpringerWienNewYork

Table of Contents

Introduction

Michael Faure and Ton Hartlief

Part I. Problem Definition

Many countries seem to be affected regularly by all kinds of catastrophes, whether these have a natural or a technological cause. Natural disasters are as old as man's existence; technological disasters have increased as the apparently unavoidable price of technological progress. Depending upon the specific characteristics of the country some are more faced with (various types of) natural disasters (earthquakes, volcanoes), whereas others have more problems with technological disasters (great fires, explosions). Nevertheless, some forms of natural disasters seem to threaten all countries. This seems especially the case for risks connected with the weather, like exceptional rainfall and flooding. 1

Today legislators increasingly have the tendency to get involved with legislation in the prevention of these catastrophes and moreover they make regulations aiming at compensating the victims of these catastrophes. It is particularly the latter aspect that will be addressed within the scope of this book. Victims nowadays apparently do not accept any longer the old saying "the loss lies where it falls" and expect to be compensated for their losses in case of a disaster. When no tortfeasor is at hand who can be held liable and when no insurance coverage is available victims will often turn to the government to claim some form of compensation. Given the large number of persons that can be victimized as a result of a catastrophe governments may have the tendency to respond to this request. This raises many interesting legal and economic questions. 2

Generally one can understand the interests of various governments in this issue: a catastrophe can lead to a large number of persons affected, a lot of attention in the media and hence to an interest by politicians, who see that many voters are affected. For a single victim on the other hand it may make little difference whether one is victimized as a result of a single victim event or as a result of a catastrophe, although the chances of special (financial) compensation by the government are larger in the latter case. 3

Although there were already many evolutions in various legal systems (more particularly concerning the compensation of the natural disasters such as flooding) the events in September 2001 have led to an increased interest in the role 4 of government in providing compensation after catastrophic accidents. With September 2001 we not only refer to the well-known September 11 events, but, in the European context, also to the explosion that took place 10 days later in Toulouse (France) in the factory Grande Paroisse AZF that killed 30 persons and injured 10,000.

5 In general there seem to be 3 different types of reactions chosen by European legislators as far as the financial compensation after catastrophes is concerned: a first possibility is that (in addition to liability law and social security which exists as basic structure in every European legal system) no specific regulatory measures have been taken. In those cases governments may provide additional compensation for victims in some cases on an *ad hoc* basis. That seems to be the case in e.g. Germany and Sweden. A second possibility is that a first party insurance solution is chosen. In this respect we do not refer to voluntary first party insurances that victims can of course take in all countries where these are available on the insurance market, but to regulatory interventions as a result of which coverage is mandatorily extended to include natural disasters. That is e.g. the case in France, will be the case in Belgium as a result of a recent legislative intervention and is discussed in both Germany and Italy. The third approach would be to have an outright compensation fund for victims of disasters that can provide for some amounts, although usually not full compensation (such as under tort law). Such a disaster fund exists *inter alia* in Belgium as a result of the Disaster Act 1976.

Part II. Goal of this Book

6 The goal of the research project which resulted in this book was, on the one hand, to identify how victims of catastrophes receive compensation in a large number of European countries and in the US. In addition the project also wished to compare the various compensation solutions from a critical perspective. Therefore attention will have to be paid to the various legal instruments that can be used to provide this compensation to victims. In that respect one can think on the one hand of private law solutions like tort law and (first party or liability) insurance, but on the other hand also at more public law oriented solutions like social security or compensation funds. Even if private law solutions (like insurance) are followed in many countries governments intervene in insurance markets, e.g. by making cover for the results of some catastrophes compulsory. Thus another goal of this project was to identify the mix of various (private and public) legal instruments that are used to provide this compensation and to identify how the coordination between the various instruments (often used simultaneously) is arranged.

7 Crucial questions underlying the optimal compensation of victims of catastrophes are on the one hand through what tools compensation to victims can be provided at the lowest possible (administrative) costs and without unnecessary side effects or negative distributional consequences. Indeed, a question related (or even preceding) the compensation issue is of course through what kind of

legal instruments catastrophes can be prevented. Although the legal instruments aiming at the prevention of catastrophes are clearly not the central focus of this book, the various contributions do of course address the prevention issue, more particularly with respect to the question whether a certain legal instrument chosen to provide financial compensation to victims may (positively or negatively) affect the prevention of catastrophes.

The ultimate goal of the book is therefore not only to provide an overview of 8
the legal rules concerning financial compensation for victims of catastrophes in various countries, but of course equally to at least give some indication of the comparative benefits and potential disadvantages of various solutions chosen. Although it may be a too ambitious aim to attempt to come up with a model for the optimal compensation for victims of catastrophes which could be applied in any legal system, we do hope that as a result of the comparison of various solutions some indications can be given of the potential benefits and disadvantages of various solutions in different countries.

Part III. Methodology

In order to be able to reach the goals set for this project (see II above) a com- 9
parative legal approach has been followed in line with the traditions of the comparative legal work executed by ECTIL and METRO. A questionnaire was drafted (it is included in annex to this book) in which the various relevant research questions were worked out in a detailed way. The questionnaire was sent to specialists in nine countries who drafted country reports. The questionnaire obviously not only contains questions concerning the legal rules with respect to financial compensation for catastrophes, but also concerning the legal practice. Thus the questionnaire explicitly addresses procedural issues, the financing of the compensation issue and empirical studies with respect to various catastrophes. The advantage of this method of working with a catastrophe is that detailed questions can be formulated and that moreover a standardised reply through the country reports can be expected. This method will thus facilitate the comparative analysis.

The countries were chosen because they all have a special relevance for the fi- 10
nancial compensation of catastrophes. More particularly they all already had interesting regimes representing one of the three possible responses (*ad hoc* solutions, compulsory insurance or funds). Thus Austria and Belgium were interesting candidates because both have experience with funds for the compensation of victims of catastrophes. France is today considered an example for many European countries (or is at least critically discussed at the occasion of any reform) since it introduced already in 1982 a mandatory additional cover for the damage caused by natural disasters. That model now seems to be followed in some other countries as well, like Belgium (moving away from the catastrophes fund) and (at least in reform proposals) Italy. At the other end of the spectrum the United Kingdom provides an interesting example of very limited government intervention (neither on an *ad hoc* basis, nor structural via

a fund), but an apparently well functioning insurance system for flooding. Germany and Sweden are interesting in the sense that they seem to rely solely on *ad hoc* solutions. Insurance for e.g. flooding seems today hardly used in Germany, but on the other hand the government generously compensated victims, e.g. after the large Elbe flood in 2002. The Netherlands is interesting since traditionally natural disasters were considered as uninsurable by the Dutch insurers, leading the government to adopt a specific act which allowed *ad hoc* compensation for victims of catastrophes. However, also today in the Netherlands this act is under critical review and insurance solutions are offered as well. Finally attention of course has to be paid to the US where the question concerning the optimal compensation of victims of catastrophes already was an issue after devastating hurricanes like Andrew, but was of course especially discussed not only in the literature, but also resulting in legislative action, after 9/11. Thus the various countries chosen for the comparative analysis seem to represent a nice mix of the seemingly quite different solutions in some European legal systems. The experts from different countries have thus been asked to report on the way the damage caused by catastrophes is dealt with in their particular country from the angle of tort law, social security, insurance or alternative compensation mechanisms (such as compensation funds), following a standardised questionnaire.

11 In addition to the country reports it seemed important to address competition law issues as well. Indeed, some insurance solutions, such as the French system of mandatory coverage, may collide with principles of European competition law. It is an issue that was explicitly raised by the Italian cartel authority at the occasion of the revision of the Italian legislation. Thus specific attention will have to be paid to competition law.

12 Finally financial compensation in case of catastrophes has also been addressed in a rich economic literature with respect to this issue. The general insights provided in this economic literature can be quite helpful in analysing the efficiencies of various solutions and proposals. However, instead of providing a separate chapter, summarising the economic literature, in the comparative chapter the law and economics literature will be used to critically review some of the solutions discussed in the various legal systems. Thus the economic approach can be used to critically discuss the different approaches presented in the country reports.

Part IV. Framework of the Project

13 Originally the Maastricht European Institute of Transnational Legal Research (METRO) was commissioned a research project by the Netherlands Ministry of Internal Affairs. In that first phase (the report was presented to the Ministry in January 2004) only reports from Belgium, France, Germany and Sweden were included. However, additional support was provided *inter alia* through the shifts in governance programme on "compensation for damage: the shift from civil law to public funding and vice versa" which allowed an enlarge-

ment of the project with country reports from Austria, Italy, the Netherlands, the United Kingdom and the United States. A draft of the papers was presented at a conference on 20–21 January 2005 in Maastricht. Afterwards rewritten versions of the papers were submitted.

The publication of this book is the result of a cooperation between METRO, the European Centre of Tort and Insurance Law in Vienna (ECTIL) and the Research Unit for European Tort Law of the Austrian Academy of Sciences (ETL). 14

Part V. Collaborators in this Project

The academic responsibility and coordination for this project lay with Prof. Dr. Michael G. Faure LL.M. (Maastricht) and Prof. Ton Hartlief (Maastricht). Michael Faure is both director of the Maastricht Institute for Transnational Legal Research (METRO) and of the European Centre of Tort and Insurance Law in Vienna. Ton Hartlief is professor of private law at the law faculty of Maastricht University. 15

The country reports are drafted by experts in the various countries. The following academics have drafted the country reports: 16

Prof. Dr. Bernhard A. Koch (University of Innsbruck and ECTIL) and Dagmar Hinghofer-Szalkay (Austria), Dr. Isabelle Durant (University of Louvain-la-Neuve, Belgium), Prof. Dr. Olivier Moréteau, Michel Cannarsa and Fabien Lafay (Université de Jean Moulin Lyon 3, France), Prof. Dr. Ulrich Magnus (Max Planck Institute for foreign and international private law, Germany), Prof. Dr. Alberto Monti and adjunct-professor Filippo Andrea Chiaves (Institute of comparative law, Bocconi University, Italy), Prof. Dr. Michael G. Faure and Prof. Ton Hartlief (Maastricht University, the Netherlands), Dr. Siv Nyquist and Dr. Erik Persson (Law faculty Umeå University, Sweden), Dr. Michael Huber and Tola Amodu (London School of Economics, United Kingdom), Prof. Dr. Robert L. Rabin and Suzanne A. Bratis (Stanford Law School, United States). The competition law perspective is provided by Prof. Dr. Roger Van den Bergh (Erasmus Universiteit Rotterdam, the Netherlands). The comparative conclusions are drafted by Prof. Dr. Michael G. Faure LL.M. (Maastricht University, the Netherlands).

Part VI. Structure of this Book

After this introduction the country reports are directly provided in alphabetical order, starting with Austria and ending with the United States. A final chapter provides the comparative and policy conclusions. In all the country reports a numbering has been followed to which the comparative report will refer. The questionnaire is provided in annex to this volume. 17

A list of references is provided at the end of every chapter, allowing the reader to obtain an overview of the relevant literature with respect to the financial compensation for victims of catastrophes in that particular country. 18

Part VII. Words of Thanks

19 We would like to express our thanks to the Ministry of the Interior of the Netherlands for financing the initial project, to the Netherlands Organisation for Scientific Research and the Netherlands Ministry of Justice for providing additional funding and for the collaborators of both ECTIL and METRO for their most valuable help with the editing of this book. In that respect we especially wish to express our gratitude to Marina Jodogne, Martin McGann, Marjo Mullers and Donna Stockenhuber.

Maastricht, December 2005

M. Faure
T. Hartlief

Country Reports

Austria

Dagmar Hinghofer-Szalkay and Bernhard A. Koch

Part I. Introduction

According to § 1311 of the *Allgemeines Bürgerliches Gesetzbuch* (Austrian Civil Code, ABGB), the fundamental rule of tort law is *casum sentit dominus*.[1] Only if there is a convincing reason to shift the loss can the victim ask for compensation by somebody else. This basic norm is, of course, bound to fall into oblivion in Austria as it is anywhere else in the world, where risk awareness has turned into compensation awareness. It is almost heretical nowadays to cite this principle if someone is harmed in a situation apparently not (yet) covered by any tort law rule. It seems to be no longer the question "why" someone else should bear the loss of another – this is almost presupposed as a given necessity; instead one shall only ask "who" shall indemnify the victim as quickly and as generously as possible. While this is a natural position to be taken by the media, unfortunately also more and more lawyers and legal scholars join that chorus. 1

This does not mean that someone who suffers a loss has no other chance to seek support but via tort law. Austria has a well-developed social security system,[2] so that harm to the most fundamental interests (life and bodily integrity) will almost always and to a very large extent be covered by such funds rather than the victim's own pockets. To a much lesser degree, but not entirely negligible, the state may also step in and award at least some financial help (in particular through a rather effective system of social assistance, which is administered by the *Länder*,[3] if not through any specific other regime).[4] 2

[1] This is expressed by the following wording: "Der bloße Zufall trifft denjenigen, in dessen Vermögen oder Person er sich ereignet. …"

[2] See *infra* Part II.II.

[3] Social assistance (*Sozialhilfe*) is granted according to the subsidiarity principle, so that all other possible means of support (including family income or assets) have to be consumed first. Social assistance mostly consists of cash benefits (between € 400 and € 500 per month), whose total volume is lower than in most other highly-developed EU states (approximately 0.2% of the

3 Nevertheless, if no third party can be identified who is by law obliged to (and can afford to) pay compensation, victims may face a more or less substantial gap between the total loss they have suffered and the aggregate amount of cover contributed by other sources (unless they have made provision for such a scenario by taking out insurance themselves beforehand). In case of a catastrophe, its nature (in particular, whether it is man-made or not) predominantly determines the size of this gap.

Part II. Information on Specific Compensation Systems

I. Tort

A. *Fault Liability*

4 Traditionally, tort liability in Austria is fault-based liability.[5] Under the standard rules of §§ 1293 *et seq.* ABGB, someone is entitled to receive compensation from another if the latter has wrongfully caused the former's harm and was thereby at fault (whether he acted negligently or intentionally).[6]

5 At least in theory, Austrian law still adheres to the subjective theory of fault, so that the personal abilities of the tortfeasor are decisive for his liability. However, there is an exception to this general rule already in the Code: According to § 1299 ABGB, the negligence of an expert is to be assessed according to an objective standard. This applies to everyone who carries out an activity which from an objective point of view requires special knowledge or abilities (including, for example, car drivers): If she fails to have them or to apply them, she has to respond to such failure irrespective of any personal reasons therefor. Another important rule worth mentioning in this respect is § 1298 ABGB, which reverses the burden of proving fault if the tortfeasor did not abide by some particular obligation vis-à-vis the victim, which – apart from contractual obligations – includes protective norms aimed at avoiding the type of harm suffered. This may be of specific importance in establishing liability for man-made catastrophes, as the typical scenario may include violations of, for example, administrative law rules prescribing certain safety standards.

6 Austrian tort law aims at full compensation of the victim. However, unlike most other legal systems, Austria's law of remedies provides for different compensation standards depending upon the degree of fault (§ 1324 ABGB): If the tortfeasor has to respond for slight negligence, she only has to indemnify the "ac-

GDP): Federal Ministry of Social Security, Generations and Consumer Protection (ed.), *Social Protection Systems in Austria* (2003), 69 available online at <http://www.bmsg.gv.at/cms/site/attachments/6/5/0/CH0339/CMS1064306288445/sozialschutzsystemengl.pdf> (in the following cited as "Social Protection Systems").

4 See *infra* Part II.III.

5 See, e.g., the overview by B.A. Koch/H. Koziol, Schadenersatz für Körperverletzung in Österreich, in: B.A. Koch/H. Koziol (eds.), *Compensation for Personal Injury in a Comparative Perspective* (2003), 4.

6 § 1295 subs. 1 ABGB therefore reads: "Everyone is entitled to demand compensation from the person who did him harm by fault".

tual loss", but neither lost profits nor non-pecuniary harm. Furthermore, property damage will only be assessed objectively on the basis of the market value (§ 1332 ABGB). These limitations do not apply in case of gross negligence or intent. However (and most importantly), in case of bodily injury, the heads of damage compensable are the same irrespective of the degree of fault: The tortfeasor therefore always has to cover costs of medical care and loss of earnings as well as damages for pain and suffering (§ 1325 ABGB). Fault liability is neither limited by a *de minimis* rule nor by any caps or mitigation provisions.

B. Strict Liability

While the ABGB only provides for a few cases of liability with presumed or without fault, there are quite a few separate statutes introducing strict liability for particular risks.[7] All statutes allow the recovery of damages for pain and suffering in case of bodily injury, but some of them limit compensation by setting maximum amounts. 7

Strict liability attaches, for example, to motor vehicles and railways (EKHG), airplanes (ground damage: §§ 146 *et seq.* LFG), nuclear facilities (AtomHG 1999), mains for electricity and gas as well as installations for their distribution (§ 1a *Reichshaftpflichtgesetz* [Reich Liability Act, RHPflG] 1943), pipelines (*Rohrleitungsgesetz* [Pipelines Act, RohrLG] 1975), mines (*Mineralrohstoffgesetz* [Mineral Resources Act, MinroG] 1999), installations emitting air-pollution which are dangerous for forests (§§ 53 *et seq. Forstgesetz* [Forestry Act, ForstG] 1975), and to facilities for genetic engineering (§ 79a *Gentechnikgesetz* [Gene Technology Act, GTG]). 8

Austrian courts cautiously allow analogy to the statutory strict liability schemes, both specifically as well as to all singular regimes seen as a whole category. Court practice has, for example, declared fireworks, factories emitting toxic fumes, or ammunition producers to be equally dangerous activities as to justify no-fault liability.[8] 9

Strict liability is typically subject to a *force majeure* defence, which is understood to be some elemental force which could not have been avoided even by utmost care and is no typical operational hazard. Some statutes allow the related defence of the so-called "unavoidable event", which focuses more on the ability of the keeper to avoid the harm.[9] Most no-fault regimes therefore will not apply if the trigger of the catastrophe is some natural disaster. 10

[7] On strict liability in Austria, see B.A. Koch/H. Koziol, Austria, in: B.A. Koch/H. Koziol (eds.), *Unification of Tort Law: Strict Liability* (2002), 9.

[8] OGH in SZ 46/36; SZ 31/26; SZ 25/84.

[9] See, e.g., § 9 EKHG, § 53 para. 4 ForstG or § 164 para. 2 MinroG. On these defences, B.A. Koch/H. Koziol (*supra* fn. 7), no. 1 *et seq. Force majeure* is no defence under the AtomHG (so that the operator of a nuclear power plant is strictly liable even in cases of war or natural disasters). The same is true for §§ 146 *et seq.* LFG.

11 Even though some laws provide for unlimited strict liability,[10] others allow only a certain maximum amount of compensation (though never as a single flat sum, but rather in a progressive scheme depending on the kind of damage). Under the EKHG, for example, strict liability for personal injury caused by motor vehicles must not exceed € 800,000 (or an annual rent of € 48,000). In case of multiple victims, the combined maximum award is set at € 2,400,000[11] (otherwise payments for each victim are reduced proportionately), so that in an accident involving many victims, they may have less problems establishing liability than collecting full indemnification. Property damage is only compensated up to € 400,000. This is also true under the RHPflG, where personal injury damages are not limited at all, however (though compensation for loss of earnings or increased need has to be paid out in periodic payments not exceeding an annual rent of € 48,000). Compensation for ground damage caused by aircraft depends on its type; the caps per accident given by § 149 LFG range from € 872,000 to € 65.4 million.

12 Under most strict liability regimes, the keeper has to provide some sort of cover.[12] Some statutes, particularly those which include liability caps, require a certain minimum insurance,[13] or at least some other cover "as usual in reasonable dealings".[14]

C. State Liability

13 Under the *Amtshaftungsgesetz* (Austrian Statute on State Liability, AHG), the state can be liable for negligent behaviour by one of its officials acting within their authority (though not necessarily in a leading position). The standard of negligence is objective, as they have to be considered experts in their field pursuant to § 1299 ABGB. Compensation follows standard rules of fault liability. It is therefore very well possible that the state has to indemnify victims of a natural catastrophe which was triggered by, say, the omission of a civil servant who was in charge of controlling a certain source of risk but failed to do so (e.g. issued a construction permit in a zone where avalanches or floodings are highly likely and where construction by individuals is therefore prohibited by law).[15]

[10] This is true for liability under the AtomHG 1999, the ForstG, the MinroG, and the ProdHG.
[11] There are qualifications, however, for busses and similar vehicles which allow higher aggregate awards.
[12] Such an obligation has not been provided for by the ForstG, the MinroG, and the RHPflG. Motor vehicle keepers have to take out insurance pursuant to § 59 *Kraftfahrgesetz* (Motor Vehicles Act, KFG) in the amount of € 3 million (§ 9 KHVG).
[13] See § 6 AtomHG 1999 (no caps, coverage at least € 407 million per event for operators of nuclear facilities, € 41 million for research or test reactors or for transportation of nuclear material); § 163 LFG (Austrian license of the insurer not required for foreign airlines, § 167 subs. 4 LFG); § 13 RohrlG. Compulsory third party insurance is regulated by §§ 158b *et seq.* *Versicherungsvertragsgesetz* (Law on Insurance Contracts, VVG).
[14] § 16 ProdHG.
[15] See also *infra* no. 85–86.

D. Procedure

Tort claims are handled in a regular civil procedure. Victims have to file their claims at the competent court. Legal aid is available, of course. The court system is typically quite efficient and rather fast in comparison to other jurisdictions. Class actions are not possible, though multi-victim cases may be handled together. There is a certain cost risk upon the victims, however, inasmuch as the losing party has to pay the costs of the other, which some see as a deterrent in particular for smaller claims (unless the claimant has taken out legal expenses insurance). 14

II. Social Security

97.6% of all Austrians are covered by social security.[16] Social health insurance as well as accident insurance are financed almost entirely by contributions of the insured, whereas unemployment insurance is co-financed by the employers.[17] 15

In contrast to tort law, social insurance law does not aim at full compensation, but at the reduction of social risks.[18] Both benefits in kind (such as medical treatment or hospital care) as well as financial awards are granted.[19] If the insured is unable to work during an illness, social health insurance covers a certain percentage of her income (between 50 and 75%) for a maximum duration of 52 weeks after her employer has discontinued payment.[20] 16

Work-related accidents and certain occupational diseases are covered by social accident insurance,[21] which also grants annuity payments in case of lasting or permanent impairment of the ability to work. Compensation for immaterial harm up to a certain maximum is only available for injuries suffered due to grossly negligent violations of employee protection rules (unless the victim has a claim in tort law).[22] 17

Unless payments out of the pension scheme are available, someone severely handicapped may be eligible for invalidity or disability pension (the latter in case of work-related accidents), depending on the number of years she has contributed to the social security system.[23] 18

[16] Hauptverband der österr Sozialversicherungsträger (ed.), *Die österreichische Sozialversicherung in Zahlen* (14th edn. 2004), 13.

[17] On details see Social Protection Systems (*supra* fn. 3), 11–12.

[18] W. Holzer, The Interaction of Tort Law and Social Security under Austrian Law, in: U. Magnus (ed.), *Tort Law and Social Law* (2003), 7 (no. 6).

[19] K. Grillberger, *Österreichisches Sozialrecht* (5th edn. 2001), 32–36; Social Protection Systems (*supra* fn. 3), 45 *et seq.*

[20] K. Grillberger (*supra* fn. 19), 36–38.

[21] K. Grillberger (*supra* fn. 19), 51–56.

[22] K. Grillberger (*supra* fn. 19), 66 (65).

[23] On details, see Social Protection Systems (*supra* fn. 3), 31–35.

19 Social security benefits are paid out irrespective of the cause of the insurance case.[24] If the health impairment triggering social security payments has been caused by some third-party tortfeasor, however, the victim's claims under tort law are assigned by law to the social security carrier to the extent the latter has paid out benefits (§ 332 *Allgemeines Sozialversicherungsgesetz* [General Social Security Law, ASVG]).[25] Employers are exempted from such recourse action, however (so-called employers' privilege), but for cases of gross negligence or intent (though then as a direct claim rather than by way of subrogation).[26]

III. The Austrian Fund for Catastrophes

A. *Introduction*

20 The federal *Katastrophenfondsgesetz* (Statute on a Fund for Catastrophes) of 1996 created an administrative fund which shall cover preventive measures and state aid contributions to compensate damage resulting from catastrophes. This fund is called *Katastrophenfonds* (Austrian Fund for Catastrophes).[27]

21 The afore-mentioned statute includes guidelines for the proper use of the fund's resources. A certain share is to be used to indemnify extraordinary damage caused by flooding, avalanches, landslides, earthquakes, hurricanes, debris flow, or hail. A percentage thereof is reserved for the repair of infrastructure, the rest can be distributed by the Austrian provinces (*Länder*) to individuals. Further shares are to be used to support the acquisition of alarm equipment, vehicles for fire brigades, and to indemnify financial losses in the course of mad cow disease and droughts.[28]

22 There is no legal claim for payments out of the fund, which are entirely discretionary.[29]

B. *Financing of the Fund*

23 The basic monetary resources for the fund are to be taken out of revenues from income and corporation taxes according to the *Finanzausgleichsgesetz* (Statute on Revenue Equalization, FAG). A certain percentage of these monies are be transferred monthly to the fund and are to be invested profitably into the fund.[30]

24 When damage caused by catastrophes is to be compensated, the provinces, which are in charge of making actual payments to individuals, receive a

[24] W. Holzer (*supra* fn. 18), no. 11, 20.
[25] W. Holzer (*supra* fn. 18), no. 13.
[26] W. Holzer (*supra* fn. 18), no. 14 *et seq.*
[27] § 1 subs. 1 *Katastrophenfondsgesetz* 1996.
[28] For a fund description see § 3 *Katastrophenfondsgesetz* 1996.
[29] See, e.g., Lower Austrian Directive (*infra* fn. 32), no. 8.8.
[30] § 2 *Katastrophenfondsgesetz* 1996.

Katastrophenfonds grant that covers 60% of their expenses. The remaining 40% is to be paid out of monies contributed by the provinces themselves.[31]

C. *Two Examples*

The Austrian provinces have passed directives[32] on what basis financial aid is to be provided to whom and on what grounds. The following details thereon focus especially on the directives of the provinces of *Niederösterreich* (Lower Austria) and Salzburg, which suffered significantly from the flooding of 2002.[33] 25

1. Lower Austria

In the province of Lower Austria, financial aid is granted according to the *Richtlinie für die Förderung der Behebung von Katastrophenschäden*[34] (Directive on Supporting Compensation of Damage Due to Catastrophes). According to the *Katastrophenfondsgesetz*, such aid is reserved for property damage due to natural catastrophes as defined by this statute (and cannot be used to indemnify personal injuries). The damaged objects for which compensation is sought may not be located on land that is in danger of being struck by one of the catastrophes covered.[35] 26

Financial aid is granted under the following conditions: 27

- damage occurred to objects that were kept in good condition and were usable,
- damage exceeds € 1,090.09[36] and is not eligible for compensation by some other source,

[31] Bundesministerium für Justiz (Federal Ministry of Justice, ed.), *Vom Hochwasser betroffen – was nun, So kommen Sie zu Ihren Recht* (3rd edn. 2002, in the following: Ministry Information Folder), 10, available online at <http://www.bmj.gv.at>; Amt der Niederösterreichischen Landesregierung, Gruppe Land und Forstwirtschaft – Abteilung Landwirtschaftsförderung, Katastrophenschaden 2002, e-mailed to the authors by this authority (in the following: NÖ Katastrophenschaden 2002), 2.

[32] Amt der Niederösterreichischen Landesregierung (ed.), *Richtlinie für die Förderung der Behebung von Katastrophenschäden*, <http://www.noel.gv.at/service/LF/LF3/Katastrophen.htm> (in the following: Lower Austrian Directive); Amt der Salzburger Landesregierung (ed.), *Richtlinien für die Gewährung einer finanziellen Beihilfe des Landes zur Behebung von Katastrophenschäden im Vermögen natürlicher und juristischer Personen mit Ausnahme von Gebietskörperschaften*, <http://www.salzburg.gv.at/themen/lf/foerderungen_lf/foerderung_katfonds.htm> (in the following: Salzburg Directive); Amt der Oberösterreichischen Landesregierung (ed.), *Richtlinie für die Vergabe von Elementarschadensbeihilfen* (Katastrophenfondsgesetz 1996), <http://www.ooe.gv.at/formulare/Katastrophen/Richtlin_Katfonds.pdf>; Amt der Steiermärkischen Landesregierung (ed.), *Richtlinien betreffend Katastrophenschäden im Vermögen physischer und juristischer Personen*, <http://wwww.agrar.steiermark.at/cms/dokumente/10032540/4978797b/schadr.pdf>; Amt der Vorarlberger Landesregierung (ed.), *Richtlinien für die Gewährung von Beihilfen zur Behebung von Elementarschäden*, <http://www.vorarlberg.at/doc/richtlinieelementarschade.doc.

[33] Details *infra* at Part III.I.A.

[34] Lower Austrian Directive (*supra* fn. 32).

[35] Lower Austrian Directive (*supra* fn. 32), no. 3.2.

[36] In exceptional cases of special hardship, financial aid for damages below that threshold can nevertheless be granted.

- the damaged object has a valid permit[37] according to the state of its construction,
- the object is not covered by insurance or any other third party coverage, and
- the loss imposes a significant financial burden upon the victim.

28 In order to obtain support, an application form has to be submitted within six months after the damage has been sustained.[38] A special local commission (*Schadenserhebungskommission*) then has to assess the loss.[39]

29 In general, a basic compensation payment up to 20% of damage to buildings and furniture is available, in cases of hardship up to 50% (if caused by landslides or mudflow even up to 70%). The social and economic situation of each victim is to be assessed before compensation is provided.[40] Compensation under this regime is meant to serve as a quick and effective first-hand help, in particular for clean-up measures or the like, whereas full indemnification is not a goal (and cannot be in light of the limited available means collected by the funds).

2. Salzburg

30 Also in Salzburg, according to the province's *Richtlinien für die Gewährung einer finanziellen Beihilfe des Landes zur Behebung von Katastrophenschäden*[41] (Directives on Governmental Support for Compensation of Damage Due to Catastrophes), financial aid is granted for extraordinary property damage caused by catastrophes as defined by the *Katastrophenfondsgesetz* 1996.[42]

31 In Salzburg, financial aid is granted under the following further conditions:

- damage exceeds € 1,000,
- it is a noticeable burden to the victims, and
- it was either uninsurable or taking out insurance was not reasonable.[43]

32 Legal entities can also claim compensation, but unless they are SMEs, there must be an imminent threat to their economic viability.

33 Harm to luxury goods, such as secondary homes, swimming- pools and so on, cannot be compensated. In any case, an application form has to be submitted

[37] "Behördliche Bewilligung".
[38] Lower Austrian Directive (*supra* fn. 32), no. 8.2.
[39] The commission in Lower Austria is formed by members of the municipality, which generally is the mayor or his representative, a member of the municipal council and a technical expert; for fund information on the commission see Lower Austrian Directive (*supra* fn. 32), no. 4.
[40] 10% bonus for category C (water in the basement), 20% bonus for category B (water in living or business space but no existential danger); 25% bonus for category A (existential danger), NÖ Katastrophenschaden 2002 (*supra* fn. 31), 2.
[41] Salzburg Directive (*supra* fn. 32), no. 1.
[42] Salzburg Directive (*supra* fn. 32), no. 1.1.
[43] Salzburg Directive (*supra* fn. 32), no. 1, 5.

within six months after damage has been sustained. In exceptional cases compensation can be provided for damage below the € 1,000 limit.

Victims of catastrophes can be awarded up to 30% of their damage. This percentage may be higher in cases of hardship. If certain machinery has to be used in order to repair damage, 80% of those costs are refundable.[44] The maximum amount of financial aid is € 500,000 (which can only be paid out in cases of extreme hardship). A commission gives recommendations to the provincial government for distributing the monies available.[45] 34

D. Summary

1. Procedure

The examples of Lower Austria and Salzburg demonstrate the following procedure for compensation out of the Austrian *Katastrophenfonds*: Damage due to catastrophes, such as floods, avalanches, landslides, earthquakes, hurricanes, debris flows, or hail can be partly compensated out of public money vested in the *Katastrophenfonds*.[46] The victims of a catastrophe have to fill out an application form of the province of their residence and submit it within half a year after the harm occurred. In both examples, damage must exceed a certain threshold. A special commission determines the total amount of money eligible for financial aid, and the victims are ultimately compensated in the amount of a certain percentage of the damage sustained.[47] For indemnification by the *Katastrophenfonds,* there is no claim for equal treatment, but the provinces have to establish commissions for complaints from victims who have doubts that they have been treated fairly.[48] 35

2. Heads and Amount of Damages

There is a lower threshold of about € 1,000; damages below this amount can only be considered in cases of special hardship. Apart from further qualifications, only a certain percentage of the damage can be indemnified with monies drawn out of the *Katastrophenfonds*, ranging from 20 to 50%, in extraordinary cases even higher. Salzburg has set a cap of € 500,000 on total financial aid available under this regime to a single victim. 36

3. Rules Preventing Cumulation

If private insurance or any other third party covers the loss, payments out of the *Katastrophenfonds* are unavailable. On the other hand, compensation out 37

[44] For a fund description see Salzburg Directive (*supra* fn. 32), no. 2.

[45] For details see Salzburg Directive (*supra* fn. 32), no. 1, 5.

[46] See *infra* Part III.I.A.

[47] In Salzburg for instance, 30% of the damage is generally compensated, see Salzburg Directive (*supra* fn. 44).

[48] Bundesministerium für Justiz (*supra* fn. 31), 13.

of public money, in particular out of the fund, cannot be considered by the private insurers and must not reduce the victim's claim against them.[49]

IV. Private Insurers

A. *First-Party Insurance*

38 According to Statistics Austria, about one third of the Austrian people took out (supplementary) private health insurance in the year 2000, which not necessarily means better treatment, but free choice of doctor (not only those in contract with their social security carrier) and more pleasant conditions during a hospital stay.[50] In 2003, health insurance premiums in Austria totalled € 1.3 billion (about 10% of the aggregate insurance premiums[51] or approximately 0.6% of the GDP), whereas € 957 million was paid out by the insurers. Furthermore, total accident insurance premiums added up to roughly one half of the health insurance amount.

39 In the area of non-life insurance, the aggregate amount of premiums rose to € 2.904 billion (22.2% of all premiums; 1.3% of the GDP). Fire insurance contributed € 497 million thereto, household insurance € 461 million, storm-and-tempest insurance € 168 million. While awards paid out amounted to roughly 60–65% of the collected premiums in almost all lines of insurance, certain years show remarkable differences (particularly in the storm-and-tempest insurance, where payments rose to more than 250% in 2000 and to 183% in 2002).[52]

40 While there are only few statutory rules prescribing insurance cover,[53] banks and other financers exert factual pressure to take out first-party insurance for objects they financed or which serve as security: Any standard contract of lien requires the owner of the object to buy insurance (and to name the bank as the beneficiary in case of a loss covered by the policy).

41 While harm caused by natural disasters was typically not covered by an average building policy, major catastrophes such as the flooding of 2002 have had a significant impact on such products. Insurers now offer broader cover also for such catastrophes, though with new qualifications.[54]

42 In the case of large-scale multi-victim losses such as those arising out of catastrophes, insurers typically waive their right to investigate every single claim in detail and therefore pay out compensation for minor claims as filed, if only for

[49] Bundesministerium für Justiz (*supra* fn. 31), 7.
[50] Social Protection Systems (*supra* fn. 3), 95.
[51] As far as total collected insurance premiums in relation to the GDP is concerned, the Austrian percentage stays at about 5.8%, whereas the equivalent ratio in Germany is 6.8% (UK 14.8%, Netherlands 9.5% – data from 2002).
[52] Source: Austrian Association of Insurance Companies (VVO, <http://www.vvo.at>).
[53] But see *supra* no. 12.
[54] On details, see *infra* no. 57 and no. 76–77.

the practical reason that not enough experts are available to assess all such losses.

According to § 67 subs. 1 of the Insurance Contract Act (*Versicherungsvertragsgesetz*, VersVG), any claim against a third party that has caused the victim's loss is subrogated by law to the insurer to the extent the latter has paid out compensation. 43

B. Third-Party Insurance

Apart from the afore-mentioned mandatory liability insurance examples,[55] most household insurance packages include cover for liability up to a certain amount or percentage of the insured risk. 44

Of the € 536 million collected on general liability insurance contracts in 2003, 77.3% went back to the insured as compensation payments.[56] 45

C. Catastrophe Management

1. Catastrophe Management in General

While all large insurance companies have internal guidelines for handling mass accidents and other extraordinary loss cases, there is only one single scenario for which all insurers on the Austrian market have provided for a joint handling procedure, and this is a mass collision of 20 cars or more (see *infra* no. 47 *et seq.*). Apart from this simplified clearing mechanism, at least major insurers individually appoint *ad hoc* claims managers who supervise the administration of claims in large-scale loss incidents. Typically, they are also competent to provide for simplified filings or loss assessment.[57] 46

2. Mass Collisions in Particular

Establishing the exact causal connection of mass car accidents, even if experts are appointed, is very difficult or even impossible. According to the prevailing view of the *Oberster Gerichtshof* (Austrian Supreme Court, OGH), the person causing the first accident leading to a mass collision can be held solely liable if at fault (apart from strict liability, which also comes into play in cases of car accidents). Presumably, her insurance cover is quickly exceeded and the lack of possibilities to seek recourse against other drivers involved in the collision may lead to her insolvency.[58] 47

In 1981, the *Verband für Versicherungsunternehmen* (Austrian Association of Insurance Companies, VVO) introduced a regulatory proceeding for mass car 48

[55] See *supra* no. 12.
[56] Source: Austrian Association of Insurance Companies (VVO, <http://www.vvo.at>).
[57] As expressed to the authors by a senior representative of one of the largest Austrian insurers.
[58] W. Posch, Multikausale Schäden in modernen Haftungsrechten, in: A. Fenyves/H. Weyers (eds.), *Multikausale Schäden in modernen Haftungsrechten* (1988), 173.

accidents (pile-ups). According to an agreement made by the insurance companies, this regulatory proceeding can be conducted if 20 vehicles or more which have Austrian insurance coverage are involved in a single mass accident. However, sometimes collisions with fewer vehicles can also be managed by this special regulatory procedure.[59]

49 The regulatory proceedings adhere to the following guidelines: After a pile-up, a steering commission including representatives of five major insurance companies is nominated and convenes in the VVO. Based on the facts collected by a regional investigation commission, consisting of representatives of car insurance companies from each province, the steering commission establishes whether the given case is to be treated as a mass collision according to the regulatory proceeding agreement, and if so, which insurance company will act as the central office to be contacted by the victims. Furthermore, they agree on how to distribute the damages and costs to the various insurance companies according to the number of cars insured with each company.[60]

50 The core principle of the regulatory proceeding is that fault is only of importance if it can be clearly established. In any other case, according to the rules of this simplified proceeding, 50% of the damages are compensated. An example: The driver of the first car reduced its speed according to traffic law regulations, and consequently the driver following immediately behind him crashes into the first car, and so do the cars following subsequently, so that each car crashes into the one in front of it. The driver of the last car therefore only caused damage at the rear end of the car in front of him. In a simplified regulatory proceeding, the owner of the first car receives full compensation, the owner of the last car none at all, and all the others get 50% of the damage they have incurred.[61]

51 This procedure is prone to work in favour of the victims of mass collisions, but those unhappy with its results still have the opportunity to seek compensation in the courts. According to experts working with this procedure, it not only saves money but is also widely accepted by the insured.[62]

[59] W. Posch (*supra* fn. 58), 173–174, citing *Verband der Versicherungsunternehmen Österreichs* Akt Nr. 4909, Ausg. Nr. 5449/81 of 21.5.1981.

[60] G. Kozak, Austrian Association of Insurance Companies, E-Mail to the authors of 7.6.2004; see further W. Posch (*supra* fn. 58), 174.

[61] G. Kozak (*supra* fn. 60).

[62] G. Kozak (*supra* fn. 60).

Part III. Detailed Information on Specific Catastrophes

I. Natural Catastrophes

A. *Galtür Avalanche 1999*

On 23 February 1999 steady snowfall in Galtür prevented tourists from skiing and therefore an entertainment programme was conducted in the village. Suddenly, three avalanches came down on the centre of this Tyrolean village. Several houses were damaged and more than 50 people were immediately buried beneath the snow. About 40 were gravely injured and 38 were killed.[63] 52

The province of Tyrol was confronted with 124 claims for compensation amounting to a total of € 7.45 million,[64] € 7.11 million of which was ultimately paid out.[65] The Federal Armed Forces intervened with considerable help given by foreign helicopters, the cost of which was about 30 million Schillings (€ 2,180,185).[66] The costs for transporting the deceased and further motor vehicle transports were estimated to be 1.5 million Schillings (approx. € 110,000).[67] 53

The Austrian government additionally provided 100 million Schillings (€ 7.3 million) for avalanche protection and other infrastructure measures.[68] 54

The Galtür avalanche also provoked a modification of the *Katastrophenfondsgesetz*, which until then had stated that the *Katastrophenfonds* only covered direct damages. After its modification, losses of earnings resulting from business disruptions, costs of evacuations, rescue operations as well as the transfer of dead bodies can now also be compensated with monies out of the fund.[69] 55

[63] *Der Standard*, 24.2.1999 ("Lawinenunglück: Retter kamen nicht zu den Opfern"); *Der Standard*, 24.2.1999 ("Lawinenkatastrophe in Galtür"); *Der Standard*, 17.3.1999 ("Sammlungen für Unglücksorte").

[64] As confirmed to the authors in a letter by the competent authority; see also *Tiroler Tageszeitung*, 12.12.2001 ("Naturkatastrophen durch Treibhauseffekt?, TIROLER-Expertensymposium: 'Naturkatastrophe durch globale Erwärmung – Wie gefährdet ist der Alpenraum?'"), stating that about 70 million Schillings (€ 5,087,089.40) of damage was sustained; see also *Tiroler Tageszeitung*, 14.12.1999 ("BH erfasste 430 Geschädigte und Schäden von 260 Millionen durch Muren und Lawinen 1999; Katastrophenjahr in Zahlen") stating that the total amount of damages caused by the Galtür avalanche is estimated to be 108 million Schillings (€ 7,848,666); *Der Standard*, 17.3.1999, ("Sammlungen für Unglücksorte"), estimates that damages are estimated to be around 150 million Schillings (€ 11 million).

[65] As confirmed to the authors in a letter by the competent authority.

[66] *Tiroler Tageszeitung*, 19.3.1999 ("Kosten für Evakuierungsaktion nach Galtür – Lawine mit 30 Millionen Schilling beziffert; Alpen bleiben gefährlich").

[67] *Landeskommission für Elementarschäden* (*Katastrophenfonds*), Jahresbilanz 1999 – Bericht, 7, attachment to a letter to the authors by the competent authority of 6.7.2004; *Die Presse*, 10.4.1999 ("Bund zahlt bei Katastrophe").

[68] *Der Standard*, 2.3.1999 ("Lawinenkatastrophen kein Fall für die Justiz").

[69] *Landeskommission für Elementarschäden*, Jahresbilanz 1999 – Bericht (*supra* fn. 67), 7; *Die Presse*, 10.4.1999 ("Bund zahlt bei Katastrophe").

56 18 million Schillings of charitable donations were collected for the victims.[70] Furthermore, a benefit concert was organized for the victims of Galtür, and other donation money was collected, for instance, by two athletes who ran a benefit race across Austria.[71] A committee responsible for the allocation of donation money according to particular need was formed.[72] Also, private donation operations were started: In a village in Bavaria 50 German Marks (€ 25) from the profits of each one-week-vacation booked there was given to the affected restaurant owners in Tyrol, who had suffered significantly from a major drop in bookings after the avalanche catastrophe in February 1999.[73]

57 Concerning insurance money, those damaged by the Galtür avalanche mainly depended on normal building insurance, which usually covered only a very small amount of the damages accrued.[74] After the Galtür avalanche, insurance companies started modifying their insurance packages, mainly developing new products covering insurance for natural disasters, such as offering instant support in cases of total loss caused by avalanches. Those offers (again) differ significantly: Some insurance companies focus on avalanches, others on flood or earthquakes.[75]

58 Some companies explicitly exclude regions in which natural catastrophes are prone to happen, and damage caps are generally fairly low.[76] Furthermore, additional clauses concerning cumulation of damage were introduced by many companies in which the insurance company defines a maximum amount payable to all victims of a single damaging incident combined.[77]

59 The purpose of many business insurance contracts is to avoid bankruptcy for those businesses which depend on weather conditions. Most packages cover fixed costs and loss of profit for the business. Others also cover costs for expired train and aeroplane tickets, and costs for room and board if tourists are

[70] *Landeskommission für Elementarschäden (Katastrophenfonds)*, Jahresbilanz 1999 – Bericht (*supra* fn. 67), 6.

[71] *Die Presse*, 7.4.1999 ("Benefizkonzert für die Opfer von Galtür"); *Die Presse* 21.8.1999 ("Benefiz-Lauf für Galtür").

[72] *Der Standard*, 17.3.1999 ("Sammlungen für Unglücksorte").

[73] *Der Standard*, 9.3.1999.

[74] *Tiroler Tageszeitung*, 31.3.1999 ("Manche Versicherer bieten Produkte an, die Folge von zuviel oder zuwenig Schnee berücksichtigen, Rettung vor dem Ruin bei Lawinenunglücken").

[75] *Tiroler Tageszeitung*, 12.12.2001 ("Naturkatastrophen durch Treibhauseffekt?, TIROLER Expertensymposium: 'Naturkatastrophe durch globale Erwärmung – Wie gefährdet ist der Alpenraum?'"), mentioning the insurance conditions offered by a Tirolean insurance company, the Tiroler Versicherung; *Konsument*, 3/2000, 15 ("Katastrophenversicherungen, Limitierter Schutz"), <http://www.konsument.at>.

[76] *Infra* no. 77.

[77] *Tiroler Tageszeitung*, 12.12.2001 ("Naturkatastrophen durch Treibhauseffekt?, TIROLER Expertensymposium: 'Naturkatastrophe durch globale Erwärmung – Wie gefährdet ist der Alpenraum?'"). Insurance policies are frequently formulated in a tricky way. In cases of avalanches for instance, some policies only cover roof avalanches, but not dust avalanches or ice avalanches, *Konsument*, 3/2000, 14–15 ("Katastrophenversicherungen; Limitierter Schutz"), <http://www.konsument.at>.

forced to stay at holiday resorts longer than planned due to weather conditions.[78]

The criminal investigations in this case were dropped, and the public prosecutor stated that avalanches of a catastrophic dimension like the one experienced in Galtür were not predictable. The responsible persons had acted promptly and in due time. Furthermore, it was said that it had been exceedingly difficult for the avalanche commission to judge that extreme powder avalanches would get down to the village.[79] Therefore, also no liability in tort had been established. 60

B. Flood 2002

1. Action by the Federal Government

In August 2002, heavy rainfalls led to a flood in the northeast of Austria, causing several deaths and severe destruction of thousands of houses and tens of thousands of hectares of area under cultivation. This flood was considered the most severe national catastrophe since 1945. The aggregate amount of damage is estimated to have been € 7.5 billion. This total consists mainly of harm to houses, premises, agricultural grounds and to infrastructure such as telecommunications and transport.[80] 61

The Austrian government instantly approved € 500 million as compensation out of public funds – money which was to be taken out of the federal *Katastrophenfonds*. This fund had already existed before this particular flood, as mentioned earlier.[81] In addition to the fund, which then was endowed with € 275 million, the *Hochwasseropferentschädigungs- und Wiederaufbau-Gesetz*[82] (Statute on Compensation for Victims of Floods and Reconstruction, HWG) was passed to increase the fund money. It furthermore stated that € 250 million was to be used for damage to property of private citizens and businesses and € 250 million for the reconstruction of the infrastructure such as streets and public buildings.[83] Of the latter € 250 million, € 28 million was spent on facilities for flood protection. Another € 50 million was used to restore harm 62

[78] *Tiroler Tageszeitung*, 31.3.1999 ("Manche Versicherer bieten Produkte an, die Folgen von zuviel und zuwenig Schnee berücksichtigen, Rettung vor dem Ruin bei Lawinenunglücken"); *Tiroler Tageszeitung*, 19.3.1999 ("Kosten für Evakuierungsaktion nach Galtür – Lawine mit 30 Millionen Schilling beziffert; Alpen bleiben gefährlich").

[79] *Der Standard*, 11.1.2001; *Die Presse*, 11.1.2001 ("Galtür: Kein Verfahren").

[80] Ministry Information Folder (*supra* fn. 31), 1–2; see further *Die Presse*, 24.8.2002 ("Hochwasser verursachte € 7,5 Milliarden Schaden").

[81] See already above Part II.III; Ministry Information Folder (*supra* fn. 31), 10.

[82] *Hochwasseropferentschädigungs- und Wiederaufbau-Gesetz* 2002, HWG BG 4.10.2002 BGBl I 155.

[83] *Bundesministerium für Finanzen* (Federal Ministry of Finance), *Bewältigung der Flutkatastrophe*, <http://www.bmf.gv.at/Budget/AktuellesThema/ArchivAktuelleThemen/Bewltigungder Flutka637/_start.htm>.

to water supply installations and sewage disposal installations. € 100 million was paid out to businesses.[84]

63 Furthermore, the Federal Ministry for Economy and Employment launched a project to help struggling businesses to recover and to protect jobs. It granted € 100 million in subsidies for businesses, along with a total credit volume of € 1 billion. Those subsidies consisted mainly of EPR loans and direct benefits of the *Arbeitsmarktförderung* (employment promotion service) and were available for business investments, warehouses and expenses necessary to re-establish basic conditions for businesses in areas highly affected by the flood.[85]

64 Accordingly, upon determination of their overall damages, businesses received 20% instant compensation out of the *Katastrophenfonds* and then had to file an application for subsidies to their own bank. This bank then assessed the credit volume for which subsidies could be granted: the total amount of damages minus money already received out of the *Katastrophenfonds* or insurance benefits was considered as a basis for subsidies out of public monies. Those subsidies consisted of an allowance for interests on loans. The 10 year credit granted was free of interest and redemption for three years, with an interest rate of 4%.[86]

65 Also the Austrian Ministry on Social Issues created a fund for family hardships. Out of this fund as well as others (such as one on water economy), another € 60 million was spent on damage compensation and reconstruction.[87]

66 € 134 million was given to Austria out of the European Union's Solidarity Fund.[88] This fund is endowed with € 1 billion every year and was created to provide money for the reconstruction of damaged infrastructure, including communication, traffic, energy supply, water supply, health, education, financing emergency services, safeguarding protection devices, protection of cultural goods and cleaning of damaged land.[89]

[84] Federal Ministry of Finance (*supra* fn. 83), *Die Presse*, 20.8.2002 ("Erste Bilanz: 10.000 Häuser beschädigt").
[85] As confirmed to the authors in an e-mail by the competent authority; see also *Der Standard*, 14.8.2002 ("Bund schürt Hilfspaket ohne Steuererhöhungen").
[86] As confirmed to the authors in an e-mail by the competent authority.
[87] *Die Presse*, 20.8.2002 ("Erste Bilanz: 10.000 Häuser beschädigt"); *Der Standard*, 14.8.2002 ("Bund schürt Hilfspaket ohne Steuererhöhungen").
[88] On this fund see <http://europa.eu.int/scadplus/leg/en/lvb/g24217.htm>. For further information see http://europa.eu.int/scadplus/leg/de/lvb/g24216.htm>.
[89] As confirmed to the authors in an e-mail by the competent authority.

2. Details on Lower Austria

a) Private Damage

The Section of Agricultural Promotion of the Lower Austrian provincial government received 17,600 reports of damages and 5,200 motions for higher compensation, for a total damage amounting to € 594 million, mainly damage to private households, businesses, agriculture and forestry.[90] 67

According to the province's directive on compensation for catastrophes[91] and the *Katastrophenfondsgesetz,* victims were eligible for compensation out of the *Katastrophenfonds* in the case of this flood. Financial aid was granted pursuant to the rules contained in the province's directive.[92] 68

Altogether the province distributed € 184.4 million among the victims of the catastrophe out of public money, of which the province paid 40%, while 60% were covered by the *Katastrophenfonds*. Furthermore, the province paid for the reconstruction of residential buildings, grants for business development and flood protection.[93] 69

b) Public Damage: Provinces and Municipalities

In Lower Austria the flood caused damage in the amount of € 16.9 million to infrastructure such as roads, asylums and schools. The provincial parliament approved an excess budget of € 20 million in support.[94] 70

253 municipalities suffered a total loss of € 58.6 million. The Federal Ministry of Finance provided extra grants: 20% of the damage were paid as instant help to the municipalities and up to 50% compensation was granted if receipts were submitted. The money was also taken out of the *Katastrophenfonds*, whose budget had been increased as mentioned before.[95] 71

In order to be eligible for compensation, a municipality was required to give notice of its damage before 30 November 2002, stating where the harm occurred, the precise time it occurred and the cause of the damage. The damage had to be assessed by an approved expert, and an approximation or estimate of costs had to be submitted. For damage already compensated by the fund or by insurance companies, no further compensation was provided.[96] 72

[90] As confirmed to the authors in an e-mail by the competent authority.
[91] Lower Austrian Directive (*supra* fn. 32).
[92] *Supra* Part II.III.C.1.
[93] As confirmed to the authors in an e-mail by the competent authority.
[94] For further information see *Beschluss des Landtages* of 11.9.2002, 1018/V-9/101-2002.
[95] *Supra* fn. 82.
[96] As confirmed to the authors in a letter by the competent authority.

3. Details on Salzburg

73 In Salzburg private damage caused by the flood amounted to approximately € 37.6 million.[97] Governmental aid was granted for extraordinary damage caused by catastrophes mentioned by the *Katastrophenfondsgesetz* 1996 and further specified by the Salzburg directive.[98]

74 All in all, 2,820 applications for compensation were made, and € 21.8 million have been paid out to victims to date, € 8.7 million of which by the province itself. Furthermore, the victims have received donations from various charitable organizations, from the European Community, money from the various municipalities. It is estimated that 90% of the damage sustained could be compensated.[99]

4. Private Compensation

a) Private Insurers

75 According to two of the largest insurance companies, € 25.5 million and € 50 million respectively were paid out in compensation of the flooding.[100] According to the application forms submitted to the province of Lower Austria, where compensation by third parties has to be declared, insurance companies had by then already paid around € 52 million.[101]

76 As far as insurance on buildings or contents is concerned, for example, a standard Austrian policy at the time would not cover damage caused by flooding. Home owners therefore had to be covered by a special additional rate offered on the Austrian market since about 1997 (*Luxustarif*).[102] The extent of cover for such loss varied from company to company; an average policy including this extra rate would have a cap amounting to € 7,500 (though one company offered cover up to € 72,000).[103] In order to obtain payment, the insured had to file their claims within three days after the loss occurred according to the terms of their contract (though all companies waived this tight time limit in the particular case). Payments from other sources such as the *Katastrophenfonds* were not deducted (though insurance payments were considered in the reverse case). However, many insurance companies had provided clauses for cumulative damages in cases of massive losses such as those resulting from a natural catastrophe in order to minimize their financial risk. This means that the insurer had set a maximum amount payable to all persons who had incurred damage from the same catastrophe, so that many victims of the flood received only a share of the compensation agreed on in the insurance contract.[104]

97 *Die Presse*, 21.2.2003 ("Hochwasser: Mehr Schaden").
98 *Supra* Part II.III.C.2.
99 As confirmed to the authors in an e-mail by the competent Salzburg authority.
100 Uniqa, *Konzernlagebericht* 2002, 93; Wiener Städtische, *Geschäftsbericht* 2002, 43.
101 As confirmed to the authors in an e-mail by the competent authority.
102 Ministry Information Folder (*supra* fn. 31), 4.
103 Ministry Information Folder (*supra* fn. 31), 8 (table based on data as of November 2002).

After the flood many Austrian insurers started to adapt their insurance products. 77
On the one hand, new offers covering insurance for natural disasters have been introduced – some focus on avalanches, others on floods or earthquakes.[105] On the other hand, certain insurers now specifically exclude regions altogether where certain natural catastrophes are prone to happen, or at least curtail the maximum cover available for such areas. While some products cover catastrophic losses up to 50% of the amount insured (typically coupled with an overall maximum), others have fairly low caps altogether, even irrespective of any particular risk proneness.[106] Furthermore, insurers have tightened clauses about cumulative damage.[107]

b) Charitable Donations

Right after the flood, in response to a call by the Austrian national television 78
network, € 72 million were raised for the victims of the flood, of which € 18 million were contributed by the Austrian government. Private businesses contributed object donations worth € 10 million.[108] Caritas, a charitable organization, raised another € 11 million of extra donation money which was distributed among the victims.[109] Furthermore, a donation account was opened in Lower Austria and a commission for fair distribution of donation money was founded, which distributed € 4.4 million.[110] Switzerland contributed € 1.3 million to the restoration of damage due to the flood.[111]

[104] *Der Standard*, 31.10.2002 ("Versichert, doch nach der Flut ernüchtert"); Kfz-Kaskoversicherung (Comprehensive Car Insurance Coverage) in general covered all damage to motor vehicles if no cost sharing was agreed upon, Ministry Information Folder (*supra* fn. 31), 4.

[105] See the overview given by <http://www.konsument.at/konsument/detail.asp?category=Geld+%2B+Versicherung&id=15582>.

[106] Some policies are, for example, capped at € 3,630 for contents and indemnify damage to the building only up to € 7,270.

[107] Also, not all types of harm caused by water is compensated. It is frequently distinguished between damage due to flooding, damage due to flooding resulting from deluge, damage due to high ground water or due to high surface water. Therefore, the person taking out insurance has to pay close attention to which product he is finally purchasing, *Konsument* 3/2000, 15 ("Katastrophenversicherungen; Limitierter Schutz"), avilable online at <http://www.konsument.at>. After the 2002 flood, most consumers complained that it became nearly impossible to get insurance coverage since most insurance companies changed their policies and no longer accept, for instance, to contract with those living in dangerous regions, e-mail by G. Riener, Verein für Konsumenteninformation, 15.6.2004; see also *Der Standard*, 14.6.2003 ("Versicherungen stecken in der Zwickmühle").

[108] *Caritas Spenderinfo* 8/2003, 5, available at Caritas Österreich, office@caritas-austria.at: 8,000 families were provided with instant payments. Upon application, families were awarded between € 600 and € 33,000 for rebuilding, depending on need. All in all € 1.6 million were spent in August immediately after the flooding, € 6.3 million for rebuilding projects. In October another € 39.3 million were spent on rebuilding projects. 2,200 households with exceptional needs were provided another € 20 million, € 2.6 million were given to those wanting to move away from the flood area, and € 1.4 million were spent on advisory services for construction and counselling. Furthermore € 500 grants for energy costs were awarded.

[109] *Caritas Spenderinfo* (*supra* fn. 108). € 3.4 million were spent on instant help, counselling, advisory service on leaving the area, advisory services on reconstruction, € 4.9 million for exceptional needs, consultancy, prevention, and reconstruction service and € 2.7 million for extra exceptional needs.

[110] As confirmed to the authors in an e-mail by the competent authority.

[111] As confirmed to the authors in an e-mail by the competent authority.

c) Tax Benefits

79 In 2002, right after the devastating flood causing an extremely wide amount of damage to Austrian citizens, their property and infrastructure, the afore-mentioned *Hochwasseropferentschädigungs- und Wiederaufbau-Gesetz* 2002[112] included changes to the *Einkommenssteuergesetz* (Income Tax Statute, EStG), the *Körperschaftssteuergesetz* (Statute on Corporation Tax, KStG) and the *Bundesabgabenordnung* (Statute on general provisions and procedure in tax matters, BAO).[113]

i) Donations of Money and in Kind within Business Expenses

80 According to the *Hochwasseropferentschädigungs- und Wiederaufbau-Gesetz* 2002, money donations and donations in kind given by businesses to direct victims, to the community, or to a charitable organization in compensation of damage after a catastrophe, including floods, avalanches and landslides, are deductible if spent for publicity purposes. The latter is evidenced by media reports or in-house advertising, such as advertisement posters at the counter mentioning the donations. Donations of private persons, on the other hand, still remain non-deductible.[114]

81 Donations received are neither subject to income tax, nor to corporation or wage tax. Furthermore, if they were received by 30 June 2003, they were also exempt from gift tax.[115]

ii) Extraordinary Expenses – Private Sphere

82 According to the changes in the law in 2002, extraordinary private expenses for restoration after catastrophes such as floods, avalanches and landslides are deductible. For primary residences, fixtures and common clothing, the current original price is to be considered, for motor vehicles, the cash value is to be considered.[116]

[112] *Supra* fn. 82.

[113] Art. 7–9 of the *Hochwasseropferentschädigungs- und Wiederaufbau-Gesetz* 2002, HWG BG 4.10.2002 BGBl I 155; For a fund description see K. Hilber, Hochwasserhilfe im Steuerrecht durch das HWG 2002, [2002] *ecolex*, 792; also B. Renner, Abzugsfähige und nicht abzugsfähige Spenden aus Sicht der Gesetzes- und der Verwaltungspraxis, Zum Jahresende: Reduzierung der Steuerlast durch "noble Gesten"?, Spenden im Ertragssteuerrecht, [2002] *Steuer- und Wirtschaftskartei* (SWK), 790; A. Schellner, Steuerliche Behandlung von Aufwendungen für Katastrophenschäden und Absetzbarkeit von Spenden an Hochwassergeschädigte, [2002] *Zeitschrift für Wirtschaftstreuhänder* (VWT) H 5, 22.

[114] K. Hilber (*supra* fn. 113), 792 on new regulations on deductibles in the law of income tax: § 4 subs. 4 EStG; see also Ministry Information Folder (*supra* fn. 31), 11.

[115] K. Hilber (*supra* fn. 113), 792; see also Ministry Information Folder (*supra* fn. 31), 11.

[116] In depth K. Hilber (*supra* fn. 113), 794-79 on new regulations on deduction of exceptional expenses according to § 34 abs. 6 ESTG; R. Beiser, Außergewöhnliche Belastungen für Hochwasseropfer, Anmerkungen zum geplanten Ausbau der außergewöhnlichen Belastungen iSd § 34 EStG, [2002] SWK, 719; G. Gaedke, Aufwendungen zur Beseitigung von Katastrophenschäden, Zur Neuregelung des § 34 Abs. 6 EStG 1988, Wirtschaftsgüter im Privatvermögen, [2002] SWK, 689.

iii) Advance Deduction of Replacements due to Catastrophes

For business replacements after 31 May 2002 and before 1 January 2004 due to catastrophes, deductions can be made in advance. Replacement in this context includes expenditures on the reconstruction of a building or the acquisition of an economic good with the same function. An advance deduction of 12% for buildings and 20% for economic goods can be made.[117] 83

iv) Fees and Transaction Tax

With the *Hochwasserkatastrophe-Erlass* (Decree on Flooding Catastrophes),[118] the Federal Ministry of Finance announced that, according to § 206 lit a BAO, no fees shall be charged for alternative issuances of official documents such as passports or for documents needed for determination, liquidation and compensation of damage due to the flood. Furthermore, fees were also waived for credit agreements and loan contracts that were concluded in connection with the 2002 flood. To be released from the duty to pay such fees, one had to give notice to the local tax authorities, stating what kind of fees he would have had to pay.[119] 84

5. State Liability

According to § 1 subs. 1 AHG, the state is liable for damage which its executive bodies cause due to their unlawful behaviour when enforcing the law.[120] Various factors have to be considered to assign liability to the state: First of all, an act of an executive body, which is to be assigned to the federal body, must exist. Secondly, the act has to consist of a conduct or omission within the sovereign power of the state. Third, the act or omission of the executive body has to have caused the damage and has to be unlawful and faulty.[121] 85

Soon after the flood, lawyers started to examine whether public legal entities such as the federal republic were liable for damages resulting from this catastrophe. In this case, the *Wasserrechtsgesetz* (Statute on Water Rights, WRG) and regulations based thereupon are of interest, according to which governmental agencies are responsible for the construction of protection and regulation devices if a flood has already been experienced or is likely to be experienced in the future in certain regions. They can do so, for instance, by establishing water rights commissions.[122] The executive organs of the state would have violated 86

[117] K. Hilber (*supra* fn. 113), 793–794, on § 10c ESTG and § 108d ESTG.

[118] *Hochwasserkatastrophe-Erlass betreffend Gebühren und Verkehrssteuern*, 6.9.2002 GZ 10 0101/8-IV/10/10/02.

[119] Federal Ministry of Finance, *Hochwasserkatastrophen-Erlass betreffend Gebühren und Verkehrssteuern*, <http://www.bmf.gv.at/steuern/weitersteuern/gebuehrengesetz/hochwasser/hochwasser-ertl.htm>; K. Hilber, [2002] *ecolex*, 796. Furthermore the victims of the flood were dispensed of contributions to clean-up operations: Federal Ministry of Finance, Bewältigung der Flutkatastrophe, <http://www.bmf.gv.at/Budget/AktuellesThema/ArchivAktuelleThemen/BewaeltigungderFlutka637/_start.htm>.

[120] See *supra* no. 13.

[121] H. Mayer, Amtshaftung für Hochwasser, [2002] *ecolex*, 797.

[122] H. Mayer (*supra* fn. 121), 797–798, focusing on §§ 43, 76, 88b WRG.

this act if they had failed to act accordingly and if it could have been proven that the regions damaged by the flood of 2002 had obviously been destined to suffer such a flooding. The organs thereby would have neglected their duty to provide for safety measures to prevent damage.[123] In one case, a home owner sued the Republic of Austria claiming € 80,000 for damage sustained from the flood in 2002. The plaintiff's lawyer contended that water from a nearby powerhouse had not been released in time, the water basins had been brim full, and the water had not been able to flow through an overflow drain. It was claimed that the state had breached its duty of supervision. The action was dismissed, however.[124]

II. Man-Made Catastrophes

A. *Lassing Mine Collapse 1998*

87 On 17 July 1998 substantial amounts of water started to leak into the mines of Lassing (Styria). This happened because the rock in which groundwater flows consists of two different layers: an upper layer consisting mainly of gravel and grit, and a layer deeper down of sand and grit. Working on the mines a layer further down broke through and several craters opened in the gravel layer. Due to these craters, the upper layer caved in. When the mud suddenly collapsed, a miner was trapped 60 metres below ground. Another tremendous collapse of mud buried a group of nine miners and a geologist below mud and water. Due to the collapse a huge crater opened up in Lassing and another village nearby. Nine days later the miner trapped 60 metres below ground in the mine's lunchroom was saved, but the other nine miners and the geologist were declared dead.[125]

88 The operator of the mines, *Luzenac Naintsch*, paid € 23.63 million for compensation.[126] They also paid for consequential damages, which were around 31 million Schillings (€ 2.25 million) to the province of Styria and 3.5 million Schillings (approx. € 254,000) to the municipality of Lassing. A settlement was reached that, after having received those payments, the province and the municipality would not claim any more compensation from the operator of the mine.[127]

89 The operator had insurance coverage,[128] also the houses dragged into the crater held various building and contents insurance contracts.[129] The insurance company which had issued most of those policies announced that their estimated

[123] H. Mayer (*supra* fn. 121), 798.
[124] OGH 24.6.2005 1 Ob 285/04z.
[125] *Der Standard*, 10.8.1998 ("Chronologie"); *Der Standard*, 16.7.1999 ("Von der Katastrophe zur 'Lex Lassing'"); *Der Standard*, 4.8.2000 ("Forscher liefern Beweise für Gerichtsprozesse"); *Die Presse*, 17.7.2003 ("Chronologie der Katastrophe").
[126] *Die Presse*, 17.7.2003 ("Gedenken in Lassing").
[127] *Die Presse*, 27.7.2001 ("Einigung über Entschädigungsforderungen").
[128] *Erste Allgemeine* insurance company.
[129] *Wiener Städtische* insurance company.

total of compensation payments was between 15 and 20 million Schillings (between about € 1.1 million and € 1.5 million) and that they would immediately seek recourse from the operator's insurance company after paying out on their own policies.[130]

The Republic of Austria granted € 15 million donation money, and the province of Styria awarded € 70 million, of which € 55 million were for damage to the infrastructure. Also, the capital of the province of Styria granted € 1 million. Even a local radio-station donated 750,000 Schillings (€ 54,500).[131] Moreover, 32.5 million Schillings (€ 2.4 million) of charitable donations were collected by the Austrian Red Cross and were distributed among the victims.[132] 90

The director of the mines, the mine fireman and a civil servant, charged with *fahrlässige Gemeingefährdung* (negligently posing danger to the public), were convicted on appeal.[133] After those convictions in the criminal court, it is estimated that a total of about € 72.7 million could be claimed in the civil court.[134] 91

B. Bergisel Panic 1999

On 4 December 1999, after a snowboard competition, an award ceremony was to be held in the Bergisel Sport Stadium in Innsbruck, in the province of Tyrol. Since many guests of the festival were already heading towards the exits, planning to attend parties in the city centre, a crowd of people was moving towards the west exit. Suddenly people started to jostle, and when people were blocked within the crowd, some started panicking. Gates were broken, some persons were pushed down to the floor, others slid down the slope. Five people died that night, 38 were injured, five have remained nursing cases and one of those five died 5 years after the incidence.[135] 92

Those possibly liable to pay compensation were the insurance company of the organizer,[136] the insurance company of the city of Innsbruck,[137] the Austrian 93

[130] *Der Standard*, 28.7.1998 ("Bergwerkgesellschaft haftet für die Schäden").
[131] *Der Standard*, 6.8.1998 ("Millionenspenden für Lassing"); *Der Standard*, 19.8.1998 (Lassing und die Kosten").
[132] *Die Presse*, 30.10.1998 ("32,5 Millionen für Lassing-Opfer aufgeteilt"); *Der Standard*, 28.8.1998 ("Länderchronik – Steiermark"); *Der Standard*, 22.8.1998 ("Beach-Volleyball für Lassing").
[133] *Die Presse*, 17.7.2003 ("Gedenken in Lassing"); *Der Standard*, 19.3.2003 ("Lassing endet mit Gefängnis"); *Der Standard*, 29.1.2003 ("Lassing: Neuer Prozess in Wien").
[134] *Der Standard*, 11.1.2000 ("Nach Lassing-Prozess Milliardenabrechnung").
[135] *Der Standard*, 6.12.1999 ("Opfer berichten: 'Sind gefallen wie Dominosteine'"); *Die Presse* 6.12.2003 ("Bergisel Prozess: Freispruch für Sicherheitschef").
[136] Uniqa, the insurer of the organizers of the snowboard festival, immediately opened a fund offering psychological help for relatives and friends of the victims of the catastrophe, <http://www.uniqagroup.com/uniqagroup/cms/de/press/press_release/archive/pa_bergiselkatastrophe.jsp> (23.06.2004).
[137] *Generali* insurance company.

Republic, the head of the security company employed by the organizers and the leaseholder of the stadium.[138]

94 The five gravely injured victims brought claims against the city of Innsbruck and the province of Tyrol. In November 2002, the city of Innsbruck and the province of Tyrol were ordered at first instance to pay compensation, including pensions, lost earnings and intensive care costs for the five severely injured girls who were now depending on lifelong intensive care.[139] The province of Tyrol was held liable pursuant to the *Amtshaftungsgesetz*.[140] The court stated that the *Veranstaltungsbehörde* (public authority responsible for mass events) should not have approved of the festival to be conducted in the stadium. According to the court, the public authority had thereby acted with fault, and therefore the province could be held liable for acts of a federal agency applying a provincial statute.[141]

95 The city of Innsbruck, the province of Tyrol and the organizer's insurance company thereafter agreed upon a settlement with the five gravely injured victims to pay a total of € 10 million to the victims as well as surviving family members.[142] The insurance company of the organizer accepted to pay about € 8 million of those € 10 million to be paid to the victims.[143] The province of

[138] *Tiroler Landtag, Regierungsantrag*, 12.12.2002, 4, *Bericht und Antrag*, 23.1.2003, 1, both available online at <http://www.tirol.gv.at> (go to *Landtag, Parlamentarische Materialien, Gastzugang, Ausschussvorlagen, 31. Sitzung der 13. Periode vom 5.–7. Februar 2003 – Bericht und Antrag* and *Regierungsantrag*). Compensation payments of the province are to be made out of budgetary money, the city of Innsbruck has insurance coverage, see *Tiroler Tageszeitung*, 4.12.2002 ("Opfer sollen von Streit nicht betroffen sein; Stadt und Land im Bergisel-Clinch").

[139] *Die Presse*, 12.11.2000 ("Bergisel-Drama: Gericht verurteilt Stadt und Land"); *Die Presse*, 20.11.2003 ("Bergisel Drama: Nachspiel für die Republik"); *Die Presse*, 19.11.2003 ("Bergisel-Drama: Millionenklage gegen Republik"); *Tiroler Tageszeitung*, 13.11.2002 ("LH Herwig van Staa will die Haftungsfrage nach dem Bergisel-Drama bis zum Obersten Gerichtshof ausjudizieren"); see also *Der Standard*, 13.11.2002 ("Petra, ein Opfer vom Bergisel, braucht Hilfe").

[140] See also *Tiroler Tageszeitung*, 13.9.2001 ("Bergisel: Stadt droht Klage").

[141] *Regierungsantrag* (*supra* fn. 138), 3; *Tiroler Tageszeitung*, 4.12.2002 ("Opfer sollen von Streit nicht betroffen sein; Stadt und Land im Bergisel-Clinch"); The city of Innsbruck was held liable according to § 1319 of the *Allgemeines Bürgerliches Gesetzbuch* (Austrian Civil Code, ABGB). It states that the owner of a building or a utility is liable to compensate damage to person or property caused by parts of the property collapsing if the owner is not able to prove that he acted with all due care in preventing danger. Therefore the city of Innsbruck, owner of the stadium, can be held liable if it can be proven that it did not apply all due care preventing the danger. In a letter the *Bundespolizeidirektion* (head office of the Federal Police Department) had warned against conducting events at night in the stadium of Bergisel because accidents were prone to happen in light of far too small exits, *Tiroler Tageszeitung*, 6.12.2003 ("Sicherheitschef Falger vom Vorwurf der Gemeingefährdung freigesprochen – Urteil nicht rechtskräftig, Bergisel – Drama nicht vorhersehbar"); *Tiroler Tageszeitung*, 13.9.2001 ("Bergisel: Stadt droht Klage"); *Tiroler Tageszeitung*, 24.6.2000 ("Staatsanwalt plant die Einvernahme von weiteren Zeugen – Ermittlungsende nicht absehbar, Bergisel: Neues Gutachten nötig").

[142] *Regierungsantrag* (*supra* fn. 138), 3; *Die Presse*, 20.11.2003 ("Bergisel Drama: Nachspiel für die Republik"); *Die Presse*, 19.1.2003 ("Bergisel-Drama: Millionenklage gegen Republik").

[143] *Die Presse*, 20.11.2003 ("Bergisel Drama: Nachspiel für die Republik"); *Die Presse*, 19.11.2003 ("Bergisel-Drama: Millionenklage gegen Republik").

Tyrol reached a settlement with the insurance company, agreeing to pay € 1.2 million for that matter under the provision that the insurance company would not claim any compensation from the province and would cover all claims for damages and recourses.[144]

Finally, the insurance company of the organizers of the festival sued the Republic of Austria in November 2003 claiming € 2.7 million (about one third of what they had paid to the victims), stating that the Republic of Austria was also liable according to the *Amtshaftungsgesetz*, in this case because the *Bundespolizeibehörde Innsbruck* (Innsbruck office of the Austrian Federal Police, a federal security body) was partly responsible for deficient safety arrangements with respect to the catastrophe in the Bergisel sports stadium. Furthermore, they claimed that the police officer who was in charge of granting the permit for the festival at the Bergisel stadium was incapable of performing this task properly.[145] The case is still pending, and its outcome is uncertain. 96

The criminal case against the organizers of the snowboard festival was dropped.[146] The head of the security company on duty had been charged with *fahrlässige Gemeingefährdung* (negligently posing danger to the public) but was acquitted by the criminal court.[147] 97

C. Kaprun Ski Train Fire 2000

On 11 November 2000, a Kaprun ski train left the valley station of Kaprun with 180 people on board, entering into the 3.3 km long tunnel leading to the Alpine centre station which is located 2,446 metres above sea level. Having passed 600 metres inside the tunnel the train suddenly stopped. By radio communication the driver of the train notified the valley station that fire had broken out in the train, and it was spreading rapidly to the whole train. The people onboard tried to escape, some by breaking the windows of the compartments to get to the emergency stairways.[148] The majority of the people onboard ran towards the mountain top, were rapidly caught by the cloud of smoke and ultimately died from suffocation. Also, the driver of the second ski train, going down when the first set was going up, was found dead. Even three people working at the mountain station of the ski train were not able to save themselves from the cloud of smoke and also died from suffocation. Only the 12 people who had decided to run downwards were able to escape death. Because of the tremendous clouds of smoke and the heat, the rescue team had not been able to get into the tunnel and extinguish the fire more quickly.[149] 98

[144] For precise conditions of the settlement see *Regierungsantrag* (*supra* fn. 138), 4–5.

[145] *Die Presse*, 20.11.2003 ("Bergisel Drama: Nachspiel für die Republik"); *Die Presse*, 19.11.2003 ("Bergisel-Drama: Millionenklage gegen Republik"); see also *Der Standard*, 28.6.2000 ("Kein Verfahren gegen Air&Style-Veranstalter").

[146] *Die Presse*, 28.6.2000 ("Tod am Bergisel: Kein Prozess").

[147] *Die Presse* 6.12.2003 ("Bergisel Prozess: Freispruch für Sicherheitschef").

[148] *Der Standard*, 13.11.2000 ("Letzte Fahrt des 'Gletscherdrachens'"); *Der Standard*, 20.2.2004 ("Chronologie").

[149] *Der Standard*, 13.11.2000 ("Letzte Fahrt des 'Gletscherdrachens'").

99 The federal government offered instant support to the family members and to the business region around Kaprun. It provided 15 to 20 million Schillings (€ 1.1 million to € 1.5 million) for that purpose.[150] Furthermore, the insurance company of the operator of the ski train agreed to pay 50 million Schillings (€ 3.6 million) as instant help, which means that when the victims gave notice of their damage claims the insurance company would pay for imminent maintenance, funeral costs, transferral costs and down payments.[151] The operator's insurance company announced immediately after the accident that it would waive the applicable deadline of three days for the notification of damage.[152]

100 Sixteen people were charged with *fahrlässige Gemeingefährdung* (negligently posing danger to the public) and *fahrlässige Herbeiführung einer Feuersbrunst* (negligently bringing about conflagration). In February 2004 a criminal court found all of them not guilty.[153] The court held that a manufacturing defect or a defect in the material of the fan heater in the driver's cabin on the end of the train had caused the catastrophe. The heater had caught fire, and as a result the hydraulic line exploded and oil was sprayed into the flames. This was the reason why the flames had spread so quickly.[154] An appeal against this acquittal was unsuccessful.[155] The catastrophe in Kaprun has led to a discussion of whether criminal responsibility for legal entities should be introduced into Austrian law.[156]

101 Moreover, about 92 civil actions involving 243 people against the Gletscherbahnen AG, which is the operator of the ski train, have been brought before the *Landesgericht Salzburg* (Civil Court of the Province of Salzburg). The total sum in dispute is estimated to be about € 9.5 million. The 155 surviving family members of the persons who died in the ski train accident claim pensions, maintenance, other compensatory damages and damages for pain and suffering.[157]

102 The operator has already acknowledged strict liability under the EKHG.[158] Liability under this statute is capped, however, and (at the time) could not exceed € 292,000 lump sum or an annual rent of € 17,520 per individual victim.[159]

[150] *Die Presse*, 1.12.2000 ("Kaprun: Soforthilfe des Bundes").
[151] *Die Presse*, 29.11.2000 ("Kaprun: 50 Millionen Schilling Soforthilfe").
[152] *Der Standard*, 15.11.2000 ("156 und maximal 160 Todesopfer – Seilbahnbetreibern drohen Millionenklagen, Anwälte wollen Betreiber in den USA klagen").
[153] This was appealed by the public prosecutor in September 2004 with respect to eight of the accused.
[154] *Der Standard*, 20.2.2004 ("Kaprun: Katastrophe ohne Schuldige").
[155] *Der Standard*, 21.2.2004 ("Prozesslawine nach den Freisprüchen").
[156] *Der Standard*, 21.2.2004 ("Kollektive Straftäter").
[157] *Der Standard*, 19.2.2004 ("Gerichte noch lange beschäftigt"); *Der Standard*, 25.2.2004 ("Kaprun – Zivilverfahren sind ruhend gestellt"); *Der Standard* 21.2.2004 ("Prozesslawine nach den Freisprüchen"); see further *Salzburger Nachrichten*, 13.11.2003 ("Millionen-Klagen") stating that the sum in dispute in each claim is between € 10,500 and € 263,000.
[158] See *supra* no. 8.
[159] For current amounts, which have been increased substantially recently, see *supra* no. 11.

The operator is insured against third party risks; the limit of indemnity being 320 million Schillings (€ 23.3 million).[160] To date the operator's insurance company has already paid out € 4.5 million for damages resulting from the ski train accident. This includes funeral costs, travelling costs for those wanting to participate at the funeral of their relatives, mourning clothes, and property damage.[161] Furthermore, the insurance company has made maintenance and annuity payments of € 16 million.[162] 103

The operator and its insurance company agreed to pay € 7,267 in compensation for pain and suffering to each family member. A total of € 460,000 has already been paid to the 60 family members of 32 victims of the ski train fire.[163] Many family members of the deceased are claiming between € 22,000 and € 36,000 in compensation for pain and suffering, declaring that the afore-mentioned sum of € 7,267 was inadequately low. The operator has rejected those claims as being too excessive.[164] 104

On 25 February 2004, the Federal Minister of Justice instituted an *ad hoc* compensation board which shall endeavour to mediate or settle the claims in a comprehensive manner. While it is already deplorable that the Minister thereby effectively intervened in pending court cases, it is entirely unacceptable that the task of this commission has been expressly defined as "to try to help the bereaved irrespective of existing substantive or procedural law".[165] The only possible explanation for such a (hopefully unique) measure can be found in the Minister's strive to gain positive media attention. 105

A class action against several companies involved in the production, maintenance and operation of the train is pending before the Southern District of New York, not only on behalf of American victims, but also including plaintiffs of other nationalities (in a strive for forum – or windfall profit compensation – shopping). The judge there has already announced obiter that she will apply Austrian tort law to this case.[166] 106

More than 2 million Schillings (€ 145,345) of charitable donations were given to the relatives of those deceased in the ski train fire. A commission in charge with the distribution of these monies was formed.[167] 107

160 *Der Standard*, 16.12.2000 ("Generali blickt auf ein schadensreiches Jahr").

161 *Der Standard*, 8.11.2003 ("Angehörige klagen auf Schadenersatz"); *Der Standard*, 29.8.2003 ("Frist für Angehörige läuft ab"); *Salzburger Nachrichten*, 22.12.2000 ("Erstes Geld für Opfer").

162 *Salzburger Nachrichten*, 13.6.2002 ("4,4 Mill. Euro für Angehörige – Aktenstau bei Behörde").

163 *Salzburger Nachrichten*, 13.6.2002 ("4,4 Mill. Euro für Angehörige – Aktenstau bei der Behörde").

164 *Der Standard*, 6.2.2004 ("Flut an Schadenersatzklagen"); *Salzburger Nachrichten*, 8.11.2003 ("Tragödie Kaprun: Klagsflut").

165 <Http://www.justiz.gv.at/service/content.php?nav=65&id=214>.

166 *In re Ski Train Fire in Kaprun, Austria, on November 11, 2000*, 230 F.Supp.2d 376, 388 (S.D.N.Y. 2002).

167 *Salzburger Nachrichten*, 4.1.2001 ("2 Mill. S gespendet"), those 2 million Schillings of donation money also included US $ 30,000 donated by the Coca Cola Company.

Part IV. Conclusions

108 Compensation for catastrophes in Austria depends upon the source of the harm, in particular on whether it is man-made or a natural disaster. In any case, however, the picture will show an overlap of several layers of funding:

109 In particular, the quite efficient and still working system of social security will invariably step in first in all cases of bodily injury or death and thereby absorb the most pressing needs of the victims (though limited to those insured, which, for example, did not apply to many victims of the Kaprun fire). Only as a second step will the social security carrier pursue a recourse action against a third party if liable.

110 In case of large-scale losses, particularly in case of natural disasters, the state will also step in and offer *ad hoc* help, though at least in part institutionalized by the *Katastrophenfonds* system to the extent applicable. Indirect help may be offered by way of tax benefits.

111 The third layer will be funded by private insurers who have to contribute on the basis of first-party or third-party insurance.

112 Tort law may step in immediately, but very often only upon subrogation of the claim, as mentioned. While fault liability may be preferential to victims as far as the amount of possible compensation is concerned, strict liability regimes may prove easier to pursue, though often limited by statutory caps which can be particularly restrictive in case of multi-victim losses.

113 Additional help may come from charitable funds, which are not meant to compensate, but nevertheless very often fill certain gaps left by the other layers. Austria has a very impressive (in particular recent) history of private donations by individuals in campaigns launched after catastrophes in the past, so the availability of such funds is by no means extraordinary or exceptional. There is of course no legal claim for such support.

114 All in all, this multi-layer system seems to be workable to a large extent. So far, the media are not (yet) calling for an alternative, more victim-friendly system, which is at least some indication for public sentiment in this respect. However, the amounts of compensation, in particular non-pecuniary loss for surviving relatives, has been a hot topic in the tabloids after Kaprun (though, surprisingly, no one took notice of the outrageous German award to the daughter of Princess Caroline for the mere publication of her photograph).[168]

115 However, catastrophes quite often trigger *ad hoc* legislation, which per se is not always desirable. On the other hand, disasters are singular events, so that

[168] The German *Bundesgerichtshof* has recently confirmed an award exceeding € 76,000 in compensation for the publication of private picture of the five-year old daughter of princess Caroline of Monaco (VI ZR 255/03).

certain tailor-made rules regulating compensation in this specific case may even be helpful. Some of the catastrophes mentioned have at least led to rather significant legislative changes, which were long overdue: The Kaprun accident, for example, will most likely lead to the introduction of criminal liability for legal persons, and as far as tort law is concerned, it has finally led the way to a substantial increase of the caps of the EKHG.[169]

Even though catastrophes are just that, in particular for their victims, the question whether or not (and if so, to what extent) the public at large should contribute to make the losses good cannot be solved easily, as the answer thereto has to be a compromise between the principle *casum sentit dominus* on the one hand and social welfare and solidarity on the other. 116

It is not even easy in cases where the loss can be shifted to a person liable under tort law, as the latter may be unable to pay full or at least partial compensation, which is quite likely in catastrophes, so that the remainder still effectively lies with the victim. 117

There seems to be no obvious concept that might resolve this Gordian knot, as a stroke with the sword of an all-encompassing compensation fund is neither affordable nor necessarily desirable to society. 118

List of References

Information by the Federal or Provincial Government or Other Authorities

Amt der Niederösterreichischen Landesregierung (ed.), *Richtlinie für die Förderung der Behebung von Katastrophenschäden*, <http://www.noel.gv.at/service/LF/LF3/Katastrophen.htm>.

Amt der Salzburger Landesregierung (ed.), *Richtlinien für die Gewährung einer finanziellen Beihilfe des Landes zur Behebung von Katastrophenschäden im Vermögen natürlicher und juristischer Personen mit Ausnahme von Gebietskörperschaften*, <http://www.salzburg.gv.at/themen/lf/foerderungen_lf/foerderung_katfonds.htm>.

Amt der Oberösterreichischen Landesregierung (ed.), *Richtlinie für die Vergabe von Elementarschadensbeihilfen (Katastrophenfondsgesetz 1996)*, <http://www.ooe.gv.at/formulare/Katastrophen/Richtlin_Katfonds.pdf>.

Amt der Steiermärkischen Landesregierung (ed.), *Richtlinien betreffend Katastrophenschäden im Vermögen physischer und juristischer Personen,* <http://wwww.agrar.steiermark.at/cms/dokumente/10032540/4978797b/schadr.pdf>.

Amt der Vorarlberger Landesregierung (ed.), *Richtlinien für die Gewährung von Beihilfen zur Behebung von Elementarschäden,* <http://www.vorarlberg.at/doc/richtlinieelementarschade.doc>.

Bundesministerium für Justiz (ed.), *Vom Hochwasser betroffen – was nun, So kommen Sie zu Ihrem Recht* (3rd edn. 2002, available online at <http://www.bmj.gv.at>).

Bundesministerium für Soziale Sicherheit, Generationen und Konsumentenschutz (ed.), *Social Protection Systems in Austria* (2003, available online at <http://www.

[169] Compare *supra* no. 11 with no. 102.

bmsg.gv.at/cms/site/attachments/6/5/0/CH0339/CMS1064306288445/sozialschutz-systemengl.pdf>).
Hauptverband der österr Sozialversicherungsträger (ed.), *Die österreichische Sozialversicherung in Zahlen* (14th edn. 2004).

Literature

R. Beiser, Außergewöhnliche Belastungen für Hochwasseropfer, Anmerkungen zum geplanten Ausbau der außergewöhnlichen Belastungen iSd § 34 EStG, [2002] SWK, 719.
G. Gaedke, Aufwendungen zur Beseitigung von Katastrophenschäden, Zur Neuregelung des § 34 Abs. 6 EStG 1988, Wirtschaftsgüter im Privatvermögen, [2002] SWK, 689.
K. Grillberger, *Österreichisches Sozialrecht* (5th edn. 2001).
K. Hilber, Hochwasserhilfe im Steuerrecht durch das HWG 2002, [2002] *ecolex*, 792.
W. Holzer, The Interaction of Tort Law and Social Security under Austrian Law, in: U. Magnus (ed.), *Tort Law and Social Law* (2003), 7.
B.A. Koch/H. Koziol, Schadenersatz für Körperverletzung in Österreich, in: B.A. Koch/H. Koziol (eds.), *Compensation for Personal Injury in a Comparative Perspective* (2003), 4.
B.A. Koch/H. Koziol, Austria, in: B.A. Koch/H. Koziol (eds.), *Unification of Tort Law: Strict Liability* (2002), 9.
H. Mayer, Amtshaftung für Hochwasser, [2002] *ecolex*, 797.
W. Posch, Multikausale Schäden in modernen Haftungsrechten, in: A. Fenyves/H. Weyers (eds.), *Multikausale Schäden in modernen Haftungsrechten* (1988), 173.
B. Renner, Abzugsfähige und nicht abzugsfähige Spenden aus Sicht der Gesetzes- und der Verwaltungspraxis, Zum Jahresende: Reduzierung der Steuerlast durch "noble Gesten"?, Spenden im Ertragssteuerrecht, [2002] SWK, 790.
A. Schellner, Steuerliche Behandlung von Aufwendungen für Katastrophenschäden und Absetzbarkeit von Spenden an Hochwassergeschädigte, [2002] VWT H 5, 22.

Belgium

Isabelle C. Durant

Part I. Introduction

This report comes within the scope of a general research project about financial compensation provided to victims of catastrophes. Under catastrophes, one has to understand misfortunes or serious accidents which affect a large number of persons *at the same time*. These catastrophes have their origin in a natural and spontaneous phenomenon, like a storm or an earthquake, or in a human activity, like the explosion of a factory or arson. Moreover it is sometimes difficult to rank the damaging event among one of these categories. It is namely the case when the damage is the direct consequence of a natural phenomenon but also at the same time the indirect consequence of a policy concerning regional development. It can also be the case when a forest fire is the consequence of the throwing of a cigarette butt in an exceptionally dry environment. 1

According to the Anglo-Saxon terminology, one could say that the present report concerns certain types of mass torts, namely situations in which one single event makes many victims at the same time, but also situations in which the damage is the consequence of the presence of toxic products which are at a particular place (where they were buried, thrown or stored). This reference to the idea of mass torts leads nevertheless to two remarks. On the one hand, all kinds of mass torts will not be examined. For example, situations in which a lot of people suffer after having taken or inhaled the same product do not fall within the scope of this paper.[1] In these situations, most of the time, harm is not caused *at the same time* to all victims. On the other hand, some situations will be examined which are generally not always described as constituting mass torts. It is namely the case of natural phenomena which arrive suddenly, like earthquakes.

Do the victims of catastrophes receive compensation? In which way and to what extent do they obtain it? This paper is devoted to these questions.

[1] We are thinking about the Dutch case concerning DES or about the cases concerning asbestos.

Part II. Method

2 As far as possible the above mentioned questions will be answered by means of the questionnaire drawn up by Prof. Dr. T. Hartlief and Prof. Dr. M. Faure.

Part III. General Scope of the Compensation System

I. Patchwork of Regulations

3 In Belgium, there is no general legislation which would be applicable specifically in cases of catastrophes and which would grant to victims full compensation. Nevertheless this does not mean that victims will not receive any compensation.

Indeed, compensation for damage can be obtained totally or partially by means of several mechanisms. These mechanisms can be cumulated:

- tort law (fault based liability and strict liability);
- insurance law (liability insurance but also others);
- various branches of the social security system;
- solidarity which is expressed notably by means of financial interventions of the Belgian State (for example through the setting up of national funds supplied by the taxpayers), of the Regions or of other persons.

One can speak about a patchwork of means. However, despite the increase of compensation mechanisms, it is not yet certain that victims will receive compensation or that they will receive full compensation. Under each of these mechanisms, various conditions have to be met. In principle, concerning the fulfilment of these conditions, the burden of proof lies upon the victim's shoulders. Moreover, the procedures usually take a long time.

The note drawn up by Prof. H. Claassens after the industrial catastrophe of Ghislenghien[2] illustrates clearly this introductory settlement. In his note concerning compensation of the victims, he refers to mutual insurance, to liability insurance, to car insurance, to fire insurance, to employer's liability insurance, to life insurance, to insurance for loss of profits, to bodily accident insurance, to hospitalization insurance, etc.[3]

We can say that quite often, victims of catastrophes experience not only pain and suffering but also financial problems.

II. First Overall Survey of the Various Rules

A. Tort Law

4 Victims of catastrophes can found their claim on tort law with the aim of obtaining compensation. Tort law tends to compensate damage indeed, at least to compensate some damage, namely that which is causally linked with the dam-

[2] About this catastrophe, see *infra* no. 10.

[3] H. Claassens, Schadevergoeding voor slachtoffers bij gasramp te Gellingen-Ghislenghien – 30.7.2004. Enkele praktische tips inzake verzekeringen, published at <http://www.brandwonden.be/ghislenghien/20040811-Stichting-Gellingen-Fr.pdf>.

aging event. Belgian tort law remains individualistic, which means that each victim has to sue the tortfeasor separately. There is no class action under Belgian tort law.

Tort law has become one of the most commonly used mechanisms to obtain compensation due to the development of liability insurance.

Providing that conditions for obtaining compensation are fulfilled, tort liability remains an adequate mechanism considering that it should lead to full compensation. However, the legislator departed from the principle of full compensation in some acts which introduced strict liability. Both of the following techniques are generally used: Either the legislator provided for a maximum compensation (limitation of the amount) – this is namely the case in the Act of 9 August 1963 concerning the liability of the operator of atomic ships,[4] in the Act of 22 July 1985 concerning nuclear energy (art. 7 and 19)[5] and in the Act of 30 July 1979 concerning the prevention of fire (art. 8)[6] – or the legislator arranged for a limitation of the heads of damage which may be compensated – this is namely the case in the above mentioned Act of 30 July 1979 which excludes compensation for moral damage (art. 8) or in the Convention on damage caused by foreign aircraft to third parties on the surface signed in Rome on 7 October 1952 which leaves away indirect damage (art. 1, 1).[7] 5

B. Insurance Law

Insurance law obviously plays a considerable role in obtaining compensation. This role is played in two ways. 6

On the one hand, there are situations in which the potential victim subscribes to insurance contracts on his/her own account. This can be the case when a fire insurance policy is taken out. 7

In this case, a real estate is for example covered against risks such as damage or destruction due to fire or connected perils (lightning, explosion, implo-

[4] Art. 2 of the Act of 9 August 1963 concerning the liability of the operator of atomic ships (*Belgian Official Journal* of 8 October 1963).

[5] According to art. 7 of the Act of 22 July 1985 concerning legal liability in the field of nuclear energy, as modified by art. 3 of the Act of 11 July 2000 (*Belgian Official Journal* of 4 October 2000): "Het maximale schadebedrag waarover de exploitant aansprakelijk is, bedraagt voor ieder kernongeval 12 miljard frank" (€ 300,000,000). Nevertheless, the amount of the compensation which is allowed to victims may exceed the amount of BEF 12 billion. The Belgian State and the other signatory countries intervene once the maximum ceiling of BEF 12 billion is reached. One can speak about international solidarity (*Parl. Doc.*, Kamer, doc. 50-0560/002, 6).

[6] Concerning this Act of 30 July 1979, cf. *infra* no. 8.

[7] Art. 1: "Any person who suffers damage on the surface shall, upon proof only that the damage was caused by an aircraft in flight or by any person or thing falling therefrom, be entitled to compensation as provided by this Convention. Nevertheless there shall be no right to compensation if the damage is not a direct consequence of the incident giving rise thereto, or if the damage results from the mere fact of passage of the aircraft through the airspace in conformity with existing air traffic regulations".
In Belgium, this international convention was ratified by an Act dated 14 July 1966 (*Belgian Official Journal* of 27 September 1966).

sion, fall of planes, etc.).[8] The fire insurance contract must compulsorily cover the consequences of fire, explosion or implosion which are caused by some kinds of attacks (for example, terrorist attack) or by industrial disputes.[9] Since 1995,[10] the risk against *storm* (including hail, ice pressure and snow pres-

[8] Fire insurance is regulated by the Act of 25 June 1992 on terrestrial insurance contracts, by the decrees providing the enforcement of this Act, and by the Royal Decree of 24 December 1992 concerning fire insurance and insurance against other dangers (*Belgian Official Journal* of 31 December 1992). Fire insurance, which is non life indemnity insurance, covers material losses.

[9] Art. 3, section 1 of the Royal Decree of 24 December 1992 concerning fire insurance contracts (*Belgian Official Journal* of 31 December 1992).

[10] Royal Decree of 16 January 1995 amending art. 3, section 1 of the Royal Decree of 24 December 1992 concerning fire insurance contracts (*Belgian Official Journal* of 11 April 1995). The appendix of the Royal Decree of 24 December 1992, as modified by art. 2 of the Royal Decree of 16 January 1995 gives a definition of the storm:
"Onder storm verstaat men de orkanen of andere stormwinden, die:

* binnen een straal van 10 km rond het aangeduide gebouw vernieling, breuk of beschadiging veroorzaken aan:
  - hetzij tegen deze winden verzekerbare constructies,
  - hetzij andere goederen die aan die winden een weerstand bieden gelijkwaardig aan de weerstand van de verzekerbare goederen;

of

* op het dichtst bijgelegen waarnemingsstation van het Koninklijk Meteorologisch Instituut een topsnelheid van minstens 100 km per uur bereiken".

According to art. 3, section 1, subsection 2 of the Royal Decree, the covering of some damage may be excluded, as damage caused:

- "aan de inhoud, die zich bevindt in een constructie, die niet vooraf beschadigd werd door storm, hagel, sneeuw- of ijsdruk;
- aan elk voorwerp dat zich buiten een constructie bevindt;
- aan constructies en hun eventuele inhoud die gemakkelijk verplaatsbaar of uiteen te nemen zijn of die bouwvallig zijn of afgebroken worden;
- aan alle ruiten, met inbegrip van spiegelglas en doorschijnend onroerend plastiek materiaal;
- aan alle afsluitingen en omheiningen van om 't even welke aard;
- aan de volgende goederen en hun eventuele inhoud:
  1. constructies waarvan de buitenmuren voor meer dan 50% van hun totale oppervlakte samengesteld zijn uit plaatijzer, asbest en cementagglomeraten, gegolfde platen en lichte materialen zoals onder meer hout, plastiek, spaanplaten en dergelijke;
  2. constructies waarvan de dakbedekking voor meer dan 20% van haar totale oppervlakte samengesteld is uit hout, spaanplaten of dergelijke, asfaltpapier, plastiekmateriaal en andere lichte materialen, uitgezonderd echter kunstleien, kunstdakpannen, riet en roofing. Als licht materiaal wordt beschouwd, elk materiaal waarvan het gewicht per m^2 lager is dan 6 kg;
  3. constructies die, geheel of gedeeltelijk, open zijn;
  4. constructies die in opbouw zijn, worden niet beschouwd als in opbouw:
     - constructies in verbouwing of herstelling, mits zij bewoond blijven tijdens deze werkzaamheden;
     - constructies in opbouw, verbouwing of herstelling, die definitief zijn uitgesloten met afgewerkte en definitief geplaatste deuren en ramen, en definitief en volledig gedekt zijn;
  5. torens, klokkentorens, uitkijktorens, watertorens, windmolens, windmotors, openluchttribunes, vergaarbakken in open lucht;
  6. voorwerpen en materialen die buiten aan een constructie zijn vastgemaakt zoals onder meer: antenne, metalen schoorsteen, verlichtingsinstallatie en -toestel, reclamebord, uithangbord, rolgordijn, zonnetent, buitenbekleding van muren door op latten vastgemaakt materiaal, met uitzondering van de schade aan dak- en hanggoten en hun afvoerbuizen, aan kroonlijsten met hun bekleding alsmede aan rolluiken;
- door terugvloeien of overlopen van water, lek in leidingen of riolering".

sure)[11] is compulsorily included in fire insurance policies, at least concerning real estate for which the insured amount does not exceed approx. € 0.75 million.[12] Since 2004, the insurer and the insured may agree on an excess.[13]

On the other hand, there are situations in which the insured risk consists in tort liability. Moreover, in such situations, the taking out of an insurance policy is sometimes compulsory. The obligation to sign liability insurance is not rare, especially in cases of strict liability. Some examples can be given. 8

1. Federal Legislation

1° The Act of 30 July 1979 concerning the prevention of fire and explosion in public buildings and concerning compulsory insurance of civil liability in such cases.[14]

This Act, which was voted after a dramatic accident had occurred in a disco, imposes a strict liability for any bodily and material damage to third parties caused by fire and explosion in buildings which are usually open to the public. The operators of these buildings can be held strictly liable. The liability insurance is compulsory. The Royal Decrees providing the conditions of application of this Act were adopted and published nearly twelve years later (!).

One of these Royal Decrees aims at the setting of categories of buildings which fall within the scope of the Act.[15] The following categories are notably mentioned: discos, restaurants, bars, hotels, retail traders, cinemas, theatres, sport halls, hospitals, schools and courts.[16]

This strict liability is limited to a maximum amount by another Royal Decree.[17] Per event, the liability is limited to a maximum of Belgian francs (BEF) 600 million (approx. € 15 million) for bodily damage and to a maximum of BEF 30 million (approx. € 0.75 million) for material damage.[18] These amounts follow the consumer price index.[19] At the end of the year

[11] Art. 1, section 1 and art. 4, section 1 of the Royal Decree of 24 December 1992 concerning fire insurance contracts.

[12] One speaks about "ordinary risks" (*risques simples/eenvoudige risico's*). The definition of "ordinary risks" is laid down in art. 5 of the Royal Decree of 24 December 1992 concerning the enforcement of the Act of 25 June 1992 (*Belgian Official Journal* of 31 December 1992). The amount of BEF 30,000,000 (approx. € 743,680) is raised to BEF 965,000,000 (approx. € 24 million) considering some kinds of buildings (blocks of flats, musical conservatories, libraries, hospitals, old people's homes, etc.).

[13] Art. 6, section 1 of the Royal Decree of 24 December 1992 concerning fire insurance contracts as amended by art. 1 of the Royal Decree of 4 July 2004 (*Belgian Official Journal* of 22 July 2004, 2nd edn.).

[14] *Belgian Official Journal* of 20 September 1979.

[15] Royal Decree of 28 February 1991, *Belgian Official Journal* of 13 April 1991.

[16] According to Prof. H. Claassens, the Act of 30 July 1979 would not be applicable to owners or operators of pipelines and other underground pipes (<http://www.brandwonden.be/ghislenghien/20040811-Stichting-Gellingen-Fr.pdf>). Consequently, this Act would not be applicable to the catastrophe that happened in the industrial park of Ghislenghien on 30 July 2004 (concerning this catastrophe, see *infra* no. 10).

[17] Royal Decree of 5 August 1991, *Belgian Official Journal* of 30 August 1991.

[18] Art. 1 of the Royal Decree of 5 August 1991.

[19] Art. 14 of the Royal Decree of 5 August 1991.

2002, both amounts rose to € 18,303,531.74 and € 918,176.59.[20] According to one author, the existence of a limitation can postpone the effective compensation.[21] The definitive damage of each victim has first to be set, then, the total amount of the whole damage can be evaluated and finally the liquid assets are divided between victims (proportionally to the extent of their damage). Those who are liable for the damaging event, according to the fundamental principles governing liability in Belgian tort law (art. 1382 *et seq.* of the Civil Code), do not benefit from the regulation and may not claim any compensation.[22]

2° Compulsory liability insurance for activities consisting in the destruction, neutralization or treatment of toxic waste.[23]

3° Compulsory liability insurance (or other financial guarantees) in the field of nuclear energy resting with the operator.[24]

4° Compulsory liability insurance (or other financial guarantees) in the field of marine oil pollution resting with the oil tanker's owner.[25]

2. Flemish Legislation

1° Compulsory insurance in the field of the collecting and transporting of waste.[26]

[20] H. Claassens, La responsabilité objective et l'assurance obligatoire en cas d'incendie ou d'explosion frappant des établissements habituellement accessibles au public, in: *Mélanges offerts à Marcel Fontaine* (2003), 613, fn. 22.

[21] Ph. Colle, *Handboek bijzonder gereglementeerde verzekeringscontracten* (2001), 59, no. 110.

[22] Art. 4 of the Royal Decree of 5 August 1991.

[23] Art. 6 of the Royal Decree of 9 February 1976 concerning the general regulation of toxic waste (*Belgian Official Journal* of 14 February 1976).

[24] Art. 8 of the Act of 22 July 1985 concerning legal liability in the field of nuclear energy.

[25] Act of 20 July 1976 ratifying the International Convention on Civil Liability for oil pollution damage, agreed upon in Brussels, 29 November 1969, and the Act of 10 August 1998 ratifying the Protocol of 1992 to amend the International Convention on Civil Liability for oil pollution damage, 1969, agreed upon in London, 19 November 1992.

[26] Art. 5.1.2.2. *Vlaams Reglement voor Afvalvoorkoming en Beheer* (Flemish Regulation for Waste Prevention and Management, Vlarea, which implements several provisions of the Waste Decree):
"Om als ophaler erkend te kunnen worden dient voldaan te worden aan de volgende vereisten:
1. natuurlijke personen:
   a. de burgerlijke en politieke rechten bezitten;
   b. de laatste acht jaar voorafgaand aan de aanvraag, geen effectieve strafrechtelijke veroordeling hebben opgelopen voor een inbreuk op de wetgeving op het vlak van milieuhygiëne in België noch, wanneer het een persoon betreft die niet van Belgische nationaliteit is, in de staat waarvan hij of zij onderdaan is;
   c. nuttige kennis en/of ervaring kunnen aantonen met betrekking tot de ophaling van afvalstoffen waarvoor de erkenning wordt aangevraagd;
   d. zich ertoe verbinden een verzekeringscontract af te sluiten ter dekking van de schade die kan voortvloeien uit de voorgenomen ophaalactiviteiten;
2. rechtspersonen:
   a. opgericht zijn conform de Belgische vennootschapswetgeving of de overeenstemmende wetgeving van een andere EU-lidstaat, met maatschappelijke zetel binnen de EU;

2° Compulsory insurance in the field of treatment of wrecks or obsolete vehicles.[27]

b. de natuurlijke personen, die de vennootschap kunnen verbinden, dienen hun burgerlijke en politieke rechten te bezitten;
c. de natuurlijke personen, die de vennootschap kunnen verbinden, mogen, de laatste acht jaar voorafgaand aan de aanvraag, geen effectieve strafrechtelijke veroordeling hebben opgelopen voor een inbreuk op de wetgeving op het vlak van milieuhygiëne in België noch, wanneer het personen betreft die niet van Belgische nationaliteit zijn, in de staat waarvan zij onderdaan zijn;
d. ten minste één lid van het orgaan of één natuurlijke persoon die de vennootschap kan verbinden, dient nuttige kennis en/of ervaring te kunnen aantonen met betrekking de ophaling van afvalstoffen waarvoor de erkenning wordt aangevraagd;
e. zich ertoe verbinden een verzekeringscontract af te sluiten ter dekking van de schade die kan voortvloeien uit de voorgenomen ophaal activiteiten".

[27] Art. 5.5.4.4.:
"Om als centrum erkend te kunnen worden dient voldaan te worden aan de volgende vereisten:
1. natuurlijke personen:
a. de burgerlijke en politieke rechten bezitten;
b. de laatste acht jaar voorafgaand aan de aanvraag, geen effectieve strafrechtelijke veroordeling hebben opgelopen voor een inbreuk op de wetgeving op het vlak van milieuhygiëne in België noch, wanneer het een persoon betreft die niet van Belgische nationaliteit is, in de staat waarvan hij of zij onderdaan is;
c. een inrichting uitbaten of beroep doen op een vergunde inrichting, vergund overeenkomstig het decreet van 28 juni 1985 betreffende de milieuvergunning, voor de opslag en mechanische behandeling van voertuigwrakken, die bovendien moet voldoen aan de code van goede praktijk;
d. nuttige kennis en/of ervaring kunnen aantonen met betrekking tot de verwerking van afgedankte voertuigen;
e. zich ertoe verbinden een verzekeringscontract af te sluiten ter dekking van milieu en andere schade die kan voortvloeien uit de bedrijfsactiviteiten;
f. zich ertoe verbinden bij een financiële instelling een bankgarantie te stellen in functie van de geraamde kosten van een ambtshalve verwijdering van de afgedankte voertuigen;
2. rechtspersonen:
a. opgericht zijn overeenkomstig de Belgische vennootschapswetgeving of de overeenstemmende wetgeving van een andere EU-lidstaat, met maatschappelijke zetel binnen de EU;
b. de natuurlijke personen, die de vennootschap kunnen verbinden, dienen hun burgerlijke en politieke rechten te bezitten;
c. een inrichting uitbaten of beroep doen op een vergunde inrichting, vergund overeenkomstig het decreet van 28 juni 1985 betreffende de milieuvergunning, voor de opslag en behandeling van voertuigwrakken die bovendien moet voldoen aan de code van goede praktijk;
d. de natuurlijke personen, die de vennootschap kunnen verbinden, mogen, de laatste acht jaar voorafgaand aan de aanvraag, geen effectieve strafrechtelijke veroordeling hebben opgelopen voor een inbreuk op de wetgeving op het vlak van milieuhygiëne in België noch, wanneer het personen betreft die niet van Belgische nationaliteit zijn, in de staat waarvan zij onderdaan zijn;
e. ten minste één lid van het orgaan of één natuurlijke persoon die de vennootschap kan verbinden, dient nuttige kennis en/of ervaring te kunnen aantonen met betrekking tot de verwerking van afgedankte voertuigen;
f. zich ertoe verbinden een verzekeringscontract af te sluiten ter dekking van milieu- en andere schade die kan voortvloeien uit de bedrijfsactiviteiten;
g. zich ertoe verbinden bij een financiële instelling een bankgarantie te stellen in functie van de geraamde kosten van een ambtshalve verwijdering van de afgedankte voertuigen".

3° Insurance or bank guarantee for costs of transporting, eliminating or treatment of waste resting with exporters or importers of waste.[28]

4° Compulsory liability insurance resting with operators of plants in the field of treatment of waste.[29]

5° Insurance or guarantee resting with operators of warehouses.[30]

6° Compulsory liability insurance relying on producers of lacquers, paintings, print inks, colours, pigments.[31]

7° Compulsory liability insurance resting with operators using covering products (paints, lacquers, inks, powders, etc.).[32]

8° Compulsory liability insurance relying on operators in the field of thermal treatment of things covered with special kinds of covering products (paints, lacquers, inks, powders, etc.).[33]

3. Brussels Legislation

1° Compulsory insurance in the field of the collecting, transporting and treatment of waste.[34]

2° Compulsory insurance in the field of treatment of obsolete vehicles.[35]

3° Compulsory insurance or banking guarantee concerning importers and exporters of waste.[36]

[28] Art. 6.5. Vlarea.

[29] Art. 5.2.1.8. § 2 *Vlaams Reglement op de Milieuvergunningen* II (Flemish Regulation on the Environmental License, Vlarem): "De exploitant is er toe gehouden een voldoende verzekering aan te gaan inzake burgerlijke aansprakelijkheid".

[30] Art. 5.2.4.7.1. § 2 Vlarem II: "De financiële zekerheden kunnen de volgende aannemen, afzonderlijk of in combinatie:
- een verzekering;
- een garantie van een financiële zekerheid;
- een andere persoonlijke of zakelijke zekerheid".

[31] Art. 5.4.2.3*bis* § 3 Vlarem II: "De exploitant is er toe gehouden een voldoende zekerheid inzake burgerlijke aansprakelijkheid aan te gaan".

[32] Art. 5.4.3.4. § 6 Vlarem II: "De exploitant is er toe gehouden een voldoende zekerheid inzake burgerlijke aansprakelijkheid aan te gaan".

[33] Art. 5.4.4.2. § 8 Vlarem II: "De exploitant is er toe gehouden een voldoende zekerheid inzake burgerlijke aansprakelijkheid aan te gaan".

[34] Art. 13 of the Brussels Order of 7 March 1991.

[35] Art. 14, section 3 of the Decree of the Government of the Brussels Region of 6 September 2001 concerning operators managing centres in the field of obsolete vehicles ("Besluit van 6 september 2001 van de Brussels Hoofdstedelijke Regering betreffende de erkenning van de exploitanten van verwijderingscentra voor afgedankte voertuigen die ertoe gemachtigd zijn een vernietigingsattest af te geven en betreffende de exploitatievoorwaarden van die centra").

[36] Art. 5 of the Decree of the Government of the Brussels Region of 7 July 1994 concerning international import and export of waste. The insurance or guarantee has to cover the costs of transporting or disposal according to art. 27 of the Council Regulation (EEC) no. 259/93 of 1 February 1993 on the supervision and control of shipments of waste within, into and out of the European Community.

4° Compulsory liability insurance in the field of Polychlorobiphenyls (PCBs) disposal.[37]

5° Compulsory liability insurance in the field of oil waste disposal.[38]

6° Compulsory liability insurance in the field of dangerous waste disposal.[39]

7° Compulsory insurance in the field of waste packing.[40]

4. Walloon Legislation

1° Compulsory guarantee of equivalent insurance in the field of import or export of waste.[41]

2° Compulsory liability insurance resting with operators of warehouses.[42]

3° Compulsory insurance in the field of waste packing.[43]

4° Compulsory liability insurance resting with operators in the field of toxic and dangerous waste.[44]

5° Compulsory liability insurance in the field of the collecting and transport of toxic and dangerous waste.[45]

6° Compulsory liability insurance resting with operators in the field of the collecting and transport of used oil.[46]

C. *Social Security*

In addition to tort law and insurance law, the social insurance system plays an important role for the compensation of victims. According to some authors, one could say that the health insurance (a branch of the social insurance sys- 9

[37] Art. 7 of the Decree of the Government of the Brussels Region of 19 September 1991 concerning the disposal of PCBs.

[38] Art. 9 of the Decree of the Government of the Brussels Region of 19 September 1991 concerning the disposal of oil waste.

[39] Art. 11 of the Decree of the Government of the Brussels Region of 19 September 1991 concerning the disposal of dangerous waste.

[40] Art. 12 of the Cooperation Agreement of 30 May 1996 ("Samenwerkingsakkoord van 30 mei 1996 betreffende de preventie en het beheer van verpakkingsafval, goedgekeurd bij Ordonnantie d.d. 30 januari 1997").

[41] Art. 8 of the Decree of the Government of the Walloon Region of 9 June 1944 implementing the Council Regulation (EEC) no. 259/93 of 1 February 1993 on the supervision and control of shipments of waste within, into and out of the European Community.

[42] Art. 4, 28 and 29 of the Decree of the Government of the Walloon Region of 23 July 1987 concerning warehouses.

[43] Art. 12 of the Cooperation Agreement of 30 May 1996 ("Samenwerkingsakkoord van 30 mei 1996 betreffende de preventie en het beheer van verpakkingsafval, goedgekeurd bij Decreet d.d. 16 januari 1997").

[44] Art. 9 and 47 of the Decree of the Government of the Walloon Region of 9 April 1992 concerning toxic and dangerous waste.

[45] Art. 32 of the Decree of the Government of the Walloon Region of 9 April 1992 concerning toxic and dangerous waste.

[46] Art. 8–10 of the Decree of the Government of the Walloon Region of 9 April 1992 concerning used oils.

tem) is the common legal means concerning compensation of victims.[47] This mechanism plays a role in all cases, regardless of the existence of an opponent who could have committed a tort or not. Nevertheless, the social security system does not offer any complete compensation contrary to tort law.[48]

D. Solidarity

10 Finally, compensation can also result from solidarity. This solidarity can take various forms.

The most common means of expression of national solidarity is the creation of funds, which are supplied by taxpayers, at least indirectly. Two examples can be given here, applicable in case of the occurrence of a catastrophe. First, the Act dated 12 July 1976 concerning the repair of damage caused to private personal properties or private real estate as a result of natural disasters.[49] This Act is based on the principle of national solidarity towards victims of natural catastrophes. Under certain conditions, the fund for victims of disasters intervenes in favour of these victims.[50] The same principle lies at the basis of the Act dated 12 July 1939 which set up a compensation fund in favour of the victims of mining activities. This fund intervenes in case of insolvency of the one who is liable.

Recently, another means of expression of solidarity has been used, probably for the first time. On 30 July 2004, an accident occurred in the industrial park of Ghislenghien. A pipeline transporting gas from Norway to France exploded. This gas pipeline was run by the company which runs the whole Belgian network of pipelines. Apparently, the explosion was directly caused by a gas leak. More or less thirty minutes after the leak had been observed, the explosion occurred precisely in the building where tools for working natural stone were sold. For the moment, the exact causes of the leak are not yet (openly) known. More than 20 persons died and more than 120 persons were injured, some of them very seriously. It appears that most of the victims were insured in the scope of their work contract. As developed below, the employer has to take out personal insurance for the benefit of his employees providing cover in the event of an industrial accident. Seeing that the accident occurred in an industrial park, a lot of victims were at work. Nevertheless, about 30 victims could not claim any compensation from a work insurer (for example because they were not at work).[51]

With the aim of helping these (in this case not insured) victims financially, the Belgian Federal Government decided to create a foundation, which is managed by representatives of the Government with the help of experts (*Fon-*

[47] D. Simoens, *Buitencontractuele aansprakelijkheid. Deel II. Schade en schadeloosstelling* (1999), 6.

[48] Except in some provisions having created strict liability and having provided for a maximum compensation. Cf. *supra* no. 5.

[49] This Act was initiated after the tornado which ravaged the city of Oostmalle and the region called "Westhoek" in 1967.

[50] See *infra* no. 24 to 27.

[51] See *infra* no. 13.

dation Ghislenghien/Gellingen Stichting).[52] What is interesting in this case is that this foundation, created on the initiative of the Government, is supplied by the professional union of the insurers on the express request of the Government (*Assuralia – Union professionnelle des entreprises d'assurances/ Beroepsvereniging van verzekeringsondernemingen*). The insurers, which make up the union, paid sums on request of the government and not in accordance with contractual obligations. The professional union made a humanitarian donation of € 1.2 million and Fluxys, the transport operator, made a donation of € 1 million. The persons who were or are still hospitalized received a first lump sum of € 1,500 or € 3,000 depending on the duration of the hospitalization. They have now to submit a request if they want to obtain a second payment, with written proof.

In addition, several other solidarity funds were spontaneously created, some of them under the form of non-profit making organizations.[53]

Moreover, the Ministry of Justice looked after the victims' interests by giving some more technical means for the preliminary examination and by providing assistance to the examining magistrate.[54]

It is difficult to say whether this new means of expression of solidarity will be used again in the future. One has here to mention the point of view of the professional union of insurers (*Assuralia*) which expressly refused to consider this "experience" as a precedent and is of the opinion that the Government does not have to knock at the door of the insurers each time there is a catastrophe or a terrorist attack.[55]

[52] The statutes of the private foundation created on initiative of the Federal Government are published in the *Belgian Official Journal* of 24 September 2004. The founding members are seven Ministers of the Belgian Federal Government. The purpose of the foundation is described in art. 4 of the statutes, according to which:
"De stichting heeft tot doel de financiële bijstand die verband houdt met de uitzonderlijke en dringende behoeften van de 'niet-arbeidsrechtelijk' verzekerde slachtoffers van de ramp te Gellingen op dertig juli twee duizend en vier of hun rechthebbenden.
Het nastreven van deze doelstelling(en) wordt inzonderheid verwezenlijkt door de volgende activiteiten:
1. het in ontvangst nemen van geld, giften en legaten, private of officiële subsidies, bijdrages en het sluiten van enige betaalde of andere samenwerkingsovereenkomst in het kader van het maatschappelijk doel;
2. het toekennen van geldsommen die een schadeloosstelling vormen voor de uitzonderlijke en dringende behoeften ven de 'niet-arbeidsrechtelijk' verzekerde slachtoffers van de ramp te Gellingen op dertig juli twee duizend en vier of hun rechthebbenden.

Ze kan alle handelingen vervullen die rechtstreeks of onrechtstreeks verband houden met haar doel. Ze kan inzonderheid medewerking verlenen en aandacht schenken aan iedere met haar doel verwante activiteit".

[53] See for example the non-profit making organizations "A.S.B.L. Solidarité Ghislenghien", created on 2 September 2004, the statutes of which were published in the *Belgian Official Journal* of 14 September 2004.

[54] Information about the assistance to the victims is published on the website of the Ministry of Justice (<http://www.just.fgov.be/ghislenghien>).

[55] In *Assur-info*, October 2004, III and IV: "Wij weigeren hier een precedent in te zien en aanvaarden niet dat de overheid bij ons komt aankloppen telkens als er zich een ramp of een terroristische aanslag zou voordoen. Het idee van een fonds is overwogen. Voor Assuralia is het duidelijk dat er in de situaties van een nationale ramp een beroep op de nationale solidariteit moet worden gedaan. Talrijke externe adviezen hebben zich in die zin uitgesproken".

Part IV. More Detailed Information

11 Below, more detailed information is provided on some aspects of the social security system (Part IV.I), on some aspects of tort law (Part IV.II) and on the Act concerning natural disasters (Part IV.III).

I. Social Security System

A. *Workmen's Compensation Law*

12 When an industrial accident occurs, the first law to be applied (before the others) is the Workmen's Compensation Act of 10 April 1971.[56] One recalls that an industrial accident is an accident which happens during the time of and due to the execution of a labour contract and which causes damage to an employee (art. 7).

Moreover,

- when an accident occurred during the time of the execution of a labour contract, one presumes that it happened due to the execution of it (art. 7, section 2);
- when an accident occurred on the way to or from the workplace, it is considered as an industrial accident (art. 8);
- when the victim (or his/her relatives) proves the existence of a lesion and the existence of a sudden event, one presumes that the lesion is due to this sudden event (art. 9).

13 The Act concerning industrial accidents is based on the following principles:

- every employer must take out an industrial accidents insurance policy with a private recognized insurer;[57] the employer which does not sign any contract is automatically affiliated to the Fund for the victims of industrial accidents (*Fonds des accidents du travail/Fonds voor arbeidsongevallen*);[58]
- when an industrial accident occurs, the victim may always claim compensation;
- the system of insurance compensates only the material professional damage (in case of death, work incapacity or medical care), including compensation for the additional efforts and, according to some authors only, compensation for post-professional damage;
- the compensation is provided on a fixed basis;
- in principle, the employee may not sue his employer or his co-employees on the basis of tort law (principle of "civil immunity" of the employer);

[56] There is a similar law concerning the public sector (Act of 3 July 1967 "betreffende de preventie van of de schadevergoeding voor arbeidsongevallen, voor ongevallen op de weg naar en van het werk en voor beroepsziekten in de overheidssector").

[57] Art. 49 of the Workmen's Compensation Act.

[58] Art. 57 of the Workmen's Compensation Act.

- the workmen's compensation insurer can take a recourse against the tort-feasor.[59]

Since 1978,[60] it has no longer been possible for the victim to make a choice between workmen's compensation law and tort law; the option was abrogated.[61] Compensation for bodily damage, such as it is covered under the Act of 10 April 1971, may only be obtained on the basis of this Act, which means on a fixed basis. 14

Nevertheless, tort law remains applicable to obtain compensation for damage other than bodily damage. The Act concerning industrial accidents has priority and common law is subsidiary to it. For example, tort law remains applicable for compensation of moral damage,[62] property damage and non-professional damage. But tort law remains also applicable for compensation of bodily injuries which are not covered by the fixed amount.[63] When there is talk of the application of tort law, it means the application of it towards the third party which is liable for the accident and not towards the employer: considering the decisions of the Supreme Court, one has to admit that the principle of civil immunity of the employer (and of the co-employees) is also applicable concerning damage which is not covered by the Act of 10 April 1971.[64]

In principle, to obtain full compensation, the victim has to take two proceedings: on the one hand, he/she has to sue his/her employer to obtain the fixed amount determined by the Act of 10 April 1971; on the other hand, he/she has to sue the third party who caused the damage to obtain compensation of the damage which does not fall within the scope of the Act of 1971. His/her claim is divided and both judicial proceedings are normally not taken before the same court.

The most important provisions of the Act of 10 April 1971 are reproduced. 15

> Arbeidsongevallenwet 10 april 1971
>
> Afdeling 6 – Burgerlijke aansprakelijkheid.
>
> Art. 46. § 1. Ongeacht de uit deze wet voortvloeiende rechten blijft de rechtsvordering inzake burgerlijke aansprakelijkheid mogelijk voor de getroffene of zijn rechthebbenden:

[59] The private recognized insurer can take legal civil action in the same way as the victim or his/her relatives and is subrogated in the rights of the victim or his/her relatives with respect for the legal provisons (art. 47 of the Act of 10 April 1971).

[60] *Belgian Official Journal* of 12 October 1978.

[61] In the Act of 3 July 1967 applying in the public sector, the option has not been abrogated. See also the decision of the *Cour d'arbitrage/Arbitragehof* (Constitutional Court) of 21 October 1998, *Belgian Official Journal* of 1 December 1998, 2nd edn.

[62] All kinds of moral damage: damage resulting from pain, *pretium doloris, pretium affectionis*, etc.

[63] The so-called "surplus".

[64] There is not any immunity when the employer misbehaved intentionally. D. Simoens (*supra* fn. 47), 342, no. 182.

1° tegen de werkgever die het arbeidsongeval opzettelijk heeft veroorzaakt of die opzettelijk een ongeval heeft veroorzaakt dat een arbeidsongeval tot gevolg heeft;

2° tegen de werkgever wanneer het arbeidsongeval schade aan goederen van de werknemer heeft veroorzaakt;

3° tegen de lasthebber of aangestelde van de werkgever die het arbeidsongeval opzettelijk heeft veroorzaakt;

4° tegen de personen, andere dan de werkgever, zijn lasthebbers of aangestelden, die voor het ongeval aansprakelijk zijn;

5° tegen de werkgever, zijn lasthebbers of aangestelden, wanneer het ongeval zich voordoet op de weg naar en van het werk;

6° tegen de werkgever, zijn lasthebbers of aangestelden, wanneer het ongeval een verkeersongeval betreft. Onder verkeersongeval wordt verstaan ieder ongeval in het wegverkeer waarbij één of meer al dan niet gemotoriseerde voertuigen zijn betrokken en dat verband houdt met het verkeer op de openbare weg;

7° tegen de werkgever die de wettelijke en reglementaire bepalingen inzake arbeidsveiligheid en -hygiëne zwaarwichtig heeft overtreden en die de werknemers aan het risico van arbeidsongevallen heeft blootgesteld, terwijl de ambtenaren die zijn aangewezen om toezicht te houden op de naleving van die bepalingen, hem schriftelijk hebben gewezen op het gevaar aan hetwelk hij deze werknemers blootstelt.

De schriftelijke ingebrekestelling vermeldt de overtredingen op de veiligheids- en hygiënevoorschriften die werden vastgesteld, het specifieke risico voor arbeidsongevallen dat hierdoor wordt gecreëerd, de concrete te nemen preventiemaatregelen alsmede de termijn waarbinnen deze moeten worden gerealiseerd, op straffe waarvan de mogelijkheid van een burgerlijke aansprakelijkheidsvordering bij gebeurlijk ongeval openstaat voor de getroffene of diens rechthebbenden.

De burgerlijke aansprakelijkheidsvordering wordt niet toegelaten tegen de werkgever die bewijst dat het ongeval mede is toe te schrijven aan de niet naleving door de getroffen werknemer van de hem voorafgaandelijk door de werkgever schriftelijk ter kennis gebrachte veiligheidsinstructies terwijl de nodige veiligheidsmiddelen hem ter beschikking werden gesteld.

§ 2. Onverminderd de bepalingen van § 1, is de verzekeringsonderneming verplicht de vergoedingen, die voortvloeien uit deze wet te betalen binnen de bij de artikelen 41 en 42 gestelde termijn.

De volgens het gemeenrecht toegekende vergoeding, die geen betrekking kan hebben op de vergoeding van de lichamelijke schade zoals zij gedekt is door deze wet, mag samengevoegd worden met de krachtens deze wet toegekende vergoedingen.

Art. 47. De verzekeringsonderneming en het Fonds voor arbeidsongevallen kunnen een rechtsvordering instellen tegen de voor het arbeidsongeval aansprakelijke tot beloop van de krachtens artikel 46, § 2, eerste lid, gedane uitkeringen, de ermee overeenstemmende kapitalen, alsmede de bedragen en kapitalen bedoeld bij de artikelen (…), 51*bis*, 51*ter* en 59*quinquies*.

Zij kunnen die burgerlijke vordering instellen op dezelfde wijze als het slachtoffer of zijn rechthebbenden en worden gesubrogeerd in de rechten die de getroffene of zijn rechthebbenden bij niet-vergoeding overeenkomstig, artikel 46, § 2, eerste lid, krachtens het gemene recht, hadden kunnen uitoefenen.

Art. 48. De bij deze wet bepaalde vergoedingen zijn niet verschuldigd, wanneer het ongeval door de getroffene opzettelijk is veroorzaakt.

Geen vergoeding is verschuldigd aan diegene van de rechthebbenden die het ongeval opzettelijk heeft veroorzaakt.

B. Health Insurance

The health insurance provisions concern two kinds of damage, namely the cost of medical and paramedical care (based on fixed tariff) and, on the other hand, the decrease of the earning capacity following work incapacity (decrease of at least two thirds). 16

These provisions are based on the idea that the other compensation mechanisms have first to be used and that the health insurance is subsidiary. Benefits will be refused if the victim may obtain compensation through other mechanisms (for example on the basis of tort law or on the basis of the Workmen's Compensation Law).

However, the health insurance institution intervenes *anticipatory* (*anticipativement/in afwachting*). As long as the socially insured has not received any real compensation, he/she will receive benefits from the health insurance funds. Real compensation means that the payment has to be effective. Consequently, the so-called anticipatory compensation constitutes a protection against the insolvency of the one who is liable. The socially insured has to give the health insurance organism information which is necessary to take recourse.

When the amounts paid on the basis of compensation mechanisms other than the health insurance are lower than the health insurance benefits, the socially insured may claim the difference from the health insurance organism.[65]

The most important provisions are reproduced. 17

Gecoördineerde wet d.d. 14 juli 1994 betreffende de verplichte verzekering voor geneeskundige verzorging en uitkeringen

[65] This is the so-called "difference rule" (*verschilregel*).

Art. 136. § 2. De bij deze gecoördineerde wet bepaalde prestaties worden geweigerd indien voor de schade voortvloeiend uit ziekte, letsels, functionele stoornissen of overlijden, krachtens een andere Belgische wetgeving, een vreemde wetgeving of in het gemeenrecht werkelijk schadeloosstelling is verleend. belopen de bedragen welke krachtens die wetgeving of het gemeenrecht worden verleend evenwel minder dan de prestaties van de verzekering, dan heeft de rechthebbende recht op het verschil ten laste van de verzekering.

Voor de toepassing van deze paragraaf is het bedrag van de door de andere wetgeving verleende prestaties gelijk aan het bruto bedrag verminderd met het bedrag van de sociale zekerheidsbijdragen welke op die prestaties worden ingehouden.

De prestaties worden, onder door de Koning bepaalde voorwaarden, toegekend in afwachting dat de schade effectief wordt vergoed krachtens een andere Belgische wetgeving, een vreemde wetgeving of het gemeenrecht.

De verzekeringsinstelling treedt rechtens in de plaats van de rechthebbende; deze indeplaatsstelling geldt, tot beloop van het bedrag van de verleende prestaties, voor het geheel van de sommen die krachtens een Belgische wetgeving, een buitenlandse wetgeving of het gemeenrecht verschuldigd zijn en die de in het eerste lid bedoelde schade geheel of gedeeltelijk vergoeden.

De overeenkomst die tot stand gekomen is tussen de rechthebbende en degene die schadeloosstelling verschuldigd is, kan niet tegen de verzekeringsinstelling worden aangevoerd zonder haar instemming.

Degene die schadeloosstelling verschuldigd is, verwittigt de verzekeringsinstelling van zijn voornemen om de rechthebbende schadeloos te stellen; hij maakt aan de verzekeringsinstelling, indien deze geen partij is, een kopij over de tot stand gekomen akkoorden of gerechtelijke beslissingen. De verzekeringsmaatschappijen burgerlijke aansprakelijkheid worden gelijkgesteld met degene die schadeloosstelling is verschuldigd.

Indien degene die schadeloosstelling verschuldigd is, nalaat de verzekeringsinstelling in te lichten overeenkomstig het vorige lid, kan hij tegen laatstgenoemde de betalingen die hij verrichte ten gunste van de rechthebbende niet aanvoeren; ingeval van dubbele betaling blijven deze definitief verworven in hoofde van de rechthebbende.

De verzekeringsinstelling heeft een eigen recht van terugvordering van de verleende prestaties tegenover het Gemeenschappelijk waarborgfonds bedoeld in artikel 49 van de wet van 9 juli 1975 betreffende de controle der verzekeringsondernemingen in de gevallen bedoeld bij artikel 50 van diezelfde wet.

K.B. 3 juli 1996 tot uitvoering van de wet betreffende de verplichte verzekering voor geneeskundige verzorging en uitkeringen, gecoördineerd op 14 juli 1994

Art. 295. § 1. De in artikel 136, § 2, van de gecoördineerde wet bedoelde toekenning van prestaties is afhankelijk van de voorwaarden dat degene die, voor hem persoonlijk of voor de personen te zijnen laste, om verzekeringsprestaties verzoekt, zijn verzekeringsinstelling in de mogelijkheid stelt het in dat artikel bedoelde recht uit te oefenen en haar het volgende mededeelt:

1° dat de schade waarvoor dat verzoek wordt gedaan, kan gedekt worden door het gemeenrecht of door een andere Belgische of buitenlandse wetgeving;

2° alle gegevens of omstandigheden waardoor kan worden uitgemaakt of de schadeloosstelling moet geschieden krachtens het gemeenrecht of een andere wetgeving, met inbegrip van de gerechtelijke informaties of handelingen waarvan hijzelf of de personen te zijnen laste in verband met de schade het voorwerp zouden zijn;

3° elke ingestelde vordering of andere procedure ter verkrijging, voor hem persoonlijk of voor de personen te zijnen laste, van de schadeloosstelling krachtens het gemeenrecht of een andere wetgeving.

II. Tort Law

If the victim wants to obtain compensation on the basis of tort law, three basic requirements must be fulfilled which concern: first, the damaging event, secondly, the damage and finally the link, more precisely the causal link, between the first two elements (Part IV.II.A). Once tortious liability has been established, the victim is normally entitled to full compensation (Part IV.II.B). 18

A. Three Basic Requirements

1. Damaging Event

The damage for which the victim claims compensation must have been caused by a damaging event. This event can be a faulty conduct (act or omission) or a no-fault event. 19

Fault still plays a considerable role in Belgian tort law. The Civil Code contains a general principle of fault liability expressed in art. 1382: "Any act whatever of man, which causes damage to another, obliges the one by whose fault it occurred, to compensate it".[66] This provision is a fundamental principle governing liability in tort law. The faulty conduct can consist in the violation of the general rule of careful behaviour. To say if someone has violated his duty of care, the judges compare his conduct with the conduct of the *bonus pater familias* in the same circumstances. In other words, the faulty conduct is a departure from the conduct of the good and reasonable man and the slightest

[66] Translation by G. Rouhette, with the assistance of A. Berton and published on the official website of the French Government: <http://www.legifrance.gouv.fr/html/codes_traduits/code_civil_textA.htm>.

departure constitutes negligence. The faulty conduct can also consist in the breach of a regulatory provision which imposes a specific conduct.

Concerning strict liability, there is not any general principle. It means that strict liability is always based on a specific provision. These specific provisions are to be found in the Civil Code or, most of the time, in specific statutes outside the Civil Code.[67] Although the concept of mass torts remains unknown under Belgian law, two authors pointed out that the introduction of strict liability rules can very often be justified by the idea of mass torts. It is namely the case when the national or international legislator developed special liability regulations considering the risk of a large number of victims that could be made by the same accident or by the same product.[68]

Strict liability has been developed in various areas. A lot of activities are concerned: mining,[69] atomic ships,[70] transportation of natural gas,[71] damage on the ground caused by aeroplanes,[72] toxic waste,[73] storage of natural gas,[74] marine oil pollution,[75] groundwater,[76] nuclear reactors,[77] etc.[78] Some of the strict liability rules could be applied in case of catastrophe. It is for example the case of the provisions concerning transportation of gaseous products or the act concerning legal liability in the field of nuclear energy.

[67] For example, cf. *supra* no. 8, the Act of 30 July 1979 concerning the prevention of fire and explosion in public buildings and concerning the compulsory insurance of civil liability in such cases. See also the Act of 22 July 1974 concerning toxic waste.

[68] I. Moreau-Margrève/M. Vanwijck-Alexandre, Les 'mass torts' en droit belge?, in: *Liber Amicorum Yvon Hannequart & Roger Rasir* (1997), 259, no. 6.

[69] Act of 15 September 1919 concerning mines, diggings and pits, *Belgian Official Journal* of 3 March 1920 ("Wet op de mijnen, de graverijen en de groeven"). This Act is no longer applicable in all the Regions.

[70] Act of 9 August 1963 concerning the liability of the operator of an atomic ship, *Belgian Official Journal* of 8 October 1963 ("Wet tot vaststelling van de aansprakelijkheid van de exploitant van een atoomschip").

[71] Act of 12 April 1965 concerning the transportation of gaseous products and others by means of pipelines ("Wet betreffende het vervoer van gasachtige produkten en andere door middel van leidingen"). This Act is no longer applicable in all the Regions.

[72] Act of 14 July 1966 ratifying the Convention on damage caused by foreign aircraft to third parties on the surface signed in Rome on 7 October 1952, *Belgian Official Journal* of 27 September 1966.

[73] Act of 22 July 1974 concerning toxic waste, *Belgian Official Journal* of 1 March 1975. This Act is no longer applicable in all the Regions.

[74] Act of 18 July 1975 concerning the prospect for and the exploitation of underground storage capacity in situ for the storage of gas, *Belgian Official Journal* of 14 August 1975. This Act is no longer applicable in all the Regions.

[75] Act of 20 July 1976 ratifying the International Convention on Civil Liability for oil pollution damage, agreed upon in Brussels, 29 November 1969, and the Act of 10 August 1998 ratifying the Protocol of 1992 to amend the International Convention on Civil Liability for oil pollution damage, 1969, agreed upon in London, 19 November 1992, *Belgian Official Journal* of 13 April 1977.

[76] Act of 10 January 1977 concerning damage for harm caused by the extraction of sub-soil water, *Belgian Official Journal* of 8 February 1977. This Act is no longer applicable in all the Regions.

[77] Act of 22 July 1985 concerning legal liability in the field of nuclear energy, *Belgian Official Journal* of 31 August 1985.

[78] For a brief description of these special statutes: H. Cousy/D. Droshout, Belgium, in: B.A. Koch/H. Koziol (eds.), *Unification of Tort Law: Strict Liability* (2002), 43–74.

Concerning strict liability, one has also to mention two articles of the Civil Code which could be used in case of catastrophes.[79]

Firstly, according to art. 1384, section 1 of this Code, "A person is liable not only for the damages he causes by his own act, but also for that which is caused by the acts of persons for whom he is responsible, or by things which are in his custody".[80] This provision is used to impose liability of the guardian of a defective thing for the damage caused by the defect of that thing.[81] No fault has to be demonstrated by the victim, but he/she has to demonstrate that the thing was defective and that his/her damage was caused by the defect. According to the Supreme Court, a defect is an abnormal feature that is deemed to cause damage.[82] The guardian is not necessarily the owner. Most generally, the guardian is the one who uses the thing for its own account, who is in possession of it or keeps it, with control on it.[83]

Secondly, according to art. 544 of the Civil Code, "Ownerships is the right to enjoy and dispose of things in the most absolute manner, provided they are not used in a way prohibited by statutes or regulations".[84] Although this provision only just defines the right of ownership, it was used (and is still used) to found the doctrine of nuisance or *equilibrium* theory (*troubles de voisinage/ burenhinder*). When the activities on a real property affect another real property, the owner of the first one (or the lessee or the holder of a limited right to use the property) has to compensate the damage suffered by the second one *in so far as* there is *excessive* nuisance.[85] The disturbance must exceed what is normal in the region to lead to compensation.[86]

2. Damage

The victim has not only to prove the existence of a faulty conduct or of a no- 20
fault damaging event to obtain compensation. He/she has also to prove the existence of his/her damage, for which he/she claims compensation.

Simoens describes the damage as the negative difference between two situations: the situation in which the victim is after the tort was committed and

[79] One thinks about the explosion of the gas pipeline that happened in the town of Ghislenghien on 30 July 2004 (see *supra* no. 10).

[80] Translation by G. Rouhette, with the assistance of A. Berton and published on the official website of the French Government: <http://www.legifrance.gouv.fr/html/codes_traduits/code_civil_textA.htm>.

[81] One has to notice that in 1804, the first section of art. 1384 was inserted in this article as an introduction to the other sections of the provision. In 1904, the *Cour de cassation/Hof van Cassatie* "discovered" in this first section the expression of a general principle of liability for defective things (Cass. 26 May 1904, *Pas.*, I, 246).

[82] Cass. 12 April 2002, C.01.0310.N; 30 January 2003, C.00.0726.F; 12 September 2003, C.02.0242.N. The decisions of the Belgian Supreme Court which are followed by the letter C, S or P are available on the official website of the Belgian judicial power (<http://www.juridat.be>).

[83] Cass. 25 March 1999, C.96.0404.N; 20 March 2003, C.02.0437; 22 March 2004, C.03.0109.F.

[84] Translation by G. Rouhette, with the assistance of A. Berton and published on the official website of the French Government: <http://www.legifrance.gouv.fr/html/codes_traduits/code_civil_textA.htm>.

[85] Cass. 24 April 2004, C.01.0371.F.

[86] See for example M. Faure, Environmental liability in Belgium, in: K. Deketelaere/M. Faure (eds.), *Environmental Law in the United Kingdom and Belgium from a Comparative Perspective* (1999), 213–215.

the situation in which the victim would have been without this tort.[87] Present and future damage can be compensated. Anyway, the damage must be certain to be compensated (it is not the case when the damage is hypothetical).

3. Causal Link

21 Finally, the victim has to prove the existence of a causal link between the faulty conduct (or no-fault damaging event) and the damage.

According to decisions of the Supreme Court, there is a causal link between the faulty conduct (or the no-fault damaging event) and the damage when this damage would not have happened as it did *in concreto* without the faulty conduct (or without the no-fault damaging event). In other words, each faulty conduct is a cause of the whole damage if the concrete damage would not have occurred without this conduct, without any other requirement. The Belgian causal approach is a one stage approach. No further selection is made among the different *conditiones sine qua non*. That is the reason why it is generally said that Belgian courts apply the doctrine of equivalence of conditions.

B. Compensation

1. General Rule: Compensation of the Entire Certain Loss

22 Art. 1382 of the Civil Code, which still remains the statutory basis of Belgian tort law, obliges the one who is liable to compensate the damage, which is generally described as the negative difference between two situations: the real situation and the situation which would have existed without the damaging event.[88] The victim has to be replaced in the situation wherein he/she would have remained without the faulty conduct.[89]

The concrete damage has to be entirely compensated.[90] Compensation has to be full and adequate.[91] The economic position of the victim and the severity

[87] L. Cornelis, Ongeschikt voor gevoelige juristen: over de intieme verhouding tussen schade en causaal verband, in: B. Tilleman/I. Claeys (eds.), *Buitencontractuele aansprakelijkheid* (2004), 249; D. Simoens (*supra* fn. 47), 51, no. 25.

[88] Cf. *supra* no. 20.

[89] Cass. 3 December 2003, P.03.0367.F; 7 September 2004, C.04.0315.N: "Overwegende dat de artikelen 1382 en 1383 Burgerlijk Wetboek degene die door zijn fout een ander schade berokkent, verplichten die schade te vergoeden; dat dit impliceert dat de benadeelde teruggeplaatst wordt in de toestand waarin hij zou gebleven zijn zonder de fout".

[90] Belgian tort law ignores the concept (the wording) of "pure economic loss". Nevertheless, it does not mean that the damage which is called "pure economic loss" in other countries never leads to compensation under Belgian tort law. Art. 1382 of the Civil Code, the statutory basis of tort law, has always been regarded as not containing any limitations neither on the scope of protected interests, nor on the scope of protected persons. See for example M. Bussani/V.V. Palmer, *Pure Economic Loss in Europe* (2003), 131–132; J.M. van Dunné, Liability for pure economic loss: rule or exception? A comparatist's view of the civil law – common law split on compensation of non physical damage in tort law, [1999] *European Review of Private Law* (E.R.P.L.), 412; C. von Bar/U. Drobnig, *The Interaction of Contract Law and Tort and Property in Europe. A comparative Study* (2004), 28–31 ("An average French, Belgian, Luxembourgian or Spanish lawyer, in turn, will most probably not even understand the concept: *a damage purement économique* is a category completely alien to him").

[91] Cass. 19 November 2003, P.03.0890.F; 3 December 2003, P.03.0367.F. J. Ronse (with the cooperation of L. De Wilde/A. Claeys/I. Mallems), *Schade en schadeloosstelling* (2nd edn. first part, coll. A.P.R. 1984), 173, no. 230.

of the faulty conduct are not taken into account. Nevertheless, specific provisions rule out the possibility of full compensation. In some cases, the legislator has limited compensation.[92]

Damage has normally to be evaluated precisely (mathematically). Nevertheless, if it is not possible to evaluate the damage mathematically, the judge may award a lump sum *ex aequo et bono*.

2. Heads of Damage

There are various ways to present heads of damage. In the present paper, the presentation generally made by Prof. Dr. B. Dubuisson is followed to a great extent.[93] 23

a) Personal Damage

i) Damage Resulting from Temporary Work Incapacity[94]

(a) Material Damage (Pecuniary Loss)

a. Loss of income (when the victim had an income).
   The degree of unfitness for work is expressed in a percentage which is applied to the wage.
b. Payments made to the victim by the employer (one week's salary or one month's salary is usually automatically paid to the employee) or by social security institutions are normally taken into consideration (it means that these payments have to be deducted from the compensation the injured party has to receive).
c. Additional efforts (when the victim carries on working).
   Economic value of domestic work. The valuations of this head of damage vary a lot from one court to another.[95]
e. Loss of a year's study (when the victim is a student).[96]
f. Damage consisting in incurred costs.
   The most common incurred costs are medical costs, care costs, clothing costs, transporting costs (incurred by the victim or by the relatives), prosthesis costs, the costs made to adapt the house, etc.

[92] Cf. *supra* no. 5.

[93] Cf. B. Dubuisson, *Obligations extra contractuelles* (course book Université catholique de Louvain, 2003–2004).

[94] "Work incapacity" means total or partial impossibility to do one's ordinary job in a normal way.

[95] In 1994, Prof. J.-L. Fagnart pointed out that the valuations can vary from BEF 250 to 910 per day (from € 6.2 to € 22.56). Cf. J.-L. Fagnart, L'évaluation et la réparation du préjudice corporel en droit commun (principes généraux – accidents mortels), [1994] *Revue Générale des Assurances et des Responsabilités* (R.G.A.R.), no. 12268(2), no. 46.

[96] D. de Callataÿ, L'évaluation et la réparation du préjudice corporel en droit commun (accidents non mortels), [1994] R.G.A.R., no. 12286(5). According to case law, compensation can vary from BEF 75,000 (€ 1,859.2) to BEF 200,000 (€ 4,957.87) (depending on the types of study: technical or university study).

(b) Moral Damage (Non-Pecuniary Loss)

a. Moral sorrows, namely all daily annoyances and worries, like anxiety, fear for the future, feeling of psychological or physical decrease.[97]
b. *Pretium doloris*, namely damage resulting from physical pain.[98]

ii) Damage Resulting from Permanent Work Incapacity

(c) Material Future Damage

a Loss of income
b. Economic value of domestic work
c. Aid by third persons
d. Incurred damage

(d) Moral Damage

a. Feeling of psychological or physical reduction
b. Aesthetic damage
c. Loss of pleasure and delight
d. Sexual damage
e. Damage resulting from the suffering

iii) Damage Resulting from Death[99]

(a) Damage Resulting from the Burial

(b) Economic Damage Suffered by the Relatives (who benefited from the professional income of the deceased) and the Economic Value of Domestic Work

(c) Moral (non-pecuniary) Damage Suffered by the Relatives (moral damage by repercussion)[100]

[97] D. de Callataÿ, [1994] R.G.A.R., no. 12286(3)*verso*. According to case law, compensation can vary from BEF 350 (€ 8.68) to BEF 2,500 (€ 61.97) per day.

[98] D. de Callataÿ, [1994] R.G.A.R., no. 12286(3)*verso*. According to case law, compensation can vary from BEF 50 (€ 1.24) to BEF 100 (€ 2.4) per day and per point (on a scale of 7 points). One can doubt whether the *pretium doloris* has to be compensated in addition to the compensation for moral suffering (D. Simoens, (*supra* fn. 47), 284–287, no. 146, 147). Both heads are here separately presented because it is sometimes the case in case law, especially when the victim is seriously injured. The opportunity to distinguish the *pretium doloris* from the moral suffering is not met in the indicative tariff (cf. *infra* no. 39, about this unofficial tariff).

[99] Under Belgian law, death in itself is not a damage.

[100] Cf. J.L. Fagnart, [1994] R.G.A.R., no. 12268(5). Prof. J.-L. Fagnart mentions namely the followings features:
– loss of husband or wife: from BEF 150,000 (€ 3,718.40) to BEF 400,000 (€ 9,915.74), often BEF 250,000 (€ 6,197.34);
– loss of cohabiting father or mother: from BEF 100,000 (€ 2,478.94) to BEF 250,000 (€ 6,197.34);
– loss of cohabiting child: from BEF 100,000 (€ 2,478.94) to BEF 300,000 (€ 7,436.81);

b) Property Damage

III. Natural Disasters

A. General Overview

An Act of 12 July 1976 concerns the repair of certain damage caused to private property by natural disasters.[101] This Act is based on the idea of national solidarity towards the victims of natural catastrophes. 24

According to art. 1 of this Act, the direct certain material damage to private personal property or private real estate is the occasion for financial aid under legal conditions, when it occurred on Belgian soil and is caused by certain natural phenomena.

A distinction is made between public disasters (*calamités publiques/algemene rampen*) and natural disasters (*calamités naturelles/landbouwrampen*).

The *public disasters* are natural phenomena which show an exceptional feature or which are unexpectedly intense or which cause important damage, in particular earthquakes or earthmovings, tidal waves and other disastrous floods, hurricanes or furies of the winds (art. 2, section 1, 1).[102]

The *natural disasters* are natural phenomena which show an exceptional feature or which are specially intense, or massive and unforeseeable action of noxious organisms having only caused important and generalized destruction to lands, cultivations or crops, and also exceptional diseases and poisonings having caused important and generalized losses of animals useful for agriculture by death or compulsory cutting down (art. 2, section 1, 2).

It is important to note that the recognition of the damaging disasters has to be carried out for each event by a Royal Decree. This Decree describes the geographical area in which the law will be applied.

The existence of a specific Act on natural disasters does not keep the victim from suing the Belgian State on the basis of tort law (art. 1382 of the Civil Code) if a faulty conduct of the State would also have caused the damage.[103] In

- loss of non-cohabiting child: from BEF 60,000 (€ 1,487.36) to BEF 200,000 (€ 4,957.87);
- loss of cohabiting brother or sister: from BEF 40,000 (€ 991.57) to BEF 100,000 (€ 2,478.94);
- loss of non-cohabiting brother or sister: from BEF 10,000 (€ 247.89) to BEF 50,000 (€ 1,239.47);
- loss of grandson or granddaughter: from BEF 15,000 (€ 371,84) to BEF 75.000 (€ 1,859.20).

[101] This Act was initiated after the tornado which fell on the city of Oostmalle and the region called "Westhoek" in 1967.

[102] This provision was modified by an Act of 21 May 2003, which has not entered into force (*Belgian Official Journal* of 15 July 2003), as follows: "De natuurverschijnselen met uitzonderlijk karakter of van een niet te voorziene hevigheid, of die belangrijke schade hebben veroorzaakt, inzonderheid de aardbevingen of aardverschuivingen, de vloedgolven of andere overstromingen met rampspoedig karakter, de orkanen of andere stormwinden".

[103] Art. 1, section 2 of the Act of 12 July 1976: "Onder voorbehoud van het bepaalde in artikel 10, § 1, 5°, a), betreffende de bedragen in te houden op de vergoeding, en in artikel 50, betreffende de indeplaatsstelling van de Nationale Kas voor Rampenschade, ingesteld bij artikel 35, kan de verkrijging van de vergoeding bepaald bij deze wet niet worden tegenworpen aan de

that case, the financial aid based on the Act of 1976 will be reduced taking into account the amounts paid to the victim by the State according to tort law.

Below, some more details are given first about public disasters (Part IV.III.B), then about natural disasters (Part IV.III.C) and finally about the weaknesses of the actual system and the changes expected in the coming year(s) (Part IV.III.D).

B. Summary of the Legal System Concerning Public Disasters

25 The system which is described in great detail in the Act of 1976 can be summarized in eight points.

a) A Royal Decree has to recognize the existence of the disaster and its geographical area (art. 2 of the Act).[104] The Royal Decrees are published in the Belgian official journal (*Moniteur belge/Belgisch Staatsblad*).[105]
b) The direct, material and certain damage caused on Belgian soil to certain private property can lead to financial aid. In case of public disaster, the following private property is concerned:

   1° built real estates;
   2° forested plantings;
   3° mobile homes;
   4° personal property which is used daily or by a family and which is listed by the King;
   5° other material personal[106] or real property, with the exception of funds and cash, but on the condition that it is used:
   – for the running of companies or factories;
   – for the exercise of a job;
   – for the activities of public utilities or non-profit-making organizations (art. 3 of the Act of 1976).

Nevertheless, the damage caused by a risk which normally can be covered by an insurance policy does not lead to any financial aid (fire and connected per-

belanghebbende die krachtens de artikelen 1382 tot 1386*bis* van het Burgerlijk Wetboek eveneens aanspraak maakt op vergoeding van de schade bepaald in § 1 hiervoor door de Belgische Staat of andere openbare besturen in het geding te brengen".

104 The following criteria would have been defined by the Government in 1986:
- total damage of at least BEF 50 million (€ 1,239,467);
- average amount per family of BEF 225,000 (€ 5,577);
- similar disasters happen each 20 years;

(E. van Nuffel, Financiële tegemoetkoming van de Staat bij natuurrampen (algemene rampen) in België, in: H. Cousy/H. Claassens (eds.), *Natuurrampen en verzekering* (1995), 47).

105 Example: in the *Belgian Official Journal* of 30 May 2001 two Royal Decrees of 19 April 2001 are published concerning floods and over flowings of public sewers which happened between 2 and 8 July 2000 and between 24 and 31 July 2000 on the area of several cities. These Royal Decrees recognized the floods as public disasters. In both cases, the total damage amounted to more than € 1,250,000. One of the Royal Decrees of 19 April 2001 was modified by a Royal Decree of 4 July 2004 (*Belgian Official Journal* of 12 August 2004).

106 The word "personal" (*roerende*) is missing in the Flemish version of the official text published on the website of the Belgian Ministry of Justice, but is used in the French version of the text (*mobiliers*).

ils like lightning, explosion, implosion, fall of places, etc.) (art. 4, 4° of the Act of 1976).[107] According to a decision of the Supreme Court given in 2002, the notion of "direct damage", which is used in the Act of 1976, implies the existence of a causal relationship without intermediate links between the disaster and the damage.[108] In this case, a square was covered by a lot of water (40 cm), following rain. A driver entered the square and his vehicle was damaged. According to the Court, the damage was not directly caused by the rain.[109] In another case, the Court decided that the costs incurred with the aim of painting a wall above the line to which water rose did not constitute a direct damage.[110]

c) Those who contributed to the occurrence of the damage may not benefit from the financial aid of the State in so far as the occurrence of the damage is due to their act or omission (art. 7 of the Act).

d) The Act of 1976 provides for rules of valuation and the King settles the method of estimation of the damage (art. 8 of the Act). The net amount of the damage is evaluated on the basis of the normal costs of repair or reconstruction, minus the value of the elements which are still useful and minus the depreciation. The loss of the personal property which is daily used in the house is evaluated on a fixed basis (art. 10, section 1, 1 of the Act).

   Considering that the damage has to be evaluated on the basis of normal costs of repair, reconstruction or new setting up of the damaged property, the Supreme Court quashed the decision of the court of appeal which decided that the buying of electric heaters, the hiring of gas bottles, the buying of emergency lighting material and the high electricity consumption had constituted a direct damage.[111]

[107] The official text is the following:
"Is van toepassing van de huidige wet uitgesloten de schade veroorzaakt:
4° aan de in artikel 3 bepaalde goederen, telkens de schade veroorzaakt is door risico's die normaal door verzekeringscontracten kunnen worden gedekt, namelijk:
a) de brand, de bliksem, de ontploffing, alsook de andere risico's die door de Koning aangeduid worden op voorstel van de Controledienst voor de Verzekeringen ingesteld door de wet van 9 juli 1975, uitgezonderd de beplantingen, de teelten, de oogsten te velde, de gronderven en hun aanleg of infrastructuuruitrusting;
b) de hagel, uitsluitend voor de beplantingen, teelten en oogsten te velde die uitdrukkelijk door de Koning aangeduid worden".

[108] Cass. 7 June 2000, C.00.0630.F; [2003] *Revue de jurisprudence de Liège, Mons et Bruxelles* (J.L.M.B.), 1423.

[109] "Overwegende dat het arrest vaststelt dat verweerder 'met zijn wagen [...] [het] plein is opgetreden om zich naar zijn werk te begeven [en] dat de motor van het voertuig schade opliep ten gevolge van het regenwater waarmee het plein overstroomd was';
Overwegende dat het hof van beroep, nu het op grond van die vaststellingen beslist 'dat de door [verweerder] geleden schade het rechtstreekse gevolg is van een natuurramp', de in het middel aangevoerde wetsbepaling schendt" (Cass. 7 June 2002, C.00.0630.F.; [2003] J.L.M.B., 1423).

[110] Cass. 5 October 2000, C.98.0448.F. According to the Belgian State, the painting of the part of the wall which was not damaged, with the aim of giving to it the same colour as the colour of the repainted part of the damaged wall, is to be considered as an indirect damage, and even perhaps as a sumptuary expense.

[111] Cass. 3 June 1993, [1993–1994] *Rechtskundig Weekblad* (R.W.), 550.

Tables containing fixed settlements of valuation and quantity of movable goods subject to compensation are published.[112] More or less 250 goods (including vehicles) are listed and evaluated.[113]

Compensation (financial aid) is calculated on the basis of the net amount of damage. There is an excess of € 250 (art. 10, section 1, 2° of the Act).[114]

If the amount of the damage exceeds the excess, compensation (financial aid) is calculated by tranches of the total net amount of the damage.[115]

Tranches of the total net amount of the damage (in Euro)	Coefficient of compensation
0 to 250	0.0
250 to 2,500	0.8
2,500 to 15,000	1.0
15,000 to 25,000	0.8
25,000 to 37,000	0.6
37,000 to 250,000	0.4
More than 250,000	0.0

If the damage amounts to € 250,000, the compensation will thus amount to € 114,700 at the most.

The compensation can possibly be increased (for example, due to fees and costs of experts)[116] or decreased (for example, in case of intervention of an insurer).[117]

[112] See the Royal Decree of 29 September 1998 having amended the Royal Decree of 20 August 1976 concerning compensation of the damage caused to personal property which is daily used in the house, published in the *Belgian Official Journal* of 20 October 1998 (Royal Decree "betreffende de vergoeding der schade aangericht aan roerende goederen van dagelijks of huiselijk gebruik door natuurrampen (algemene rampen)").

[113] Examples:
- Hall: coat stand (approx. € 25), mirror (approx. € 37), umbrella stand (approx. € 12.4), etc.
- Living room: armchair (max. approx. € 173), coffee table (approx. € 148), lights (approx. € 148), books (max. approx. € 124), etc.
- Dining room: chair (approx. € 75), stove (max. approx. € 620), etc.
- Study room: computer hardware (max. approx. € 744), office furniture (max. approx. € 248), etc.
- Bedroom: single bed (max. approx. € 248), double bed (max. approx. € 372), etc.
- Bathroom: towels (max. approx. € 100), etc.
- Box room: washing machine (max. approx. € 446), fridge (max. approx. 87), iron (max. approx. € 37), vacuum cleaner (max. approx. € 136), etc.

[114] The main rules of the Act are here given. For example, one does not examine the provisions concerning allowances or concerning increases or decreases of the financial aid.

[115] Art. 10, section 1, 3° of the Act of 12 July 1976.

[116] Art. 10, section 1, 4° of the Act of 12 July 1976.

[117] Art. 10, section 1, 5° of the Act of 12 July 1976.
"5° de overeenkomstig de bepalingen van 3° berekende herstelvergoeding wordt verminderd:
a) met alle bedragen, door de Belgische of buitenlandse openbare machten, door internationale organismen of door natuurlijke of rechtspersonen betaald, als dekking of als, volledig of gedeeltelijk, herstel van de in deze wet bedoelde schade.
De uit dien hoofde betaalde of verschuldigde bedragen in uitvoering van verzekeringscontracten die de geteisterde heeft afgesloten tegen risico's, andere dan die bepaald in artikel 4, § 2, worden echter slechts tot een beloop van drie vierde ervan in mindering gebracht, eventueel met beperking

f) The State can also intervene by allowing "repair credit". Under certain conditions, the State partially takes charge of the interest rate on loans allowed by some recognized credit institutions (artt. 9, A and 11 of the Act).

g) The fund for victims of public disasters (*Fonds national des calamités publiques/Nationaal Fonds voor Algemene Rampen*) can be supplied by advances of the Treasury Department (*Trésor/Schatkist*) or by short term loans and possibly by contributions of the Treasury (*Ministère des Finances/Ministerie van Financiën*). The fund is also supplied by donations[118] and by incomes from investments (art. 37 of the Act).

   The Minister of the Economy summarized the situation by saying that one worries oneself about financing the fund only after a disaster has happened.[119]

   The available funds of the fund for victims of public disasters amounted to € 14,568,285.98 on 1 January 2002, to € 12,332,622.57 on 1 January 2003 and to € 2,668,439.96 on 1 January 2004. The compensation and advances paid in 2002 amounted to € 5,003,310.77 in 2002 and to € 14,805,464.61 in 2003.[120]

h) The victim, namely the owner of the damaged property, has to use the indemnity he received to repair, reconstruct or set up his/her damaged property within three years (artt. 5 and 12 of the Act). The Belgian legislation tends to repair estates.

C. *Summary of the Legal System Concerning Natural Disasters*[121]

The system which is described in great detailin the Act of 1976 can be summarized in eight points.

tot het bijkomend gedeelte van de vergoeding waartoe de betrokken schade aanleiding zou gegeven hebben, als deze niet door een verzekeringscontract gedekt was geweest".
There is no art. 4, § 2 in the Act of 12 July 1976. Probably, the legislator wanted to relate to art. 4, 4°. One recalls that damage caused by a risk which is normally covered by an insurance contract does not fall within the scope of the Act (for example: fire, lightning, explosion).

118 Donations made to recognized institutions can lead to tax exemption under certain conditions. The conditions that are to be met by the institutions to be recognized are defined by the Royal Decree of 27 August 1993 concerning tax. Art. 59 of this Royal Decree concerns the institutions which help the victims of natural disasters. Art. 59 of this Royal Decree concerns the institutions which help the victims of important industrial disasters.

119 Cf. the parliamentary documents ("Verslag namens de commissie voor het bedrijfsleven uitgebracht door S. Creyf en M. Gerkens op 13 maart 2003, *Parl. Doc.*, Kamer, doc. 50-1007/1008, 4").

120 *Belgian Official Journal* of 5 May 2003 (2nd edn.) and 18 June 2004 (2nd edn.).

121 Concerning natural disasters, one examines only the federal legislation. Nevertheless, there are also some regional regulations. For example, the Flemish Region provides for compensation of damage caused by natural disaster by allowing loans with a reasonable interest rate or by allowing subsidies or guarantees. Victims have to introduce their request to a special fund (*Vlaams Landbouwinvesteringsfonds*). For more details, see the Decree of the Flemish Government of 24 November 2000, *Belgian Official Journal* of 14 February 2001 ("Besluit van de Vlaamse Regering betreffende steun aan de investeringen en aan de installatie in de landbouw").

a) A Royal Decree has to recognize the existence of the disaster and its geographical area (art. 2 of the Act). The Royal Decrees are published in the Belgian official journal (*Moniteur belge/Belgisch Staatsblad*).[122]
b) The direct, material and certain damage caused on Belgian soil to certain private property can lead to financial aid. In case of natural disaster, the following private property are concerned:

   1° land used for agriculture or horticulture;
   2° cultivations;
   3° crops;
   4° animals which are useful to agriculture.

   Nevertheless, the damage caused by a risk which normally can be covered by an insurance policy does not lead to any financial aid (hailstorms) (art. 4, 4° of the Act of 1976).

c) Those who contributed to the occurrence of the damage may not benefit from the financial aid of the State in so far as the occurrence of the damage is due to their act or omission (art. 7 of the Act).

d) The Act of 1976 provides for rules of valuation (art. 8 of the Act). The damage which is taken into account is evaluated: 1° for cultivations, crops and animals, on the basis of the real loss calculated according to market prices of the day of the disaster; 2° for land used for agriculture and horticulture, on the basis of the restoration to a normal fertile state.

   Moreover, the King determines the method of estimation of the damage. For example, the method to evaluate the damage caused to cultivations by heavy rains which fell in September 2001 was published in September 2003.[123]

[122] Example: in the *Belgian Official Journal* of 20 September 2002 a Royal Decree of 9 August 2002 was published concerning heavy rain which fell in October and November 2000 on the area of several cities and which caused damage to cultivations. This Royal Decree recognized the heavy rain as a natural disaster. This Royal Decree was amended by a new Royal Decree of 11 July 2003 published in the *Belgian Official Journal* of 21 August 2003.

[123] Royal Decree of 11 July 2003 (*Belgian Official Journal* of 12 September 2003).
"Art. 3. De schadeloosstelling wordt toegekend op basis van de volgende bedragen aan 100% schade per hectare:

– vlas (*flax*)	€ 1,916;
– aardappelen (*potatoes*)	€ 2,873;
– wintertarwe (*winter wheat*)	€ 1,167;
– zomertarwe (*summer wheat*)	€ 932;
– wintergerst (*winter barley*)	€ 968;
– zomergerst (*summer barley*)	€ 775;
– haver (*oats*)	€ 799;
– triticale (*triticale*)	€ 874.

(...)
De schadeloosstelling wordt berekend volgens het percentage van de te gelegener tijd geraamde schade, of volgens het schadepercentage berekend op basis van de stavende stukken. Indien er geen schadepercentage is geraamd of op basis van de stavende stukken kan berekend worden, wordt de schadeloosstelling berekend op basis van het gemiddelde van de betrokken gemeente, of bij ontstentenis daarvan, van de streek.
Indien het te gelegener tijd vastgestelde schadepercentage op een bedrijf kleiner is dan 30% van de normale productie per teelt, of 20% in de probleemgebieden, wordt er geen schadeloosstelling betaald voor dat bedrijf. (...)".

e) The compensation, possibly reduced or increased,[124] is awarded taking into consideration an excess. No compensation is awarded if the total net amount of the damage does not exceed 30% of the value of the damaged part of the damaged property. This percentage amounts to 20% when the damaged property lies in a problematical area which is determined by the Walloon Government.[125]

f) The State can also intervene by allowing guarantees or by taking charge of the interest and costs of "repair credits".[126]

g) The fund for victims of natural disasters (*Fonds national des calamités naturelles/Nationaal Fonds voor Landbouwrampen*) can be supplied by advances of the Treasury Department (*Trésor/Schatkist*) or by short term loans and possibly by contributions from the Treasury (*Ministère des Finances/Ministerie van Financiën*). The fund is also supplied with donations[127] and income from investments.[128]

   The credit balance amounted to € 1,185,954.60 on 1 January 2002, to € 5,895,330.91 on 1 January 2003 and to € 5,573,173.36 on 1 January 2004. The compensation and advances paid in 2002 amounted to € 1,077,482.05 in 2003.[129]

h) The victim, namely the farmer, has to use the indemnity he received to repair, reconstruct or set up his damaged property within three years (artt. 5 and 12 of the Act).

D. Weaknesses of the Actual System and New Prospects

Since the fund for victims of public disasters was created, it has intervened on 26
more or less forty occasions and the total amount awarded exceeds € 250 million.[130]

[124] Examples:
- increased with the fees of experts;
- decreased with the already paid advances (Art. 10, section 1, 4° and 5° of the Act of 12 July 1976).

[125] Royal Decree of 6 May 2002 which amended the Royal Decree of 7 April 1978 concerning the settlement of the percentages (*Belgian Official Journal* of 16 July 2002) (Royal Decree "tot vaststelling van de percentages, veranderlijk per gedeelten van het netto totaal bedrag van de geleden schade, evenals van het bedrag van de vrijstelling en van het abattement voor de berekening van de herstelvergoeding van zekere schade veroorzaakt aan private goederen door landbouwrampen"). See also the Decree of the Walloon Government of 17 July 1997 concerning support to agriculture (*Belgian Official Journal* of 25 October 1997).

[126] Art. 9, B of the Act of 12 July 1976.

[127] Donations made to recognized institutions can lead to tax exemption under certain conditions. The conditions that are to be met by the institutions for being recognized are defined by the Royal Decree of 27 August 1993 concerning tax. Art. 59 of this Royal Decree concerns the institutions which help the victims of natural disasters.

[128] Art. 38 of the Act of 12 July 1976. The Act provides also for the possibility to tax the premiums relating to insurance contracts which cover damage to lands, cultures and crops.

[129] *Belgian Official Journal* of 5 May 2003 (2nd edn.) and 18 June 2004 (2nd edn.).

[130] Cf. the parliamentary documents ("Verslag namens de commissie voor het bedrijfsleven uitgebracht door S. Creyf en M. Gerkens op 13 maart 2003, *Parl. Doc.*, Kamer, doc. 50-1007/1008, 3").

Nevertheless, the actual, above described system, shows at least three weaknesses:

- all the phenomena which have a natural cause and which cause damage are not recognized by the King as being a public disaster;
- the State never compensates the damage fully;
- procedures take a long time (generally many years).[131]

27 Rather recently, after more than ten years discussion, the Act of 12 July 1976 was greatly modified, by an Act of 21 May 2003 which concerns public disasters.[132]

The new Act settles the consequences of floods by including the risk of flood in fire insurance. In case of public disaster, the Act of 1976 should no longer be applied towards property which normally can be covered by an insurance contract ruled by the new art. 68-1 of the Act of 25 June 1992 concerning insurance contracts. This provision concerns insurance contracts relating to "ordinary" risks (*risques simples/eenvoudige risico's*) (especially houses). According to the new art. 68-1, these fire insurance contracts should obligatorily cover the risk of flooding but only if the asset insured is located in a risk area.

Flooding insurance should become a compulsory part of fire insurance which is nevertheless not compulsory. The premiums of fire insurance should therefore normally increase. Nevertheless, the obligatory link between flooding insurance and fire insurance is made by law only if the asset is located in a risk zone. In the other cases, the owner who takes out fire insurance is free to also take out flooding insurance or not.

The new art. 68-2 of the terrestrial insurance contract Act of 25 June 1992 provides for a definition of the notion of flooding[133] and specifies that in certain cases several successive floods constitute only one claim (new art. 68-3 of the Act of 25 June 1992).

The new provisions should apply principally to existing property. However, the insurer is not obliged to foresee the cover against the risk of flooding if the building was built more than eighteen months after the publication in the Belgian official journal of the Royal Decree classifying buildings in risk zones.[134] The explanation for this exception is the fact that the new provisions should tend to prevent building in risk zones.[135] This purpose should probably not be achieved easily.

[131] One gives an example. Heavy rain fell from 24 to 27 December 1999. A Royal Decree was taken on 13 June 2000, recognizing the heavy rain as a natural disaster. On 29 April 2001, a new Royal Decree was taken extending the damaged area. The new Royal Decree was published in the *Belgian Official Journal* of 30 May 2001, that is to say 17 months after the disaster. For a similar example, see the Royal Decree of 25 June 2003 (*Belgian Official Journal* of 23 July 2003). Publication of the Royal Decree does not yet mean effective payment of the financial aid.

[132] *Belgian Official Journal* of 15 July 2003.

[133] Art. 68-2 of the Act of 25 June 1992 was introduced by art. 3 of the Act of 21 May 2003 (*Belgian Official Journal* of 15 July 2003).

[134] New art. 68-7 of the Act of 25 June 1992 on terrestrial insurance contracts.

[135] Cf. the parliamentary documents ("Verslag namens de commissie voor het bedrijfsleven uitgebracht door S. Creyf en M. Gerkens op 13 maart 2003, *Parl. Doc.*, Kamer, doc. 50-1007/1008, 65").

By the Act of 21 May 2003 a Fees Office (*Bureau de tarification/Tariferingsbureau*) has also been set up.[136] The task of this Office is to make sure that all owners can be insured. Each owner who has been refused by at least three insurers can go to the Office to have conditions and fees fixed under which they are entitled to insurance cover.[137] The situation of the asset in a risk zone can be taken into consideration to determine the amount of the premium. That is the reason why it is said that the new Act would perhaps imply an indirect dis-

[136] Art. 68-9 of the Act of 25 June 1992 on terrestrial insurance contracts:
"Tariferingsbureau

§ 1. Teneinde de dekking van de door deze onderafdeling bedoelde risico's te verzekeren, richt de Koning een Tariferingsbureau op met als opdracht een verzekeringsdekking tegen de overstromingen te vinden voor de risico's die geen dekking vinden en er de tariefvoorwaarden van vaststellen.
De kandidaat-verzekeringsnemer wiens risico door tenminste drie verzekeraars werd geweigerd of aan wie door ten minste drie verzekeraars een dekking werd voorgesteld waarvan de premie of de vrijstelling de maxima vastgesteld door de Koning overschrijden, omwille van het risico overstromingen, kan zich tot het Bureau wenden.
De Koning stelt de procedure en de termijnen van toegang tot het Bureau vast.

§ 2. De verzekeraar moet de kandidaat-verzekeringsnemer informeren over het feit dat hij zich in één van de gevallen bevindt als bedoeld in § 1.

§ 3. Het Bureau is samengesteld uit vier leden die de verzekeringsondernemingen vertegenwoordigen en uit vier leden die de consumenten vertegenwoordigen, benoemd door de Koning voor een termijn van zes jaar. De leden van het Bureau worden gekozen uit een dubbele lijst, voorgesteld door de beroepsverenigingen van de verzekeringsondernemingen en door de verenigingen die in aanmerking komen om de belangen van de consumenten te vertegenwoordigen.
De Koning benoemt, voor een periode van zes jaar, een voorzitter die niet bij de vorige categorieën hoort.
De Koning bepaalt de vergoedingen waarop de voorzitter en de leden van het tariferingsbureau recht hebben.
De Koning wijst eveneens voor ieder lid een plaatsvervanger aan. De plaatsvervangers worden op dezelfde manier gekozen als de effectieve leden.
Het Bureau kan er deskundigen bij nemen die niet stemgerechtigd zijn.
De Ministers bevoegd voor Economische Zaken en Binnenlandse Zaken kunnen een waarnemer naar het Bureau afvaardigen.
Tenzij de Koning er anders over beslist, oefent het Bureau zijn activiteiten uit bij de Nationale Kas voor Rampenschade, bedoeld bij artikel 35 van de wet van 12 juli 1976 betreffende het herstel van zekere schade veroorzaakt aan private goederen door natuurrampen, die er het secretariaat en het dagelijks beheer van waarneemt.

§ 4. De Koning legt de voorwaarden vast van de werking van het Bureau en de verplichtingen van de verzekeraars teneinde de dekkingsverplichting te eerbiedigen bedoeld in paragraaf 1.
De verzekeraar die de door en krachtens dit artikel bepaalde verplichtingen niet naleeft, wordt geacht niet meer in overeenstemming te zijn met de bepalingen van de wet van 9 juli 1975 op de controle der verzekeringsondernemingen.

§ 5. De door het Bureau getarifeerde risico's worden verzekerd door al de verzekeraars die in België de verzekering van de eenvoudige risico's tegen brand aanbieden. Het Bureau vertrouwt het beheer van deze risico's toe aan één of verschillende verzekeraars. Het resultaat van dit beheer alsmede de werkingskosten van het Bureau worden omgeslagen over de verzekeraars die in België de verzekering van de eenvoudige risico's tegen brand aanbieden".

[137] Cf. the parliamentary documents ("Verslag namens de commissie voor het bedrijfsleven uitgebracht door S. Creyf en M. Gerkens op 13 maart 2003, *Parl. Doc.*, Kamer, doc. 50-1007/1008, 7").

suasive effect.[138] The risks which are fixed by the Fees Office are covered by all the insurers who offer fire insurance for ordinary risks in Belgium.[139]

According to the new rules, the Act of 1976 concerning the repair of damage caused by natural disasters would still be applied in four cases:

1° when the insurer has reached its limits of intervention;[140] in that case, the national fund for the victims of natural disasters should intervene; the intervention of the fund is limited to € 125 million;[141]

2° when the damaged buildings are not insured due to the economic position of the owner;

3° when the natural disaster is a disaster other than flooding (for example, earthquake);[142]

4° when the damaged buildings do not fall in the scope of the insurance contracts acts.

This Act of May 2003 is the result of more than ten years parliamentary work. The director of a parliamentary commission noticed that at the beginning the project concerned natural disasters insurance with large solidarity in the background, but that finally the Act concerns only flooding insurance based on limited solidarity.[143] The Act of May 2003 was freshly received, especially by the insurers.

The new rules give rise to several questions.

The first problem is that risk areas have to be determined by Royal Decree in accordance with the three Regions,[144] which should take several years. Risk areas are zones in which one observes or could observe frequent and heavy floods.[145] The new provisions shall only enter into force on the day which the Royal Decree setting out the risk areas enters into force.[146] At the moment, the new mechanism is thus "ticking over".

Secondly, the premiums of the policies should increase. The amount of the increase will depend on the extent of the risk areas. The more extensive

138 *Ibidem*, 67.

139 *Ibidem*, 7 and art. 68-9, § 5 of the Act of 25 June 1992 on terrestrial insurance contracts.

140 The Act permits the insurers to put a ceiling on their obligations, with the aim of maintaining the risk and the premiums within reasonable limits.

141 New art. 34-3 of the Act of 12 July 1976 (as introduced by art. 5 of the Act of 21 May 2003).

142 Originally, the scope of the bill was more extensive and provided also for the covering for other risks such as earthquakes, earthmovings, etc.

143 Cf. the parliamentary documents ("Verslag namens de commissie voor het bedrijfsleven uitgebracht door S. Creyf en M. Gerkens op 13 maart 2003, *Parl. Doc.*, Kamer, doc. 50-1007/1008, 39").

144 The Flemish Region, the Wallon Region and the Brussels Region.

145 New art. 68-7 of the Act of 25 June 1992 on terrestrial insurance contracts.

146 Art. 8 of the Act of 21 May 2003. Nevertheless, the provision concerning the Fees Office has already entered into force. The mission of the Office is to help people who have been refused by insurers by finding cover against floods and by defining conditions and fees under which they are entitled to insurance cover. The provisions concerning the deadlines for the payments of indemnities in the scope of the fire insurance entered into force on 1 July 2004 (cf. *infra* no. 32).

the areas are defined, the less important the increase will be. If the zones are defined in a (too) narrow way, the premiums will become unbearable, according to the Minister.[147]

Thirdly, the assets which are located in a risk area will probably depreciate and the sale of such assets will probably become problematic.

In short, the Minister of the Economy recognized that the new Act was a "bad" act, useless and unenforceable, at least for two reasons: 1° the Act cannot be applied within the next months because the risk zones have to be settled; 2° the risk of flooding is only compulsory covered if the insured asset is located in a risk zone (only the "bad risks" are obliged to take out insurance).[148]

Considering the difficulties implied by the new provisions (especially the difficulty in settling the risk zones), they will very probably never come into force without any modifications.[149] Nevertheless, the old situation should not be maintained. The insurers and the Ministry of the Economy worked up a new settlement which should lead to the improvement of the previous (not entered into force) regime of 2003.[150]

The future system will be based on the following idea: all the fire insurance policies should cover compulsorily public disasters not only floodings, but also earthquakes, breaking of breakwaters, tidal waves, etc. wherever the asset is located at least if the building still exists.[151] Consequently the premiums should increase by some percent.[152]

[147] Cf. the parliamentary documents ("Verslag namens de commissie voor het bedrijfsleven uitgebracht door S. Creyf/M. Gerkens op 13 maart 2003, *Parl. Doc.*, Kamer, doc. 50-1007/008, 38 en 43"). It would be thinkable that risk areas would be definied in a less narrow way in the Flemish Region than in the Walloon Region (*ibidem*, 42).

[148] Cf. the parliamentary documents ("*Parl. Doc.*, Senaat, Handelingen nr. 3-28 van de plenaire vergadering van donderdag 11 december 2003").

[149] Nevertheless, the provision concerning the Fees Office has already entered into force. The mission of the Office is to help people who have been refused by insurers to find cover against floods, by defining conditions and fees under which they are entitled to insurance cover. The provision concerning the deadlines for payments of indemnities in the scope of the fire insurance are entered into force on 1 July 2004 (cf. *infra* no. 32).

[150] The present report dated from December 2004 unfortunately does not include the developments of the year 2005. Nevertheless, we can refer to the recent parliamentary works ("*Parl. Doc.*, Kamer, doc. 51-1732/001-006; Senat, doc. 3-1291/1).

[151] Cf. the parliamentary documents ("*Parl. Doc.*, Senaat, Handelingen nr. 3-28 van de plenaire vergadering van donderdag 11 december 2003").

[152] According to the spokesman of the Ministry of Economy (see *La Libre Belgique* of 12 November 2004). The project of new Act was officially tabled on 25 April 2005 ("*Parl. Doc.*, Kamer, doc. 51-1732/001").

Part V. Procedures

I. Social Security System

A. *Charter of the Socially Insured*

28 If the victim is entitled to obtain compensation under one of the social security mechanisms, the time in which to make decisions and deadlines are provided in a special Act of 11 April 1995.[153]

The principles which are laid down in this Act can be summarized as follows.

1° Payments are made either automatically when this is materially possible, either on written request (art. 8).
2° Decisions of the social security organisms have to be taken within four months after receipt of the request or after the event which give rise to the automatic inquiry (art. 10, section 1).
3° If the organism cannot make any decision within four months, it informs the socially insured about the situation and mentions the reasons for this (art. 10, section 2).
4° The organism which has to examine a request collects, on its own initiative, the missing information with the aim of considering the rights of the socially insured (art. 11).
5° Payments are made within four months after the notification of the decision and at the earliest at the moment the terms of payment are fulfilled (art. 12, section 1).
6° If the payment is not made on time, the organism informs the socially insured, every quarter, about the reasons for the delay and without prejudice to the right of the socially insured to take legal action (art. 12, section 3).
7° Social security benefits bear interest automatically from the moment the payment is due and at least after the four months mentioned above (art. 20).

B. *The Workmen's Compensation Law*

29 The above mentioned Act of 11 April 1995 comes into force without prejudice to particular rules.

For example, there are specific provisions concerning payments in the Act of 10 April 1971 on workmen's compensation. According to this Act:

- compensation of funeral costs must be allowed within one month after the death of the individual who incurred the costs;[154]
- temporary indemnities have to be paid on the same dates of payment as wages;[155]

[153] Act of 11 April 1995 concerning the Charter of the socially insured (*Belgian Official Journal* of 6 September 1995) (*"Handvest" van de sociaal verzekerde*).
[154] Art. 41 of the Workmen's Compensation Act.
[155] Art. 42 of the Workmen's Compensation Act.

- the King defines the methods of payment concerning the yearly indemnities.[156]

II. Tort Law

If the victim uses the mechanism of tort law, he/she will probably have to go to law. The procedure will very probably last for many years and will be expensive. The victim bears the burden of proof. The identification of the tortfeasor, the existence of the damage and of the causal link has to be proven by the victims most of the time. 30

Concerning causation, victims have to convince the judges that without the damaging event, the damage would not have happened as it did concretely. The damaging event and the damage can be proven by all legal means. Oral testimonies are therefore authorized if necessary.

III. Insurance Law

A. *General Rule*

Art. 19 of the Act of 25 June 1992 on insurance contracts concerns the obligation to inform the insurer when a disaster has happened. The insured must inform his insurer as soon as possible and in any case within the required contractual time. 31

The insured has also to provide his insurer with all useful information and has to answer questions asked by the insurer with the aim of laying down the circumstances and the extent of the damage.[157]

Moreover, there is no legal deadline for the payment of the indemnities, except in the scope of fire insurance.

The existence of an insurance contract does not necessary guarantee that the victims will receive compensation quicker. Expert valuation must often be undertaken.

Recently, an author pointed out that the delay in compensating victims can also frequently be explained by the existence of a penal action. Most of the time, the civil action is suspended during the time of the penal action.[158] This author quotes as an example the plane crash during a show in Oostende.[159] More than five years after the fall of the plane, the victims and their relatives had not received any compensation.[160]

[156] *Ibidem*, section 2.

[157] Art. 19, section 2 of the Act of 25 June 1992 on terrestrial insurance contracts.

[158] H. Claassens (*supra* fn. 20), 624, fn. 59.

[159] On 26 July 1997, during an airshow in Oostende, a plane crashed on parked planes and on the tent of the *Croix-Rouge/Rode Kruis*. Ten people died and fifty eight were injured.

[160] See notably the nota made by Prof. H. Claassens after the catastrophe of Ghislenghien (http://www.brandwonden.be/ghislenghien/20040811-Stichting-Gellingen-Fr.pdf). As a result of this situation the "Red Cross" (*Croix-Rouge/Rode Kruis*) intervened twice to distribute humanitarian aid for the victims provided by the Flemish Region (according to the press, € 500,000). The financial aid was distributed according to a points system.

B. Fire Insurance-Property Insurance

32 Within the context of fire insurance, the Act of 25 June 1992 provides for deadlines for the payment of the indemnities.[161] Since 1 July 2004, new deadlines have been in force.[162]

Rehousing costs and other costs relating to necessities must be paid within 15 days following the notification of the claim or the provision of proof of costs incurred.

The undisputedly due amount agreed by the insurer and his insured is paid within 90 days after the notification of the claim. Nevertheless, this deadline can be delayed or postponed by a decision of the Minister of the Economy.[163]

In case of reconstruction, the insurer has to make a first payment (80% of the new value) within 30 days after the date of closing of the expert valuation or, failing that, after the date of assessment of the amount of the damage. The rest of the compensation may be paid as reconstruction work progresses.[164]

In case of replacement (buying of another building), the insurer has to pay 80% of the new value within 30 days after the date of closing of the expert valuation or, failing that, after the date of assessment of the amount of the damage. The rest of the compensation is to be paid at the moment of signing the deed before a notary.

In the other cases, compensation is to be paid within 30 days after the date of closing of the expert valuation or, failing that, after the date of assessment of the amount of the damage.

The assessment must be closed within 90 days following the notification of the claim.

If payments are not made on time, interest can be charged on the indemnity.[165]

IV. Natural Disasters[166]

33 The above mentioned Act of 12 July 1976 provides that the claim for financial aid has to be addressed to the Governor of the Province in which the damaged estate is located.[167]

The King defines the period within which claims have to be made. At the present moment, this period is defined as follows: under penalty of exclusion, a claim for compensation has to be made at the latest three months following the month during which the Royal Decree recognizing the natural disaster is

[161] Art. 67 of the Act of 25 June 1992 on terrestrial insurance contracts as modified by art. 2 of the Act of 21 May 2003.

[162] Art. 71 of the Act of 9 July 2004 modifying art. 8 of the Act of 21 May 2003, *Belgian Official Journal* of 15 July 2004.

[163] Art. 67, section 2*bis*.

[164] There are exceptions to this rule.

[165] Art. 67, section 6.

[166] A "Vade-Mecum" for the victims of public disasters is published on the website of the Federal Government. The last version dates from September 2004 (<http://www.belgium.be>).

[167] Art. 17 of the Act of 12 July 1976.

published.[168] Sometimes, the period is prolonged.[169] Moreover in some exceptional cases, claims may be introduced after this period (in case of Act of God or good faith).[170]

On his side, the Governor of the Province[171] does not have to respect any legal deadline.[172] As above mentioned, victims can wait many years before obtaining a decision. Once the decision of the Governor is notified to the victim, he/she has one month to approve it.[173] The victim and the competent Minister can appeal against the decision to the court of appeal located in the concerned Province.[174]

The victim must use the financial aid to repair, reconstruct or set up the damaged property within three years after the date of the final decision concerning it.[175]

Part VI. Combination of the Various Systems

Below, a brief summary of the preceding pages: 34

- the health insurance (branch of the social security system) intervenes anticipatory (fixed based intervention);
- the Act of 10 April 1971 on Workmen's Compensation has priority in the common (tort) law; the industrial accidents' insurer is subrogated in the victim's rights towards the third party who is liable for the damage;

[168] Art. 1 of the Royal Decree of 20 February 1995 amending the Royal Decree of 18 August 1976 concerning the way and deadline for bringing a request for action (*Belgian Official Journal* of 24 February 1995) (Royal Decree "tot vaststelling van de vorm en de termijn van indiening van de aanvragen"). Examples: art. 2 of the Ministerial Decree of 11 July 2003, *Belgian Official Journal* of 12 September 2003; art. 3 of the Ministerial Decree of 30 September 2003, *Belgian Official Journal* of 14 October 2003.

[169] Example: art. 1 of the Royal Decree of 18 December 1998, *Belgian Official Journal* of 29 December 1998 (prolongation of one month).

[170] Art. 5, section 2 of the Royal Decree of 18 August 1976, *Belgian Official Journal* of 9 September 1976.

[171] Art. 17 of the Act of 12 July 1976:

"§ 1. De aanvraag tot financiële tegemoetkoming wordt aan de gouverneur van de provincie van de plaats van de teistering gericht. Ze moet door de belanghebbende of door een advocaat worden ondertekend.
Als de geteisterde goederen afhangen van een onverdeeldheid, kan de aanvraag ingediend worden door een van de eigenaars in onverdeeldheid, namens die van zijn medeeigenaars in onverdeeldheid, die hem daartoe volmacht gegeven hebben.

§ 2. De geteisterde die in verschillende provincies schade geleden heeft, richt zijn aanvraag, betrekking hebbende op het geheel van zijn schade, aan de gouverneur van één dezer provincies, naar zijn keuze.

§ 3. De aanvraag bevat keuze van woonplaats in België.
De keuze van woonplaats is geldig voor de gehele procedure als zij niet gewijzigd wordt door een verklaring, bij ter post aangetekende brief, gericht aan de gouverneur die de aanvraag tot tegemoetkoming heeft ontvangen.

§ 4. De voorwaarden van vorm en termijn van indiening der aanvragen worden door de Koning vastgesteld".

[172] E. van Nuffel (*supra* fn. 104), 52.

[173] Art. 21 of the Act of 12 July 1976.

[174] Art. 20, section 1 of the Act of 12 July 1976.

[175] Art. 12, section 1 of the Act of 12 July 1976.

- the insurer who allowed and paid compensation to the victim according to an insurance contract is subrogated to the claim of the victim against the one who caused the damage, up to the amount of the allowed compensation;[176]
- the existence of a specific law on natural disasters does not keep the victim from suing the Belgian State on the basis of tort law (art. 1382 of the Civil Code) if the damage results from a faulty conduct of the State;[177] in that case, the financial aid based on the Act of 1976 on natural disasters is reduced taking into account the amounts paid to the victim according to tort law.

Part VII. Financing

35 When tort law is applied, one can briefly say that the estate of the one who is liable will normally use a part of his estate (patrimonium) to pay damages to the victim except if he is insured.

36 The funds managed by the social security organisms are mostly supplied by the workers, employers and the Belgian State.[178]

37 Other funds are specifically supplied. For example, the fund for natural risks is mostly supplied by the Belgian State (and indirectly by taxpayers).[179]

Part VIII. Amounts of Damages

38 One refers mostly to Part IV of this paper.[180] Nevertheless, concerning tort law, two additional points are detailed.

39 First of all, one has to mention that damage has to be evaluated concretely (*in concreto*) and precisely (mathematically). Nevertheless, if the existence of the damage is certain, but if the extent of this damage cannot be evaluated *in concreto* because exact criteria to evaluate it are missing, the victim may propose

[176] Art. 41 of the Act of 25 June 1992 on terrestrial insurance contracts.

[177] Art. 1, section 2 of the Act of 12 July 1976: "onder voorbehoud van het bepaalde in artikel 10, § 1, 5°, a), betreffende de bedragen in te houden op de vergoeding, en in artikel 50, betreffende de indeplaatsstelling van de Nationale Kas voor Rampenschade, ingesteld bij artikel 35, kan de verkrijging van de vergoeding bepaald bij deze wet niet worden tegengeworpen aan de belanghebbende die krachtens de artikelen 1382 tot 1386*bis* van het Burgerlijk Wetboek eveneens aanspraak maakt op vergoeding van de schade bepaald in § 1 hiervoren door de Belgische Staat of andere openbare besturen in het geding te brengen".

[178] Art. 22 of the Act of 29 June 1981 concerning the general regulation of the social security for employees:
"§ 1. De geldmiddelen van de sociale zekerheid komen voort uit:
- de solidariteit van de werkgevers en de werknemers in de vorm van sociale zekerheidsbijdragen;
- de nationale solidariteit in de vorm van rijkstoelagen;
- de inkomsten te bepalen door of krachtens de wet;
- de legaten, leningen, interesten van kapitalen".

[179] Cf. *supra* no. 25.

[180] Especially no. 23 and 25.

an evaluation *ex aequo et bono*. In this case, the judge may award a lump sum *ex aequo et bono*, which means according to equity.[181] When the judge awards a lump sum even when the claimant has proposed a method of calculation, he has to mention the reasons for which he could not admit this method and has to notice the impossibility to evaluate the damage mathematically.[182]

The granting of a lump sum has to be considered as a subsidiary technique, which may only be used if it is not possible to evaluate the damage in another way. It is, for example, the case when the judge has to assess the economic value of a student. There is no compulsory tariff that has to be used to grant lump sums. For this reason the National Unions of first instance judges (*Union nationale des magistrats de première instance et Union royale des juges de paix et de police/Nationaal Verbond van de Magistraten van Eerste Aanleg en het Koninklijk Verbond van Vrede- en Politierechters*) took the initiative to elaborate an indicative tariff (*tableau indicatif/indicatieve tabel*). The latest version of this tariff, the fourth one, dates from May 2004.[183] In publishing this tariff, the first instance judges want to promote the standardization of case law and to furnish the judges with a work instrument.[184] The tariff was elaborated within the scope of traffic accidents.

40 Secondly, some information can be given concerning the types of compensation. In tort law, compensation comes generally as a sum of money. This financial compensation is awarded as a one-off payment or as periodic payments (capital or index-linked annuities). The choice between the types of compensation is exercised by the judges. Most of the time they award index-liked annuities only to severely injured victims.[185]

Part IX. Empirics

41 In the opinion of some authors, catastrophes happen quite rarely in Belgium. According to Prof. Dr. I. Moreau-Margrève and Prof. Dr. M. Vanwijck-Alexandre, one can explain this situation by the smallness of the country, by the geographical location and by the "developed civilization".[186]

Nevertheless, in the last few years the situation seems to have changed.[187] According to the OFDA/CRED International Disaster Database,[188] five natural

[181] According to some authors, the evaluation *ex aequo et bono* still remains a concrete evaluation, because in both cases the evaluation aims to put the victim, as far as possible, in the conditions where he/she would have been had the act entailing liability not been committed.

[182] Cass. 20 February 2004, C.02.0527.F.

[183] The tariff is freely available on the website of the review *Nieuw Juridisch Weekblad*: <http://www.njw.be>.

[184] W. Peeters, De 'Indicatieve tabel' als antwoord op de noden van de praktijk, in: M. Van den Bossche (ed.), *De indicative tabel. Een praktisch werkinstrument voor de evaluatie van menselijke schade* (2001), 9.

[185] D. Simoens (*supra* fn. 47), 184, no. 97.

[186] I. Moreau-Margrève/M. Vanwijck-Alexandre (*supra* fn. 68), 276, no. 37.

[187] Ph. Hoyois/D. Guha-Sapir, *Three decades of floods in Europe: a preliminary analysis of EMDAT data*, <http://www.cred.be/docs/publications/FLOOD-EUR.pdf>. These authors observe that "During the last three decades (1973–2002), the reported number of disasters caused by floods and registered in the EMDAT database which remained more or less stable

disasters happened in Belgium in the last two years killing or affecting more than 2,500 people[189] while one industrial disaster killed or affected 131 people.[190]

If floods seem to be the most "frequent" natural disasters in Belgium, earthquakes would imply more damage than floods over a long period time, according to Prof. J. Van Dyck.[191]

42 Concerning the public disasters that happened in Belgium between 1976 and 1995, the general director of the service in charge of the natural disasters gave the following features (updated to 31 July 1994) in a study published in 1995:

- 35 disasters were recognized as public disasters (earthquake, floods, windstorms) since the Act of 12 July 1976 came into force;[192]
- 50,936 decisions to award compensation were made;
- financial aid was furnished for a total amount of € 188,869,844 (BEF 7,618,990,492).

After the earthquake which happened in the city of Liège in 1983,[193] the financial aid amounted to BEF 1.7 billion (BEF 1.9 billion according to the insurers) (respectively € 42,141,900 and € 47,099,770). After the storm which happened in the spring of 1990, the aid amounted to more or less BEF 3.5 billion (in the Walloon Region the storm mostly affected forests) (€ 86,762,730).[194]

during the first two decades increased progressively during the last decade and knew an exponential growth in the last three years. (…) In Western Europe, small disastrous floods are more frequently reported for Belgium, France, Switzerland. In France, however, big disastrous floods occurred several times during the period. The Netherlands and Germany offer more contrasted figures with apparently lower frequency of floods but with more severe ones reported proportionally".

188 CRED: Centre for Research on the Epidemiology of Disasters. This centre was established in 1973 as a non-profit institution, with international status under Belgian law. It is located within the School of Public Health of the Université catholique de Louvain (UCL). The country profiles for natural and industrial disasters are available on the website of the CRED (<http://www.cred.be>). In order to list a disaster into the EM-DAT database at least one of the following criteria has to be fulfilled:
- 10 or more people reported killed;
- 100 people reported affected;
- a call for international assistance;
- declaration of a state of emergency.

189 Four disasters are floods (January, February, August and December 2002) and one is the extreme temperature of August 2003.

190 The catastrophe of Ghislengien (see *supra* no. 10).

191 The conclusions of a recent study of Prof. J. Van Dyck are briefly presented on the website of Aon Corporation (provider of risk management services, insurance and reinsurance brokerage) (<http://www.aon.com/be/en/about/news/catnat_fr_300904.jsp>).

192 According to art. 62 of the Act of 1976, the Act applies to events which happened from 1 January 1976.

193 Having killed two persons and affected more than 1,000 people (EM-DAT).

194 E. van Nuffel (*supra* fn. 104), 84.

Part X. General Comments

In Belgium, there is no general legislation which would be applicable specifically in cases of catastrophes and which would grant to victims full compensation. 43

In accordance with the circumstances, the victims use one or several mechanisms with the aim of obtaining compensation: tort law, insurance law, several branches of the social security system, or call on solidarity. Within the scope of one catastrophe, all victims are not necessarily compensated in the same way.[195] Moreover, in some circumstances, the final amount which is awarded to each victim may depend on the total number of victims (the more numerous the victims are, the less compensation they will receive).[196]

The great advantage of tort law is that it provides full compensation, at least theoretically. This mechanism seems attractive. Nevertheless, one should not forget that:

- the victim has to prove the existence and the extent of his/her damage as well as causation;
- the unavoidable legal proceedings can last many years;
- the victims will not receive any compensation in case of insolvency of the party who is liable for the damage (except in case of existence of an insurance);
- the legislator sometimes neglects the principle of full compensation (by limiting the amount of the compensation or by limiting the heads of damage).

Insurance law plays a considerable role in compensating the victims in two different ways:

- either the victims have taken out an insurance contract for their own benefit (fire insurance, hospitalization insurance, car insurance, etc.); since 1995, the risk against *storm* is compulsorily included in fire insurance policies;
- either the civil liability is the subject matter of the insurance contract; sometimes the conclusion of such an insurance contract is compulsory (for example, for the risk of explosion in some public establishments); if tort law remains one commonly used mechanism to obtain compensation, it is certainly due to the development of liability insurance.

Except in the scope of fire insurance, there is no legal deadline for the payment of the indemnities by the insurer.

Social security is also a mechanism frequently used to compensate the damage. In this case, the compensation is mostly provided on a fixed basis. Nevertheless, tort law is still applicable towards the third party who caused the

[195] For example, in tort law, the amounts of compensation vary from one court to another, which can be explained by the fact that the damage is evaluated by the judge supremely. Moreover, some victims are insured, other are not.

[196] Cf. *supra* no. 8 (Act of 30 July 1979).

damage. In principle, the lump sum, which is sometimes allowed "anticipatory", can be obtained within reasonable time.

Finally, compensation can also be obtained thanks to national solidarity. The Act of 12 July 1976 concerning the repair of damage caused to private personal property or private real estate as a result of natural phenomena has especially to be mentioned. This Act concerns "public disasters" (damage to built real estates and personal property) and "natural disasters" (damage to land, cultivations, crops and some animals).

The mechanism which is stated in great detail in the Act of 1976 is applicable when the damage is caused by an exceptional natural disaster. Nevertheless, it shows several weaknesses: the King has to recognize the natural disaster as a disaster; compensation occurs on a fixed base and the procedure takes a long time. At the beginning of November 2004, an agreement was settled by the Ministry of the Economy and the insurers concerning the extension of the scope of fire insurance to damage resulting from public disasters. In the future, all fire insurance policies should compulsorily cover public disasters. The parliamentary work should begin as soon as possible and a new Act should be voted within the next months[197]. Should the damage resulting from public disasters be compensated in the scope of fire insurance, one could not speak any more at the first sight about solidarity, except obviously if one is of the opinion that the insurance mechanism is founded on the idea of solidarity.[198]

In brief, a patchwork of mechanisms exists; nevertheless, the victim is never guaranteed to obtain full compensation of his/her damage. As said in the beginning of this report, quite often, victims of catastrophes are confronted not only with pain and suffering but also with financial, proceedings and legal problems.

List of References

C. von Bar/U. Drobnig, *The Interaction of Contract Law and Tort and Property in Europe. A comparative Study* (2004), 28–31.

M. Bussani/V.V. Palmer, *Pure Economic Loss in Europe* (2003), 131–132.

D. de Callataÿ, L'évaluation et la réparation du préjudice corporel en droit commun (accidents non mortels), [1994] *Revue Générale des Assurances et des Responsabilités* (R.G.A.R.), no. 12286(5).

[197] On 7 and 14 July 2005, the new regime based on this idea was adopted by the Belgian Parliament. The regime adopted in 2005 is not detailed in the present report dated from December 2004.

[198] The Ministry of the Economy is of the opinion that the new suggestions remain the expression of national solidarity. Cf. the parliamentary documents ("*Parl. Doc.*, Senaat, Handelingen no. 3-28 van de plenaire vergadering van donderdag 11 december 2003"); *Assur-info*, October 2004, V: Over het wetsontwerp betreffende de natuurrampen: "Technisch gezien, is dit ontwerp klaar. Het heeft tot doel de wet van 21 mei 2003 grondig te wijzigen, zodat die wet op technisch vlak operationeel kan worden. De verplichte dekking van de brandverzekering wordt uitgebreid tot alle rampen (naast overstromingen en stormen ook aardbevingen, dijkbreuken, vloedgolven, grondverschuivingen en -verzakkingen) en tot alle brandverzekerden. Op die manier wordt er een algemene solidariteit ingevoerd die de dekking tegen het risico van natuurrampen voor iedereen toegankelijk zal maken".

H. Claassens, *Schadevergoeding voor slachtoffers bij gasramp te Gellingen-Ghislenghien – 30.7.2004. Enkele praktische tips inzake verzekeringen*, published on <http://www.brandwonden.be/ghislenghien/20040811-Stichting-Gellingen-Fr.pdf>.

H. Claassens, La responsabilité objective et l'assurance obligatoire en cas d'incendie ou d'explosion frappant des établissements habituellement accessibles au public, in: *Mélanges offerts à Marcel Fontaine* (2003), 613, fn. 22.

Ph. Colle, *Handboek bijzonder gereglementeerde verzekeringscontracten* (2001), 59, no. 110.

L. Cornelis, Ongeschikt voor gevoelige juristen: over de intieme verhouding tussen schade en causaal verband, in: B. Tilleman/I. Claeys (eds.), *Buitencontractuele aansprakelijkheid* (2004), 249.

H. Cousy/D. Droshout, Belgium, in: B.A. Koch/H. Koziol (eds.), *Unification of Tort Law: Strict Liability* (2002), 43–74.

B. Dubuisson, *Obligations extra contractuelles* (course book Université catholique de Louvain, 2003–2004).

J.M. van Dunné, Liability for pure economic loss: rule or exception? A comparatist's view of the civil law – common law split on compensation of non physical damage in tort law, [1999] *European Review of Private Law* (E.R.P.L.), 412.

M. Faure, Environmental liability in Belgium, in: K. Deketelaere/M. Faure (eds.), *Environmental Law in the United Kingdom and Belgium from a Comparative Perspective* (1999), 213–215.

J.-L. Fagnart, L'évaluation et la réparation du préjudice corporel en droit commun (principes généraux – accidents mortels), [1994] R.G.A.R., no. 12268(2), no. 46.

Ph. Hoyois/D. Guha-Sapir, *Three decades of floods in Europe: a preliminary analysis of EMDAT data*, <http://www.cred.be/docs/publictions/FLOOD-EUR.pdf>.

I. Moreau-Margrève/M. Vanwijck-Alexandre, Les 'mass torts' en droit belge?, in: *Liber Amicorum Yvon Hannequart & Roger Rasir* (1997), 259, no. 6.

E. van Nuffel, Financiële tegemoetkoming van de Staat bij natuurrampen (algemene rampen) in België, in: H. Cousy/H. Claassens (eds.), *Natuurrampen en verzekering* (1995), 47.

W. Peeters, De 'Indicatieve tabel' als antwoord op de noden van de praktijk, in: M. Van den Bossche (ed.), *De indicative tabel. Een praktisch werkinstrument voor de evaluatie van menselijke schade* (2001), 9.

J. Ronse (with the cooperation of L. De Wilde/A. Claeys/I. Mallems), *Schade en schadeloosstelling* (2nd edn. first part, coll. A.P.R. 1984), 173, no. 230.

D. Simoens, *Buitencontractuele aansprakelijkheid. Deel II. Schade en schadeloosstelling* (1999), 6.

France

Michel Cannarsa, Fabien Lafay, and Olivier Moréteau

Part I. Introduction

France may well be described as a Welfare State. Of the three words engraved above the front door of all public buildings, *liberté, égalité, fraternité* (liberty, equality, fraternity), the third expresses the social value on which national solidarity is based. French citizens expect State assistance in many events of their existence. 1

Catastrophes, be they natural or industrial, are typical events generating a strong expectation for national solidarity. In 1976, French citizens found it acceptable to pay an additional tax to subsidise farmers victim of a severe drought. In 2003, a significant proportion of the population seemed ready to accept working an additional day (sacrificing a public holiday rather than questioning the *droit acquis* to work 35 hours a week) every year in order to improve the situation of the older generation: 15,000 elderly people had died as a direct or indirect consequence of the most severe heat-wave in recent history.

The French mentality is more willing to see compensation to the victims of catastrophes as a manifestation of national solidarity than the redress of a wrong by a party liable in tort. Compensation may come from the social insurance system, compulsory first party insurance coverage or compensation funds, in any case the risk is to a large extent socialised.[1]

In 1946, the principle was given constitutional value. The Preamble to the Constitution of 1946, referred to in the Preamble to the present Constitution of 1958, states "the solidarity and equality of all French people as to the charge resulting from national calamities".[2] This report surveys the vast amount of legislation and regulation tailored to enforce this principle,[3] commenting on 2

[1] The combination of liability and socialisation of risks is emphasised in a recent report of the *Conseil d'Etat* (highest administrative court, CE), *Rapport public 2005, Responsabilité et socialisation du risque*, La Documentation française, 2005. This report deals *inter alia* with compensation of victims of catastrophes and contains interesting comparative data.

[2] 12th paragraph: "la solidarité et l'égalité de tous les Français devant les charges qui résultent des calamités nationales".

[3] The CE indeed ruled that this Preamble may not serve as an independent cause of action: CE 29 November 1968, *Tallagrand*, Rec., 607.

its main features and recent evolution. It will focus on social compensation rather than giving details on tort liability, the latter being of limited importance as far as catastrophes are concerned, whether natural or created by human interference.

Compulsory compensation schemes have been flourishing in recent years, following a number of catastrophes at home or abroad, including Seveso (1976), Bhopal (1984), Mexico (1985), Tchernobyl (1986), the landslide in Grand Bornand (1987) and more recently the devastating tempest of December 1999 and the explosion of the AZF factory in Toulouse in September 2001. A number of terrorist attacks in 1986, 1995 and 1996, followed with the threat of more devastating events after 11 September 2001 also caused terrorism to be taken into account as a cause of major catastrophes. A new statute was enacted in July 2003, dealing with the environmental, material and human health effects of industrial activities as well as of natural catastrophes.[4]

3 The French system favours universal social insurance coverage (*Sécurité sociale*, hereafter called Social Security), non-compulsory first party insurance (yet including compulsory coverage of catastrophes) and, in respect of terrorist attacks, recourse to a compensation fund. Reassurance with State coverage is also provided for. Seldom do victims have to face the complexity of court actions against tortfeasors. Such actions are not eliminated but are usually exerted by insurance companies and compensation funds subrogated into the victim's rights after having paid compensation. The report shows that the system is victim friendly but does not make life easy for subrogated payees, who have to cope with a complex tort law, combining fault based liability and strict liability on the one hand, and a dual private law and public law tort system on the other hand.

In addition to compensation schemes, French law makes provision to organise public help in case of emergencies (Plan ORSEC, meaning *organisation des secours*) and also to prevent major risks, industrial and natural.[5]

Part II. General Scope of the Compensation System

4 Physical injury and damage to property are not compensated in the same way. Here is an outline of the French system.

I. Physical Injury

5 The victim of physical injury and the dependants of a deceased person are entitled to partial compensation by the Social Security system. Social protection was known to be minimal and largely insufficient in case of death and perma-

[4] See Law No. 2003-699 of 30 July 2003 relating to the prevention of technological and natural risks and the compensation of damage. For an overview of the new Act, see C. Gory, L'assurance des risques technologiques et naturels, [2003] *Gazette du Palais* (Gaz. Pal.), 3.

[5] Law No. 2003-699 of 30 July 2003 relating to the prevention of technological and natural risks and the compensation of damage. Most provisions are embodied in the *Code de l'environnement* (Environment Code). Those relating to the compensation of victims, amending the *Code des assurances* (Insurance Code), will be surveyed in this report.

nent incapacity. Victims had to rely on tort law in order to receive full compensation.

The creation in the year 2000 of a new insurance system, called *garantie accidents de la vie* (meaning guarantee for accidents of life), offers at a minimal cost (starting as low as € 15 per month for full family coverage) almost full coverage of the consequences of death (for the dependants) or physical injury when such damage occurs in the following circumstances: accidents occurring in the course of private life, whether at home or outside, consequences of natural or technological catastrophes, consequences of crimes and terrorist attacks and consequences of a medical risk. The accident must always have been caused by some outside event, which normally excludes the compensation of the consequences of a heart attack. The compensation is usually limited to a maximum amount of € 1 million. It also covers the compensation of economic loss, loss of amenity and pain and suffering. The *garantie accidents de la vie* is almost a novelty in France. Two major mutual insurance companies offered similar and yet not as extended coverage in the past. It is unprecedented in Europe. 6

Victims of terrorist attacks may also be compensated by a compensation fund, providing full compensation for physical injury and mental suffering. 7

II. Damage to Property

Damage to property is in most cases covered by first party insurance. As explained below, insurance companies may not exclude the coverage of risks such as natural catastrophes and terrorist attacks. However, in the case of natural catastrophes, the insured may not be compensated in all cases unless the event is declared a "natural catastrophe" by government decision. Most people in France benefit from such contracts, when they live in rented premises or own their house or apartment. 8

A prevention fund for major natural risks was created in 2002 to compensate people who have to be displaced and expropriated when they happen to live in high-risk zones.[6] 9

One may say that the victims will usually be satisfied with the compensation received from their insurance company in addition to what they receive from Social Security. Tort actions are usually made by insurance companies and the compensation fund (in case of terror attacks) that are subrogated in the victims' rights. Only people not having subscribed to the *garantie des accidents de la vie* or *assurance individuelle accident* may be tempted to sue in tort, but it is difficult to find a natural or legal person answerable in the case of a natural catastrophe. 10

[6] Law No. 2002-276 of 27 February 2002, art. 159.

Part III. More Detailed Information

11 The system combines a general or universal Social Security system, private (non-compulsory) insurance with extensive coverage, compensation funds and ultimately tort law, with recourse to different courts and different rules depending on whether the defendant is a private person or a State or public authority.

I. Social Security

12 All French citizens and people residing in France, including their dependants (spouse or partner, children under 18), benefit from Social Security. The system was created in 1945 and has been improved ever since[7] so as to be accessible to everyone, even to those who may not contribute financially to the funding of the system. Most people contribute to and benefit from the general regime of Social Security (*régime général de la sécurité sociale*). In 1999, a statute extended protection and coverage to everyone not benefiting from the general regime, under the name of universal health coverage (*couverture maladie universelle*).[8] Everyone is now entitled to medical care, even the poorest victims, that is to say those victims who have not earned sufficiently to be liable to pay social contributions. Minimal coverage is available for all kinds of disease or injury, whatever the cause. Victims of accidents or natural catastrophes will indeed turn to Social Security for coverage of their medical expenses.

Health insurance covers the expenses within a statutory percentage, usually 70% of a statutory cost (*base de remboursement*). The uncovered part left to be borne by the insured is supposed to moderate and refrain a consumer attitude towards health benefits (*ticket modérateur*). Some may benefit from 100% coverage, which is typically the case with pregnant women, disabled people and patients suffering from a long disease.

13 The Social Security system also has a fund for the purposes of sickness payments where the injured has suffered a loss caused by days off work.[9] Any employee involved in an accident at work has a right to be compensated for the incapacity resulting from the injury.

14 More frequently than not, the insured will benefit from a complementary insurance subscribed to either by employers or by themselves, and usually administered by mutual insurance. The purpose is to cover the *ticket modérateur*, partly or in full, and to offer additional benefits, especially when the statutory cost of a given medical expense is fixed far below the actual cost. This is typi-

[7] Ordinance of 4 October 1945 and *Code de la sécurité sociale*. See J.-P. Chauchard, *Droit de la Sécurité sociale* (2nd edn. 1998); J.J. Dupeyroux/R. Ruellau, *Droit de la Sécurité sociale* (13th edn. 1998); D.C. Lambert, *L'Etat providence en question* (1990).

[8] Law No. 99-641 of 27 July 1999, in *Code de la sécurité sociale* (Social Security Code) article L.380.1; F. Taquet, Premières réflexions sur la loi du 27 juillet 1999…, [1999] Gaz. Pal., 21.

[9] See article L. 323-1 and R. 323-1 *Code de la sécurité sociale*.

cally the case for dental appliances and eyeglasses, which are assessed at about a tenth or a fifth of the actual cost.

Benefits may be provided by way of direct payment to hospitals or health providers (*tiers payant*), or by way of refund (*remboursement*). There is a tendency to generalise direct payments by Social Security to health providers, a system facilitated by the general use of an electronic health identification card (*carte vitale*), tendered by patients to general practitioners, chemists, hospitals and other health providers. In this case, the patient only pays the extra part not covered by health insurance (*ticket modérateur*). In some cases, no payment is due by the patient. This applies to those benefiting from a 100% coverage but also to people covered by complementary insurance when the latter is substituted to Social Security for the management of the system. This is the case with most civil servants. For instance, people employed by the public education system may benefit from a one-stop service arranged by the *Mutuelle générale de l'éducation nationale*. 15

Hospital expenses are usually paid directly by Social Security, which covers 80% of the expense in the case of public hospitals and also private hospitals when having entered into an agreement with the Social Security (*cliniques conventionnées*). In addition, the patient also has to pay a further lump sum (for daily services such as food) which amounts to a little more than € 10 per day. 16

General practitioners and specialists may also enter into an agreement with Social Security (*médecins conventionnés*). In that case, medical fees are fixed by such agreements (often on the basis of units) and are covered, to the exclusion of the *ticket modérateur*. The doctor may exceed this amount (*droit au dépassement*) in which case there is no refund for the excess. A majority of specialists do operate under a free fee basis which goes far beyond the Social Security agreed amounts. 17

A long stay in hospital, especially where surgery is needed, may be quite costly when the patient is bound to pay 20% of a high bill. This is why many people subscribe to an additional "individual" insurance (*assurance individuelle accident*) or the new insurance, *garantie accidents de la vie*.

II. Insurance

French law operates on the basic assumption that most citizens subscribe to first party insurance to cover possible damage to their property. However, it is to be noted that such insurance is not compulsory. Recent catastrophes revealed that approximately up to 15% victims of major disasters are not insured.[10] 18

Regarding damage to property, all persons living in rented premises subscribe to an insurance called *multirisque habitation*, covering most risks to the

[10] See *infra* no. 81.

building, its contents, and the consequences of tortious acts committed by the insured or his dependants. It is common practice for a landlord to request the prospective tenant to give evidence of such insurance before signing the lease. Private house and apartment owners also subscribe to such insurance, especially when the property is mortgaged.

A. *Insurance Cover of Natural Catastrophes*

19 Under such policies, including also first party car insurance for the insured value of the car and property left in it,[11] insurance companies are bound by law to insure damage resulting from natural catastrophes.[12] The Insurance Code gives the following definition.[13]

> "Non-insurable direct material damage whose determining cause was the abnormal intensity of a natural agent, when normal measures to be taken to protect against such damage have been unable to prevent the occurrence thereof or could not be taken shall be deemed to be natural disasters within the meaning of this chapter".

This must be an unusual phenomenon, a natural one not provoked by human activity. The phenomenon must be abnormal. This may mean unusual, because of exceptional intensity or duration. For instance, continuous rain has nothing exceptional but may become so if occurring over a very long period. An unusual change in the ecosystem may also qualify. Last, it should be unavoidable, in the sense that the consequences may not be avoided by the taking of normal care. It may be compared to *force majeure*.[14]

According to the Insurance Code itself, as quoted above, the damage must be "uninsurable", a paradoxical word from the moment the risk must be compulsorily insured. However, where an exceptional risk (one of those traditionally excluded before the creation of the compulsory system) is nonetheless covered by insurance, the more favourable coverage will of course apply.

Another feature that appears in legal literature (though not expressly in the above-mentioned statutory definition) is that the disaster should be perceived as intolerable, in such a way that the collective consciousness compels it to be described as a natural catastrophe. Floods, landslides, snowfalls and droughts usually qualify. Tempests are usually covered by assurance but, as explained below in this paragraph, they today qualify when of outstanding magnitude.

20 According to the Insurance Code, natural catastrophes also include landslides due to subterranean cavities, natural or man-made, except in the latter case

[11] Third party car insurance is compulsory. People may in addition subscribe to first party insurance to cover damage caused to their car and property transported in the car.

[12] Law No. 82-600 of 13 July 1982 relating to the compensation of victims of natural catastrophes, presently *Code des assurances*, article L 125-1 to L 125-6. See P. Segur, La catastrophe et le risque naturel, essai de définition juridique, [1997] *Revue Générale du Droit des Assurances* (RGDA), 1693.

[13] Article L 125-1 par. 3, translation Legigrance (<http://www.legifrance.gouv.fr>).

[14] *Première chambre civile de la Cour de Cassation* (Cass. Civ. 1ère), 7 July 1998, RGDA, 1998, 841, note Vincent.

when caused by past or present exploitation of a mine.[15] A clause in the contract must indicate that natural disasters are covered and the contract may not exclude the coverage for any property insured under the contract.[16] All contracts are presumed to include such a clause and every exclusion clause must be disregarded.[17]

The contract may not exclude "the reimbursement of the cost of geotechnics studies rendered necessary prior to repairing constructions affected by the effects of a natural disaster".[18] Victims may only be compensated for the consequences of such risks under the compulsory scheme where the Government recognises and declares that there is a "natural catastrophe". This is done by way of administrative order, stating the geographic zone and times affected by the natural catastrophe and the nature of the damage to be covered by the insurance.[19] This causes victims and local authorities to put the State government under pressure every time a disaster happens. Ministers, and even the President of the Republic, will promptly appear on the scene and promise an immediate declaration, so that the victims may be quickly compensated.

The compulsory coverage in case of natural disaster does not apply to some categories of damage: "damage caused to non-gathered crops, cultivation, soil and livestock outside premises", "damage sustained by the hulls of air, marine, lake and inland waterway vehicles as well as goods in transit".[20] All excluded types of damage are covered otherwise,[21] free from the additional contribution levied on insurance policies for the coverage of natural catastrophes.[22]

Where no declaration of "natural catastrophe" is made, the insured may only benefit from coverage of the risks expressly covered under the insurance policy.

In 1990, compulsory coverage was extended to damage caused by tempests, hurricanes and cyclones for every policy covering the risk of fire.[23] Such coverage may not be excluded and applies where no declaration of "natural catastrophe" has been made. However, this does not apply where the winds "have reached or exceeded 145 kilometres an hour on average over ten minutes or 215 kilometres an hour in gusts",[24] in which case compensation is not due under the contract but exclusively if a declaration of a "natural catastrophe" has been made. 21

[15] Article L 125-1 §§ 1 and 5.
[16] Article L 125-2 §§ 1 and 2.
[17] Article L 125-3.
[18] Article L 125-4.
[19] Article L 125-1 § 4, as amended by Law No. 92-665 of 16 July 1992.
[20] Article L 125-5.
[21] Law No. 64-704 of 10 July 1964 as amended, organising a cover scheme against agricultural disasters, to be found in *Code rural* (Rural Code) article L 361-1 to 21 and described in *infra* no. 28.
[22] As explained *infra* no. 28.
[23] Law No. 90-509 of 25 July 1990, article L 122-7 *Code des assurances*.
[24] Article L 122-7.

There is no specific provision regarding floods. This means that damage caused by flooding may only be covered by the effect of an express stipulation in the contract or, failing express coverage, if the devastating event has been declared a "natural catastrophe".

B. Insurance Cover of Man-made Catastrophes

22 Insured victims of damage to property caused by terrorist attacks or bombing perpetrated on French territory will benefit from full insurance coverage. Indeed, article L 126-2 of the Insurance Code makes such coverage compulsory: "Property insurance contracts may not exclude the insurer's cover for damage as a result of terrorist attacks or bombing perpetrated on the national territory. Any clause to the contrary shall be deemed non written". This reference to "property insurance contracts" includes housing insurance (*multirisque habitation*) as well as first party motor vehicle insurance.

Regarding personal injury, pain and suffering and other personal damage, victims of terrorist attacks will benefit from the Compensation Fund for the victims of terrorist actions and other offences.[25] They may also call upon a special insurance policy (*couverture individuelle accident; garantie des accidents de la vie* etc.) but, as explained below, may not be compensated twice for the same damage.[26]

23 Wherever an industrial disaster occurs, for reasons not linked to a terrorist attack, the following rules apply. A new Act was enacted in July 2003, dealing with the environmental, material and human health effects of industrial activities as well as for natural catastrophes.[27] The Act came in response to a disaster which occurred on 21 September 2001, when the explosion of a chemical plant called AZF (owned by Total Fina Elf) located in Toulouse killed 30 people, injured another 5,000 and devastated thousands of private and public buildings.[28] Admittedly, this disaster was not caused by a terrorist attack.

The new Act intends to extend first party insurance coverage like the one called *multirisque habitation*, to damage caused by such industrial catastrophes. Though some of the victims in the AZF case (15% of them) were uninsured since the *multirisque habitation* insurance is not mandatory, insurance companies had to cope with 70,000 claims (*déclarations de sinistres*) linked to the Toulouse catastrophe. Insurance companies have provided compensation for nearly all these claims.

24 For uninsured victims, the only way to obtain redress was to sue the owner of the chemical plant in tort. As mentioned below, the new law of 2003 allows compensation of the uninsured victims of technological catastrophes by a Compensation Fund.[29]

[25] *Infra* no. 29.
[26] *Infra* no. 69–77.
[27] Law No. 2000-699 of 30 July 2003.
[28] For more details, see *infra* no. 81.
[29] See article L. 421-16 *Code des assurances*, *infra* no. 27 and 42.

The new articles L. 128-1 to 128-4 of the Insurance Code set the framework of the new mechanism. Article L. 128-1 of the Code gives a definition of the "*situation of technological catastrophe*" which will stem from an accident occurring in a specific plant (what is called *installation classée*), causing damage to a large number of buildings. An official statement will recognise the catastrophe situation. Article L. 128-2 of the Insurance Code specifies that the coverage of first party motor vehicles and housing insurance (*multirisque habitation*) extends to risks linked to technological catastrophes. This new article applies to undergoing first party insurance contracts.[30] It should be underlined that the new articles do not set up a mandatory first party insurance (though the majority of people subscribe to such insurance). The Act does not apply to third party insurance: damage caused by natural or technological catastrophes are not covered by third party insurance. 25

The new provisions apply to all victims, whether they are private persons or businesses. Its financing has not been regulated yet.

Only property damage is within the scope of the 2003 Act, personal injuries being left aside, as it is the case in the field of natural catastrophes. Here again, the general tort system will have a role to play in the compensation of such injuries. 26

The insurance companies, in case of a technological catastrophe, are bound to make a compensation proposal within three months after the victim asked for this compensation or after the official statement declaring the catastrophe.

The new Article L. 128-3 of the Insurance Code refers to the subrogation of the insurer to the plaintiff's right against the party at fault, where compensation has been provided by the insurer according to the new Article L. 128-2.

It is to be noted that the new scheme for technological catastrophes is not meant to cover technological disasters caused by terrorist attacks. As explained above, in such a case, compensation of victims covered by first party insurance is compulsory and immediate and does not depend on an official statement recognising the catastrophe situation. However, in case of doubt as to the cause of the catastrophe, one may expect government authorities to be urged by the media and the public to make such recognition in order to facilitate prompt compensation.

III. Compensation Funds

A *fonds de garantie automobile* was created in 1951 to compensate victims of road traffic accidents where the tortfeasor has not been identified or is insolvent.[31] As explained below,[32] this Fund may only intervene in a subsidiary 27

[30] See article 81 III, Law of 30 July 2003.

[31] *Code des assurances*, article L 421-1: "A guarantee fund has been established to compensate victims of personal injury as a result of an accident in which a motor vehicle as well as its trailers or semi-trailers is involved, to the exclusion of railways and tramways running on dedicated tracks, when the person liable for the loss is unknown or is not insured, apart from a legal dispensation from compulsory insurance, or when its insurer is entirely or partly insolvent. The guarantee fund shall pay the indemnities allocated to the victims or their assigns that cannot be covered in any other respect, when the accident entitles them to compensation".

[32] *Infra* no. 42.

way, in the following situations: the tortfeasor was not identified or, where he was, damages may not be recovered due to the tortfeasor's insolvency. The fund also intervenes in the case of the insurer's total or partial insolvency.

The Law 30 July 2003 extends coverage by this fund to uninsured victims of technological catastrophes.[33]

28 Another compensation fund was created in 1964 to compensate farmers in case of damage to property (*fonds national de garantie des calamités agricoles*): this Fund covers non-insurable damage of exceptional importance caused by variations of abnormal intensity of a natural element.[34] It covers damage to growing crops, cultures and chattel, land and buildings, wherever used for agricultural purposes.[35] Only farmers sufficiently insured against normal insurable risks may benefit from the fund.[36] Coverage may not exceed 75% of the suffered damage and insured victims may also obtain loans, the fund covering part of the interest for two years when the damage exceeds 60% of the value of the damaged property.[37] As a consequence of the exceptional heat-wave of summer 2003, farmers could benefit from special four-year or seven-year loans with an interest rate of 2.5% per annum, reduced in some cases to 1.5%.[38] This is to repair damage to the crops and chattel.

29 A Compensation Fund for the victims of Terrorist Action and other Offences (as presently called) was created by a law of 9 September 1986 (art. 9), a year when France was the subject of a number of terrorist attacks.[39] Victims of terrorist attacks had organised themselves as a pressure group (*Association SOS Attentats*), requesting the legislature to intervene. The purpose was to obtain within weeks and without complex and lengthy proceedings full compensation of personal injury, including pain and suffering, as well as of the economic loss suffered by the victims' dependants. This was afforded by the creation of the new compensation fund. The request relating to the compensation of damage to property was dealt with by the medium of first party insurance, which must cover damage caused by terrorist attacks.[40] The Compensation Fund was improved by a law of 6 July 1990. Funding is provided by a levy on the premiums paid to insurance companies insuring damage to property (€ 3 per contract in 2003).

The Fund compensates all French citizens victim of a terrorist attack in France or abroad, as well as foreign victims of a terrorist attack in a French territory.

[33] See article L. 421-16 *Code des assurances*.
[34] Law No. 64-706 of 10 July 1964, to be found in *Code rural* article L 361-2.
[35] Article L 361-6 *Code rural*.
[36] Article L 361-6 *Code rural*.
[37] Article L 361-13 *Code rural*.
[38] Arrêté of 9 September 2003.
[39] For further details, see O. Moréteau/F. Lafay, Liability for Acts of Terrorism Under French Law, in: B.A. Koch (ed.), *Liability for Acts of Terrorism in a Comparative Perspective* (2003), 29–46.
[40] *Supra* no. 22.

The Fund provides full compensation for physical injury, pain and suffering and any consequential loss, but does not cover damage to property. In case of death, the victim's dependants are compensated for their economic loss. Compensation includes the coverage of all medical expenses as well as all additional expenses arising from physical impairment such as medical appliances and special fittings, costs related to nursing and assistance with housework, in addition to welfare benefits. The victim may also claim additional compensation for damage to or loss of clothing, within certain statutory limits.

By way of subrogation, the victim's entire claim is assigned to the Fund.

Some important exceptions are made in order to afford better and more efficient protection to some basic principles of French law. The fact that the Fund must pay compensation, even though the terrorists have been identified and prosecuted, reveals a national duty of solidarity.

The law of 1990 grants the victims of terrorism the status of civil victims of war (*victimes civiles de guerre*), with all the rights and advantages inherent in such status. This includes totally free medical care and the benefit of a pension, in addition to compensation.

IV. Tort Law

The central point to be grasped here is that the victim is seldom under pressure 30
to fight a compensation claim in court against a tortfeasor. This may be necessary in cases where the victim did not contract for sufficient insurance cover. However, most tort claims are made by Social Security, insurance companies and compensation funds subrogated in the victim's rights after having paid compensation.

A. *Private Law*

Until the twentieth century, French jurisprudence required proof of fault in ac- 31
cordance with art. 1382 of the French Civil Code (this article makes provision for general liability as follows: "Anyone who, through his act, causes damage to another by his fault shall be obliged to compensate the damage"), except in the case of industrial accidents where the injured workman benefited from the law of 9 April 1898 which released him from the necessity of proving fault.

The central change in personal injury law doctrine has been the development of a robust regime of liability without fault. Damage caused by things (since the famous *Teffaine* decision of the *Cour de cassation* in 1896)[41] has been governed by art. 1384 paragraph 1 which provides that a person is responsible for damage caused by things which are under his control (art. 1384 states: "[Man] is liable not only for the damage which he caused by his own act, but also for that which is caused by the act of persons for whom he is responsible, or by things which he has in his keeping…").

In certain circumstances, fault-based liability is still relevant. In these cases the plaintiff must establish fault, and the conduct of the defendant will clearly be relevant. Below, we describe how the two differing regimes on lia-

[41] Cass. Civ., 16 June 1896, [1897] *Sirey* (S.), I, 17, note A. Esmein.

bility (liability for fault and strict liability) apply, before briefly setting out the specific no-fault schemes.

1. Liability Based on Fault

32 Liability based on fault or negligence can arise due to an act or an omission. The tortfeasor may create a risk for the victim whether by an act or by an omission. Under art. 1382 of the Civil Code, the person who caused an event to happen, and who was at fault, is liable for it. Art. 1383 stipulates that liability is also established where conduct manifests itself in the form of an omission.[42] Misconduct occurs where the defendant acts in breach of a statutory duty or the rules of conduct derived from the general principle of *neminem laedere*.[43] The courts evaluate whether the individual exercised the degree of care expected of the reasonable man in the particular circumstances.

The existence, content and scope of the relevant duty of care depend upon a variety of issues. For some causes of action, compensation will be awarded only where the plaintiff is able to prove negligence on the part of the defendant.

2. Strict Liability

33 The development in the interpretation of classical rules on liability (for fault) has placed considerable emphasis on the protection of life, bodily integrity and health.

In the landmark *Teffaine* decision,[44] the *Cour de cassation* ruled that art. 1384 paragraph 1 could be interpreted as a general stand-alone provision providing for a presumption of responsibility where damage is caused by things of whatever sort.

This article has been used ever since as the principal tool for the application of strict liability in tort. The courts use the article to impose liability on the sole basis of the "use, direction and control"[45] by the defendant of the thing which caused the damage. We can speak of strict liability since it is no

[42] "Everyone is responsible for the damage caused not only by his act but also by his negligence or carelessness".

[43] B. Starck/H. Roland/L Boyer, *Droit civil, Obligations, Responsabilité délictuelle* (6th edn. 1998), no. 28; G. Viney, *La responsabilité: conditions* (2nd edn. 1998), no. 48; F. Terré/Y Lequette/P. Simler, *Les obligations* (7th edn. 2002).

[44] F. Bénac-Schmidt/Ch. Larroumet, V Responsabilité du fait des choses inanimées, [1990] *Encyclopedie Juridique Dalloz: Répertoire de droit civil* (Dalloz Rép. civ.); J. Carbonnier, *Droit civil* (vol. IV. Les obligations 2000), no. 255 *et seq.*; G. Viney (*supra* fn. 43), no. 628 *et seq.*; F. Terré/Ph. Simler/Y Lequette (*supra* fn. 43), no. 714 *et seq.*

[45] *Chambres réunies de la Cour de Cassation,* (Cass. Ch. réun.), 2 December 1941, [1942] *Dalloz* (D)., note G. Ripert; [1941] S., 1, 217, note H. Mazeaud; P. Roubier, L'arrêt des Chambres réunies du 2 décembre 1941 et la théorie générale de la responsabilité civile, [1942] *La Semaine Juridique: Juris Classeur Périodique* (JCP), I.257; B. Goldmann, *La détermination du gardien responsable du fait des choses inanimées* (1946); B. Goldman, Garde de la structure et garde du comportement, in: *Mélanges en l'honneur de Paul Roubier* (vol. II 1961), 51 *et seq.*; A. Tunc, La détermination du gardien dans la responsabilité du fait des choses inanimées, [1960] JCP, I.1592, no 11.

defence for the keeper (*gardien*) to show that he took all the precautions which a prudent and diligent man would have taken.[46]

Three conditions must exist in order for such liability to be imposed: 34

A thing must have caused the damage. The principle applies to things which are hazardous such as liquid oxygen, for example,[47] explosives,[48] bullets,[49] and to ordinary objects such as a chair,[50] bicycle,[51] as well as very big things like ships.[52]

The act of the thing must be an intervention. Art. 1384.1 does not apply in cases where the thing has been "purely passive" in the production of damage. If a moving object has caused harm by colliding with the plaintiff's person or his property, the presumption of responsibility means that the plaintiff need prove only causation.[53] But if the thing was stationary, or normal, it must be established that the object was the *cause génératrice*, the "generating cause" of the accident.[54]

The defendant must have had "guard" of the thing. To have guard is normally to have the use, direction and control of the thing (including also the power to direct and control: the employer has control of any thing used by his employees). The owner, of a chemical plant for example, is usually the *gardien* unless he has lost or transferred the use, direction and control of the thing to someone else.

Admissible defences are *cas fortuit* and *force majeure* (damage must have been inevitable).[55] The onus placed on the defendant is said to create an "objective theory of created risk".

[46] Cass. Ch. réun., 13 February 1930 (*Jand'heur* case), S. 1930.I.121. This decision is said to be the first by virtue of which art. 1384 was transformed into a general and autonomous strict liability regime for things of all kinds. It indeed clearly extended strict liability to damage caused by things activated by man, such as a driven car. A separate law to facilitate the compensation of victims of road traffic accidents, based on strict liability, was later adopted: Law No. 85-677 of 5 July 1985.

[47] *Deuxième chambre civile de la Cour de Cassation* (Cass. Civ. 2ième), 10 June 1960, [1960] D., Jur., 609, note R. Rodière.

[48] *Ville de Montigny-lès-Metz v Sté Cardem et autres*, [1994] D., Jur., 80.

[49] Cass. Civ. 2ième, 29 March 1984, [1984] Gaz. Pal., 2, pan. 264, note F. Chabas.

[50] Cass. Civ. 2ième, 8 March 1995, [1995] D., somm. 232, note Ph. Delebecque.

[51] Cass. Civ. 2ième, 18 November 1987, [1988] Gaz. Pal., I, pan. 29.

[52] *Chambre mixte de la Cour de Cassation* (Cass. Ch. mixte), 4 December 1981, [1982] JCP, II.19748, note H. Mazeaud.

[53] Cass. Civ. 2ième, 29 May 1964, [1965] JCP, II.14248, note J. Boré; Cass. Civ. 2ième, 13 May 1981, [1981] Gaz. Pal., 2, pan., 353, note F. Chabas; Cass. Civ. 2ième, 28 November 1984, [1985] JCP, II.20477, note N. Dejean de la Bâtie.

[54] Cass. Civ. 2ième, 7 March 1979, [1980] D., I.R., 35, note Ch. Larroumet (fragility of the glass); Cass. Civ. 2ième, 19 May 1976, D. [1976], I.R., 233 (abnormal position of a car).

[55] F. Chabas, Vo Force Majeure (Dalloz Rép. Civ.); Cass. Civ. 3ième, 29 June 1988, [1988] D., I.R., 216; Cass. Civ. 2ième, 21 June 1966, [1966] D., 645, note A. Tunc (black ice); Cass. Civ. 2ième, 5 January 1994, [1994] JCP, IV.608 (the event must be unforeseeable and unavoidable).

B. Public Law

35 The liability of the State and of certain public authorities is governed by administrative law and falls within the jurisdiction of separate administrative courts. Like most continental countries, France has two court systems which generates problems of jurisdiction. In addition, administrative courts do not apply the Civil Code to disputes within their jurisdiction.

Two non-contractual liability regimes for public authorities exist under French administrative law. The first is fault-based, and liability applies whenever any administrative action is found by administrative courts to be unlawful. The second is a no-fault regime applicable in certain circumstances and which is based on the principle of equality before public burdens. Liability for fault, which includes negligence, is divided into two categories: liability for "simple" fault (*faute simple*) and liability for gross negligence (*faute lourde*). Only those acts which are so serious as to evidence a complete lack of responsibility constitute gross negligence. This was aimed at preserving the autonomy of those engaged in so-called complex activities.

36 It is remarkably difficult to make the State liable for breach of a duty to ensure safety in public places. Evidence of gross negligence (*faute lourde*) needs to be adduced.[56] For instance, the fact that the State did not manage to reduce the number of terrorist attacks in Corsica may not be considered as gross negligence generating State liability.[57] An insufficient number of police is no ground for action, nor is the fact that a protective fence was not high enough.[58] Where a suspicious parcel has been found, gross negligence of the police must be proved to make the State liable. If the police injures a person when trying to arrest terrorists, the State may be declared liable by the civil courts, since the police is no longer acting in the course of its administrative functions but within its so-called judicial activity, a subtlety that even a French lawyer might find hard to understand.[59]

In the case of terrorist actions as well as natural catastrophes, a tendency has been observed to create new compensation regimes such as those described above rather than stretching the possibility of making the State or public administration liable.[60]

37 However, being subrogated into the victims' rights, insurance companies do not hesitate to sue the State or local authorities for gross negligence for failure to anticipate a foreseeable risk. It is indeed the duty of local authorities to give notice of the existence of certain risks and to take any reasonable step to prevent such risks. The disastrous flooding at Grand-Bornand on 14 July 1987,

[56] CE 26 January 1968, *Dame Maron*, 69, [1968] *Actualité juridique Droit Administratif* (A.J.D.A.), 293: attacks against the Ambassador of Turkey; police protecting the ambassador held not to be negligent.

[57] *Cour administrative d'appel* (Administrative Court of Appeal, CAA) Marseille, 5 July 2001, no. 98 MA01316, unreported.

[58] CAA Marseille, 23 November 2000, unreported.

[59] *Le Tribunal des Conflits* (TC), 7 June 1951, *Dame Noualek*, 636, S. [1952], 3.13.

[60] Ph. Le Tourneau/L. Cadiet, *Droit de la responsabilité et des contrats* (2002), no. 238.

which caused 23 persons to die in addition to important damage to property, affords a good example.[61] A summer thunderstorm in the mountains surrounding the valley where the village of Grand-Bornand is located caused two rivers to surge very rapidly and wash away camping grounds located nearby the river. When sued, the State and the local authorities argued that this was a *force majeure* case excluding any possible liability. Both were made jointly liable. The State because of lack of care in authorising the development of a camping ground in an area likely to be flooded by the mountain torrent, without serious preliminary ground studies. The municipality because the mayor, being responsible for public safety, was bound to give warnings of possible dangers. The ground was damp at that time due to a very rainy summer season and a severe thunderstorm was forecast. Also, there was no *force majeure* since devastating floods had already occurred in the area.

All the various regimes surveyed in this paragraph go far beyond a simple recognition of the victim's damage. French law operates under a clear purpose: offering the victim full compensation of every damage sustained. The socialisation of risks also tends to limit the use of traditional court proceedings. 38

Part IV. Procedure

A well-insured victim will obtain full compensation without the cost and bother of going to court. Court actions based on the law of tort will be initiated by third-party payers (Social Security, insurance companies or compensation funds) subrogated in the victim's rights. It may sometimes be in the victim's interest to sue in tort, to get full or additional compensation. Third-party payers are likely to join such actions. 39

I. Insurance Schemes

This paragraph concentrates on claims made under the specific insurance scheme relating to insurance for consequences of natural catastrophes, described in the previous section.[62] Other cases depend indeed on the stipulations of the insurance policy and ordinary rules of insurance law. 40

The first step is the declaration of a "natural catastrophe", to be made by government authorities. This declaration is regarded as an administrative decision, which may be declared void by a court decision.[63] As a consequence of such annulment, all compensation paid under the scheme has to be reimbursed to the insurance companies. The State may be made liable for negligence in case of failure to declare that there is a "natural catastrophe" in a situation where it should have been declared.[64]

[61] CAA Lyon (Administrative Court of Appeal), 13 May 1997, *Droit administratif* (Dr. adm.) July 1997, 7.
[62] *Supra* no. 18–26.
[63] There is a *Conseil d'Etat* judgment on the point: CE 12 March 1999, [2000] RGDA, 199, note Vincent.
[64] CE 10 February 1993, *Ets. Jean Diant et Cie*, [1993] AJDA, 580.

Within ten days following the publication of the declaration in the official gazette (*Journal officiel*), the insured must report his damage to the insurance company. This time limit is longer than the ordinary one (five days following the damage, also where caused by tempest, or two days in case of theft). The time limit is stretched to thirty days for claims related to business interruption (*pertes d'exploitation*). Insurance companies have created local co-ordination units to facilitate the relationship between insurance companies, the insured, government and local authorities and the media.

The application made to the insurance company must include a statement of all direct damage to property. All relevant documentation, including photos and videos must be submitted.

Non-compliance with the time limits may exclude the right to compensation, with the exception of cases where they may be suspended by *force majeure* (case of the insured that had to stay in hospital during the weeks following the event). The purpose of these strict time limits (which may be suspended at the insurer's discretion or in case of *force majeure*) is to press the victim to act with due care and diligence and allow the experts sent by the insurance company to investigate the damage as early as possible.

41 The Insurance Code imposes on insurance companies a legal duty to pay the compensation "within three months as from the date of the submission of the estimate of damaged property or losses sustained, without prejudice to more favourable contractual provisions".[65] Non-compliance with the three-month rule makes the insurance company liable to pay additional compensation, such as a high interest on the compensation offered. Any more favourable stipulation in the insurance policy must indeed supersede the statutory regime.[66] A provisional payment must be made within two months from the above-mentioned date.[67]

It is to be noted that compensation proposed by the insurance company is nothing more than an offer. The insured may reject such an offer and negotiate for a higher compensation. Any attempt to reach a compromise (transaction) is governed by art. 2044 and following of the Civil Code. Such an attitude of the insured will inevitably postpone the compensation. In practice, the insured seldom refuses the offered amount.

II. Compensation Funds

42 The *Fonds de garantie automobile* was created in 1951 to compensate victims of road traffic accidents where the tortfeasor has not been identified or is insolvent as well as in the case of the insurer's insolvency.[68] As a rule, this Fund may only intervene in a subsidiary way, in the following situations: the tortfeasor was not identified or, where he was, damages may not be recovered due

[65] *Code des assurances*, article L 125-2.
[66] Cass. Civ. 1re, 7 March 1995, *Bulletin des arrêts de la Cour de Cassation, chambres civiles* (Bull. Civ.) I, no. 110.
[67] Article L 125-2, final paragraph.
[68] *Supra* no. 27.

to the tortfeasor's insolvency. This means that the victim may only apply to the Fund where the tortfeasor is unknown. Otherwise, the tortfeasor must first be found liable and then proved insolvent.

However, the law of 30 July 2003 creates a new situation where this Fund has to pay.[69] The uninsured victim of a technological catastrophe is entitled to compensation by the Fund under similar conditions as to the insured victim, which includes compliance with all requirements and limitation periods mentioned above.[70] This means that compensation must be paid within three months following the application, like for the insured victim.[71] This applies to all damage to property that could be covered by first party insurance, relating to motor vehicle or housing. However, a maximum amount is due to be fixed by way of regulation, since this regime is only meant to protect indigent people living under precarious circumstances: they are more likely to lose everything but not much in value by comparison to others. They may indeed have no car and no permanent housing. There is no reason indeed to afford free and full compensation to those who neglected to insure their property!

The national fund for agricultural disasters may not be called upon until a statement is made by a government authority recognising the catastrophe as an agricultural disaster.[72]

Also, as explained above, in case of terrorist attacks, victims may claim com- 43
pensation from the Compensation Fund for the victims of Terrorist Action and other Offences.[73] The victims, or dependants in case of death, may file a compensation claim to the Fund directly, by means of registered letter.[74] The period of limitation is ten years from the event and a new claim may be introduced within the same ten-year period should the victim's situation deteriorate. The claim must identify the victim and give detailed information as to the date, place and nature of the terrorist attack and include the police report and statements by witnesses. Medical certificates and any evidence relating to the injury must be enclosed. Information relating to welfare coverage must also be included as well as the quantum of social benefits already received. Indications that the injury may have been caused by an industrial accident must also be supplied.

Within three months of receipt of the claim, the Fund must make an offer of compensation. Where the victim accepts the offer, there is a binding and directly enforceable agreement, compromising any existing or future action (*transaction*).[75] Payment will be made shortly thereafter, but an interim payment to cover existing costs will be made not later than one month after the application.[76] If the victim rejects the offer, a registered letter must be sent

[69] *Supra* no. 27.
[70] *Supra* no. 40.
[71] Article L 421-16 and 17, referring to article L 128-2 and 3 for requirements and conditions.
[72] *Code rural* (Rural Code), article L 361-3.
[73] *Supra* no. 25. This paragraph is based on O. Moréteau/F. Lafay (*supra* fn. 39), no. 10–11, 32.
[74] A special form is provided at <http://www.fgti.fr>.
[75] As provided for in art. 2044 *Code Civil* (Civil Code, CC).
[76] Complete information is supplied on the Compensation Fund website: <http://www.fgti.fr>.

within fifteen days and the victim may start proceedings before the civil courts.

III. Tort Law

44 Ordinary rules of civil procedure, to be found in the Code of Civil Procedure, apply to tort claims filed before ordinary courts. Other rules apply to claims before administrative courts.

Two points will be stressed here: the possibility to use interlocutory proceedings in order to obtain urgent relief or interim payment, on the one hand, and limitation periods which may affect tort actions, on the other hand.

A. Interlocutory Proceedings

45 The *référé* can be described as a special procedure, which allows one party to refer a case to a single judge, thus asking him to make a provisional order within a short period of time.[77] The other party must be informed and can appear before the judge. In case of extreme urgency, this can be achieved within a few days, even hours. The term *référé d'heure à heure* indicates that only a few hours may run between the time of the application and the time when the judicial order is made.

As a rule, jurisdiction belongs to the president of the main civil court, the *tribunal de grande instance*. Exception is made to the principle that a bench of three normally tries cases. However, the essence of the order made in *référé* is to be temporary and provisional, which means that the matter may be discussed again, at a later time, in front of the full court. The *référé* may also be used before the administrative courts. There, it is limited to urgent matters and does not allow the president of the *tribunal administratif* to suspend an administrative decision. This procedure is not regulated by the Code of Civil Procedure but by special statutes.[78]

46 Before civil courts, the *référé* is no longer limited to cases of urgency. According to art. 809 of the Code of Civil Procedure, the president of the court may order by way of *référé* some "indispensable measures of conservation or repairing, either to prevent an imminent damage or to stop an obviously unlawful disorder". Also, according to art. 809 paragraph 2, the judge may grant by way of *référé* a provisional payment to the creditor. However, this is possible only when the existence of the obligation cannot be seriously disputed. The administrative courts may not grant such an injunction.[79] It usually takes between two and four weeks to obtain such an order and to have it enforced.

In a controversial case, the *Cour de cassation* admitted that the provisional payment might cover the total amount of the debt when this amount cannot be

[77] See P. Estoup, *La pratique des procédures rapides* (1990); J. Vincent/S. Guinchard, *Procédure civile* (27th edn. 2003).

[78] Law of 28 November 1955, modified by Decree of 10 April 1959.

[79] CE 20 June 1980, [1980] *Gazette de France, Recueil* (Gaz de France, Rec.), 284 concl. Rougevin-Laville.

disputed.[80] However, this was a contract case and the amount of damages to be paid in case of breach was stipulated in the contract (*clause pénale*).[81] The payment remains provisional in the sense that the order is not final and may be challenged during the subsequent regular proceedings before the full court … if this ever happens. It is common practice to obtain 80% of what may be regarded as a fair compensation, in which case the plaintiff will abandon the main claim and be satisfied with the provisional order.

According to art. 5-1 of the Code of Criminal Procedure,[82] when the plaintiff brought a civil action before a criminal court, it remains possible to act by way of *référé* before the civil court for any provisional measure whenever the existence of the obligation cannot be seriously disputed.

As a matter of principle, when proceedings have been initiated, parties may ask a pre-trial judge (*juge de la mise en état*) to order measures helping to find evidence, called *mesures d'instruction*. The pre-trial judge may even make such orders on his own motion. This can cover examination of parties or witnesses, discovery of documents (although this is far less effective than in common law jurisdictions), or expert opinions. 47

But one party may need such investigations before starting the action when there is a danger that the evidence may disappear, for instance, when it is urgently necessary to repair the consequences of a disaster. Since one relies more and more upon expert opinions in French civil cases, it has been felt necessary to allow the aggrieved party to obtain by way of *référé* the appointment of an independent expert.[83] According to art. 145 of the Code of Civil Procedure,

> "where there is a legitimate reason before the proceedings to keep or establish evidence of facts which may be relevant to the settlement of a dispute, permissible measures for an investigation may be ordered by way of *requête or référé*, at the request of any interested person".

Urgency is not required.[84] This sort of *référé* is also allowed before the administrative courts.

B. Limitation Periods

The first period of limitation upon the expiry of which the claim is barred is the thirty-year period, which operates as a default rule.[85] However, there is a special time limit of ten years in the case of tort disputes.[86] 48

[80] *Cour de Cassation, chambre commerciale* (Cass. Com.) 20 January 1981, [1981] Gaz. Pal., note Bertin, [1981] *Revue trimestrielle de droit civil* (R.T.D.Civ.), 679 obs. J. Normand.

[81] Cass. Civ. 2ième, 10 July 1978, [1980] JCP, II.1935 note Bey.

[82] Law No. 83-608 of 8 July 1983.

[83] It is common practice in French civil procedure to ask the judge to appoint an independent expert, chosen out of an official list, rather than to rely on expert witnesses chosen by the parties.

[84] Cass. Ch. mixte, 7 May 1982, [1982] D., 541. Concl. Cabannes, [1982] RTD. Civ., 785 obs. R. Perrot.

[85] Art. 2262 CC.

[86] Art. 2270-1 CC.

There are other special periods in respect of some causes of action. Where a claim is brought against a public body, the limitation period is four years.[87] In the case of an action against an airline, the plaintiff must initiate proceedings within two years from the date of disembarkation (art. 29 of the Warsaw Convention). The victim of an accident at work has two years to initiate proceedings.[88]

According to art. 8 of the Paris Convention of 29 July 1960, in the case of a nuclear accident, the limitation period is ten years (or three years from the moment that the plaintiff knew of his injury and the identity of the defendant).

In the field of tort, the limitation period does not run until the injury emerges. Prior to 1985, the courts used to consider that the limitation period did not start to run until the plaintiff knew of his injury.[89] The law of 5 July 1985 provides for the starting point of the limitation period: it is the "manifestation" of the damage or its aggravation. Thus the starting point is neither the date of the wrongful act nor the date when the victim knew of his injury.[90] However, the solution does appear to depend upon the knowledge of the injured person.[91]

49 If there is an event that makes it impossible to commence proceedings, the limitation period does not start running[92] (the notion of "impossibility" refers principally to *force majeure*). However the impossibility can also stem from the existence of a first set of proceedings upon which the second claim depends for compensation.[93] It can also stem from ignorance of the identity of the defendant, or his insurer.[94] In these cases the plaintiff is entitled to commence proceedings outside the normal limitation period. Where the defendant knowingly wastes time, in an attempt to extinguish the right of action, the judge has a discretion to allow the plaintiff to bring proceedings even where the principal limitation period has expired.[95]

Time does not run in relation to minors. There is therefore a suspension of the running of time for the duration of the minority.[96]

The solution is the same in relation to persons with a disability. If the injured person is under the charge of someone capable of taking proceedings on his behalf, the person with a disability will no longer benefit from the suspension but will have an action against his guardian (*tuteur*) if the latter was neg-

[87] Law No. 68-1250 of 31 December 1968.

[88] Article L. 431-2 *Code de la sécurité sociale*.

[89] Cass. Civ. 11 December 1918, [1921] S., 1, 161.

[90] See M. Bruschi, *La prescription en droit de la responsabilité civile* (1997), 225.

[91] Cass. Civ. 2ième, 28 May 1990, [1990] Gaz. Pal., pan. 156: the negligence of a surgeon led to a second operation; time started to run from the second operation, that is to say when the knowledge of the injured person was established.

[92] *Cour de Cassation, Chambres des Requêtes* (Cass. Req.), 22 June 1853, [1855] S., 1, 511; Civ., 28 June 1870, [1871] S., 1, 137; Cass. Civ. 1re, 22 December 1959, [1960] JCP, II.11494.

[93] Cass. Civ. 1re, 4 February 1986, [1987] 1987, II.20819, note Boyer; Cass. Civ. 3e, 17 February 1964, Bull. civ. III, no. 78.

[94] Cass. Civ. 1re, 7 October 1992, [1993] *Droit et Patrimoine*, législation et jurisprudence, no. 33.

[95] See A. Sériaux, *La faute du transporteur* (1984), no. 380.

[96] Art. 2252 CC. The age of majority is 18 years.

ligent.[97] A person with a disability is a person considered by law as being unable to use some of his rights.[98]

Part V. Financing

The system described in the previous paragraphs is funded by contributions and premiums paid by the insured. Reassurance plays an important role, with apparently unlimited coverage by the State. So far, the compensation funds have been financed at a minimum cost. 50

I. Social Security Contributions and Insurance Premiums

The Social Security system is financed by contributions from beneficiaries, a percentage on the salary or the income fixed by law. There is no evidence that the rising number of natural catastrophes has affected the level of such contributions in recent years. 51

Private insurance is financed by the premiums paid by the insured. The annual rate of the premium or contribution corresponding to the guarantee against the effects of natural catastrophes is fixed as follows:[99]

- on property insurance contracts, the initial rate was 5.5% in 1982. It was raised to 9% the following year and to 12% in the year 2000;
- on automobile insurance, 6% of the premium covering theft and fire and 0.5% of premiums relating to damage insurance.

For the new insurance coverage of technological catastrophes created by the law of 30 July 2003,[100] an additional premium of € 5 per year and per contract will be levied after 1 January 2004. On the basis of the 50 million contracts existing at present, this means € 250 million in anticipation of the coverage of this risk. This is controversial. Unlike the case of natural catastrophe, a liable party can be identified there, and third party insurance may have been a better option. It is odd to levy the amount necessary for the compensation on the victims themselves rather than on the industry. However, the insurers say, one is dealing with first party insurance there, and victims will be covered even where the owners of the defective plants are insolvent.[101]

II. Reassurance and State Guarantee

Reassurance is provided through the *Caisse centrale de réassurance* (hereafter CCR), fully controlled by the State.[102] Half the premiums levied to cover the consequences of catastrophes go to the CCR, which will always cover half the 52

[97] See M. Bruschi (*supra* fn. 90), 207.
[98] *Ibidem.*
[99] *Code des assurances*, article A 125-2.
[100] *Supra* no. 23–26 and *infra* no. 68.
[101] "Les assureurs vont faire payer aux particuliers le risque industriel", *Le Monde*, 9 September 2003.
[102] See P. Bidan, Le régime d'indemnisation des catastrophes naturelles a-t-il un avenir?, [2001] RGDA, 243.

damage insured and pay for it. This way, the CCR is acting as a mutual fund, under a very simple 50% rule, which balances the risk of catastrophes among all insurance companies. The CCR also acts as a reinsurer for the French insurance companies; a victim may not call directly on the CCR. The CCR also protects insurance companies for the share they themselves are supposed to cover, through a stop-loss system. The CCR is itself covered by the State, which provides unlimited guarantee.[103] In the year 2000, for the first time in its history, the CCR had to call for the guarantee of the State. This was due to the combined cost of a drought, severe flooding in the South and the tempest of December 1999.

In 2003, A.M. Best Co. announced that it has affirmed the "A" (Excellent) financial strength rating of CCR, with a "positive" outlook. The following is a quote from the *Insurance Journal*:[104]

> "The rating reflects the company's superior risk-based capitalisation, its leading position in the domestic (state guaranteed) catastrophe reinsurance sector and the excellent underwriting performance in this segment", said Best. "The main offsetting factor is the historically weak operating result of its traditional (non-guaranteed) book of business; but its recent and projected improvement has led to a change of the outlook from stable to positive".

Best noted that

> "On a risk-adjusted basis, CCR has a superior capital base benefiting from another year of robust retained earnings. In addition, CCR further increased its 2002 equalisation reserves by a substantial € 224 million (US $ 259 million)",

and A.M. Best expects

> "a further strengthening in 2003. The French government provides unlimited guarantee for natural catastrophe and terrorism risks by securing the company's equalisation reserves".

It also described CCR as "the only French reinsurer providing unlimited cover for catastrophe perils, supported by the unlimited guarantee of the French government". The company also writes life and non-life reinsurance in the open market (36% of total gross premium), both in France and other European countries, and has plans to "further expand its open market business".

> "Despite the inherent volatility of its catastrophe risk portfolio, CCR achieved an excellent combined ratio of 55.8% in 2002, down from 56.7% in 2001", said Best. "Underwriting results of its open market reinsurance book are improving, with a 3.3% fall in combined ratio to 117.6% at year end 2002". Best said it "expects this improvement to continue in 2003 and 2004 as a result of selective underwriting and the with-

[103] *Code des assurances*, article L 431-10.
[104] *Insurance Journal*, 24 June 2003.

drawal from unprofitable risks, bringing greater stability to bottom line results".

Another French initiative in the field of reinsurance for risks of terrorism 53
should be mentioned here. In 2002, the French insurance companies and the companies authorised to carry on direct insurance business on French territory created a pool called GAREAT (*Gestion de l'assurance et de la réassurance des risques attentats et actes de terrorisme*),[105] for one year. The Pool GAREAT was renewed in 2003 and is still in force in 2005. It reinsures damage to property caused by terrorist attacks. It covers enterprises, local authorities, large buildings (for instance hospitals) and technological risk where the insured capital exceeds € 6 million. The system is organised in layers. The CCR appears at the third and fourth layers, with unlimited State cover through the CCR.

III. Funding the Compensation Funds

The amount of yearly contributions to the various funds is fixed by adminis- 54
trative order. The Compensation Fund for the victims of Terrorist Action and other Offences is funded by a levy on the premiums paid to insurance companies insuring damage to property (€ 3 per contract in 2003).

The *Fonds de garantie automobile*, also covering uninsured victims of technological accidents, is funded as follows:[106]

- insurance companies contribute to 12% of the total expenses of the Fund;
- uninsured tortfeasors owe a contribution to the Fund, corresponding to 10% of the amount of damages they have to pay;
- 2% of the premiums paid by the insured;
- a 50% addition on the fine imposed on those who do not comply with compulsory insurance.

Apparently, recovery based on subrogation into the victims' right count for a substantial part of the funding.[107]

The fund created in 2002 for the prevention of major natural risks compensates owners of expropriated property located in zones of major natural risk.[108] Funding is levied on the additional contribution covering the risk of natural catastrophe, with a 4% limit. Financial management of this fund is operated by the CCR (*Caisse centrale de réassurance*). This fund may be authorised, by specific statutory provision, to provide additional compensation to insured victims having made a claim under the above-mentioned system.[109] In 2003, it was allowed to do so for the victims of floods and landslides declared

[105] <http://astre.scor.com/astrehelp/fr/qualif/env/GAREATPool_terrorisme_vers_déf_april_Engl_.pdf>.
[106] *Code des assurances*, article R 421-27 and 28.
[107] <http://www.fga.fr>.
[108] Law No. 2002-276 of 27 February 2002, art. 159.
[109] *Supra* no. 19–20.

"natural catastrophe" on 31 August 2002, within a limited amount of € 15 million.[110]

Last, the national fund for agricultural disasters[111] is financed by an 11% contribution levied on insurance premiums covering farming enterprises, to which the State adds a contribution at least equal to the amount levied on the insurance premiums.[112] This fund is managed by the CCR.[113]

Part VI. Heads and Amounts of Damages

55 Under tort law alone or through a combination of Social Security benefits, insurance and sometimes a compensation fund, the victim may obtain full compensation of any kind of damage. Although the victim is likely to rely on Social Security and insurance benefits rather than on a tort action, it is best to look at heads of damages under tort law first just to show that French law does allow for full compensation of pecuniary and non-pecuniary damage.

I. Under Tort Law

56 The cornerstone of the French system is full compensation of any possible loss. Payments may be made under different forms.

A. Recoverable Losses

57 The victim shall be placed in the same position that he would have been in had the accident not occurred. This principle is known as the principle of full compensation (*principe de réparation intégrale*).[114] Full compensation shall be awarded for all injuries and losses to legitimate interests suffered by the victim. The principles which apply in relation to losses caused by a breach of duty are: compensation for the whole injury; nothing but the injury,[115] and only the real injury.[116] Generally, the judge will declare that, having regard to art. 1382, a tortfeasor must make full reparation for the damage he has caused. Losses must be made good in their entirety, that is to say both material and non-material losses. The compensation must be proportionate to the damage suffered. Its assessment is traditionally based on objective considerations (medical expenses, loss of income, occupational disability, permanent total or

[110] Law No. 2002-1576 of 30 December 2002, art. 75.

[111] *Supra* no. 28.

[112] *Code rural*, article L 361-5 as amended by Law No. 2000-1352 of 30 December 2000.

[113] *Code des assurances*, article L 431-11.

[114] Cass. Civ. 2ème, 28 October 1954, [1955] JCP, II.8765, note Savatier ("Le propre de la responsabilité est de rétablir aussi exactement que possible l'équilibre détruit par le dommage, et de placer la victime, aux dépens du responsable, dans la situation où elle se serait trouvée si l'acte dommageable n'avait pas eu lieu"); Cass. Civ. 2ème, 18 January 1973, Bull. civ. II, no. 27, 20; Cass. Civ. 2ème, 19 November 1975, Bull. civ. II, no. 302, 243; Cass. Civ. 2ème, 9 July 1981, Bull. civ. II, no. 156, 101.

[115] Cass. Civ. 1re, 15 January 1957, [1957] D., 161; Cass. Crim. 15 mai 1984, Bull. crim. no. 176; Cass. Civ. 2ème, 14 February 1985, Bull. civ. II, no. 40, 28; Cass. Crim. 22 August 1995, Bull. crim., no. 266, 743.

[116] Y. Lambert-Faivre, *Droit du dommage corporel* (4th edn. 2000), no. 87.

partial incapacity) and subjective considerations (pain, aesthetic detriment and loss of amenity).

1. Property Damage

Property damage as well as loss of profit are recoverable losses under tort law. Damages are to be paid in respect of loss of income consequential on property damage, such as loss of profit on property damages as a consequence of a tortious act. 58

2. Pecuniary Losses (past, actual and future)

Damages are awarded for the injury actually sustained by the victim, and for all the consequential losses and expenses which flow from the injury. Pecuniary loss may be classified under two different headings: the first concerns the loss of earnings and other benefits which the injured person would have received but for the accident (*lucrum cessans*); the second concerns the additional expenses incurred as a result of the accident. In principle, the measure of damages or pecuniary loss will reflect the exact amount of money which the victim has lost, or has spent, in consequence of the injury (the injured person should be placed in the same financial position, as far as can be done by an award of money, as he would have been had the accident not happened) (*damnum emergens*). 59

3. Damnum Emergens

French law provides compensation for medical expenses incurred by the injured person in treating his condition and restoring him to health. Social Security provisions enable the victim to obtain coverage of medical needs within the limits explained above.[117] 60

The items which may be claimed as medical expenses are many and diverse.[118] The costs of nursing care at home can also be claimed. A plaintiff is equally entitled to recover future expenses as well as those already incurred at the time the court makes its award.[119]

4. Lucrum Cessans

The victim may be awarded compensation for temporary loss of earnings (*Incapacité temporaire totale*). Where the victim used to work, he will be com- 61

[117] *Supra* no. 12–17.

[118] *Cour de Cassation, Chambres Sociale* (Cass. Soc.) 28 April 1981, Bull. civ. V, no. 348, 261 and Cass. Soc. 16 January 1985, Bull civ. V, no. 33 (artificial limb); (transportation to and from hospital); Cass. Crim. 28 January 1969, Bull. crim., no. 52, 116, Cass. Soc. 11 June 1980, Bull. civ. V, no. 515 (professional rehabilitation); Paris, 1 February 1973 (cost of a guide dog); Cass. Soc. 21 November 1984, Bull. civ. V, no. 528, 319 (adaptation of the home).

[119] *Cour de Cassation, Assemblée Plénière* (Cass. Ass. plén.), 9 June 1978, [1978] Gaz. Pal., 2, 557; Cass. Soc. 30 May 1973, Bull. civ. V, no. 354, 17; Cass. Civ. 2ème, 20 June 1990, Gaz. Pal., 28 December 1990, 19.

pensated for any loss of earnings as a result of having to give up work.[120] The calculation of loss will be carried out by comparing the previous level of earnings and the level of earnings during the temporary incapacity (after deductions of sick payments and Social Security benefits).[121] Where the employer has continued to pay the victim, the former can recover the losses from the tortfeasor.[122] Even if the victim did not work at the time of the injury, compensation may not be precluded.[123]

5. Non-Pecuniary Losses

62 All matters which amount to a disturbance in one's living conditions may be the subject of a claim for compensation. Victims are entitled to recover damages not only for pecuniary but also non-pecuniary losses. There are no limits on the recoverability of non-pecuniary damages; art. 1382 and following do not contain any restrictions in this respect. Thus, both pecuniary and non-pecuniary damages are recoverable so long as they are a direct and immediate consequence of the tortious act. Usually, courts award a global sum for the non-pecuniary loss but divide the award into specific categories of loss.

The element of physical pain is placed within the category of *pretium doloris*. It is recognised as an element of non-pecuniary loss. This item was fully established as a head of damages in awards made by the courts long before the more sophisticated head of *dommage moral* appeared.

It shall be noted that this head of damages is protected from the recoupment of benefits by Social Security.[124] The sums awarded under this head are rather modest (from € 1,000 to € 15,000).

63 The head of loss called *préjudice d'agrément* represents loss of amenity.[125] The courts have devised numerous sub-categories of loss of amenity within the scope of the head of *préjudice d'agrément*. According to the *Cour de cassation*, loss of amenity results from the "loss of quality of life",[126] which concerns not only the future impossibility of doing a particular activity or sport[127] and does not require specific proof that the victim had in fact carried out the sport or other activities prior to sustaining the injury.[128] This injury is included

[120] Cass. Soc. 28 March 1984, Bull. civ. V, no. 115, 89; Cass. Civ. 2ème, 7 February 1979, Bull. civ. II, no. 41 (compensation shall be awarded even where the victim kept on working but suffered psychological problems).

[121] The assessment may also be made by an expert (Cass. Civ. 2ème, 16 June 1961, Bull. civ. II, no. 462, 330).

[122] Cass. Civ. 2ème, 22 April 1966, Bull. civ. II, no. 467, 331 and art. 16 of Law No. 85-677 of 5 July 1985 on road traffic accidents.

[123] For example in the case of a housewife: Colmar, 15 May 1956, [1956] D., 614 (reference will be made to the minimum statutory wage, the *Salaire Minimum de Croissance*).

[124] Law No. 73-1200 of 27 December 1973.

[125] L. Cadiet, *Le préjudice d'agrément* (1983); P. Jourdain, Jurisprudence Française en Matière de Droit Civil, Obligations et Contrats Spéciaux, Responsabilité Civile, [1995] *Revue trimestrielle de droit civil* (RTD civ.), 893.

[126] Cass. Civ. 2ème, 19 March 1997, [1998] D., Jur., 59, note Y. Lambert-Faivre.

[127] Cass. Crim. 26 May 1992, [1992] JCP, I.3625, note G. Viney.

[128] Cass. Civ. 2ème, 20 May 1978, Bull. civ. II, no. 131, 105; Cass. Crim., 14 June 1978, [1978] Gaz. Pal., 2, 550, note L.-H. Thomas; Cass. Crim., 9 March 1982, Bull. crim. no. 71, 183.

within the head of damage known as *dommage moral*, and is different from mere physical injury.[129]

Aesthetic damage may constitute a separate injury in itself of some importance (leading to a loss of career, or causing the victim to avoid social occasions), or it can be a trivial mark left after a minor accident. In order to assess such damage, the medical expert applies a scale graduated from 0 to 7, which does not take into consideration the age and the sex of the plaintiff.[130]

French courts deal with mental injury and related claims under the general heading of *dommage moral*. The question whether the harm caused had a physical or psychological impact is irrelevant: the courts do not consider the issue to be of any significance in the context of art. 1382 of the *Code civil*. The French courts have a liberal attitude towards awarding damages for anguish suffered. Compensation includes the mental suffering caused by the accident, including the fright of the accident and any mental reaction, any fear of future incapacity, whether in respect of physical or mental health or the capacity to earn.[131] 64

There is no particular law which governs personal injury caused by pollution.[132] In the case of ecological disaster, where no physical or psychological injury has been suffered, a victim may nevertheless claim compensation for the anxiety suffered whether under the tort of *trouble de voisinage* (nuisance) or under the general cause of action for damage caused by things,[133] so long as the damage suffered was direct and certain.

B. Lump Sums, Periodical Payments, Interim Payments

The judge has a discretionary power to award a lump sum or periodical payments.[134] The sum can be divided into two parts: one part to be given by means of a lump sum and the other by means of periodical payments.[135] The judge is not bound by the plaintiff's claim (he can award periodical payments even though the plaintiff has asked for a lump sum).[136] Periodical payments are usually preferred where the plaintiff is a minor or suffers the consequences of serious incapacity as a result of the injury. The award may also be turned into capital, by applying an earnings ratio (*taux de capitalisation*).[137] There is no 65

[129] Cass. Crim. 5 March 1985, Bull. crim., no. 105, 1°, 275.

[130] Y. Lambert-Faivre (*supra* fn. 116), no. 144.

[131] Y. Lambert-Faivre (*supra* fn. 116), no. 139.

[132] Y. Lambert-Faivre (*supra* fn. 116), no. 697; G. Viney, Les principaux aspects de la responsabilité civile des entreprises pour atteinte à l'environnement en droit français, [1996] JCP, I.3900; J. Huet, Le développement de la responsabilité civile en droit de l'environnement en France, [1993] *Revue Internationale de Droit Comparé* (RIDC), 235; G. Viney, Le préjudice écologique, [1998] *La responsabilité civile et les assurances* (RCA), 6.

[133] Y. Lambert-Faivre (*supra* fn. 116), no. 698.

[134] Cass. Civ. 2ème, 17 February 1972, Bull. civ. II, no. 50, 36; Cass. Civ. 2ème, 13 June 1979, Bull. civ. II, no. 178, 124.

[135] CA Paris, 11 May 1968, [1968] Gaz. Pal., 2, 118.

[136] Cass. Crim., 19 June 1996, Bull. crim., no. 261, 785.

[137] This earnings ratio is to be found in the Decree No. 86-973 of 8 August 1986 *fixant les modalités de conversion en capital d'une rente consécutive à un accident*, [1986] D., L. 461. However the judge may choose other more recent ratios (See Y. Lambert-Faivre (*supra* fn. 116), no. 124).

general rule as to the choice between a lump sum and periodical payments, and it mostly depends on the age and the incapacity of the plaintiff. Nevertheless, courts are more accustomed to making global awards.

II. Recoverable Losses under Specific Regimes

66 Under the various insurance schemes presented above, the following heads of damage may be compensated:

- personal injury and medical expenses;
- disability payments;
- damage to property;
- loss of earning, also when due to business interruption.

Limitations may be applied under various Social Security regimes and also under insurance policies.

67 Where a disaster is declared a "natural catastrophe", the insured must bear a share of the loss, which remains uninsured (*franchise*). Since 1 January 2002,[138] the insured bears € 380 for private housing (yet € 1,520 if the damage is due to a drought), vehicles and other property used for private purposes. The uninsured share is 10% of the damage with a minimum of € 1,140 for any property used for the purpose of business, industry or agriculture (yet € 3,050 if due to a drought). It corresponds to three days of activity for the loss of income due to business interruption, with a minimum of € 1,140. In municipalities not having adopted a "prevention of risk plan" (*plan de prévention des risques*), the uninsured share gets higher every time there is a declaration of natural catastrophe: twice as much the third time, three times as much the fourth time and four times as much the following times. This is an incentive on the local population to press the municipality to adopt a prevention plan or to move to safer places.

Last but not least, economic loss such as cost of temporary housing is not compensated in case of natural catastrophe except where expressly provided for in the insurance policy. Indeed, this insurance scheme only covers direct damage to property and loss of earning for business interruption.

68 In case of technological disaster and in such a case only, the new article L. 128-4 of the Insurance Code introduces a limitation to the insurance coverage, made compulsory by the new law of 30 July 2003 where the existence of a technological catastrophe has been officially recognised.[139] Insurance coverage will be excluded in special areas recognised in a prevention plan of technological risks (*plan de prévention des risques technologiques*) as causing a serious risk for human life,[140] for all buildings erected in this area after the plan has been published. Insurance coverage is also excluded where a building is erected in violation of administrative rules, where the purpose of such rules is to prevent damage caused by a technological catastrophe. This is a clear in-

[138] *Code des assurances*, article A 125-1 (arrêté 3 September 2001).
[139] *Supra* no. 23–26.
[140] *Code de l'environnement*, article L 515-15 to 26 (especially article L 515–16).

centive not to build in these special danger zones, where expropriation may be decided, or to comply with protective administrative rules. Where no expropriation has been decided, insurance coverage in the special zones will only be granted to building existing before the publication of the plan.

Lost profits are compensated, with a special time limit of 30 days to file the claim (instead of 10 or 5 for other heads of damages). Unless the contract stipulates for full coverage, loss of income is only covered where a direct consequence of the catastrophe. The loss of value of a business may not be regarded as a direct damage.

In case of flooding, property damage will include expenses relating to pumping, cleaning and disinfecting. Compensation by the insurance company must cover all direct damage, such as damage to a building caused by the fall of a tree. However, damage caused by the loss of supply in electricity following a natural catastrophe is not regarded as direct. Some special rules relating to damage caused to buildings need be mentioned. Under a rule made mandatory by the Insurance Code, monies paid to compensate the destruction or deterioration of a building may not be used for any other purpose than rebuilding or repairing, in a way compatible with the environment.[141] This obligation is excluded wherever rebuilding is banned "insofar as a prevention plan for foreseeable natural disasters is applicable to the area".[142] However, in such a case, no compensation may be given for the value of the land itself, which may, in exceptional cases, be covered by the State.[143] The contract may provide for a compensation "refurbishment value" taking into account pre-existing decay, or may be extended so that to cover all expenses for full renewal.

In case of natural and technological disasters, damage such as personal injury is covered by Social Security, complementary insurance, insurance *garantie des accidents de la vie* and *individuelle accident* etc. Occasionally, like in the case of terrorist attacks, compensation of personal injury is made by a compensation fund.[144]

Part VII. Rules Preventing Cumulative Benefits

The French legal system is encouraging victims to apply first for Social Security, insurance benefits and compensation by a fund at least in the case of terrorist attacks, before having recourse to tort law. In a majority of cases, the tort action is exerted by a subrogated third-party payer. However, there is room for a direct tort action by the victim who tries to get additional compensation, especially for those heads of damage not covered by Social Security, insurance and compensation funds. Circumstances may exist where the victim may be compensated twice for the same damage, which allows for a bonus but not double compensation.[145] 69

141 Article L 121-17.
142 Article L 121-16.
143 N. Lesage, Les inondations, à chacun sa responsabilité, *Petites Affiches* (PA) 27 April 1994, 53.
144 *Supra* no. 29.
145 See *infra* no. 77.

I. Social Security Benefits

70 Nowadays, an injured person often continues to receive his pay, in whole or in part, for the period he is unable to work. There is statutory sick pay, which the employer is required by law to pay during the first few weeks of sickness or disability. In respect of disability, the Social Security system provides substantial income replacement benefits, for a reasonably high proportion of lost wages. As explained above,[146] a significant percentage of medical treatment and hospital care costs is paid directly by the appropriate Social Security institution. Non-pecuniary losses are outside this specific scheme.

Where no person is liable, the victim will be compensated by the Social Security system. Although the Social Security system provides an injured person with only limited compensation, the victim will be automatically and immediately indemnified for the injuries he has suffered. The law of 27 July 1999[147] provides everyone with an entitlement to medical care, even for the poorest victims (that is to say even for victims who have not earned sufficiently to be liable to pay social contributions).

As explained above,[148] the Social Security system offers the victim of catastrophes two categories of benefits. Firstly, generally, injuries which give rise to significant medical expense are for a great part covered by the Social Security payments. Secondly, any employee involved in an accident at work has a right to be compensated for the incapacity resulting from the injury.

71 The Social Security bodies are the principal third-party payers entitled to recover expenses sustained through subrogation. According to art. 29 Law of 5 July 1985, the expenses which the Social Security body is entitled to recover are those dealt with above: hospital fees, drugs, treatments[149] and sickness benefits.[150] As far as compensation for non-pecuniary losses is concerned, these are beyond the scope of the right of subrogation.[151] Non-pecuniary losses are not covered by Social Security benefits. However, before 1973, the subrogation right concerned the whole amount of compensation: it was not unusual to see a victim left without compensation after the subrogation recourse (especially when there was contributory fault on the part of the plaintiff). The law of 27 December 1973 limited the right of recourse, by excluding non-pecuniary losses (for example *préjudice d'agrément, préjudice esthétique, pretium doloris*).

[146] *Supra* no. 12-17.
[147] *Supra* no. 12.
[148] *Supra* no. 12-17.
[149] See Art. 29-3, Law of 5 July 1985.
[150] See Art. 29-5, Law of 5 July 1985.
[151] J. Bedoura, Les incidences de la loi du 27 décembre 1973 sur les concepts traditionnels relatifs au préjudice, [1980] D., 139; Y. Lambert-Faivre, Les droits de la victime et les recours de la Sécurité sociale, [1998] JCP, I.110.

II. Insurance Companies Benefits

For a given risk, one victim may be covered by multiple insurance policies. Benefits may accumulate when subscribed independently. In other cases there may be co-insurance when several insurers pool resources to cover a given risk.[152] A party subscribing to multiple insurance must inform the other insurers involved. French law does not allow a compensation that would go beyond the full compensation of the damage.[153] 72

The plaintiff is not prevented from bringing proceedings against an insurance company.[154] Where the initial claim was made only against the defendant, the plaintiff may still bring proceedings against the liability insurer up until ten days prior to the hearing. The plaintiff may prefer to proceed directly against the insurer (*action directe*). The claim is based on art. 1166 of the Civil Code which regulates the *action oblique*, connected with article L. 124-3 of the Insurance Code which provides that the exclusive destination of the amount of money payable is to the injured person. 73

The *action directe* was first admitted by the Court of Cassation in 1939.[155] The limitation period could either be that provided for in the insurance contract (two years according to article L. 114-1 of the Insurance Code) or under the general provisions concerning civil liability. In the decision of 1939, the *Cour de cassation* stated that the limitation period applicable to the *action directe* is the same as the one applicable to the proceedings against the wrongdoer (ten years for tort and thirty years in contract for the two most common situations).

The insurer's duty to compensate the plaintiff for the injury stems from the insurance contract: according to article L. 112-6 of the Insurance Code, the insurer is entitled to rely as against the plaintiff upon any defence which would be available against the other party to the contract.[156] If some risks are not covered by the insurance contract, the injured person is not entitled to claim compensation from the insurer.[157] Any ceiling on the amount of compensation provided for in the contract must also be taken into consideration.[158] 74

If the victim has the benefit of insurance, the sum received will be prescribed in the insurance policy (this is the situation where the plaintiff has sub-

[152] Y. Lambert-Faivre, *Droit des assurances* (11th edn. 2001), no. 540, 389.

[153] *Code des assurances*, article L 121-1: "Insurance in respect of property is a compensation contract. The compensation that the insurer owes to the insured may not exceed the amount of the value of the insured property at the time of the loss".

[154] According to the Law of 8 July 1983, the plaintiff can claim for compensation from the insurance company, even if the case is before a criminal court.

[155] Cass. Civ. 28 March 1939, [1939] D., 1.68, note E. Picard.

[156] "The insurer may invoke, against the policy bearer or a third party who claims under the policy, exclusions invocable against the initial policyholder".

[157] Cass. Civ., 26 April 1972, [1973] *Revue Generale des Assurances Terrestres* (RGAT) 51; Cass. Civ. 1re, 1 October 1980, [1981] RGAT, 201.

[158] Cass. Civ. 1re, 15 February 1977, [1977] JCP, II.18737; Cass. Civ., 7 October 1975, [1976] RGAT, 379; Cass. Civ. 1re, 7 July 1992, [1992] RCA., no. 428; Cass. Civ. 1re, 9 June 1996, [1996] D., 610, note Y. Lambert-Faivre.

scribed to a specific capital fund managed by the insurance company).[159] In such a case, there is no subrogation of the sums paid out to the plaintiff's rights.[160] Therefore the plaintiff will still be able to claim full compensation against the party at fault since the sum he has received from the insurance company was due, and provided for in the contract.[161]

According to art. 33 of the Law of 5 July 1985,[162] there is a subrogation of the insurer to the plaintiff's right against the party at fault where the sums received by the plaintiff are considered to be sums which have been advanced. The subrogation is usually provided for by the insurance contract and the insurance company is not entitled to recover any monies due until the plaintiff has been compensated. If there is no third party to blame, the plaintiff will be compensated by the insurance policy and no subrogation will lie. If there is a finding of contributory fault on the part of the plaintiff, this does not affect the sum he is entitled to receive under the insurance contract.

III. Benefits Received from Compensation Funds

75 As a rule, a compensation fund will only compensate in situations where there is no identified third party liable. This is the case of the above-mentioned *Fonds de garantie automobile*,[163] compensating victims of road traffic accidents where the tortfeasor has not been identified or is insolvent. Payments by the Fund may only be made in the two following situations: the tortfeasor was not identified or, where he was, damages may not be recovered due to the tortfeasor's insolvency. In the latter case, the tortfeasor must have been declared liable, damages must be assessed and evidence must be adduced of the tortfeasor's insolvency.[164]

76 The Compensation Fund for the victims of terrorism operates quite differently. As explained above,[165] the victims (or dependants in case of death) may claim to the Fund even before any court action is started, to receive interim and then full compensation for physical injury or for the loss suffered as a consequence of the victim's death. The Fund is then subrogated in the victim's rights and may recover through tort action.

77 A case has been reported where the victim of a terrorist attack, after having received, supposedly, full compensation from the Fund, claimed additional compensation from the terrorist by means of a civil action (tort claim introduced before the criminal court whereby the victim of the crime seeks compensa-

[159] See article L. 131-1 *Code des assurances*: "En matière d'assurance sur la vie et d'assurance contre les accidents atteignant les personnes, les sommes assurées sont fixées par le contrat".

[160] See article L. 131-2, al. 1 *Code des assurances*: "Dans l'assurance de personnes, l'assureur, après paiement de la somme assurée, ne peut être subrogé aux droits du contractant ou du bénéficiaire contre des tiers à raison du sinistre".

[161] See Y. Lambert-Faivre (*supra* fn. 116), no. 309.

[162] Art. 211-15 *Code des assurances*.

[163] *Supra* no. 27 and 42.

[164] See Ph. Le Tourneau/L. Cadiet (*supra* fn. 60), no. 2565.

[165] *Supra* no. 29 and 43.

tion).[166] Such a situation should not occur under normal circumstances, since the compensated victim assigns all claims to the Fund, by way of subrogation. The Fund should be the only party with a claim in damages against the terrorist. In this case, the *Cour d'assises spéciale de Paris* sentenced to life imprisonment a member of the terrorist group *Action Directe*, directly involved in a bloody bomb attack on the central criminal police station in Paris in July 1986. The victims had already been compensated by the then newly created Compensation Fund. Nevertheless, some of them initiated a civil action before the criminal court, which was more generous than the Fund in granting higher damages. The case went up to the Court of Cassation, the highest French court for civil and criminal cases. In a judgment of 20 October 1993,[167] the *Cour de cassation* held that granting higher damages to those victims who took civil proceedings before the criminal court did not aggravate the Fund's position, since only the amount paid in excess of agreed compensation benefits the victims, without causing loss to the Fund.

This ruling raises an interesting question concerning the legal status of the agreement made between the victim and the Fund. Such an agreement is a settlement (*transaction*), enforceable as a final judgment. As such, prima facie, it extinguishes the victim's cause of action, since the object of the settlement is to grant the victim full compensation. However, French law considers settlements to be a category of contract. The principle of privity of contract (*effet relatif du contrat*) therefore applies, but settlements are also binding on third parties. According to the *Cour de cassation*, the extinctive effect of settlements is limited to the parties to the agreement, namely the Fund and the victim. It has the effect of discharging any claim the victim may have against the Fund, but not any claim which the victim may have against the tortfeasor (a euphemism for a terrorist), who is not a party to the agreement. The victim's right to a civil action against the terrorist is not extinguished.[168]

It is to be noted that even in that case, the victim did not receive more than what the court perceived a fair compensation. The danger of a double claim and of a judge granting double compensation being in ignorance of the previous compensation is purely hypothetical. The judge (and, of course, the tortfeasor) will always be informed of a previous compensation paid by the Fund to the victim. Being subrogated into the victim's right, the Fund will also sue the tortfeasor to recover the compensation paid. Since these cases are brought before criminal courts by way of civil action, the prosecution services will keep the Fund informed of any prosecution against a terrorist. Insurance companies having compensated the victim of damage to property are also subrogated and therefore likely to intervene.

Part VIII. Empirics

A brief survey of four recent catastrophes will illustrate how the French system works and keeps developing by reaction to incoming events. 78

[166] Cass. Crim., 20 October 1993, [1994] D., 280, note Anne d'Hauteville.
[167] *Ibidem.*
[168] For further comments, see O. Moréteau/F. Lafay (*supra* fn. 39), no. 16–20.

I. The Tempests of December 1999

79 On 26 and 27 December, a severe tempest (called in France *la grande tempête*) hit France and a number of European countries, causing the fall of millions of trees (115 million cubic metres of wood corresponding to two and a half years of normal exploitation) and devastating the electricity power lines. A declaration of natural catastrophe was quickly made,[169] facilitating compensation of pecuniary damage by the insured victims, and less than one year later, the Insurance Code was amended to provide for compulsory coverage by every insurance contract covering the risk of fire.[170] The total damage caused by *la grande tempête* is estimated at € 6.86 billion. € 200 million of public money was made available in the next four months and a national solidarity fund was created to support municipalities where forests offer the main resource (*Fonds national de solidarité pour les communes forestières*). The existence of this *ad hoc* fund is justified by the fact that municipalities who happen to be the owners of vast forest resources may not benefit from the above-mentioned existing funds. Also, municipalities were entitled to an almost immediate refund of the VAT paid on the works undertaken as a consequence of the tempests.

II. The Sinking of the Tanker Erika

80 The tanker Erika split in two off the French Atlantic coast in severe weather on 12 December 1999 and spilled 15,000 tonnes of her heavy fuel oil cargo. The entire crew of 26 was airlifted to safety. The two sections, with a further 15,000 tonnes of fuel oil remaining in the cargo tanks, sank in 120 metres of water about 100 km from the mouth of the River Loire. The spilt cargo was blown east towards the coast and on 25 December the first oil washed ashore. By early January various stretches along a 400 km length of French coastline had been polluted, and thousands of seabirds had been oiled.

A French fund called POLMAR (*Fonds d'intervention contre les pollutions marines accidentelles*) was used to cover some € 125 million of public works to clean up, to which the government added another € 100 million for renovation purposes. This disaster revealed that the International Oil Pollution Compensation Funds based on the 1992 international convention (in French called FIPOL and in English IOPC Funds) provides for insufficient coverage. Only six months later, in July 2000, did the IOPC Funds fix a compensation rate covering 50% of the victims' damage. One year later, the Fund had paid not more than € 6 million. The State quickly organised a compensation system to provide victims with substantial cash advances on the expected compensations. On 11 September 2000, cash advances were transformed into additional compensation to allow victims to receive full compensation. Meantime, the State had organised, through the banking system, similar cash advances to enterprises having suffered from the pollution, especially in the tourism sector. Ever since France has pressed the IOPC Funds to increase its coverage to € 2 billion.

[169] Arrêté of 29 December 1999.
[170] Article L 122-7 as amended by Law No. 2000-1207 of 13 December 2000, *supra* no. 21.

III. The Toulouse AZF Explosion

81 As a consequence of the explosion of a chemical plant called AZF (owned by Total Fina Elf) located in Toulouse, 30 people died, 5,000 suffered personal injury and thousands of private and public buildings were damaged, as if a large part of suburban Toulouse had been bombed.[171] The total cost of the accident was considered to amount of € 1,800 million. The cost of the catastrophe was covered only in part by the insurance system. The owner of the chemical plant, Total Fina Elf, was burdened with 52% of the total cost, paid by way of transactions. It should be underlined that some of the claims may not be settled yet as regard to personal injuries, physical or immaterial, and economic losses (*pertes d'exploitation*). The insurance companies have had to cope with 70,000 claims (*déclarations de sinistres*) and have so far provided compensation for nearly all these claims.

It appeared that a substantial number of victims, approximately 15% of them, were not insured. As explained above, the *Multirisque habitation* insurance is not mandatory. For these uninsured victims, the only way to obtain redress was to sue in tort the owner of the chemical plant. The extension of the benefit of the compensation fund for victims of automobile accidents (*Fonds de garantie automobile*) in 2003 to all uninsured victims of natural and industrial disasters may be seen as an appropriate answer.

82 The AZF catastrophe has stressed several problems in the field of prevention of damage in case of such events and among them the question of housing in risky zones. Specific legislation tends to prevent the construction of housing in the neighbourhood of dangerous plants, which is strengthened by the implementation measure of the Seveso II directive.[172] The European Commission is working on a modification of the Seveso directive, in part because of the events of Baia Mare and Enschede.[173] A recent survey proved that no less than 10 million people in France live in the neighbourhood of dangerous plants.[174]

The existing provisions apply to the building of new housing, and do not apply to existing housing in dangerous zones. However the new article L. 515-16 of the Town Planning Code (*Code de l'urbanisme*) (modified by the law of 30 July 2003, also making substantial amendments to the Environment Code) empowers the public entities, when an area has been affected by a "prevention plan", to expropriate, with compensation by a special compensation fund.[175] Other prevention measures can be undertaken if needed, like the creation of "an exclusion zone" (see article L. 515-16 IV *Code de l'urbanisme*). The cost of these measures is shared by the State and by the industries located in the dangerous area. The spirit of the new provisions tends to the collaboration be-

[171] F. Henri, *Toulouse: Chronique d'un désastre annoncé* (2002).

[172] Directive No. 96/82 of 9 December 1996, JOCE no. L 10 of 14 January 1997, implemented by an *arrêté ministériel* of 10 May 2000.

[173] See COM(2000) 624 final. See also C. London, Risques industriels d'accidents majeurs: de la non-application du principe de prévention?, PA, 29 April 2002, no. 85, 7.

[174] See "AZF, un an après", *Le Monde*, 21 September 2002, 13 *et seq.*

[175] *Supra* no. 54.

tween the administration and the industries in the setting of prevention measures.

IV. The Rhone Flood of December 2003

83 During the first week of December 2003, following intense and unusually long-lasting rain, the river Rhone reached, in its lower part, its highest level in a hundred years with some 15,000 cubic metres per second. This caused prolonged flooding in the Arles region, causing thousands of people to leave their homes and hundreds of enterprises to suffer extensive damage all around the Rhone delta. National and international help was welcome, especially for the pumping of huge amounts of water over a period of more than ten days. The estimated losses reached € 800 million. A total of 80,000 claims, 90% of which were filed by private individuals, had to be dealt with by insurance companies.[176] Provincial authorities (*Conseil général des Bouches-du-Rhône*) immediately levied a € 15 million fund and the Region Provence-Alpes-Côte d'Azur announced an emergency plan to help victims, with € 20 million. The State was called to intervene and the President of the Republic, accompanied by a number of ministers, visited Marseilles and other devastated areas to promise immediate help and national solidarity. The state of "natural catastrophe" was to be declared on 11 December to allow victims to call immediately on property insurance. Special financial help was provided to re-establish the supply of drinkable water, electricity and the train service. The catastrophe is also due to be recognised as an agricultural disaster to allow farmers to benefit from the special fund.

The government announced a vast plan to repair the dykes protecting the delta region, with a € 24 million subsidy. A public report made in 2002, which had so far remained unnoticed, was indeed urging the State to provide for better control of the 250 km of dykes protecting the region, since they were found inadequate in case of severe flooding. Part of the problem is that there is no central agency to control and co-ordinate the security of the dykes, which belong here to municipalities, there to the national Railway Company or to other authorities.

Part IX. Conclusion

84 France maintains a complex and extensive legal system (different regimes depending on the type of catastrophe) for dealing with the environmental and human health effects of industrial and natural catastrophes. This legal framework has developed piecemeal, primarily out of necessity. As the *Conseil d'Etat* noted in its Annual Report for 2005,[177] the recent tendency is to extend the coverage, combining in diverse ways insurance, liability and solidarity.

Although the environmental regulatory system is impressive and plays an important role, there may be a need, in the long-term, for a unified "catastrophes law",[178] to get rid of sometimes useless complexity, causing perplexity to the lawyer and additional distress to victims. Regarding personal injury, the

[176] RCA, December 2004 (no. 12), 4.
[177] CE, *supra* note 1.
[178] See C. Lienhard, Pour un droit des catastrophes, [1995] D., 91; see also Y. Lambert-Faivre (*supra* fn. 116), no. 642 *et seq*.

system has the advantage of affording minimal protection to everyone, with a possibility for potential victims to increase their protection by way of personal insurance, such as complementary social insurance and *garantie des accidents de la vie*. Regarding damage to property, the existence of compensation funds complements an efficient but non-mandatory insurance system. The system is efficient but often too complex. For instance, the (non-) specialist has a hard time to understand the extent of insurance coverage and in how far it may be affected by governmental declarations recognising that there has been a natural or industrial catastrophe. The terminology is sometimes confusing: why call "uninsurable" (a term appearing in the Insurance Code, cases and legal literature) a risk that the law makes insurable by compulsory coverage?

Recent disasters reveal that there are always some people who suffer from a lack of coverage because they are not properly insured. In such cases, local authorities are often more responsive than the Welfare State. So far, the social coverage of natural, human and technological risk has been achieved at a reasonable and affordable cost.

The French system certainly deserves approval wherever it makes a link be- 85
tween compensation and prevention of risks. This is the case where insurance compensation for damage to property is limited by a higher franchise because people keep living in areas where natural disasters are frequent and do not press local authorities to adopt a prevention plan.[179] This is also the case where insurance coverage is denied because people violated the law when building in a special area recognised in a prevention plan of technological risks as causing a serious risk for human life.[180] And last, it is again the case where the national fund for agricultural disasters only covers insured victims.[181] But this is not the case where uninsured victims may get compensation from a fund in case of damage to property by a technological catastrophe, a new plan which may only be acceptable where limited to people living in precarious conditions.[182]

State regulation may be felt heavy and questionable from a purely market 86
economy perspective. However, regarding the compensation of damage to property, it is worth noting that the system offers a subtle combination of voluntary insurance and compulsory coverage, reinsurance with a back up by the State, and clear incentives to reduce the risks or move out of risky areas. There may be some *ex ante* distortions to free competition in this model, as well as unequal treatment of victims whether the damage is triggered by an individual or collective event. However, in countries favouring the development of market solutions, the State nonetheless intervenes in case of major catastrophes, also bringing inequality of treatment and possibly creating *ex post* distortions to strictly defined competition rules. The authors of the present report leave the question open to economists and politicians: how should the creed of mar-

[179] *Supra* no. 67.
[180] *Supra* no. 68.
[181] *Supra* no. 28.
[182] *Supra* no. 27 and 42.

ket economy be reconciled with collective reaction to national emergencies? The South Asian Tsunami of December 2004 revealed that no one seems to object to *ex post* solidarity. Should we therefore blame preventive solidarity?

List of References

J. Bedoura, Les incidences de la loi du 27 décembre 1973 sur les concepts traditionnels relatifs au préjudice, [1980] D., 139.

F. Bénac-Schmidt/Ch. Larroumet, V Responsabilité du fait des choses inanimées, [1990] *Encyclopedie Juridique Dalloz: Répertoire de droit civil* (Dalloz Rép. civ.).

P. Bidan, Le régime d'indemnisation des catastrophes naturelles a-t-il un avenir?, [2001] *Revue Générale du Droit des Assurances* (RGDA), 243.

J. Carbonnier, *Droit civil* (vol. IV. Les obligations 2000), no. 255 *et seq.*

J.-P. Chauchard, *Droit de la Sécurité sociale* (2nd edn. 1998).

B. Goldmann, *La détermination du gardien responsable du fait des choses inanimées* (1946).

B. Goldman, Garde de la structure et garde du comportement, in: *Mélanges en l'honneur de Paul Roubier* (vol. II 1961), 51 *et seq.*

C. Gory, L'assurance des risques technologiques et naturels, [2003] *Gazette du Palais* (Gaz. Pal.), 3.

J.J. Dupeyroux/R. Ruellau, *Droit de la Sécurité sociale* (13th edn. 1998).

P. Estoup, *La pratique des procédures rapides* (1990).

J. Huet, Le développement de la responsabilité civile en droit de l'environnement en France, [1993] *Revue Internationale de Droit Comparé* (RIDC), 235.

P. Jourdain, Jurisprudence Française en Matière de Droit Civil, Obligations et Contrats Spéciaux, Responsabilité Civile, [1995] *Revue trimestrielle de droit civil* (RTD civ.*)*, 893.

D.C. Lambert, *L'Etat providence en question* (1990).

Y. Lambert-Faivre, Les droits de la victime et les recours de la Sécurité sociale, [1998] JCP, I.110.

Y. Lambert-Faivre, *Droit des assurances* (11th edn. 2001), no. 540, 389.

N. Lesage, Les inondations, a chacun sa responsabilité, *Petites Affiches* (PA) 27 April 1994, 53.

C. Lienhard, Pour un droit des catastrophes, [1995] D., 91.

O. Moréteau/F. Lafay, Liability for Acts of Terrorism Under French Law, in: B.A. Koch (ed.), *Liability for Acts of Terrorism in a Comparative Perspective* (2003), 29–46.

P. Segur, La catastrophe et le risque naturel, essai de définition juridique, [1997] RGDA, 1693.

B. Starck/H. Roland/L Boyer, *Droit civil, Obligations, Responsabilité délictuelle* (6th edn. 1998), no. 28.

F. Taquet, Premières réflexions sur la loi du 27 juillet 1999…, [1999] Gaz. Pal., 21.

F. Terré/Y Lequette/P. Simler, *Les obligations* (7th edn. 2002).

Ph. Le Tourneau/L. Cadiet, *Droit de la responsabilité et des contrats* (2002), no. 238.

A. Tunc, La détermination du gardien dans la responsabilité du fait des choses inanimées,[1960] JCP, I.1592, no 11.

J. Vincent/S. Guinchard, *Procédure civile* (27th edn. 2003).

G. Viney, Les principaux aspects de la responsabilité civile des entreprises pour atteinte à l'environnement en droit français, [1996] JCP, I.3900.

G. Viney, *La responsabilité: conditions* (2nd edn. 1998), no. 48.

G. Viney, Le préjudice écologique, [1998] *La responsabilité civile et les assurances* (RCA), 6.

Germany

Ulrich Magnus

Part I. Introduction

This paper is not concerned with what could be termed the almost forgotten daily catastrophe, namely the number of 18 people statistically killed each day on German roads and of another 1305 people who are more or less severely injured each day in traffic accidents.[1] Though these accidents and also accidents at work or on other occasions affect many more people and cause much higher property losses each year than those catastrophes which this paper addresses they are not regarded as catastrophes in the normal sense of the word. For, the distinguishing element is lacking that one single event unexpectedly causes damage to many people at the same time. Nevertheless it is worth to remind us at the outset of this exercise of the "normal" accidents and their consequences when the question is discussed whether and to which extent victims of "real" catastrophes are, and should be, compensated for their damage. 1

Moreover, it has to be stressed that the term "catastrophe" is ambivalent insofar as it may only relate to unavoidable events like earthquakes or other natural catastrophes for which no other person could be made liable so that the victim, unless insured against such events, had to bear the damage him- or herself. The term may, however, also include man-made catastrophes like explosions and the like which can be avoided with reasonable care and for which a tortfeasor is responsible. Under the aspect of tort law it regularly makes an important difference in which sense the term is used since unavoidable external incidents normally do not attract tortious liability nor liability insurance. The following text, unless otherwise indicated, uses the term "catastrophe" in its wide sense which includes not only natural disasters but also cases of catastrophic ("mass") damage caused by negligent or even intentional conduct.

The last years have seen a number of such major catastrophes affecting Germany. In August 2002, the flooding (*Jahrhundertflut*) of the Elbe and some minor rivers caused the loss of about 30 lives and property damage in the amount of several billion Euro.[2] In July 2000, 100 German citizens died in

[1] See B. Harenberg (ed.), *Aktuell 2004* (2003), 442 relying on figures released by the *Statistisches Bundesamt* for 2002. In 2002, 6,842 people were killed and 476,413 were injured through traffic accidents (88,382 with severe injuries).

[2] As to the consequences of that flood see specifically the *Bericht der Sächsischen Staatsregierung zur Hochwasserkatastrophe im August 2002* (2003).

the Concorde air-crash near Paris.[3] In the same year 37 German citizens[4] lost their lives in an accident in Kaprun/Austria when a fire in a glacier train broke out while the train was in a tunnel.[5] In 1998, the tragic derailing of a high-speed-train near the town of Eschede/Germany caused the loss of almost 200 lives.[6] Another *Jahrhunderflut* occurred already in 1997 when the river Oder flooded parts of Brandenburg/Germany and caused large property damage. A further dramatic catastrophe still remembered is the death of 67 people and the injury of another 450 when in 1988 at an air-show at Ramstein/Germany Italian airplanes collided and crashed into the crowd. Many more similar instances could be mentioned.[7] Fortunately, thus far almost no terrorist attacks have occurred in Germany which caused catastrophic damage.[8] But it might only be a question of time until such attacks happen also in Germany.

2 All of these catastrophes raise the question of tortious liability as well as of insurance benefits or of specific state aid for the victims and/or their dependants. Not infrequently do they also raise the question of the applicable law – an aspect that is, however, not pursued in the following paper.[9] German law does not provide a single remedy in these cases of catastrophic damage but follows a mixed approach which combines different sources of compensation.

But it has also to be stressed that Germany puts greatest importance on the aspect of prevention of catastrophic damage. Prevention as far as possible is the overriding aim of any protection against catastrophes. This is particularly effected by requiring extended preventive measures and precautions as far as private or public operators of installations, plants, trains, planes, sports events etc. are concerned. These operators etc. are required to provide reasonable preventive safety measures even against natural disasters such as flooding, storm, fire and the like – measures which have to be taken in advance. Moreover, the German Federation and the *Länder* have established specific institutions, agencies and measures whose task it is to protect the population against catastrophic risks.[10] If, nevertheless, a catastrophe occurs, then regularly rapid help by these state agencies against the immediate consequences is to be, and is, organised in order to avoid at that stage further worsening of the damage as far as possible.

[3] See thereto R. Schmid, Der Concorde-Absturz: Welche Lehren können Reiseveranstalter und Versicherer daraus ziehen?, in: H. Koch/A. Willingmann (eds.), *Modernes Schadensmanagement bei Großschäden* (2002), 109 *et seq*.

[4] And further 118 people from other nations.

[5] See thereto E. Eybl, Das Gletscherbahn-Unglück von Kaprun am 11. November 2000 aus der Sicht des Haftpflicht-Versicherers, in: H. Koch/A. Willingmann (*supra* fn. 3), 81 *et seq*.

[6] Compare thereto O.E. Krasney, Aufgaben eines ‚Ombudsmannes' für die Opfer von Massenunfällen – Möglichkeiten und Grenzen, in: H. Koch/A. Willingmann (*supra* fn. 3), 67 *et seq*.

[7] In particular a number of bus accidents in the summer 2003.

[8] But more than 20 Germans were killed by a terrorist attack in Djerba/Libya in April 2002.

[9] See with respect to mass damages: U. Magnus, Kollisionsrechtliche Fragen grenzüberschreitender Schäden, in: H. Koch/A. Willingmann (eds.), *Großschäden – Complex Damages* (1998), 129 *et seq*.

[10] See the (federal) *Zivilschutzgesetz* (Civil Protection Act) of 25 March 1997, [1997] *Bundesgesetzblatt* (Federal Journal for Statutes, BGBl), I 726 which defines the tasks of the *Zivilschutz*.

Part II. General Scope of the Compensation System

3 In this part, a first overall survey shall be given how present German law reacts in general to catastrophic damage and how it provides for compensation in such cases. At the outset it must be stressed that the notion "catastrophe" has no specific meaning in relation to compensation of damage. Nevertheless, one finds the term "catastrophe" legally defined as "a state of necessity where life, health or the absolutely necessary supply for a great number of persons or important property values are endangered or substantially impaired".[11] But this definition is used in connection with prevention of, and protection against, catastrophes. With respect to the law of compensation, the term is unfamiliar; here it has no specific bearing.[12] Here the normal notion of damage is used which regularly disregards whether the damage resulted from a catastrophic or non-catastrophic incident. Only the amount of non-pecuniary damages depends under German law among other factors also on the circumstances under which the damage was suffered. Therefore, non-pecuniary damages, as far as they are due, tend to be higher if the damaging incident was of a catastrophic, particularly horrifying nature.[13]

As already indicated there is no single instrument dealing exclusively with the compensation of damage caused through catastrophes. In some cases – like in the case of the 2002 flood – the Federal Republic of Germany enacted an *ad hoc*-basis specific legislation on the compensation for victims – in that case for the victims of that flood.[14] The Act (*Flutopferhilfesolidaritätsgesetz*) established a fund in order to support the victims of this very catastrophe. But at present no general act exists which explicitly and generally provides for compensation in all cases of a catastrophic nature. Instead, many provisions of a considerable number of different statutes can apply to such a situation.

4 Besides the already mentioned *ad hoc* statutes like the *Flutopferhilfesolidaritätsgesetz* there are some specific statutes of rather limited ambit which can achieve relevance here: First, the *Opferentschädigungsgesetz* (Act on Victims' Compensation, OEG)[15] has to be mentioned. It entitles bodily injured victims of illegal attacks to claim compensation from the state.[16] Terror attacks with

[11] See, e.g., § 1 par. 2 *Katastrophenschutzgesetz* (Act on the Protection against Catastrophes) of the Bundesland Sachsen-Anhalt of 5 August 2002: "Ein Katastrophenfall im Sinne dieses Gesetzes ist *ein Notstand, bei dem Leben, Gesundheit oder die lebenswichtige Versorgung einer Vielzahl von Personen oder erhebliche Sachwerte gefährdet oder wesentlich beeinträchtigt werden* und zu dessen Abwehr oder Eindämmung der koordinierte Einsatz der verfügbaren Kräfte und Mittel unter einer gemeinsamen Gesamtleitung erforderlich ist" (the translated part in cursive). Each Bundesland has enacted a *Katastrophenschutzgesetz* similar to the one of Sachsen-Anhalt.

[12] It is remarkable that the index of the leading textbook on the law of damages does not even mention the word: see H. Lange/G. Schiemann, *Schadensersatz* (3rd edn. 2003), 769.

[13] This has been so decided particularly with respect to the conduct of the liable person: see, e.g., *Bundesgerichtshof* (Federal Civil Court – BGH), [1993] *Neue Juristische Wochenschrift* (NJW), 1531.

[14] See the *Flutopferhilfesolidaritätsgesetz* (Act on Solidarity with the Victims of the Flood) of 20 September 2002, [2002] BGBl, I 3651.

[15] Act of 11 May 1976, [1976] BGBl, I 1181 with later amendments.

[16] For further details see *infra*.

catastrophic consequences would therefore fall under this Act.[17] Victims of such specific catastrophes could avail themselves of the advantages of this Act. In a similar way, the *Atomgesetz* (Nuclear Energy Act, AtomG)[18] could render protection in cases of damage of this specific kind. The Act provides that the operator of a nuclear power plant is strictly liable for damage caused by the nuclear power of his plant even if in turn the nuclear incident had been caused by an "armed conflict, invasion, civil war, insurrection, or a grave natural disaster of an exceptional character".[19] On the other hand, a considerable number of strict liability statutes relieves the operator or keeper of the installation or the like from liability if a natural or other catastrophic event – *force majeure* (*höhere Gewalt*) – led to the damage.[20]

Besides the mentioned statutes the general rules of tort law apply which deal with compensation of damage as such irrespectively of whether or not the damage is the consequence of a catastrophe. Except where strict liability statutes can be invoked German tort law requires that the tortfeasor acted negligently; only then is his or her liability incurred.[21] That is also true in case of state liability for tortious acts of state officials. This fault principle leads to the general consequence that, if the catastrophic damage could not have been avoided by reasonable care, no compensation under general tort law can be claimed. Tort law – be it fault or strict liability – can therefore rather rarely than often found a claim for compensation of catastrophic damage.

5 A further source of compensation for – even catastrophic – damage is social security law. The entitlement to social security benefits does, however, not depend on the nature of the damage. Therefore, it does not matter whether or not the damage was the result of a catastrophe. As far as benefits for illness and injury through accidents are concerned, what matters here is the fact that the injured person must belong to the protected categories of persons who enjoy such benefits. As a rule the protected categories include all persons who are dependently employed as well as their next family members.[22] But further classes are also included.[23] The benefits regularly cover the basic needs of the entitled person but do not provide full compensation; in particular, non-pecuniary damage – pain and suffering – is not compensated. As far as property damage is concerned, social security law provides only some financial support under special circumstances namely where persons lack a sufficient economic basis for life (*ausreichende wirtschaftliche Lebensgrundlage*).[24]

[17] See thereon U. Magnus, Liability for Acts of Terrorism under German Law, in: B.A. Koch (ed.), *Liability for Acts of Terrorism* (2004), 47 *et seq.*
[18] Act of 23 December 1959, [1959] BGBl, I 814 with later amendments.
[19] § 25 par. 3 AtomG.
[20] See for details *infra* Part III.II.A.
[21] See the central tort provision § 823 par. 1 *Bürgerliches Gesetzbuch* (Civil Code – BGB).
[22] For a survey see J. Fedtke/U. Magnus, The Impact of Social Security Law on Tort Law in Germany, in: U. Magnus (ed.), *The Impact of Social Security Law on Tort Law* (2003), 86 *et seq.*
[23] See § 2 *Sozialgesetzbuch* IV (Social Code – SGB; Book IV).
[24] § 30 *Bundessozialhilfegesetz* (Federal Social Aid Act – BSHG).

A further means of compensation is private insurance coverage of catastrophic damage. However, in case of first party insurance many insurance policies exclude those catastrophic risks which result from natural catastrophes like earthquake.[25] 6

If a victim of a catastrophic damage can claim compensation from different sources, the general rule is that where there is a liable tortfeasor s/he should finally bear the loss. Those who grant state aid or social or private insurance benefits then regularly acquire the victim's tort claim to the extent they support the victim. Greater difficulties arise where there is no liable tortfeasor but where the victim can claim benefits from different social or private (insurance) sources. Here the general rule is that state funded aid is granted as a subsidiary measure only. The victim therefore must first exhaust the private insurance resources. Only when they do not cover the entire damage may s/he approach state funded resources. If the victim is entitled at the same time to different kinds of state aid, these measures cannot be cumulated if they concern the compensation of the same damage.[26]

Part III. Specific Regulations

The following part describes in greater detail under which conditions and to which extent the different sources provide compensation for catastrophic damage. 7

I. *Ad hoc* Legislation

The most recent legislative Act which deals with compensation for catastrophic damage is the already mentioned *Flutopferhilfesolidaritätsgesetz* of 2002.[27] This Act can be regarded as a model of how Germany reacts in cases of catastrophes of national importance. The Act was enacted by the Federal Parliament only just a month after the 2002 flood had occurred. The Act is only concerned with the consequences of the 2002 flood. It has no application for catastrophes in general. But it is very likely that the Federal legislator would react in a rather similar way if other catastrophes of comparable size occurred. 8

The *Flutopferhilfesolidaritätsgesetz* established a *Solidaritätsfonds „Aufbauhilfe“* (a solidarity fund "Reconstruction Aid"). The purpose of the Fund is to give some first and limited financial assistance on a preliminary level (*Soforthilfe*) and then to finance measures for the removal of the damage caused by the 2002 flood and for the reconstruction (*Aufbauhilfe*).[28] Moreover, though not of interest here, the Act provides substantial financial support to the local authorities to reconstruct the damaged infrastructure. With respect to private losses the Act explicitly prescribes that private households and enterprises which have suffered damage because of the 2002 flood should be financially assisted "insofar as neither insurance companies nor other third persons grant

[25] In case of fire insurance even the respective statute provides for such exclusion: see § 84 *Versicherungsvertragsgesetz* (Insurance Contract Act – VVG).
[26] The subsidiarity principle is for instance expressly mentioned in § 2 BSHG.
[27] See *supra* fn. 14.
[28] Art. 5 § 2 par. 1 *Flutopferhilfesolidaritätsgesetz*.

compensation".[29] As far as claimants are also entitled to receive compensation from others, for instance from insurers but have not in fact already received such compensation they are obliged to assign their respective claims to the Flood Fund.[30] It is further prescribed that for the distribution of the financial means of the fund it has to be taken into consideration whether and to which extent the victims had to bear differently important losses (*unterschiedliche Schadensbelastungen*).[31] This means that it has to be taken into account that the loss of the same thing – for instance a car – may not count in the same way for a wealthy enterprise as for a poor family household.

The financial means of the fund amount to € 8.1 billion. They were – and still are – borne to one half by the Federation and to one half by the *Länder*.[32] A specific Regulation prescribes further details of the distribution of the means of the fund.[33] The practice of distribution is discussed below.

Further provisions of the *Flutopferhilfesolidaritätsgesetz* concern tax provisions or relieve those who became insolvent because of the 2002 flood from certain time requirements in connection with their insolvency.[34]

In essence the *Flutopferhilfesolidaritätsgesetz* created the possibility to grant victims of the flood rapid and effective financial assistance to overcome the situation the flood had caused. The Act is specifically designed to compensate for property damage. Since the 2002 flood caused property losses which in several ten thousands of cases exceeded the individual capacity to bear the loss, the solidarity of the public at large had to step in.

II. Tort Law

9 Compensation under tort law presupposes that a tortfeasor is liable either under a strict liability statute or under the general fault rule. Therefore victims of catastrophic damage can generally rely on tort law only if somebody can be made liable for the catastrophe or for insufficient prevention against it. As a consequence mere natural catastrophes rarely attract tortious liability.

A. Strict Liability

10 In Germany strict liability is regulated by specific statutes which the courts are not allowed to extend to other situations by way of analogy.[35] It is only the legislator who may introduce new kinds of strict liability. Apart from international conventions, which are left aside here, the practically most important strict liability statutes are the *Straßenverkehrsgesetz* (Road Traffic Act, StVG), the *Haftpflichtgesetz* (Liability Act, HaftPflG), the *Produkthaftungsgesetz* (Product Liability Act, ProdHG), the *Luftverkehrsgesetz* (Air Traffic Act, LuftVG),

[29] Art. 5 § 2 par. 2 no. 1 *Flutopferhilfesolidaritätsgesetz*.

[30] See § 2 par. 5 no. 2 Verordnung nach § 2 Abs. 6 des *Aufbauhilfefondsgesetzes* (*Aufbauhilfeverordnung* – AufbauhfV) of 24 June 2003, [2003] BGBl, I 962.

[31] Art. 5 § 2 par. 3 *Flutopferhilfesolidaritätsgesetz*.

[32] See Art. 5 § 4 *Flutopferhilfesolidaritätsgesetz*.

[33] Verordnung nach § 2 Abs. 6 des *Aufbauhilfefondsgesetzes*.

[34] Art. 6 *Flutopferhilfesolidaritätsgesetz*.

[35] See in particular BGHZ 55, 229 (234).

the *Umwelthaftungsgesetz* (Environmental Liability Act, UmweltHG), the AtomG and the *Gentechnikgesetz* (Genetechnic Act, GenTG).[36] The statutes have introduced strict liability mainly for the operation of means of transportation and energy installations and for activities which pollute the environment. There is, however, no strict liability of enterprises as such or for example of enterprises or single persons who store fireworks or explosives or run a switchback at a fair.[37]

The liability under the mentioned statutes is incurred when the damage is the result of the very risk against which the statute is designed to protect. The damage must be due to the operation (*beim Betrieb*) of the installation, plant, vehicle or the dangerous activity that caused the damage. Some of the catastrophic events envisaged in this paper are in principle covered by strict liability statutes – for example the derailed train (Eschede) as well as the burning train in the tunnel (Kaprun, if that had happened in Germany).[38] The same would be true for major bus accidents with many victims.[39] There the operation of the train or bus has led to the damage and – subject to possible excuses – the operator or keeper is strictly liable for the damage.

The true reasons for these accidents are often not clear. If "internal" causes – a broken wheel, bursting tyre or the like – were responsible, strict liability would be incurred. But the chain of causation between the specific risk and the damage would not necessarily be interrupted if the specific risk materialised even if it in turn had been set in motion by an external catastrophic cause. Then it depends on the respective strict liability statute whether nonetheless the person creating and controlling the risk – the operator or keeper – is primarily liable irrespective of fault.

Several of the strict liability statutes (in particular for road or rail accidents) 11
exempt the liable person from liability if s/he proves that the damage was caused by *force majeure*.[40] *Force majeure* has been defined as

> "von außen kommende betriebsfremde Eingriffe ... (die) mit zumutbaren Mitteln auch durch die äußerste, vernünftigerweise zu erwartende Sorgfalt nicht verhindert werden können" ("interferences from outside being not internal causes ... [which] cannot be avoided with reasonable means by even the utmost care which can be reasonably expected").[41]

[36] Further statutes which provide for strict liability are the *Wasserhaushaltsgesetz* (Waterhousehold Act, WHG), the *Bundesberggesetz* (Federal Mining Act, BBergG), the *Arzneimittelgesetz* (Pharmaceuticals Act, AMG).

[37] For a survey on strict liability under German law compare J. Fedtke/U. Magnus, Germany, in: B.A. Koch/H. Koziol (eds.), *Unification of Tort Law: Strict Liability* (2002), 147 *et seq.*

[38] § 1 HaftPflG provides for strict liability of the operator of the train unless s/he is excused because of *force majeure*.

[39] § 7 par. 1 StVG (again with the possible *force majeure* excuse).

[40] See § 7 par. 2 StVG, § 1 par. 2 HaftPflG, § 22 par. 1 and 2 WHG, § 4 UmweltHG.

[41] [1988] BGH NJW, 2733. It may be added that the European Directive on package travel, package holidays and package tours of 13 June 1990 (No. 90/314/EC) contains a legislative definition of *force majeure* (see Art. 4(6)(b)(ii) of the Directive): "force majeure, i.e. unusual and unforeseeable circumstances beyond the control of the party by whom it is pleaded, the consequences of which could not have been avoided even if all due care had been exercised".

Unforeseeable and unavoidable natural forces or unforeseeable and unavoidable acts of third persons constitute *force majeure* and relieve from liability.[42] For example, terrorist attacks on busses or on electric power installations would be causes which exempt the keeper of the bus or the operator of the power installations from liability for the ensuing damage through the misuse unless the keeper or operator negligently enabled the misuse.[43]

On the other hand, a considerable number of strict liability statutes do not exempt the liable person even in case of *force majeure*. Neither catastrophic external events nor unexpected acts of third persons then exclude the keeper's or operator's liability. Besides the already mentioned example of the Nuclear Energy Act[44] this is true for instance for the keeper of an aircraft who is strictly liable for damage even through a malfunction of the plane which was due to *force majeure*; anyhow, the keeper remains liable if s/he has enabled the misuse of the plane by third persons.[45] Also the person who produces or works with genetically modified organisms cannot rely on the excuse of *force majeure* when those organisms cause damage to third persons.[46] As a further example, mining enterprises can also not invoke the excuse of *force majeure* when certain mining activities cause damage to third persons.[47] The underlying reason for this "very strict" liability appears to be the particularly high or incalculable risk of the respective installation or activity as is especially the case with nuclear power or genetically modified organisms.

12 If strict liability is established, the liable person is obliged to compensate any damage to body and to property of the victim. In case of bodily harm, any consequential damage (lost income etc.) but also non-pecuniary damage is to be compensated.[48] However, mere economic loss is not compensable.[49] Most though not all strict liability statutes provide for some maximum limit of the compensable damage.[50] Beyond the prescribed limit compensation can only be claimed where the liable person acted negligently or intentionally thus meeting the fault requirement of general tort law. At present the limits which have been unified to a certain extent for the strict liability statutes in 2002[51] are the following:

[42] See for instance the case that acts of sabotage caused the damage: [1988] BGH NJW, 2733.

[43] See § 7 par. 3 StVG; § 2 par. 3 no. 3 HaftPflG (unless the damage is caused by falling electric wires; then the operator is liable even if this happens through *force majeure*).

[44] Compare § 25 par. 3 AtomG as discussed *supra*.

[45] See § 33 par. 2 LuftVG

[46] See thereon J. Kohler, Buch 3: Umwelthaftungsrecht, in: J. von Staudinger (ed.), *Kommentar zum Bürgerlichen Gesetzbuch mit Einführungsgesetz und Nebengesetzen. Umwelthaftungsrecht* (2002); §§ 32, 34–5, 37, GenTG no. 40.

[47] See J. Kohler (*supra* fn. 46), § 114 BBergG no. 40.

[48] See § 253 par. 2 BGB in general and specific provisions in the strict liability statutes, for example § 11 sent. 2 StVG.

[49] The only exception is § 22 WHG according to which also mere financial loss can be claimed where water has been polluted.

[50] In particular the strict liability of the keeper of household animals (so-called luxury animals) is unlimited, see § 833 BGB.

[51] By the *Zweites Gesetz zur Änderung schadenersatzrechtlicher Vorschriften* (Second Act on the Amendment of Provisions on Damage) of 19 July 2002, [2002] BGBl, I 2674.

As far as personal injury or death is concerned: Some statutes like the Road Traffic Act or the Liability Act provide in case of death or bodily injury of a single person for maximum amounts of € 600,000 as lump sum or – alternatively – € 36,000 as yearly rent;[52] these maximum amounts apply also where the killed or injured person leaves behind several dependants who can claim maintenance. Other statutes like the Product Liability Act, the Environmental Liability Act or the Genetechnic Act do not fix the amounts a single person can claim but set a maximum overall limit of € 85 million.[53] The reason for this distinct solution seems to be that these statutes refer to cases where numerous victims are more likely than for example in case of traffic accidents.

Certain statutes like the Road Traffic Act provide for still another maximum amount: if several persons are killed or injured, then the prescribed maximum is € 3,000,000 (lump sum) or € 180,000 (rent) for all persons entitled to compensation.[54] If the maximum amount does not suffice to meet all justified claims – as will often be the case with catastrophic incidents concerning road accidents – then each claimant gets a proportionate share only. This proportionality rule applies also where the high overall amount set by some statutes[55] does not suffice to satisfy all claimants.[56]

As far as property damage is concerned: some statutes fix the maximum 13
amount for such damage at € 300,000 irrespective of whether there are one or several victims.[57] Other statutes set the limit at € 85 million.[58] The different approach can be attributed to the presumably higher risk potential which these last mentioned statutes concern.

All strict liability statutes contain the general rule that a claim can be reduced because of the victim's contributory negligence.[59]

In sum, strict liability statutes do not render satisfactory protection in cases of 14
catastrophic damage. First, there are situations which can result in catastrophic damage where no strict liability statute applies at all. One example is the storage of explosives in the neighbourhood of densely inhabited flats. But also in case of flooding or other natural catastrophic events no liability statute as such applies. Secondly, in cases of external catastrophic events strict liability can often not be invoked due to the *force majeure* excuse. Thirdly, even where victims can rely on strict liability, the maximum amounts prescribed by the various strict liability statutes further restrict satisfactory compensation at least when catastrophes with extended losses occur. It is likely that in such cases the victims can successfully claim only a proportional part of their damage.

[52] Compare for instance § 12 par. 1 no. 1 StVG, § 9 HaftPflG, § 117 par. 1 no. 1, § 88 sent 1 no. 1 AMG, § 46 par. 1 LuftVG.
[53] See § 10 ProdHG, § 33 sent. 1 GenTG, § 15 sent. 1 UmweltHG.
[54] § 12 par. 1 no. 2 StVG.
[55] See § 10 ProdHG, § 33 sent. 1 GenTG, § 15 sent. 1 UmweltHG.
[56] See § 10 par. 2 ProdHG, § 15 sent. 2 UmweltHG.
[57] Compare § 12 par. 1 no. 3 StVG, § 10 HaftPflG.
[58] § 15 sent. 1 UmweltHG, § 33 GenTG.
[59] See for instance § 9 StVG, § 4 HaftPflG, § 11 UmweltHG.

B. Fault Liability

15 Under general tort law a person is liable to compensate any damage if s/he has wrongfully caused damage to body, health or property and if s/he was at fault (§ 823 par. 1 BGB). The fault requirement means that the tortfeasor acted either intentionally or negligently. The negligence requirement is met when the tortfeasor has neglected that standard of care that s/he could be reasonably expected to observe in the circumstances of the case. If the activity of the tortfeasor him- or herself has caused the damage and if the activity was dangerous in itself, then also the standard of care corresponds to this specific risk and requires a particularly high level of care. Therefore the standard of care is particularly high where the tortfeasor for example stores liquids which are dangerous for the public[60] or where s/he organises a big public firework display.[61] Only when the tortfeasor has taken all reasonable precautions in such a case in order to avoid damage will s/he not then be held liable. In practice the courts tend to hold the tortfeasor liable if the consequences of some activity are disastrous. It is not formally presumed that the tortfeasor was at fault; but the courts then regularly raise the level of care and require further precautionary measures which the tortfeasor should have applied to prevent the damage. And since the tortfeasor in fact did not apply these measures s/he is at fault and will be held liable.

If on the other hand an unexpected and unavoidable catastrophic event like an earthquake, a flood, storm or any other natural source causes the damage, private persons are normally not liable for any of the damaging consequences because they then have neither caused the damage nor are they at fault in respect of the ensuing damage. Therefore tort liability based on fault will regularly be excluded if events which qualify as *force majeure* have caused the damage.

However, this result will be different if the person was specifically obliged to render protection against the specific natural risk. For instance, if an architect had to construct a building in an earthquake area s/he can be made liable by those who are injured when the building collapses due to a "normal" earthquake in that area since it was the architect's obligation to construct the building earthquake-safe. The negligent violation of this obligation would render the architect liable in tort even towards third persons with whom no contractual bonds exist.[62] Likewise, even if lightning set a store of explosives on fire by which neighbours and third persons are damaged then nonetheless the owner of the store might be liable if s/he did not take all reasonable steps in advance to prevent catastrophic consequences of such an unexpected but possible event. Cases of this kind may particularly often happen when state authorities are obliged to prevent damage. Whether and when state liability is then incurred will be discussed below under Part III.IV.A

If tortious liability is established, the tortfeasor has to compensate the full damage. German law does not know of any possibility to reduce the tortfea-

60 [1986] BGH NJW, 1182.
61 [1965] BGH NJW, 199.
62 See, e.g., BGHZ 68, 169; [1991] BGH NJW, 562.

sor's burden because of the mere fact that the heavy consequences would overburden the tortfeasor. Compensation for bodily harm includes consequential damage (loss of income etc.) and non-pecuniary loss as well.[63] Damage to property entitles one to the cost of repair or of a substitute where necessary.[64]

Generally a claim can be reduced where the victim contributed to the damage.[65] The extent of the reduction depends on the circumstances and in particular on how far each party had contributed to the causation of the damage and had neglected their own obligations.

In essence, the general, fault-based tort law regularly grants protection in case of catastrophic damage if an individual tortfeasor has caused this damage by his or her activity. Then only rarely will the courts deny that the tortfeasor was at fault. In case of damage through natural catastrophes general tort law normally does not lead to liability of individual tortfeasors unless they violated their obligation to protect third persons against damage of the kind that happened. This will however rarely be the case.

III. Insurance Law

A. *Private Insurance Law*

Since in many cases of catastrophic damage tort law renders no protection and since an individual tortfeasor, if liable at all, alone will often not be able to satisfy all claims for which s/he is liable, private insurance is of particular importance to victims of catastrophic damage. This insurance may take the form of first party or third party insurance. 16

Private health or life insurance contracts regularly do not specifically exclude catastrophic risks – except war risks – but sometimes do not cover injuries through particularly risky activities.[66] (It is likely but thus far it has not been decided by the courts that the exclusion of war risks does not extend to terror risks as well.) However, some accident insurers have now begun to exclude from their policies coverage for bodily injury through terrorist attacks by way of specific means like ABC weapons[67] or even in general.[68]

More often property insurance policies do not cover property damage which was caused by catastrophic events (*Elementarschäden*). As already mentioned, the relevant German statute provides for instance that fire insur-

[63] See §§ 253, 842 BGB.

[64] For details compare H. Heinrichs, in: O. Palandt (ed.), *Bürgerliches Gesetzbuch* (64th edn. 2005), § 249 no. 11 *et seq.* with extensive references.

[65] § 254 BGB.

[66] Normally the life insurance contract excludes the case of suicide only, see also § 169 VVG.

[67] For instance, the following clause is used: "In Abänderung von § 2 (which defines the extent of the coverage) sind jegliche Schäden oder Kosten bei einem Unfall als Fluggast, die direkt oder indirekt verursacht werden durch terroristische Handlungen, die das Benutzen von nuklearen, chemischen oder biologischen Massenvernichtungswaffen mit sich bringen, wie auch immer diese in Umlauf gebracht oder kombiniert werden und unabhängig von anderen Ursachen oder Ereignissen, die gleichzeitig oder in anderer zeitlicher Reihenfolge zu diesem Schaden oder diesen Kosten beitragen, ausgeschlossen" (Axa-Versicherung).

[68] See, e.g., the General Conditions of Innova Versicherung.

ance contracts need not cover the risk that the fire was caused by an earthquake or by war.[69] But, as always in private insurance law, the coverage depends on the specific terms of the respective policy. In case of the 2002 flood about 50% of those households which suffered damage were insured against the risk of property damage through natural sources.[70]

17 In reaction to the September 11 events a special insurance company (*Extremus Versicherungs AG*) has been established in Germany in order to grant coverage in cases of huge damage caused by terror attacks. This initiative was taken by the insurance industry. *Extremus Versicherungs AG* is a direct insurer founded by industry insurance companies. The shares of *Extremus Versicherungs AG* are held by 17 insurance companies, among them *Allianz Versicherung, Münchener Rück* und *Swiss Re Germany*.[71] The admission of this new company to the insurance market received the approval by the respective state authority by the end of 2002.[72] The new company offers direct insurance protection to enterprises and individuals. It insures against terror damage to property and through business interruption, but only in cases where this damage exceeds the amount of € 25 million, because up to this sum coverage is regularly provided for by the normal insurance policies. *Extremus* therefore insures those losses which are higher than € 25 million up to an overall maximum limit of € 3 billion; however, the maximum damage within a single year which a policyholder can insure with *Extremus* is limited to € 1.5 billion.[73] Beyond the limit of € 3 billion the German state will provide additional coverage up to the amount of further € 10 billion.[74] Until spring 2003 *Extremus* had concluded 855 insurance contracts with an overall insured value of € 558 billion.[75]

As far as liability insurance contracts are concerned, the insurer is in principle not obliged to satisfy claims if the insured person intentionally and wrongfully caused the damage.[76] The insurer is however not relieved if the insured person caused catastrophic consequences but did not act intentionally. The insurer is then obliged up to the amount which was agreed in the policy.

B. Social Insurance Law

18 Social insurance law aims at a basic protection of every member of society in order to enable everybody a dignified and self-organised existence.[77] Social insurance law renders specific protection against the consequences of personal

[69] § 84 VVG.

[70] See *Bericht der Sächsischen Staatsregierung zur Hochwasserkatastrophe im August 2002* (2003), 45.

[71] See *Frankfurter Allgemeine Zeitung* (FAZ) of 1 April 2003, 16. The starting capital had been € 60 million.

[72] See the report in FAZ of 4 September 2002, 11 ("Terrorversicherung Extremus gegründet").

[73] See FAZ of 1 April 2003, 16 with further details.

[74] See FAZ of 1 April 2003, 16.

[75] See FAZ of 1 April 2003, 16.

[76] § 152 VVG.

[77] See the main aims of social security law as formulated in Art. I § 1 par. 1 SGB I.

injuries.[78] Today more than 90% of the German population is protected by social security schemes against the consequences of illness, accidents and invalidity.[79] The protection does not depend on whether illness, accident or invalidity resulted from catastrophic or non-catastrophic events. Even in case of catastrophic events – for which no-one or someone is liable – the benefits have to be granted if the general requirements for the entitlement are met, in particular that the claimant belongs to the protected group of persons.

The benefits cover the necessary costs for medical treatment and rehabilitation measures. Where the entitled person's earning capacity has been impaired temporary or permanent payments become due which correspond to the degree of impaired earning capacity. Social security benefits do not aim at a full and precise compensation of the concrete loss. They are calculated in a rather general and abstract way and are generally lower than compensation under tort law would be. This is due to the fact that the protection granted by social security law is subject to various restrictions, caps and deductions which the insured have to bear themselves. Moreover social security benefits do not include any compensation for immaterial loss. And they regularly do not cover property loss. As already mentioned above only where a person is lacking a sufficient economic fundament to secure the own existence by own activity can some financial assistance (*Sozialhilfe*) be granted by the social aid agency.[80] This support has to aim at securing the building up of an own existence.

In sum, in most cases of even catastrophic events, the general social security law protects rather effectively against the consequences of personal injuries. Here it offers reasonable basic protection though not complete compensation. But it normally does not grant protection against property damage.

IV. Further Possible Sources

A. *Liability for Acts of State Officials*

As a further source of protection against catastrophic damage state liability for 19
acts of state officials has to be taken into account. The state is liable according to § 839 BGB and Art. 34 *Grundgesetz* (Fundamental Act, GG) if its officials have intentionally or negligently violated their official duties (*Amtspflichten*) and have thereby caused damage to the claimant. But this liability is subject to some restrictions.

[78] This is mainly achieved by the *Gesetzliche Krankenversicherung* (Legal Health Insurance) against the consequences of illness, the *Gesetzliche Unfallversicherung* (Legal Accident Insurance) against the consequences of (employment) accidents, the *Gesetzliche Rentenversicherung* (Legal Pension Insurance) against the consequences of invalidity and retirement and the *Pflegeversicherung* (Care Insurance) against the consequences of becoming a person who needs special attendance.

[79] See the figures quoted by J. Fedtke/U. Magnus (*supra* fn. 22), 91 *et seq.* and by H. Kötz/G. Wagner, *Deliktsrecht* (8th edn. 2001), 84 *et seq.*

[80] § 30 BSHG.

First, state liability is only incurred if the purpose of the relevant duty was to protect persons like the claimant.[81] The various state agencies which are concerned with the protection against catastrophes have the general duty to take reasonable preventive measures. This duty is also designed to protect private persons who are otherwise endangered. However, the courts have decided that this general duty does not comprise measures against catastrophes which re-occur only over great time spans, for instance every 50 years.[82]

Moreover, the respective state agencies have the duty to maintain any existing protection – for instance protective walls, dykes or the like – in good condition. The state agencies are liable under general tort law (§ 823 BGB) when they have at least negligently violated their so-called *Verkehrssicherungspflicht* with respect to the safety of these protective precautions.[83] But in case of unforeseen and unavoidable "real" catastrophes it will always be questionable and difficult to prove whether and to which extent better safety could have prevented the damage that in reality ensued. The burden of proof of that fact falls on the claimant unless principles of prima facie evidence apply.

The state agencies are also under a duty to warn endangered persons as early and quickly as possible of any imminent danger.[84] In case of catastrophes which tend to happen unexpectedly and at once there is generally little time for such warnings. Nevertheless state officials are obliged to react immediately and with foresight. Therefore depending on the circumstances of the case, liability of the state can sometimes be based on the negligent neglect of the duty to warn in time.[85]

If state liability is established, then the extent of compensation is the same as under general tort law.

B. Further Possible State Liability

20 It has been discussed under constitutional aspects whether victims of catastrophes are generally entitled to compensation by the state beyond the extent that is already foreseen but which does not cover all such damage.[86] But it is accepted that the legislator has a wide discretion concerning the extent and the organisation of state assistance in case of catastrophic events. The legislator has exercised its discretion in an admissible way by enacting legislation on social aid (*Sozialhilfe*). The basic protection provided for by the *Sozialhilfe* is

[81] See thereto H. Thomas, in: O. Palandt (ed.), *Bürgerliches Gesetzbuch* (6th edn. 2005), § 839 no. 47 *et seq.* with numerous references.

[82] See *Oberlandesgericht* (OLG) Celle, [1989] *Versicherungsrecht* (VersR), 484 (485) with respect to the protection against flooding.

[83] See for example BGH, [1964] *Monatsschrift für deutsches Recht* (MDR), 399 (with respect to the safety of a dyke). For further references compare W. Ewer, Ersatz-, Entschädigungs- und Ausgleichsansprüche wegen Hochwasserschäden – erste Bestandsaufnahmen nach der Katastrophe, [2002] *Neue Juristische Wochenschrift* (NJW), 3497 *et seq.*

[84] See thereto W. Ewer (*supra* fn. 83), 3500.

[85] See W. Ewer (*supra* fn. 83), 3500.

[86] See thereto *Bundesverfassungsgericht* (Federal Constitutional Court – BVerfG) BVerfGE (Decisions of the BVerfG) 40, 121; BVerfGE 82, 60; BVerfGE 102, 254; further W. Ewer (*supra* fn. 83), 3501 *et seq.*

sufficient state aid.[87] Victims of catastrophic events are therefore not entitled in law to require the legislator to enact legislation that grants further and more far-reaching assistance.

Part IV. Procedural Questions

I. Distribution of Means under the *Flutopferhilfesolidaritätsgesetz*

The *Bericht der Sächsischen Staatsregierung zur Hochwasserkatastrophe im August 2002* (2003) describes in detail how the means of the Fund for Flood Victims (2002) were distributed in Saxonia. From this Report it can also be gathered how the other affected regions proceeded since they followed a similar practice. The other but much less affected regions were: Bavaria, Brandenburg, Lower Saxonia, Mecklenburg-Vorpommern, Saxonia-Anhalt, Schleswig-Holstein and Thuringia. The form and amounts of compensation there had also to follow the rules and procedure regulated in outline by Federal enactments. 21

The means of the 2002 Flood Fund (in total € 8.1 billion) are mainly distributed by the administration of the local communities in an administrative procedure. A specific (Federal) statutory Regulation[88] which was however enacted only a year after the 2002 flood gives some broad guidance for the distribution of the financial means. The main principle is that losses can be compensated up to their full amount though the local administrative authorities have a certain discretion in that respect.[89] In exerting their discretion they shall take into account to which extent the involved persons and enterprises are afflicted by the damage („*Bei der Verteilung der Mittel und der Gewährung der Hilfen sind die unterschiedlichen Schadensbelastungen der Betroffenen zu berücksichtigen*“).[90] This is to mean that the authorities shall take into consideration how severely applicants were affected by their loss with respect to their remaining means.[91] Moreover, the administrative authorities are bound by the general principle of equality (Art. 3 Basic Law) that like cases have to be treated alike. But in general the authorities are obliged to grant persons who have suffered flood damage full compensation for their loss.[92] Courts are not involved in the distribution unless a claimant seeks relief when support is unjustifiably denied.

The Fund is mainly directed at the compensation of property damage caused by the 2002 flood. Claimants who suffered through the 2002 flood have to apply for financial support and can receive first a limited immediate payment (*Soforthilfe*) and then a middle-term reconstruction support (*Aufbau-*

[87] BVerfG, decision of 12 January 1991 – 1 BvR 540/91, juris.

[88] Verordnung nach § 2 Abs. 6 des Aufbauhilfefondsgesetzes of 24 August 2003, [2003] BGBl, I 962.

[89] See § 2 par. 5 no. 1 sent. 1 Verordnung nach § 2 Abs. 6 des Aufbauhilfefondsgesetzes; see thereto *supra*.

[90] § 2 par. 3 *Aufbauhilfefondsgesetz* (which is part [Art. 5] of the *Flutopferhilfesolidaritätsgesetz*).

[91] See already *supra* Part III.III.A.

[92] See *supra* fn. 70, 53.

hilfe).[93] The reconstruction support is intended to cover in particular the cost of the reconstruction of private houses and of enterprises while the *Soforthilfe* shall satisfy the first basic needs of any kind. Private claimants could get € 500 (per person) as *Soforthilfe* and further immediate support to enable them to move back into their homes. Enterprises could receive as *Soforthilfe* € 500 per employee and additional € 15,000 per enterprise.[94] On the contrary the amount of the *Aufbauhilfe* depended on the concrete extent of the damage suffered in the individual case.

The means of the Fund which are granted to private persons or enterprises can amount to full compensation of the entire property damage;[95] nonetheless a certain deduction (*Eigenanteil*) is intended.[96] The sums of financial support are however calculated according to the full costs the repair or substitution of the damaged buildings or things would amount to.[97] This will often exceed the temporary value (*Zeitwert*) of the building which is generally less and which normally sets the limit for compensation. The aim of this high level of compensation was to render specific protection to the eastern parts of Germany and not to impede the general process of reconstruction underway there.[98] In line with this general aim the prescribed deductibles, though no precise figures are available, are reported to be "relatively low".[99] The goal of the deductible is to avoid wrong incentives for private persons and enterprises who otherwise might also in future rely on state aid in case of natural catastrophes instead of taking own precautionary measures as for instance taking out insurance against such events.[100]

Applicants need not necessarily fully prove their damage. Sufficient probability and personal assurance of the damage can suffice.[101] The granting of the *Soforthilfen* was very informal and speedy.[102] But if applicants applied for

93 See *supra* fn. 70, 52 *et seq.*

94 See *supra* fn. 70, 56 *et seq.*

95 § 2 par. 5 no. 1 sent. 1 Verordnung nach § 2 Abs. 6 des Aufbauhilfefondsgesetzes: „Aus den Mitteln des Fonds können für individuelle Schäden … Leistungen bis zur Höhe des entstandenen Schadens … gewährt werden".

96 See *supra* fn. 70, 53.

97 *Supra* fn. 70, 52 *et seq.*

98 See *supra* fn 70, 53.

99 *Supra* fn. 70, 53.

100 *Supra* fn. 70, 53: „Von dieser hohen Förderung darf jedoch keine präjudizierende Wirkung ausgehen, die falsche Anreize für Unternehmen und private Haushalte setzt. Vielmehr stellt sie eine einmalige Reaktion auf ein Ausnahmeereignis dar. Deshalb muss klar sein, dass es in der Eigenverantwortung der Bürger, Unternehmen und Kommunen bleibt, künftigen Schäden auch durch Versicherungen gegen Elementarschäden zu begegnen. Schließlich soll der Grundsatz der Eigenvorsorge gerade verhindern, dass der Steuerzahler insgesamt für mangelnde individuelle Risikovorsorge in Anspruch genommen wird.
Der notwendige Anteil an Eigenmitteln – und damit an Eigenverantwortung – soll etwaigen Fehlinvestitionen und Fehlleitungen der Fördermittel vorbeugen. Eigenanteile haben somit auch eine **ordnungspolitische Funktion**" (emphasis of the original).

101 See § 2 par. 5 no. 3 Verordnung nach § 2 Abs. 6 des Aufbauhilfefondsgesetzes: „Der jeweilige Nachweis der Angaben der Geschädigten kann durch die Glaubhaftmachung und Versicherung der Richtigkeit der Angaben erbracht werden. Diese schließt auch nachträgliche Überprüfungen und Anforderungen von Nachweisen insbesondere bei Schäden von großem Umfang nicht aus".

102 See *supra* fn. 70, 55.

Aufbauhilfen, in particular when sums exceeding € 1 million were demanded, the procedure of examining and granting was more formal and careful and lasted significantly longer.[103]

The distribution of *Soforthilfen* was successfully finished by the end of 2002.[104] The same was true for most of the *Aufbauhilfen* for the reconstruction of private houses.[105] The middle-term financial assistance (*Aufbauhilfen*) granted to enterprises was, however, only partly distributed by that time. Where the sum which was applied for exceeded € 1 million, in only less than half of these cases payments – apart from the *Soforthilfen* – had already been made by spring 2003, eight months after the flood. Evidently the examination of the entitlement takes longer in cases of important damage.[106]

II. Normal Tort Law Procedure

Under tort law the regulation of catastrophic damage generally needs some time; rather often the courts have finally to decide whether or not tort liability is established.[107] The main reasons are that in these cases the often difficult questions of causation, further of the extent of the damage and adequate damages and, if necessary, of fault cannot otherwise be clarified and finally be decided. Moreover the fact that many victims – sometimes of different classes: directly and indirectly affected victims, bystanders – are involved also increases the complexity of these cases. And if there are many victims, they do not rarely form an "interest group" which – probably more effectively than a single victim – can pursue all victims' rights.[108] 22

Thus far, there are no specific procedural forms of dealing with such complex tort cases in Germany. It is neither required that mediation procedures are used nor does German law provide instruments like the class action of US origin for normal tort cases.[109] However, sometimes, as in the case of the train disaster in Eschede, specific forms, in this case an ombudsman, are voluntarily used by both parties in order to enable easier negotiations.[110]

If tortious liability is doubtful, the tortfeasor is not obliged to pay anything before his or her obligation is at least stated by a judgment of first instance which then can be executed on a preliminary basis. However, some tortfeasors offer prepayments even without obligation in order to avoid further loss of im-

[103] See *supra* fn. 70, 55.
[104] *Supra* fn. 70, 56 *et seq.*
[105] See *supra* fn. 70, 57.
[106] See *supra* fn. 70, 59.
[107] See the reports of O.E. Krasney/W.D. Müller-Rostin/E. Eybl/R. Schmid, in: H. Koch/A. Willingmann (*supra* fn. 3), which concern most of the catastrophic accidents mentioned above under Part I.
[108] See the information given by O.E. Krasney (*supra* fn. 6), 67 *et seq.* Krasney was "ombudsman" in the case of the Eschede train disaster.
[109] As to the class action see J. Basedow *et al.* (ed.), *Die Bündelung gleichgerichteter Interessen im Prozess* (1999); H. Koch, *Kollektiver Rechtsschutz im Zivilprozeß* (1976); J. Zekoll, Prozessrechtliche Instrumente bei der Bewältigung von Großschäden in den USA, in: H. Koch/A. Willingmann (*supra* fn. 9), 219 *et seq.*
[110] See O.E. Krasney (*supra* fn. 6), 67 *et seq.*

age of their enterprise.[111] For the same reason these enterprises, for instance big travel agencies, airlines, shipping companies, railway companies follow the strategy of a "client oriented" "damage management".[112] They try to inform as openly and quickly as possible; they try to provide first support even through psychologists and to compensate any damage in case of doubt rather generously instead according to strict juristic standards.[113] The aim of the strategy is to give future potential clients the impression that even in case of catastrophic accidents, which never can be entirely avoided, the best is done to ease the consequences.

As far as proof and evidence in tort cases are concerned the general rule is that the claiming victim must prove all facts which evidence causation, fault and damage. Only in particular circumstances is this burden reversed, for instance where there is – strong – prima facie evidence that the tortfeasor must have caused the damage or must have been at fault.

III. Private Insurance Regulation Procedure

23 It appears that today almost all catastrophic damage cases are dealt with and regulated by insurance companies.[114] In some cases insurance coverage is mandatory and then includes also catastrophic risks. Thus, in some *Bundesländern* owners were obliged to insure their buildings against fire.[115] More common is mandatory liability insurance, for instance in case of nuclear power plants[116] or motor cars.[117] However, a general legal duty obliging everybody to insure against damage through natural sources does not exist and would be hardly reconcilable with the general freedom to act as granted by the Constitution (Art. 2 Basic Law). It is likewise not suggested to introduce such mandatory insurance in regions which are particularly endangered by elementary forces. Indirectly there is nevertheless a strong incentive to take such insurance since where flooding or like natural catastrophes become normal, it is for the persons settling in that region to be aware of the risk or insure it. They cannot expect to be protected at the expense of the ordinary tax-payer.[118]

Private insurers regularly organise the regulation of the damage at first and as far as possible according to their own in-house procedures and try to avoid court procedures. But if nonetheless cases go to court, the preceding remarks on the normal tort law procedure in courts apply.

[111] See the information provided by R. Schmid (*supra* fn. 3) 109 *et seq.* (Schmid was concerned with the regulation of the Concorde desaster 2000 in Paris); in the same sense P. Kiesgen, Vermeidung von Zielkonflikten durch integratives Krisenmanagement, in: H. Koch/A. Willingmann (*supra* fn.3), 103 *et seq.*

[112] See particularly thereto P. Kiesgen (*supra* fn. 111).

[113] See P. Kiesgen (*supra* fn. 111); R. Schmid (*supra* fn. 111), 109 *et seq.*

[114] C. Hinsch, Regulierungspraxis der Versicherer bei Großschäden und die Rolle des Haftungsrechts, in: H. Koch/A. Willingmann (*supra* fn. 9), 69 *et seq.*

[115] Though this practice has mainly been abolished.

[116] §§ 13, 14 AtomG.

[117] § 1 PflVersG.

[118] See also *supra* fn. 70, 53, cited above in fn. 100.

However, insurance companies also increasingly seem to follow the modern unbureaucratic "damage management" approach described above[119] though still less intensively than touristic or transportation companies.[120] In particular, the practice of rather prompt prepayments even in cases of doubt gradually seems to be gaining ground.

According to general insurance law, the policyholder is obliged to give immediate notice (*unverzüglich*) after the insured event has occurred (§ 33 VVG). But the holder will lose insurance coverage only if he or she wilfully neglects this duty (§ 6 par. 3 VVG).[121] In case of catastrophic damage it is likely that the requirement of immediate notice will be handled with reluctance anyhow.

IV. Social Insurance Regulation Procedure

The compensation procedure under social insurance law is regularly an administrative process which is formalised to a certain extent. But for reasons of rationality, the formal elements are reduced to the necessary minimum. That is in principle also true for the proof of the victim's damage. Normally it suffices that the victim of a – catastrophic or non-catastrophic – damage presents the doctor's bills or that the dependants of a deceased victim present their claim for maintenance. 24

Courts – special social courts – come onto the scene only if claimants feel that their claims for social security benefits have unjustifiedly not been satisfied. The procedure before these courts is less expensive and less formal when compared with the procedure before the civil courts which treat the normal tort law cases.[122] Moreover, a tendency to favour the claimant with respect to procedural matters because s/he is normally less familiar with the procedure is inherent in the suits before the social courts.[123]

Part V. Cumulation of Claims?

As a rule the various claims under which victims of catastrophic damage can be entitled to compensation cannot be cumulated as far as they concern the same damage. 25

Therefore, the *Flutopferhilfesolidaritätsgesetz* and the accompanying Regulation explicitly prescribe that the financial assistance that may be granted under the Act is subsidiary to benefits and payments by third persons, especially by insurers.[124] If such claims against third persons exist, the amount of the compensation is to be reduced respectively. And generally Fund payments shall be made under the reservation that they have to be repaid if third persons

[119] See the information on the regulation of the train disaster in Kaprun presented by E. Eybl (*supra* fn. 5), 81 *et seq.*

[120] See the remarks by R. Schmid (*supra* fn. 111), 109 et seq.

[121] See thereto H.-L. Weyers, *Versicherungsvertragsrecht* (2nd edn. 1995), 214 *et seq.*

[122] See H. Bley/R. Kreikebohm/A. Marschner, *Sozialrecht* (8th edn. 2001), 362, 364.

[123] H. Bley/R. Kreikebohm/A. Marschner (*supra* fn. 122), 362.

[124] Art. 5 § 2 par. 2 no. 1 *Flutopferhilfesolidaritätsgesetz* and § 2 par 5 no. 1 Verordnung nach § 2 Abs. 6 des *Aufbauhilfefondsgesetzes*.

afterwards compensate the damage.[125] But if justified claims against third persons cannot be expected to be realised in the short term, then the victim is entitled to full compensation through the Flood 2002 Fund but must assign these claims to the Fund.[126]

A similar solution prevails in private and social insurance law. Where private or social insurers are obliged to pay and have paid benefits they acquire by way of legal assignment (*cessio legis*) those claims which the insured has against a tortfeasor.[127] The assignment works when, and to the extent that, the insurer has compensated the insured's damage for which the tortfeasor is liable as well. In the end it is the tortfeasor and not the insurer who should bear the loss. The victim is, however, free to choose whom to approach. Rather often the insured victim of a tort will, on the one hand, claim the insurance benefits from the insurance and, on the other hand, approach the tortfeasor for those parts of the damage which are not covered by the insurance, for instance for compensation of pain and suffering which is not covered under social security law.

Part VI. Financing

26 It has already been mentioned that the Flood 2002 Fund is financed both by the Federal Republic of Germany and by the *Bundesländer* to the same degree.[128] Therefore in essence all tax-payers bear these catastrophic losses.

Where tort liability is established, the tortfeasor, unless a large company with sufficient assets or being sufficiently insured, will often not be able to satisfy all claims which can arise from catastrophic accidents. Unless an insolvency procedure is initiated there is no equal treating of all claims. That means: the claimants who come first are fully paid. If the tortfeasor's means are exhausted, those who come late get nothing. Because of this unhappy consequence it has been suggested that the distribution of insufficient means of a tortfeasor should follow the model of an insolvency procedure where all claimants – at least in theory – get equal shares.[129] A minimum solution could

[125] § 2 par 5 no. 1 sent. 2 and 3 Verordnung nach § 2 Abs. 6 des *Aufbauhilfefondsgesetzes*: „Leistungen Dritter zum Ausgleich des Schadens und für denselben Schaden gewährte Soforthilfen sind beim Ausgleich des Schadens zu berücksichtigen. Die Auszahlung an Private und Unternehmen ist unter Rückforderungsvorbehalt insbesondere für den Fall zu stellen, dass Leistungen durch Dritte erbracht werden und hierdurch eine Überkompensation des Schadens bewirkt wird".

[126] § 2 par 5 no. 2 Verordnung nach § 2 Abs. 6 des *Aufbauhilfefondsgesetzes*: „Schadensausgleichsansprüche gegenüber Dritten, insbesondere Versicherungen, können bei der Berechnung und Gewährung der Mittel des Fonds … vorerst außer Betracht gelassen werden, soweit die Ansprüche trotz Erfolgsaussicht nach Einschätzung der bewilligenden Stelle nicht kurzfristig von Geschädigten realisiert werden können. In diesen Fällen sind die Ansprüche nach Einschätzung der bewilligenden Stelle jedoch bis zur Höhe der bewilligten Mittel an diese abzutreten. Im weiteren Verfahren ist bei Konkretisierung der Sachlage über eine dann gegebenenfalls erforderliche Rückabtretung zu entscheiden".

[127] See § 67 VVG (for private insurers); § 116 SGB X (for social insurers).

[128] See Art. 5 § 4 *Flutopferhilfesolidaritätsgesetz*.

[129] Compare C.G. Paulus, Das Insolvenzmodell, in: H. Koch/A. Willingmann (*supra* fn. 3), 117 *et seq*.

be that, in case of insufficient means, at least those claimants enjoy priority who have suffered personal injuries over claimants who have suffered only property damage.[130]

The same problem of possibly unequal distribution arises where an insurance policy does not cover all justified claims but only part of them. Again, it seems preferable that equal treatment at least of equal classes of victims is aimed at instead of a mere priority principle.

Where victims receive social security benefits, those benefits are financed by contributions from different sources, namely by contributions of the insured, of their employers and third persons, by state subsidies and other sources.[131]

Part VII. Heads and Amounts of Damages

The Flood 2002 Fund covers property damage. It is designed to enable reconstruction measures concerning buildings and to compensate for the loss of, or damage to, immovable or movable goods (household goods, machinery, stored goods etc.).[132] Lost profits, lost income, pure economic loss, compensation for personal injury or pain and suffering are not dealt with by the Fund and cannot be granted under it. 27

Under tort law all heads of damage except pure economic loss can be compensated. The general principle is full and concrete compensation; compensation should bring the victim into the position s/he would have been in if the tort had not occurred.[133] In case of personal injury all necessary medical expenses, adequate indemnification for pain and suffering and lost income have to be paid. Where the victim has received sickness payments or the like either from the employer or from a social security agency, the respective part of the victim's tort claim then passes by way of legal assignment to the employer or social security agency which can claim that amount from the tortfeasor.[134] The loss of mere earning capacity (which is not exploited and causes no actual economic loss) does, however, not entitle one to compensation.[135] Sums for pain and suffering are more or less standardised; for instance, the complete loss of sight (total blindness) has been indemnified with sums between € 75,000 and € 250,000.[136] In case of death of the victim, the dependants who were legally entitled to be maintained by the deceased can claim their lost maintenance from the tortfeasor.[137] Where the victim has suffered lasting impairments through the personal injury resulting in reduced income or increased needs, compensa-

[130] See U. Magnus, in: H. Koch/A. Willingmann (*supra* fn. 3), 161.

[131] See the general provision of Art. I § 20 SGB IV; see further J. Fedtke/U. Magnus (*supra* fn. 22), 86 *et seq.*

[132] See *supra* fn. 70, 45 *et seq.*

[133] See § 249 BGB and thereto H. Heinrichs (*supra* fn. 64), § 249 no. 2 *et seq.*; H. Lange/G. Schiemann (*supra* fn. 12), 212 *et seq.*

[134] Compare already above under Part III.II.A.

[135] Compare OLG Celle, [1988] NJW, 2618; H. Heinrichs (*supra* fn. 64), § 249 no. 36; H. Lange/G. Schiemann (*supra* fn. 12), 378 *et seq.*

[136] OLG Stuttgart, [1994] VersR, 313; OLG Frankfurt, [1996] VersR, 1509.

[137] See § 844 par. 2 BGB.

tion has to be in the form of a rent.[138] Only if special reasons require that the victim be awarded one single sum – for instance to build up a basis for regular income – is a lump sum then due.[139] As far as property damage is concerned, the general measure of compensation in tort law is the necessary market cost for repair or substitution. General fault-based tort law does not provide for any caps or limits of the compensation while most strict liability statutes prescribe maximum amounts.[140]

Compensation under private insurance law follows rather strictly the requirements set by tort law subject to specific conditions agreed upon in the insurance contract. Heads and amounts of damages correspond to those available under tort law.

As indicated earlier, social security benefits do not aim at full compensation of the damage that ensued but shall enable that a basic protection for a person in need is granted and secured.[141] Therefore the calculation of benefits is much more abstract and rationalised due also to the great number of cases which have to be dealt with by social security agencies. The main protection of social security law is directed against the consequences of personal injuries. Cost of medical treatment and of rehabilitation measures are borne as well as loss of income (sickness allowance) and of earning capacity (social pensions). But these benefits are standardised in the sense that, for instance, the loss of the right hand of a right-handed person generally means a reduction of earning capacity by about 60% thus justifying a rent in the amount of 60% of the last average income.[142] Pain and suffering is not a head of damage that can be granted under social security law. Also lost profits – other than the reduction of income – are not recoverable. Compensation in the strict sense is also excluded under social security law for property damage. However, the *Sozialhilfe* steps in where victims of catastrophic events have lost their belongings and lack sufficient financial means and prospects to ever substitute them.

Part VIII. Empirics

28 There are some statistics highlighting how the extensive losses caused by the most recent catastrophic event, the 2002 flood, have been dealt with.[143] The statistical material refers to the Bundesland Saxonia alone where most of the damage (about 2/3) was suffered but it gives a picture that can be regarded as representative also for the other affected regions. In Saxonia the flood caused the loss of 21 lives and injuries to 110 people. The property damage with whose removal the Flood Fund is only concerned reaches the amount of € 6.196 billion. This sum comprises the following heads (lost profits etc. are not included):

[138] § 843 par. 1 BGB.
[139] § 843 par. 3 BGB.
[140] See thereto *supra* Part III.II.A.
[141] See also J. Fedtke/U. Magnus (*supra* fn. 22), 86 *et seq.*
[142] Compare B. Schulin/G. Igl, *Sozialrecht* (7th edn. 2002), 247 *et seq.*
[143] See in particular *supra* fn. 70.

- damage to inhabited buildings (€ 1.706 billion; 27.5% of all property damage);
- damage to enterprises, their buildings, machinery, stores etc. (€ 1.420 billion; 22.9%);
- damage to household belongings (€ 529 million; 8.5%);
- damage to state buildings, infrastructure etc. (€ 2.541 billion; 41.1%).[144]

25,652 private homes were damaged; about 70% of them were severely damaged, but only 3% were a total loss. For the removal of that damage in spring 2003 an amount of about € 140 million was paid out to involved persons and a further amount of € 180 million has been approved though not yet paid.[145]

With respect to the property damage, *Soforthilfe* in the amount of about € 150 million was paid out until spring 2003 to around 11,000 enterprises.[146] The middle-term assistance (*Aufbauhilfe*) was at that time only partly approved and paid depending on the applied amounts of assistance:

- If the damage was below € 100,000, 8,265 enterprises were awarded the total amount of € 87 million. Of that sum an amount of € 55 million has already been paid out to 5,693 enterprises.
- If the damage was between € 100,000 and € 1 million, 866 enterprises were awarded € 110 million. Of that sum € 62 million was paid out to 598 enterprises.
- If the damage was higher than € 1 million, 38 enterprises were awarded € 44 million. Of that sum an amount of € 21 million has been paid out to 22 enterprises.[147]

Evidently, the bulk of enterprises which suffered damage were smaller ones and their damage was relatively minor, namely less than € 100,000. Around two thirds of those enterprises received their "flood" compensation within the first eight months after the catastrophe. The same was true for enterprises which had suffered losses up to € 1 million. And even more than 50% of those enterprises which had suffered damage of over € 1 million received payments reasonably quickly after the catastrophic event.

Part IX. Reform Proposals; Criticism

I. Reform Proposals

Mass torts (*Massenschäden*) have been the subject of intensive discussion in recent years in Germany.[148] The discussion culminated in 1998, when the 62nd *Deutsche Juristentag* aired the question whether specific legislative measures should be taken in case of mass torts. Christian von Bar prepared a report on the matter[149] and recommended few modest amendments. In particular, he suggested that, in case of traffic accidents with several cars involved, it should 29

[144] *Supra* fn. 70, 43 *et seq.*
[145] See *supra* fn. 70, 57.
[146] See *supra* fn. 70, 46 and 58.
[147] See *supra* fn. 70, 59.

be presumed that each car contributed an equal share and that the car keepers should be held jointly liable unless different shares of contribution could be proven. The plenary meeting of the *Juristentag* supported this proposal on the one hand but denied on the other a general necessity of legislative measures in the field of mass torts. Thus far the legislator has not introduced a provision of the suggested kind.

However, the German legislator reacted to the general critic which was also advanced and strongly supported by von Bar and the *Juristentag* that the strict liability statutes should no longer exclude the compensation of non-pecuniary damage. In 2002 this restriction was abolished. At the same time the maximum amounts of compensation prescribed by the various strict liability statutes were considerably raised and unified.[150]

The most recent legislative initiatives concern administrative measures for a better protection against catastrophes and for the coordination of protective measures. A Draft of an Act on the Establishing of a Federal Agency for the Protection of the Population and for Aid in Case of Catastrophes (*Entwurf eines Gesetzes über die Errichtung eines Bundesamtes für Bevölkerungsschutz und Katastrophenhilfe*) has reached the parliamentary stages.[151] The purpose of the Draft is to institute a new agency on the federal level which is authorised to initiate and coordinate measures of protection and rapid help when catastrophes of national importance are threatening or impending.[152] The focus of the Draft is therefore on better protection against catastrophes and their immediate consequences. The Draft does not deal with the compensation of the damage caused by such catastrophes nor is there any actual legislative initiative in that direction.

II. Criticism

30 Criticism concerning the present practice and law of the regulation of catastrophic incidents which evidently happen each year has been raised in that in "medium size" catastrophes like air crashes or derailing trains etc. no equal treatment of the victims and/or of different classes of victims is prescribed.[153] Generally the principle of priority applies here. In case of limited funds, that principle may lead to a race among different victims to be the first.

[148] See, e.g., C. von Bar, *Empfehlen sich gesetzgeberische Maßnahmen zur rechtlichen Bewältigung der Haftung für Massenschäden?* Gutachten A zum 62. Deutschen Juristentag Bremen 1998; H. Koch, Haftung für Massenschäden – Recht, Abwicklungspraxis, rechtspolitischer Handlungsbedarf, [1998] *Juristenzeitung* (JZ), 801 *et seq.*; see further the contributions in: H. Koch/A. Willingmann (*supra* fn. 9); H. Koch and A. Willingmann (*supra* fn. 3); P. Winkler von Mohrenfels, Bewältigung von Großschäden, in: H. Koch (ed.), *Herausforderungen an das Recht* (1997), 223 *et seq.*

[149] C. von Bar (*supra* fn. 148).

[150] See *Zweites Gesetz zur Änderung schadenersatzrechtlicher Vorschriften* (Second Act on the Amendment of Provisions on Damage) of 19 July 2002, [2002] BGBl, I 2674.

[151] See *Bundesrat-Drucksache* 825/03 of 7 November 2003.

[152] See the *Begründung* (reasoning) of the Draft, *Bundesrat-Drucksache* 825/03 of 7 November 2003, 4.

[153] See in particular C.G. Paulus (*supra* fn. 129), 117 *et seq.*

Moreover, for a long time it has been criticised that German law does not allow for the indemnification of pain and suffering of dependants.[154]

Part X. Concluding Remarks

When the question has to be answered how a legal system should react to catastrophic damage affecting many persons and enterprises, any general answer remains difficult. It is certainly a possible way to provide on an *ad hoc*-basis protection and indemnification for those who have become victims of such a catastrophe. However, this way has the disadvantage that any legislative action depends on whether the catastrophe is politically regarded as being "worthy" of a reaction. Many "smaller" catastrophes – like in Germany the Eschede train disaster and the air show in Ramstein – will fall short of any such legislative "interest". On the contrary a general statute which provides for compensation for catastrophic damage has also to define the borderline between those catastrophes where the public as a whole should bear the damage or at least large parts of it and those catastrophes where the damage still remains with the victim alone. Moreover, a general statute might support the attitude that, in any case of catastrophic damage, society as such should step in. This could contribute to an undermining of the sense of self-responsibility that is desirable in society. In my view the disadvantages of the *ad hoc* legislation are less than the disadvantages of a general statute. 31

List of References

J. Basedow *et al.* (eds.), *Die Bündelung gleichgerichteter Interessen im Prozess* (1999).

H. Bley/R. Kreikebohm/A. Marschner, *Sozialrecht* (8th edn. 2001), 362, 364.

C. von Bar, *Empfehlen sich gesetzgeberische Maßnahmen zur rechtlichen Bewältigung der Haftung für Massenschäden?* Gutachten A zum 62. Deutschen Juristentag Bremen 1998.

W. Ewer, Ersatz-, Entschädigungs- und Ausgleichsansprüche wegen Hochwasserschäden – erste Bestandsaufnahmen nach der Katastrophe, [2002] *Neue Juristische Wochenschrift* (NJW), 3497 *et seq.*

E. Eybl, Das Gletscherbahn-Unglück von Kaprun am 11. November 2000 aus der Sicht des Haftpflicht-Versicherers, in: H. Koch/A. Willingmann (eds.), *Modernes Schadensmanagement bei Großschäden* (2002), 81 *et seq.*

J. Fedtke/U. Magnus, Germany, in: B.A. Koch/H. Koziol (eds.), *Unification of Tort Law: Strict Liability* (2002), 147 *et seq.*

J. Fedtke/U. Magnus, The Impact of Social Security Law on Tort Law in Germany, in: U. Magnus (ed.), *The Impact of Social Security Law on Tort Law* (2003), 86 *et seq.*

B. Harenberg (ed.), *Aktuell 2004* (2003), 442.

C. Hinsch, Regulierungspraxis der Versicherer bei Großschäden und die Rolle des Haftungsrechts, in: H. Koch/A. Willingmann (eds.), *Großschäden – Complex Damages* (1998), 69 *et seq.*

T. Kadner, Schmerzensgeld für Angehörige – Angemessener Ausgleich immaterieller Beeinträchtigungen oder exzessiver Ersatz mittelbarer Schäden?, [1996] *Zeitschrift für Europäisches Privatrecht* (ZEuP), 135 *et seq.*

[154] See, e.g., T. Kadner, Schmerzensgeld für Angehörige – Angemessener Ausgleich immaterieller Beeinträchtigungen oder exzessiver Ersatz mittelbarer Schäden?, [1996] *Zeitschrift für Europäisches Privatrecht* (ZEuP), 135 *et seq.*

P. Kiesgen, Vermeidung von Zielkonflikten durch integratives Krisenmanagement, in: H. Koch/A. Willingmann (eds.), *Modernes Schadensmanagement bei Großschäden* (2002), 103 *et seq.*

H. Koch, *Kollektiver Rechtsschutz im Zivilprozeß* (1976).

H. Koch, Haftung für Massenschäden – Recht, Abwicklungspraxis, rechtspolitischer Handlungsbedarf, [1998] *Juristenzeitung* (JZ), 801 *et seq.*

H. Koch/A. Willingmann (eds.), *Großschäden – Complex Damages* (1998).

H. Koch/A. Willingmann (eds.), *Modernes Schadensmanagement bei Großschäden* (2002).

J. Kohler, Buch 3: Umwelthaftungsrecht, in: J. von Staudinger (ed.), *Kommentar zum Bürgerlichen Gesetzbuch mit Einführungsgesetz und Nebengesetzen. Umwelthaftungsrecht* (2002).

H. Kötz/G. Wagner, *Deliktsrecht* (8th edn. 2001), 84 *et seq.*

O.E. Krasney, Aufgaben eines ‚Ombudmannes' für die Opfer von Massenunfällen – Möglichkeiten und Grenzen, in: H. Koch/A. Willingmann (eds.), *Modernes Schadensmanagement bei Großschäden* (2002), 67 *et seq.*

U. Magnus, in: H. Koch/A. Willingmann (eds.), *Modernes Schadensmanagement bei Großschäden* (2002), 161.

W.D. Müller-Rostin, Der Krisenfall: Vorbereitende Maßnahmen und Maßnahmen zu seiner Abwicklung in: H. Koch/A. Willingmann (eds.), *Modernes Schadensmanagement bei Großschäden* (2002).

O. Palandt (ed.), *Bürgerliches Gesetzbuch* (6th edn. 2005), § 839 no. 47 *et seq.*

C.G. Paulus, Das Insolvenzmodell, in: H. Koch/A. Willingmann (eds.), *Modernes Schadensmanagement bei Großschäden* (2002), 117 *et seq.*

R. Schmid, Der Concorde-Absturz: Welche Lehren können Reiseveranstalter und Versicherer daraus ziehen?, in: H. Koch/A. Willingmann (eds.), *Modernes Schadensmanagement bei Großschäden* (2002), 109 *et seq.*

H.-L. Weyers, *Versicherungsvertragsrecht* (2nd edn. 1995), 214 *et seq.*

P. Winkler von Mohrenfels, Bewältigung von Großschäden, in: H. Koch (ed.), *Herausforderungen an das Recht* (1997), 223 *et seq.*

J. Zekoll, Prozessrechtliche Instrumente bei der Bewältigung von Großschäden in den USA, in: H. Koch/A. Willingmann (eds.), *Großschäden – Complex Damages* (1998), 219 *et seq.*

Italy

Alberto Monti and Filippo Andrea Chiaves

Part I. Introduction

According to a recent report published by the European Environment Agency (EEA), Italy ranks very high among the 31 EEA member countries in terms of overall exposure to natural disasters.[1] In particular, the Italian territory proved to be especially vulnerable to floods, landslides, earthquakes, forest fires, volcanic eruptions and drought. Up to 40% of the Italian population lives in seismic areas where 64% of buildings are not constructed according to anti-seismic rules and where over 120,000 people have died from earthquake-related causes in the last century.[2] Almost two million people are exposed to volcanic risks in Italy, where there have been as many as 5,400 floods and 11,000 landslides and avalanches over the past 80 years. Victims of hydro-geological risks in the last 50 years have reached 3,448, while the overall costs for natural disasters in this country have been estimated at approximately € 100 billion in the last two decades.[3] 1

In the third millennium disasters are no longer caused by natural events only: man-made industrial and technological accidents, financial risks,[4] computer- 2

[1] *Mapping the impacts of recent natural disasters and technological accidents in Europe*, Environmental Issue Report no. 35, EEA, (2004). The EEA report brings together information about natural disasters and technological accidents that have occurred across Europe in the period 1998–2002 and their impacts on the environment and society. The natural disasters covered are floods, storms, forest fires, droughts, landslides, snow avalanches and earthquakes. Among technological accidents, oil spills, industrial accidents and mining accidents are considered. The report does not deal with biological hazards (e.g. epidemics), social hazards (terrorism, war) or certain types of technological risks such as nuclear accidents. Nor does it cover hazards related to chronic exposure to harmful substances or transport accidents other than those involving dangerous substances.

[2] Source: *Servizio Nazionale di Protezione Civile* (National Service of Civil Protection). Pursuant to Law no. 225 of 24 February 1992, the National Service of Civil Protection is coordinated by the President of the Cabinet of Ministries. See also: *Catastrophes and Insurance in Italy*, Report by Aldo Marzano, (Italian National Association of Insurance Companies, ANIA) Conference – Milan, 11 November 2003.

[3] Source: *Servizio Nazionale di Protezione Civile* and ANIA.

[4] Financial risks include sanctions, devaluations and financial losses incurred by world industries and enterprises involved in global scandals such as Enron, WorldCom, Tyco, Parmalat, etc. amounting to more than US $ 300 million.

related issues and international terrorism are increasingly affecting businesses and persons; the total insured losses caused by the September 11 terrorist attacks to the World Trade Center in New York, for instance, amount to approximately US $ 35 billion. In the year 2003 Sigma recorded 142 natural catastrophes and 238 man-made disasters across the world,[5] causing a total damage of approximately US $ 70 billion (including insured losses of US $ 18.5 billion) and thus continuing the trend towards an increasing number of events in both categories that has been observed during the part 30 years.[6] All such events affect perspective evaluations as to the opportunity of changing and adapting the Italian model to future challenges.

3 From the point of view of citizens in Italy, catastrophes – may they be natural or caused by man – are events generating a strong expectation of State intervention and aid. The traditional Italian idea of State, which developed in the last three centuries and especially after World War II (State based on the principle of solidarity, fully recognized in art. 2 of the Italian Constitution), brings people to unconsciously rely upon the State for any unexpected, unaffordable, unbearable matter, which implies that persons expect Government intervention as a right and demand full restoration of damages whenever a disaster occurs. This of course is extremely cumbersome for the State in terms of costs.[7]

4 In Italy most often man-made catastrophes may be classified as torts or crimes and thus fall under the related legal qualifications and proceedings.[8] However, although victims will seek legal protection from alleged wrongdoers, they will equally be expecting the State to provide some sort of compensation for the damages occurred. This mentality, far from leading to efficient or even satisfactory results, is very difficult to overcome.

5 The State on its part has never spared its aid: according to recent statistics, in the last 10 years the government has spent over € 35 billion for damages caused by natural catastrophes, and yearly expenses are progressively growing. Governmental expenditures in this field could be thoroughly reduced should an insurance mechanism covering losses from natural disasters be in-

[5] Swiss Reinsurance Company (2003), *Natural catastrophes and man-made disasters in 2003* (Swiss Re SIGMA series 1, 2004). According to SIGMA, of the total amount of approximately US $ 70 billion, US $ 58 billion worth of damage was caused by natural catastrophes (including insured losses of US $ 16.2 billion).

[6] See also: Munich Re, *TOPICS geo 2003. Annual Review: Natural Catastrophes in 2003* (2004).

[7] This problem is common to other Western democracies: in the United States government funding of natural catastrophes has become an increasingly serious issue, also considering that very often the funds are not used to recover the damages arising from the disaster but for other unrelated purposes, as occurred in 1993 with funds indemnified to local victims of hurricane Andrew. See G. Priest, The Government, the Market and the Problem of Catastrophic Loss, [1993] *Journal of Risk and Uncertainty* 12, 219. See also: K.A. Froot (ed.), *The Financing of Catastrophe Risks* (1999).

[8] Sometimes human misconduct combines with natural phenomena generating catastrophic losses and, thereby triggering liability in tort as well as under criminal law. This is the case, for instance, of the Vajont disaster, discussed in Part VIII.I.

troduced on the basis of a partnership between the public and private sectors.[9]

Part II. The General Framework of Disaster Law in Italy

Italy belongs to those countries which have dealt with disaster-related issues by following their traditional legal institutions. No organic legislation was ever enacted to cover the issue of natural catastrophes. In this framework, disasters are handled on a case-by-case basis, whereby the government intervenes in emergencies by providing *ex post* financial aid and enacting *ad hoc* laws (so-called emergency legislation). 6

From a strictly legal perspective, natural and industrial/technological catastrophes are most often classifiable as torts or crimes and imply damage recovery both under civil and criminal law, and practically always have victims sought legal protection and loss recovery. From an insurance viewpoint, Italy remains an exception among modern Western democracies: as of today, very few catastrophe risks are being privately insured, and there is no such thing as a compulsory disaster insurance coverage system. However, in most recent times several proposals to develop a more efficient model were presented by ANIA (National Association of Insurance Companies), the Government and other public institutions; this trend may eventually lead to the establishment of a national insurance system covering natural disaster risks and providing a combination of private insurance and State aid. 7

Part III. Legislation, Rules and Regulations

Under Italian law catastrophes and disasters, whether man-made or natural, are generally treated from a legal standpoint just like any other event and thus follow the general rules outlined by the legal system for events causing damage to persons or things. Hence, certain behaviours may fall under the penal provisions and be classified as crimes or misdemeanours, and may thus imply criminal liability; at the same time, if they generate material or moral losses, they may be classified as torts and may imply civil, tortious liability. 8

Based upon the foregoing, in order to examine existing rules and regulations in the field of natural and man-made disasters in Italy, one may do nothing other than examine the general framework of criminal and tort liability, and make a few specific remarks on the so-called dangerous activities, refer to nuisance issues, and to disaster-related matters regarding moral damages, as well as to some particular instances such as smoking and mass infections. Finally, some procedural aspects will be analyzed to complete the picture. 9

[9] For a comparative overview of different institutional approaches involving a public/private partnership for the coverage of natural catastrophe risks, see: A. Monti, *Environmental Risks and Insurance. A Comparative Analysis of the Role of Insurance in the Management of Environment-Related Risks*, Policy Issues in Insurance No. 6, Paris, OECD Publications (2003).

I. The Law of Torts

10 The law of torts in Italy is a set of provisions and general models which are combined in various ways so as to generate a family of single, diverse, specific rules. Thus, there is no such thing as a definition of "tortious liability" under Italian law. According to legal scholarship, tortious liability is "the condition of being subject to a civil tort", the latter being "an event violating certain interests which are protected by the law in human relationships". The term "civil liability" (*responsabilità civile* in Italian) is used when referring to the rules of private law liability provided by artt. 2043-2059 of the Italian Civil Code, as opposed to criminal liability (*responsabilità penale*) which is regulated by the Penal Code.

11 The Italian Civil Code of 1942 encompasses rules on tortious liability under artt. 2043-2059. The basic principle is contained in art. 2043 which states that whoever causes wrongful damage to others is liable for such damage, literally: "any intentional or negligent fact causing wrongful damage to others obliges he or she who committed the fact to compensate the damage".[10] The very general rule contained in art. 2043 is nothing but a modern version of the Roman *neminem laedere* principle providing that one should not harm others, and if so, the victim should be redressed for the harm incurred.

12 After the general clause on tort, Italian law contemplates several forms of vicarious liability which are often invoked in disaster-related issues. Vicarious liability is the imposition of liability on one person for the actionable conduct of another, based solely on the relationship between the two persons, such as the liability of an employer for the acts of an employee, or of a tutor for the acts of a pupil. The Italian Civil Code regulates several cases of vicarious liability under artt. 2047-2049, namely: tutor's responsibility for acts carried out by the person (usually of minor age or of unsound mind) being under his care (art. 2047 of the Civil Code); liability of parents, teachers, masters for torts caused by trainees or pupils under their custody (art. 2048 of the Civil Code); employer's liability for injury to person or property of another resulting from acts of the employee done within the scope of his employment in the employer's service (art. 2049 of the Civil Code).

13 Among the other relevant rules set forth by the general tort provisions of the Civil Code, we find art. 2053 of the Civil Code, entitled "Collapsing of Buildings", providing that:

> "(t)he owner of a building or other construction is liable for the damage caused by their collapse, unless he or she proves that the latter is not the result of lack of maintenance or construction defects". [our translation]

[10] See: G. Iudica/P. Zatti, *Language and Rules of Italian Private Law: An Introduction* (2003). See also U. Mattei/J. Lena, *Introduction to Italian Law* (2002).

According to this rule, owners of buildings are liable for any damage caused to third parties by the total or partial collapse of their buildings.

Furthermore, the Code encompasses specific strict liability rules concerning things and animals. Under art. 2051 of the Civil Code, entitled "Damage Caused by Chattels Under One's Custody", "(e)very person is liable for damage caused by chattels under his or her custody, unless he or she proves the occurrence of a fortuitous event". Liability for things under one's custody is not based upon fault, but is a form of strict liability. Basically, the rule encompassed in art. 2051 of the Civil Code was established to cover cases where the guardian of a chattel or thing causing injury to third parties would not be liable under the general rules on torts, because the damage was indeed caused by something under his or her custody, but not as a result of the custodian's direct action on the object or chattel. Moreover, under art. 2052 of the Civil Code, 14

> "(t)he owner of an animal or the person using it for the time when it is given for use, is liable for the damage caused by the animal, both if it was under the person's custody and if it escaped or was lost, unless the person proves the occurrence of a fortuitous event".

Beyond the general tort provisions set forth by artt. 2043 to 2059 of the Civil Code, the Code provides for specific rules of liability related to various areas of the law which may often be invoked in disaster situations, such as professional liability (art. 2236 of the Civil Code). Generally speaking, professionals are required to exercise their activity with due care and reasonable diligence, and are thus very often called in disaster-related issues to answer for their negligence and lack of skill in evaluating geological data relating to a site where a catastrophe subsequently occurred, or in failing to prevent a natural event from occurring or in wrongly considering the environmental status of a disaster site. Under art. 43 of the Penal Code, professional fault may arise out of negligence, lack of skill, lack of prudence, as well as from failure to abide to existing professional laws and regulations. Professionals do not ensure a positive result of their activity, but they must ensure that their activity is carried out with ability and professional competence. Professional liability is regulated by artt. 2229 *et seq.* of the Civil Code: under art. 2236 of the Civil Code, if a professional activity implies solving technical issues characterized by particular difficulty, professionals are not liable for damages except for fraud or gross negligence. However, courts generally require an increasing degree of care and expertise by professionals: the more the professional is specialized in a field (such as geology or water, soil or construction engineering), the higher will his or her expected expertise be, so that the level of diligence required to avoid liability basically increases together with the level of difficulty of the activity carried out. 15

Another important point regards liability of public authorities. Indeed, unless otherwise provided by specific statutory provisions, public agencies and governmental bodies are civilly liable under the ordinary principles encompassed 16 in artt. 2043 *et seq.* of the Civil Code. This widely accepted principle is today undisputed. Most often in disaster-related issues are local authorities held responsible, such as towns, provinces, regional governments, as well as the national authorities. Public offices may be called to respond under several counts for tortious liability: for instance a local Department of the Environment, of Forests, of Water Handling may be held liable for having failed to duly provide safety measures or preventive measures to reduce the risk of a natural catastrophe; equally, the Building and Construction Department of a public authority may be held responsible for *culpa in vigilando*, i.e. for having failed to duly supervise the construction of buildings in areas subject to seismic risk or to specific poor soil conditions. Examples of the above may be found in the Seveso disaster, in the Stava catastrophe and in the cases regarding floods which are examined in Part VIII.

17 Several statutes specifically deal with civil liability in disaster-related issues, namely in the following matters:

- damage in the execution of public works (Art. 46 Law no. 2359 of 25 June 1865);
- liability of civil servants (D.P.R. no. 3 of 10 January 1957) and public workers (Act no. 90 of 5 March 1961);
- liability for enterprises running nuclear installations (Act no. 1860 of 31 December 1962);
- liability for accidents caused by automobile driving (Act no. 990 of 24 December 1969);
- liability in nuclear energy production matters (Act no. 109 of 12 February 1974; D.P.R. no. 519 of May 10, 1975);
- liability in public transportation matters (train, bus, tramways, etc.) (Act no. 131 of 5 March 1975; Act no. 381 of 28 April 1976);
- liability for damage caused by space objects (Act no. 23 of 25 January 1983);
- liability for environmental damage (art. 18 of Act no. 349 of 8 July 1986);
- defective product liability (D.P.R. no. 224 of 24 May 1988 implementing EC Directive no. 85/374) and product safety (D.L. no. 115 of 17 March 1995);
- damage redress to victims of transfusions, vaccinations and inoculation of hemo-derivatives (Act no. 210 of 25 February 1992 and Law no. 238 of 25 July 1997).

II. Dangerous Activities

18 Catastrophes, whether natural or man-made, may often be deemed as torts arising out of faulty conduct by persons (i.e. act or omission which was negligent, imprudent or simply violated a specific rule of conduct), or out of strict liability (i.e. situations where a person or entity is held responsible for an event regardless of fault). Under Italian tort law, fault liability occurs each time the plaintiff must prove the damage, the causal connection, and other facts showing the defendant's behaviour diverging from an ideal, model be-

haviour of reference depicted by the law. Strict liability regards cases where the legal system imposes liability upon a certain party as a matter of policy, and thus the defendant may not avoid liability by showing he had been diligent, and often he or she may avoid liability only by proving that the damage was not a result of his or her own activity. The Italian legal system also contemplates a further, intermediate form of liability (*prima facie* liability or *culpa in re ipsa*), which occurs when the plaintiff may only prove the damage and causal connection, but the defendant may avoid being held liable by proving that certain preventive requirements were met beforehand.

This leads us to analyse rules enacted by the Italian legislator in terms of dangerous activities which most often lead to catastrophic events or disasters. Dangerous activities[11] are not regulated by the general rule of art. 2043 of the Civil Code, but under the specific provision of art. 2050 of the Civil Code: 19

> "whoever causes damage to others upon performing an activity being dangerous by its nature or for the nature of the means employed to perform it, is liable for damages, unless evidence is brought that all possible measures had been taken to avoid the damage". [our translation][12]

This rule, which is recognized as being a strict liability rule, is aimed at regulating activities which are socially useful and thus *per se* considered lawful, although they are very likely to cause damage to third parties.

The notion of "dangerous activity" was defined by the Supreme Court of Cassation in the *Angelici*[13] case, where the court found that: 20

> "an activity is dangerous if qualified as such by statute, or if its dangerousness is inherent with the means used to perform it or with their own nature. An activity is not dangerous if the dangerousness arises out of mistaken or improper use". [our translation]

Dangerous activities are continued, organized activities (such as business activities), consisting of a series of acts: isolated, dangerous acts do not fall under the scope of art. 2050, but are rather censurable under the general rule encompassed in art. 2043 of the Civil Code.

[11] See P. Recano, *La responsabilità civile da attività pericolose* (2001); R. Zuccaro, Sulla responsabilità per l'esercizio di attività pericolose, [2001] *Giurisprudenza Italiana* (Giur. It.), 2275; M. Bianca, *Diritto civile, V, La responsabilità* (1994), 704 *et seq.*; P. Ziviz, Le attività pericolose, in: P. Cendon (ed.), *La responsabilità civile a cura di Cendon* (1988), 543 *et seq.*; M. Comporti, *Esposizione al pericolo e responsabilità civile* (1965), 271 *et seq.*

[12] As mentioned above, the Civil Code also provides a specific rule (art. 2051 of the Civil Code) for liability of persons holding or possessing objects, devices or other movables which cause injuries to third parties, the difference with art. 2050 of the Civil Code being the latter will apply if the object or device is started or run by the person exercising a dangerous activity, whereas in all other cases of damage caused by said object, art. 2051 will apply.

[13] *Angelici v C. Terni*, *Corte di Cassazione* (Italian Supreme Court, Cass.), 23 February 1983, no. 1394, [1983] *Massimario della Giurisprudenza Italiana* (Mass. Giur. It).

21 "Dangerousness" implies a potential degree of injury beyond normal. There may be two concurrent criteria: (*i*) the frequency of damage habitually caused by the activity at issue, and (*ii*) the severity of the prejudice threatened. Therefore, an activity qualifies as dangerous if it statistically causes many accidents and it threatens to cause very serious ones. However, an activity may also be considered dangerous, pursuant to art. 2050, if it entails a low probability and high consequences (LPHC) risk of loss. Beyond applying a general dangerousness standard, Italian courts tend to apply a dangerousness test based upon the actual circumstances in which the activity was performed.[14]

22 The most dangerous activities are regulated by statutory law, such as running nuclear energy plants (Act no. 1860 of 1962 and D.P.R. no. 519 of 1975), air carriers (the Navigation Code), automobile traffic (art. 2054 of the Civil Code), and specific professional activities such as surgery, etc., which fall under the scope of art. 2236 of the Civil Code. Art. 2050 applies to all other activities, such as the production and distribution of electric energy, methane and liquid gas, as well as any easily inflammable, combustible liquids such as raw oil through an oil duct or transported by ships, and inflammable mineral oils. Pyrotechnic activities are equally considered dangerous, as well as all activities dealing with weapons and explosives. Producing and distributing venoms, poisons and infective substances is similarly considered dangerous. Building, construction and road traffic works are all dangerous activities; some agricultural activities are considered dangerous, such as cutting trees. Work with mechanic saws, cranes, hoists and lifts for goods have at times been qualified as dangerous. Some medical therapies such as using X-rays, are considered dangerous, and some sports are considered dangerous activities: chairlifts for cross-country and downhill skiing are considered dangerous and have been qualified as such upon the occurrence of disasters.[15]

23 According to art. 2050, any victim having incurred damage as the result of a dangerous activity is entitled to sue. The protection granted by art. 2050 thus extends to persons exercising a dangerous activity, persons not exercising such an activity, and persons providing services in connection with the dangerous activity.

24 The damage must be somewhat connected to the dangerous activity: courts tend to point out that the rule encompassed in art. 2050 of the Civil Code covers accidents connected to the peculiar nature of the activity performed, and excludes all accidents which are not directly connected with the risky nature of the activity at issue.[16] However, the plaintiff needs not prove a causal connection between the damage and a specific action or omission by the defen-

[14] *Negri v Manzoni*, Cass. 5 June 2002, no. 8148, in [2002] *Massimario del Foro Italiano* (Mass. Foro it.), *Responsabilità civile*, 5760, 24.

[15] See Tribunale (Trib.) Savona, 20 December 1965, [1966] Giur. It., I, 2, 557; *Menghini v Soc. Funivie Saslong Seilbahnen AG*, Cass. 10 May 2000, no. 5953, [2002] *Diritto ed economia assicuraz* (Dir. ed economia assicuraz.), 1233.

[16] *Brenna v Grigato*, Cass. 30 March 1967, no. 702, [1967] Mass Giur. it.

dant: it is enough to provide evidence that the damage is causally connected with the generic exercise of the defendant's dangerous activity at issue.[17] The causal connection is interrupted either by a concurrent action by the victim or a third party bystander, or by a fortuitous event or *force majeure*. The defendant will thus avoid being held liable either by proving that the damage was caused by events not ascribable to him, or by proving having adopted all possible measures to avoid the injury, i.e. having abided by all rules of due care, diligence and prudence suggested by ordinary technical knowledge and common experience.[18] This requirement is practically the same as proving the occurrence of a fortuitous event. If this provision applies, very often in case of man-made accidental disasters, liability under art. 2050 is generally excluded for natural catastrophe-related issues, due to the fact that damage is caused by *force majeure* or by a fortuitous event, such as an earthquake or flood.

III. Nuisance

In the section dedicated to the protection of private property and the right of ownership, the Civil Code provides under art. 844 that: 25

> "the owner of a parcel of land may not prevent smoke emissions, odours, noises, shakings, and similar outcomes from the neighbouring land, unless they go beyond normal tolerability having also considered the conditions of the premises. Upon applying this rule, the court must balance the expectations of production with any existing proprietary interests. Priority of a certain customary practice may be kept into consideration". [our translation]

The mechanism outlined by this rule is very simple: emissions below a certain level of tolerability are allowed, whilst emissions above the tolerability level are forbidden; however, if the emissions are caused by an activity responding to the requirements of national production and it is impossible to reduce or eliminate any such emissions by adopting technical measures which are not excessively cumbersome, the victim will no longer be entitled to an interim cease-and-desist order, but will only be indemnified according to the decrease in value of its parcel of land as a consequence of the emissions.

While intolerable emissions violating proprietary rights are protected as above, intolerable emissions affecting health and thereby damaging persons imply the possibility for the victim to seek compensation for biological damage (in Italian: *danno biologico*), i.e. damage to health and physical integrity, under the general clause of art. 2043 of the Civil Code.[19] In all such cases, the court will also issue a cease-and-desist order barring the company from any further discharging.[20] Since this second remedy does not imply indemnifica- 26

[17] *Soc. Ultragas v Liverani*, Cass. 28 October 1980, no. 5799.

[18] *Paolillo v Caramico*, Cass. 21 November 1984, no. 5960, [1984] Mass Giur. It.

[19] *Palmieri v Pasqualini*, Cass. 19 July 1985, no. 4263, [1986] Giust. civ., I, 128.

[20] *Menni e Palladini v Ditta Menni*, Trib. Milan 21 October 1999, [1999] *Responsabilità civile a prevdenza* (Resp. civ. e prev.), 1335.

tion, victims will most often sue claiming protection under both art. 2043 of the Civil Code (for health injuries) and art. 844 of the Civil Code (for violation of proprietary rights). Damage recovery may also be sought for intolerable electromagnetic emissions.[21]

27 Italy has enacted several special laws containing statutory provisions on atmosphere pollution, water pollution and soil pollution. As opposed to the variable criteria provided by art. 844, these statutes introduce fixed parameters beyond which contamination and pollution are held as unlawful and intolerable. This has led several authors,[22] commentators and courts[23] to oppose the automatic replacement of the general rule by the special laws: if the emission exceeds the parameters provided by the special statute, it is certainly to be deemed intolerable; however, if the emission respects the fixed, detailed parameters prescribed by the special legislation, it may equally be intolerable according to the general rule outlined by art. 844 of the Civil Code.[24]

IV. Moral Damages

28 An interesting issue regards recovery of moral damages in disaster situations. This matter may be traced back to one of the most relevant catastrophes which occurred in Italy in the last decades, i.e. the Seveso accident, which is described in detail in Part VIII.IV. Basically, after an explosion in the ICMESA factory located in the town of Seveso (north of Milan), a cloud of dioxin was dispersed in the surrounding atmosphere, and eventually much of the local population was evacuated, isolated or quarantined and suffered other severe limitations of their freedom.

29 Insofar as the legal issues connected to this catastrophe are concerned, the first essential element was that as late as 1997, i.e. more than eleven years after the accident, there was no direct proof that dioxin is harmful to health although there had been an incredible number of inspections, experiments, research and studies on persons, animals and soil throughout the years. The absence of reported scientific evidence of the harmfulness of dioxin prevented inhabitants of the affected area from suing for damage to health because any attempt to connect any incurred pathology to the dioxin cloud would not have proved credible.

[21] *Genovese v ENEL*, Cass. 27 July 2000, no. 9893, annotated by De Marzo, Inquinamento elettromagnetico e tutela inibitoria, [2001] *Diritto e Responsabilità* (Dir. e Resp.), 37; see also D. Chindemi, Le immissioni elettromagnetiche: limiti di liceità e danni risarcibili con particolare riguardo al danno esistenziale, [2001] Resp. civ. e prev., 1051.

[22] C. Salvi, *Le immissioni industriali. Rapporti di vicinato e tutela dell'ambiente* (1979), 397 *et seq.*; G. Visintini, Il divieto di immissioni e il diritto alla salute nella giurisprudenza odierna e nei rapporti con le recenti leggi ecologiche, [1980] *Rivista di diritto commerciale* (Riv. dir. civ.), II, 262 *et seq.*; F. Di Giovanni, *Strumenti privatisticie tutela dell'ambiente* (1982), 142 *et seq.*

[23] *Scannapieco v Califri*, Cass. March 16, 1988, no. 2470; *Soc. Eridania Zuccherifici Nazionali v Amoretti*, Cass. March 12, 1987, no. 2580.

[24] *Aveline v Società Cementerie Siciliane*, Cass. 28 March 1980, no. 2062, [1980] Giur. It., I, 1, 1871; *Società Dai v Società Bonifiche Sarda*, Cass. 18 July 1986, no. 4633, [1987] Giur. It., I, 1,452.

Nevertheless, an action was initiated in 1981, and claims for personal injury damages were added in 1983. The appeals case ended in 1995, at a time when very little was known of the effective harmfulness of dioxin. The case was eventually resolved with a settlement agreement which was thoroughly encouraged by local and national authorities and political leaders of the time. The Prime Minister was actually deemed competent[25] to approve the protocol for the settlement between the State and local authorities (the Lombardy Region in this case) and the companies in charge of the industry (ICMESA and Givaudan). Ordinary courts dealt with residual instances connected with the indemnification of non-economic losses: the grounds for the action were connected to the circumstance that the inhabitants of the Seveso area who were affected by the dioxin cloud suffered strong emotional distress due to an initial lack of information on the events having occurred, whereby authorities had minimized the effects of the toxic cloud. Subsequently, the local population learned that taking no precautions due to the lack of information and to the reassuring press releases issued by local authorities could have additionally jeopardized their health without it being possible to evaluate to what extent this might have incremented the dangers connected to the dioxin exposure. 30

The scenario depicted by plaintiffs was that of an emotional distress which instead of decreasing as years went by, progressively increased as the victims learned more information on dioxin and the risks of seriously affecting their health increased. As the lawyers put it upon pleading the plaintiffs' case, on the one hand the population suffered an indubitable psychological uneasiness (i.e. they led their life with the fear of getting ill) which is directly proportional to the number of years having elapsed from the event, on the other hand it is impossible to determine whether any person falling ill for any reason may at any rate ascribe the illness to the dioxin cloud or if any proximity may be found thereto. 31

In Italy until 2003 moral damages and generally non-pecuniary compensation could be awarded only if they were the consequence of a crime (former interpretation of art. 2059 of the Civil Code). In the case at issue, the losses due to psychological distress could certainly be connected to the commission of crimes. Indeed, the criminal proceeding in the Seveso case[26] had been concluded in first degree on 24 September 1983[27] whereby five directors of the ICMESA industry involved in the production process had been indicted for 32

[25] Corte dei Conti, *Sezione Centrale de Controllo di Legittmità su atti del Governo e della Amministrazioni dello Stato* (Sez. Contr), decision no. 1175 of 26 June 1981, [1981] *Il Consiglio di Stato* (Cons. Stato), II, 1122.

[26] On the criminal aspects of the case, see D. Feola, Il caso "Seveso" e la risarcibilità dei Danni non patrimoniali alla collettività vittima di un disastro ambientale, [1995] Resp. civ. e prev., 143 *et seq.*; A.G. Cianci, Danno evento e danno conseguenza: la distinzione se ne va in soffitta, [2002] *Diritto e Giurisprudenza* (Dir. e giust.), n. 11, at 20.

[27] Trib. Monza (Crim. Div.), decision of 24 September 1983, in [1983] *Rivista giuridica del lavoro* (Riv. Giur. Lav.), IV, 19; the criminal court decision is commented by C. Piergallini, Il concorso apparente di norme nella sentenza sui 'fatti' di Seveso, [1985] Riv. giur. lav., IV, 19.

having omitted to provide precautionary measures to prevent industrial accidents (art. 437(2) of the Penal Code), intentional disaster (art. 449 of the Penal Code) and negligent disaster (art. 434 of the Penal Code), all aggravated by the fact that the event was foreseeable (art. 61(3) of the Penal Code). In the appeals case, two of the five persons initially accused were found guilty of the crime of negligent disaster aggravated by the fact that the event was foreseeable.[28] The appeals decision was confirmed by the Supreme Court of Cassation by decision no. 112 (ruling issued on 23 May 1986, entire judgment filed on 7 February 1987). This decision also confirmed the recoverability in a civil action of the losses claimed by the victims.[29]

33 The disputed question in the civil proceeding was: can pure moral damages be awarded to a victim having suffered strong emotional distress without there being any material losses or diminution to the victim's health? After long debate, the Supreme Court reversed its previous decisions nos. 5530/1997 and 4631/1997 and solved the dilemma by a final decision rendered in plenary session on 21 February 2002 (decision no. 2515 of 2002),[30] stating that moral damages for emotional stress may be recovered also in the absence of material damage to the victim's health. Most recently, the Court of Milan, following the ruling of the Supreme Court, awarded moral damages in the equitable amount of € 5,000 to each individual plaintiff.[31]

34 An interesting case where moral damages were awarded to public authorities as a consequence of a disaster is the *Vajont* case, where as a result of the landfall and flood that hit several villages in the Vajont area, some towns and villages were practically obliterated from the face of the earth with over 90% of the buildings having collapsed or having been seriously affected. The towns of Vajont and Castellavazzo were awarded moral damages by the court for non-pecuniary loss in consideration of their historical, cultural, political and social identity being seriously affected (if not completely annihilated) by the disaster.[32]

35 Another case where moral damages were awarded as a consequence of events affecting the environment can be traced to a 1996 decision of the Supreme Court of Cassation relating to a servitude imposing a power line on a beautiful landscape in the Tuscan countryside, whereby the owners of the land where the power line was installed sued on grounds that a particularly beautiful area was being ruined by the power line.[33]

[28] Appeals Court of Milan (Crim. Div.), decision of 14 May 1985, [1986] *Giustizia penale* (Giust. pen.), II, 171.

[29] Court of Cass. (Crim. Div.), decision no. 122 of 23 May 1986, in *Rivista penale* (Riv. pen.), 1987, 1004.

[30] *Corte Suprema di Cassazione* [2002] *Danno e Responsabilità* (Danno e resp.), 499; [2002] Resp. civ. e prev., 726.

[31] *Aggujaro et alii v Icmesa Spa*, Court of Milan, Sec. I, June 9 2003, [2004] *Danno e Responsabilità*, 73.

[32] Decisions by the Supreme Court of Cassation no. 5650 of 1996 and 3807 of 1998.

[33] Court of Cass. decision no. 2959 of 29 March 1996, [1996] *Guida al Diritto – Il Sole 24 Ore*, May 11, 36.

V. Specific Issues: Mass Infections

Courts dealt with mass disasters caused by defective products in the *Crinos* case,[34] where a pharmaceutical industry had marketed a medical substance without previously screening it, and the substance contained infected gamma-globulins which had infected several patients, who had been treated with the medicine, with Hepatitis B. The court established that production of medicines is to be classified as a "dangerous activity", and as such the related manufacturer was asked to comply with the latest, most recent technology known in the field or even only abstractly possible at the time when the product was manufactured. The same approach should be adopted in the case of AIDS infection-related issues.[35] In the *Maritano* case,[36] a nurse was accidentally covered by an HIV patient's blood spurting out of a defective machine applied to the patient, and was infected with AIDS. The Director of the Division of the hospital, as well as the manufacturer of the machine were held liable for damages for having failed to instruct the hospital's personnel on how to use the machine and for having omitted to provide precautionary measures in using the machine. The court held that managers and employers have a duty to keep up-to-date and seek information on the dangers which may arise in a working place, by duly supervising it and by acquiring the necessary technical knowledge and skills. The court also found that the manufacturer of a device has a duty to inform persons who will use the device of the related risks connected to the device, by providing instructions containing all relevant information. 36

Based upon the foregoing principles and the conclusions reached in the *Crinos* case, we may say that HIV infection due to blood transfusions may be covered by art. 2050 of the Civil Code concerning dangerous activities, provided that using test tubes, medical machinery and transfusion devices may be classified as a dangerous activity, although subsequent court decisions have partially disagreed, adopting the *culpa in vigilando* approach:[37] the court held that victims of blood transfusions with infected blood seeking damage redress may sue the Ministry of Health, whose liability is based upon *culpa in vigilando* doctrine (for failure to supervise its officers and civil servants). At other times, courts have referred to the doctrine of negligence: in 2000 a hospital was held liable for having negligently ignored a recommendation by the Ministry of 37

[34] *Ferriello v Società Crinos*, Trib. Milan 19 November 1987, [1988] *Il Foro Italiano* (Foro it.), I, 144.

[35] As regards AIDS victims infected after sexual intercourse with persons with HIV, such issues may be classified under the general *neminem laedere* principle of the tort clause established by art. 2043 of the Civil Code.

[36] *Maritano*, Pret. Turin 22 March 1989, [1990] Foro it., II, 58.

[37] *X v Ministero della Sanità*, Trib. Rome, 14 June 2001, annotated by V. Carbone, Danni da sangue infetto: il Ministero della Sanità risponde per omessa vigilanza e non per esercizio di attività pericolosa, [2001] *Il Corriere Giuridico* (Corriere giur.), 1204. See also U. Izzo, La responsabilità dello Stato per il contagio di emofiliaci e politrasfusi: oltre i limiti della responsabilità civile, [2001] Dir. e resp., 1067; U. Izzo, *La precauzione nella responsabilità civile. Analisi di un concetto sul tema del danno da contagio per via trasfusionale* (2004).

Health to make virus checks before transplants, after a patient underwent a bone tissue transplant with tissue infected with Hepatitis C.[38]

38 Finally, it must be said that Law no. 210 enacted on 25 February 1992 and Law no. 238 enacted on 25 July 1997 contain rules governing the State compensation scheme for damage arising out of compulsory vaccinations, blood transfusions or the use of blood derivates,[39] once again following the traditional trend tending to refer to the State for any loss recovery connected to mass disasters.

VI. Specific Issues: Smoking

39 Smoking-related issues[40] have led to increasing litigation in recent times in Italy. Tobacco products have long been distributed in Italy through the State monopoly and recently the marketing of several brands of cigarettes was privatized. Victims claiming smoking-related injuries base their arguments on the violation of the general protection of health clause encompassed in art. 32 of the Italian Constitution and of the general tort liability clause of art. 2043 of the Civil Code; plaintiffs also attempt to qualify smoking as a "dangerous activity" falling under the provision of art. 2050 of the Civil Code. At other times, smokers found their claims on failure by the State monopoly to inform consumers of the risks of smoking in past years, based upon recent legislation enacted in the 1990s requiring manufacturers to place health warnings on cigarette packets (Law no. 233 of 6 August 1990 and Ministerial Decree no. 425 of 30 November 1991). So far, although several cases have been filed against tobacco manufacturers claiming damage to health as a result of long-term heavy smoking, most claims have been dismissed and courts have not yet come to a unanimous view on these issues, which are still to be considered heavily debatable especially because cigarettes have long been a significant source of income for the State. Furthermore, although the advertising of tobacco is banned in Italy (Act no. 165 of 10 April 1962), another debated issue regards the misleading,

[38] *Ronchi v ASL 30 Desio*, Trib. Monza, 14 October 2000, [2001] Dir. e resp., 816.

[39] See A. Castelnuovo-Pintus, Infezione da HIV: il ristoro del danno tra indennizzo e risarcimento, in: P.G. Monateri/M. Bona/F. Peccennini/P. Tullini (eds.), *Il danno alla persona* (2000), I, 439.

[40] See V. d'Antonio, Pubblicità ingannevole e prodotti da fumo leggeri, [2003] Danno e resp., 1170 *et seq.*; A.G. Cianci, Discovery e danni da fumo: gestione dei documenti aziendali, tecniche di difesa e violazione del fair trial, [2003] Danno e resp., 587; AA.VV, Il divieto della pubblicità di prodotti da fumo non vale se il marchio ha acquistato autonomia, [2001] *Guida al diritto*, 10, 74; Sarlo, Sigarette e pubblicità ingannevole, [2002] *Diritto e Giustizia* (D&G), 2002, 38, 52; L. Nava, La responsabilità del produttore di sigarette in Italia, Francia e Stati Uniti d'America, [2002] *Diritto & Diritti – rivista giuridica on line*, <http://www.diritto.it>; Iannantuono, Camel ha fatto strada: ora evoca viaggi e non la pubblicità vietata delle sigarette, [2001] D&G, 10, 63; G. Giacchero, Fumo attivo e responsabilità civile del produttore di sigarette, [2001] Giur. It., 1643; M. Pacifico, Il risarcimento del danno da fumo attivo (Annotation of *Schiaratura v Philip Morris Corporate Sewrvices Inc.*, Trib. Rome, 11 February 2000), [2000] *Corriere Giurisprudenza* (Corriere giur.), 1639; *Giacalone Stalteri v Monopoli Stato, Corte di Appello* (App.) Rome, 2 October 2000, annotated by G. Giacchero, Causalità e danni da fumo attivo, [2001] Dir e resp., 853; G. Facci, Brevi considerazioni in tema di danno da fumo, [1999] *Contratto e Impresa*, 944.

deceptive nature of the wording "lights" formerly placed on packets of several cigarette brands. Starting from 30 September 2003, all such wording was required to be deleted from cigarette packets under Legislative Decree no. 184 of June 24, 2003 (implementing EC Directive 2001/37), but there are many pending cases where smokers claim that in the past they opted for light cigarettes rather than quitting because they were led to believe that "light" cigarettes were less harmful to their health than ordinary cigarettes. Although this argument has been mostly rejected, courts have not yet resolved this issue and the few decisions upholding plaintiffs' claims are now on appeal.

In 1991, the Constitutional Court was asked to judge the constitutionality of 40
several provisions regarding smoking in public places, and found[41] that damages from passively inhaling dangerous substances as a result of cigarettes smoked by others are recoverable as a result of the violation of art. 2043 of the Civil Code (general tort clause) and art. 32 of the Italian Constitution protecting health and the environment. But the Court also held that although the injury caused is wrongful and unjust (which is an essential requirement for art. 2043 to apply), no damages may be liquidated because the law does not forbid smoking except in certain working places and public facilities. A recent case involving injuries arising from passive smoking regards a bank clerk who was adjudicated damages by a first degree court in Milan for inhaling passive smoke at her work post and suffering consequential physical injury. The outcome of the case – on appeal since 2004 – is uncertain after a court expertise identified other factors such as pollen as contributing to injury in passive smoking issues. Today the entire matter is subject to deep reform: legislation was passed in 2002 basically forbidding smoking in all public facilities including restaurants and cafés: from 29 December 2004 smoking is strictly banned in all enclosed public spaces except in separate, isolated areas specifically reserved for smokers which restaurants, bars and hotels are now bound to provide with appropriate ventilation After almost one year from the entry into force of the law, the ban seems to work effectively and is equally appreciated by smokers and non-smokers.

VII. Class Actions?

Traditionally, the solution to mass torts, i.e. torts characterized by a plurality 41
of victims, is typically handled differently by the common law and civil law tradition. The common law tradition contemplates the instrument of class actions. Class actions are characterized by the fact that a single plaintiff, usually a law firm, seeks to bring a suit pleading the claims of single components of a group of victims without it being necessary that each member of the group grant a specific power of attorney for this purpose. The law firm usually anticipates the court fees and expenses, and in case of defeat, it may not recover

[41] *De Russis v Candidi, Corte Costituzionale* (Corte Cost.), 7 May 1991, no. 202, [1991] Foro it., I, 2312. On passive smoking issues, see also G. Ponzanelli, Fumo passivo e tutela nei luoghi di lavoro, [1997] Danno e resp., 174; Zoani, Fumo da tabacco e tutela della salute dei lavoratori, [1995] *Massimario di giurisprudenza del lavoro* (Mass. giur. lav.), I, 180.

any costs from the single members of the group.[42] From an economic efficiency point of view, therefore, the profitability of the entire operation is closely connected to the probability of achieving a victorious case.

42 On the contrary, in the legal systems based on the Romanist tradition such as Italy, traditionally mass torts are handled by allowing consumer associations, non-profit bodies, guilds and societies representing the collective interests of a group to have legal standing in court and to sue to recover damages (so-called *Verbandsklage* model).[43] This approach is based upon the idea that certain tortious behaviours violating the rights of wide groups of persons not only affect their individual interests, but also clash with common, collective, supra-individual interests. All such interests are not referable to single individuals nor to the community as a whole, and thus can only be claimed in court by intermediate entities such as representative associations. This approach may soon be abandoned after the presentation of a bill in Parliament in 2004 for the introduction of class actions in Italy, allowing consumer associations and national representatives of users standing to sue in the event of tortious acts against a large number of consumers or users. The bill was approved by the House on 21 July 2004 and is now being examined by the Senate. The bill amends the existing consumer protection act (Law no. 281 of 30 July 1998) by introducing new provisions entitling consumers, consumer associations, investors associations, professional societies and chambers of commerce to file direct claims for damages on behalf of single consumers having incurred losses as a result of tortious liability arising from legal relationships regarding business-to-consumer agreements finalized with pre-printed standard forms (so-called contracts *en masse*). Following publication of the court ruling, individual consumers may bring a suit against the tortfeasor asking the court to verify that they possess the requisites identified in the aforesaid ruling and to assess the exact amount of the damages or indemnity awarded thereunder. The final decision is thence enforceable against the tortfeasor. Several large consumer associations (including Codacons, Italy's largest) have voiced their dissatisfaction as to the current text of the bill, claiming that a two-phase mechanism such as the one contemplated in the bill would force consumers to wait several years before obtaining damage redress for small amounts. Beyond this, class actions are likely to further overcharge Italian courts – which are already well past saturation – with extra work. Moreover, if the bill should be approved in its current version by Parliament, this would certainly require a substantial modification of several provisions of Italy's legal system.

43 Prior to presentation of the class actions bill, in Italy the primary issue involving injury to public interests shared by large classes of people was always

[42] A. Giussani, Mass torts e tutela giurisdizionale: modelli di azione giudiziaria collettiva a confronto sotto il profilo della efficienza economica, [2002] Resp. civ. e prev., 315 *et seq.*

[43] B.A. Koch, Die Verbandsklage in Europa, [2000] *Zeitschrift für Zivilprozess* (ZZP), 413 *et seq.*; G. Cappelletti, Finding an Appropriate Compromise: A Comparative Study of Individualistic Models and Group Rights in Civil Procedure, [1983] *Civil Justice Quarterly* (C.J.Q.) 2, 111 *et seq.*

(whether and) to what extent associations, societies or public bodies representing said persons are entitled to sue for damages and whether or not they may be classified as victims of a tort. Indeed, in all such cases damages are exorbitant taken as a whole, but each victim suffers rather small losses and is often discouraged to sue for such a little amount, especially considering legal costs connected to filing an action, whereas associations representing classes of victims may very well be encouraged to sue for larger amounts. In Italy, this issue has mostly arisen in connection with civil actions in a criminal proceeding. The leading approach was offered by the Criminal Division of the Supreme Court of Cassation: in several cases, the Court held that not all persons having incurred damage arising out of the perpetration of a crime are entitled to file a civil action in a criminal proceeding, but only persons having suffered a loss directly and immediately deriving from the crime have standing to sue.[44]

In the past, Italian courts have widely accepted and admitted civil actions 44
brought in criminal proceedings by town authorities and other public bodies,[45] as well as entities representing State property and public demesne.[46] On the contrary, private associations have rarely accomplished this aim in past times, and when they have there has been much debate over their acceptance. For instance, in 1986 local environmental associations were accepted in a criminal proceeding involving water pollution.[47] In other fields, such as in penal proceedings for crimes involving the environment, it is customary for courts to admit civil actions by national and international environment associations such as the World Wildlife Fund (WWF), *Italia Nostra, Lega per l'Ambiente* and the World Nature Fund (*Fondo Mondiale per la Natura*).[48]

VIII. Rules of Procedure

Leaving aside any issues connected to the bill on class actions mentioned in 45
the previous chapter, it may be interesting to examine existing Italian rules of procedure. Actions for damages in Italy may consist of two separate proceedings, one aimed at generally awarding damages to the plaintiff and condemning the defendant, the other at assessing the exact amount of redress to be paid by the injuring party (so-called action for *quantum*). The first action only requires the ascertainment by the court of a fact which is potentially damaging, while evidence of the actual occasioning of damages and of their entity are

[44] See, *inter alia*, *Di Gregorio* case, Cass. (Crim. Division), 16 May 1980, in [1981] Riv. pen., 102.

[45] Cass. (Crim. Division), 6 February 1981, in [1982] *Massimario Cassazione Penale* (Mass. Cass. pen.), 1057; Court of Cassation in Plenary Session (Cass. SS.UU.) 21 April 1979, [1979] Mass. Cass. pen., II, 356.

[46] *Seganfreddo* case, Cass. (Crim. Division), 21 March 1980, [1981] Riv. pen., 87.

[47] *Casentino* case, *Pretore* (Pret.) (Crim. Div.) Vibo Valentia, 24 November 1986, [1988] Foro it., II, 48.

[48] *Vasm* case, Pret. (Crim. Div.) Sestri Ponente, 7 February 1986, [1986] Foro it., II, 323; Pret. Rome 5 February 1980, [1980] *Rivista Cassazione Penale* (Riv. Cass. pen.), 694; Pret. Trento 1 December 1978, [1979] Foro it., II, 234.

matters regarding the second proceeding.[49] The plaintiff having been awarded damages to be assessed in the further course of the proceeding may ask that any such assessment be made in a separate proceeding on *quantum* (art. 278, section 1, Code of Civil Procedure), as long as the defendant agrees.[50]

46 In the first proceeding, aimed at awarding damages in general, courts have traditionally required the plaintiff simply to prove that some damage occurred in general, without the need to provide actual, specific evidence of the damage suffered.[51] Once the first proceeding has come to a decision and such decision becomes *res judicata*, there may be no further question as to the unlawfulness of the facts examined. However, the further action on *quantum* may bring the court to ascertain that there was no actual prejudice to the victim, or that there was no causal connection between the defendant's wrongful conduct as ascertained in the first proceeding, and the damage occurred to the plaintiff.[52]

47 According to Italian civil procedure, the court may require technical experts to deliver a report on specific issues of the case. In disaster-related loss recovery cases, the expert reports on the entity of the disaster and causes thereof have proven fundamental and essential for the final outcome of the case. This matter is regulated by art. 61 *et seq.* of the Italian Code of Civil Procedure: the expert is considered an advisor of the court, giving advice on non-legal matters and technical issues which may not be known to the court, and delivers a motivated report to the judges: any conclusions contained in such report are not binding for the court, although most often will the expert's opinion be held in high consideration.

48 As regards the relationship between civil and criminal actions, under artt. 75, 651 and 652 of the Code of Penal Procedure of 1988, civil actions and criminal actions regarding the same factual circumstances are generally independent from one another.[53] Criminal decisions have no prevalence over civil courts, except in specific cases provided by artt. 651-54 of the Code. The ascertainment of criminal liability is binding for civil courts if it is encompassed in a decision on the merits issued by a criminal court and having become *res judicata*. Moreover, if a civil action is initiated within a criminal proceeding, any penal decision on liability issues will be binding in the subsequent civil action for *quantum* initiated by the victim for the assessment of damages awarded.

[49] *Boschieri v Comune di Cornuda*, Cass. 7 December 1994, no. 10501, [1994] Mass. Foro it.

[50] *Barbugian v Fusetto*, Cass. 10 March 1987, no. 2468, [1987] Mass. Foro it.

[51] *Quinteri v Quinteri*, Cass. *Sezioni Unite* (S.U.) 11 March 1932, no. 878, [1932] Mass. Foro it.

[52] *Monti v Banco Lariano*, Cass. 11 April 1987, no. 3603, [1987] *Archivio Civile* (Arch. civ.), 988; see also *Cassan v Rizzi*, Cass. 9 February 1965, no. 201.

[53] See *inter alia* A. Chilberti, *Azione civile e nuovo processo penale* (1993); P. Della Sala, Natura giuridica dell'azione civile nel processo penale e conseguenze sul danno, [1989] *Rivista Italiana di Diritto Procedura Penale* (Riv. it. Dir. E Proc. pen.), 1079; R. Pennisi, Azione (azione civile nel processo penale), [1988] *Enciclopedia del diritto* (Enc. Giur.) IV, 1988; G. Giannini, *L'azione civile per il risarcimento del danno e il nuovo codice di procedura penale* (1990).

A criminal decision having become *res judicata* implies that the following elements are binding for any civil court: ascertainment of facts (i.e. author's behaviour, criminal event, causal connection between the two), qualification of facts as a crime, ascertainment that said facts were perpetrated by the accused. The civil court will thus be bound to the factual circumstances ascertained by the penal court and will have to stick to the ascertainment of fault or fraud made by the penal court: however, the civil court may interpret such circumstances by giving them a different legal qualification. 49

Regarding evidence brought in a criminal or civil proceedings, generally speaking all elements of proof examined in one proceeding should lawfully be used in the other proceeding. Evidence gained in a civil proceeding may be used in criminal proceedings only if the civil decision is *res judicata* and the evidence may not otherwise be repeated, and the parties agree to any such use. The penal court may evaluate the evidence independently, regardless of any evaluation made by the civil court. Evidence gained in a criminal proceeding may only be used in a civil proceeding if the evidence was originally examined in adversary process, i.e. if the party against whom the evidence is brought was actually allowed to counter-examine such evidence during the criminal proceeding. 50

Part IV. Mass Torts and Environmental Protection Issues

I. Mass Torts

Only recently did Italian courts employ tortious liability principles to mass torts: disasters such as the Chernobyl, Bhopal, Three Miles Island, or the Amoco-Cadiz, Exxon-Valdez and – most recently in 2002 – Prestige oil vessels, or the asbestos issue and the like are late, common experiences of the Western legal tradition.[54] In the United States, mass torts are strictly connected with the issue of class actions. We have already seen that the Italian approach is different. Mass torts characterized by losses to a large number of victims caused by a single event do not imply particular legal issues and fall under the traditional tort law approach, although some matters may be quite complex, especially in automobile accidents involving many vehicles. Chain losses caused by defective products may imply more serious problems: in all such cases, the causal connection issue and the question regarding inappropriate use of the product by the victim imply that all such matters are to be treated individually. The problem of causation is even more essential in issues connected to damage caused by toxic substances and events affecting the environment, where it often may be very difficult to identify each wrongdoer's degree of fault in the chain of events having caused the injury. 51

[54] *Three Miles Island Litigation*, Federal District Court for the District of Pennsylvania, 27 February 1985, [1986] Foro it., IV, 134; *Amoco Cadiz*, Fed. Distr. Court for the District of Illinois, 18 April 1984, [1985] *Il Diritto Marittimo* (Dir. maritt.), 904; *Exxon Valdez*, State Jurisdictions (USA), Alaska, 13 May 1994, [1995] Dir. maritt., 528.

52 In the past, authors have claimed that insurance is not an adequate instrument in issues regarding losses connected to mass torts. Indeed, in all such cases indemnification for losses may be so exorbitant that insurance companies may not be able to afford coverage and may be led to go bankrupt, as occurred to several asbestos producers and to the Lloyds Syndicates after the asbestos disaster. Hence, several Western legal systems enacted legislation aimed at limiting the amount of redress for damages connected to mass torts: for instance, the Convention for Oil Liability in Oil Pollution was reached in 1969 after the Amoco-Cadiz disaster. Equally, international treaties such as the Warsaw Convention of 12 October 1929 were specifically aimed at limiting liability for companies operating nuclear plants and aircraft. Moreover, EC legislation provides for limitations of liability for defective products.

53 Regarding the issue of limiting redress for damages incurred in mass disasters, in Italy the Constitutional Court established in the *Turkish Airlines* case[55] that rules limiting liability are not justifiable in case of loss of human life, and thus declared that several law provisions enforcing art. 22 of the Warsaw Convention limiting liability of air carriers in case of accidents, are unconstitutional.

54 In mass torts as in other matters, the future is destined to lead to a mixed system where the private insurance sector cooperates with the State in determining and solving any compensation schemes.

II. Environment Protection

A. The Environment Act (Law No. 349 of 1986)

55 Italian authors and commentators have for long shown much interest in environmental damage issues.[56] The theories born in the United States at the beginning of the 70s with the creation of the Environmental Policy Act (EPA) only reached the Italian shores in the 80s. A specific law on the environment was enacted in 1986 (so-called Environment Act, Law no. 349 of 1986) introducing a private law regime aimed at granting direct protection to the environment in Italy. Art. 18 of Law no. 349 of 1986, in fact, imposes civil liability on

[55] *Soc. Turkish Airlines v Coccia*, Corte Cost., 6 May 1985, no. 132, [1985] *Rivista Cassazione Penale* (Riv. CP), 537.

[56] See, *inter alia*, B. Pozzo, *Danno ambientale ed imputazione della responsabilità* (1996); P. Trimarchi/B. Pozzo/A. Gambaro/G. Villa/G. Bagnetti/E. Moretti/L. Rimini, *Per una riforma della responsabilità civile per danno all'ambiente* (1994); G. Alpa/M. Bessone/V. Carbone, *Atipicità dell'illecito, III, Diritti reali – Tutela dell'ambiente* (1994); T. Ballarino, Azioni di diritto privato per il risarcimento di danni da inquinamento transfrontaliero, [1990] *Rivista Diritto Internazionale* (Riv. Dir. Int.), 849; A. Albamonte, *Danni all'ambiente e responsabilità civile* (1989); F. Giampietro, *La responsabilità per danno all'ambiente – Profili amministrativi, civili, penali* (1988); C. Castronovo, Il danno all'ambiente nel sistema di responsabilità civile, [1987] *Rivista Trimestrale di Diritto e Procedura Civile* (Riv. Dir. e Proc. civ.), 511; P. Cendon/P. Ziviz, L'art. 18 legge 349/86 nel sistema della responsabilità civile, [1987] Riv. Dir. e Proc. civ., 521.

the causer of pollution for damage to the environment, and the State is entitled to receive compensation on behalf of the citizens.

The provisions set forth by the Environment Act include specific rules prescribing the remedies imposed by the court to cope with environment disasters, the primary remedy being an order to proceed with restoring the environment to its original conditions (*restitutio in integrum*). Under art. 18, 56

> "[...] if no specific assessment of the loss is possible, the court will liquidate damages according to equitable reasonableness, considering the degree of individual fault, the costs necessary to restore the original situation, and the profits gained by the wrongdoer [...]. If possible, [...] the court orders the liable person to restore the affected sites to their previous situation". [our translation]

The law also grants the right to certain relevant, representative environment protection associations and societies to take part in the legal proceedings connected to environment losses, as is better explained below. 57

As one may see, under art. 18 of the Environment Act, courts are granted broad powers in defining the interests protected by the Act, as well as the damage assessment criteria connected thereto. Certainly, courts have affirmed that the environment is a primary interest, and any violation of statutory rules regarding the environment is considered in itself a tort; moreover, any damage to the environment is certainly considered an economic loss.[57] Courts have also recognized that in environment issues it is actually impossible to provide full and precise evidence of the loss occurred:[58] which is why damage assessment must be made on the basis of equitable fairness, justice and reasonableness.[59] Said assessment shall be made considering the criteria provided by art. 6 of the Act, i.e. considering the degree of individual fault, the costs necessary to restore the original situation, and the profits gained by the wrongdoer.[60] 58

In the absence of a definition of the concept of "environment" (Act no. 349 of 1986 indeed provides several forms of protection without defining the object of said protection), the term "environmental damage" was construed by Italian 59

57 *Tavanti, Greco et alii v proc. gen. Corte dei Conti*, Constitutional Court decision no. 641 of December 31, 1987, [1988] Foro it., I, 694.

58 *Mattuizzi*, Court of Cass. (Crim. Div.), January 11, 1988, [1989] Riv. pen., 515 (river pollution by a paint and dilution manufacturer).

59 *Associazione Cacciatori Provincia di Trento v Cemin Sperandio*, Cass. May 26, 1992, no. 6289, [1993] *Diritto e Giurisprudenza Agraria e dell'Ambiente* (Dir. Giur. Ambiente), 93; (animals unduly killed in a forest assigned by the State to a hunting society); *Ministero marina Mercantile v Patmos Shipping Corporation*, App. Messina December 24, 1993, [1994] *Diritto dei Trasporti* (Dir. T.), 585.

60 For a recent application of such criteria, see: Tribunal of Venice, Office of the Monocratic Judge, Penal Section, 27 November 2002, no. 1286, [2003] *Rivista Giuridica dell'Ambiente* (Riv. Giur. Ambiente) no. 1, 164.

thinkers as including both detriment to elements of the environment which are *res nullius*, and to elements of the environment which pertain to or are owned by public authorities, or are considered part of the public demesne, and to elements belonging to private parties. The term is broadly interpreted so as to also include the effects of pollution upon physical health and the consequences affecting the economic and business activities carried out in the area affected by the environmental loss. This led authors and commentators to criticize the Act:[61] most authors qualified environmental damage as non-pecuniary losses because they differ from physical damage to material things and they generally violate the right of ownership.[62] Moreover, environmental damage is generally considered public in the sense that it does not imply the violation of individual rights of persons but rather losses "pertaining to the State" as courts have stated several times.[63]

B. Other Statutory Provisions

60 More recent statutes are to be coordinated with the Environment Act, namely in the field of water pollution (art. 58 of Legislative Decree no. 152 enacted 11 May 1999 implementing EC Directive no. 91/271/CEE on urban water treatment and EC Directive no. 91/676/CEE on protection of waters from pollution due to agricultural nitrates), and waste (art. 17 of Legislative Decree enacted 5 February 1997 implementing EC Directives nos. 91/156/CE on waste and 91/689/CE on dangerous wastes and 94/62/CE on packing and packing disposal).

61 Under art. 58 of Legislative Decree no. 152 of 1999 (water pollution), protection is granted against any act or omission wilfully or negligently causing damage to waters, soil, subsurface and other environment resources, and any actual danger jeopardizing the environment. The mere violation of these provisions is in itself considered a tort. There are three kinds of sanctions and remedies: *(i)* the wrongdoer may be ordered to proceed with reclaiming and decontaminating the land or soil and providing safety measures, beyond bringing back the polluted areas to their original status, and to bear all costs thereof; *(ii)* the victim may be awarded damages to be redressed by the wrongdoer, and if damage assessment is impossible, it is presumed to be determined according to art. 18 of the Environment Act; *(iii)* failing to reclaim or decontaminate the water or soil and to and bring it back to its original pre-disaster status after having caused damage to the environment is a misdemeanour involving criminal liability.

[61] G. Alpa, Progetti comunitari sulla assicurazione del danno ambientale, [2001] Resp. civ. e prev., 1091; M. Comporti, Profili generali di responsabilità ripristino dello stato dei luoghi e liquidazione dei danni ambientali, in: E. Cesaro (ed.), *Danno ambientale e tutela giuridica* (1987), 31.

[62] G. Bigliazzi, A proposito di danno ambientale ex art. 18 legge 8 luglio 1986, n. 349, e di responsabilità civile and M. Libertini, Le nuove frontiere del danno risarcibile, [1987] *Contratto e Impresa*, 122 *et seq.*

[63] Order by the Corte dei Conti issued on 1 December, 1986, [1987] Riv. giur. Ambiente, 65; see also Corte dei Conti in plenary session, decision no. 107 of 21 October 1986, [1986] Giust. civ., I, 3271.

Under art. 17 of Legislative Decree enacted 5 February 1997 (so-called Ronchi Act after the minister who implemented it), whoever exceeds – whether wilfully or accidentally – the level of waste acceptability in soils, surface waters or underground waters (or causes an actual risk of exceeding said level) is strictly liable for the clean-up costs. 62

C. Legal Qualification of Environmental Damage as Health Injuries

Personal injuries and health related damage have been the object of great discussion by legal Italian legal scholars. They include biological damage (i.e. detriment to physical and psychic integrity), pecuniary losses (i.e. medical expenses incurred and diminution of the victim's specific working capacity), moral damage (i.e. pain and suffering), and the latest trends have extremely extended the concept and scope of health damage. Within this broad notion of personal injury, one may certainly think of moral damage which is not connected with any detriment to physical (or mental) integrity, but however implying an alteration of the victim's existence which amounts to biological damage. With regard to losses arising out of environmental pollution issues, some recent cases have opened the doors to this kind of damage. In the *Seveso* case for instance, although the victims did not suffer any detriment to their health, they were awarded moral damages amounting to € 5,000 each for having suffered restrictions to their freedom and existence (due to contact with contaminated things and animals) and being forcibly subject to ongoing sanitary control. This issue is examined in Part III.IV. 63

Another future issue may regard collective moral damages, as could be imagined in cases similar to the 1963 Vajont disaster, where a landslide caused an enormous mass of rock and debris to fall in the Vajont artificial basin spilling water and mud downhill over the adjacent villages below and causing 1,900 deaths. The disaster was due to human error, i.e. having built a dam in the wrong place, having elevated the level of the artificial lake beyond safety limits, and not having warned the population when the disaster was known to be imminent (this disaster is examined in Part VIII.I). Beyond the criminal issues connected with this case, which were all examined and resolved, no sufficient attention was brought at the time to possibly seeking moral damage redress to be awarded to the entire population affected as a community. If the tragedy had occurred thirty years later, this issue could certainly have led to an outstanding outcome. 64

D. Nature of Liability. Standing to Sue

The environmental liability regime introduced by Law no. 349 of 1986 is based on fault, although several authors and commentators have vividly criticized this approach[64] mainly agreeing that in most cases environmental pollution liability should be strict. From an insurability viewpoint, in fact, under 65

[64] P. Trimarchi, *Per una riforma della responsabilità civile per danno all'ambiente* (1994).

certain conditions, a strict liability regime is preferable to a fault liability regime.[65]

66 In case of unilateral accidents, where the injured party has substantially no control over the risk of loss, it suffices to control the behaviour of the potential tortfeasor (i.e. the potential polluter). A strict liability standard, imposing a full internalisation of the negative externalities, forces the potential tortfeasor to consider all variables influencing risk (i.e. both the level of care and the level of activity) generating incentives to behave in an efficient manner.[66] Strict liability allocates the risk of loss to the party who is better able to control it and, therefore, who is the least cost avoider of the harm. Environmental pollution events, in the vast majority of cases, are unilateral accidents. Hence, in order to achieve an efficient level of deterrence, strict liability proves to be more appropriate than negligence, at least with respect to dangerous activities.[67]

67 Beyond these strictly theoretical assumptions, as far as *locus standi* and legal standing to take part in civil proceedings is concerned in environment-related issues, the Environment Act (Law no. 349 of 8 July 1986) allows relevant environmental protection associations not to sue independently, but rather to take part in a pending civil action for environmental damages aside the main plaintiff and to provide aid and cooperation to the latter's claims (i.e. to intervene *ad adiuvandum*). Otherwise, environmental protection associations may only sue government entities and public authorities before the Regional Administrative Tribunals by opposing or attacking any issued administrative orders or decrees deemed unlawful.

68 Courts have confirmed an approach traditionally shared with authors and commentators, i.e. that claims for environmental damages do not prevent other persons from filing claims for damages for infringements of rights connected with the environmental disaster or pollution. Basically, this view entitles several victims to take part in the proceedings, including persons who have suffered health injuries, damage to private property and also government agencies having incurred public property losses, as long as the damages claimed are in some way connected to the environment issue.

69 Furthermore, most recently courts have opened the way to a new approach concerning the capacity of environmental protection associations to sue or initiate proceedings or take part therein. Indeed, courts have claimed that the

[65] M. Faure/D. Grimeaud, *Financial Assurance Issues of Environmental Liability* – Report, Follow up study commissioned by the European Commission, 2000. See also: M. Faure (ed.), *Deterrence, Insurability and Compensation in Environmental Liability. Future Developments in the European Union* (2003); G. Alpa, [2001] Resp. civ. e prev., 1099.

[66] "The failing of the negligence rule that is under discussion can be regarded as resulting from an implicit assumption that the standard of behavior used to determine negligence is defined only in terms of care. Were the standard defined also in terms of the activity level, injurers would make sure not to engage in their activity to an excessive extent", S. Shavell, *Economic Analysis of Accident Law* (1987), 25.

[67] See P. Trimarchi, *Rischio e responsabilità oggettiva* (1961).

purpose of ordering the defendants to bring back the environment to its original conditions prior to the disaster is to provide some sort of redress to local residents who would otherwise not be entitled to sue for environment damages. This indirectly implies that only environmental associations could be entitled to any such environment-connected rights and interests. Subsequently, the powers of these associations within civil proceedings for environmental disasters were further defined by courts: in an unpublished decision by the Court of Milan regarding sea pollution due to discharging by a chrome manufacturing industry, the court denied any title or capacity to sue to small entities such as the Naval Association (*Lega Navale*) and the Breeders' Society (*Assicurazione Allevatori*) and other similar groups who had jointly initiated a civil action against the polluting industry and the town authorities who had authorized the discharge at sea.[68]

In another decision issued by the Administrative Tribunal of the Lombardy Region (*Tribunale Amministrativo Regionale della Lomabardia,* TAR),[69] whereby the court had to deal with the construction of modern exhibition structures at Villa Erba, a 17th century villa overlooking Lake Como, local environmental protection associations sued the town authorities before the Administrative Tribunal, claiming that the building permit issued by the authorities was to be deemed unlawful because it ruined the beauty of the villa that was subject to town planning restrictions to protect its unique setting. The judges held that the environment is a common heritage jointly owned by the community and by single citizens. In this regard, the Tribunal held that environmental protection associations are certainly entitled by the Environment Act (Law no. 349 of 1986) to sue public authorities by questioning any administrative acts (such as licenses or permits) deemed unlawful, as long as they pertain to the environment such as hydro-geologic or landscape matters. But in the case at issue, given the very notion of "environment" provided by Law no. 349 of 1986, the plaintiffs were not allowed to attack an administrative order such as the construction permit which did not directly regard the environment, but rather pertained to town planning restrictions for archaeological, zoning, historical or artistic purposes. 70

Part V. State Subsidizing. Special Laws and Extraordinary Government Contributions

Notwithstanding the above mentioned rules on tortious liability, every year the Italian Government spends on average € 3.5–4 billion to indemnify damages caused by catastrophic events. For instance, after the river Po's banks broke in 1951 causing the death of 84 people and incommensurable damage to farms in the Po Valley (14–19 November 1951), the Government paid the equivalent of € 934 million (Lire 1.86 billion) for economic losses; similarly, the floods which occurred on 3–4 November 1966 which caused 113 deaths and serious- 71

[68] Cited by G. Alpa, [2001] Resp. civ. e prev., 1100.
[69] TAR Lombardia, Section II, decision no. 105 of 15 July 1988.

ly affected the cities of Florence and Venice led the State to compensate as much as € 5.15 billion; in more recent times, on 28 July 1987 Mount Coppetto collapsed on the village of St. Antonio Morignone, in the Valtellina area in the Alps between Milan and Switzerland (75 dead): public funding of the disaster reached € 5.5 billion, and in 1994 roughly the same amount was spent by the Italian Government to cover losses due to floods in Piedmont (4–7 November 1994, 75 dead). Many other examples could be made and will be referred to during the course of this report. Less than a year ago, upon presenting a State funding for 2002 of € 101 million for agricultural losses, the Italian Minister of Agriculture stated that:

> "aid requests and petitions for damages to agriculture have more than tripled in 2002. Risk insurance in this field shall be an important issue upon approving the next finance bill".[70]

72 The above is evidence of how much disaster recovery affects the State budget every year. The issue should be dealt with more efficiently by involving the private insurance sector in this field, as we shall very shortly see.

73 In most cases, State indemnification of disaster losses follows a routine procedure. Whenever a natural catastrophe involves a given area, the Regional government proposes the declaration of a state of emergency for that particular area, which may involve the territory of a town, of a province or of an entire region according to the extent of the disaster. The Cabinet of Ministries must approve the proposal for the state of emergency to be officially declared. Approval opens the way to government intervention. In November 2002,[71] for instance, the Cabinet approved the declarations of the state of emergency proposed by: the Liguria, Piedmont, Lombardy, Veneto, Friuli Venezia Giulia and Emilia Romagna regions for adverse weather conditions having caused disasters in the provinces of Savona, La Spezia, Cuneo, Genoa, Turin, Pistoia and Lucca (for flooding having occurred between May and October 2002); the city of Modica in Sicily for losses caused by a tornado in September 2002; the towns of Loiano and Monzuno in the Province of Bologna for collapse of mountainside; the Competent Ministry to cover losses due to industrial pollution in the Lake Maggiore. As one may see, the state of emergency may very well be declared for all sorts of man-made and natural catastrophes affecting the population, public and private property and the environment.

74 A relevant share of the State's yearly budget is devoted to restoring damage incurred as a result of catastrophes. In the absence of an organic set of rules of reference and legal guidelines, State funding is basically inspired by provisions aimed at covering emergency situations connected to specific, unexpected disastrous events, so that *ad hoc* provisions were enacted which varied consistently in time and were characterized by being excessively discretional. Unexpected, concentrated and extremely exorbitant expenses were often

[70] Excerpt taken from the newspaper *La Repubblica*, 21 September 2003 edition.
[71] See *Official Journal* of the Republic of Italy of no. 290 of 11 December 2002.

granted without there being any prevention plans to avoid future similar disasters.[72] At the same time, the enactment of special laws and provisions indemnifying the owners of properties affected by single disasters generated a sort of reliance on the Government by Italian citizens, who know they may always count on the State for recovery, which is one of the reasons why private insurance covering natural disasters has never fully developed in Italy.

Part VI. The European Union Solidarity Fund

In addition to *ad hoc* State budget allocations, funding for disasters occurring in Italy is also provided by the European Union Solidarity Fund (EUSF). Established by Council Regulation (EC) no. 2012/2002 of 11 November 2002,[73] the EUSF aims at enabling the Community to express its solidarity rapidly, efficiently and flexibly with the population of a Member State that has suffered a major disaster. The Fund is aimed at intervening mainly in cases of major natural disasters with serious repercussions on living conditions, the natural environment or the economy in one or more regions. 75

Pursuant to the regulation, a disaster is considered as "major" if it results in damage estimated either at over € 3 billion (2002 prices), or at more than 0.6% of the affected State's gross national income. By way of exception, the Fund may also be mobilised for extraordinary regional disasters resulting in damage inferior to this threshold, affecting the major part of its population, with serious and lasting repercussions on living conditions and the economic stability of the region. In this context, particular attention is paid to remote and isolated regions, for example the outermost and island regions. Assistance from the Fund takes the form of a single and global grant, with no necessary co-financing, complementing the public efforts of the beneficiary State. Intended to finance measures alleviating non-insurable damage in principle, the urgent actions eligible for the Fund are the following: (*i*) immediate restoration to working order of infrastructure and plants in the fields of energy, drinking water, waste water, telecommunications, transport, health and education; (*ii*) providing temporary accommodation and funding rescue services to meet the immediate needs of the population concerned; (*iii*) immediate securing of preventive infrastructures and measures of immediate protection of the cultural heritage; (*iv*) immediate cleaning up of disaster-stricken areas, including natural zones. No later than ten weeks after the first damage caused by the disaster, the State affected should submit an application to the Commission for assistance from the Fund. It should provide all possible information on the damage caused by the disaster and its impact on the population and the economy. It must estimate the cost of the foreseen assistance and indicate any other sources of national, Community and/or international funding. Beneficiary Member States must seek all possible reimbursement from third parties. 76

[72] See e.g. the Report by Prof. Giovanni Manghetti, former President of ISVAP, at the Conference on "Catastrophic Events and Connected Consequences. The Insurer's Approach and the Role of Brokers", Rome, 31 October 2000.

[73] *Official Journal* L 311 of 14 November 2002.

77 With regard to the above, it is worth noting that in July 2003 the European Commission proposed the mobilisation of € 47.6 million under the EU Solidarity Fund to compensate the direct damage caused by the earthquake which occurred in Molise and Apulia on 31 October 2002 and by the volcanic eruption of Mount Etna in Sicily of 26 October, 2002.

Part VII. Private Insurance

78 The conditions for insurability of catastrophic risks and extreme events is a matter of intense academic debate.[74] The traditional insurance and reinsurance mechanisms, in fact, encounter significant problems in coping with such risks, since risk predictability, the ability to spread the risk both geographically and over time and the financial capacity of the market are severely limited. The risk of accumulation is quite high in the primary market, since the same catastrophic event can cause losses involving many different insured properties and infrastructures at the same time, giving rise to immense claims burdens in a single policy period. Adverse selection is another problem that may negatively affect the ability of an insurance company to spread the risk of loss geographically, even on a national market. Effective risk spreading, therefore, can be performed only on a global scale, through a series of international reinsurance arrangements.

79 In Italy, insurance coverage of risks related to natural catastrophes is and remains basically limited to private insurance on a voluntary basis. At present, this kind of insurance coverage is fairly infrequent and it mostly concerns the industrial sector, covering devices, machinery, installations and ancillary services.

80 The private insurance market in Italy is placed under the supervision of *Istituto per la Vigilanza sulle Assicurazioni Private e di Interesse Collettivo* (ISVAP), a government body established by law (Act no. 576 of 12 August 1982) whose purpose is to supervise insurance and reinsurance companies as well as other entities subject to private insurance legislation, such as insurance agents and brokers. ISVAP operates in compliance with the insurance guidelines provided by the Government.

[74] See e.g.: D. Jaffee/T. Russell, Markets Under Stress: The Case of Extreme Event Insurance, in: R. Arnott/B. Greenwald/R. Kanbur/B. Nalebuff (eds.), *Economics for an Imperfect World: Essays in Honor of Joseph E. Stiglitz* (2003); K.A. Froot, The Market for Catastrophe Risk: A Clinical Examination, [2001] *Journal of Financial Economics* (J. Finan. Econ.) 60, 529–571; M. Faure, The Limits to Insurability from a Law and Economics Perspective, [1995] *Geneva Papers on Risk and Insurance* (G.P.R.I.I.P.), 454–462; C. Camerer/H. Kunreuther, Decision Processes for Low Probability Events: Policy Implications, [1989] *Journal of Policy Analysis and Management* (J. Pol'y Analysis & Mgmt.) 8, 565–592.

I. Private Insurance and Environment Issues

The complex relationship between environmental risks and insurance is currently an issue for debate at an international level.[75] Among various environment-related risks, one may distinguish between: 81

- the environmental pollution risk (the risk associated with industrial and commercial activities that may adversely affect the environment, cause human health problems, damage property, contaminate natural resources and affect biodiversity) and
- the natural catastrophe risk (the risk associated with the occurrence of natural disasters, such as earthquakes, floods, hurricanes or other extreme environmental conditions).

In recent times, professional risk carriers have been facing environmental pollution liability risk with a new approach.[76] In order to guarantee particularly cumbersome levels of coverage in pollution issues, there has been a growing tendency for several large-sized insurance companies to group together into insurance company pools to face loss recovery which in case of environmental damage may amount to exorbitant sums which single insurance companies could hardly face if they were to provide payment by themselves. In Italy, for instance, the *Pool RC Inquinamento* was established in 1979. The Pool offers coverage for certain aspects of the liability risk associated with environmental pollution, while it should be noted that it does not cover the property risks associated with natural catastrophes.[77] 82

Not always do insurers possess the statistical figures of the risk of occurrence of events: indeed, with society progressing much, much faster than in the past, the ongoing technological evolution of all fields of production defines scenarios which could hardly be compared to those of the old times. Insurance companies have faced this issue by introducing preventive inspections in businesses before stipulating insurance policies with them. Beyond ascertaining the status of the machinery in order to verify compliance with technical standards and existing rules and regulations, the purpose of the inspection is to identify the necessary amendments and updates to ensure a safer industrial process. Often the changes in the working cycle, or the storing process, or the industrial systems or machinery become a condition for the insurance company to execute the insurance policy. 83

Pollution damage is often defined in insurance policies as any damage occurring as a consequence of air, soil and water contamination. Thus, any direct 84

[75] See A. Monti, (*supra* fn. 9).

[76] See A. Monti, L'assicurabilità del rischio ambientale in prospettiva europea, in: B. Pozzo (ed.), *La nuova responsabilità civile per danno all'ambiente* (Quaderni della Rivista Giuridica dell'ambiente. N. 12, 2002); B. Pozzo/A. Monti, *Responsabilità delle imprese in campo ambientale* (1997).

[77] The availability of private insurance coverage for natural catastrophe risks is at present quite limited in Italy, and the demand in any case appears to be extremely low.

detriment which does not occur through air, water or soil contamination may not fall under the insurance coverage provided by the policy, but is to be included in the general civil liability clause covering all business risks. Covered losses include damage to person or limb, to chattels, things, including "suspension or interruption of business operations in the field of industry, agriculture and provision of services, and, generally speaking, the impossibility to use goods which are found in the environment" which is being polluted. The direct and indirect consequences of environmental pollution accidents, indeed, are complex and manifold: suffice it to think of events such as the *Seveso* accident, where a polluting cloud dispersed by a chemical industry spread in the atmosphere causing the evacuation of an entire town and the interruption of all kinds of business activities in the entire area.

85 Another fundamental aspect of insurance applied to environmental pollution risk is its role not only as a loss recovery instrument, but also as a device to stimulate prevention.[78] On the one hand, insurance guarantees loss recovery in case of damage; on the other, it encourages risk evaluation, it implements the introduction of preventive measures aimed at risk reduction, and stresses premium differentiation according to the degree of risk introduced in society by the insured, to the extent that coverage will be denied if such risk is intolerable for the entire community. In view of all such legitimate expectancies, one must keep in mind that an insurance business carries on its business profitably by balancing premiums and losses: this explains why recently, beyond the development of insurance policies guaranteeing pollution coverage, there has been a growing demand for risk evaluation systems which allow insurance companies to better assess the probability and severity of events so as to analyze at best the relationship between insurance coverage provided by the insurer and premium paid by the insured.

86 New challenges for insurers are now posed by the recent approval of Directive 2004/35/CE of 21 April 2004 on environmental liability with regard to the prevention and remedying of environmental damage, whose art. 14 states that:

> "Member States shall take measures to encourage the development of financial security instruments and markets by the appropriate economic and financial operators, including financial mechanisms in case of insolvency, with the aim of enabling operators to use financial guarantees to cover their responsibilities under this Directive".[79]

[78] A. Monti, Environmental Risk: a Comparative Law and Economics Approach to Liability and Insurance, [2001] *European Review of Private Law* (ERPL) 1, 51–79.

[79] Pursuant to the II paragraph of art. 14, "the Commission, before 30 April 2010 shall present a report on the effectiveness of the Directive in terms of actual remediation of environmental damages, on the availability at reasonable costs and on conditions of insurance and other types of financial security for the activities covered by Annex III. The report shall also consider in relation to financial security the following aspects: a gradual approach, a ceiling for the financial guarantee and the exclusion of low-risk activities. In the light of that report, and of an extended impact assessment, including a cost-benefit analysis, the Commission shall, if appropriate, submit proposals for a system of harmonised mandatory financial security".

II. Private Insurance and the Costs of Catastrophes

In 2003 natural catastrophes caused most of the losses covered by insurance, amounting world-wide to US $ 16.2 billion (US $ 11.4 billion in 2002; US $ 10 billion in 2001).[80] As many as 51,500 persons died as a consequence of natural catastrophes in 2003, causing direct financial losses amounting to US $ 58 billion. Man-made technical disasters caused US $ 2.3 billion of insured losses, with the main contributors being industrial fires and loss of satellites. 87

Floods were the greatest source of insured losses in 2002: they counted for US $ 4.1 billion in 2002 as opposed to US $ 1.1 billion in 1990, of which US $ 3.2 billion in connection with the floods that hit Europe in the summer of 2002 (July and August).[81] Another outstanding issue remains that of terrorism risk insurance,[82] although several countries (including Italy) have set up special compensation funds for victims of terrorism or other violent crimes, covering certain terrorism-related losses.[83] 88

Is it possible to identify the areas where risk is potentially higher? In the last few years insurance companies have been touched by myriads of new issues connected to technology (such as cyber-liability), to asbestos, to frequent floods and, last but not least, to terrorism. Some of these issues literally surprised the insurance industry and could seriously have affected their profits if insurers had not been ready to react by implementing an appropriate risk management. For instance, most recently in the case of floods, insurance businesses have attempted to reduce the risks connected to these events by making pressure on the government to introduce adequate safety measures. 89

New issues include potential health hazards connected to the use of cellular phones and venous thrombosis. 90

Part VIII. The Major Italian Disasters and Catastrophes

We shall now proceed with a description of some of the major disasters which have occurred in Italy from post World War II until present day. The para- 91

[80] Swiss Reinsurance Company (*supra* fn. 5).

[81] Swiss Reinsurance Company (2002), *Natural catastrophes and man-made disasters in 2002* (Swiss Re SIGMA series 2/2003).

[82] See H. Kunreuther/E. Michel-Kerjan, *Dealing with Extreme Events. New Challenges for Terrorism Risk Coverage in the U.S.*, The Wharton School of the University of Pennsylvania – Center for Risk Management and Decision Processes, Working Paper no. 14 (June 2004); *Terrorism Insurance – Pools & Market Solutions in Europe*, PartnerRe (2004); Munich Re, *TOPICS 1/2004*, Munich, 2004.

[83] B.A. Koch (ed.), *Terrorism, Tort Law and Insurance. A Comparative Survey* (2004). At an international level, the European Convention on the Compensation of Victims of Violent Crimes was signed in Strasbourg on 24 November 1983. More recently, the Council of the European Union adopted a Directive on compensation to crime victims on 29 April 2004, on the basis of a proposal from the Commission [COM(2002) 562 final], whose enactment had been called for by the European Council in the "Declaration on Combating Terrorism" of 25 March 2004.

graphs below are limited to a factual reconstruction of events: legal issues and insurance-related considerations regarding these catastrophes are dealt with in other sections of this report.

I. The Vajont Disaster (9 October 1963)

92 On 9 October 1963 at 10.39 p.m. an enormous landfall detached over 270 million cubic metres of rock and debris from Mount Toc crumbling into the Vajont artificial basin, causing a gigantic wave that flooded the underlying area and in a few minutes obliterated an entire portion of territory below the dam including the town of Vajont and several buildings of other nearby villages. There were 1,909 deaths.

93 The disaster was mainly due to three fatal human mistakes: the dam had been built in a geologically unsuitable valley; the level of water in the artificial lake was beyond the safety level; although indicia of the disasters were clear when the accident was imminent, the inhabitants of the area were not warned in time and were not evacuated.[84]

94 The criminal proceedings for the disaster were initiated on 25 November 1968 and the case was closed in third insance on 25 March 1971 recognizing that the flood was foreseeable and indicting the accused for involuntary multiple manslaughter. It is noteworthy to point out that as a result of the civil action for damages initiated by several plaintiffs including direct victims and local authorities, the towns of Vajont and Castellavazzo were awarded non-pecuniary damages for loss of their historical, cultural political and social identity:[85] the towns were indeed entirely obliterated as a result of the flood.

II. The Asti Flood (4 September 1948)

95 In September 1948 the Asti area in the Western portion of the Po valley in the Piedmont Region was subject to heavy rains that poured millions of cubic centimetres of water on the land. On 4 September 1948 between noon and 1.00 p.m. the waters of the Borbore and Tanaro rivers flooded and invaded the city of Asti and nearby towns and crop fields. The rains reached 62 millimetres in one hour against a yearly average of 900 in the area. A new flood hit the area one week later, and several landfalls were registered in the hilly areas around the city causing the collapsing of several buildings. As recorded by documents dating from the period,[86] 42 houses and buildings were entirely destroyed, 70

[84] Literature on the Vajont disaster: comment by Colonna, *Enel S.p.A. v Comune di Vajont*, Court of Cassation decision no. 5650 of 19 June 1996, [1996] Danno e Resp., 693; <http://www.stava1985.it/>.

[85] Decisions by the Supreme Court of Cassation no. 5650 of 1996 and 3807 of 1998: see B. Pozzo, Il caso Seveso e la risarcibilità del danno morale, [2002] Riv. giur. Ambiente 6, 947 *et seq*.

[86] *Nubifragio ed alluvione*, in City of Asti, *L'amministrazione del Comune dal 1946 al 1951*, report edited by the City of Asti, Asti, 1951; Archivio Storico del Comune di Asti, Le alluvioni ad Asti dal XIV secolo ad oggi, [1995] *Palinsesto* 10, no. 1.

were condemned as unfit for use, 90 were seriously damaged and 70 were slightly damaged. Sixteen people died as a result of the flooding and landfalls, four hundred inhabitants lost their dwellings and damage amounted to over 5 billion Lire (€ 2.5 million).

Local records note that a First Aid Committee was established by local town authorities that beyond providing first aid and emergency facilities, granted indemnities to all individual citizens affected by the disaster, ranging from the equivalent of today's € 2,000 to € 10,000. The local Chamber of Commerce reportedly paid an initial lump sum (the equivalent of € 1 million) to craftsmen and small businesses affected by the disaster. Contributions and aid by private individuals and charities were enormous. The State and local authorities granted a first indemnification to 334 families between November and December 1948, and a second set of indemnifications was granted in June 1949. At the end of 1949 local town authorities and private donors had indemnified as much as the equivalent of € 30 million. More than a third of the entire amount of indemnifications came from town governments. After the emergency was coped with, the reconstruction phase started. The main instrument used to cover expenses and costs was Legislative Decree no. 1010 of 1948 that authorized the Ministry of Public Works in case of natural catastrophes to provide monies to execute emergency construction works and to restore damaged buildings. 96

III. The Cermis Accidents (9 March 1976 and 3 February 1998)

The Cermis ski-resort in the Eastern Alps is sadly known in Italy for its fatal accidents.[87] On 9 March 1976, due to strong swinging, the two traction cables of the Cermis cableway had overlapped and one had cut the other, thereby causing one of the cabins of the cableway to detach from its support cable and tumble to the ground, causing the death of 42 persons. The criminal proceedings revealed that the persons in charge of handling the cableway had shut off the security device that would automatically start the emergency brake each time the two traction cables should collide. 97

Subsequently, on 3 February 1998, during a training flight, an airplane of the United States Marines Corps cut the support cable of the Cermis cableway, causing the fall of one of its cabins and 20 deaths. The pilot and the navigator of the plane were acquitted by the United States Martial Court holding jurisdiction over the Marines involved in the disaster, although the Investigation Commission appointed by the Italian Parliament to inquire into the disaster issued a report clearly revealing the responsibility of the crew of the U.S. fighter plane that had recklessly carried out dangerous acrobatic manoeuvres under the cableway, and of their chiefs, who had tolerated similar acrobatic behaviours in the past. 98

[87] <http://www.stava1985.it>.

IV. The Seveso Dioxin Cloud (10 July 1976)

99 On 10 July 1976 at 12.37 p.m. there was an explosion in the ICMESA factory located in the town of Seveso, located between the Milan northern suburbs and the Brianza area. The accident occurred in the area of the factory dedicated to the production of tri-chlorine-phenol, a chemical compound necessary to manufacture cosmetics and hospital disinfectants. As a consequence of the explosion, the substance was heated to 300° C and turned into a highly toxic compound known as tetra-chlorine-di-benzo-p-dioxin, or dioxin. After about an hour, the dioxin accumulated in the tanks started spilling out after the breakdown of a security disc and also started spurting out from the vents of the system. Since it was Saturday, there was no staff present in the factory but there were some independent workers building the purification tanks of the system who immediately activated the cooling system to bar the steam from being dispersed through the roof of the plant. This was eventually judged as a very intelligent move that avoided a larger disaster from occurring.[88]

100 The first symptoms of the dioxin cloud felt by locals were a harsh smell and an itching feeling on the skin, that were mostly ascribed to the presence of sodium hydroxide generated by a chemical reaction. A few days later several small animals, such as rabbits, who fed on fresh grass were reportedly found dead, and many children living in the surrounding area suffered skin wounds and injuries and chlorine acnes. Only nine days after the accident did the Givaudan company, the owner of the plant, admit that a certain amount of dioxin could have been released in the atmosphere as a consequence of the explosion.

101 A first report by the Prophylactic Labs of the Province of Milan distinguished three concentric areas where larger, medium-sized and slight concentration of dioxin was registered. On 24 July 1976 – 14 days after the accident – the town of Seveso issued an evacuation order for the area mostly affected by the dioxin, whilst in the other areas children and aged persons were evacuated, growing crops was prohibited, house pets were put under quarantine and fresh vegetables were destroyed. Newborn children were subject to special treatment and supervision, breast feeding was prohibited and abortion was exceptionally authorized at a time when it was still forbidden by the law.[89]

102 A Commission was appointed by the Superior Health Council and it was immediately clear that the measures taken had been excessively precautious and that the seriousness of the situation had been overestimated and the disastrous scenarios depicted in the first place would not occur, and that serious consequences to health would be highly unlikely. Nevertheless, the entire ICMESA personnel and each individual inhabitant of the affected area was subject to special supervision for the following ten years (until 1986), and special stud-

[88] The facts of the Seveso case are very well described by D. Feola, Il prezzo dell'inquietudine: il caso "Seveso" torna in Cassazione, [2002] Resp. civ. e prev. 3, 727 *et seq*.

[89] As many as 33 women aborted.

ies were carried out in the field of spontaneous abortions, sterility and cancer mortality. A study presented in 1981 analyzing the period between 1975 and 1979 confirmed there were no reported peculiar illnesses due to the dioxin cloud. The last report by the Commission issued in December 1985[90] confirmed the over-cautious initial measures taken and stated that the only reported illnesses due to the dioxin amounted to skin irritation known as chlorine acnes.

Many other studies were conducted in Europe on dioxin: the only peculiar result was that more females than males were born in the Seveso area in the period at issue. However, after a first reassuring report issued in 1985, in 1994 the United States Environment Protection Agency published a reassessment on dioxin acknowledging the following: 103

> "The draft reassessment differs significantly from the 1985 document in its evaluation of dioxin's non-cancer effects. Today we have a stronger body of evidence to suggest that at some dose, dioxin exposure can result in a number of non-cancer health-effects in humans. These effects may include developmental and reproductive effects, immune suppression, and disruption of regulatory hormones".

In 1997 the International Agency for Cancer Research of the World Health Organization included dioxin in the list of cancerous substances, but concluded that:

> "overall, the strongest evidence for the carcinogenicity of 2, 3, 7, 8-TCDD is for all cancers combined, rather than for any specific site".[91]

Still today do we not know how dangerous dioxin is or can potentially be in the long-run.

As mentioned, the legal aspects of the *Seveso* case are particularly interesting.[92] In the criminal proceeding, two of the five directors of the ICMESA industry initially accused were found guilty of the crime of negligent disaster aggravated by the fact that the event was foreseeable.[93] The civil action for damages eventually led to a settlement agreement, but a new, particularly innovative approach was adopted by the court in the action for non-pecuniary losses, whereby moral damages were awarded to the inhabitants of the areas affected by the dioxin cloud for suffering strong emotional stress, for having lived with the fear of becoming sick, and having suffered limitations to their personal freedom (such as evacuation from their homes, isolation, quarantine, ongoing medical supervision, etc.) without the victim suffering any material 104

[90] See *Official Bullettin* of the Lombardy Region of 30 December 1987.

[91] Report by the International Agency for Cancer Research, 1997.

[92] See B. Pozzo, [2002] 6, 947 *et seq.*

[93] Appeals Court of Milan (Crim. Div.), decision of 14 May 1985, [1986] Giust. pen., II, 171. The appeals decision was confirmed by the Supreme Court of Cassation by decision no. 112 issued on 23 May 1986.

losses or diminution of their health.[94] This issue is dealt with in detail in Section III.4 above.

V. The Stava – Val di Fiemme Disaster (19 July 1985)

105 On 19 July 1985 the embankment walls of the decanting basins of the Prestavel mine, located in the Val di Fiemme alpine area near Trento in North-eastern Italy, crushed to pieces. The inhabitants of the surrounding area were invaded by a huge mud avalanche that covered entire villages killing 268 persons.

106 The origin of the disaster may be traced down to the works carried out years before in the Prestavel fluorite mine.[95] In order to "enrich" the fluorite extracted in the mine, in 1961 a flotation plant was installed in the mine. The flotation proceeding, which separates fine crushed materials through a process requiring the creation of foam in water, requires an enormous quantity of water that was brought to the Prestavel mine through an aqueduct pipeline. The residual debris of the process, which is basically a watery mud made up of 5% of rock debris and of 95% of water, was transferred to several decanting and discharge basins. Every month the basins were filled with 1,340 tons of solid scrap materials and 24,000 cubic metres of water.

107 On 19 July 1985 the embankment walls of the upper basin crushed to pieces, and the mud spilled over the lower basin smashing its embankment walls as well. A huge cloud of rock particles followed by an enormous mass of mud (180,000 cubic metres plus an additional 40–50,000 generated from the erosion process) precipitated down the mountain at a speed of 90 km/h, destroying trees, buildings and everything it hit on its way, affecting an area of 435,000 sq. m. until it eventually flowed into the Avisio river. The mud fall destroyed 53 houses, 3 hotels, 9 buildings and eradicated hundreds of trees. There were 268 victims, of whom 28 were children under the age of 10, and 31 between 10 and 18 years old.

108 The first aid operations were efficient and showed an enormous solidarity by private individuals and authorities. On 30 July 1985 the Provincial Government of Trento funded € 1.5 million for first aid, and the Italian Government issued a decree on 24 September 1985 (implemented into Law no. 662 of 21 November 1985) funding € 15 million for the reconstruction of the area. An additional € 2.5 million were granted by the Provincial Government to indemnify local families on 28 November 1987. All contributions were assigned on the basis of the volume and space of each destroyed building, with the duty to reconstruct the buildings and to file the documentary evidence of said reconstruction. Town building plans were revised so as to conciliate reconstruction and environment protection requirements. In this specific instance, public authorities anticipated these amounts as contributions of the damages that would

[94] Cass. Civ., no. 2515 of 21 February 2002.

[95] <http://www.stava1985.it/>.

be liquidated in the court proceedings, and subrogated into the rights of the victims to claim such damages. The environment recovery and reconstruction were completed over a period of fifteen years, bringing back the Val di Stava area to its original splendour. The only memories of the former Val di Stava are nothing but old photographs.

The criminal proceedings lasted 7 years and the ten persons accused were in- 109
dicted for involuntary disaster and involuntary multiple manslaughter. The court found that the persons responsible for managing the mine could have foreseen the collapse by using ordinary diligence, but in over 20 years the discharge basins had never been subject to stability checks by the licensees of the mine extraction nor by local authorities. Thus, the following persons were criminally indicted: those responsible for the construction and management of the embankment walls of the upper basin between 1969 and 1985, the director of the mine, and the officers of the Mine District Authority of the Provincial Government of Trento for having omitted to carry out periodical supervisory checks. The 194 civil actions for damages involved over 1,000 parents of victims, and the Provincial Government of Trento was held civilly liable as well as the companies who were licensees of the mine extraction during the entire period at issue, i.e. Montedison S.p.A., Industria Marmi e Graniti Imeg S.p.A, Snam S.p.A. and Prealpi Mineraria S.p.A. So far, 183 of the 194 actions have been settled or resolved. Total damages awarded amount to € 245,810.00.

VI. Floods, Fires, Earthquakes, Droughts and Oil Spills

Upon monitoring the evolution of disasters in Europe in the last few years, the 110
European Environment Agency (EEA) reported that between 1998 and 2002 the highest number of earthquakes, floods and fires in Europe occurred in Italy.[96] In 2003, floods and landslides occurred between 24 and 27 January in the Molise, Apulia, Abruzzi and Basilicata regions caused one death and total damage exceeding € 839 million. On 29–30 August 2003 floods caused by heavy rain affected the Val Canal and Canal di Ferro areas in the Friuli region causing 3 deaths and a total of € 519 million in damage.

Almost half of the Italian cities are subject to landfall risks, which have great- 111
ly increased in the second half of the 20th century due to heavy urbanization. One of the most serious problems is connected to floods, which are grossly indemnified by the State through funding amounting to 0.02% of the GDP.

Italy together with France, Spain, Greece and Portugal are heavily subject to 112
fires. Although the Mediterranean lands represent only 14% of the entire European territory, 62% of the fires in Europe occurred in this area. Earthquakes are another serious issue: several areas of Italy (especially Sicily, Sardinia, Apulia and the Naples area) are subject to seismic risk and have been hit by

[96] See *Mapping the impacts of recent natural disasters and technological accidents in Europe*, Environmental Issue Report no. 35, EEA, (2004).

terrible earthquakes in the past (in 1908 the City of Messina was entirely destroyed by a terrible earthquake that killed over 100,000 persons). The latest earthquake in 2002 in San Giuliano di Puglia (in the Apulia region) caused several deaths and serious damage.

113 Drought and forest fires are also widespread in the summer, mostly on the coasts and in Central and Southern Italy where many areas are characterized by dry, Mediterranean climate. Droughts are also an increasing problem. Between June and September 2003 droughts caused severe damage to agricultural crops throughout Italy, France, Germany, Spain, Switzerland, Austria, Slovenia, Belgium, Bosnia and Slovakia, causing € 10.7 billion total damage.

114 Although their infrequency may be compared to that of air accidents, shipwrecks causing oil spills in the sea have an enormous impact on the media. Nevertheless, according to the most recent statistics issued by the International Tanker Owners Pollution Federation (ITOPF), oil spills dropped from 301 million tons in 1970 to 103 in 1980 and 65 in 1990 and as little as 8 in 2001, with a constant diminution trend.[97] Oil spills generally involve ships with a single hull, whereas in the last few years oil ships with a double hull account for 50% of all ships navigating the seas worldwide. Oil spills have caused several serious disasters throughout Europe. The most serious one was the *Amoco Cadiz* accident in 1978 that spilt over 223,000 tons of oil off the northern French coasts; recently, the *Sea Empress* breakdown in 1996 dispersed over 72,000 tons of oil off the British isles, and the *Prestige* disaster which occurred in Spain in 2002 discharged 76,000 tons of raw oil off the coasts of Galicia. On that occasion, victims were indemnified by the International Oil Pollution Compensation Fund (IOPCF-FIPOL) for over € 155 million and the ship insurer indemnified € 25 million.

115 Italy was involved in one sole major accident in 1991 when the *Haven* ship spread over 144,000 tons of oil in the sea off the coast of small town resorts nearby Genoa. Also on this occasion was indemnification once again partially provided by the International Oil Pollution Compensation Fund.[98]

Part IX. Future Perspectives in the Italian Disaster Recovery System

I. Shared Views

116 Due to its geological conformation, its seismic characterization and its geographic position, Italy is indubitably a country particularly exposed to natural catastrophes such as earthquakes, landfalls and floods. Having to face such ongoing, unexpected, cumbersome perils, the Government has attempted to solve emerging issues mostly by providing first aid, emergency compensation and long-term State funding to victims of disasters. The country is yet to de-

[97] <http://www.itopf.com/>.

[98] The accident led to a legal action: *International Oil Pollution Compensation Fund v Comune di Varazze*, App. Genoa March 30, 1996, [1996] Dir. e resp., 720.

cide which road to follow to best solve these issues in the future, although recent proposals seem to favour one solution. According to several thinkers and commentators, Italy should take inspiration from the French model based upon the so-called solidarity principle, i.e. on a compulsory insurance system whereas the insurance premium paid by private individuals is established by the State and is in substance the same for all of the insured: this way, citizens of areas not particularly subject to risks contribute to financing actual insurance costs of the areas subject to higher risk.

This was indeed the focus of the discussion in Parliament on the *Camoirano* reform bill presented during the Thirteenth Legislature and which is examined in Part IX.IV.A. This draft statute aimed at establishing an insurance system characterized by feasible premiums for the insured and financial equilibrium. This mechanism, where citizens of areas less exposed to risks are to pay equal premiums as those imposed upon citizens of areas more exposed to risks, would of course function only in the presence of a compulsory insurance system: the adverse aspects of such a system are connected to the indifferent attitude which necessarily arises towards risk prevention policies in such situations. Indeed, if all citizens are covered by insurance (and must pay the premiums), individuals, communities and public authorities will be discouraged from adopting safety measures and prevention steps beyond the legal requirements since they are already covered by compulsory insurance. Thus, the system must be balanced by adequate corrective measures aimed at urging communities and individuals to take responsible steps towards prevention, as is apparently done in France. 117

Others view the possibility of establishing a compulsory insurance system through the establishment of pools or consortiums grouping insurance companies that would apply a "partial" fixed premium mechanism by adopting personalized criteria aimed at imposing higher premiums exceeding the risks in areas less subject to catastrophe risks, which would offset the imposition of premiums below average in areas subject to frequent catastrophe risks. Such a system would of course function only in the presence of an adequate data base providing full information on pure premiums and specific risk management expertise.[99] 118

Regarding the nature of goods and assets forming the object of a hypothetical compulsory insurance system, the first step could be to impose insurance coverage on land, civil buildings and houses only, thus excluding movables and chattels present within the insured constructions. This would allow the establishment of more accurate statistical data, thereafter proceeding by subsequent approximations. Furthermore, it would be easier to assess damage considering that when it comes to real property, damage assessment techniques are much faster than in case of chattels and movables. 119

[99] *Supra* fn. 72, 9.

120 Several thinkers believe that the French model should be taken as an example also insofar as reinsurance issues and State backing are concerned. From this perspective, the adoption of the French model implies that at least in the starting phase there should be a form of guarantee by the State in case of exceptional events: this is of course routine in Italy in case of disasters, hence it should be easily achieved as a form of continuity with the past. The French model thus seems to be the future example for Italian legislation in this field. On the contrary, in the view of several thinkers, the experience based on the model adopted in the United States, centred around the concept that insurance is not compulsory but *voluntary* and that premiums are substantially "pure", seems to have failed to provide satisfactory results and to generate a wholly-independent insurance coverage system. Indeed, according to this approach, the purpose of a mandatory insurance system is to face and solve the problem of adverse selection which leads only individuals subject to high risks to seek insurance coverage.

121 Other instruments to implement natural disaster risk coverage could include the adoption of fiscal measures. In France, for instance, persons insured may deduct the premiums paid from their taxes, and insurers may set up tax-exempt technical reserves for the corresponding premium amounts. Otherwise, tax rates on premiums could be reduced, considering that in most European countries they are already lower than in Italy (especially in relation to insurance policies providing fire coverage). The lower amounts of taxes collected would be offset by the lower funding that State authorities should provide to victims in the occurrence of a disaster.

122 Another direction where thinkers believe steps should be taken is to plan a national mapping of the risks of natural catastrophes. Costs for such a mapping project would not be exorbitant and there reportedly would be experts available who would be ready to carry out the work in reasonable time. A complete mapping of risks would encourage insurance companies to agree with the proposed compulsory insurance system, beyond allowing insurance appraisers and assessment experts to better define premium rates and to adopt preventive measures and policies both on a local and on a national scale.[100]

II. The "Mixed" System: Foreign Models

123 Coping with issues related to natural catastrophes and man-made disasters has led to the establishment of different "mixed" models where State funding is accompanied by the implementation of particular (public or private) insurance coverage systems and by other instruments, the trend being indeed to organize "mixed" models where several measures are established both on a public and on a private scale to cope with disasters, and they coexist and interact with one another.

[100] *Supra* fn. 72, 2.

In the United States, for instance, costs for State compensation of catastrophes have been thoroughly reduced by the implementation of a voluntary-based insurance system. Basically, State funding is limited to a fixed portion of the overall damage suffered by victims of disasters: the rest is left to private insurance, and individuals exposed to risks may choose to seek insurance coverage or not to do so. In States such as California and countries like Japan, the entire system is based upon a fully private insurance system, and non-insured citizens are considered civilly liable for the damage incurred. In California insurance companies are only required to quote the risk in a free market regime. 124

As we have already discussed, France has also adopted a "mixed" system. Whenever individuals take out an insurance policy to cover property risks, an additional premium amount is imposed upon the insured which represents the insurance premium for catastrophe risk coverage which insurance companies must compulsorily provide to all citizens. 125

In Norway, by law all insurance policies covering fire risks have an automatic extension covering risks of natural catastrophes. The same applies in New Zealand, where all residential property owners who buy fire insurance from private insurance companies automatically acquire EQCover, the Earthquake Commission's seismic disaster insurance cover.[101] EQCover premiums are added to the cost of the fire insurance and passed on to EQC by the insurance company. EQC's administration of the natural disaster insurance scheme involves: collecting premiums via insurance companies; processing and meeting claims by insured people; administering a disaster fund; investing the fund in accordance with Government directions; organizing reinsurance as a potential supplement to the fund; accounting to its shareholder (the Government). 126

Shortly we will see that many of these solutions were taken as a model in adopting suggested reform bills and proposals in Italy. 127

III. ISVAP's Proposals

In order to develop a market for risks arising from natural catastrophes, insurance companies must be encouraged to develop increasing mutuality and sufficient funds in premium collection. In 1997 Italy's insurance supervisory body ISVAP (*Istituto per la Vigilanza sulle Assicurazioni Private e di Interesse Collettivo*) drafted a reform schedule and submitted it to the Ministry of Industry and to the Treasury Department, proposing to establish a compulsory insurance system to cover the risk of occurrence of natural catastrophes in 128

[101] The EQC is a Crown Entity, wholly owned by the government of New Zealand and controlled by a board of commissioners. Crown Entities are not Government departments or State-owned enterprises but nevertheless belong to the Government and are subject to public sector finance and reporting rules. EQC administers the Natural Disaster Fund. The Government guarantees that this fund will meet all its obligations. Perils insured by the EQC catastrophe coverage are: earthquake, natural landslip, volcanic eruption, hydrothermal activity, tsunami and, in the case of residential land, also storm or flood.

connection with fire risk coverage clauses contained in insurance policies. According to this scheme, it would not be mandatory but rather voluntary for citizens to stipulate this further insurance coverage upon taking a fire insurance policy, but insurance companies would be obliged to guarantee this sort of coverage upon request by any insured. The project was based upon the simple assumption that fire insurance coverage is traditionally very common in Italy not only in the industry but also among families who most often seek this kind of insurance for their houses and private belongings.

129 ISVAP's draft also included the possibility for the insured to partially bear the risks of occurrence of a disaster by introducing a discount, deductible and franchise mechanism which basically allowed the insured to reduce the premium in proportion to the amount of risk they were willing to bear themselves. The State would also concur or integrate the insured's premium.

130 The purpose of the ISVAP proposal was to achieve a generalized, minimum-sized insured portfolio which would allow the implementation of an individual prevention system. The ISVAP proposal was very much considered and formed the basis for subsequent reform bills drafted by the Italian Parliament.

IV. Law Reform Bills Introducing Mandatory Insurance Coverage for Disasters

131 Following the generalized trend throughout the rest of Europe, several reform bills have been proposed within the Italian Parliament in the last fifteen years in the field of natural catastrophes, disaster insurance and indemnification.

A. *Reform Bill No. 1164/1993*

132 The first attempt to introduce a natural catastrophe risk coverage system dates back to 1993. On the initiative of Senator Cesare Golfari, a draft reform bill was presented to the Senate (no. 1164/93) and was subsequently proposed to the House of Deputies by Dep. Andriollo Camoirano (no. 800/94) thus becoming the so-called *Camoirano* draft. Art. 1 of the draft established the creation of a National Private Insurance Fund. A 1% increment in the local property taxes would have funded this newly established body, incremented by an additional 0.5% in case of a particularly serious disasters (art. 4.1h). The law prescribed the compulsory formation of insurance consortiums grouping large insurance companies. Since in Italy property taxes are collected by towns, each town would have stipulated an insurance policy for its own inhabitants with a pool of insurance companies. In exchange, 85% of losses incurred by citizens and arising out of natural catastrophes would be covered, whilst the initial 15% of the loss would be borne by the insured victims.

133 The key element of the system, which would apparently allow it to function properly and independently, was of course its mandatory nature. The critical point of this reform was that the insurance policy was being entered into by the town authorities and by the pool of insurance companies, not between a

private insured party and the insurer: this of course would affect the benefits arising from the introduction of market economy principles in the system, namely the insurance company's power to check the actual damage suffered by the insured, and the personalization of insurance premiums on the basis of the preventive measures adopted by the insured. Moreover, the town's role in the operation was quite ambiguous, as it acted both as supervisory body and as entity subject to supervision. Indeed, it was the town who stipulated the insurance policies, who collected the insurance premiums and conveyed them to the pool (art. 4.1c), but it was also the town who was in charge of declaring any state of emergency in the occurrence of a disaster in its territory (art. 3), and it was the town who was in charge of evaluating damage claims by victims, assessing damages (art. 4.1n), and supervising State indemnification procedures. The pool's role was equally criticized because it was practically vested with all tasks once ascribable to the insurance companies, including premium assessment, liquidation of indemnifications, and executing reassurance contracts, thereby depriving insurance companies of all their original functions except that of cashing in their returns, with an overall loss of efficiency in the indemnification system.[102]

The *Camoirano* draft generated great debate on these issues in and out of Parliament.

B. ANIA's Mapping Plan

In 1996 the National Association of Insurance Companies (*Associazione Nazionale fra le Imprese Assicuratrici,* ANIA) drafted a mapping plan to classify 134
the entire Italian territory.[103] Although it was limited to flood-related issues, the plan divided the Italian territory into areas of low, medium and high risk of flood and identified six thousand towns particularly subject to floods. With this study, ANIA suggested that a system providing insurance coverage against natural catastrophes should be preceded by a careful evaluation of actual risks in relation to the Italian territory. ANIA's work was another step in the direction of an organic reform in the field.

C. Reform Bill No. 235/1996

After ISVAP's proposed draft,[104] the Government in 1999 presented a bill in- 135
tending to regulate the entire natural catastrophe insurance subject. The bill was to be adopted in the form of a law authorizing the Government to enact a reform in the field of natural catastrophes and related insurance, and was thereafter included in the Finance Act for 1999 and then transposed into an independent reform bill (no. 5809-*ter*) assigned for discussion to the Environment Commission, and subsequently presented before the House of Deputies

[102] G. Mureddu, *Calamità naturali intervento pubblico e copertura assicurativa* (1997), 90.

[103] ANIA, *Progetto di classificazione del territorio italiano ai fini della garanzia alluvione* (1996), 1–10.

[104] See Part IX.III.

on 22 February 2001, the general reporter of the draft being Deputy Casinelli, thus becoming the so-called *Casinelli* draft (reform bill no. 235/1996).[105]

136 The draft authorized the Government to enact provisions regulating insurance covering natural catastrophes (art. 2). The rules were based on the French model: the *Casinelli* draft, in fact, provided for an extension to natural catastrophes of the insurance coverage provided by fire insurance policies, following also the Norwegian approach, and it was characterized by several peculiarities. In order to implement demand for insurance coverage, the bill provided that all victims of natural catastrophes would be indemnified for the first five years from the enactment of the law regardless of the fact that they had or had not sought insurance coverage against natural catastrophes. However, after this initial 5-year term, the draft provided for a limitation (of 30% to 60%) of State contributions to private victims of disasters whose assets were not covered by insurance against natural catastrophes. The 30–60% range depended upon the economic status of the victim hit by the disaster. This should imply a general increase of insurance policies (and related amount of taxes for the State) in the fire/disaster field, and a general increase in the number of persons and entities insured. The establishment of consortiums grouping insurance companies was being allowed only for the purpose of facilitating catastrophe reinsurance.

137 Insurance premiums would be determined by the Government according to the different areas of risk present on the national territory, and would be published by the Ministry of Industry based upon an initial average premium defined by the market (art. 2c). Furthermore, the draft provided for a premium cap for disaster coverage, which should not exceed 50% of the premium for fire coverage. Of course, this provision was highly criticized because establishing premiums and insurance policy terms and conditions common to all insurers was and is contrary to existing Italian and European rules on competition, beyond clashing with EC law on insurance coordination, which liberalized all insurance tariffs starting from 1994. Moreover, technically speaking there is no connection between the premium for fire insurance and the premium for natural catastrophe coverage, provided that entirely different elements and data are taken into consideration in order to determine the related tariffs. This could of course affect the terms and conditions for the fire insurance, leading insurers to impose exorbitant deductibles which would clash with the very purpose of the new rules.

138 The Antitrust Authority expressed its dissenting opinion on the extension to natural disasters of fire insurance policies, claiming that this would affect competition in the fire insurance business.[106] Furthermore, by grouping fire in-

[105] Disegno di Legge 235/1996, assegnato alla VIII Commissione permanente della Camera, in sede referente, in data 11 marzo 1999. The entire text of the draft (in Italian) may be found in the official website of the Italian Parliament: <http://www.parlamento.it/att/dll/home.html>.

[106] *Antitrust Authority Bulettin*, no. 13–14 of 26 April 1999, 95.

surance (i.e. a non-regulated market) and natural catastrophe insurance (i.e. a market subject to specific regulation), the fire insurance would inevitably be affected by the competition restrictions necessary for natural catastrophe insurance to fully operate. However, the Authority also held that adopting the alternative solution, i.e. an entirely *mandatory* insurance system covering natural disasters, would certainly ensure an outstanding collection of premiums but could lead the community to interpret the new compulsory insurance as an indirect form of taxation.[107]

The draft was never approved by Parliament, but led most political parties to agree on the necessity of promptly adopting a reform in the natural catastrophe field. 139

D. Reform Bill No. 533/2001

In 2001 Senator Manfredi presented before the Senate Reform Bill no. 533 dated 26 July 2001 entitled "General Law for Damage Redress and Reconstruction Following Disasters or Catastrophes".[108] The bill was very simply aimed at authorising the Ministry of Industry to enter into a memorandum of understanding with private insurance companies to regulate indemnification of damage incurred by private citizens as a consequence of natural disasters. 140

E. ANIA's 2003 Proposals and Government's Current Reform Plan

At a congress held in Milan on 11 November 2003 Mr. Aldo Marzano, speaking for ANIA, drew a very clear picture of the Italian situation stressing several typical factors connected to natural disasters:[109] firstly, in Italy there is no official database for catastrophic risks; secondly, the country is characterized by a strongly diversified natural environment; thirdly, insurers have a very limited experience in the field of natural catastrophe risk coverage and there is limited insurance and reinsurance market capacity; fourthly, citizens have a strong expectation for government intervention in the occurrence of a disaster. Based upon the foregoing, ANIA proposed to include a reform in the Financial Law for 2004 introducing a true risk partnership between Government, the insurance market and the insured. The reform should provide for compulsory extension of fire coverage to coverage for catastrophes. The law should give a full definition of the term "catastrophe" and strictly list catastrophes to which the law applies. The reform should also provide for different risk index individuation, and for specific, clear parameters to determine the value of the assets damaged by the disaster. Retentions should be defined in detail, together with compensation limits. At last, the law should regulate and implement the establishment of a co-reinsurance pool between insurers, providing for general yearly limits to the involvement of the pool. 141

[107] *Supra* fn. 72, 6 *et seq.*
[108] <http://www.parlamento.it/att/ddl/home.htm>.
[109] ANIA, *Catastrophes and Insurance in Italy* (2003).

142 The current Government has announced that it intends to regulate insurance coverage of natural disasters once and for all by implementing a mixed system conciliating principles of solidarity and victim indemnification with technical requirements, in full compliance with applicable competition rules and regulations and existing insurance legislation. Following ANIA's suggestions, the Government intended to include provisions regulating natural disaster insurance coverage in the Financial Law for 2004. The text of the proposed provision (art. 40), which had been previously approved by the Balance Commission on 4 November 2003, is very similar (if not almost identical) to the ANIA 2003 proposals.

143 The text provided for a compulsory extension of natural catastrophe insurance coverage to all and any new fire insurance policies entered into by private businesses and individuals after the enactment of the new law, with a gradual extension to all previously existing fire insurance policies (art. 40(a) of the draft). Insurance coverage under the mandatory catastrophe extension would be triggered by the declaration of a state of emergency by the Cabinet of Ministries. According to the bill, the law would have to provide detailed parameters of reference to determine the value of goods and assets damaged by natural catastrophes (art. 40(c) of the draft) and unauthorised buildings would not be entitled to any form of compensation. Insurance premiums would be defined also on the basis of different risk indexes characterizing different areas of the nation (art. 40(e) of the draft), thus encouraging a system based on retentions and indemnification limits (art. 40(g) of the draft). The draft also implemented a strict definition of catastrophes falling under the applicability of the law (art. 40(f) of the draft), and excluded State indemnification for any buildings and assets not covered by insurance (art. 40(h) of the draft). The draft also provided for rules regulating co-reinsurance, by imposing the establishment of a co-reinsurance consortium or pool grouping insurance companies and responsible for the collection of premiums paid for natural catastrophe risk coverage (art. 40(i) of the draft). At last, the law would define the co-reinsurance consortium's yearly maximum indemnification cap, beyond which the State would cover any residual compensation, including any amounts paid to non-insured victims of natural catastrophes (art. 40(l) of the draft). The text also provided for more detailed provisions to be encompassed in a Regulation to be enacted within the following 3 months.

144 Ultimately, the draft was not approved in December 2003 because it did not find full convergence by all political parties involved within the framework of the enactment of the Financial Law for 2004. Moreover, the Italian Antitrust Authority voiced another negative opinion on the draft.[110] The Authority was especially concerned with the provisions calling for: (*i*) compulsory extension of catastrophe coverage to all fire insurance policies (assuming that it would

[110] Antitrust Authority Decision AS270 of 20 November 2003, Bulletin no. 47/2003. The opinion expressed by the Authority does not appear to be entirely consistent and may be subject to criticism.

constitute an illegitimate tie-in);[111] (*ii*) strict regulation of the terms of coverage;[112] (*iii*) mandatory participation of all insurers in a single co-reinsurance pool; (*iv*) harmonised minimum pricing mechanisms. Apart from the detailed reasons that may support the negative outcome of this opinion, the Italian Antitrust Authority seems to be in principle against the idea of a public/private partnership in the management of catastrophe risks:[113] this, of course, appears to be completely at odds with the most recent trends observed at an international level.

Part X. Conclusions

An insurance system covering natural catastrophe risks is in itself not only feasible, but is probably the most efficient solution to the issue of indemnification to victims of natural disasters allowing the State to spend its budget destined for this purpose not only to indemnify victims, but also to implement disaster prevention and to encourage soil and water protection measures. Several issues must be taken into careful consideration, including: pricing mechanisms, pooling and reinsurance options, and State backing. 145

From an insurance point of view, the efficiency of a "mixed" system providing voluntary or compulsory insurance coverage against natural catastrophes will also depend on the professional expertise of insurers both in the underwriting and in the claims handling phases. Moreover, since natural disasters imply potential damages which may go beyond the financial capacity of Italian insurance companies, State backing and reinsurance become essential instruments for the system to function properly. In order to appear feasible to the international reinsurance market, Italian insurers and authorities must implement a rigorous risk mapping system as well as prevention and coordination plans so as to encourage the establishment of credible insurance pools between large insurance companies. In this framework, a well designed reinsurance programme may help to cope with unexpectedly high losses arising from increasingly frequent natural disasters. The role of the State could then be to act as a "re-insurer of last resort", stepping in only in case of disasters causing damage that exceeds the allocated private sector capacity. 146

For the future, Italy must put aside the traditional indemnificatory position of the State and develop a new system whereby the private insurance sector plays a significant, primary role, complemented by State intervention. The various bills proposed by the recent Governments seem to go in this direction, with a 147

[111] The antitrust problem with tie-ins is that the leverage generated by economic power in one market is used by the seller to accomplish sales in another. This, however, would not certainly be the case with regard to the proposed compulsory catastrophe insurance extension.

[112] This argument proves too much, since it would also be applicable to compulsory motor third party liability (MTPL) insurance.

[113] "In conclusion, the Authority hopes that the Parliament and the Government, with a view to reforming the current system of compensation for natural catastrophes losses, will make a clear decision between public and private intervention". Antitrust Authority Decision AS270 of 20 November 2003, Bulletin no. 47/2003, last sentence.

view to promoting a solid partnership agreement between public authorities and the private insurance sector. The way is traced. The target is not far from being achieved.

List of References

AA.VV, Il divieto della pubblicità di prodotti da fumo non vale se il marchio ha acquistato autonomia, [2001] *Guida al diritto,* 10, 74.

A. Albamonte, *Danni all'ambiente e responsabilità civile* (1989).

G. Alpa, Progetti comunitari sulla assicurazione del danno ambientale, [2001] *Responsabilità civile a prevdenza* (Resp. civ. e prev.), 1091.

G. Alpa/M. Bessone/V. Carbone, *Atipicità dell'illecito, III, Diritti reali – Tutela dell'ambiente* (1994).

ANIA, *Progetto di classificazione del territorio italiano ai fini della garanzia alluvione* (1996), 1–10.

V. d'Antonio, Pubblicità ingannevole e prodotti da fumo leggeri, [2003] *Danno e responsabilità* (Danno e resp.), 1170 *et seq.*

T. Ballarino, Azioni di diritto privato per il risarcimento di danni da inquinamento transfrontaliero, [1990] *Rivista Diritto Internazionale* (Riv. Dir. Int.), 849.

M. Bianca, *Diritto civile, V, La responsabilità* (1994), 704 *et seq.*

G. Bigliazzi Geri, A proposito di danno ambientale ex art. 18 legge 8 luglio 1986, n. 349, e di responsabilità civile, [1987] *Contratto e Impresa.*

C. Camerer/H. Kunreuther, Decision Processes for Low Probability Events: Policy Implications, [1989] *Journal of Policy Analysis and Management* (J.Pol'y Analysis & Mgmt.) 8, 565–592.

G. Cappelletti, Finding an Appropriate Compromise: A Comparative Study of Individualistic Models and Group Rights in Civil Procedure, [1983] *Civil Justice Quarterly* (C.J.Q.) 2, 111 *et seq.*

A. Castelnuovo-Pintus, Infezione da HIV: il ristoro del danno tra indennizzo e risarcimento, in: P.G. Monateri/M. Bona/F. Peccennini/P. Tullini (eds.), *Il danno alla persona* (2000), I, 439.

C. Castronovo, Il danno all'ambiente nel sistema di responsabilità civile, [1987] *Rivista Trimestrale di Diritto e Procedura Civile* (Riv. Dir. e Proc. civ.), 511.

P. Cendon/P. Ziviz, L'art. 18 legge 349/86 nel sistema della responsabilità civile, [1987] Riv. Dir. e Proc. civ., 521.

A. Chilberti, *Azione civile e nuovo processo penale* (1993).

A.G. Cianci, Danno evento e danno conseguenza: la distinzione se ne va in soffitta, [2002] *Diritto e Giurisprudenza* (Dir. e giust.), no. 11, at 20.

A.G. Cianci, Discovery e danni da fumo: gestione dei documenti aziendali, tecniche di difesa e violazione del fair trial, [2003] Danno e resp., 587.

D. Chindemi, Le immissioni elettromagnetiche: limiti di liceità e danni risarcibili con particolare riguardo al danno esistenziale, [2001] Resp. civ. e prev., 1051.

M. Comporti, *Esposizione al pericolo e responsabilità civile* (1965), 271 *et seq.*

M. Comporti, Profili generali di responsabilità ripristino dello stato dei luoghi e liquidazione dei danni ambientali, in: E. Cesaro (ed.), *Danno ambientale e tutela giuridica* (1987), 31.

F. Dominique, Il prezzo dell'inquietudine: il caso "Seveso" torna in Cassazione, [2002] Resp. civ. e prev. 3, 727 *et seq.*

M. Faure, The Limits to Insurability from a Law and Economics Perspective, [1995] *Geneva Papers on Risk and Insurance* (G.P.R.I.I.P.), 454–462.

M. Faure (ed.), *Deterrence, Insurability and Compensation in Environmental Liability. Future Developments in the European Union* (2003).

M. Faure/D. Grimeaud, *Financial Assurance Issues of Environmental Liability* (Report, Follow up study commissioned by the European Commission, 2000).
K.A. Froot (ed.), *The Financing of Catastrophe Risks* (1999).
K.A. Froot, The Market for Catastrophe Risk: A Clinical Examination, [2001] *Journal of Financial Economics* (J. Finan. Econ.) 60, 529–571.
G. Giacchero, Fumo attivo e responsabilità civile del produttore di sigarette, [2001] Giur. It., 1643.
F. Giampietro, *La responsabilità per danno all'ambiente – Profili amministrativi, civili, penali* (1988).
G. Giannini, *L'azione civile per il risarcimento del danno e il nuovo codice di procedura penale* (1990).
F. Di Giovanni, *Strumenti privatisticie tutela dell'ambiente* (1982), 142 *et seq.*
A. Giussani, Mass torts e tutela giurisdizionale: modelli di azione giudiziaria collettiva a confronto sotto il profilo della efficienza economica, [2002] Resp. civ. e prev., 315 *et seq.*
Iannantuono, Camel ha fatto strada: ora evoca viaggi e non la pubblicità vietata delle sigarette, [2001] D&G, 10, 63.
G. Iudica/P. Zatti, *Language and Rules of Italian Private Law: An Introduction* (2003).
U. Izzo, La responsabilità dello Stato per il contagio di emofiliaci e politrasfusi: oltre i limiti della responsabilità civile, [2001] Dir. e resp., 1067.
U. Izzo, *La precauzione nella responsabilità civile. Analisi di un concetto sul tema del danno da contagio per via trasfusionale* (2004).
D. Jaffee/T. Russell, Markets Under Stress: The Case of Extreme Event Insurance, in: R. Arnott/B. Greenwald/R. Kanbur/B. Nalebuff (eds.), *Economics for an Imperfect World: Essays in Honor of Joseph E. Stiglitz* (2003).
B.A. Koch, Die Verbandsklage in Europa, [2000] *Zeitschrift für Zivilprozess* (ZZP), 413 *et seq.*
B.A. Koch (ed.), *Terrorism, Tort Law and Insurance. A Comparative Survey* (2004).
H. Kunreuther/E. Michel-Kerjan, *Dealing with Extreme Events. New Challenges for Terrorism Risk Coverage in the U.S.* (Working Paper no. 14, June 2004).
M. Libertini, Le nuove frontiere del danno risarcibile, [1987] *Contratto e Impresa*, 122 *et seq.*
U. Mattei/J. Lena, *Introduction to Italian Law* (2002).
A. Monti, Environmental Risk: A Comparative Law and Economics Approach to Liability and Insurance, [2001] *European Review of Private Law* (ERPL) 1, 51–79.
A. Monti, L'assicurabilità del rischio ambientale in prospettiva europea, in: B. Pozzo (ed.), *La nuova responsabilità civile per danno all'ambiente* (Quaderni della Rivista Giuridica dell'ambiente. N.12, 2002).
A. Monti, *Environmental Risks and Insurance. A Comparative Analysis of the Role of Insurance in the Management of Environment-Related Risks* (Policy Issues in Insurance no. 6, 2003).
Munich Re, *TOPICS 1/2004*, Munich, 2004.
Munich Re, *TOPICS geo 2003. Annual Review: Natural Catastrophes in 2003* (2004).
G. Mureddu, *Calamità naturali intervento pubblico e copertura assicurativa* (1997), 90.
L. Nava, La responsabilità del produttore di sigarette in Italia, Francia e Stati Uniti d'America, [2002] *Diritto & Diritti – rivista giuridica on line*, <http://www.diritto.it>.
M. Pacifico, Il risarcimento del danno da fumo attivo, [2000] *Corriere Giurisprudenza* (Corriere giur.), 1639.
PartnerRe, *Terrorism Insurance – Pools & Market Solutions in Europe* (2004).
R. Pennisi, Azione (azione civile nel processo penale), [1988] *Enciclopedia del diritto* (Enc. Giur.) IV, 1988.

Ponzanelli, Fumo passivo e tutela nei luoghi di lavoro, [1997] Danno e resp., 174.
B. Pozzo, *Danno ambientale ed imputazione della responsabilità* (1996).
B. Pozzo/A. Monti, *Responsabilità delle imprese in campo ambientale* (1997).
G. Priest, The Government, the Market and the Problem of Catastrophic Loss, [1993] *Journal of Risk and Uncertainty* 12, 219.
P. Recano, *La responsabilità civile da attività pericolose* (2001).
P. Della Sala, Natura giuridica dell'azione civile nel processo penale e conseguenze sul danno, [1989] *Rivista Italiana di Diritto Procedura Penale* (Riv. it. Dir. E Proc. pen.), 1079.
C. Salvi, *Le immissioni industriali. Rapporti di vicinato e tutela dell'ambiente* (1979), 397 *et seq.*
Sarlo, Sigarette e pubblicità ingannevole, [2002] *Diritto e Giustizia* (D&G) 38, 52.
S. Shavell, *Economic Analysis of Accident Law* (1987), 25.
Swiss Reinsurance Company (2003), *Natural catastrophes and man-made disasters in 2003* (Swiss Re SIGMA series 1, 2004).
P. Trimarchi, *Rischio e responsabilità oggettiva* (1961).
P. Trimarchi, *Per una riforma della responsabilità civile per danno all'ambiente* (1994).
P. Trimarchi/B. Pozzo/A. Gambaro/G. Villa/G. Bagnetti/E. Moretti/L. Rimini, *Per una riforma della responsabilità civile per danno all'ambiente* (1994).
G. Visintini, Il divieto di immissioni e il diritto alla salute nella giurisprudenza odierna e nei rapporti con le recenti leggi ecologiche, [1980] *Rivista di diritto commerciale* (Riv. dir. civ.), II, 262 *et seq.*
P. Ziviz, Le attività pericolose, in: P. Cendon (ed.), *La responsabilità civile a cura di Cendon* (1988), 543 *et seq.*
Zoani, Fumo da tabacco e tutela della salute dei lavoratori, [1995] *Massimario di giurisprudenza del lavoro* (Mass. giur. lav.), I, 180.
R. Zuccaro, Sulla responsabilità per l'esercizio di attività pericolose, [2001] *Giurisprudenza Italiana* (Giur. It.), 2275.

The Netherlands

Michael Faure and Ton Hartlief

Part I. Introduction

1 The Netherlands have, in the past decennium, been the victim of various types of catastrophes. In some cases it concerned natural disasters (more particularly an earthquake in Southern Limburg, flooding in South-East Netherlands and heavy rains); more recently there were also "man-made" disasters that led to a lot of attention in the media. In this respect more particularly the explosion of a fireworks factory in Enschede, the large fire in a café in Volendam and a legionella epidemic in Bovenkarspel were incidents that hit many victims. In all of these cases the question of course arose what legal instruments could be used to provide compensation. In this respect primarily the possibilities of tort law were examined. That was the case both as far as natural disasters were concerned (whereby for instance the question arose whether flooding was caused by negligence on the side of the water board) but more particularly in case of man-made disasters.

A common feature with all of these disasters is that victims, the press, but also many lawyers will often try to address the government for compensation. In some cases attempts will be undertaken to make the government liable for the catastrophes.[1] Victims will often address the government with a claim on compensation and this is more particularly the case when the damage cannot be compensated through the "normal" way (first party insurances, tort liability or liability insurance). In that case victims will often call on the government to claim compensation from the public budget.

2 The literature in the Netherlands has often pointed at the difficulties that victims will encounter in their attempts to obtain compensation for the financial

[1] See concerning the government liability for the consequences of catastrophes the various contributions in E.R. Muller/C.J.J.M. Stolker (eds.), *Ramp en Recht* (2001) and more particularly the special issue of the *Nederlands Juristenblad* (NJB) concerning liability of public authorities for failing supervision (E.R. Muller/C.J.J.M. Stolker, Overheidsaansprakelijkheid en toezicht, [2001] NJB, 1647 *et seq.*). The arrangements concerning the financial compensation of victims after catastrophes in the Netherlands has also been sketched in a research report by D.A. van den Wall Bake and others, *Eindrapportage. Inventarisatie van financiële voorzieningen na rampen in Nederland* (Utrecht, 1 March 2004) written on the request of the Commission for the Compensation in Case of Catastrophes and Incidents.

consequences of catastrophes through the "normal" ways. For instance, the possibility to apply tort law in case of natural disasters (such as flooding or earthquake) will often be difficult for the simple fact that a liable injurer may often be lacking.[2] Also in the case of e.g. air pollution, the number of victims may be that widespread and the damage may come from unknown sources that this inhibits the use of liability law.[3] But also in cases where tort law can theoretically be applied it does not mean that victims will also be compensated. One problem is that liability coverage is often excluded if the damage was caused with intent.[4] In addition, the problem often arises that the injurers are often not or only to a limited extent insured. Therefore it is logical that in those cases victims will often address the only solvent debtor: the government. This is moreover the case when damage occurs for which victims would have liked to seek insurance coverage, but where that coverage was unavailable. That was more particularly for a long time the case concerning damage as a result of natural disasters (earthquakes, flooding and heavy rain).[5]

3 This issue has thus given rise to various occasions where the Dutch government has indeed intervened with public budget to provide *ad hoc* compensation to the victims, albeit that the legal arrangements in that respect are not unified and that the arrangements have been the subject of criticism. As we will sketch below, a specific Act (*Wet Tegemoetkoming Schade bij Rampen en Zware Ongevallen*, WTS) was created with the aim to provide compensation to the victims of catastrophes. However, in practice it appeared that this Act could often not be applied to cases where many victims suffered harm as a result of a disaster. Therefore one could notice that in addition to the statutory arrangement in the WTS the Dutch government (and other organizations) have also created *ad hoc* solutions for specific victims. Some of the problems with respect to the insurability of disasters and the solutions via these collective arrangements will be addressed below. However, it is not possible within the scope of this report to discuss all of these arrangements in detail; therefore we will mainly focus on the most important arrangements from the perspective of the compensation of victims of catastrophes.[6]

For the reasons mentioned above (more particularly the fact that the government still often had to intervene on an *ad hoc* basis, notwithstanding the existence of the statutory basis in the WTS) the system in the Netherlands has been

[2] See T. Hartlief, Schadefondsen en de rol van de overheid, in: *Kring van aansprakelijken bij massaschade* (2002), 61 *et seq*.

[3] M. Faure/T. Hartlief/M. Hertoghs, *Evaluatie van het Fonds Luchtverontreiniging* (2000), 12–16.

[4] See for the problems in that respect H. Vos, De opzetclausule in: T. Hartlief/M.M. Mendel (eds.), *Verzekering en maatschappij* (2000), 57 *et seq*.

[5] See in this respect the contributions of M. Faure/T. Hartlief, Vergoeding van rampschade, in: E.R.Muller/C.J.J.M. Stolker (eds.), *Ramp en Recht* (2001), 151 *et seq*. and J.E. van de Bunt, Voorgeschiedenis van de WTS. Beschouwing over verschillende regelingen ter vergoeding van rampschade, in: E.R. Muller/C.J.J.M. Stolker (eds.), *Ramp en Recht* (2001), 176 *et seq*.

[6] Therefore more general arrangements, like a specific fund for the compensation of victims of crime and a specific fund to compensate victims of air pollution will not be discussed within the scope of this report for the simple reason that these compensation arrangements do not specifically address catastrophes.

subject to much criticism and is now in full revision. A specific committee has received the task of addressing alternative compensation solutions for the victims of catastrophes and it is likely that the recommendations of this committee may lead to legislative changes in the near future. Some of these recent developments, criticisms and proposals for reform will be addressed as well.[7]

Part II. General Scope of the Compensation

In the introduction we already sketched on what systems the victims of catastrophes in the Netherlands will generally rely to obtain compensation for their damage. Usually a combination of legal instruments will be used, whereby largely a distinction can be made between personal injury on the one hand and property damage on the other hand and the case of the natural disasters on the one hand and the case of man-made disasters on the other hand. In that respect, the general structure of the compensation system in the Netherlands is relatively compatible to solutions in other legal systems. 4

Indeed, as far as personal injury is concerned, victims will primarily be able to rely on the social security system that will provide them with a basic guarantee against income losses as a result of disability; social security will moreover also take care of the medical bills and health care expenses (depending on whether one has private insurance or not this coverage will be more or less very generous). However, social security usually only covers a part of the damage. For instance the top of one's income will usually not be compensated under social security, nor will there be compensation for the non-pecuniary losses. In that respect, the victim will just have to look for additional compensation mechanisms whereby tort and insurance are the primarily indicated systems.[8] 5

Tort can obviously only be used when a liable injurer can be found. In that respect a distinction can generally be made between natural disasters and man-made disasters. In case of natural disasters it will usually not be the case that a liable injurer can be found (except in the case of liability of public authorities), whereas with most man-made disasters an injurer can usually be identified.[9] If the injurer can be held liable and is solvent (or has liability insurance to cover his obligations), the victim can receive coverage through tort law.

If this is not the case, the victim can, in some cases, call on a personal accident insurance that might provide compensation for personal injury. Most of these accident insurances provide for lump sum payments (and sometimes additional coverage of lost income for the part not covered under social security) to cover the damage resulting from personal injury. However, these personal accident insurances are not mandatory and the scope of coverage therefore very much depends upon the policy conditions. Note that with these personal

[7] Within the scope of this contribution we could only take into account recent evolutions until 1 November 2004.

[8] In that respect it is sometimes argued that social security provides an *Existenzsicherung*, whereas tort law provides the "luxury" of full coverage. See M. Faure/T. Hartlief, Economic perspectives, in: U. Magnus (ed.), *The Impact of Social Security Law on Tort Law* (2003), 228–229.

[9] Again with some exceptions, for instance when pollution caused personal injury damage and the source cannot be identified.

accident insurances coverage will usually take place for personal injury damage irrespective of the source of the damage. As far as personal injury is concerned, these insurances may thus cover both in case of natural as well as in case of man-made disasters.

If there is no liable injurer and no first party insurance covering the damage, the victim might call on specific compensation regimes if these apply to his particular situation. For instance if he is a victim of crime, the victim may call on the crime compensation fund. In other cases he may call on specific *ad hoc* compensation mechanisms if the government (for political reasons) decided that for that particular risk compensation needed to be made available.

6 A similar structure governed the situation of the victim of property damage although there are a few important differences. A victim of property damage will not be able to call on social security. He will thus have a larger need to use alternative compensation mechanisms like tort or private insurance. As far as tort law is concerned the same possibilities and limits apply as with personal injury damage: there may be possibilities in case of man-made disaster (provided that a solvent liable injurer can be found), but less so in case of natural disasters. An additional difficulty is that, in case of property damage, insurance coverage may be particularly difficult and until recently to a large extent even not available. Dutch insurers indeed considered the damage caused by natural disasters as uninsurable and as a result of that they had excluded damage resulting from risks such as earthquake, flooding or heavy rain from coverage. This *de facto* led to the situation that those victims suffering property damage as a result of natural disasters could only call on *ad hoc* solutions through government (or other) aid to obtain compensation of their damage. Some victims, more particularly farmers or owners of greenhouses suffering crop damage as a result of heavy rainfall, were relatively successful. They indeed sometimes succeeded in convincing the government to apply the specific statutory solution (WTS) that provides additional indemnification for specific victims of natural disasters.

Part III. More Specific Information

I. Liability Law

7 As already indicated above liability law can in principle in the Netherlands be used by victims of a catastrophe in order to obtain financial compensation. Of course the conditions for liability according to Dutch tort law then have to be fulfilled.[10] In the Netherlands recently a debate has been going on concerning

[10] We are not going to discuss the details of Dutch tort law within the framework of this contribution on the financial compensation of victims of catastrophes. It seems more interesting to generally sketch the possibilities and limits of tort law in this respect. The reader interested in a more detailed analysis of recent evolutions in Dutch tort law, also taking into account case law can consult the various contributions to the Yearbooks on European tort law, the most recent one being M. Faure/T. Hartlief, The Netherlands, in: H. Koziol/B.C. Steininger (eds.), *European Tort Law 2003* (2004), 278–315.

the goals of tort law. Where traditionally in the Netherlands tort law was mainly seen as a system to compensate victims, nowadays other functions are stressed as well. In that respect increasing attention is paid to the preventive effects of tort law.[11] In addition to mentioning the preventive effect, others also point at the fact that liability rules could play an important role in recognizing the damage that has been suffered by the victim.[12] Finally it is also stressed that tort law has an important function in order to contribute to a correct allocation of the costs of accidents.

However, differently than in the economic analysis of law, traditional Dutch tort lawyers still have difficulties accepting a preventive function of the traditional tort rules like the negligence based art. 6:162 *Burgerlijk Wetboek* (Civil Code, BW).[13] This notion certainly also played a role at the occasion of the introduction in 1995 of certain specific strict liabilities for damage caused as a result of dangerous substances and waste sites (art. 6:175 of the Civil Code).[14]

From this brief introduction to the functions of Dutch tort law it follows that 8
the literature recognizes (with different accents) various functions in (Dutch) tort law, like prevention, compensation and the correct allocation of costs. However, these theoretical discussions of course do not guarantee that in a specific case a victim of a catastrophe will effectively be able to use tort law in order to obtain compensation. The problem is indeed that, no matter what function one wishes to see in tort law, generally tort liability always requires some shortcoming on the side of the wrongdoer.[15] Indeed, generally liability is possible either in case of (1) an attributable wrongful act of a third party, (2) the attributable wrongful act of someone other than the liable party or (3) a liability for damage caused by objects. There are of course differences between these three general types of liability in Dutch tort law (some are based on negligence, whereas others are more strict liabilities). The common denominator is, however, that in all of these cases some form of shortcoming on the side of the defendant will have to be proven by the victim. In the literature it has been pointed out that, as a result, tort law is (also in the Netherlands) primarily considered as a system that steers the behaviour of the potential injurer.[16] A consequence of this main focus of tort law on the behaviour of the injurer is that as such tort law is a problematic legal remedy for the victim who wishes to achieve compensation. Indeed, in order to obtain compensation for the finan-

[11] See for instance C.C. van Dam, *Zorgvuldigheidsnorm en Aansprakelijkheid* (1989), 199 *et seq.*, T. Hartlief, *Ieder draagt zijn eigen schade* (1997), no. 8 *et seq.* and S.D. Lindenbergh/A.R. Bloembergen, *Schadevergoeding: algemeen, deel 1*, monografie NBW (2nd edn. 2002), no. 8.

[12] See in this respect more particularly the contributions to G.E. van Maanen (ed.), *De rol van het aansprakelijkheidsrecht bij de verwerking van persoonlijk leed* (2003).

[13] Some of the more recent literature is, however, more positive concerning preventive effects of tort law. See *inter alia* W.H. van Boom, *Structurele fouten in het aansprakelijkheidsrecht* (2003).

[14] See *inter alia* W. Snijders, Aansprakelijkheid voor milieuverontreiniging: het verzekeringsaspect, [1993] *Aansprakelijkheid en Verzekering* (A&V), 1 *et seq.*

[15] So T. Hartlief (*supra* fn. 11), no. 22 *et seq.*

[16] See for instance J.M. Barendrecht, Aansprakelijkheid en welzijn, [2002] NJB, 612.

cial damage caused by the catastrophe, the victim will have to satisfy relatively stringent conditions. Other systems (like private and social insurances) have considerably lower thresholds and are therefore, as it has often been held in the literature, better able to compensate damage. As a consequence, only a relatively small part of damage that is caused in society is compensated by using tort law.[17] This is generally true but certainly also as far as the compensation of damage caused by catastrophes is concerned. As far as compensation is concerned, tort law will often lose the competition with other systems (like social security and insurance).[18]

9 As was already indicated, tort law will more particularly play only a modest role in the compensation of victims of catastrophes for the simple reason that more particularly with natural disasters a liable injurer can often not be identified. The only cases where liability law could thus play a role are either the man-made disasters or the natural disasters where there could be liability of public authorities. On the occasion of several floodings at the beginning of the 1990s the possibilities of the liability of public authorities were examined.[19] In that respect various shortcomings of public authorities were mentioned, more particularly:

- lack of maintenance of rivers, canals and mechanisms to prevent flooding;
- late warning for flooding;
- issuing licenses to build in flood prone areas;
- failure to act whereas there was reason to take measures based on previous floodings.

10 The case law will judge the liability of the water board on the basis of various criteria.[20] Elements that play to the advantage of the public authorities are generally the fact that the authority has discretionary power to act and usually only limited means at its disposal. This may lead the judge to a restrictive application of liability of public authorities, but that is far from certain.

Liability of public authorities may not only play a role in case of failure to prevent natural disasters. Also in case of man-made disasters (and we indicated in the introduction that in recent years the Netherlands has been confronted with many) the question has been asked whether shortcomings of public authorities have contributed to the accident risk. For instance, on the occasion of some of the recent disasters the following shortcomings were mentioned:

[17] See R.R. Bloembergen, *Schade lijden en schade dragen* (1980), 16–17.

[18] So it was orderly held by H. Drion, *Verzekering en aansprakelijkheidsrecht* (inauguration address 1955) (1959), 4–5.

[19] See more particularly T. Hartlief, Vergoeding van watersnoodschade, [1995] NJB, 311 *et seq.* and T. Hartlief, Vergoeding van watersnoodschade, in: M. Faure/F. Stroink (eds.), *Recht in het water. De juridische aspecten van watersnood* (1995), 131–142 as well as M. Hertoghs, Hoogwater in Den Haag: de rol van de Rijksoverheid, in: M. Faure/F. Stroink (eds.), *Recht in het water. De juridische aspecten van watersnood* (1995), 35–62.

[20] As determined by the *Hoge Raad der Nederlanden* (Dutch Supreme Court, HR) in HR 9 October 1981, [1982] *Nederlandse Jurisprudentie* (NJ), 332 with case note by C.J.H. Brunner, HR 8 January 1999, [1999] NJ, 319 with case note by A.R. Bloembergen.

- as far as the legionella infection in Bovenkarspel was concerned, the question was raised whether the authorities could be made liable for a lack of adequate regulation and/or a lack of enforcement of existing regulations;
- on the occasion of the catastrophic New Year's Eve fire in the café in Volendam the question was again asked whether the regulations concerning the prevention of fires had been sufficiently enforced;
- on the occasion of the explosion of the fireworks factory in Enschede various shortcomings of different authorities may have contributed to the risk. For instance, the central government was blind to the fact that nothing had been done with the information acquired at the occasion of a previous explosion of a fireworks factory a few years before in Culemborg. However, blame was equally addressed to local authorities for failing to control regulations and permit conditions.

In all those cases the liability of public authorities is theoretically possible. However, it will of course depend on the assessment by the courts whether this liability will effectively be accepted or not.[21] For instance as far as a liability for a lack of control and enforcement is concerned, until recently legal doctrine held that there is no formal duty of public authorities to enforce legislation, so that it is highly questionable whether a lack of enforcement can indeed give rise to liability. Moreover the victim may also be confronted with causation problems since the question can of course be asked in what respect a shortcoming of public authorities can be considered the cause of the victim's loss.

The reason victims often seek (or at least discuss) the possibilities of public 11
authorities are of course linked to the fact that victims of catastrophes may often not be compensated through the liable injurer or through first party insurances. Indeed, the problem with a liability claim on direct injurers has already been mentioned. In case of natural disasters there simply may not be a liable injurer; in case of man-made disasters this may be the case, but a lack of (or limited) liability insurance and limited solvency of the injurer may make a liability claim on the direct injurer not very effective. This explains why victims increasingly seek recovery through liability of public authorities although it is until now still doubtful that the case law in the Netherlands will also award those claims. However, the call on public authorities giving the lack of compensation through other instruments is a reality and some have therefore held that, in case of catastrophes, authorities may well be inclined to organize *ad hoc* compensation for victims also to reduce the likelihood of liability claims.

II. Social Security

As indicated earlier social security will play a primary role in the compensa- 12
tion of damage suffered as a result of personal injury, but less so as far as property damage is concerned. Without going into detail it should be men-

[21] See in this respect W. van Boom/I. Giesen, Civielrechtelijke overheidsaansprakelijkheid voor het niet voorkomen van gezondheidsschade door rampen, [2001] NJB, 1676.

tioned that (although there have been important changes in recent years) the scope of protection of social security law in the Netherlands is still relatively broad, at least as far as personal injury damage is concerned.[22] For instance, a national insurance covers in principle all citizens against the loss of maintenance caused by the death of a breadwinner. However, strict income thresholds apply and the number of beneficiaries is reduced. The effects of personal injury on employees' income are covered through a variety of complicated arrangements. Indeed, employees generally receive a higher protection than other groups of the population (like self-employed individuals).

13 Generally it is important to remember that – also in the Netherlands – social security thus provides relatively easy (although with more stringency in recent years) coverage, but the amount of compensation is limited. The easy character of the compensation lies in the fact that the victim usually only has to prove a certain illness or other condition that satisfies the statute, but the cause of the event is generally irrelevant and the contributory negligence of the victim is not taken into account in social security systems.[23] However, as a result of these low thresholds, the compensation provided as a result of social security will necessarily be limited. It therefore thus plays a role in compensating (part of) health care expenses and income losses, but it does not provide compensation for non-pecuniary losses, nor for the (luxury of) compensating the top of one's income, nor for property damage. For those heads of damage the victim will therefore have to rely on other systems like tort or private insurance.

III. Insurance

14 Above we already made clear that accident insurances may play a role in providing additional coverage for personal injury damage. This may be important for the parts of damage not covered under social security. In that case it usually concerns first party insurances taken out by the victim for which the victim himself pays a premium *ex ante*. Depending on the formulation in the insurance policy, the insurance will provide cover irrespective of the cause of the accident. In that sense a first party accident insurance may also provide cover when damage occurred as the result of a catastrophe. Thus first party accident insurances may have benefited those victims who suffered personal injury losses as a result of the recent (man-made) disasters in Volendam and Enschede. As we already indicated, the situation of victims of natural disasters, especially those suffering property damage, may be more problematic since for a long time the damage caused by natural disasters such as flooding, heavy rain or earthquakes was excluded from insurance coverage.

[22] For details see C.E. du Perron/W.H. van Boom, The Netherlands, in: U. Magnus (ed.), *The Impact of Social Security Law on Tort Law* (2003), 153–155.

[23] There are, however, some exceptions as a result of which contributory negligence may equally limit the victim's right on compensation in social security. See in that respect S. Klosse, Vergoeding als noodverband?, [2003] *Aansprakelijkheid Verzekering en Schade*, (AV&S), 25–33 and W.H. van Boom, Waarheen leidt de weg … van werknemersschade?, [2003] AV&S 2003, 33–40.

In the 1950s Dutch insurers made so-called binding decisions which apply to all of their members prohibiting them from insuring flood and earthquake risks (the latter being relatively small in the Netherlands with the exception of the area around Southern Limburg).[24] The argument of the insurers was that these risks were technically not insurable and that therefore all its members should refrain from covering them.[25] This point of view of the Dutch insurers association was of course remarkable: those who ran the risks of being hit by those natural disasters could thus simply not receive any coverage as the result of the simple fact that the insurers had agreed not to cover those risks. The Dutch insurers claimed that they feared a large damage (a natural disaster could cause an accident with billions of Euro in damage) and also claimed to have too little statistical material to calculate the premiums and thus feared adverse selection. The latter risk related to the danger that insurers claimed that only those who would largely be exposed to the risk would have a demand for insurers; good risks would have no demand for coverage.[26] Insurers therefore claimed that if good risks had no demand for insurance, there would be adverse selection and coverage would be impossible. 15

However, as a result of an earthquake close to Roermond in 1992 and the flooding of the river Maas in 1993, the binding decisions not to cover the damage costs as a result of natural disasters came under increasing political pressure. As a result, the binding decision concerning earthquakes was quickly withdrawn. Moreover, the pressure on insurers also to abrogate the binding decision not to cover flooding increased. This had on the one hand to do with political pressure on insurers,[27] but also with the fear that the European competition authorities may dislike the binding agreement. The latter fear was correct since the binding decisions clearly violated the conditions of regulation 3932/92.[28] Consideration 8 preceding the exemption clearly states that standard policy conditions may in particular not contain any systematic exclusion of specific types of risk without providing for the express possibility of including that cover by agreement. This is repeated in art. 7 (1) (a) of the exemption. In its report to the European Parliament of 12 May 1999,[29] the Commission explicitly discusses these binding decisions.[30] The report states that,

[24] See for the contents of this binding decision T. Hartlief (*supra* fn. 19), 142–143.

[25] For details see M. Faure/T. Hartlief, *Insurance and expanding systemic risks* (2003), 223–225.

[26] During the parliamentary proceedings (see *Kamerstukken* (Documents of the Second Chamber of Representatives) *II* 1993–1994, 23 564, no. 3, 15) it was argued by Minister Andriessen that only approximately 13% of the population would have a demand for an insurance against the risk of flooding.

[27] See for instance the questions that were posed to the government in *Kamerstukken II* 1993–1994, 23 564, no. 3.

[28] Regulation no. 3932/92 of 21 December 1992 on the application of art. 85 (3) of the Treaty to certain categories of agreements, decisions and concerted practices in the insurance sector, *Official Journal* L 398/7 of 31 December 1992. For comments on this exemption regulation see G. Levie/H. Cousy (eds.), *La politique Européenne de concurrence en matière d'assurance* (1994).

[29] Report of the Commission to the European Parliament and to the Council concerning the operation of the exemption regulation 3932/92 (COM(1999) 92 final).

[30] See report, no. 18, 9.

as a result of the questions asked by the Commission, the Dutch association of insurers decided to bring its binding decisions in line with art. 7.1 sub. a by simply converting it into a non-binding recommendation, leaving each insurer free to extend cover to flood risks. However, this example shows that non-competitive practices are apparently not an exception in Dutch insurance practice.

As a result of this in the 1990s, discussions took place between insurers and the Dutch government to come to a new system of coverage for natural disasters whereby the French model played an important role. These debates finally led to the introduction of the WTS 1998 which provides compensation in case the damage is uninsurable. We will discuss the contents of this WTS below.[31]

16 Important is that, as a principle, the specific public compensation under the WTS only takes place when the damage is considered uninsurable. Therefore the question still arises in what respect damage resulting from natural disasters can be considered insurable. This has meanwhile become more important since the mentioned binding decisions have, as the result of the mentioned pressure from the European competition authorities, been abrogated. In the literature it has been held that the arguments of insurers concerning adverse selection (which would make the risk uninsurable) would be simply wrong. It was held that the traditional remedy against adverse selection, being risk differentiation, can of course be applied to insurance of natural disasters as well. Some citizens may not have a demand for coverage at all, in which case there is no point in making coverage for them compulsory. Others may be exposed e.g. to the risk of flooding, but the risk may be a minor one whereas again others (those living in riskier areas) may be exposed to a higher risk. Classic principles of insurance then teach that an adequate differentiation between those risks (with corresponding differentiated premiums) can provide an adequate remedy to adverse selection and thus make the risks caused by natural disasters insurable as well.[32]

This increasing pressure on insurers seem to have worked since by the end of the 1990s the Dutch insurers changed their attitude and for instance stated that they were prepared to cover damage as a consequence of heavy rains.[33] Also damage to crops as a result of heavy rains would now be considered insurable by the Dutch insurers. The fact that the public funding mechanism offered under the WTS 1998 clearly was not applicable in all cases where risks would in principle be insurable played an important role in this respect. This of course increased pressure on insurers to actually provide this coverage as well.

[31] See *infra* Part III.IV.

[32] This has been argued by M. Faure/T. Hartlief, *Nieuwe risico's en vragen van aansprakelijkheid en verzekering* (2002), 187–189 and M. Faure/T. Hartlief, Schade als gevolg van natuurverschijnselen: de betekenis van de WTS, [2001] *Milieu en Recht* (MenR), 240–246.

[33] See the letter of the Secretary of State of Internal Affairs, De Vries, *Kamerstukken II* 1999–2000, 24 071, no. 55 *et seq.*

This story makes clear that although there are undoubtedly great benefits in cooperation between insurers in the case of the Netherlands the binding decisions indicate that this cooperation may effectively also limit or even exclude coverage. Even when the binding decisions were abrogated in fact the negotiations between the government and the monopolistic Dutch association of insurers determined the conditions under which coverage of damage caused by (natural) disasters would be possible. According to legal doctrine, this shows that an effective competition policy is highly indicated in order to increase a wide and differentiated supply of insurance policies.[34] 17

Meanwhile, after these binding decisions were withdrawn, various negotiations took place between the government authorities and the insurers concerning the possibility of providing insurance for agricultural damage caused by water, more particularly by heavy rain. As a result of these negotiations, the insurers reached already in 2002 an agreement with the government whereby they agreed to offer agricultural water damage insurance through a pool. The pool would cover the damage up to an amount of € 50 million. If the damage were higher, the central government would provide a guarantee for an amount between € 50 and € 100 million. Moreover, a deductible of 25% would apply.[35] The insurance is especially meant to cover crop damage as a result of heavy rain. As a result of the deal the agricultural sector also agreed that, in case of damage caused by heavy rain, they would not additionally call on compensation from the government on an *ad hoc* basis. However, the already mentioned WTS 1998 would still remain applicable, for instance in case of damage caused by flooding.[36] However, since the guarantee by the central government principally constitutes State Aid the European State Aid procedure had to be followed[37] and on 15 October 2003 the subsidy provided by the central government (in the form of a guarantee) was approved by the European Commission.[38] At that moment it became possible for the market to start developing these crop damage insurances. As a result two pools were instituted, called Agriver and LTO Aquapol, which both applied for the subsidy in the form of a guarantee by the central government. On 18 March 2004 the government signed the guarantee agreement with Agriver and LTO[39] and since 19 March 2004 the insurer Agriver has offered insurance for crop damage against consequences of heavy rain, subsidised with a guarantee by the central government.[40]

Here one can therefore note an intervention of the government to facilitate the insurability of the risk caused by a catastrophe, more particularly the crop

[34] So M. Faure/R. van den Bergh, Restrictions of competition on imprudence markets and the applicability of EC antitrust law, [1995] *Kyklos*, 65–85 and for an application on the Netherlands M. Faure/R. van den Bergh, Aansprakelijkheidsverzekering, concurrentie en ongevallenpreventie, in: T. Hartlief/M.M. Mendel (eds.), *Verzekering en maatschappij* (2000), 315–342.

[35] See *Kamerstukken II* 2002–2003, 24071, no. 59, 1.

[36] *Kamerstukken II* 2002–2003, 24 071, no. 59, 2.

[37] See the letter of the Minister of Agriculture of 11 April 2003 (*Kamerstukken II* 2002–2003, 24 071, no. 60).

[38] *Kamerstukken II* 2003–2004, 24 071, no. 63.

[39] See *Kamerstukken II* 2003–2004, 24 071, no. 64.

[40] *Kamerstukken II* 2004–2005, 24 071, no. 65.

damage caused by heavy rainfall. A similar construction whereby the government also intervenes to facilitate insurability is also followed in the Netherlands as far as the terrorism risk is concerned. On 1 July 2003 the Dutch reinsurance society for terrorism damage was created.[41] It is a private enterprise in which two hundred insurance companies participate. Coverage is provided in various layers.[42] Insurers bring together an amount of € 400 million for a first layer; a second layer is provided by reinsurers for € 400 million and the central State provides an additional third layer of € 200 million, which brings the total capacity of the reinsurance pool for terrorism to € 1 billion. Criticism has been formulated in the literature on the intervention of the State for the terrorism risk. It was held in legal doctrine that the State should not intervene to provide reinsurance and thus intervene in the insurance market. Scholars hold that it would have been better to provide a structural solution (in the form of government compensation) by applying the WTS 1998 to the terrorism risk also.[43]

IV. WTS 1998

18 As we already mentioned, in the 1990s an intense debate took place in the Netherlands concerning the compensation for victims of catastrophes, more particularly of flooding, also on the occasion of the debate concerning the so-called binding decisions of the insurers not to cover natural disasters. Remarkably the Dutch government first contemplated introducing the French model of a compulsory additional coverage for natural disasters. Originally the government argued against the French solution since it was feared that the free consumer choice would be limited and that this compulsory system would lead to increased costs for the citizen.[44] Later the government apparently considered these problems as less important since it introduced a draft largely similar to the French solution: a fund would be installed financed through a tax on housing insurances. All insured (bad or good risks) would have to pay the tax. However, the Dutch Council of State formulated a negative advice concerning this draft. The Council argued that it would be more likely to let the government finance this risk; moreover the Council of State held that it would be likely that the risk of flooding could be insured.[45] The criticism of the Council of State was considered that serious that the government decided to withdraw the draft. In a next phase the Belgium example of the catastrophes fund of 1976 suddenly seemed appealing and this Act became the model for the so-called WTS, an Act concerning compensation of damage in case of catastrophes and large accidents. The goal of the WTS was to offer a more structural solution to the compensation of victims of catastrophes instead of the until then applicable system of *ad hoc* solutions. The WTS provides a right to

[41] *Nederlandse herverzekeringsmaatschappij voor terrorismeschaden NV* (NHT).

[42] For details see V.C. Ammerlaan/W.H. van Boom, De Nederlandse herverzekeringsmaatschappij voor terrorismeschaden, [2003] NJB 2330–2339.

[43] See for this criticism V.C. Ammerlaan/W.H. van Boom, [2003] NJB, 2334–2337.

[44] See *Kamerstukken II* 1993–1994, 23 400 VII, no. 34, 2 and for a further discussion of this parliamentary debate see M. Faure/T. Hartlief (*supra* fn. 32), 185–186.

[45] *Kamerstukken II* 1995–1996, 26 640, no. 1, 2–3.

compensation of damage and lays down the main principles of compensation.[46] The WTS is applicable in case of flooding as a result of fresh water or earthquakes that are considered a catastrophe or large accident in the sense of the WTS. However, art. 3 of the WTS in addition provides that the WTS can be declared applicable through a Royal Decree, which can only be the case if the government considers the incident as a catastrophe or large accident. The parliamentary proceedings make clear that such an accident at least requires that many governmental organisations and services of various disciplines must have intervened in a coordinated way and that the accident has endangered the health of many persons and moreover caused substantial damage.[47]

The WTS clearly has a subsidiary character which is made clear in the Act itself. Art. 4 for instance provides that the victim will receive compensation for particular heads of damage, like damage to a dwelling, commercial loss and property damage. Also other heads of damage can be declared to fall under the scope of the WTS, but pure economic loss will not be compensated since this is considered as a normal business risk.[48] Very important is that art. 4, 3 of the WTS stipulates that the victim is not entitled to compensation under the WTS when the damage was reasonably insurable or when the victim was able to obtain compensation from another source. The parliamentary proceeding made clear that a damage is considered as reasonably insurable when it is not generally excluded from coverage and that it is generally insurable without limiting conditions or excessively high costs. It is therefore explicitly mentioned that for instance damage to motor vehicles will not be compensated through the WTS since that type of damage is insurable.[49] If, however, insurance were theoretically possible, but victims would *de facto* not have used this possibility since the premium charged would not be proportional to the coverage provided, the WTS may be applicable again.[50] 19

The subsidiary nature of the WTS also has consequences for the relationship to liability law. Indeed, a consequence of art. 4, 3 is that the damage should not be recoverable from another source. The practice has shown that, as a result, the WTS may not be applicable in all cases of man-made disaster where in principle the damage can be claimed from a liable injurer. During the parliamentary proceedings the question was asked whether the WTS could be applied in case of damage caused by an airplane crash; immediately the government indicated that in such a case liability law would apply, so that the WTS would not be applicable.[51] The WTS therefore only can be applicable in case of damage as a consequence of natural disasters.[52] The subsidiary nature

[46] For details see F.J. de Vries, Vergoeding van Rampschade, [1998] NJB, 1908–1913, M. Faure/T. Hartlief (*supra* fn. 5), 149–172 and J.F. de Groot, Na de ramp. Een beschouwing over de toepassing van de WTS, [2004] *Overheid en Aansprakelijkheid* (O&A), 141–152.

[47] *Kamerstukken II* 1996–1997, 25 159, no. 3, 4–5.

[48] See *Kamerstukken II* 1996–1997, 25 159, no. 5, 25–26.

[49] See *Kamerstukken II* 1996–1997, 25 159, no. 3 15.

[50] *Kamerstukken II* 1996–1997, 25 159, no. 5, 7.

[51] *Kamerstukken II* 1996–1997, 25 159, no. 5, 3.

[52] See in this sense also M. Faure and T. Hartlief, [2001] MenR, 241 *et seq.*

of the WTS can appear from two circumstances: either the WTS is applicable, but certain heads of damage are recoverable from another source and therefore not covered under the WTS or the WTS is not applicable at all, given the claim possibilities in tort law. The recent events in Enschede and Volendam made painfully clear how limited in fact the impact of the WTS is for catastrophes that are not natural disasters. In these cases the government has financially intervened in a very generous way, but not through the WTS. This may show that the legislator has not succeeded in its (at least implicit) attempt to create with the WTS an exclusive arrangement for government contributions in case of catastrophes.

20 Indeed, recent overviews show that the WTS mainly applies to damage caused as a result of heavy rain.[53] De Groot claimed in a paper published in October 2004 that in its six years of existence the WTS was merely applied four times.[54] The first two times it was applied also concerned heavy cases of rain. Since in both cases the heavy rain did not concern a formal flood in the sense of art. 1 of the WTS, the WTS needed to be declared applicable by Royal Decree. It is of course a remarkable result that this statutory arrangement, which was specifically created by the legislator to compensate victims of catastrophes, has in fact merely been applied in case of damage caused by heavy rainfall (thus mainly touching the agricultural sector) but not in case of serious man-made disasters with heavy personal injuries like in the cases of Volendam and Enschede. It is therefore not surprising that this WTS has been the subject of criticism in the literature and is now most likely undergoing a serious revision.

V. Compensation Funds

21 In the Netherlands a debate has also taken place on the function of compensation funds. Some have, in the literature, advanced an increasing use of compensation funds, arguing that funds would be able to provide a remedy for all the shortcomings of liability law.[55] Others have been far more critical.[56] This call in legal doctrine for an increasing use of compensation funds has various sources. In some cases one argues that the compensation fund should intervene when the damage cannot be insured (more particularly in case of flooding and earthquakes), in other cases the fund should intervene to solve problems of tort liability (like lacking proof of a causal link or latency problems) and in some cases the fund should remedy insolvency problems. In some cases

[53] E. van der Schans, Regen als ramp. Wateroverlast en de WTS, [2000] *Tijdschrift voor Milieuaansprakelijkheid* (TMA), 13 *et seq.*

[54] J.R. de Groot [2004] O&A, 152.

[55] See for instance L. Dommering-Van Rongen, *Schade vergoeden door fondsvorming* (1996), L. Dommering-Van Rongen, Een schadefonds voor asbestslachtoffers, [1996] TMA, 97–101 and E. Bauw, Tussen traditie en efficiëntie; na een wettelijke regeling voor de afwikkeling van massaschade, [1995] NJB, 622–630.

[56] See *inter alia* M. Faure/T. Hartlief, Een schadefonds als alternatief voor aansprakelijkheid en verzekering?, [1998] *Rechtsgeleerd Magazijn Themis* (RM Themis), 211–228.

the funds have an *ad hoc* character, whereas in other cases the compensation funds are more or less structural.

Of all of these cases examples can be found in Dutch law. For instance *ad hoc* compensation took place after a flood in 1995 in Limburg with as background the fact that insurance for flooding was at the time not available. A more or less structural arrangement took place for victims of mesothelioom to deal with the problems of latency and insolvency of an employer. The structural fund to compensate victims of violent crime has a similar background: it aims to provide compensation in case of an unidentifiable or insolvent injurer. The compensation fund for damage caused by air pollution on the other hand primarily aims at solving problems in tort liability, like causation problems. Compensation after the catastrophes in Enschede and Volendam did not directly take place via a normal fund, but through the so-called national catastrophes fund which in fact is a private initiative, although the government provided substantial funds as well. Again it is remarkable that most of these arrangements took place outside of the scope of the earlier mentioned WTS 1998, although this arrangement was precisely created to provide a structural arrangement for the victims of catastrophes.

Of course we will not discuss all of these already existing compensation funds[57] since some of these may be of help to victims of some catastrophes, but most of them have not been erected with the particular goal to assist victims of catastrophes. This is for instance the case for the compensation fund for victims of violent crime[58] which provides compensation for personal injury damage caused by an intentional violent crime which caused serious personal injury to the victim. This is a subsidiary fund (social security and private insurance have priority over the fund) that provides some compensation to the victim based on equity. The maximum for property damage is € 22,700 and the maximum for non-pecuniary losses is € 9,100. The fund is financed through the general public budget. Only between 4,000–5,000 victims apply to this fund on a yearly basis, whereas the potential group of victims that could use the fund would be between 20,000 and 30,000.[59] In recent years there has been an increasing number of demands and compensation awards. This is partially due to the fact that insurers exclude all damage from coverage that has been caused intentionally.[60] The fund can of course be used by some victims of crimes that could qualify as "catastrophes" although the conditions are rather restrictive: the fact that the damage must have been the result of an 22

[57] There is moreover in the literature discussion to introduce compensation funds for other types of damage as well. This is more particularly the case for environmental damage, where the introduction of a compensation fund has been suggested as well.

[58] See for an analysis of this fund M.S. Groenhuijsen, Schadefondsen in Nederland en in het buitenland: supra nationale normen, rechtsvergelijkende en empirische beschouwingen, [2001] *Delikt en Delinkwent* (DD), 930–947.

[59] See *Kamerstukken II* 2000–01, 27400 VI, no. 59, 1–3.

[60] See on these highly debated insurance issues, J.H. Wansink, De aansprakelijkheidsverzekering en opzettelijk veroorzaakte schade: Een Januskop in beweging, [2000] AV&S, 14–17 and J.H. Wansink, Assurance oblige: de maatschappelijk verantwoord handelende verzekeraar in de 21e eeuw, [2003] AV&S, 50.

intentional violent crime may not apply to all man-made disasters (except perhaps the case of terrorism).

23 The same is probably the case for the fund for the compensation of air pollution damage. Also this fund is subsidiary in the sense that it only compensates when the victim cannot claim compensation from another source (insurance or tort law). The fund is again financed through the public budget. A recent assessment of the functioning of this fund[61] shows that:

- most of the compensation awards relate to the agricultural sector and concern damage to crops;
- personal injury damage is almost never compensated (given the availability of social security and insurances) and ecological damage is not compensated either since the fund requires that the damage must have been caused by a sudden polluting act;
- although the fund formally provides compensation based on equity, *de facto* the full loss of the successful claimant is often compensated.

On average this fund has not paid more that approximately € 100,000 on a yearly basis, which means that the importance of this fund compared to the real impact of air pollution damage can be considered as rather small. Again, this fund probably plays no significant role at all for damage caused by disasters.

24 As mentioned above, many *ad hoc* compensation funds could be mentioned as well.[62] For instance after a catastrophic air crash with an El Al plane that flew into an apartment building in the Amsterdam neighbourhood "Bijlmer" the government instituted the *Stichting Hulpfonds Gedupeerden Bijlmer ramp* (Foundation Compensation Fund to Victims of the Bijlmer Catastrophe) as a result of a demand of the parliament to provide help to those victims who, after several years, still suffer financial and psycho-social problems as a result of the catastrophe. Victims received a lump sum payment of 4,000 Guilders (approximately € 2,000) if it could be proven that he/she suffered psycho-social problems as a result of the catastrophe.

After it appeared that the damage caused by the so-called legionella epidemic in Bovenkarspel (North Holland) could not be recovered through liability law, the Dutch government erected a fund that was compatible to this Bijlmer catastrophes fund. The government made an amount of 2,000,000 Guilders (approximately € 1,000,000) available to a foundation that provided compensation to victims: they received a lump sum payment of 4,000 Guilders (€ 2,000) and descendants of a deceased received an amount of 10,000 Guilders (€ 5,000).

[61] See M. Faure/T. Hartlief/M. Hertoghs (*supra* fn. 3), 89 *et seq.* and M. Faure/T. Hartlief/M. Hertoghs, Evaluatie van het fonds luchtverontreiniging, [2000] MenR, 64–69.

[62] For an overview see T. Hartlief (*supra* fn. 2).

Whereas these are examples of *ad hoc* compensation funds related to particular incidents, a more structural arrangement has been created for the victims of mesothelioom. We will not discuss this fund in detail here since it relates to damage caused as a result of exposure to asbestos and is thus probably further related from the catastrophes as discussed in this book. It is, however, interesting that for the particular case of victims of asbestos a specific structural arrangement was brought into life. A victim can receive (again financed through the public budget) a lump sum payment of € 15,882 under the following conditions: 25

- he/she had to be alive on 6 June 1997;[63]
- that he/she incurred so-called maligne mesothelioom as a result of exposure to asbestos during work;
- no financial compensation from an employer was obtained and
- no possibilities of a claim against the employer exist either because the employer cannot be identified, thus no longer exists, is insolvent or because the statute of limitations has passed.[64]

If one would summarize certain trends when addressing all of these various compensation funds, one could argue that most of them have, in principle, a subsidiary nature, meaning that only that damage will be compensated which in principle cannot be compensated from any other source (social security, private insurance or tort law). However, one can also notice that the legal basis for creating a compensation fund for this particular type of victims is in every case different. In general one can notice that the government usually simply wants to make a gesture towards the victim as an expression of the solidarity of the community towards the victims. Only the compensation fund for air pollution damage is nowadays subject to much criticism, since apparently only the agricultural sector benefits from this fund, whereas one can equally doubt whether the types of damage that are today compensated through this fund are truly uninsurable. Thus it has been suggested recently in the literature whether this fund should probably not be abrogated and replaced by an arrangement whereby the agricultural sector itself would finance its compensation.[65] 26

Finally it should be mentioned that in the literature many critical voices have been heard as far as the existence of compensation funds is concerned. The crucial question that is always asked in this literature is why the government 27

[63] This was simply the date that the government took the decision to install the compensation arrangement.

[64] See on these arrangements also M. Faure/T. Hartlief, Een asbestfonds als alternatief voor aansprakelijkheid van de werkgever?, [1996] *Sociaal Recht*, (SR), 37 *et seq.* and J.P. Hustinx/C.J.J.M. Stolker, Massaschade en fondsvorming, [1997] *Verzekeringsarchief* (VA), 58–66 as well as A.E. Dek, Asbestontwikkelingen. Oprechte tegemoetkomingen of doekjes voor het bloeden?, [1999] TMA, 61–62.

[65] So E.H. Hulst, Actualiteiten milieuaansprakelijkheid. Schadelijk water en schadefonds, pleidooi voor adequate oplossingen!, [1999] TMA, 33 *et seq.* and M. Faure/T. Hartlief/M. Hertoghs (*supra* fn. 3), 98–99.

would install a particular compensation fund for the particular type of victims. This, so it is held, always means that a certain category of victims will receive preferential treatment, for which the legal basis seems to be doubtful. Of course it is argued that the compensation fund will never provide the "luxury of tort law", being full compensation, but only a "gesture of solidarity". The community cannot provide a full guarantee of the individual wealth of all of its citizens.[66] As long as a victim cannot successfully call on tort law, one can of course defend an intervention from the public budget based on a feeling of national solidarity (although the choice in this respect will always depend upon political will and thus be arbitrary). A consequence is, however, that also when a compensation fund exists will the victim, in most cases, still have to carry part of the damage itself.[67]

Part IV. Heads of Damage and Accumulation of Compensation

28 Already in discussing the details of the various compensation mechanisms under III we have sketched what the differences are concerning the heads of damage that can be compensated under the various systems and how the systems relate to each other. However, in order to promote the uniformity and comparability of the reports we summarize briefly the earlier findings.

As far as the heads of damage are concerned, we already made clear that, also in the Netherlands, tort law is the only system that awards the luxury of full compensation and guarantees a right to the victim of a *restitutio ad integrum*. This means that not only all pecuniary losses are compensated but also pure economic losses and non-pecuniary losses. However, we also indicated that the threshold for applying tort law is still relatively high since it only applies if some kind of shortcoming on the side of the injurer can be proven.

The opposite is true for the system of social security: in that case the thresholds are relatively low and the source of the illness or disability is not examined in detail. However, as indicated above, social security does not provide full compensation.[68] It rather provides a minimum and basically only covers the consequences of personal injury damage, not property damage. As far as the limits are concerned, usually compensation for the financial consequences of disability is also standardized (and thus limited) and social security will generally not compensate for non-pecuniary losses.

For the heads of damage not compensated under social security, the victim may try to call on private insurance. The heads of damage and the level of compensation in those cases of course largely depend upon the availability of insurance (which is, as we indicated, a problem in case of natural disasters) and upon the level of compensation provided for in the insurance policy. Accident insurance policies generally provide lump sum payments if the condi-

[66] See J.A.J. Peeters, Rampschade, [1980] NJB, 503–504. See also J.A.J. Peeters, Rampschade, in: M.J.P. Verburgh/A.R. Bloembergen/G.J. de Groot *et al.* (eds.), *Schade lijden en schade dragen* (1980), 59–84.

[67] So M. Faure/T. Hartlief [1998] RM Themis, 228.

[68] Although also in the Netherlands in recent years there has been an increasing pressure on the social security system. See in that respect M. Faure/T. Hartlief (*supra* fn. 8), 241–248.

tions of the policy (an accident) are fulfilled. Usually first party insurance policies in the Netherlands do not compensate non-pecuniary losses;[69] so far the Netherlands does not know a *garantie des accidents de la vie* as it exists in France that equally compensates for non-pecuniary losses. However, some may of course argue that the lump sum payments under accident insurances could represent some compensation for non-pecuniary losses as well. Also the part of one's lost income as a result of disability which is not compensated under social security can, again depending upon the policy conditions, be covered under first party insurance. Coverage of property damage is, however, more problematic, more particularly in the case of natural disasters.

As far as the various funds that we discussed are concerned, we indicated that the amounts awarded will largely depend upon the specific arrangement. However, with the exception of the (rather odd) fund for the compensation of air pollution damage most (*ad hoc* or structural) compensation funds only provided a lump sum payment that merely symbolizes a gesture towards the victims, but does not aim at providing full compensation. Also as far as the WTS 1998 is concerned (in the rare cases that is applies), it should be mentioned that it, in principle, covers pecuniary losses, but not pure economic losses since they are supposed to belong to the normal entrepreneurial risks. Property damage like damage to a dwelling is compensated, but a deductible and a maximum amount can be introduced. 29

As far as the combination between the different potential systems is concerned, it is important to stress that, like in other countries, also in the Netherlands are social security and private insurances the systems that will in principle generally pay out the compensation due as far as either the statutory (social security) or contractual (first party insurances) conditions are fulfilled and this irrespective of possibilities to recover in tort as well. Thus a social insurance carrier or first party insurer may be subrogated in the rights of the victim against the injurer and exercise a right of redress against the injurer, using tort law. Given the high costs of those redress actions these kind of actions are, however, not very popular in the Netherlands today.

Note that the other compensation systems, more particularly the various compensation funds and the WTS 1998 clearly declared to have a subsidiary character. In those cases one will therefore first principally examine whether the victim could obtain compensation via insurance or tort law from the injurer. The WTS goes even a step further by excluding all damage that was "reasonably insurable" (even if insurance may *de facto* not be available). These additional systems only intervene after the primary systems (social security, tort and insurance) have been exercised.

In addition we should briefly mention that the legal basis and possibilities of exercising the already mentioned rights of subrogation provide a rather complicated picture since every specific social security act has (in some cases dif- 30

[69] This is of course different with the third party liability insurance of the injurer that may have to intervene for the non-pecuniary losses suffered by the victim.

ferent) subrogation arrangements whereby also some limitations apply. It would lead us too far to discuss these complicated arrangements in detail within the scope of this paper; we will therefore limit ourselves to some general notions.[70]

First of all there is a general provision that applies to the first party insurer who is subrogated in the rights of the victim on the basis of art. 284 of the Commercial Code. In addition various social security acts provide separate subrogation rights to the institutions that paid the victim. The employer who had to pay the income of the victim during his disability also receives a right of redress against the liable injurer based on art. 6:107a of the Civil Code. If there is no statutory basis for a subrogation, the paying institution is dependant upon the formal transfer of the victim's claim against the liable injurer to the paying institution.[71] Again, within the framework of this chapter it is not useful to provide a detailed overview of these subrogation rights. We will therefore mainly point at some headlines.

There is relatively little debate on the subrogation right of the first party insurer on the basis of art. 284 of the Commercial Code. However, this article only applies to insurers that compensated the damage to the victim. A distinction is made with an insurer of a specific sum (like a life insurer); those do not enjoy a subrogation right.

31 Until recently the subrogation rights in the social insurances were relatively limited. An important role in that respect was the fact that, in the Dutch literature more particularly Bloembergen (former member of the Hoge Raad), has voiced severe criticism of subrogation rights.[72] He argued that it would be meaningless to transfer money from one collectivity to the other, thus the exercise of a subrogation right would have no sense at all. However, in the 1990s the approach changed, with an important argument that the exclusion of subrogation rights would lead to an incorrect allocation of costs. Thus a government report argued that also social insurance carriers should be able to exercise redress rights since otherwise an incorrect pricing of socially dangerous activities would take place. This reasoning has again given rise to much criticism.[73] Notwithstanding the criticism in legal doctrine, the subrogation rights

[70] For a further more detailed analysis see G.E. van Maanen/P. Römers, *De tijdelijke regeling verhaalsrechten, verhaalsmogelijkheden voor verzekeraars en uitkeringsinstanties* (1994), S.P. de Haas/T. Hartlief, *Collectivering en institutionalisering van regres* (1996) and especially the recent dissertation of E. Engelhard, *Regres. Een onderzoek naar het regresrecht van particuliere en sociale schadedragers* (2003).

[71] Based on art. 3:94 in combination with 3:84 of the Civil Code.

[72] See A.R. Bloembergen, Het verhaalsrecht van de risicodrager in de algemene wet zware geneeskundige risico's, [1996] *Sociaal Maandblad Arbeid* (SMA), 329–330 and A.R. Bloembergen, Aansprakelijkheidsrecht en sociale verzekering: nieuwe ontwikkelingen, [1970] SMA, 74–80.

[73] *Inter alia* again by A.R. Bloembergen, Het SER-rapport over regresrechten: een fout verhaal, [1994] NJB, 117–123, T. Hartlief/G.E. van Maanen, Regres bij volksverzekeringen. De dader heeft het gedaan, [1994] *Nederlands Tijdschrift voor Burgerlijk Recht* (NTBR), 75–78 and G.E. van Maanen, Permanente beperking van verhaalsmogelijkheden van particuliere en sociale schadeverzekeraars, [1994] A&V, 94–97.

have been expanded, with as effect that almost all social security institutions can now exercise a right of redress against the liable injurer.

Interesting is that since the employer is forced to pay the income of the employee who has a disability to work as a result of an accident (at least for a certain period), art. 6:107a of the Civil Code now grants a right of the employer to recover this income paid from a liable third party.[74] An important aspect in this respect is that the legislator realized that an increasing financial risk will have to be paid by the employer. Moreover, the subrogation by the employer does not increase the liability of the third party. It only means that the injurer will now (for the lost income) not be sued by the victim but by the employer who paid the income during the period of disability. Of course the subrogation right of the employer is limited to the amount that the victim could have claimed himself from a liable third party. This is also referred to as the "civil limit". There are, however, in practice, many difficulties in correctly assessing the limits and scope of this so-called "civil limit".[75]

There is one final recent evolution that is worth mentioning, being the fact that 32 the increasing (administrative) costs of subrogative actions have led to so-called institutionalization and collectivization of redress actions. The bottom line of this tendency is that for instance social insurance carriers and liability insurers agree not to exercise redress any longer on an individual basis, but to do so collectively. This simply means that a standardization takes place as a result of which liability insurers agree, e.g. on a yearly basis, to pay a fixed lump sum to social insurance carriers, corresponding with the amount they could approximately have claimed through redress.[76]

Part V. Empirical Evidence

It of course was within the scope of this report impossible to discuss all the ca- 33 tastrophes that have hit the Netherlands in detail. Some of them have already been mentioned in the introduction, more particularly the man-made disasters of Enschede and Volendam. The flooding has already been mentioned at the occasion of the discussion on insurability. We will briefly discuss the legionella case in Bovenkarspel (Part V.I), the flooding (Part V.II), Enschede (Part V.III) and Volendam (Part V.IV).

[74] See for further details R.Ph. Elzas, Regresrecht: ANW en veegwet, [1996] *Verzekeringsrechtelijke berichten* (Vrb), 4 *et seq.*, N. Frenk, Regresrecht voor werkgevers voor doorbetaald loon, [1996] A&V, 6–7 and W.H. van Boom, Het verhaalsrecht van de werkgever ex art. 6: 107a BW, [1995] *Weekblad voor Privaatrecht, Notariaat en Registratie* (WPNR) 6202, 863 *et seq.*

[75] For details see W.H. van Boom/H.M. Storm, Het verhaalsrecht van verzekeraars en risicodragers, [1995] A&V, 157 *et seq.*

[76] See on this collectivization also S.P. de Haas/T. Hartlief (*supra* fn. 70) and M. Faure, Regres in rechtseconomisch perspectief, in: W.H. van Boom/T. Hartlief/J. Spier (eds.), *Regresrecht. Afschaffen, handhaven of uitbreiden?* (1996), 45–71.

I. Legionella in Bovenkarspel

34 In 1999 an exhibition was organized by the West Friese Flora where apparently some legionella bacteria were present in whirlpools. As a result, many of the visitors of the exhibition, referred to as the West Friese Flora, suffered from the infection with the legionella bacteria, also know as the veteran disease. In the end 28 persons died as a result of the infection with legionella.[77] A claim was made against *inter alia* Mr. Jong, who had a whirlpool stand at the exhibition. The victims originally also brought a suit against the organizing institution, West Friese Flora in a summary proceedings, but the case against Jong continued to the *Hoge Raad*. It was indicated that the most likely source of the infection was that the whirlpool of Jong contained infected water. The contamination usually takes place when contaminated water is emitted in the form of very small particles which are subsequently inhaled by the victims. Known sources of contamination are all water circuits with a temperature under 50°C such as fountains, whirlpools, bathing areas and air-conditioning.

A procedure was initiated against an enterprise Jan Jong Holding BV who had exhibited a whirlpool at the time of the Flora which had bubbling water all the time at approximately 37.5°C. The Court of Appeal of Amsterdam[78] held that from a reasonable and careful dealer in whirlpools it can be expected that he should be aware of the normal dangers connected to the use of whirlpools and that he should be aware of the preventive measures that should be taken. The Court held that the dealer knew or should have known that in the water of a whirlpool a growth of the number of bacteria could take place and that therefore devices should be applied which could have stopped this process. The Court therefore holds that the dealer did not take sufficient safety measures to reduce the risk and is therefore held liable on the basis of the general article in tort law 6:162 of the Dutch Civil Code.

Interestingly enough the Court clearly stresses that the risk caused by bacteria in whirlpools was not unknown or unforeseeable and that moreover, this risk could have been prevented by taking adequate (and not too expensive) measures. Interesting as well is the fact that the dealer defended himself by arguing that there was no causal link between his whirlpool and the damage suffered by the victims (there were possibly other sources of legionella at the exhibition as well). This defence is, however, rejected precisely because the so-called reversal rule, just discussed, is applied: the dealer has violated a safety norm and has therefore acted wrongfully against the victim. When the risk then materialises, the causal link between the violation of the norm and the damage is therefore in principle given, unless the dealer could have proven that the damage would also have occurred without a violation of the safety norms.[79]

[77] Various contributions to the volume *Aansprakelijkheid en schadeverhaal bij rampen* (A.J. Akkermans/E.H. Brans (eds.), *Aansprakelijkheid en schadeverhaal bij rampen* (2002)) discuss the details of this case and the liability of all possible persons involved in this catastrophe.

[78] Court of Amsterdam, 4 January 2001, [2001] *Kort Geding* (KG), 40.

[79] For a comment on this case and for possibly other legal foundations see B. Maat, De legionella-affaire in Bovenkarspel en mogelijke toepasselijkheid van de aansprakelijkheid voor gevaarlijke stoffen, [2000] *Verkeersrecht* (VR), 353–358.

The dealer was therefore held liable and a subsequent appeal to the *Hoge Raad* was rejected.[80] It is, however, questionable whether this can be considered as a real victory since it appeared that the dealer only had liability insurance coverage to an amount which may not be sufficient to cover the claim.

In addition to this summary proceedings a case was also filed before the Civil Court of Alkmaar by the Consumer Union (*Consumentenbond*) against the firms who exhibited the whirlpools at the exhibition, against the State and against the West Friese Flora. A judgment was issued on 12 December 2002.[81] In this judgment the Civil Court of Alkmaar clearly benefits from the earlier mentioned summary proceedings. The Civil Court denies the claims against the State and the Flora, but sustains two claims against the whirlpool sellers. In that respect the Court followed the construction of the Court of Appeals of Amsterdam concerning the fact that an unwritten safety norm would have been violated.

This epidemic in the North of Holland has not only led to serious consequenc- 35
es in tort law, which we already discussed. The case also led to a changing of the regulation and to the erection of a fund for the victims of the legionella epidemic.[82] The government decided on 18 February 2002 to (again) make a gesture to the victims and the descendants in the form of a lump sum payment from a fund and this irrespective of any liability of the State. An amount of 2,000,000 old Dutch Guilders was made available which is managed by a foundation and the argument for this financial gesture was *inter alia* that the legionella epidemic in 1999 concerned a unique event and that the unforeseeable nature, the shocking emotional effects and the large number of victims made this epidemic so exceptional that it warranted financial intervention by the State. The victims (or the descendants) could receive a lump sum payment of 4,000 Guilders; in case of the death of the victim the descendants received 10,000 Guilders.[83]

As a comment on this case legal doctrine indicated that apparently regulation 36
should be able to prevent these kinds of disasters and that the intervention of the legislator after the epidemic once more showed the importance of regulation. Moreover, the case also showed that Dutch tort law can be used also in these cases of new risks that create a dangerous situation. But apparently (given the high number of victims) a financial contribution by the State was unavoidable as well, although the amount can probably still be considered as relatively limited.[84]

[80] See HR 29 November 2002, [2003] NJ, 549 with case note by JBM Vranken. For a discussion of this legionella case in Bovenkarspel see also M. Faure/T. Hartlief (*supra* fn. 32), 61–66.

[81] Civil Court of Alkmaar 12 December 2002, [2003] NJ, 68. For a comment M. Frenk, [2003] *Tijdschrift voor Pensioenvraagstukken* (TVP), 48 *et seq.*

[82] For a more detailed discussion of all of the legal consequences of this case see M. Faure/T. Hartlief (*supra* fn. 32), 61–66.

[83] These rules have been laid down in the so-called *Uitkeringsregeling Fonds Slachtoffers Legionella Epidimie*, [29 June 2000] *Staatscourant* (Stcrt.) no. 123, 11.

[84] See M. Faure/T. Hartlief (*supra* fn. 32), 66.

II. Flooding

37 Above we already discussed at various stages the flooding that hit the Dutch province of Limburg (and many other parts of the Netherlands) twice in the early nineties. Above we already mentioned that all of the various possible compensation mechanisms played a role in that respect. Hence we can be brief here. First of all the liability of public authorities was examined from different angles,[85] although there was actually not one claim filed against them.

In addition, particularly the floodings in the early nineties triggered the whole debate on the insurability of the consequences of natural disasters. Indeed, on the occasion of the floodings it became clear that the consequences of natural disasters were excluded from insurance coverage in the Netherlands based on a cartel agreement between insurers not to cover those risks.[86] Moreover, the absence of insurance coverage for these risks thus led to a debate on the compensation of victims of catastrophes which was precisely the reason for the introduction of the WTS 1998.[87]

38 However, all of these plans may help future victims; the victims of the flooding in the early nineties were still confronted with uncompensated losses and hence, also on the occasion of the floodings in the early nineties the Dutch government intervened with *ad hoc* compensation measures basically financed through the public purse.

III. Enschede

39 An already often mentioned example of a true catastrophe is the explosion of a fireworks factory in Enschede on 13 May 2000.[88] It concerns here the consequences of explosions that took place after a fire in the fireworks factory of S.A. Fireworks. As a result, many lost their lives and several were injured and a whole neighbourhood was more or less extinguished. The damage amounted at least to several hundred million Euros. The question of course arises how that damage has in practice been compensated. Of course a claim could and has been filed against the liable company based on tort law. However, it became immediately clear that this corporation was only to a limited extent able to compensate the damage: the total amount of insurance available compared to the total amount of the damage is hardly worth mentioning. A claim in tort will therefore never lead to compensation of the victims. As a result, again the question was asked whether other mechanisms could be used to compensate the victims.

The catastrophe in Enschede is interesting since it shows very clearly the limited scope of the specific Act that should provide compensation to victims of catastrophes, the WTS 1998. This Act was not declared applicable to the

[85] See *supra* no. 9.
[86] See *supra* no. 15.
[87] See *supra* no. 18.
[88] See for the legal consequences and compensation arrangements after this catastrophy also J.J. van der Helm, Tegemoetkomingregelingen na de vuurwerkramp, [2003] TVP 40–44.

catastrophe in Enschede for the simple reason that the government argued that it concerned largely insurable damage. As far as victims are concerned, one can of course think of various first party insurances that have or could have covered the losses of the victim; as far as corporate damage is concerned one can again think about various corporate insurances that would have covered the losses. However, although the WTS 1998 was not declared applicable the government argued that as far as the damage was not insured victims could receive some compensation through a national catastrophes fund (*Stichting Nationaal Rampenfonds*, NRF).[89] The latter is an interesting construction: it is in principle a private initiative and thus a privately run fund to which the government (generously) donates funds.

In this specific case the community of Enschede provided first aid and paid funeral costs and other related costs. For victims who were not (sufficiently) insured the community received a contribution from this NRF.[90] For corporations a specific fund was created to make advance payments and provide loans.[91] The already mentioned NRF thus provided compensations for the citizens; companies could not call on help from the NRF.

40 After the disaster the community of Enschede created the so-called commission for the financial settlement of the fireworks disaster (*Commissie Financiële Afwikkeling Vuurwerkramp*, CFA). In this commission there were representatives from the community and province as well as from the insurers and the NRF. The central government only acted as "observer". The task of this CFA was to make an inventory of the damage and to determine to what extent some victims were not or were underinsured.[92] The CFA then had to formulate disposals for additional compensation to the community of Enschede. This CFA proposed various arrangements for non-insured damage, which were also largely implemented. As far as the damage of individual citizens is concerned they dealt *inter alia* with[93] compensation for lost furniture, compensation for damaged cars (that were not insured) and compensation for specific costs caused by the unusual circumstances. All these heads of damage were compensated through the already mentioned NRF. The central government made a lump sum payment of 6.2 million Guilders to the fund.[94]

In November 2001 an arrangement for companies was worked out specifically for damage caused by the fireworks catastrophe, consisting *inter alia* in[95]

- a compensation for not and underinsured material damage (60% of the value with a 10% deductible);

[89] See *Kamerstukken II* 1999–2000, 27 157, no. 1, 4–5.
[90] See *Kamerstukken II* 1999–2000, 27 157, no. 2, 17–19.
[91] See *Kamerstukken II* 1999–2000, 27 157, no. 5, 7–8.
[92] *Kamerstukken II* 1999–2000, 27 157, no. 5, 9–10.
[93] See *Kamerstukken II* 1999–2000, 27 157, no. 10, 5–7.
[94] *Kamerstukken II* 1999–2000, 27 157, no. 10, 5.
[95] See *Kamerstukken II* 2000–2001, 27 157, no. 12, 1–2 and *Kamerstukken II* 2000–2001, 27 157, no. 13, 4–5.

- a compensation for not and underinsured commercial losses (70% of the lost profits compared to 1999 with a deductible of 30%) under condition that the assets of the corporation are lower than € 225,000;[96]
- a compensation in case of the shut down of a company with a maximum of three times the annual profit in 1999 under condition that the companies' own assets were lower than € 225,000;
- a compensation of maximum € 2,500 for legal, fiscal and accountancy assistance.

This consisted in total of an amount of approximately 90,000,000 Guilders which was paid by the Ministry of Economic Affairs to a foundation Financial Aid Fireworks Catastrophe (*Financiële Hulpverlening Vuurwerkramp*).[97] The government estimated that more than 90% of the companies concerned in the disaster area could – with this aid – continue their enterprise in an acceptable manner.[98]

IV. Volendam

41 Relatively shortly after the events in Enschede the Netherlands was again confronted with yet another major catastrophe: on New Year's Eve between 31 December 2000 and 1 January 2001 a large fire took place in a café, "De Hemel" in Volendam. Many young victims died and many suffered serious injuries as a result of the fire. Also in this case the question of adequate compensation and the role of government was raised. A major difference with the fireworks explosion in Enschede was that in Volendam it concerned mainly personal injury damage, whereas in Enschede in addition to personal injury there also was large property damage and there were economic losses. Just as with the case of Enschede also in the case of Volendam, in addition to social security payments to the victim the possibilities of using tort law were examined. This mainly concerned the owner of the café. The basis for liability did not seem to be the major problem: there were no adequate fire escapes and various regulations (also concerning permits) were violated. However, although the owner of the café may be the primary individual responsible, victims probably also look at other potential defendants given, again, the insolvency problem. The owner only had insurance coverage for a relatively limited amount and thus victims would probably seek recovery from other sources as well. In a recent paper Barendrecht showed that the Volendam case is typically one where multiple tortfeasors have acted together and have all contributed to the risk and he therefore suggests that in those cases a division of liability should take place on the basis of the contribution of each of the tortfeasors (and victims!) to the risk.[99]

[96] This limit was introduced in order to indicate that companies that can carry the damage themselves should indeed take the financial consequences themselves as well. However, in reality the large majority of the corporations were apparently below the limit. See *Kamerstukken II* 2000–2001, 27 157, no. 15, 10.

[97] *Kamerstukken II* 2000–2001, 27 157, no. 12, 2.

[98] *Kamerstukken II* 2000–2001, 27 157, no. 13, 5.

[99] See J.M. Barendrecht, Verdeling van verantwoordelijkheid als het fout gaat. Volendam en aandelenlease als voorbeelden, [2004] NJB, 2180–2191.

Nevertheless formal law suits against public authorities did not take place and in the end a group of victims reached an agreement with the owner of the café, Mr. Veerman. With the help of the community of Volendam, (which also invested a substantial amount in a fund) a settlement was reached whereby Veerman decided to sell his café which was purchased by the community. The sum received by the Volendam community for the real estate was then made available (via a fund) for victim relief.

However, also other forms of support were discussed on the occasion of this disaster. The WTS 1998 was – again – declared not applicable. The reason was that it concerned insurable damage.[100] However, the government donated shortly after the disaster an amount of 3.5 million Guilders to two foundations that took care of the victims with serious burns, more particularly the *Nederlandse Brandwondenstichting* (Netherlands Burns Foundation) and the *Stichting Slachtoffers Nieuwjaarsbrand* (Foundation Victims New Year's Eve Fire).[101] It was explicitly mentioned that this payment was made as a gesture of national solidarity with the victims and not as a recognition of some kind of government liability. In addition substantial amounts were paid by the central government as well, for instance the compensation of the costs made by the Edam-Volendam community and the compensation of costs for a specific research committee that examined the sources of the disaster and for the compensation of various other costs.

A Committee more particularly formulated several advice papers concerning the compensation that the central government should provide as well for the Volendam victims. In that respect many comparisons were made with the arrangement for the victims of the fireworks factory explosion in Enschede. The suggestion was made to provide an amount of € 150,000 to the Volendam victims, whereas the amount provided to the Enschede victims was only € 120,000. The arguments made (by the specific Committee) were *inter alia* that specifically in the case of Volendam many young victims were involved whereby the incident damaged their future perspectives; also the serious burns would lead to a very long and slow recovery process.[102] On the basis of these proposals the central government would have made a total amount of € 30.1 million available for the victims.[103] This is remarkable since initially the idea of the central government was to merely provide compensation of direct costs, but in the end apparently large amounts of *ad hoc* compensation were provided as well.

[100] So *Kamerstukken II* 2001–2002, 27 575, no. 6, 50.

[101] See *Kamerstukken II* 2000–2001, 27 575, no. 2, 8 and no. 5, 42.

[102] See a letter of the Secretary of State of Internal Affairs to the Second Chamber (*Kamerstukken II* 2001–2002, 27 575, no. 18, 1–3).

[103] See *Kamerstukken II* 2002–2003, 27 157 and 27 575, no. 51, 9.

Part VI. Criticisms and Reform

I. Criticism

42 The Netherlands has, as the previous section showed, recently been hit by many disasters. In some cases it concerned natural disasters, but the most striking recent events were man-made. In all of the cases just discussed one could notice that there were a large number of victims and that hence the total amount of the damage was enormous. In all of these cases the question arose what legal instruments could be used to pay compensation to the victim and initially always attention was given to tort law, but given the inherent limits of this system, to other compensation systems as well.

One can notice that as a result of various calls for intervention on the Dutch government different *ad hoc* compensation funds were created. Sometimes these funds had to solve problems of liability law, as in the case of natural disasters; in other cases the fund only needed to provide a "gesture" as a sign of solidarity with the victims as in the cases of Enschede, Volendam and Bovenkarspel. The major criticism of all of this of course concerns the fact that the attempt of the government to provide a structural compensation arrangement for victims, being the WTS 1998 largely failed since this instrument was not applicable to the major disasters that hit the Netherlands in recent years. Therefore the entire system of compensation of victims of catastrophes has been seriously criticized in the literature from various perspectives.[104]

43 There is *first* of all criticism of the fact that the government on an *ad hoc* basis intervenes with specific funding for victims of catastrophes. This preference for victims of catastrophes (compared to victims of other accidents) has been criticized from the angle of the equality principle.[105] *Second*, legal doctrine also held that, if specific compensation needs to be provided for victims of catastrophes, it would be more desirable to have a structural solution instead of the current *ad hoc* solutions. In that respect the WTS 1998, which apparently did not serve that goal, would have to be revised. *Third* it is also stressed that there might be reasons to increase duties of potential tortfeasors to guarantee their solvency. Both in Volendam and in Enschede large damage was caused by activities for which no compulsory insurance applied. Hence it was argued that a duty to seek insurance coverage might be introduced on a larger scale or, where it exists, the amounts should be increased.[106] *Fourth*, it seems logical to increase the possibilities of first party insurance also. Now that the prohibited cartel agreements not to cover the consequences of natural disasters have been withdrawn, it seems logical that insurance policies covering those risks would

[104] For a summary of this criticism see T. Hartlief (*supra* fn. 2), 61–103.

[105] See already A.R. Bloembergen, Een schadefonds geweldsmisdrijven?, in *Bloembergens werk* (1992), 51 *et seq.* and J.M. Polak, Schade en schadevergoeding bij incidentele calamiteiten. Een vervolg, [1997] NJB, 1093–1094.

[106] Compare in this respect W.H. van Boom, De strategische verzekeringsplicht, [2001] AV&S, 165 and J.H. Wansink, De verzekering van rampschade, in: A.J. Akkermans/E.H.P. Brans (eds.), *Aansprakelijkheid en schadeverhaal bij rampen* (2002), 131 *et seq.*

be brought on the market. This is apparently, as we described, the case now for agricultural damage caused by heavy rainfall.

II. Reform

It should first of all be mentioned that, on the occasion of both the fireworks disaster in Enschede and the fire in Volendam, specific committees were instituted to examine both the causes and the compensation arrangements. In some of the conclusions of these committees also some opinions were formulated concerning an optimal compensation of the victims. However, these usually applied to the specific cases of these particular disasters. But for instance the commission instituted on the occasion of the fireworks explosion in Deventer (Commissie Oosting) had also formulated proposals to come to a more structural financial arrangement for victims of catastrophes.[107] However, the government did not follow that proposal since it considered that the Netherlands already had a structural arrangement in the WTS 1998. Moreover, the central government had provided generous support to both the *Nationale Rampenfonds* (a private initiative) and the *Stichting Financiële Hulpverlening Vuurwerkramp*, so that the government felt that it had satisfied its duty to provide a gesture of national solidarity towards the victims.[108] 44

Nevertheless the government has installed a committee with the specific task of providing an assessment of the WTS 1998. Indeed, a so-called *Commissie Tegemoetkoming bij Rampen en Calamiteiten* – CTRC, (Commission for the Compensation in Cases of Catastrophes and Incidents) was asked to provide advice to the government on the optimal compensation in case of catastrophes.[109] The committee had to examine first of all what the existing possibilities of compensation were, but second also to formulate proposals for additional compensation that should probably be made available.[110] 45

A draft version of the report of the CTRC was presented in The Hague in November 2004 and, *inter alia* based on experience abroad (more particularly in France, Belgium, Germany and Sweden) the commission formulates several interesting suggestions:

- tort law needs to be amended in order to manage mass torts more easily and to reduce trials; alternative dispute resolution should be stimulated;
- insolvency guarantees for injurers need to be introduced or increased;
- for catastrophes where no liable injurer can be identified, the commission suggests an increasing use of first party insurances. The proposal is followed not to make the purchase of disaster coverage mandatory (like in France), but to facilitate the insurability of risks on the one hand by letting

[107] See *Kamerstukken II* 2000–2001, 27 157, no. 20, 59.
[108] *Kamerstukken II* 2000–2001, 27 157, no. 20, 60.
[109] *Kamerstukken II* 2001–2002, 27 157, no. 44, 4.
[110] The Commission has been installed by formal decision of the Secretary of State of Internal Affairs of 3 April 2003, which also specifies its formal task (see [7 April 2003] Stcrt. no. 68, 9).

the State act as reinsurer (if necessary) and by pursuing an active information policy;

- change the WTS into a national solidarity fund that would, on the basis of clear rules and structures, provide various types of compensation, *inter alia* for the case of uninsurable damage.

It is today, of course, too early to provide an educated guess of whether these proposals will be accepted at the political level. One can only mention that most of these proposals of the committee are in line with was has been suggested in the legal doctrine as well as far as the revision of the compensation of victims of catastrophes is concerned. In any event it is clear that within the next few years also in the Netherlands an important revision of the compensation system will take place.

List of References

A.J. Akkermans/E.H. Brans (eds.), *Aansprakelijkheid en schadeverhaal bij rampen* (2002).

V.C. Ammerlaan/W.H. van Boom, De Nederlandse herverzekeringsmaatschappij voor terrorismeschaden, [2003] *Nederlands Juristenblad* (NJB) 2330–2339.

J.M. Barendrecht, Aansprakelijkheid en welzijn, [2002] NJB, 612.

J.M. Barendrecht, Verdeling van verantwoordelijkheid als het fout gaat. Volendam en aandelenlease als voorbeelden, [2004] NJB, 2180–2191.

E. Bauw, Tussen traditie en efficiëntie; na een wettelijke regeling voor de afwikkeling van massaschade, [1995] NJB, 622–630.

A.R. Bloembergen, Aansprakelijkheidsrecht en sociale verzekering: nieuwe ontwikkelingen, [1970] *Sociaal Maandblad Arbeid* (SMA), 74–80.

A.R. Bloembergen, *Schade lijden en schade dragen* (1980), 16–17.

A.R. Bloembergen, Een schadefonds geweldsmisdrijven?, in: *Bloembergens werk* (1992), 51 *et seq.*

A.R. Bloembergen, Het SER-rapport over regresrechten: een fout verhaal, [1994] NJB, 117–123.

A.R. Bloembergen, Het verhaalsrecht van de risicodrager in de algemene wet zware geneeskundige risico's, [1996] SMA, 329–330.

W.H. van Boom, De strategische verzekeringsplicht, [2001] *Aansprakelijkheid Verzekering en Schade* (AV&S), 165.

W.H. van Boom, *Structurele fouten in het aansprakelijkheidsrecht* (2003).

W.H. van Boom, Waarheen leidt de weg ... van werknemersschade?, [2003] AV&S, 33–40.

W. van Boom/I. Giesen, Civielrechtelijke overheidsaansprakelijkheid voor het niet voorkomen van gezondheidsschade door rampen, [2001] NJB, 1676.

W.H. van Boom, Het verhaalsrecht van de werkgever ex art. 6:107a BW, [1995] *Weekblad voor Privaatrecht, Notariaat en Registratie* (WPNR) 6202, 863 *et seq.*

W.H. van Boom/H.M. Storm, Het verhaalsrecht van verzekeraars en risicodragers, [1995] *Aansprakelijkheid en Verzekering* (A&V) 6, 157 *et seq.*

J.E. van de Bunt, Voorgeschiedenis van de WTS. Beschouwing over verschillende regelingen ter vergoeding van rampschade, in: E.R. Muller/C.J.J.M. Stolker (eds.), *Ramp en Recht* (2001), 176 *et seq.*

C.C. van Dam, *Zorgvuldigheidsnorm en Aansprakelijkheid* (1989), 199 *et seq.*

A.E. Dek, Asbestontwikkelingen. Oprechte tegemoetkomingen of doekjes voor het bloeden?, [1999] *Tijdschrift voor Milieuaansprakelijkheid* (TMA), 61–62.

L. Dommering-Van Rongen, *Schade vergoeden door fondsvorming* (1996).
L. Dommering-Van Rongen, Een schadefonds voor asbestslachtoffers, [1996] TMA, 97–101.
H. Drion, *Verzekering en aansprakelijkheisdrecht* (inauguration address 1955) (1959), 4–5.
R.Ph. Elzas, Regresrecht: ANW en veegwet, [1996] *Verzekeringsrechtelijke berichten* (Vrb), 4 *et seq.*
E. Engelhard, *Regres. Een onderzoek naar het regresrecht van particuliere en sociale schadedragers* (2003).
M. Faure, Regres in rechtseconomisch perspectief, in: W.H. van Boom/T. Hartlief/J. Spier (eds.), *Regresrecht. Afschaffen, handhaven of uitbreiden?* (1996), 45–71.
M. Faure/R. van den Bergh, Aansprakelijkheidsverzekering, concurrentie en ongevallenpreventie, in: T. Hartlief/M.M. Mendel (eds.), *Verzekering en maatschappij* (2000), 315–342.
M. Faure/R. van den Bergh, Restrictions of competition on imprudence markets and the applicability of EC Antitrust law, [1995] *Kyklos*, 65–85.
M. Faure/T. Hartlief, Een asbestfonds als alternatief voor aansprakelijkheid van de werkgever?, [1996] *Sociaal Recht* (SR), 37 *et seq.*
M. Faure/T. Hartlief, Een schadefonds als alternatief voor aansprakelijkheid en verzekering?, [1998] *Rechtsgeleerd Magazijn Themis* (RM Themis), 211–228.
M. Faure/T. Hartlief, Vergoeding van rampschade, in: E.R.Muller/C.J.J.M. Stolker (eds.), *Ramp en Recht* (2001), 151 *et seq.*
M. Faure/T. Hartlief, Schade als gevolg van natuurverschijnselen: de betekenis van de WTS, [2001] *Milieu en Recht* (MenR), 240–246.
M. Faure/T. Hartlief, *Nieuwe risico's en vragen van aansprakelijkheid en verzekering* (2002), 187–189.
M. Faure/T. Hartlief, Economic perspectives, in: U. Magnus (ed.), *The impact of social security law on tort law* (2003), 228–229.
M. Faure/T. Hartlief, *Insurance and expanding systemic risks* (2003), 223–225.
M. Faure/T. Hartlief, The Netherlands, in: H. Koziol/B.C. Steininger (eds.), *European Tort Law 2003* (2004), 278–315.
M. Faure/T. Hartlief/M. Hertoghs, *Evaluatie van het Fonds Luchtverontreiniging* (2000), 12–16.
M. Faure/T. Hartlief/M. Hertoghs, Evaluatie van het fonds luchtverontreiniging, [2000] MenR, 64–69.
N. Frenk, Regresrecht voor werkgevers voor doorbetaald loon, [1996] A&V, 6–7.
M.S. Groenhuijsen, Schadefondsen in Nederland en in het buitenland: supra nationale normen, rechtsvergelijkende en empirische beschouwingen, [2001] *Delikt en Delinkwent* (DD), 930–947.
J.F. de Groot, Na de ramp. Een beschouwing over de toepassing van de WTS, [2004] *Overheid en Aansprakelijkheid* (O&A), 141–152.
S.P. de Haas/T. Hartlief, *Collectivering en institutionalisering van regres* (1996).
T. Hartlief, Vergoeding van watersnoodschade, in: M. Faure/F. Stroink (eds.), *Recht in het water. De juridische aspecten van watersnood* (1995), 131–142.
T. Hartlief, Vergoeding van watersnoodschade, [1995] NJB, 311 *et seq.*
T. Hartlief, *Ieder draagt zijn eigen schade* (1997), no. 8 *et seq.*
T. Hartlief, Schadefondsen en de rol van de overheid, in: *Kring van aansprakelijken bij massaschade* (2002), 61 *et seq.*
T. Hartlief/G.E. van Maanen, Regres bij volksverzekeringen. De dader heeft het gedaan, [1994] *Nederlands Tijdschrift voor Burgerlijk Recht* (NTBR), 75–78.
J.J. van der Helm, Tegemoetkomingregelingen na de vuurwerkramp, [2003] TVP 40–44.

M. Hertoghs, Hoogwater in Den Haag: de rol van de Rijksoverheid, in: M. Faure/F. Stroink (eds.), *Recht in het water. De juridische aspecten van watersnood* (1995), 35–62.

E.H. Hulst, Actualiteiten milieuaansprakelijkheid. Schadelijk water en schadefonds, pleidooi voor adequate oplossingen!, [1999] TMA, 33 *et seq.*

J.P. Hustinx/C.J.J.M. Stolker, Massaschade en fondsvorming, [1997] *Verzekeringsarchief* (VA), 58–66.

S. Klosse, Vergoeding als noodverband?, [2003] AV&S, 25–33.

G. Levie/H. Cousy (eds.), *La politique Européenne de concurrence en matière d'assurance* (1994).

S.D. Lindenbergh/A.R. Bloembergen, *Schadevergoeding: algemeen, deel 1*, monografie NBW (2nd edn. 2002), no. 8.

G.E. van Maanen, Permanente beperking van verhaalsmogelijkheden van particuliere en sociale schadeverzekeraars, [1994] A&V, 94–97.

G.E. van Maanen (ed.), *De rol van het aansprakelijkheidsrecht bij de verwerking van persoonlijk leed* (2003).

G.E. van Maanen/P. Römers, *De tijdelijke regeling verhaalsrechten, verhaalsmogelijkheden voor verzekeraars en uitkeringsinstanties* (1994).

B. Maat, De legionella-affaire in Bovenkarspel en mogelijke toepasselijkheid van de aansprakelijkheid voor gevaarlijke stoffen, [2000] *Verkeersrecht* (VR), 353–358.

E.R. Muller/C.J.J.M. Stolker (eds.), *Ramp en Recht* (2001)

E.R. Muller/C.J.J.M. Stolker, Overheidsaansprakelijkheid en toezicht [2001] NJB, 1647 *et seq.*

J.A.J. Peeters, Rampschade, [1980] NJB, 503–504.

J.A.J. Peeters, Rampschade, in: M.J.P. Verburgh/A.R. Bloembergen/G.J. de Groot *et al.* (eds.), *Schade lijden en schade dragen* (1980), 59–84.

C.E. du Perron/W.H. van Boom, The Netherlands, in: U. Magnus (ed.), *The impact of social security law on tort law* (2003), 153–155.

J.M. Polak, Schade en schadevergoeding bij incidentele calamiteiten. Een vervolg, [1997] NJB, 1093–1094.

E. van der Schans, Regen als ramp. Wateroverlast en de WTS, [2000] TMA, 13 *et seq.*

W. Snijders, Aansprakelijkheid voor milieuverontreiniging: het verzekeringsaspect, [1993] A&V, 1 *et seq.*

H. Vos, De opzetclausule in: T. Hartlief/M.M. Mendel (eds.), *Verzekering en maatschappij* (2000), 57 *et seq.*

F.J. de Vries, Vergoeding van Rampschade, [1998] NJB, 1908–1913.

J.H. Wansink, De aansprakelijkheidsverzekering en opzettelijk veroorzaakte schade: Een Januskop in beweging, [2000] AV&S, 14–17.

J.H. Wansink, De Verzekering van rampschade, in: A.J. Akkermans/E.H.P. Brans (eds.), *Aansprakelijkheid en schadeverhaal bij rampen* (2002), 131 *et seq.*

J.H. Wansink, Assurance oblige: de maatschappelijk verantwoord handelende verzekeraar in de 21e eeuw, [2003] AV&S, 50.

D.A. van den Wall Bake *et al.*, *Eindrapportage. Inventarisatie van financiële voorzieningen na rampen in Nederland* (Utrecht, 1 March 2004).

SWEDEN

Siv Nyquist and Erik Persson

Part I. General Scope of the Compensation System

The main rules concerning compensation for damage are laid down in the Tort Liability Act.[1] This Act specifically deals with responsibility for negligence. Tort law is of course the foundation for deciding who is liable for damages and what types and amounts of compensation should be made. However, when it comes to settling real injuries or losses it is the compulsory public social insurance schemes, to some extent the social welfare system, and the extensive coverage of various types of collective and private insurances that will remunerate losses and injuries. This means that one does not have to use the tort liability procedure to get compensation. 1

In some important areas where injuries often occur, such as road traffic and workplace injuries, traditional tort liability has been replaced by obligatory insurances, which give the injured party a right to claim compensation directly from insurance. These types of remunerations are therefore not called damages but remuneration. At least until recently, the lawmakers emphasised humanitarian and social aspects of damage compensation more than the interest to distribute losses.[2] The preventive effect of liability has also been downplayed. Lately, the idea of loss distribution has fallen out of focus. The social and protective role of insurance, and the humanitarian argument that even negligent parties to some extent should be protected against the ruinous consequences of an accident, have been somewhat replaced, and preventive considerations are regaining influence.[3]

Part II. Detailed Information

Catastrophe victims can use the tort system to get compensation if somebody can be found to have caused the event and that somebody has wilfully or negligently caused loss, injury, or damage. This fault liability is called the "culpa principle" and is the basic foundation of tort law.[4] In some areas, however, there 2

[1] Tort Liability Act (*Svensk författningssamling* 1972:207).

[2] B. Bengtsson, Torts and Insurance, in: P. Cronhult *et al.* (eds.), *Swedish Law a Survey* (1994), 156.

[3] B. Bengtsson, Torts and Insurance, in: M. Bogdan (ed.), *Swedish Law in the New Millennium* (2000), 300.

[4] B. Bengtsson (*supra* fn. 3), 301.

is extended liability, which can be strict, implying responsibility for damage irrespective of negligence. This occurs for particularly dangerous actions e.g. certain types of military actions during exercises. The most common areas for strict liability are laid down in statutes. These include losses caused by air traffic, liability for oil spillage at sea, damage caused by railway traffic, damage caused by nuclear plants and owners of high-powered electricity installations. The Environmental Code,[5] for example, imposes strict liability for all types of pollution or interference upon the use of real property in so far as the nuisance caused should not reasonably be tolerated in view of the circumstances, and in the locality or its general occurrence under comparable circumstances.

3 An interesting issue is whether victims could effectively sue the licensee of a firework enterprise that explodes, and what the limits in a particular procedure like this would be. Most of the basic losses and injuries in such an accident would be covered by the social insurance schemes and other social services provided by the Social Services Act. Furthermore, most people who are employed in Sweden are also covered by collective insurances paid by their employer, or private collective insurances via their trade union. More than 95% of the population have also a household insurance that covers most types of losses.[6] Apart from this, the licensee could have liability insurance. The extensive coverage of various insurances means that most people would get compensated for most of their injuries and losses by way of recompense, without having to use tortious litigation. If one examines the example of the discotheque fire in Gothenburg (Part IX), the insurance companies involved made standardised disbursements to victims and, in addition, *ex gratia* disbursements from insurance.[7] This means that insurance companies' settlements of claims often display a generous attitude and the incentives for going to court are thus rare.

4 The risk of taking a dispute to court is that, if the case is lost, a plaintiff has to pay the litigation costs. This means that the cost for the legal representative, the costs for the defendant's representative, and also the costs for presenting the evidence in the process must be met. This could end up as a substantial amount. If the plaintiff has household insurance, the litigation costs are covered by the insurance, excluding a minimum amount, which always has to be paid by the policyholder, for example 20% of the costs. For further information about this see *infra* Part IV.II. Another inhibiting factor may be the time the litigation might take. This could run up to maybe five years or more if it is to be tried in three instances.

The State and/or a municipality are liable to pay compensation for injuries or damage to property according to tort law on the same grounds as any other legal entity when they are acting in the civil law sphere. This means that normally negligence must have occurred. These public entities are also responsi-

[5] Environmental Code (SFS 1998:808).

[6] L. Häll, *Victims of violence and of property crimes 1978–2002* (2004), 160.

[7] Personal contact with the insurer, Folksam.

ble for culpable acts by their employees on the same basis as private employers (vicarious liability).[8] Furthermore, public entities have to pay for financial loss in connection with the exercise of public authority in carrying out functions for the performance of which the State or the municipality is responsible. Also, in case these entities have caused pure financial loss through fault or negligence when providing erroneous information or advice, and considering the circumstances, there are special reasons to grant compensation. Exercise of public authority here means an expression of powers of public organs entities to take decisions against individuals, which the individuals have to follow. In case of a flood, the State or a municipality could, for example, be held responsible if the authorities had taken a decision prescribing the building of a barrage in a certain way and it later turns out that the measures prescribed were inadequate or wrong. If their negligence caused losses, they would be liable to pay damages. However, if it is a situation where a public body has failed to act, the outcome might be different. Swedish tort law does not require anybody to act to stop others from causing damage, except if there is an obligation in a statute saying so. For example, it is an obligation for the municipality to clear snow in public places and streets and the State should keep public roads in such a condition that they can be used for transportation. Nevertheless, in most cases, neglecting to act is not a foundation for a claim. An example would be a municipality that has not built a dam around a lake, and through heavy rains, the lake floods and submerges surrounding areas. In a situation like this, it is not a matter of exercise of public authority, and the municipality would most likely not have to pay any damages.[9]

Social insurance compensates for the economic consequences of injuries or sickness in the way that it covers most of the costs for medical treatment, permanent disability and the major part of the loss of income irrespective of the cause of the injury or sickness. This means that victims of all types of catastrophes or terrorist outrage will basically be able to uphold a standard of living that is not too far from the level enjoyed before the event. In case a person is not covered by social insurance, the Social Services Act[10] obliges municipalities to cover the costs and supply of services for an injured person to sustain a basic living standard.

Private first party insurances are complementary to social insurances and could cover excesses or other costs that are not fully compensated by the public schemes. The public schemes do not compensate, for example, for pain and suffering and inconvenience that have been caused by permanent medical and occupational disability or property damage.

The policy of the group insurance from the insurer Folksam could serve as an example of a private first party insurance structure.[11] This company supplies life insurance which becomes due in case of death or sickness, and accident in-

[8] See <http://www.sverige.se/sverige/templates/page_7516.aspx> for a presentation of how the Swedish public sector works.

[9] See *Supreme Court Law Reports* (*Nytt Juridiskt Arkiv*, NJA) 1971, 468.

[10] Social Services Act (SFS 1980:620).

[11] <http://www.folksam.se/resurser/pdf/s1870.pdf>. Similar policies apply to other insurance companies.

surance for leisure time which compensates various costs and also permanent harm in the form of disfiguring scars. However, in this case no compensation for pain and suffering is disbursed. The insurance also contains an insurance against sickness and accidents for children and adolescents and a supplementary loss of income insurance that covers some of the loss of income due to sickness which is not covered by public social insurance. Depending upon what the insurance policy says, in most cases catastrophic events are not excluded from coverage. The limitations are in the form of ceiling amounts in the policy, that is, how much money can be disbursed for each case of loss.

This private first party insurance is somewhat limited if the injury occurs abroad and especially if it occurs in a country where war or warlike disturbances are in progress. However, if the wars or riots start during one's stay in the area, the insurance is valid for the first three months. Further exclusions are in case of war or conditions that are deemed by the Government as equivalent to war, the insurer has a statutory right to levy a war premium. The last limitation is injuries caused by atomic nuclear reactions and spreading of biological chemical and nuclear substances in connection with terrorist activities. These exclusions are typical for first party insurances. Other types of terrorist activities, and consequences of natural catastrophes, are not excluded from coverage.

Part III. Procedure to Obtain Compensation for Damage

I. Personal Injuries[12]

5 Available income is derived from social security fees, general pension fees, national old age pension fees, interest on the National Pension Insurance Fund, and taxation financing the National Social Insurance. In 2001 the income was approximately 367 billion SEK (€ 44.5 billion) and the total expenditure was approximately 352 billion SEK (€ 42 billion).[13]

A. Social Insurance Administration

6 The National Social Insurance Board and the social insurance offices together administer the social insurance schemes and are responsible for the greater part of society's financial safety net. The National Social Insurance Board is responsible for the central direction and supervision of activities. The national social insurance scheme provides financial security e.g. for disease, disability, and insurance benefits of this kind, including sickness insurance, basic retirement pensions, and supplementary pensions. Another social insurance benefit is housing allowance. Regional Social Insurance offices, one in each county, and their local offices, process individual cases at regional and local level and disburse benefits. Another obligation of the National Social Insurance Board is to prevent and reduce ill health by taking positive action to facilitate and co-

[12] Information about the social insurance system can be found on <http://www.rfv.se/english/index.htm> and <http://www.forsakringskassan.se/>.

[13] *Riksförsäkringsverket* (RFV) 2002, 26.

ordinate rehabilitation with a view to enabling sick and functionally impaired persons to return to work.

The Social Insurance system forms the basis of the compensation system for loss of income or ability to support dependants. It encompasses rights for medical and dental care. A person will always be compensated from this system if s/he is insured. To be fully covered by all types of benefits, the person must reside in Sweden and have acquired an income. If the person has not acquired an income s/he will not be insured against loss of income, but will still have the opportunity to receive benefits from pensions.

B. *Costs for Medical and Dental Care and Medicines from the Social Insurance*

The Social Insurance scheme covers most of the costs for consulting a doctor 7
or medical treatment both in and out of hospital. It also covers costs for physiotherapy and other additional treatment. The injured only has to pay a minor part of the cost – a patient's fee. However, there is an upper limit for these fees of 900 SEK (€ 100) per year at present. Medicines are in most cases paid according to the actual costs but there is also an upper limit here for the cost for the patient, at present 1,800 SEK (€ 200) per year.

Dental treatment is also covered by Social Insurance. For a person under the age of 20 dental care is provided free of charge. People above the age of 20 are entitled to subsidised dental care. A part of the bill is paid directly to the dentist, and the Social Insurance Office pays the rest directly to the dentist.

C. *Loss of Income*

If a person has lost income because of corporal injuries, s/he must notify the 8
employer and s/he will receive compensation – sick pay – for the first three weeks coming directly from the employer (except for the first day of the period – the waiting day). If the person has not recovered after this three week period, the employer will notify the Social Insurance Office, who will take over the responsibility for the administration of the disbursement of sickness benefits. The compensation covers 77.6% of the lost income and is disbursed as soon as the sick person has notified their employer or the Social Insurance Office. Under normal circumstances, disbursement of sickness benefits starts within 30 days.

In case a person is not entitled to receive sick pay, s/he can draw sickness benefit from the Social Insurance Office. In this case the person has to notify the Social Security Office on the day of the injury. The sickness benefit is covered by the publicly funded social security system. A doctor's certificate must be presented indicating to what extent the person is unable to work. One-quarter, half, three-quarters or full sickness benefit may be drawn. This continues as long as the person can present a doctor's certificate and the Social Insurance Office considers that the person's ability to work is either partially or fully restored. If the person has suffered an illness or injury making it difficult for him/her to return to the labour market, assistance to enable him/her to go back to work may be received. This can be employability assessment, occupational rehabilitation or training. During this period a person is entitled to a rehabilitation allowance.

Disease carrier's allowance is another benefit a person might be allowed to receive if s/he has, or is suspected of having, an infectious disease and is barred from work by a decision made under the Prevention of Infectious Diseases Act or the Foodstuffs Act, even though the person is fit to work.

If a person is permanently impaired and aged between 30 and 64, the Social Insurance Office assesses if the person is entitled to part-time or full-time early retirement pension (sickness compensation). If a person is aged between 19 and 29 and is ill for a long period and unable to work, s/he may be entitled to activity compensation on a part-time or full-time basis. This means that the injured person receives sickness benefit while attending school (including upper secondary school) or participating in activities that develop skills and increase the prospects of obtaining work.

In case a person refrains from taking gainful employment in order to care for a close relative or next of kin who is seriously ill, the carer may be entitled to time off work and may be eligible for a benefit of the same amount as sickness benefit.

Temporary parental benefit is a further benefit that entitles parents to care for a sick child under the age of 12. This also applies if parents have to visit a doctor with the child. Parents can stay at home for up to 60 days per year for each child. Under certain circumstances, an additional 60 days per child can be granted. The period can also be extended for children aged up to 15 years if the child is so seriously ill that he/she needs special care and supervision, provided that a doctor's certificate can verify this.

For children who are seriously disabled special rules apply. Parents are allowed to receive a benefit if they need to tend to their child permanently on a daily basis. The benefit is payable for a full, three-quarters, half or one-quarter day.

D. Support for the Disabled from the Social Insurance

9 Disabled persons who have reached the age of 19 and are not older than 65 and who need time-consuming assistance in order to manage their day-to-day life, work, or studies, can get a disability allowance. This benefit can also be disbursed if a person has sustained substantial extra costs.

E. Other Social Insurance Benefits in Case of Death

10 Relatives of deceased persons may be entitled to one of several social insurance benefits.

If a spouse has died, the survivor may receive a conversion pension for ten months if s/he has not reached the age of 65. An extended conversion pension of another twelve months can be allowed if the person is living with a child under the age of 18.

Children under the age of 18 are entitled to child pensions in the event of the death of one or both their parents. An extended child pension may be payable to children over 18 up to and including June of the year of the child's 20th birthday, providing the child is studying at school.

F. The Work Injuries Insurance Act

In the event that an injury occurs at work or on the way to or from work, the social security benefits are supplemented with benefits from the Work Insurance Act. This scheme not only covers injuries in conjunction with accidents but also diseases related to the work, for example skin ailments caused by contact with chemicals. 11

If a person dies as a result of an occupational injury, the surviving spouse and children will be entitled to an annuity. The size of the annuity will be co-ordinated with the survivor's pension and survivor's support for the children. The survivors are also entitled to help in meeting the funeral expenses in the event that the death has occurred due to an occupational injury. This amounts to 30% of the price base amount and for 2003 this was set at 11,500 SEK (€ 1,278).

To receive compensation for work-related injuries and diseases, the employee should notify the employer who reports to the Social Insurance Office. The Office assesses if it is a work-related injury, and also takes care of the disbursement of the benefits. The handling time for occupational compensation matters can be more than one year due to the heavy workload that usually dogs the Social Insurance Offices.

G. Support According to the Social Services Act

The Social Services Act[14] gives all residents in Sweden a right to social and financial security, care and assistance. It is the responsibility of the municipalities to grant each citizen a reasonable standard of living. This means that a person is entitled to assistance for upkeep and other living requirements. A person is not entitled to assistance if s/he is able to meet their own needs or sustain themselves through other means. The law lays down that those entitled to financial assistance, meaning social security and income support, shall be granted reasonable expenses for food, clothes and shoes, leisure time, consumable goods, health and hygiene, a daily newspaper, and telephone costs. Each year the Government establishes the standards for these costs, which apply throughout the country. A larger sum than the standard may be granted if a person has special needs, for instance dietary requirements for medical reasons. 12

The right to financial assistance also covers reasonable costs for accommodation, household electricity, work-related travel, home insurance, and membership of a trade union and unemployment funds. There is no national standard for these costs. A person can also apply for additional financial assistance for other long or short-term needs such as dental and medical care, spectacles, travel and funeral expenses.

Repayment of income support may be demanded if the disbursed amount was granted as an advance for a benefit or compensation, for example sickness benefit or pension that the party is expecting to receive. Another situation would be if a person could not access wages or assets because of circumstances beyond the person's control.

[14] See *supra* fn. 9.

The time to handle issues of income support with the Social Services Committee is short. A client should be given a time for an appointment with an official within a week.

Persons who have significant difficulties in their daily life due to physical or psychological functional disabilities have extended rights for assistance according to the Social Services Act. This could mean a specially adapted apartment with support facilities, and/or a personal assistant etc.

If a claim for support or assistance according to the Social Services Act is denied, an appeal to an administrative court can be made. This means that a person can have both the legality and the reasonableness of the decision re-examined. This would be a prioritized case with the administrative courts and judgment from the court of first instance can be expected after two to three months.

H. Compensation from Private Insurances for Personal Injuries

13 Basically, the public insurance schemes cover most of the loss of income or, if the injury was caused during the course of work, all loss of income (under certain circumstances). The loss of income that is not covered by social insurance, and the costs for medical and dental care, medicine and disability that is not covered by the public schemes, have to be covered by the person's private insurance. In order to get compensation a person must first turn to her/his own insurance company, not the liable party's insurance company. In case a person does not have any insurance, s/he must turn to the liable party's insurance company, or if possible, to the person himself or herself.

According to the Tort Liability Act chapter 5, the following items could be claimed as compensation for injuries:

- costs for medical care and other costs or expenses, including reasonable compensation for pain and suffering to close relatives of the injured party;
- loss of income;
- pain, suffering, permanent disability and harm, as well as other inconveniences resulting from the injury;
- in case an injury has resulted in the victim's death, compensation will also cover funeral expenses and other reasonable expenses resulting from the death;
- loss of maintenance allowances or other financial support;
- personal injuries to persons who were particularly close to the deceased, and
- for serious violations of personal integrity due to criminal activity.

Some first party insurances cover pain and suffering, for example, the insurer Länsförsäkringar in their Individual Accident and Sickness Insurance policy for adults *Olycksfalls- och sjukförsäkring för vuxna* (OSV) 628:3.[15] There it is stated that, in case of an accident, the insurance compensates for pain and suffering in the event that acute treatment for the injury exceeds 30 days. The

[15] <http//www2.lansforsakringar.se>.

compensation is calculated according to a "table for the estimation of compensation for pain and suffering" laid down by the insurer and valid at the time of the disbursement. This means that an injured person is compensated during the acute recovery period. In case the person has a limb plastered, the remuneration will be paid until one week after the plaster is removed. The amount is 70 SEK (€ 7.77) per day. In case a person is hospitalised the sum is 116 SEK (€ 12.90) per day. These sums are the same as road traffic victims would get and also a court of law would probably decide roughly the same compensation if a claim for pain and suffering was put to them for adjudication. This right to compensation is subsidiary to compensation for pain and suffering from any other sources including a statutory rule or another insurance policy. This insurance does not cover accident, injuries or sicknesses caused directly or indirectly by atomic nuclear processes. Furthermore, injuries due to terrorist acts through spreading of biological, chemical or nuclear substances are not covered by the insurance.

In the household insurance policy from the insurer Folksam as of 1 January 2003 a reference to "assault protection compensation" is included. This is available if a person is exposed to a battery or other intentional violence. The insurance compensates injury claims that any claimant is entitled to according to chapter 5 of the Tort Liability Act which includes pain and suffering. If s/he is related to somebody who is killed through murder or manslaughter s/he has the right to compensation for pain and sorrow to a maximum of 25,000 SEK (€ 2,777).

Household insurance covers damage to property due to, for example, fire or theft. It also covers damage on another person's property or if one injures another person. Furthermore, household insurance covers court costs, costs in connection with assault, and costs as a result of calamity during travel, for example, extra costs due to sicknesses or travel accidents.

If one is an owner of a house, household insurance also covers damage to the house because of a fire or natural disasters like storm, hail, flood, heavy snow, damage caused by avalanche, landslide etc. (see Part III.I.H).

Household insurance is an insurance that all persons ought to have. It is, fortunately, very common for people to have it.[16] In conjunction with household insurance, one can sign additional insurance, for example for a yacht or an extended travel insurance that covers the liabilities in case one has to cancel a trip. Some insurers offer leisure accident insurance as an added extension to the household insurance while others offer accident insurance as a separate choice. In practice this does not make much difference so the conclusion is that often basic household insurance does not give any compensation for accidents to a person and a separate insurance has to be negotiated.

I. Criminal Injuries Compensation

If a catastrophe is caused by a crime, and the victims have private insurance, 14
they will get compensation for losses as well as associated pain and suffering.

[16] L. Häll (*supra* fn. 6), 60.

Normal household insurance policies, for example, cover injuries resulting from criminal assault. Many people also have collective or individual accident insurances covering personal injuries. Moreover, most employees are covered by a labour market insurance scheme, which offers compensation for loss, damage or injuries at the workplace.

The next step would be to get the perpetrator to pay compensation. However, culprits of crimes often cannot be found or, if they are found and are sentenced to pay damages by a court, they do not have any means of paying. To ensure that crime victims actually receive compensation, Parliament enacted the Criminal Injuries Compensation Act,[17] which entitles crime victims to criminal injuries compensation for personal injuries. Injury here means physical or psychological injury. This kind of compensation may be granted even in cases where no perpetrator is found, provided that a police investigation has shown that the injury is actually the result of a criminal act, rather than, for example, an accident. Compensation is paid for any violation of personal integrity according to chapter 2, art. 3 and chapter 5 of the Tort Liability Act.

15 Social security compensation based on tort law rarely covers loss or damage to property through crime. In these situations compensation will normally only be paid if the offender, when s/he committed the crime, was under police arrest, an inmate of a prison or otherwise receiving institutional treatment by the State. Damage for lost property may also be paid in cases where there are particularly distressing circumstances.

The Crime Victim Compensation and Support Authority administers Criminal Injuries Compensation.[18] If there is no court ruling on the damage issue, because no perpetrator was found, this authority decides on the compensation. In the authority there is also a Crime Victim and Support Authority Board that is the appeal instance for decisions by the Authority. Furthermore, the Board, as the first and only instance of redress, decides on matters of principle or of otherwise greater importance. These decisions have no right of appeal. The chairman of the board must be an ordinary judge.

If a court has adjudged damages, especially if it is a court of appeal or the Supreme Court, the Authority still decides the compensation independently but usually follows the judgment. Reasons to deviate from the court ruling would include an incorrect application of the law or if the level of damages as adjudged deviates from prevailing practice. The reference decisions by the Authority are published and are frequently used by insurance companies and the courts, and reference is made in their *ratio decidendi*. This means that in areas where the Supreme Court has not made any rulings, the decisions of the Authority serve as precedents.

[17] Criminal Injuries Compensation Act (SFS 1978:4139).
[18] <http://www.brottsoffermyndigheten.se>.

II. Compensation for Property Damage

For property damage there are few public schemes or insurances covering losses apart from those that are discussed in Part III.III. Normally a person would in this case initially have to rely on private insurance. Most people have some kind of insurance that covers damages and loss, for example, a household insurance, and also many have additional collective and individual insurances. 16

Exclusions for natural catastrophes and terror-like situations could be formulated like this example from the insurer Folksam's insurance for Holiday Cottages as of 1 January 2003. In the policy it is laid down that the insurance does not cover damage in conjunction with war and warlike situations, civil war, revolutions, and riots. Further, exclusions exist for injuries caused by atomic nuclear reactions, spreading of biological chemical and nuclear substances in connection with terrorist activities, and finally, damage due to flooding because of the failure to build a barrage. Other types of terrorist activities and consequences of natural catastrophes are not excluded from coverage.

III. Particular Compensation Mechanism for Catastrophes

In Swedish law there are different types of special mechanisms that are of special interest, such as those that handle environmental and natural catastrophes. These are the Environmental Damage Insurance and the Environmental Clean-up Insurance in the Swedish Environmental Code, the rule on damaged wood in the Income Tax Act, the Swedish Nuclear Liability Act, the law concerning extraordinary occurrences during peacetime in the municipality and county council, the Reformed Rescue Service Act, and the Motor Traffic Damage Act. 17

Compensation that is covered by these special cases are principally taken care of by the social insurance schemes and the ordinary insurance system, and, to a minor supplementary extent, by the tort system.

Compulsory liability insurance exists for motor traffic vehicles and railway services. The obligatory traffic insurance covers injuries to the driver, passengers and others and damage to all other things except goods on insured vehicles. At the most 300 million SEK (€ 33 million) can be disbursed from the insurance of any one vehicle. In case this amount is not enough for all claims, compensation for injuries to persons will be paid before property damage. The insurance does not cover injuries or property damage due to war and warlike occurrences, civil war and revolutions rebellion and riots (Motor Traffic Damage Act).

Strict liability also applies to rail traffic both for passengers and goods and injuries and damage to third parties according to the Railway Traffic Act.[19] However, there is an exclusion for *force majeure*. The railway is free from liability if the injury or damage is caused by circumstances which cannot be referred to the running of the railway itself and which the railway could not have avoided or provided against even if the railway had taken all measures that could reasonably be demanded of them. The Railway Safety Act section 4 (last para-

[19] Railway Traffic Act (SFS 1985:192).

graph) lays down that a railway operator must, through insurance or another equivalent way, cover the liabilities that can arise from their operations. The Railway Inspectorate requires that a railway operator must have a liability insurance that covers injuries and losses up to 300 million SEK (€ 33 million) for passengers and goods. The insurer makes exclusions in their liability insurance policies for terrorist acts in the form of spreading of biological chemical or nuclear substances. However, for liability insurance with the highest ceiling amounts (that is, 300 million SEK or more) they make exemptions for all types of terrorist activities since this is a requirement from reinsurers in other countries.

In Sweden the National Railway Administration is responsible for the railway infrastructure and they have insurance covering claims up to 500 million SEK (€ 56 million). However, since the National Railway Administration is a state body and therefore has almost unlimited assets, the Administration can be obliged to pay compensation exceeding 500 million SEK if they are found liable to do so according to tort law.

Air operators are also subject to strict liability towards third parties according to the Aviation Liability Act[20] and liability is unrestricted. The operators must be "sufficiently" insured according to EC regulation 2027/97.

The legislator has not made any proposals to force insurers to include or exclude catastrophic events from coverage in insurance policies due to, and after, the terrorist attack upon the USA on 11 September 2001.

A. *Insurances According to the Swedish Environmental Code*[21]

18 Environmental Damage Insurance and Environmental Clean-up Insurance are compulsory, and are financed by those who pursue environmentally hazardous activities, for which a permit must be obtained, or notification submitted pursuant to the Environmental Code. The contribution depends on the size of the enterprise but is of a minimum 400 SEK (€ 43). Those enterprises that must have a notification to operate will not contribute to the insurance in 2004.

It is important to point out that these insurances are not a protection for the enterprise but for any persons who suffer damage therefrom.

The insurance company AIG Europe AS manages the insurance premium and Marsh Försäkringsmäklare AB in Stockholm handles the administration. A board with members from enterprises, government etc. sets the terms of insurance.[22]

1. Environmental Damage Insurance

19 Environmental Damage Insurance came into force in 1989 as a result of a number of environmental catastrophes, for example, an accident in the southern part of Sweden in the seventies, where buried barrels with environmentally hazardous waste products were found.

[20] Aviation Liability Act (SFS 1957:297).
[21] See *supra* fn. 5.
[22] <http://www.aigeurope.com/miljoe/main.html>. See also SFS 1998:1473.

Chapter 32 in the Swedish Environmental Code states that persons who suffer loss caused by any activity pursued on a property can get compensation for bodily injury, material damage and pecuniary loss. Compensation can be payable for damage caused by:

- pollution of water areas;
- pollution of ground water;
- changes in the ground water level;
- air pollution;
- land pollution;
- noise;
- vibration;
- similar disturbances.

Liable for compensation are any companies that pursue a harmful activity or cause such an activity to be pursued in their capacity as property owners or land leaseholders.

Persons who suffer loss caused by environmentally hazardous activities, and are entitled to compensation according to chapter 32, can get compensation from the Environmental Damage Insurance according to chapter 33 of the Environmental Code if:

- the liable party is insolvent (not just refuses to pay),
- the right to demand compensation has lapsed or
- it cannot be established who is liable for the injury or damage.

This insurance gives compensation to the claimants for bodily injury and material damage. The application must be sought in writing within three years of the injury/damage.

Persons who suffer loss can get compensation for medical treatment, loss of income, damage for pain and suffering, disability and other inconveniences. The compensation is a maximum of 5 million SEK (€ 550,000) per person. For any one injury the total amount payable is 100 million SEK (€ 11 million). Material damage is compensated with a maximum of 50 million SEK (€ 5.5 million).[23]

According to AIG,[24] only a few people have received compensation from the Environmental Damage Insurance. In those cases the usual amount has been about 100,000 SEK (€ 10,900).[25]

2. Environmental Clean-up Insurance

In Sweden the county administrative boards and the municipalities are two of 20
the authorities that supervise and ensure compliance with the objectives of the Environmental Code. If a person who is liable is not able to pay for the damage caused by the environmentally hazardous activity, the supervisor can get compensation for the clean-up cost from their Environmental Clean-up Insurance.

[23] Ministry of the Environment 2002.
[24] Personal contacts with the insurer AIG.
[25] Personal contacts with Niklas Skår at Svenskt Näringsliv.

This insurance covers urgent clean-up costs and costs for actions to prevent future damage and any effects on human beings, property or the environment. The insurance also covers the costs for inspections of the extent of the damage. However, the insurance does not compensate clean-up costs if the liable party is unknown. According to the government bill 1997/98:45 to the Environmental Code, the consequences of this eventuality are difficult to estimate. It may also be difficult to define the cases that should be compensated.

The insurance does not compensate accidents caused by nuclear events or occurrences that are generally included in the concept of *force majeure*. Further, clean-up costs caused by earthquake, landslide, or flood are not compensated nor are costs caused by rescue action according to the Rescue Service Act.[26] The latter costs are not compensated since these are seldom clean-up costs. Finally, no or reduced compensation is paid if the supervisors have not taken measures against an activity that did not fulfil its obligations according to the regulations of the Environmental Code if the supervisor knew or ought to have known about these circumstances.

Compensation can be paid if the cost is more than 58,000 SEK (€ 6,300). The maximum compensation for each clean-up case is 50 million SEK (€ 5.5 million).[27]

Environmental Clean-up Insurance was introduced in 1999 when a new Environmental Code came into force. According to the government bill 1997/98:45, one reason for introducing a clean-up insurance was to reduce the costs for the Government, but it was also considered reasonable that those who pursue hazardous activities should contribute to the clean-up costs. According to AIG,[28] this clean-up insurance has been used more often than the damage insurance. The compensation has normally been above 1 million SEK (€ 109,000).

B. *Income Tax Act*

21 Chapter 21 of the Income Tax Act[29] states that a sole proprietor with income from forestry may, if certain conditions are fulfilled, not have to pay tax directly for income from damaged wood. This income is put in a special bank account and the taxation is payable when the money is withdrawn. In that way the marginal tax rate can be decreased since the income is spread out over several years.

To be able to benefit from this taxation rule some conditions must be fulfilled:

- the income must come from forestry in an agricultural activity;
- the income comes from catastrophes such as storms, fires, or insect outbreaks;
- more than one third of the forest has to be felled earlier than planned;

[26] Rescue Service Act (SFS 1986:1102).
[27] Ministry of the Environment 2002.
[28] See *supra* fn. 5.
[29] Income Tax Act (SFS 1999:1229).

- the main part (75%) of this particular year's income must come from damaged wood.

The deduction is a maximum of 80% of the year's forestry income including insurance compensation if the income derives from felling rights and 50% of the income comes from wood products. That is to say, the deduction is less if the manager sells wood products since the payment is also a compensation for work. A deduction is allowed if the deduction sum is more than 50,000 SEK (€ 5,500) and it does not create a deficit.

The taxation is payable when the money is withdrawn from the bank and the minimum withdrawal each time is 1,000 SEK (€ 110). The account must be concluded within 20 years.

The Act states that storm, fire, insect outbreaks and similar occurrences are examples when the regulation can be used. The National Tax Board gives more examples of other occurrences that may allow deductions. Examples are drought, fungus attack, flood, and damage from industrial emission. The Board points out that the damage must not solely come from natural catastrophes.

The damaged wood regulation came into force in 1982. During the 1970s a large part of growing forest was destroyed because of a fungus attack. This was in turn a result of some major storms in the 1960s. The possibility of decreasing the marginal tax rate gave forest owners more money to finance their forestry activities and to repair the damage. The Government also claimed that the high marginal tax could cause the owners to neglect the protection of the forest.[30]

A total picture of the extent of damaged wood is rather difficult to obtain. A storm in January 2002 in the southern part of Sweden felled 2 million m^3 of forest.[31] This can be compared to the total amount of Swedish forest – 3 billion m^3. According to the Swedish National Tax Board, there are no separate statistics about the use of this particular tax regulation.

C. *The Nuclear Liability Act*

There are four nuclear power plants in Sweden; Ringhals, Forsmark, Oskar- 22
shamn and Barsebäck. These provide nearly half of the Swedish energy production.

The Nuclear Liability Act[32] from 1968 prescribes the compensation for nuclear catastrophes. This act follows international conventions – the Paris Convention and the Brussels Convention.

The owner/operator of a nuclear plant must compensate any nuclear damage caused by a nuclear accident in the plant. The owner/operator of the plant also compensates nuclear damage caused by a nuclear accident during transportation if the transportation consists of atomic substances. However, the owner/operator is not responsible for a nuclear accident if it is a direct conse-

[30] *Propositioner* (Prop.) 1978/79:81, 7.
[31] <http://www.svo.se>.
[32] Nuclear Liability Act (SFS 1968:45).

quence of an act of war, civil war, revolt etc. or if it is caused by a serious natural catastrophe of an extraordinary kind.

The compensation that a person can receive because of nuclear damage is set by the general tort regulations. The matter must be reported within 3 years after the nuclear accident and any claim for compensation must be raised against the possessor of the plant within 10 years from the date of the accident. The maximum amount paid for each nuclear accident is 175 million "drawing rights" (in currency stipulated by the International Monetary Fond).

The owner/operator of the nuclear plant in Sweden must take out third party insurance and the Government must approve the insurance. This Act has never been used.[33]

D. Law on Extraordinary Occurrences in Peacetime in the Municipality and County Council

23 The Local Government Act[34] states that the public sector in the county council and in the municipality is divided into different operational fields. Each field has a managing board accountable for the activity. No board has, in peacetime, overall responsibility or the right to make decisions above the other boards. It is therefore difficult to co-ordinate the activity in case of extraordinary occurrences. This fact became especially obvious after some major accidents in Sweden – an accident when building a railway tunnel, a fire at a discotheque, flooding etc. All those occurrences were extraordinary and put special and high demands on the public sector.

As a result of this, a new law came into effect in 2003[35] that states that a special "crisis management board" shall exist in each municipality and in the county council. This board handles extraordinary occurrences that cause a severe disturbance, or an immediate risk of severe disturbance, and where an urgent effort is needed. Each municipality and county council must establish a plan concerning how the extraordinary occurrences shall be managed. It is then the task of the chairman of the board to judge whether the board must act.

Since this law is rather new no experience is available for consideration. A discussion about financing this new engagement is currently taking place between the Government and the Swedish Association of Local Authorities. The law states that municipalities may assist other municipalities and that they have a right to equitable compensation for this assistance from the municipality in need. This municipality can in turn demand compensation from the State according to the law on protection against accidents. See the following chapter.

E. The Reformed Rescue Service Act

24 In the Rescue Service Act[36] from 1986 the municipality's responsibility and duty in rescue service was regulated. Rescue service here meant the rescue

[33] Personal contact with The Swedish Nuclear Power Inspectorate.
[34] Local Government Act (SFS 1991:980).
[35] Law on Extraordinary Occurrences in Peacetime (SFS 2002:833).
[36] Rescue Service Act (SFS 1986:1102).

work that the Government or the municipality was responsible for in case of accidents. Their mission was to prevent and reduce damage to human beings, property or the environment. The municipality was responsible for planning and organizing the activity so that the rescue operation could start within an acceptable time and be effective. The municipality also had to develop a rescue plan.

The Rescue Service Act gave different municipalities the possibility to co-operate and, for instance, to have a mutual rescue service. However, the Act did not provide any possibilities for overlooking the formal decision-making process stipulated in the Local Government Act, for example, the notice to attend meetings and the right of the committee to make decisions.

A new Reformed Rescue Act came into force in 2004.[37] This new Act gives the municipalities better possibilities for adjusting the service and the size of the activity to local conditions. It also prescribes an investigation of the rescue service activity after each accident and that the State has a right to appeal against a court's decision on compensation from the State to the municipality. This new right to appeal is due to the concept of "rescue service" and the actions that are included in that concept. The municipalities have a right to compensation from the State in case of discharge of oil in water and if the expenditures for this rescue operation exceed a stipulated sum or if expenditures are required for cleaning-up after emission of nuclear material. The municipality also has the right to compensation for rescue actions that have been costly and exceeded excess. The county administrative courts have, in two cases, adjudged that the municipality should have received more compensation than the Swedish Emergency Management Agency had paid. (The Swedish Emergency Management Agency co-ordinates, by order of the Government, the rescue service in Sweden). The new Act explains more clearly that expenditures that occur after the rescue actions will not be compensated.

F. The Motor Traffic Damage Act

According to the Motor Traffic Damage Act,[38] motor traffic damage insurance 25
is statutory but is operated by private insurers. The insurance is compulsory. The insurance compensates for injuries and damage from traffic with motor driven vehicles. Compensation is paid for injuries to drivers, passengers or other persons. This means that the compensation is paid independent of liability. The motor traffic damage insurance compensates damage to another person's vehicle or for material damage. Damage to the guilty party's vehicle or material are not compensated. Insurance is here paid by the private insurance.

G. Responsibilities for Dams at Hydroelectric Power Stations

Nearly half of Swedish energy production comes from hydroelectric power. 26
There are, therefore, many regulated water areas and around 900 dams for hy-

[37] Law on Protection against Accidents etc. (SFS 1993:778).
[38] Motor Traffic Damage Act (SFS 1975:1410).

droelectric power. Of these 143 are classified as high dams i.e. more than 15 m in height. Three are higher than 100 m and the highest is 122 m.[39]

An accident when a dam breaches can of course lead to severe damage, since a great volume of water is dammed up behind it. Two major accidents occurred in 1973 and in 1985. The first was a breach of a smaller dam that caused one death, and the latter caused forestry damage. In 1994 a group that co-ordinates information about high flow, The Co-ordinating Group for High Flows, was established. This group consists of representatives from interest groups from six major rivers, five county administrative boards, the rescue service, SOS Alarm, the police, the Swedish Meteorological and Hydrological Institute, the Swedish National Road Administration, and the Swedish Armed Forces. The task of this group is also to give recommendations so that the effects of high flow can be minimized. Furthermore, this group assists with information in case of a dam breach. The major rivers also have special groups with the task of collecting knowledge about the specific river, which is of importance if an accident is imminent.[40]

Chapter 11 of the Environmental Code regulates water operations. An amendment to the law was made in 1997, which prescribes that the person who is responsible for maintaining a dam for water regulation is also strictly liable for damage caused by failure of the dam. This person is often the owner, but can also be the user or the person who has the responsibility for maintaining the dam. The liability applies even if the damage is not caused by the person responsible for maintenance or by a person for whom the former is responsible. However, a person is not responsible if the damage is caused by an act of war or similar act in connection with an armed conflict, civil war or riots.

The Government claimed, in the government bill (Prop. 1997/98:45) that it is logical that the person who is running the activity also, as a cost for the activity, runs the risk of the damage that may occur. Another reason for the strict liability is that the costs of damage are more likely to be lowered if the person who carries the burden of the costs also controls the risk. That is, it is the enterprises that should be responsible for the risks that they can manage, for the persons who suffer from the damage have limited possibilities of controlling these risks. The Government stated that it is important that the persons who may suffer damage can get sufficient protection and do not have to prove the guilt of others in order to claim successfully.

Part IV. Administrative Procedure and Appeals

27 The Social Insurance Office has an obligation to assist and investigate any case so that the report is as comprehensive as possible to form a correct decision. If a person is not satisfied with the Social Insurance Office's decision, the Office can be asked to reconsider the matter. The Office will then review the case and deliver a new decision. In some instances the Office can be demanded to re-evaluate its decision, for example, a decision to withdraw a sick-

[39] <http://www.vattenreglering.se>.

[40] T. Madell, *Dammägaransvar. En skadeståndsrättslig studie om ansvar vid dammgenombrott* (1992), 7.

ness benefit. If it is a question of pension, the appeal goes directly to a County Administrative court. The judgments of the courts can be appealed to an Administrative Court of Appeal and to the Supreme Administrative Court (SAC). However, review permission is needed from the two last courts to get the case heard. The SAC only considers those few cases involving important matters of principle or precedence, or where the lower instance courts have made flagrant mistakes. The procedure is in writing and the courts have an obligation to assist and advise the complainants. This means that the court should inform the complainant if, for example, a certain type of evidence is needed. The court can also invoke evidence *ex officio*. This means that a complainant will not lose their case because of ignorance of any formal requirements, so in most cases legal aid is not granted and legal counsel is not needed.

The formal requirements for the appeal petitions are very low and the petition should be interpreted in favour of the appellant. It should also be noted that Swedish administrative courts examine the administrative acts in all aspects, not only the legality, as in many other countries. This means that the court both tries the legality and the appropriateness of the decisions and puts itself in the same position as the administrative authority. There are no costs for the individual, neither with the administrative authority, nor at the court. This means that there are no court fees or other compensation to be paid if applicants are not successful with their claims.

I. Elements of Proof

A dispute over responsibility for damage and any claim for compensation in 28
connection with a catastrophe usually ends up in a general court system and starts in a district court. The procedure here is laid down in the Code of Judicial Procedure. One important principle of this Code is the application of free evaluation of evidence. This means that anything, including oral statements of any kind and by anybody, can be used as proof during the litigation, even if it is illegally acquired evidence. It is then up to the court to determine to what extent the facts have been proved by a conscientious examination of everything that has occurred during the main hearing. In a compensation case, the plaintiff has to prove that it was probable that damage was caused by the event or that they were the owner of a specific piece of property. Oral testimony of the value of lost or damaged property can be used, and in this sense the process is rather informal. In a civil case a party can ask to be heard under oath, which also means that the party is criminally liable for untrue statements. Normally it is up to the party that makes a claim to prove its existence. If the value of a claim cannot be objectively calculated, the court will make a discretionary estimate of the value.

The same level of proof is put on the claim brought before an insurance company since the formal requirements of the evidence here can of course be no higher than those that a court would demand, as the dispute eventually might end up there if not settled beforehand.

If a dispute over compensation has reached the court, legal counsel would be necessary and the individual would be entitled to legal aid. During initial negotiations with an insurance company no legal aid would be necessary. If a conflict arises, legal assistance could be needed and legal aid could be granted.

Receipt of a prepayment would only be possible if it was undisputed that the party was entitled to compensation, but the amount was in dispute. If a party is in a state of destitution and has no means of her/his own because of some catastrophe, s/he is entitled to welfare assistance from the Municipal Social Welfare Committee. This would cover immediate requirements such as housing and other basic needs such as food, clothes, furniture and household utensils.

II. Public Legal Aid and Private Legal Expenses Insurance

A. Private Legal Expenses Insurance

29 If a person has insurance with insurance protection that covers legal expenses, s/he cannot obtain legal aid. The possibility of obtaining legal aid is restricted to damages that are payable under liability insurance, or compensation under the Motor Traffic Damages Act. Legal protection insurance is automatically included in all Swedish home, house and summerhouse insurance, and furthermore in comprehensive insurance of boats, and also comprehensive and partial insurance of cars. This means that more than 95% of the population is covered by such insurance. If a party "ought to have" private legal protection insurance, that is, has sufficient economic means or has no excuse for not having such a policy, public legal aid will not be granted. A person who cannot afford home insurance will get public legal aid. Applications to utilise legal protection insurance are made to the person's own insurance company.

Primarily, a person must, as a rule, rely on legal expenses coverage in insurance policies whenever s/he needs financial help in a legal dispute. The legal expenses coverage is intended to cover part of the expense of the insured for retaining a lawyer in disputes of a private nature. If a person does not have legal expense insurance, and there is no valid reason for this, no State assistance, as a rule, will be available for the legal expenses.

Litigation insurance covers the expenses of, amongst other things, a legal representative. It also covers the costs a losing party may be obliged to pay to the winning party. The litigation insurance is normally constructed such that policyholders are obliged to pay 10 to 20% of the costs incurred, with a minimum amount of, for example, 1,200 SEK (€ 140). Many insurance companies have also restricted the total sum of their compensation to around 100,000 SEK (€ 11,000). Regard is not given to the financial situation of the policyholder.

B. Public Legal Aid

30 Legal aid is a form of social security for persons unable to obtain legal assistance in any other way. Subject to certain conditions, one can obtain legal aid from the State if the dispute does not come within the legal expenses coverage of insurance policies. Whether a person can obtain legal aid depends, amongst other things, on their financial circumstances. In addition, it must be found

reasonable for the State to contribute towards the cost, and the person must be in need of legal aid representation.

Public legal aid can only be given to individuals and not to legal entities, with the exception of a deceased person's estate. Legal aid can be provided in various forms, i.e. legal advice, general legal aid in civil cases, and aggrieved party counsel. Lawyers at advocates' offices and other law practitioners can provide legal aid under the Legal Aid Act. However, they are not obliged to do so.

In order to be granted legal aid, a person must, as a rule, begin with one hour's consultation with an advocate or some other lawyer who grants legal aid. Advice may be given, for example, on the rules applicable to interpretation of contracts, how one should proceed if dissatisfied with a decision of a court, other public authority or private insurance company. Advice under the Legal Aid Act may not take more than two hours. If assistance is needed with more complex issues, which take longer time, legal aid may in some cases be obtained. Assistance can also be obtained from an aggrieved party counsel. Advice is provided for a fixed fee and for, at most, two hours. One hour's advice costs, as of 1 January 2000, 1,075 SEK, (€ 118). In certain cases, the fee may be reduced by half. This consultation must, as a rule, be paid for out of the person's own pocket.

If the party granted legal aid loses the case, s/he will have to reimburse the winning party its litigation costs, as these cannot be covered by the legal aid. S/he will have to cover those costs herself or himself although the main part of these costs might be covered by a legal expense insurance connected to home insurance and car insurance, which more than 95% of the population in Sweden are covered by.

Legal aid means that a person can obtain assistance with part of the costs in matters that cannot be dealt with within the advice time, for example settlement negotiations with insurance companies or preparation for court action. Legal aid covers part of the costs for a lawyer or other expert. Help can also be obtained with expenses for presenting evidence and other disbursements, for example, expenses for appearing in court.

In order to obtain legal aid, and for a person to receive one hour's advice under the Legal Aid Act, s/he must not have a financial base exceeding 260,000 SEK (€ 28,500) per annum. Should there be a need for legal counsel, it should be reasonable for the State to contribute to the expenses in the matter. If legal aid is granted, a lawyer is appointed and paid for by the State up to a maximum of 100 hours. A person who is granted legal aid must contribute to the costs by paying a legal aid charge, which is fixed as a percentage of the costs of counsel (2–40% of the costs). The State pays the rest. The amount of the charge depends on how high the income is, the maintenance obligations, her/his wealth and debts (that is to say, the financial base). The charge may never be greater than the costs for the legal aid. The charge is collected continuously in pace with the work done by the counsel handling the matter.

The lawyer the party approaches should help to apply for legal protection or legal aid. The court grants legal aid if the court is already dealing with the legal case when the party applies for legal aid. In other cases, the Legal Aid Authority decides on legal aid.

If the party loses a case at court, s/he will normally pay her/his own legal aid costs (i.e. advice and legal aid charge) and also the other party's costs, even if s/he has legal aid. If the party wins, the losing party should reimburse the costs.

An aggrieved party counsel, who is an advocate or trained lawyer, will protect the interests and should provide support and assistance. An aggrieved party counsel may, for example, present the claim for damages in a criminal prosecution if the prosecutor does not do this. A person can obtain aggrieved party counsel if s/he is a victim of crime (aggrieved party) for any offence under the Penal Code for which imprisonment may be imposed. The court appoints aggrieved party counsel. The court can only do this when the preliminary investigation has been initiated. The aggrieved party counsel is paid by the State irrespective of the income of the applicant.

Part V. Coordination or Cumulation

31 Coordination means that the benefit an injured party has received is deducted from damages. If there is no deduction, but an injured party receives compensation from various sources for the same injury, the benefits are said to cumulate. There are basically three main alternatives as far as coordination and cumulation are concerned:

- In the Tort Liability Act Chap. 5 Art. 3 it is laid down that, when deciding compensation for loss of income or for other financial maintenance support, deduction shall be made for any such benefits the person suffering the loss is entitled to obtain. It can be compensation from compulsory social insurances, pension, sick-pay which is payable by an employer under the terms of an employment contract, or any insurance paid by the employer. There is no recourse for the society or the employer. Consequently the compensation that the tortfeasor otherwise would have been obliged to pay will be covered by the taxpayer or the employer. The purpose of this is to reduce transaction costs by diminishing the number of actions for recourse. As a result, a large proportion of the costs related to traffic injuries are covered by society and not by car insurers. There is a current discussion concerning whether these costs for traffic injuries should be transferred to car insurance or remain with the state.

- From the tortfeasor's point of view, this compensation principle means that his or her obligation to pay is diminished accordingly. As far as compensation for personal injuries is concerned, this is the main principle. This means that social insurance benefits, benefits from collective private insurances, and benefits from other insurances are coordinated. The received damages from the tortfeasor will be reduced with the benefits that already have been received e.g. from the social insurance, such as sickness benefits, etc.

  If it is a matter of property damage, the same result will, in practice, often be the same as above. That is, if the person entitled to damages uses his insurance, which would be the simplest way to get compensation, then the tortfeasor cannot be liable to pay damages. A person should not get more compensation than that which covers the actual loss, and should not be able to make a profit. The insurer in this situation has a right to recourse from the tortfeasor only in cases of gross negligence or intentional acts.

- Compensation from applicable insurance is deducted from the damages, but the insurer has a right to recourse against the tortfeasor according to the Insurance Contract Act section 25. This is usual with insurance against damages where recourse would be of a great economic importance, for example for marine insurance. If the recourse would be directed towards a private person, insurance companies often refrain from exercising their rights. This section, however, is non-compulsory and insurance companies often do include a clause in their standard-form contracts that they should have a right to recourse for all types of negligence in this situation. The right to damages is transferred to the insurance company. When it comes to property insurance, insurers normally demand a right to recourse. In recent years, recourse has been more frequent against companies. Tort law in Sweden at present focuses on the injured person's possibilities for compensation, and pays less attention to who will ultimately cover the costs of the loss. This means that especially the social insurance system covers a substantial part of the losses. It is a characteristic trait of Swedish tort law that insurances to a large extent cover the compensation instead of awards of damages. The reparative function of damages has been emphasised before the preventive function. There have been some proposals that the right to recourse should be extended, but these have not yet led to any changes in the law.
- In some areas, the law allows indemnity to cumulate with damages, i.e. compensation does not affect the damages. This leads to an over-compensation, but it is accepted in those cases where injured parties themselves have paid the insurance fee, for example, for private accident and life insurance. From the tortfeasor's point of view this means that the damages will not be reduced owing to the injured person being compensated from an insurance of his own for the same injury. For these insurances, the rule is that there is no right for recourse for the insurer against the tortfeasor.

A priority order for receiving compensation for personal injuries would be 32
first to rely on the social insurance and social welfare system for the immediate needs for medical treatment and compensation for loss of income. If an income cannot be received from the social insurance system, a person can turn to the social welfare committee for support according to the Social Services Act. However, the Social Services Act is coordinated with the social insurance system, in the sense that if economic support is disbursed later from the social insurance, then this money could be directed to the Social Welfare Committee to cover the payments that have already been made. This means that no-one can be overcompensated from the public support schemes for their upkeep. Victims do not have to use tort law before they can turn to either the social security or the specific compensation mechanisms. This means that the victim will get compensated almost immediately after the event.

For additional compensation outside the social insurance and welfare systems, persons must turn to their private insurance. This would be step number two. This means that for injuries and losses that are not covered by social insurance, a person will be reimbursed by the insurance policies, for example for property losses, extra costs for accommodation, or non-financial damage, pain and suffering, etc. The responsible entity for nuclear plants or dams should be insured according to rules laid down in law. In practice this means that the injured person turns to the tortfeasor's insurance for compensation. S/he could also turn to the tortfeasor's liability insurance for those types of compensation where cumulation is allowed.

The next step, and often also the last resort for claims of compensation, would be to use the tort system itself if there is a party with sufficient means possible to negotiate with, and eventually sue. This way is seldom used, since the systems described above cover most of the costs that the injured person would have accumulated. Compensation according to insurance policies is decided against the background of what a formal tort law dispute would mean if brought to court. Furthermore, there is a substantial risk that tort litigation would take a very long time before finally being settled, which is an inhibiting factor, since it may take five years or more if appeals are made.

In case a catastrophe is caused by a criminal action, the last resort for compensation would be the criminal injuries compensation described above.

Part VI. Discussion

33 A Swedish Government Committee Report has been assigned to review the rules on coordination of damages, compensation from public insurance schemes and compensation from other types of insurances in connection with personal injuries.[41] This report has not yet led to any Government bill.

Part VII. Heads and Amounts of Damages

34 The basic principle for calculation of damages for compensation is that the injured parties should be put in the same position as if the injury or damage had not happened. The Tort Liability Act regulates the heads of damage. Compensation due to personal injury covers:

- costs of medical care and other costs or expenses, including reasonable compensation to persons who are particularly close to the injured;
- loss of income;
- pain and suffering;
- disability and harm.

Where personal injury has resulted in the victim's death:

- compensation is paid for funeral expenses and other expenses to the extent that it is deemed reasonable as other expenses resulting from the death;
- loss of maintenance allowance or other financial support;

[41] *Statens offentliga utredningar* (SOU) 2002:1, 265–273.

- compensation for personal injury for a person who was particularly close to the deceased victim.

For property damage, the Act states that compensation should be paid for:

- the value of the property or for repair expenses, together with the diminution of value;
- other expenses incurred as a result of the loss or damage;
- loss of income or infringements on professional activities.

There is no ceiling amount laid down in the Tort Liability Act. A characteristic Swedish trait is that opinions on the amount of damages for personal injuries are regularly given by advisory boards comprising judges or former judges, insurance officials usually with legal training and with great experience in loss adjustment, and laymen. The opinions are only consultative but have a considerable influence by virtue of the composition and competence of the board. The most important of these boards is the Road Traffic Injuries Commission established in 1936. The purpose of the Commission is to ensure that the compensation is reasonable and as just and uniform as possible. The Commission also evaluates injuries and makes a proposal for the calculation of the compensation. The Government has stipulated that the insurance companies settling motor car claims regarding personal injuries must consult the Commission for an advisory opinion before the insurer reaches a final settlement with a claimant if the claims are of a certain proportion (10% invalidity). The insurance company is also, in a number of other cases, obliged to send the claim to the Commission. If there is a dispute, the injured person can also refer it to the Commission. The Commission's opinion is only advisory and the parties may settle the case in accordance with the Commission's recommendations, agree on some other solution or bring the case to court. In more than 90% of cases, the parties agree to settle in accordance with the Commission's recommendations.

To uphold the uniformity of compensation, the Commission issues guidelines on how they consider various types of injuries should be compensated. This is often done in the form of a table with various parameters. Formally the Commission only handles claims according to the Swedish Traffic Damage Act. However, the practices of the Commission have an influence on the whole tort law and insurance area. On request from courts and authorities it also issues recommendations on how claims should be settled. The tables are frequently used in the Swedish law society, and the Supreme Court has, on several occasions, adjudicated according to these tables.

As an example, the Commission has issued a guiding table for determining compensation for pain and suffering. According to the table for 2003, one should get 4,800 SEK (€ 533) as long as one is hospitalised for a serious injury. However, if the hospital treatment continues for longer than six months, the amount is somewhat diminished to 3,500 SEK (€ 389). A serious condition could for example be severe paralytic conditions or total or near total incontinence. The Commission also issues guidelines for compensation of various forms of amputations. For example, in 2003 an amputation of a hand should normally be compensated with 75,000 SEK (€ 8,333) for a 25 year old person.

The procedural rules must be approved by the Government which also appoints the chair. The other members are appointed by the Swedish Financial Supervisor Authority. The chairman and five deputy chairmen are highly qualified judges. Twelve members of the Commission are laymen representing professional organisations and twelve members represent the insurance companies. The normal quorum is six people, two lawyers, two laymen and two representing the insurance companies. The Commission has access to highly qualified medical experts who may be consulted in cases concerning medical matters. The Commission handles about 3,500 cases every year. Traffic insurances cover the costs for the Commission and there are no costs for the injured person.

Pure economic loss or financial loss that is economic damage, which arises without any person having concurrently sustained loss of life, personal injury or loss of or damage to property, is only compensated if it is caused by a crime. That is the rule according to the Tort Liability Act. However, pure economic loss can be compensated if the State or a municipality has caused damage by a wrongful act or omission in connection with the exercise of public authority or if these bodies have supplied incorrect information or advice and there are particular reasons for liability. Particular statutes sometimes also allow compensation for pure financial loss, such as the Environmental Code e.g. for reduced value of real property or loss of profit in a business.

There are ceiling amounts that the Crime Victim and Support Authority can compensate and it is, for property damage, 10 times the price base amount (according to an index linked base amount fixed by the Government for one year at time on the basis of figures provided by Statistics Sweden). This is adjusted annually. Various social security benefits and allowances are calculated from this amount. For 2003 this amount is 38,600 SEK (€ 4,289). This means in this case 386,000 SEK (€ 42,889). Damages for personal injuries cannot exceed 20 price base amounts, that is 772,000 SEK (€ 85,778) and to this sum one may add compensation for violation of personal integrity, with a ceiling of 10 price base amounts.

I. Third Party Insurance

35 Many insurance companies do not cover third party interests in connection with personal injuries, apart from a smaller amount to close relatives for "sorrow and regret" in connection with pain and suffering. The main rule according to Swedish tort law is that third party losses due to bodily injuries or damage to another person do not entitle this third party to any compensation. That means that an employer, for example, cannot claim any damage if one of his employees is killed or injured.

Part VIII. Empirics

I. Discotheque Fire in Gothenburg

At the end of October 1998, a discotheque in Gothenburg was set ablaze by arsonists and 63 people died, about 200 people were seriously injured and around 450 people were considered as aggrieved parties. Four people were subsequently convicted for the crime.[42] 36

Gothenburg Municipality, a few days after the fire, paid a lump sum of 20,000 SEK (€ 2,220) to each family who lost a child in the fire. This disbursement was paid *ex gratia* by the municipality without support by the Swedish Local Government Act or the Social Services Act. Actually both Acts prohibit stereotyped disbursements to individuals without an examination of the circumstances in each and every case. These decisions would probably have been questioned if somebody had appealed to the County Administrative Court. The disbursements were supposed to cover unspecified costs for the relatives especially in connection with funeral expenses. Many of the victims were immigrants with different religious backgrounds and some of these religions require a rapid funeral after a death and also many of these were considered to be in need of financial support. There was no time to make individual evaluation of needs and the municipality therefore made these "stereotyped" disbursements without seeking support under the Social Services Act.

If victims' families had additional costs outside this, they could apply for assistance according to the Social Services Act and then an ordinary individual evaluation could have been made. The reason for making the disbursements could also have been influenced by the stir and state of shock that arose due to the extent of the catastrophe and the fact that the politicians wanted to show determination and made statements that they later felt obliged to fulfil. Social Insurance covers most costs for medical treatment and the major part of one's loss of income but not funeral costs.

Gothenburg municipality calculated that their extra costs after the fire were 120 million SEK (€ 13 million). This money was for the most part used to finance wages for 120 people who were engaged in various social support programmes, for example in schools where survivors of the victims studied. The Government has paid *ex gratia* in this case 90 million SEK (€ 10 million) to the Municipality to cover some of its costs.

Most of the claims for compensation were dealt with by two insurance companies. It was either the assault protection in the household insurance of the victims, or the liability insurance of three of the four perpetrators that covered this. Liability insurances, however, do not cover intentional acts. This rule notwithstanding, the liability insurers of the tortfeasors in this case made disbursements *ex gratia* for goodwill reasons etc, as if they had been obliged to do so (Kulans). The tortfeasors were convicted of arson, an intentional crime, but the courts did not consider them to have had intent to injure any persons.

[42] Judgment by the Court of Appeal for West Sweden (*Hovrätten för Västra Sverige*) 28 May 2004, T3338-03.

Therefore the insurer Folksam made disbursements from the liability insurances.

However, these insurance policies had ceiling amounts for liability, which meant that some people could not receive damages from the insurance companies. The ceiling amount for the three liability insurances was 5,000,000 SEK (€ 555,555). Only three perpetrators out of the four had liability insurance which means in total 15 million SEK (€ 1,666,666). If these three liability insurers had decided not to make any disbursements, the subsidiary responsibility of the Crime Victim and Support Authority would have compensated the victims.

Those who were inside the room where the fire raged received a general compensation of 100,000 SEK (€ 11,100) for violation of their personal integrity, 25,000 SEK (€ 2,800) for pain and suffering, and 2,000 SEK (€ 220) for unspecified costs. Those who stayed in the stairwell received 25,000 SEK (€ 2,800) for violation of their personal integrity. The insurance companies gave stereotyped disbursements to avoid litigation over damage claims. The sum of 100,000 SEK for violation of one's personal integrity is equivalent to what the insurance companies would have disbursed for a victim of an attempted murder. In this case the amounts of € 11,100 were taken from liability insurance. Other types of compensation were disbursed by the Crime Prevention and Support Authority because the compensation payments were greater than the total ceiling amounts in the three liability insurances. This was the case with a stereotyped compensation of 25,000 SEK (€ 2,777) which was paid to the close relatives of the deceased according to the Tort Liability Act chapter 5 art. 2 for the psychological injury they suffered (pain and sorrow). This amount was decided by the Crime Victim and Support Authority and they considered that it reflected the standardised compensation to relatives in the case of death. It corresponds to pain and sorrow compensation for one year of sick leave according to tort law practice. If a party can show that they are unable to work for a longer period, the amount could be higher. Some of the relatives sued the tortfeasors in a civil litigation and claimed that the compensation should be 100,000 SEK (€ 11,111). The District Court awarded the plaintiffs 50,000 SEK (€ 5,555) but, in that case, the plaintiffs had been unable to work for more than one year. An appeal is now pending in the Court of Appeal.

The amount of 100,000 SEK (€ 11,100) was a compensation for violation of the victims' personal integrity which, according to Swedish tort law, is a ground for compensation in conjunction with crimes. The Tort Liability Act chapter 2 art. 3 and chapter 5 art. 6 lay down that when deciding compensation, one should take into account if the perpetrator's deed was likely to cause serious fear for life or health. The amount was standardised. As a result one could probably assume that some people were overcompensated.

"Pain and suffering" refers to personal physical and/or psychological suffering during the acute medical treatment period and normally the injured person should be on the sick-list. The period continues until the injured person returns to work, or permanent disability conditions have set in.

The assault protection in household insurances for relatives contains a clause covering "sorrow and regret" in the case of a close relative who is killed through murder or manslaughter. In one insurance policy as of 1 January 2003, for example, this protection amounted to 25,000 SEK (€ 2,777) and in another policy covered 30,000 SEK (€ 3,333). In case a relative has household insurance, this could cover pain and sorrow. However, if the courts or the Crime Prevention Authority rules that the compensation should be higher than 25,000 SEK, then the Crime Prevention and Support Authority will disperse the difference between the ceiling amounts in the insurances and what the court might decide.

In the Gothenburg fire case, the insurance companies chose to make a favourable interpretation of insurance conditions, which led to more generous compensation than victims were really entitled to, according to tort law and the strict terms of the insurance policy. The reasons for this are probably that insurance companies generally like to avoid litigation over the amount of the compensation and thereby incur costs and loss of goodwill. This process was probably also affected by an extensive media interest in the fire and its aftermath. If the insurance companies had chosen to interpret the insurance conditions strictly according to the conditions in the insurance policy, some of the injured would have been without compensation, which would have given the companies bad publicity. Apart from the general compensation, victims who were seriously injured also received individual compensation according to regular insurance standards under other heads of damage, such as disability and lost income. The legal counsellors to the parties in their dealings with the insurance companies were given a fee equivalent to two hours of work by the insurance companies.

Those injured who were not covered by insurance compensation could turn to the Crime Victim Compensation and Support Authority to receive criminal injuries compensation instead of insurance remuneration, since the fire was a catastrophe caused by a criminal act. In this case the insurance companies and the authority had negotiated in advance what to disburse to avoid discrepancies in the compensation levels.

After the Crime Victim and Support Authority received a claim from the injured parties, 80% of the parties received their compensation within four months. In November 2003, five years after the accident 19 people are still waiting for some types of indemnity to be finally settled. This is because the insurance companies or the Authority are, for example, waiting for testimonials concerning permanent disability. One case is pending because of a tort law dispute in court.

According to the insurer Folksam neither the Gothenburg accident nor the 11 September attack have led to any changes in the terms of insurance.

II. The Ferry Estonia

Another major catastrophe occurred in September 1994, when the ferry Estonia sunk in the Baltic Sea during a storm, and more than 800 people were missing or dead, out of a total of more than 1000 passengers and crew. To compensate for lost property for the passengers, the insurance companies (to a large extent) made standard disbursements after oral or written claims were 37 made to them. The settling of this compensation was rapid, often within a week after the claim was made.[43]

III. Chernobyl

38 When the nuclear reactors in Chernobyl collapsed in April 1986, radioactive isotopes, especially cesium 137, spread over the countryside in middle and northern Sweden. To avoid contamination of the meat of grazing animals, livestock had to be kept indoors and fodder had to be transported to the area. Reindeer, which cannot be kept inside, were contaminated, and they also had to be supplied unaffected fodder before slaughter to get cesium levels down to below the prescribed hazardous level. A substantial number of slaughtered reindeer also had to be discarded since the radioactive levels in the meat were too high. When the accident occurred, the Government promised to compensate those exposed, and this was done *ex gratia* on an *ad hoc* basis. In these cases the State, through the National Board of Agriculture, compensated farmers and reindeer owners for their losses.[44]

IV. EU Summit Meeting

39 When Sweden chaired the EU there was a summit meeting in Gothenburg. During this meeting violent demonstrations took place and the demonstrators destroyed restaurants and other businesses along the main street in the city. The enterprises that were hit made a claim to the State for damages and lost income of about 19 million SEK (€ 2.1 million). This was to compensate for losses that were not covered by insurance. One insurance company had not paid any compensation at all because it considered that the damage through violent demonstrations was excluded from coverage. The Government, after an evaluation of the claims, made an *ex gratia* disbursement of about 4.2 million SEK (€ 470,000).[45]

V. Agricultural Damage

40 Various types of catastrophes can hit farmers. Crops and forests can be damaged through all sorts of unfavourable weather conditions or destroyed by insects, diseases or fire. There was previously a State Harvest Protection Fund but it was abolished after the State considered that these issues should be taken care of by the farmers themselves through their own insurance.

Any insurance that would cover all sorts of losses of crops would be very expensive. There are, however, insurances that cover certain types of losses in crops. For example, the insurance company Agria compensates losses due to hail (from 1 April to 31 October) or if one has to re-sow new crops because of frost, drought or erosion (between 1 April and 15 of June). If unfavourable weather strikes at another time of the year, no compensation through insur-

[43] Personal contacts with the Insurers.
[44] Personal contacts with the National Board of Agriculture.
[45] Personal contacts with the Government.

ance is possible. The only way then would be if the destruction was of such a magnitude that the State *ex gratia* decides to mitigate the consequences of the catastrophe.

There are also insurances covering other types of losses of all sorts of farm property including livestock.

One type of major calamity that can strike agro business is various contagious animal diseases such as foot and mouth disease, mad cow disease or salmonella. Compensation for these types of diseases is, to a large extent, covered by State funds according to the Epizoon Act and the Zoonosis Act. Zoonotic diseases are diseases or contagion with animals that can spread from animals to humans (zoonoses) and are not considered to be covered by the Epizoon Act. The administration of these Acts is entrusted to the National Board of Agriculture and decisions by the board about compensation can be appealed to administrative courts. According to Art. 87 of the EC treaty, it is compatible with the common market to grant aid by a Member State through State resources to make good the damage caused by natural disasters or exceptional occurrences.

The Epizoon Act[46] requires that the State shall compensate losses and costs due to decisions by virtue of the Act for:

- losses due to destruction of animals or if they die because of pre-emptive inoculation or other treatment;
- costs for decontamination measures;
- falls in production;
- types of loss of income other than those stated in item 3 above.

Full compensation is paid except for falls in production which is normally paid up to 50% unless it is a serious epizootic disease outlined in a Government decree when full compensation will be remunerated. This means that the farmer has a right to compensation for certain types of diseases.

Compensation for zoonotic diseases is not obligatory for the State but can be made on a discretionary basis by the National Board of Agriculture according to rules laid down in the government decree on zoonotic diseases. Disbursements can be made for basically most types of costs and losses related to the zoonotic disease including the same types of losses and costs enumerated above according to the Epizoon Act. However, the compensation can at the most cover 50% of the losses or costs or up to 70% if the livestock were under voluntary supervision according to the Act on examination of livestock etc. If there are particular reasons, the National Board of Agriculture may exceed the limits above. There are also certain limits applying to, for example, how many broilers (maximum 5,000 per year) or pigs one may include in a claim for compensation. This decree, according to the National Board of Agriculture, gives a discretionary right for partial compensation and is aimed at mitigating the economic effects of the disease.

The rest of the losses and costs have to be covered by private insurances by farmers themselves which could cover up to 91% of the damages. The rest (minimum 9%) is an excess covered by the farmer himself or herself. In case

[46] Epizoon Act (SFS 1999:657).

one can find somebody who caused the disease, for example a deliverer of feedstuff, one could make a claim for indemnification from this party.

In June 2003, some 50 farms in the south of Sweden were contaminated by salmonella cubana. The source of the contamination turned out to be contaminated feed from a feed plant. The Board of Agriculture and other authorities concerned acted swiftly to prevent the contamination from spreading any further by destroying infected animals and feed and decontamination of the farms etc. No infected meat reached consumers. No feed from the plant that delivered the contaminated feed had been exported to any other country. Whenever salmonella is detected in Sweden, the infection or contamination is stamped out. Any food item contaminated with salmonella is deemed unfit for human consumption.[47]

The National Board of Agriculture considered that the food supplier (Lantmännen) had caused the outbreak of the disease by not having performed enough controls upon the fodder, and since the Zoonotic Act is supplementary to the Tort Law and only applicable to spontaneous outbreaks of salmonella, that Lantmännen should pay damages to the farmers.

On 16 July the Board decided to make *ex gratia* preliminary disbursements to farmers for part of their costs and losses of income. These were not based on the Zoonotic Act. These payments were made to help the farmers sustain incomes while waiting for compensation from Lantmännen. The disbursements were also made on the condition that the farmers transferred their right to damages to the National Board of Agriculture.

A number of farmers considered that there is an obligation to pay compensation according to the Zoonotic disease legislation, and they have appealed to the County administrative court.

Part IX. Conclusions

41 According to the Ministry of Justice and the Swedish Insurance Federation, there is no generalised compensation system for victims of catastrophes. However, the question might have been raised in the *Riksdag* (the Parliament) but it has not led to any legislative actions and there is not any commission working along these lines either. This means that the basic needs of victims of catastrophes will be covered according to the Social Services Act and the social insurance system which cover all types of calamities.

In addition, most people can get various types of compensation from first or third party insurance policies governing injuries and property damage. In case a catastrophe is not covered by insurance because of exclusion, for example, if there is a terrorist attack that spreads nuclear substances, compensation outside the social schemes would have to be made on an *ad hoc* and discretionary basis.

In Sweden insurances are required only in special cases. These requirements are for motor vehicles, railways, aircrafts, nuclear plants, and oil spills

[47] <http://www.jordbruksverket.se/net/SJV/Startsida/Presskontakten/Pressmeddelanden/pP.> 2003-12-17 and personal contacts with the National Board of Agriculture.

from shipping. The Environmental Damage Insurance is both insurance and a fund. Companies have to pay a fee to the fund but are not protected by this insurance if an accident happens. The persons suffering from damage on the other hand, can be compensated from the Environmental Damage Insurance (see Part III.III).

In other cases, individual insurance covers costs for damages, except for the excess. This compensation is up to an individual ceiling amount for some types of damage or up to a collective ceiling amount if many injured people are involved. For instance, in a traffic accident, the ceiling amount is 300 million SEK (€ 32.4 million).

These individual insurances cover major damage such as that caused by flood, storm etc. There are seldom any special exceptions except for dam catastrophes and nuclear accidents. On the other hand, nuclear plants must carry special insurance (see Part III.III.C) and hydroelectric power stations operate under strict liability (see Part III.III.G). Terrorist attacks are not specifically excluded in the ordinary individual insurance. However, spreading of biological, chemical, and nuclear substances in connection with terrorist activities is excluded. Insurances for firms have often more extensive regulations.

One deficiency in the Swedish compensation system is that the compensation for future loss of income is low for some young people. This happens for people without employment. Social insurance schemes require that one must have an income from which to compute a pension, otherwise one can only get a basic pension. In addition to that, the Crime Prevention and Support Authority only compensates up to 120,000 SEK (€ 12,900) over the pension.

List of References

Literature

B. Bengtsson, Torts and Insurance, in: P. Cronhult *et al.* (eds.), *Swedish Law a Survey* (1994).

B. Bengtsson, Torts and Insurance, in: M. Bogdan (ed.), *Swedish Law in the New Millennium* (2000).

L. Häll, *Victims of violence and of property crimes 1978–2002* (2004).

T. Madell, *Dammägaransvar. En skadeståndsrättslig studie om ansvar vid dammgenombrott* (1992).

Riksförsäkringsverket (RFV), *Socialförsäkringens omfattning 2002–2003* (2002).

Internet Sites

http://www.aigeurope.com/miljoe/main.html

http://www.brottsoffermyndigheten.se (The Crime Victim Compensation and Support Authority)

http://www.folksam.se (Insurance company Folksam)

http://www.forsakringskassan.se (The Social Insurance Office)

http://www.jordbruksverket.se (The Swedish Board of Agricultural)

http://www2.lansforsakringar.se (Insurance company Länsförsäkringar)

http://www.rfv.se/english/index.htm (The National Social Insurance Board)

http://www.ski.se (The Swedish Nuclear Power Inspectorate)

http://www.sverige.se/sverige (The online gateway to Sweden's public sector)
http://www.svo.se (The National Board of Forestry)
http://www.vattenreglering.se

UNITED KINGDOM

Michael Huber and Tola Amodu

Part I. Introduction

When studying compensation regimes we normally anticipate that relief will derive primarily from the state, more generally its welfare system. The UK is a welfare state that has evolved over the last six decades. Contrary to the dominant writing on the evolution of British social welfare, it does not represent a linear uninterrupted continuum from "individualism" to "collectivism" and hence towards broad, fully inclusive solidarity; instead it is characterised by *two trends* that have been conceptualised in terms of periodisation: firstly, the broad *solidarity* and collectivism concerning individual hardship and secondly, the emphasis on *individual responsibilities*. 1

The Beveridge Plan of 1942 is usually considered as the starting point from which Britain developed the features of a welfare state. This first phase was characterised by collectivism and continuous growth. James Callaghan's speech to the Labour Conference in 1976 in which he told that governments could no longer expect to spend their way out of recessions marks the end of this "classic" period of the British welfare state and opens up a second, pronouncedly individualistic phase that is tightly connected with the name of Margaret Thatcher. Her social policy aimed to limit the role of the state in terms of both public expenditure and size of bureaucracy. In the phase from 1976 to 1996 the role of the market was emphasised and individual responsibilities strengthened. With the Labour victory of 1997, the basic trend of emphasising individual responsibility has not really altered. However, when we say that British social policy focused first on the emerging collectivism, and in a second phase on individualisation, we do not claim that these foci represented exclusive reference points for social policies. We should rather talk about a mixed approach to social welfare that oscillates between solidarity and individualisation.

Taking the tension between solidarity and individualism as the societal standpoint from which to consider compensation issues, it has to be noted, however, that a general trend in the British system has been to opt for individualised solutions, *i.e. there is a strong tradition of the state distancing itself from compensation payments.* Few publicly financed compensation funds exist when emergencies occur: in the context of IRA-terrorism the state has taken specific action to act as insurer-of-last-resort (PoolRe). For natural hazards the other major exception providing minor economic support for communities (not individuals) after catastrophes that has been established is the Bellwin-scheme. This does not imply however that the political sphere or the welfare state do not influence decisions on compensation. Regulatory and legal governance exists, but – if at all avoidable – no direct resource allocation or intervention.

2 Following the guidelines of the questionnaire, we structure the report by distinguishing fundamentally two modes of compensation as decisions about financial compensation are either made in a *public* or a *private* setting. While the public setting is referred to as the state, or politics including the broad implementation of social security objectives, the private setting means essentially insurance. Law is not a third pillar but is seen instead as a complex tool for settling conflicts that mainly (but not exclusively) emerge from the private sphere that develops a dynamic of its own. Political negotiations and public inquires are often, but not solely, the main instruments used to regulate and settle conflicts emerging from the social welfare setting. This very schematic presentation of an overall compensation regime in the UK allows us to discuss legal, political and economic issues and their interrelationship. This constitutes the core of the report.

3 There are some additional features of compensation management that are interesting:

- Increasingly, if the results are unsatisfactory, the private compensation regime is exposed to claims for public compensation – and vice versa. Insurance claims are made if the welfare system fails. Conversely, political demands for state intervention are made if the private insurance system cannot provide morally acceptable outcomes. This means that the pillars of compensation not only cover complementary ground, but any articulation of the existence of a "compensation culture" can lead to irresolvable conflicts when the different compensation systems are confronted with claims by representatives of the other pillar, sometimes with pathological results.
- Compensation by welfare scheme always implies some form of redistribution. This observation points to the limitations of compensation. To what extent are the systems able to compensate for losses? Are there specific types of losses that cannot be compensated or can we observe a certain share of losses that are not insured? How can these uncompensated or under-compensated losses be accounted for? These are questions of both positive and normative significance. Here the issue of the legitimacy of compensation plays a crucial role.
- Are welfare state schemes and private insurance complementary compensations schemes? Is there a natural upper limit or equilibrium of compensation and what effect does a "compensation culture" have on the overall design?
- To what extent do public inquiries gain importance in the settlement of the essential features of compensation management?

Summarising, the UK system favours insurance solutions, i.e. individuated and privately organised attempts to manage accidents, hence insurance compensation plays a central role. Public actors play a limited role in the context of financial compensation for catastrophes. Although conceptually it is not well established what triggers such an intervention, the practical approach is quite uncontroversial. In cases of profound disagreement, the legal arena seems the very place to settle these issues.

Part II. Conceptual Concerns

In looking at the forms of financial compensation for catastrophes we have to begin with observations on the relationship between the welfare state and insurance, and the specific role of law in this context. *What constitutes financial compensation and e.g. when is it just redistribution?* From there we consider if it is possible to distinguish compensation from redistribution, so as to situate the boundary between insurance and state welfare provision. The legal system posits compensation as restitution; the social welfare system focuses on redistribution. Our focus is, of course, on catastrophe compensation. If we consider catastrophe compensation to differ from more routine ways of compensating, the question of what *disasters or catastrophes* are gains importance, as this will trigger a specific social response. Is it a certain risk level, the number of fatalities (expected or factual) or the size of damage that defines a disaster? 4

I. State, Insurance and Law

Any consideration of the role of the welfare state in the context of financial compensation supports a hypothesis about the *complementarity* of welfare state and insurance provision: a comprehensive social welfare system should result in fewer and/or smaller claims for compensation elsewhere and less dispute about size and adequacy of financial compensation. A system based upon private compensation, on the other hand, implies that more individualised responsibility can be allocated and consequently attributes greater significance to the legal arena as a forum to settle disagreements or conflicts. This hypothesis suggests the existence of a choice to either opt for private or public compensation[1] and that at the interface between the two forms *the* legal system will play a key role. Two issues arise from that: first, what is the role of law and how can we clearly distinguish compensation and redistributive policies, particularly if state institutions are involved in this process? 5

Considering the role of law in this context, we are interested in the legal principles or mechanisms that limit compensation claims. Here issues concern-

[1] The "welfare state" is guided by political concepts and ideas, its main interest will not be to identify culprits, or fault and it will try to settle disagreements in form of political negotiations. The main concern here is that victims are provided with the necessary aid and some kind of compensation as swiftly as possible. The insurance related logic is based rather *in* attributing individual fault; the main weakness of the welfare state was seen as inefficiency, lack of clarity and some form of moral hazard. The insurance regime is more efficient, flexible and able to attribute individual faults and victim status. The law is mainly concerned with the settlement of problems emerging from the insurance regime; unlike political negotiations, courts become the main arena for settling issues of compensation.

ing the construction of quantifiable losses, attribution of fault, definition of victims and the methods used to calculate financial compensation are of interest. Legal procedures help to manage compensation claims by defining the situation in which legal actions for compensation claims can be rightly made. Moral and more broadly political issues may challenge or alter legal conceptions of wrongdoing and thus the nature of liability. If the political sphere or the public find certain new claims rightful and morally acceptable, either the definition of the 'trigger' event or the legal tests to be satisfied may change over time (causing problems of accountability and in the long run with insurability), or political solutions offering alternative compensation strategies arise. Here the legal construction of accountability, fault or duty may be of less significance than political pragmatism. A use of state revenues (taxation) to compensate victims bears the hallmarks of re-distributive practices from all perspectives. However, the distinction is blurred and limited effort has been made to identify compensation as a political redistributive strategy.

II. Catastrophe, Hazard or Disaster?

6 Another question, decisively shaping the outcome of this field of research is: what is a catastrophe? Does Britain have any common definition regarding compensation claims in this respect and is a distinction drawn between man-made disasters and natural hazards? Although there is no *ex-ante* established understanding of what a catastrophe is (or rather: there have been numerous attempts), there are institutional actors having the authority to define events as catastrophes. The Environment Agency (EA) has established a four step scheme to identify floods and it has the duty to issue warnings accordingly. In the area of man-made disasters, and in particular in the case of terrorism, political or policy related decisions will play an essential role. The variability in definition leads us to expect that compensation outcomes will vary according to context.

In England and Wales the term "catastrophe" is not a term of art in the legal sense. A reference to various academic journals gives only a broad insight into any potential definition, and in general terms most authors define a catastrophe in terms of actuarial risk. Some guidance is given by the reports of commercial organisations including the Swiss Re series of *sigma* studies.[2] Regardless of the difficulties in defining catastrophes, the economic implications are substantial with the economic losses attributable to natural and man-made catastrophes in 2003 of € 60 billion. The property insurance industry bore approximately one quarter of these (€ 17 billion).[3] The *sigma* studies are useful because they define catastrophe and disaster accordingly:

[2] These *sigma* studies are published by Swiss Re's Economic Research & Consulting team based in Zurich, New York and Hong Kong approximately eight times a year (<http://www.swissre.com/>).

[3] The Report notes "...While the insured property loss figure of $ 18.5 billion is below those of recent record years, 2003 can be added to the list of costly loss years. Catastrophes have caused billions of losses in every year since the late eighties (an inflation-adjusted annual average of $ 20 billion since 1987). There are strong indications that the billion-dollar loss trend will continue, and the 2003 figures confirm this trend towards high losses, which is being driven by increasingly densely populated areas, higher concentrations of insured values and the development of endangered zones. In the long run the natural hazards will increase their share of insurance costs".

- "Natural catastrophe" *is ... an event caused by natural forces. Such an event generally results in a large number of individual losses involving many insurance treaties and insured parties. The extent of the loss resulting from a catastrophe depends not only on the severity of the natural forces concerned, but also on the human factors like construction methods or the efficiency of disaster protection measures in the effected region.*[4]
- By contrast the same Report frames human induced failure in terms of *man-made or technical disasters*, which are ... *major events arising in conjunction with human activities. Generally a large object in a very limited space is affected which is covered by a small number of insurance policies* [p. 4]. The study goes on to divide man-made disasters into a further seven categories. These include major fires and explosions, shipping disasters, rail and road disasters, mining accidents, terrorism and building collapses. The Chartered Insurance Institute (the CII) in its Fact files adopts a similar taxonomy.

The Law Society of England and Wales defines a "disaster" in terms of ... *a sudden or unexpected event ..., which adversely affects a group of individuals resulting in physical injury or death and possibly property damage.*[5] Similar definitions seem to be adopted by the EU (here the reference is made to the percentage of loss or damage in relation to GDP, or the percentage of the population affected by the catastrophe) when considering the entitlement to solidarity funds.[6] The OECD in contrast focuses on large-scale or "mega" disasters whether natural or man-made, by reference to the number of fatalities, the level of economic damage, fiscal impact and insured losses.[7]

By contrast medical professionals (especially psychiatrists and psychologists) define *traumatic events* by reference to the person and in particular a ... *capacity to evoke terror, fear, helplessness or horror in the face of a threat to life or personal injury,*[8] and "disasters" as things which ... *by definition overwhelm institutions, health care or social resources and require months or years for both individuals and communities to recover.*[9]

It seems that catastrophes are presented in terms of a specific risk category, namely events with a low probability of occurrence and high costs; the consequences of this category of events has been most vividly discussed in the context of conflicts about the use of nuclear power in the USA, Germany and the UK. However, the vagueness of criteria and the irresolvable question,

[4] Thus natural catastrophes are defined to include floods, storms, earthquakes, droughts and forest fires. *Sigma* Report, *Natural Catastrophes and man-made disasters in 2000* (2/2001), 4.

[5] Disaster Litigation, *Practice Guidelines for Solicitors* (October 2003), 1.

[6] Council Regulation 2012/2002 11 November 2002, instituting solidarity funding in the event of natural disasters (OJ L 311 14 November 2002).

[7] <http://www.oecd.org/dataoecd/48/39/21121542.pdf> *Lessons Learned in dealing with Large-Scale Disasters* SG/AU (2003)1 15 September 2003 (General Secretariat Advisory Committee on Multi-disciplinary Issues).

[8] American Psychiatric Association 1994.

[9] C.S. Fullerton/R.J. Ursano/A.E. Norwood/H.H. Holloway, Trauma, Terrorism and disaster, in: C.S. Fullerton/R.J. Ursano/A.E. Norwood (eds.), *Terrorism and Disaster: individual and community health interventions* (2003).

which costs are to be included, leaves *catastrophe* as a vague concept. The idea of a disaster or catastrophe is thus more likely in England and Wales (and probably all other European countries) *to be defined by the public sphere more specifically in political or media terms*. This in turn can have significant effects upon the handling of compensation claims, both from the perspective of conceptualising the victim and allocating risks and ultimate responsibility.

7 Fault in general and negligence in particular are based upon a conception of wrongdoing. A classification of types of torts (i.e. civil wrongs) further narrows (or clarifies) the nature and extent of liability viz. who can be a victim, what can be claimed and the nature of the relation between the wrongdoer and the victim in order to establish a prima facie case. But there are exceptions to the above, in particular where Government has decided for reasons of public policy that the victim does not need to establish each and every step of the claim to prove the case (as in the case of the imposition of strict liability). For a claim in negligence to succeed, the question of fault is further refined by a series of judicially imposed hurdles. Over centuries this has included the courts asking questions about the nature of the activity and its "riskiness". This can be deconstructed to a series of principles. In particular (a) the existence of a duty of care must first be established; if there is no duty found to be owing to the victim, a failure to take reasonable care will not give rise to liability. The idea of the existence or otherwise of a duty of care is a relative concept, but has over time been further articulated in terms of the foreseeability of harm, the proximity of the relation between the parties in question and the fairness or reasonableness in establishing the existence of a duty.[10] There is then (b) the issue of the existence of a breach of duty viz. something akin to carelessness and (c) the link between injury and the breach of that duty of care. Relevant to the issue of whether reasonable care has been taken is an objective enquiry into what reasonable measures could have been taken to minimise the risk. Finally the existence of legally recognisable damage needs to be proven. These remarks highlight the role of law and legal procedures in the establishment of compensation rights.

Part III. The General Scope of the Compensation Regime

8 There is a fundamental difference in the treatment of damage to property and injuries to the person caused by disasters. In case of injuries, the social welfare system provides (a) health services and (b) additional benefits. The limited nature of these benefits may be such as to result in court claims for damages to enhance compensation. Access to court proceedings is eased by Legal Aid programmes (a state funded system underwriting some legal proceedings) and recent institutional developments in the legal profession. While in other European countries in the case of natural disasters and man-made catastrophes (such as terrorism), the state intervenes in terms of compensation, in the UK, governments endeavour not to become involved in such payments. The UK

[10] *Capro Industries plc v Dickman* [1990] *Law Reports Appeal Cases* (AC) 2, 605.

system is *primarily* based upon individual insurance agreements. This is true for property damage as well as damage to life and personal injuries. Miscellaneous statutory powers are given to local authorities under local government legislation to alleviate emergencies or disasters, which in expenditure terms ultimately have to be underwritten by Government, and these will be discussed later in the report.

Part IV. The British Compensation Regime

9 This section outlines the main pillars of the British compensation regime, and the social security system (including more general public sponsored activities), which underpin health and property compensation. Specific compensation funds, insurance with a specific focus on terrorism and property insurance in the case of natural hazards will also be discussed. Issues of legal procedures that manage conflicts where competition arises are sketched in the next section.

I. Social Security in the UK

10 All people living in Britain are subject to the *National Insurance System*. The Social Security system in the United Kingdom operates in the form of targeting benefit payments for people who are elderly, sick, disabled, unemployed, widowed, bringing up children or on very low incomes. Some benefits depend on the payment of regular contributions by those in work, employers and the self-employed, as in the case of statutory sick pay and sickness benefit, invalidity and incapacity benefits. Others are related to a person's income. The National Health Service (NHS) provides hospital care (diagnosing and treating illnesses), family health services (local doctors, dentists, opticians and pharmacists) and community health services. Most forms of treatment, including hospital care is given free, i.e. it is financed through the tax system and treatment is independent of individual contributions. Whilst private health care thrives in the UK, three-quarters of people receiving private health care pay for it through health insurance schemes.

11 Historically, the fundamentals of the British social welfare system were laid out in the Beveridge Report of 1942. This report is mainly concerned with a national and comprehensive system of social protection (funded through progressive taxation), which should cover people 'from the cradle to the grave'. Six principles of welfare insurance were introduced: (*i*) comprehensiveness, (*ii*) classes of insurance, (*iii*) flat-rate benefits, (*iv*) flat-rate contributions, (*v*) adequacy and (*vi*) unified administration.[11] These principles were never fully

[11] The original report mentions three principles: "(i) The first principle is that any proposals for the future, while they should use to the full the experience gathered in the past, should not be restricted by consideration of sectional interests established in the obtaining of that experience. Now, when the war is abolishing landmarks of every kind, is the opportunity for using experience in a clear field. A revolutionary moment in the world's history is a time for revolutions, not for patching. (ii) The second principle is that organisation of social insurance should be treated as one part only of a comprehensive policy of social progress. Social insurance fully

realised. Still, social policy in the UK guarantees a minimum standard (or floor) of protection, including a minimum income protection in the event of insecurity. Coverage is extensive, but benefits and services are delivered at a low level consistent with the characteristics of a liberal market economy. The social protection provided is patchy, and services are tightly rationed. The sources of finance for public services are hugely varied: they include taxation, levies, borrowing, charges, commercial profits, public subscription, sales of licences, voluntary donations, labour conscription and lottery funding. As a counterbalance, the activities of public authorities also tend to be restricted by the application of special rules, which do not apply to private firms. In order to avoid distortions in the operation of the independent or private sector that may impact upon overall market conditions (and as such be anti-competitive), the activities of the public sector are closely regulated. They may not be allowed to diversify activities or their financial base.

With the election of the Labour Government in 1997, there were few initial statements of policy guiding the future of welfare in the UK. Commentators have observed[12] however a number of consistent trends or themes. Although in the early years there remained little scope for an increase in public spending resources to enhance benefits, subsequent increases have been targeted towards encouraging paid work and reducing poverty (especially of the elderly and children) through enhanced means testing of benefits. The cost of social security benefits (including tax credits) as a percentage of GDP is in decline, at approximately just below 11.5% for 2003–6. Where tax credits are not taken into account, benefits for the same period amount to approximately 10% of GDP.[13] Before Labour came to office, social security spending amounted to 11.7% of GDP for 1996–7 or £ 106 billion.[14] The real cost of social security, however, continues to rise to approximately £ 120 billion at 2002 prices. Non-contributory non means-tested benefits continue to be paid to the disabled e.g. disability living allowance and invalid care allowance, industrial disablement benefit (see below) and severe disablement allowance. It is in the area of non-contributory non means-tested benefits that the rise in spending continues and these types of benefit continue to command a greater share of public spending overall.

developed may provide income security; it is an attack upon Want. But Want is one only of five giants on the road of reconstruction and in some ways the easiest to attack. The others are Disease, Ignorance, Squalor and Idleness. (iii) The third principle is that social security must be achieved by co-operation between the State and the individual. The State should offer security for service and contribution. The State in organising security should not stifle incentive, opportunity, responsibility; in establishing a national minimum, it should leave room and encouragement for voluntary action by each individual to provide more than that minimum for himself and his family". Social Insurance and Allied Services Report by Sir William Beveridge Presented to Parliament by Command of His Majesty November 1942-3 HMSO Cmd. 6404.

12 E.g. M. Brewer/T. Clark/T. Wakefield, Social Security in the UK under new labour: What did the Third Way mean for welfare reform?, [2002] *Fiscal Studies* 23(4), 505–537.

13 M. Brewer/T. Clark/T. Wakefield, [2002] *Fiscal Studies*, 508 on statistics provided by the Government's Department of Work and Pensions.

14 M. Brewer/T. Clark/T. Wakefield (*supra* fn. 13), 509.

12 The provision of social welfare is divided between public (provision by the state), private (provision by commercial organisations), voluntary (provision on a non-profit basis), mutual aid (provision by solidarity) and informal sectors (provision by friends, neighbours and families).[15] While the National Insurance scheme is a compulsory system, over 10% of the population are insured by private health schemes too (up to seven million in the early 1990s). Furthermore, throughout the 1990s the mix of public and private cooperation increased. This mixed approach to social security plays a central role as far as individual injuries are concerned. Benefits are provided in the form of health services.

The welfare state provides the basic health services. These services mainly define the floor of compensation. Other systems of compensation comprise in the main *additional benefits* or cover against threats that are linked to the effects of injury or incapacity e.g. disablement, loss of income or reduced possibilities in general terms. Compensation claims can be categorised here by two, complementary forms: the more traditional measures to ensure compensation after accidents at work or those harms determined by public policy as warranting additional protection and the more general or diffuse claims after catastrophic events, concerned with loss of income, environmental harm and more general compensation claims. These issues are outlined in the next section.

II. Social Security Benefits and Insurance

13 In a society underpinned by a system of general welfare provision such as the UK, social security benefits are often the most certain (if limited) route to compensation. The existence of sickness and unemployment benefits may in some cases be sufficient to ward off civil actions where personal injury is of a limited scale. In the case of catastrophic events however the same cannot be said.

A. *Welfare or Social Security Entitlements for Industrial Injuries*

14 Some benefits for disablement are paid because of an accident at work, or because of one of over 70 prescribed diseases known to be a *risk* in certain types of employment (see Social Security Benefits and Contributions Act 1992). Others are payable because of the level of disability, *irrespective of employment.*

In the context of *Industrial Injuries Disablement Benefit* (IIDB), only employees rather than the self-employed can benefit.[16] IIDB is a non-contributory (in the sense that it does not rely upon National Insurance contributions paid) non means-tested benefit. People who are disabled because of an industrial accident or prescribed industrial disease may be able to receive Industrial Injuries Disablement Benefit. To obtain the basic benefit, a medical assess-

[15] As far as compensation for catastrophes are concerned, the other providers of social welfare, i.e. mutual aid, voluntary actors and family hardly play a substantial role.

[16] Members of the Armed Forces are also excluded, but there is provision for the payment of a War Pension under another statutory scheme.

ment indicating the degree of the disability (expressed as percentage) caused by the injury or disease is required. Before 1 October 1986 persons being assessed at between 1% and 19% disability received a lump sum gratuity. The size of this lump sum depended on the degree of their disability and the period of assessment. Since 1 October 1986 persons with a disability below 14% are normally excluded from benefits.[17] Alternatively, a weekly disablement pension is paid. The claimant's occupation or any loss of earnings is not taken into account in the assessment of their disability. If the claimant is entitled to other Social Security benefits, these will be paid as well as IIDB. If the claimant is awarded IIDB, it may also be possible to claim further allowances for care and assistance. Benefits for industrial injuries may, however, affect other benefits receivable if these are means-tested. There are strict rules to avoid cumulative effects.

15 There are two additional, tightly related benefits linked to long-term effects of injuries caused by industrial accidents. A Reduced Earnings Allowance (REA) is payable to a person assessed as disabled, and unable to return to their normal job or one which pays an equivalent amount. However, there is a specified maximum rate that is also less than 140% of the maximum disablement pension rate. The disability must have occurred before 1 October 1990. The amount the claimant receives is the difference between the wage in their normal job and the wage of any job they are capable of doing. For victims of industrial accidents occurring after 1 October 1990, REA is not available. Receiving REA of £ 2 a week or more, and not being in regular employment implies that, on reaching the State Pension Age, the person will be eligible for Retirement Allowance (RA) instead of REA, which is 25% of their rate of REA.

16 To fund claims by employees against their employers, a compulsory *employers' liability insurance* (EL) was introduced in 1969. It covers the employer against claims from accidents and illness caused in the workplace, except motor accidents. The regulations (revised in 1998) require the employer to be covered against claims to the sum of at least £ 5 million; practically the minimum coverage is £ 10 million. Insurance claims must be paid even if sufficient information has not been provided or health and safety regulations have not been met. This, together with increased claims, leads to a situation that EL is considered too difficult to sustain from an insurance perspective. It is still however compulsory. This raises a number of problems that (*i*) costs are spiralling and (*ii*) it is increasingly difficult to predict events – hence inadequate premiums will be set.[18] The number, type and costs of EL claims depend on whether future advances in medical science show links between certain occupational diseases and working practices. Procedural legal issues play a crucial role for the problems of the EL. Successive courts and governments have continued to extend the range of claimants entitled to compensation, the level of damage and the range of years after which the liability for diseases may be

[17] Except where the disability is caused by pneumoconiosis, byssinosis, or diffuse mesothelioma.
[18] As this criticism comes from industry, inadequate premiums means too low premiums.

claimed (reference will be made to these issues in more detail later in the paper). Further legal changes such as the reduction of the discount rate for calculating damages and the no win, no fee approach of legal firms have increased the total costs by over 40% (see also: Part X.III "Compensation culture").

B. Compensating Man-made Catastrophes extra the Benefits System

Social security and EL or IIDB are also tools for providing compensation for personal injuries and disablements in the case of larger accidents. Compensation in these cases, however, is focused mainly on insurance. Larger accidents have wider implications for compensation, which are sketched here by way of illustration. The main difference seems to lie in the higher complexity of compensation claims and the differentiation of these claims. Proof of fault becomes a necessity unlike social security. Here (semi-)public investigations and decisions about fault and duty may decide if insurance claims are triggered. The legal arena is used to establish compensation also for damage that is not necessarily covered by insurance in the first place and to settle disagreements about the attribution and sharing of fault (and the consequent allocation of responsibility for loss). The focus of this section is on the second part of compensation: litigation. 17

In both criminal and civil cases relating to large industrial accidents, courts make decisions on an adversarial rather than an inquisitorial basis. The claimant and defendant (in the case of civil proceedings) or the prosecution and defence (in criminal cases) have to test the credibility and reliability of the evidence their opponent presents to the court and the judge arrives at findings based on the evidence presented. In civil proceedings a lower burden of proof is required. Here the case must be proved on 'the balance of probabilities' viz. more likely than not.

Miscellaneous powers exist for local authorities to take steps (including the spending of money) to alleviate a major emergency or disaster within their area – one of which is section 138 Local Government Act 1972. This applies on an *ad hoc* regional basis and presumably will not have national application unless there was a major single catastrophic event affecting the whole of England and Wales. The power (viz. section 138) was used in connection with the Sea Empress disaster. The exercise of this power can result in councils incurring significant amounts of expenditure for which they will not have made provision – and potentially exceed any government set expenditure limits. For this reason the Local Government and Housing Act 1989 provides that the Secretary of State can establish a scheme giving financial assistance to those authorities which have incurred expenditure in connection with an emergency or disaster that has occurred "involving destruction or danger to life or property" where the authority has taken action to safeguard life or property or to prevent further suffering or inconvenience in their area. 18

III. Compensating Natural Hazards

19 The UK system operates under the assumption that property owners purchase private insurance cover. The main challenges are natural hazards. As floods are the greatest threat and natural hazard insurance is bundled, we focus here on flood insurance. This private coverage is *de facto* compulsory; market penetration is estimated to be between 75% and 95%.[19] Court cases are rare, here the main issues are dealt with in the political arena.

Unlike most industrialised countries, England has developed a private flood insurance scheme. It emerged in 1961 as a reaction to challenges of the 1953 flood and has remained largely unchanged ever since. The conditions of private insurance are shaped by a *Gentlemen's Agreement* that codifies a division of responsibility between the state, providing flood defences and the insurance companies, compensating in the case of flood damage. The state sets standards and procedures for decision-making in the fields of flood protection (technological fixes, resource allocation), land-use and flood warning (*protection regime*). This regime grows from attempts to decide on flood defence and can be traced back to the 16th century.[20] Table 1 below indicates the total government spending on flood protection during the period 1990–2004.

Flood protection, land-use and housing development constitute the main areas of flood related regulations – a patchwork of vaguely joined areas.[21] The main elements of the regulations can be found in the Environmental Act (1995), the Water Resource Act (1991), the Land Drainage Act (1991) and the Coastal Protection Act (1949). Flood protection is a state-task delegated to regional and local authorities.

20 Political and administrative responsibilities are therefore organised in a multilayered structure: The Department for Environment, Food and Rural Affairs (DEFRA) is responsible for the overall policy and provides most of the funding. Local authorities have the responsibility for the provision, design and construction of single projects and the maintenance of local flood protection. The Environment Agency (EA) has the responsibility of supervising all matters related to flood defence, but the implementation of its policies is delegated to regional and local authorities, i.e. the *Regional and Local Flood Defence Committees*.[22] Furthermore, the former Department of Transport, Local Gov-

[19] These estimates vary as 95% refers to mortgage lenders, 75% refers to the overall housing stock. This reflects also the fact that not all house owners have a mortgage on their property. In these cases we can expect adverse selection, i.e. only those will purchase a flood insurance that are markedly exposed to the threat.

[20] S. Elahi, *Easter Floods, UK*. Case Study report of Project on the Uninsured Elements of Natural Catastrophic Losses (2000), 9.

[21] D.J. Parker, The Institutional and Policy Context, in: J. Handmer (ed.) *Flood hazard Management. British and international perspective* (1987), 36.

[22] For more detail see DEFRA, *National appraisal of assets at risk from flooding and coastal erosion, including the potential impact of climate change* (2001). Final report July 2001, <http://www.defra.gov.uk/environ/fcd/default.htm>, 11.

Table 1. Total government spending 1990–2004

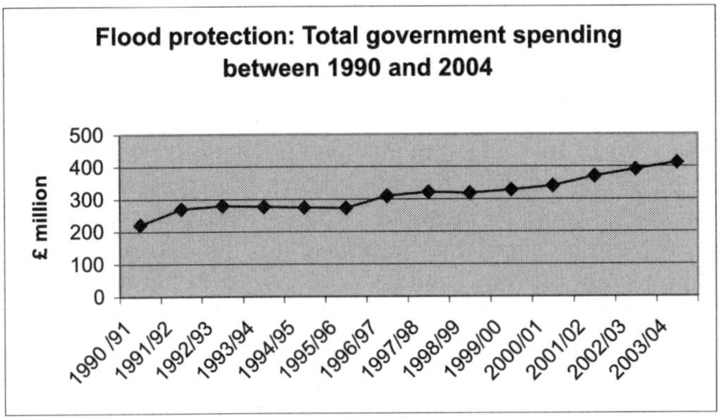

ernment, now Office of the Deputy Prime Minister (OPDM)[23] and the Regions as well as the Internal Drainage Boards hold competencies in flood management. In this fragmented system of complementary competencies, friction and difficulties in articulating and implementing a coherent policy are generated, a situation confirmed by assessments of the Environment Agency (1998) and the National Audit Office (NAO) (2000).

Land use planning control is an original area of flood related regulation too, but until recently flood played only a minor role as far as regulation was concerned. Although an increasing number of people are exposed to the risk of flooding – currently 1.85 million houses, 185,000 commercial properties and 5 million people with the trend of increasing exposure – the awareness about the economic and social consequences of land-use hardly exists in regulation. Local planning guidelines exist, but have only considered the effects of natural disasters. Only as a reaction to the floods of 2000, was *Planning Policy Guidance Note* (PPG 25) *Development and Flood Risk* developed suggesting some minor improvements in the planning processes.

Fragmentation characterises the relationship between formal regulations. However, the evident lack of detailed rules in some areas is not a random event but depends on the formation of the compensation regime and the Gentlemen's Agreement that coordinates compensation and protection.

For individual compensation, private insurance covers (virtually) all damages. 21
Private insurance depends on the state in two ways: *firstly*, as it requires a certain level of flood protection and, *secondly*, as the state has to guarantee the independence of the compensation-regime. It is important to note that there are

[23] A new Department for Transport was established to focus solely on transport issues. Most of the other responsibilities of the former Department for Transport Local Government and the Regions (DTLR) are brought into the Office of the Deputy Prime Minister and put together with his existing related responsibilities for social exclusion and the regions (including the Government Offices in the Regions).

no compensation funds for property insurance. The compensation-regime builds mainly on the decision to accept – in contrast to most other industrialised countries – that flood management should be based upon individual responsibility and insurance. Basically, flood insurance in the UK has two main features: It is a bundled *and* a compulsory system. *Bundled*, as all natural hazards, including flood, are packaged to one insurance policy; *compulsory*, to the extent that all house owners are obliged to purchase protection when applying for mortgage (see fn. 19). A number of features derive from these basic characteristics, four of which should be mentioned briefly. Firstly, the regime depends on the state as far as prevention is concerned. It is the state deciding on the level of flood protection measures and hence the threat of floods to house owners. Secondly, it can be identified by an intentional lack of formal regulation. The *compensation*-regime takes the form of private, industrial self-regulation where insurance firms and financial intermediaries like banks or building societies shape flood management. Financial intermediaries and insurance firms together implement this bundled system and are able to obtain a high insurance density. Thirdly, the regime focuses on the behavioural dimension of individual responsibility. This can, fourthly, be seen when the data-gathering dimension of this regime is analysed. Data-gathering is focused on claim histories, but little incentive is given to predict floods, provide detailed data on flood plains, weather changes or other challenges. Little is therefore known about flood risks. The reasons for this "crippled" regulatory regime can be found in the design of the Gentlemen's Agreement that is outlined and discussed in the next two sections.

22 The invisible core of flood management is constituted by an informal *Gentlemen's Agreement* that coordinates the responsibilities of state and industry: The insurance industry gave the

> "guarantee to government that for residential properties it would not refuse to offer flood insurance for any residential property, *no matter what the risk*. It further agreed that the additional premium rate would not exceed 0.5% on the sum insured"[24] (emphasis added).

"No matter what the risk" interprets the availability of protection too widely however. It fails to point to more restrictive conditions for insurance coverage:

> "Insurers and Government agreed in the late 1950s *that only in exceptional circumstances where continual, regular flooding was unavoidable*, would insurers consider withholding cover or apply especially loaded terms to reflect the higher risk"[25] (emphasis added).

Regular exposure to flooding defines a situation where insurance can be declined. It introduces an *escape clause* for industry, and a certain degree of

[24] D. Crichton, UK and Global Insurance Responses to Flood Hazard, [2002] *Water International* 27 (1), 127.

[25] R. Salthouse, Lessons to be leaned from the autumn 2000 flood disaster in the UK, [2002] *Insurance Research and Practices* 17 (1), 71.

freedom for the appraisal of the insurability of floods. At the same time, this Agreement should motivate the state to provide sufficient flood protection. No further qualification about the *sufficiency* of flood protection or related financial commitments can be found. The insured house-owners – as another stakeholder group, keenly interested in flood management and insurance coverage – play no role in this Agreement.

The main reasons to establish such division of responsibility is seen in the industrial fear for formal, restraining regulation that goes beyond immediate flood issues. John Hadmer presumes that the "fear of nationalisation and other pressure from government played a major role in prompting extension to cover during the 1960s".[26] Government refrains from regulation as it can externalise the costs and responsibilities of a highly uncertain situation to other actors.

This Gentlemen's Agreement triggered unintended and unwanted consequences. The substantial goal of flood insurance is the protection of all house-owners against all flood related damage. The Gentlemen's Agreement helps to optimise the risk spreading across all property owners and in that way to establish a sound economic basis for insurance activities. The behaviour of insurance firms, the state as well as the insured can be characterised by lax behaviour, withdrawal, negligence and irresponsibility.

Government tends to withdraw from responsibility as insurance firms accept 23
the financial responsibility for flood risks.[27] Knowing that almost all negative effects of flooding are covered, the state pursues *flood protection* in a lax way. Government has reduced investments into flood management over the years. Today, flood management is therefore considered by all relevant actors to be underfunded (e.g. NAO 2001). The withdrawal of the state has been interpreted such that a *social policy* was successfully externalised to the economy. Therefore insurance coverage was also interpreted as "free of costs". John Hadmer writes, "(f)lood insurance is automatically included in most British household policies at no extra premium".[28] But flood protection is not "free of cost". To blur the effects of payments means to trigger lax behaviour, both from the side of the house-owners, as their damage is compensated regardless of exposure from the side of insurance firms. As the state can reduce its investment into flood management with impunity, private flood management instead of being efficient, ends by generating unexpected and unwanted results. The entire regime is bound to fail if costs increase.[29] However, there seems to exist a *threshold* before the cost-problem is taken up. In the case of flood manage-

[26] J. Hadmer, *Flood insurance and relief in the US and in Britain* (1990), 21.

[27] As *The Economist* remarks: "In most rich countries, the government forks out to compensate those who suffer flood damage. That has not been true in Britain since 1961 when the Government *offloaded responsibility for flood damage to the insurance industry*" emphasis added ([17.11.2001] *The Economist*, 34).

[28] J. Hadmer (*supra* fn. 26), 21.

[29] In this section we followed the task of outlining the main features of flood insurance. The practical consequences of the Gentlemen's Agreement are discussed in section Part X.I.

ment, it seems to be transgressed when climate change was held accountable for some of the biggest floods in the history of the UK in 1998 and 2000.

Part V. Compensation Funds

24 Solutions based on state guaranteed funds are rare in the British case as the state tends to avoid financial commitments. There are two exceptions, however: The Bellwin scheme that helps economically weak communities and the PoolRe arrangement where the state figures as insurer-of-last-resort for compensation claims linked to terrorism.

I. Flood

25 The Bellwin scheme of emergency financial assistance was established in the mid-1980s and is named after the then local government minister, Lord Bellwin. The Secretary of State can activate the Bellwin scheme in the event of natural or man-made disasters of an exceptional nature which would, otherwise, impose an unreasonable burden on the local authorities involved. The Scheme of emergency financial assistance to local authorities was given a statutory basis in Section 155 of the Local Government and Housing Act 1989. Since 1983 it has been activated several times in each financial year. Shortly before the beginning of each financial year ODPM issues guidance on the terms and procedures that will apply to any Bellwin-scheme that is activated in the course of the year. In recent years the guidance has stipulated that any local authority applying for assistance under a scheme would have to have spent an amount equal to 0.2% of their budget (the "threshold") before qualifying for assistance. Grant is then paid to the local authority at a rate of 85% of eligible costs above the threshold. On two occasions there were emergencies of a wide ranging nature but in other years the number of cases arising totalled less than 10 in any one year and the amounts of grant claimed less than £ 1 million.

Amounts paid by way of Bellwin grant over the last 15 years were as follows (in several years most of the money paid was in respect of incidents reported in the previous year) in Table 2.

Table 2. Amounts paid through Bellwin scheme (1987–2001)

1987/88	£ 20 m	Severe snows and hurricane
1988/89	£ 6.2 m	Storms
1989/90	£ 0.6 m	Storms and floods
1990/91	£ 4.9 m	Floods
1991/92	£ 0.3 m	—
1992/93	£ 0	Storms
1993/94	£ 0.2 m	Storms and floods
1994/95	£ 0.6 m	Floods and landslides
1995/96	£ 0.1 m	Unexploded bomb and fire
1996/97	£ 0.2 m	Storms and flooding
1997/98.	£ 0.17 m	Storms and flooding
1998/99	£ 0.44 m	Floods
1999/00	£ 0.35 m	Floods
2000/01	£ 4.1 m	Floods, unexploded bomb and plane crash

State intervention through the Bellwin scheme is minimal, given the fact that the 1998 flood caused damage of about £ 500–700 million and the 2000 flood generated costs of £ 1.2 billion. Thus the state relies on private measures.

II. Terrorism

The other established case of state funded compensation has been for terrorism. Here the state acts as *insurer of last resort*. Here the conditions of state intervention are very difficult to meet. 26

After frequent terrorist attacks from the IRA, insurance coverage turned out to be a substantial problem. Historically, businesses operating in the United Kingdom have relied on terrorism insurance for protection. In 1992, this situation changed drastically. As a result of several costly terrorist incidents, the U.K. insurance market decided to exclude terrorism coverage from its policies.

The St. Mary's Axe bomb in 1992 generated damage of about £ 800 million. The insurance industry could no longer adequately predict the frequency and size of damage of terrorist attacks, and therefore wanted to exit the market. Furthermore, they were unable to calculate the aggregations of risk potentials in areas such as the City of London. Fearing devastating losses, reinsurers subsequently decided to cancel terrorism cover for insurance firms. In November 1992, insurance firms also retreated from insurance coverage. To resolve this difficult situation, the Association of Insurance and Risk Managers, formerly an Association of insurance Managers in industry and commerce together with the U.K. broker community and the British Insurance and Investment Brokers Association suggested a scheme that required government support: it was later discovered that the Association of British Insurers was talking to the government about a similar proposal. The outcome was PoolRe, a government-backed insurance facility in which the government through the Department of Trade (DTI) acts as a reinsurer of last resort. The first attack covered by PoolRe was a bomb at Bishopsgate in the City of London. This incident killed one, injured 44 and caused damage of at least £ 350 million.

PoolRe is a mutual company, consisting of a conglomerate of British insurance firms, Lloyd's syndicates, overseas insurers and captives. The British government reinsures the pool of insurance firms. Originally, the country is divided into two zones where zone 1 covers major city zones and zone 2 applies to everywhere else. The rates varied according to the total assets. If the assets of one firm are spread across the zones, an aggregate factor and discounted rate is established. Since July 1993, four zones have been established.[30] Currently the distribution of the burden is organised in the following way by the PoolRe: 27

- Individual customers purchase coverage at individual insurance companies.

[30] Zone A covers the centre of London, Zone B constitutes other areas in London and other cities, and Zone C is everywhere else in the British Isles except Cornwall and most parts of Scotland, which are covered by Zone D.

- In case of terrorist acts, the insurance company pays the first £ 100,000 per coverage type with no reimbursement from the government.
- Insurers contribute premiums to fully capitalize and maintain a national pool, paying out all claims directly from the pool (once the deductible is met by the insurance company).
- If losses exceed the funds available in the pool, the industry is assessed up to an additional 10% of current year premium.
- Additional losses beyond the 10% are covered by the pool's investment income.

Since the Bishopsgate bomb, most companies have experienced significant premium increases. This is also due to a government commitment as insurer of last resort, having no money to pay for losses. The increase in premiums led to a decrease in insurance density. These are not the only difficulties that PoolRe poses to insurance firms and the insured. First of all, it is highly bureaucratic. Secondly, the tendency of the British Government to abstain from being involved in compensation payments leads to a clear strategy of the state to pass costs on to the industry. In its strong tradition of distancing itself from compensation payments, Government keeps its involvement in PoolRe to a minimum. Another major problem with PoolRe concerns the definition of terrorism loss. The effects of exploding bombs were considered terrorist attacks, the subsequent looting and thefts fell under the category of traditional market losses. Questions remain about events that are not carried out by recognised terrorist groups.[31]

Part VI. Legal Procedures

28 A legal system can be defined as

> an operating set of legal institutions, procedures, and rules. In this sense there are one federal and fifty state legal systems in the United States, separate legal systems in each of the other nations, and still other distinct legal systems in such organizations as the European Economic Community and the United Nations.[32]

Unlike the Civil Jurisdictions of mainland Europe, which have their origins in Roman law, as codified in the Corpus Juris Civilis of Justinian, the legal system in England and Wales is a common law one. There is no written constitution or embedded codified system and many legal principles derive their origin from the courts as opposed to Parliament. Furthermore, no clear distinction exists between the treatment of private and public law actions. Public authorities are ostensibly subject to the same proceedings as individuals, partnerships, corporations and voluntary associations. Although there is an increasing trend to require some proceedings against public authorities to be brought in the Administrative Court of the High Court, such as judicial review actions, this applies

[31] See also: OECD, *Economic Outlook* (vol. 2002, no. 1), 71.

[32] J.H. Merryman, *The Civil Law Tradition: An Introduction to the Legal Systems of Western Europe and Latin America* (2nd edn. 1985), 1.

in a restrictive sense and does not extend to tortious liability. Court actions for negligence can be commenced in either the High Court or the lower courts. The Queen's Bench Division, of the High Court as well as the County Court (the lower provincial court in England and Wales, of which there are 220), have jurisdiction to deal with claims of negligence. Since July 1991 the county courts have jurisdiction to deal with tort cases regardless of the value of the claim. The streamlining of civil procedures by the Government's Civil Justice Reforms, which were introduced in April 1999, requires that litigation claims are started in the county court. The Civil Justice Reforms adopted the vision of Lord Woolf Master of the Rolls to make litigation less adversarial and generally more efficient. The *Access to Justice* Report of July 1996, at section 1.9 identified the following key objectives:

- to avoid litigation wherever possible;
- to make litigation less adversarial and more co-operative;
- to make litigation less complex;
- to shorten the litigation timescale and make it more certain;
- that the cost of litigation be made more affordable, more predictable, and more proportionate to the value and complexity of individual cases;
- that parties of limited financial means will be able to conduct litigation on a more equal footing;
- that clear lines of administrative and civil responsibility be put in place in the handling of cases;
- that structure of the courts and the deployment of judges will be designed to meet the needs of litigants;
- that judges be deployed effectively so that they can manage litigation in accordance with the new rules and protocols, and
- that the system be responsive to the needs of litigants.

Where the claim is defended, cases which exceed £ 15,000 in value are allocated to a multi-track procedure by the judge for case management purposes. Claims in excess of this figure can be commenced in the High Court (Queen's Bench Division) as of right.

We now set out a brief schematic outline of the rules relating to court proceedings in England and Wales. It is to be emphasised that different rules apply in Scotland and are not considered here. Personal Injury Litigation was transformed by the introduction on 26 April 1999 of the Civil Procedure Rules (CPR) because claims, which were otherwise quite straightforward, were taking a number of years to complete. Under the new rules, both sides are under a positive obligation to help the court to further the overriding objective of dealing with the case equitably. This includes ensuring that the parties are on an equal footing, saving expense and acting in ways which are proportionate. One of the key innovations introduced by the CPR (Part 36) is the ability of the injured party and his/her solicitors to make a "claimant's offer" to the other side. Part 29 of the Civil Procedure Rules sets out the rules regarding how multi-track actions will be dealt with. The court has the power to set directions as to how the action will proceed and fix what is known as a case management 29 conference (so as to deal with progressing the action) and a pre-trial review in order to handle the action as expeditiously as possible. Whilst the parties are actively involved in the processing of the case, it is for the judge to determine the appropriate proceedings after hearing representations from both parties. As the Department of Constitutional Affairs notes,[33] the hallmarks of a multi-track procedure are the ability of the court to deal with cases of widely differing complexity and values, and the flexibility which is given to the court to manage the case in a way appropriate to its particular needs. To this extent it is for the court to give directions as to how the case will proceed irrespective of whether a preliminary hearing is held, and this can include fixing a date for trial without holding a preliminary hearing, although the parties will, of course be involved in determining the trial timetable. Under CPR 24.2(a)(ii) the Court may give summary judgment against a defendant on the whole of a claim or on a particular issue if it considers that the defendant has no real prospect of successfully defending the claim or issue.

30 Lord Woolf in his final Access to Justice Report of July 1996 recommended the development of pre-action protocols: "To build on and increase the benefits of early but well informed settlement which genuinely satisfy both parties to dispute".

The aims of pre-action protocols are:

- more pre-action contact between the parties;
- better and earlier exchange of information;
- better pre-action investigation by both sides;
- to put the parties in a position where they may be able to settle cases fairly and early without litigation;
- to enable proceedings to run to the court's timetable and efficiently, if litigation does become necessary. [Department for Constitutional Affairs (DCA) *Pre-Action Protocol for Personal Injury Claims* paras 1.1 and 1.2].

The concept of protocols emerges as relevant to a range of initiatives for good litigation and pre-litigation practice. They were devised by Lord Woolf to set standards and timetables for the conduct of cases before proceedings are issued. The protocols are approved by the Head of Civil Justice after a rigorous consultation exercise of legal professional bodies, the judiciary, court users, the Association of British Insurers and representatives from industry. These are treated by the court as the normal and reasonable approach to pre-action proceedings. Failure to adhere to them could result in increased liability as to costs. The Protocols tend not to be imposed in complex claims such as multi-track proceedings where the claim exceeds £ 15,000. In its guidance the DCA notes:

> "However, the 'cards on the table' approach advocated by the protocol is equally appropriate to some higher value claims. The spirit, if not the letter of the protocol, should still be followed for multi-track type claims. In

[33] § 3.2 Practice Direction: the Multi-track.

> accordance with the sense of the civil justice reforms, the court will expect to see the spirit of reasonable pre-action behaviour applied in all cases, regardless of the existence of a specific protocol. In particular with regard to personal injury cases worth more than £ 15,000, with a view to avoiding the necessity of proceedings parties are expected to comply with the protocol as far as possible e.g. in respect of letters before action, exchanging information and documents and agreeing experts".[34]

The general substance of guidance requires early disclosure, and notification. 31
A detailed letter of claim will usually be sent to the defendant outlining in detail the nature of the claim, a clear summary of the facts and the injury and the sum claimed. The letter will ask for details of the defendant's insurer so that a copy of the letter can be sent to it. The letter must contain sufficient information to enable the defendant to consider the substance of the claim, and evaluate the risks involved. The defendant has 21 days within which to notify the claimant of his insurer. In the absence of a reply, the claimant is entitled to issue proceedings. The whole object of this procedure is to ensure that the defendant is given the opportunity to settle the claim *before* proceedings commence and so minimise the costs to both parties. Where the defendant (or his insurer) acknowledges the claim he/she has three months within which to investigate the matter. If the defendant denies liability, or admits liability but alleges contributory negligence (viz. that the claimant was in part at fault) a letter has to be sent (in a particular form, listing all documents in his possession material to the issue which the court would normally ask to be disclosed). After this date the claimant has to submit a schedule listing all special damages i.e. those specifically quantifiable, with all supporting documents. Special rules also apply to the instructing of experts whose evidence is as far as possible to be agreed.

I. The Duty of Care

If one of the main tasks of legal systems is to settle disagreements about com- 32
pensation, the establishment of fault will play a central role. The common law notion of the duty of care has no exact equivalent in European civil law jurisdictions. It is, in essence, a basis by which courts frame or fix the boundaries of liability in negligence, and it acts as an indicator to determine whether the type of loss is actionable. It is often suggested that negligence does not impose a duty to act carefully but instead imposes a duty not to act carelessly.[35] Before 1932 there was no general duty of care in negligence in England and Wales. All this was to change with the landmark decision of *Donoghue v Stevenson*,[36] where for the first time the court (in this case the House of Lords) was prepared to impose the principle that liability might accrue where foreseeable damage is inflicted upon those whom it is reasonably foreseeable are likely to be harmed by careless activity. This is sometimes known as the neighbour

[34] § 2.4 Pre Action Protocol for Personal Injury Claims.
[35] M.A. Jones, *Textbook on Torts* (8th edn. 2002), 31.
[36] *Donoghue v Stevenson* [1932] AC 562.

principle, but represents the generalised formulation of what is termed the "duty of care". The formal requirements for a duty of care to exist are that:

- foreseeability of the damage exists;
- there is a sufficiently proximate relationship between the parties (*the test of proximity*); and
- that it is fair and reasonable to impose such a duty.[37]

33 The idea or concept of a duty of care is often used to categorise compensation victims or defendants, and to settle the bounds of policy considerations. An example of this is the distinction drawn between positive acts as opposed to a failure to act (an omission). Subsequent refinements of the idea of proximity in particular have indicated that:

> Proximity requires such a relation between the parties as renders it fair, just and reasonable that liability be imposed … the policy factors should now be considered as part and parcel of the relationship of proximity.[38]

In the case of a liability for a failure to act, a duty of care is imposed only in exceptional circumstances. Further refinements on the duty principle are also used to connect the victim's loss with the defendant's actions. The existence of a breach of duty is a normative concept, essentially concerned with the normative standards that are deemed appropriate viz. the standard of care that ought to have been adopted in the given circumstances. Not only must the negligence have caused the loss in question but also if the type of damage is considered too remote i.e. such that it could not have been reasonably anticipated, it will not be recoverable irrespective of whether the defendant had caused that loss. The concepts of causation and remoteness of damage further narrow the possibility of compensation. In the case of the former there must exist a physical connection between the negligence and the victim's loss. Furthermore the idea of "remoteness" exists to place limits on a defendant's liability to the extent that notwithstanding the actions, the damage might be unusual in terms of the way in which it resulted or its type. Thus negligence can be divided into duty, breach and consequent damage.

34 Not all forms of damage are granted equal protection under the law; whilst damage to persons or property are normally within the scope of the duty, the existence of financial losses not connected to physical damage (termed in law as pure economic loss) may not be recoverable. Whilst the law recognises the existence of a duty of care in relation to pure economic losses, recovery is very limited. Liability in damages may arise by reason of negligent misstatement or negligence in the performance of a service, but only in the rare case will recovery be permitted arising from product defects or in respect of economic losses as a consequence of damage to a third party's property.

[37] *Caparo Industries v Dickman* [1990] *All England Law Reports* (All ER) 1, 798 at 803 per Bingham LJ.

[38] Per Ward J *Ravenscroft v Rederiaktiebolaget Transatlantic* [1993] All ER 3, 73, 84–5.

Even if a *duty of care* is established, it is further necessary for any claimant to establish a breach in the standard of care reasonably expected and that it was foreseeable that loss or damage would ensue. Even if damage was foreseeable it does not follow that liability can be sustained. In *Bolton v Stone*[39] it was pointed out that it is only necessary to take precautions against those risks likely to occur. Where, however, the magnitude of the risk is extensive, the greater the precautions that will be required to be taken.[40]

II. The Liability of Public Bodies

The nature of the relationship between the claimant and the defendant and the status of the parties to the claim can be of particular significance in identifying the existence of a duty of care. This is particularly so when considering the liability of public bodies in negligence. Following the enactment of the Crown Proceedings Act 1947, the immunity of the Crown in tort for the liability of its servants and employees has been almost wholly abolished.[41] Damages actions are sustainable against local government and public agencies, but these bodies are treated differently as a matter of policy, from private individuals and corporations. For this reason the liability of public bodies has to date played a minimal role in compensating catastrophes. There is nothing in principle to prevent the liability of a public body or agency, but policy considerations prevail in those difficult cases arising from a failure to act or where the damage in question does not involve personal injury. For policy reasons the courts have held that agencies deriving their powers from statute will not be treated as incurring liability in tort simply by reason of the non-performance of their statutory duty and even less so in cases of their failure to exercise a statutory power viz. for an omission rather than a positive act, and the courts strive to maintain some form of protection to public bodies in this respect. Where the body in question is charged with performing some form of discretionary activity, it will not usually be liable for the decisions taken within the parameters of that discretion unless that decision could be classified as wholly unreasonable on the basis of normal public law principles. Over time public bodies have become attractive targets for liability in part because of the resources available to them to meet substantial and significant damages claims. The courts are particularly reluctant to investigate claims relating to areas of policy, which are not properly justiciable.[42] This idea is intended to protect the autonomy or independence of a body responsible for the allocation of scarce resources, where awards of damages would have not only an impact on the resources available to the body in performing its statutory duty but could also lead to unduly defensive practices. These policy principles are also upheld where it is considered that alternative remedies may exist to give redress to claimants, (such as the existence of rights of appeal, or the availability of compensation from the Criminal Injuries Compensation Scheme, although they have limited applica- 35

[39] *Bolton v Stone* [1951] AC 850.
[40] *Glasgow Corporation v Muir* [1943] AC 448.
[41] Only the Monarch retains personal immunity outside the provisions of the Act.
[42] *X (Minors) v Bedfordshire County Council* [1995] AC 2, 633.

bility here). Certain areas of public activity still attract protection on policy grounds as in the limited liability of the police for negligence in the course of investigating crimes.[43]

III. Access

36 Compensation claims do not necessarily lead to success, they not only fail due to difficulties in assessing and attributing fault, but also due to institutional barriers of the British legal system. These can include such factors as access or the costs structure of court cases (for the claimant). Delays will add to the lack of success. Generally, it can be seen that in the case of catastrophic events or disasters the law itself is not an easy avenue for putative claimants to pursue. One example of this is the case of rail disasters. On 5 October 1999, two trains collided almost head on when a Thames Train commuter service went through a red light just outside Paddington Station. The Thames Train hit a London-bound Great Western train that was approaching the station. The combined speed on impact was thought to be in excess of 100mph. 31 people died and over 400 people were injured in the crash. A public Inquiry was subsequently held (Chaired by Lord Cullen; the *Ladbroke Grove Rail Inquiry 2001*), which criticised both the rail operator at the time (Railtrack) and the train operator. Criminal action was successfully brought in 2004 by the Health and Safety Executive (HSE), which resulted in the train operator being fined £ 2m. One firm acting on behalf of 50 of the claimants (including the relatives of some of those who had died) recovered damages of £ 6.5 million. These claims were finally settled in 2004 without proceeding to trial.

In 2002 827 personal injury actions were commenced in the Queen's Bench Division of the High Court.[44] There were 268 other negligence claims begun in the same year according to statistics provided. 54% of the court's judgments related to personal injury cases of which 60% were for sums exceeding £ 50,000. These figures do not necessarily present a full account and need to be balanced against an older study of 1976. The Oxford Centre for Socio-Legal Studies 1976 study indicated that only one in seven accident victims reached the stage of consulting a lawyer and that of these only one in seven recovered damages at all.[45]

The management of Legal Aid since 1999 falls to The Legal Services Commission (LSC) an executive non-departmental public body created under the Access to Justice Act 1999. From 1 April 2000 the Community Legal Service (CLS) replaced the civil Legal Aid Scheme. The CLS will only pay the fees of those solicitors accredited to the Scheme, thus the claimant does not have a free choice of lawyer. Claims for personal injury other than clinical negligence are not usually funded by the LSC. As one commentator noted,

[43] *Hill v Chief Constable of West Yorkshire* [1988] QB 60.
[44] Source: *Judicial Statistics* 2002 (Her Majesty's Stationery Office (HMSO)).
[45] D. Harris/M. Maclean/H. Genn/S. Lloyd-Bostock/P. Fenn/P. Corfield/Y. Brittan, *Compensation and Support for Illness and Injury* (1984).

"...Legal aid appears to focus on the severity of an injury, whereas other sources of finance such as trade unions are more likely to take account of liability. Privately financed cases were likely to be associated with high levels of defendant (perceived) liability".[46]

With the limited availability of public funding, claimants are resorting to the use of Conditional Fee Arrangements (CFA). This posits a strong link between both the legal and the insurance systems. The CFA involves the claimant entering into an arrangement with the solicitor to cover the legal fees if the action is successful through the vehicle of an after the event (ATE) insurance premium. The legal fees incurred in taking action are thus backed by an insurance policy. Concerns remain as to how far the defendant should be liable for these fees. The case of *Callery v Gray*[47] considered the reasonableness of the defendant paying the success fee under a CFA and the premium for an after the event insurance policy in a personal injury claim. Liability was not disputed and the case was settled without the need for litigation, hence only the costs were in dispute. The Court of Appeal reduced the success fee but allowed the premium payment. The case was subsequently appealed to the House of Lords. Whilst the House of Lords declined to intervene, Lord Bingham stated that responsibility for making the new funding regime work fairly and effectively lay with lawyers agreeing to act under conditional fee arrangements and insurers offering after the event cover. This system was designed to help people on low incomes gain access to the law, but some suggest that it has fuelled more speculative claims and insurers have expressed concerns on this basis. The legal professional obtains remuneration, as a percentage of the successful claim, which in theory, if not in practice, enables those not entitled to Legal Aid to pursue civil actions. 37

Whilst one of the objectives of the Civil Justice Review was to reduce the cost of litigation by making it more affordable and predictable and more proportionate to the value and complexity of the individual case, studies are equivocal as to whether this is so. The Department of Constitutional Affairs in its Report: *Further Findings: A Continuing Evaluation of the Civil Justice Reforms*, August 2002 (§ 7) remained doubtful as to whether sufficient evidence exists to provide a definitive view.

Even though an action may be successful it does not follow that the claimant will recover the full amount of the costs that he/she has incurred. It is always open to the party claimed against to challenge the level of fees and this can be done through a process known as "taxing" where a Bill of Costs is carefully scrutinised. Studies undertaken in respect of personal injury litigation indicate that where the other party questions the costs allowed, these are likely to be reduced. The mean costs allowed are indicated in the table below.[48] Most impor- 38

[46] P. Fenn/N. Rickman, *Costs of Low Value Employers' Liability Claims* (2003).

[47] *Callery v Gray* [2002] All E.R. 3, 417.

[48] Department of Constitutional Affairs, *Survey of Litigation Costs: Summary of Main Findings Annex III* (November 2003).

tantly, the duration of the procedure is extremely long which adds costs to the claimant – and might have considerable impact on the success rate of 60%.

	Mean	Median
Costs allowed	£ 19,382	£ 12,134
Claim value	£ 98,434	£ 50,000
Delay between instruction and issue	17 months	15 months
Duration	56 months	54 months
Average total counsel fees	£ 3,744	
Average total expert fees	£ 2,413	
Average costs discovery + documents	£ 5,016	
% of successful parties with legal aid	58%	

In essence costs of litigation and the availability or otherwise of Legal Aid (the state sponsored means-tested mechanism for the funding of litigation in England and Wales) are significant factors in determining whether litigation will commence.

IV. Limitation of Actions

39 It is a general principle of law that actions cannot be commenced after a certain period of time. In actions relating to claims for damages for physical injury actions cannot be brought outside the period of three years from the date the right to take action occurred or the date the claimant first had knowledge of the injury. In the case of damage to property the limitation period is six years. The limitation of actions means that civil proceedings are time-barred after a certain period for reasons of administrative convenience and fairness. It is considered, as a matter of policy, to be inequitable to allow claimants to pursue "old" claims where the defendant may have little real recognition of the event in evidential terms. This in turn would hamper the administration of a fair and reasonable system, which is fundamentally adversarial in form. Whilst for personal injury claims the limitation period is three years, this time runs from the date of the cause of action arising or the date when the person had first knowledge of the injury (its discoverability).[49] Power does however exist for the court to grant relief in the case of fraud or deliberate concealment by a defendant. In the case of tort actions this will rarely apply, although this is sometimes the case with industrial injuries. In *Cartledge v E. Jopling & Sons Ltd*,[50] the claimant contracted pneumoconiosis through inhaling dust for many years. One consequence of the disease is the gradual degeneration of lung capacity without the initial awareness of the victim. Although the employer had replaced the unsafe system of working practices well before the relevant limitation period, the House of Lords held that the cause of action had accrued at the time of the initial damage to his lungs (of which he was unaware) and that as a result the claim was time-barred. As a result of the hardship this caused parliament introduced the "discoverability" test for personal injury claims.

[49] Limitation Act 1980, §§ 11 and 14.
[50] *Cartledge v E. Jopling & Sons Ltd* [1963] AC 758.

There is a separate regime for latent defects in property in cases of negligence leading to property or financial loss, under the Latent Damage Act 1986 which inserted section 14A(4)(a) into the Limitation Act 1980. Whilst the basic rule is that the limitation period runs for six years from the date of the cause of action accruing, paragraph (b) of the section provides for an exception to this rule with regard to latent defects, and provides for a three year period from the date when the person "… had both the knowledge required for bringing an action for damages … and a right to bring the action".[51] In addition the 1986 Act also provides for a fresh cause of action to accrue to successive owners of a property with latent defects, which had not been discovered at the time of their purchase.

Part VII. The Assessment of Damages in Tort Law

Once all of the above hurdles have been surmounted a victim is entitled to re- 40
cover damages. This section describes the principles underlying an award of damages in the event of a successful legal action in negligence as they apply in England and Wales. The rules are complex and only a brief outline is given here. It is a general principle of tort law that damages are recoverable once only. This means that the claimant cannot bring multiple actions on the same facts even if the initial loss turned out to be more serious than originally thought.[52] Damages are recoverable for financial losses on a net basis in respect of pre-trial losses (i.e. with a deduction for the amount of tax and national insurance contributions that would have been paid by the victim).[53] Future losses of earnings are calculated by the courts with the assistance of the Government's Actuary's Department actuarial tables (known as the 'Ogden' Tables or with the full title *Actuarial Tables with Explanatory Notes for Use in Personal Injury and Fatal Accident Cases*). Future losses are then assessed on the basis of generating an award, which will produce when invested a sum equivalent to the claimant's loss over his/her life expectancy (known as the 'multiplier method'). Where a claimant's life expectancy is reduced, damages are also recoverable for the losses of earnings in the 'lost years'.[54] Damages are also recoverable for lost earning capacity if the victim is disadvantaged in obtaining employment as a result of the injury attributable to the accident. There is however a general principle against the recovery of excessive compensation and this can result in benefits received being taken into account in the calculation of any award of damages. In *Hussain v Taplow Paper Mills Ltd.*[55] the House of Lords held that payments of long term sickness benefit had to be deducted from any claim for loss of earnings.

[51] Section 14A(4) (b) Limitation Act 1980.

[52] *Fetter v Beal* (1701) Ld Raym 339.

[53] *British Transport Commission v Gourley* [1956] AC 185, *Cooper v Firth Brown Ltd.* [1963] *Weekly Law Reports* (WLR) 2, 418.

[54] *Pickett v British Rail Engineering Ltd.* [1980] AC 136.

[55] *Hussain v Taplow Paper Mills Ltd.* [1988] AC 514.

41 Broadly similar rules apply to claims for damage to property as those relating to personal injuries. In *Liesbosch Dredger v SS Edison*[56] the court set down some general principles. Where property is destroyed, the market value and incidental costs (e.g. transportation, and loss of profit) are recoverable. Where property is damaged but not destroyed, the loss to the claimant is the reduction in its value. Claims may be made in respect of a loss of use.

It is possible for interim payments to be awarded by the court according to the provisions of the Civil Procedure Rules (CPR 25). Guidance in the form of a Practice Direction has been issued covering this issue. Where a child or patient makes a claim for an interim payment, the sanction of the court must be obtained. An application for an interim payment of damages must be supported by details of the amount of the interim payment, the amount likely to be finally awarded at the stage of final judgment, information as to why an interim payment is being sought together with details of special damages and all past and future loss. In addition medical reports must be disclosed and any evidence upon which those challenging the application intend to rely. The court can order interim payments of this type to be paid as a lump sum or by instalments. Where judgment is ultimately given, the amount of any interim payment is to be taken into account.

I. The Recovery of Cumulative Benefits

42 As a matter of general principle collateral benefits or insurance monies are not deducted from the award. Payments made to claimants by insurance companies or through charitable or other voluntary donations as a general rule are not deducted from any award. For reasons of policy, the courts have held that only payments made by the tortfeasor (the wrongdoer) will be set against damages awards. The rules are different however, in the case of state benefits. Under the Social Security Act 1989, and the Social Security (Recovery of Benefits) Act 1997 the court is required to disregard certain specified benefits when assessing the award, but the tortfeasor must pay to the state the amount of benefits received in respect of the injury or accident. These rules are complex and extensive, with deductions being made in respect of compensation for loss of earnings, the cost of care or loss of mobility. The scheme, which was introduced in October 1997, covers compensation payments made to a person after an accident, injury or contracting a disease. The compensator, usually the insurance company, is liable to repay any benefits already received by the claimant as a result of their injury or disease. The Compensation Recovery Unit of the Department for Work and Pensions handles recovery action.

As commentators[57] note this could result in the victim being made worse off financially in principle and may result in an additional claim for the loss under the head of special damages. Payments made under the Fatal Accidents Act (1976) are excluded as are payments made under charitable trusts. The Criminal Injuries Compensation Scheme has its own rules as to recoupment.

[56] *Liesbosch Dredger v SS Edison* [1933] AC 449.
[57] B.S. Markesinis/S.F. Deakin, *Tort Law* (4th edn. 1999).

Part VIII. Procedures

Private insurance is the main source of compensation; additional compensation is provided by welfare state institutions. The legal arena is used to obtain compensation beyond the broadly welfare system and to settle disagreements on causes, effects and the size of compensation. As we mentioned at several points, the notion of a "compensation culture" indicates that the legal arena is today perceived as a cause of uncertainty and tension. 43

I. Insurance Schemes

External incidents tend to establish the occurrence of the catastrophic event. 44
This may be either political or public; e.g. the Environment Agency has established a four stage definition of flood risks. The published warning (telephone helpline and website) is the official definition of the situation. As mentioned in the introduction, generally there are no clear rules and the use media and the political system make of certain events will be a major factor in such definitions. This is of particular concern as the financial liabilities of either actor are minimal.

Claims have to be made via the insurance company and are established in the individual insurance contract. The Gentlemen's Agreement on flood insurance illustrates that contractual conditions are not met all the time. Recently, certain escape clauses for insurance firms in the event of floods have been interpreted more rigidly than during the last half century. The only way to resolve these tensions is to bring the case to court.

Elsewhere (as in the case of the Criminal Injuries Compensation Scheme) "trigger" events, defined by law, determine whether compensation becomes payable. This Scheme, which applies throughout England, Scotland and Wales is administered by a non-departmental public body, the Criminal Injuries Compensation Authority. The Scheme has, since its introduction in 1964 provided a source of compensation to victims of violent crime. Although successive governments have indicated that the state bears no primary responsibility for compensating injuries caused by others and that the main source of redress should come from the offender, the Scheme is a recognition in both political and legal terms of the policy limitations of such a premise.[58] The Scheme allows financial awards to be made:

- to recognise the injuries, physical and mental, caused by a crime of violence;
- in certain circumstances, to compensate for past or future lost earnings or special expenses caused by such a crime;
- for bereavement as a result of a crime of violence, including, in some cases, compensation for the lost earnings of the person who has been killed.

[58] *Compensation for Victims of Violent Crime: Possible Changes to the Criminal Injuries Compensation Scheme* (Home Office Consultation paper, 29 March 1999) § 11.

45 The current Scheme dates from 1 April 2001, and its awards total more than £ 200 m annually. The rules of the Scheme are fixed by Government rather than the Authority itself, which bears responsibility for applying the Scheme. The current Scheme was made by the Home Secretary, exercising his powers under the Criminal Injuries Compensation Act 1995. Prior to 1 April 1996, the Scheme was based on the common law. Applicants' cases were assessed on the same basis as for a personal injury claim in the civil courts. In 1996 the system was changed with the introduction of a tariff of injuries. The tariff is a list of fixed compensation payments for each injury and the Authority will not make awards of less than £ 1,000. In general terms legal advice is not required and the applicant is required to submit a pro forma application for compensation. The applicant has to be prepared to submit to a medical examination, if required, and must have reported the injury to the police promptly. Claims must be submitted within two years of the relevant incident. An internal appeals procedure applies in the event of the application being refused. The concepts of "criminal injury" and "crime of violence" are central to the Scheme. Thus the Scheme is of limited assistance in cases of natural disasters or hazards or indeed where personal injury results from non-criminal activities. It does however have some utility where physical or mental injury is sustained as in cases of terrorist activity as the Scheme can apply irrespective of a conviction.

II. Fund Solutions

46 Other compensation funds can be subject to political interventions also. A Bellwin scheme can be activated when a disaster occurs and, as a result, one or more local authorities incur expenditure on immediate safeguards in their area. There is no automatic entitlement to financial assistance; Ministers are empowered by Section 155 of the Local Government and Housing Act 1989 to decide whether or not to activate a scheme after considering the circumstances of each individual case. The decision of when the Bellwin scheme is to be activated is a political one. There is guidance, but this cannot cover every possible eventuality, and Ministers have to make individual decisions according to the merits of the case following each accident. Traditionally Bellwin has been seen as a response to threats caused by bad weather "beyond all previous local experience".

Normally a grant at a rate of 85% of eligible expenditure above the threshold would be paid. The threshold requires authorities to have spent 0.2% of their annual budget on works that have been reported to the department as eligible for grant. Within a month after the event the authorities have to report to the Deputy Prime Minister. Within two months of the incident the authority must complete all works in respect of which it intends to claim a grant.

In the case of terrorism the claims are made to the insurance company. State involvement concerns only reinsurance. Before PoolRe can make any payment to their members in respect to losses from acts of terrorism, PoolRe must obtain the Secretary of State's certification that the losses have been caused by an act of terrorism. The decision of the Secretary of State can be challenged at a Tribunal comprised of representatives from PoolRe and the Government whose decision shall be final and binding on the Government and PoolRe. The event, again, is defined by political pragmatism and to some extend by the terrorist organisation.

III. Natural Hazards/Insurance

In the case of natural hazards the UK government tends not to compensate for insurable risks. Only as far as damage can be dealt with under the Bellwin scheme, is the state involved. 47

Natural hazard insurance is purchased through building or household insurance. Premiums and deductibles are set on a case-to-case basis. Initially the real risks were not taken into account and an undifferentiated premium across all UK households was collected. Recently attempts to improve the knowledge base of natural hazards through e.g. flood-maps, led to more accurate pricing. There is a clear difference between private and business coverage as commercial/industrial risks are covered through the fire insurance where premiums vary according to level of exposure; costs of business interruption might be included in these kind of contracts. In domestic cases the public is either not insured or natural hazard insurance is part of a block insurance. Reinsurance is dealt with at the international market. Although flood insurance is *de facto* compulsory, only 40% of the costs of the 1998 flood in UK were covered, i.e. £ 1.2 billion (€ 1.8 billion).[59]

Part IX. Financing

As mentioned throughout the report, the compensation regime in Britain is based upon public contributions (mainly taxes) as far as social security and compensation funds are concerned, and private payments as far as insurance is concerned. 48

Effects of the increased number of events/costs have caused substantial increases in flood insurance (+4% on average, peaks of +50%) and terrorist insurance. These events had limited effect on the social security system.

Private insurance against flood protection costs – on average amounts to £ 230 per house. Recently a differentiation of fees according to exposure has been introduced but until now no systematic application of exposure can be detected.

[59] A breakdown of the costs and insurance shows, first of all, that the entire costs distribution is insufficiently understood. In the case of the 1998 floods a direct loss of £ 350 million is estimated, of which £ 137 million are covered by insurance. Additional reimbursements by local flood relief funds and Bellwin scheme amounts to £ 600,000 (250,000/350,000). Indirect losses (lack of train services) or business losses are not accounted for. Payments after the event did not occur swiftly, and households had to wait more than six months after the event to return to their homes. In the case of agriculture it was mentioned that the value in sheep and lamb fell by 5% which amounted to £ 57 million. From the Bellwin scheme £ 345,554 of compensation was paid to victims.

Part X. New Developments

49 We have chosen four aspects of compensation to illustrate current difficulties and indicate future developments. The case of flood insurance indicates *how governments are responding to the problems associated with* climate change *via* private insurance schemes. The second case we briefly touch upon is terrorism after the events of September 2001 and their effect on the PoolRe. A third comment concerns the compensation culture which has been mentioned at different points and which is expected to overload the legal system. In a last section we refer to the increasing importance of public inquiries and indicate some of the problems involved in that strategy. These new developments can be read as anecdotes on the shifting relationship between state and industry, i.e. on the balance between prevention and compensation.

I. Flood Insurance

50 The fear that floods would be more frequent and have a higher impact on insurance led to a two-year moratorium on the old Gentlemen's Agreement on flood insurance. If no new agreement had been signed within this period, the insurance industry was to exit the agreement. In late autumn 2002, a new/old Agreement between the state and insurance industry was signed. New as far as it envisaged reform in the areas of land-use planning, and the administrative organisation of the protection-regime. It also proposed more money for flood protection, i.e. increased investments into prevention to reduce the burden of compensation. The compensation regime was adapted as well. A certain differentiation of premiums was introduced. It remains, however, the old agreement as systemic moral hazard unfolds only at a higher level of engagement. Generally it was felt that those adaptations ensured the continuity in flood management.

Starting with the financial improvements, the state funding of flood protection is envisaged to increase slowly. In 1990/91 the total investment in flood protection was £ 221.4 million and grew to £ 339.8 million in the budget of 2000/01. It is forecast to be £ 411.7 million in 2003/04.[60] The increase between 2000 and 2004 is £ 71.9 million while a rise of total spending in England (including local authorities) of £ 150 million is suggested until 2006 (ABI 15.7.2002; Table 2). This supplementary funding of flood protection measures does not fully match the (higher) expectations of the insurance industry, but the state is gradually becoming more engaged. Regulatory improvements are still under debate. They concern a more efficient use of the additional resources by simplification and coordination. DEFRA and regional committees should implement administrative improvements and make more effective use of funds. As the state of flood defences is not uniform across the country, a "National Plan" to decide upon priorities seems indispensable; such a detailed plan should establish modified land use regulations that influence

[60] DEFRA, *Flood and Coastal Defence. The Autumn 2000 floods* (2002), 5 (<http://www.defra.gov.uk/environ/fcd/floodingincidents/floodinf.htm>).

housing development. Further developments are promised, but have yet to be decided upon.

The insurance industry reacted to these suggestions with a Statement of Principles that outlines its position after the end of the moratorium on 31 December 2002. Five objectives are identified: full access to a competitive market for insurance for the vast majority of house owners and small businesses; improved security for those who live and work in high-risk areas; new provisions for those who wish to sell their home and businesses, and better use of new solutions to make property insurable even in high risk areas where improvements to flood defence are not planned are also advocated as is a clear incentive for Government and local authorities to continue to invest in flood defences.[61]

Although the "old" aim of providing flood insurance to the great majority of homes and small business was maintained, the first signs of a policy shift can be observed. Industry re-assesses insurability, and it limits coverage. While the pre-2000 narrative emphasised the completeness of coverage, now coverage is turned into an issue of risk levels, state commitment and willingness to accept additional regulation. While flood insurability was presented as unconditional since the 1960s, now it is conditional. The conditionality, however, reflects not only a premium differentiation, but also issues of regulation [and] of other non-economic behaviour. The new arrangements were considered moderately successful. Industry assumed that the entire flood management has been improved as far as the containment – not the solution – of the systemic moral hazard is concerned. 51

> "We have come a long way in achieving the three improvements the industry has asked for. We asked for improvements in planning guidance and steps have been taken into that direction. We have seen more expenditure pledged by the Government on the question of flood defences. And work is now being done on how funding will be allocated in the future".[62]

The success of these negotiations refers to the reaffirmation of the state's commitment. Instead of exiting flood insurance, it seems possible to continue with a – somewhat qualified – division of responsibility and the reinvigoration of the bundled, compulsory system. This impression of continuity is challenged as insurance itself takes on the role of a regulator when it claims that "better use of new solutions to make property insurable (should be made) even in high risk areas where improvements to flood defence are not planned".[63] In order to be insured, the insured needs to take more than normal regulatory precautions. Here a previously unknown linkage of compensation and protection is made explicit for the insured. Now the clear division of responsibilities that charac-

[61] Association for British Insurers (ABI), *Insurers Announce New Principles for Flood Insurance*, press release of 26 September 2002.

[62] J. Parker (Head of General Insurance AB), [November 2002] *Insurance Age*, 30.

[63] *Supra* fn. 61.

terised the Gentlemen's Agreement seems no longer in place. If the compensation-regime assumes competencies in the field of flood protection, and competes with the protection-regime, the coordination of these regimes by the Gentlemen's Agreement no longer seems to work.

52 At first sight, the adaptation of the Gentlemen's Agreement to new conditions did not alter the regime. The robustness of the Gentlemen's Agreement to "survive" this significant crisis could be considered a sign of its suitability of natural disasters. It could be concluded that the English private flood insurance works, it covers nearly all risks and is able to adapt to changing situations within a brief period. The general construction of flood management binding two regimes together by a Gentlemen's Agreement can be used also in the case of more frequent and high impact floods. The Gentlemen's Agreement is a success-story even if challenged. This is, however, only part of the story. The Gentlemen's Agreement is altered in two essential points that massively challenge the entire construction. Firstly, in its attempt to mitigate and control *moral hazard,* UK flood insurance differentiated premiums according to levels of exposure, carried out more thorough risk assessments to identify the properties with a very regular, nearly habitual exposure to flooding and refined the assessment of insurability with a decline in solidarity. Bad risks are identified more cautiously and sorted out more rigorously. The efficiency of insurance increased, but political and legal problems emerged. If insurance weeds out bad risks, but the local authority allows the development of these areas, the properties diminish in value and are no longer marketable due to lacking insurance coverage. In addition, liability issues will arise. In this way insurance companies turn into indirect regulators as they define insurability in a way that establishes preliminary political decisions e.g. for land-use or housing developments. Furthermore, these decisions are only valid until new assessments are made and leave the direct regulator, i.e. the local authorities, with uncontrollable effects of its decisions for the future. Not only are properties turned into bad or uninsurable risks, but also the possibilities of further housing developments are limited considerably and may annul other regulatory efforts. If certain risks are no longer insurable, but coverage is socially demanded, other solutions have to be established.

53 In the Gentlemen's Agreement a division of responsibility was institutionalised. Changing the insurability of floods, not only influences flood management in an indirect (and often uncontrollable) way but it also changes the role of actors. Insurance rests on the role of a regulator of last resort. Industrial standards, however difficult it might appear to develop and implement them in a coherent way, could be decisive for flood protection and its effects on land-use, property development and insurance coverage. Although the Gentlemen's Agreement has formally survived, the role of the state and the industry has changed fundamentally. The state may be expected to act as insurer of last resort, at least for the increasing number of bad risk properties as it is politically not feasible to exclude certain flood plains from coverage especially if most of the housing development is expected to occur in these areas. This would, how-

ever, fundamentally challenge the spirit of the Gentlemen's Agreement. We can observe an *emerging* regulatory regime that brings together the *protection* and the *compensation* regime. The Gentlemen's Agreement is mutated from an *implicit* to an *explicit agreement* that not only dissolves the strict division of responsibilities but now establishes a wider actor space, which includes apart from state and industry (and the insured), also regulators (e.g. Environment Agency), experts and local authorities in a regulatory space. Although these changes are not manifest in all their consequences, a fundamental change in flood management can be perceived. Its consequences will unfold in the near future.

II. Terrorism after September 2001

PoolRe was amended in the light of 11 September 2001 as the size and expected frequency of terrorist events changed. As the expected features of these events were challenged, post 9/11 a substantial reassessment had to take place. A working group under the Department of Treasury reassessed the situation and identified changes that were put in place since January 2003. 54

PoolRe will move from the current per head of cover, per insured basis to a Treaty basis. From 2003 on, PoolRe will operate a per event retention, combined with an annual aggregate limit for each insurer, based on the overall terrorism market share of each insurer. The maximum retentions for industry are as follows:

Applying from	Per Annum	Per Event
1 January 2003	£ 60,000,000	£ 30,000,000
1 January 2004	£ 100,000,000	£ 50,000,000
1 January 2005	£ 150,000,000	£ 75,000,000
1 January 2006	£ 200,000,000	£ 100,000,000

Insurers will be free to set the premiums for underlying policies according to normal commercial arrangements, therefore introducing "competition" into the terrorism market. Reducing the restrictions on premiums opened competition among firms, but triggered also a major concern, as the benefits of PoolRe had to be compared with the advantages of general competition. While until now the cover was protecting the insurance firm only if the event could be linked to fire or explosion, a more comprehensive "all risk" approach has been established; damages caused by electronic viruses however are explicitly excluded from coverage and PoolRe will continue to only cover commercial property risks.

While the flood example pointed to a certain interest of the state to be more engaged in the management of compensation risks to insurance firms, in the case of terrorism the reaction is to shift the burden to the insurance firms respectively the insured business companies.

III. Compensation Culture

55 The legal path to compensation is not only opening the possibilities of claims from diverse actors, it is increasingly used to compensate for the failures of other parts of the compensation regime. There are two issues worth mentioning here: firstly, this can lead to increasingly more events that can be subject to compensation claims leading to the inflation of claims, which are driven by law firms. The growing idea of the existence of a "compensation culture"[64] however posits some correlation between the severity of injury and also the identification of someone at fault. In a MORI poll undertaken in 2000 (reported by the BBC, 15 November 2000) almost three in four people questioned said they would consider pursuing a personal injury compensation claim if they felt it to be someone else's fault. A survey undertaken by the Stationery Office in 2003 revealed that 96% of organisations believed the public to be more focused in obtaining compensation, with 60% of companies fearing that the existence of such a culture will gravely affect their business.

A research Report of the Centre for Policy Studies, "Courting Mistrust", estimated that the same "compensation culture" is costing the UK £ 6.8 billion per year or an estimated 1% of GDP in terms of compensation and fees, with as many as 98% of cases being settled prior to a court hearing.[65] Associations (such as Association of Personal Injury Lawyers) point to a reduction in some claims between 1998 and 2000 but a rise in the amount actually paid by insurers on each successful claim. Furthermore the manner in which successful claimants are to be compensated in the future by means of periodical payments rather than lump sums (with increases according to RPI indexation) has also raised concerns within the profession that victims will not recover full compensation.[66]

The compensation (and blame) culture affects the functioning of public services. In 1974 the National Health Service had to manage compensation claims of about £ 1 million, in 2003 the yearly compensation claims grew to £ 477 million. This money is the equivalent of 22,700 nurses; similar figures are reported from schools where claims are up to £ 200 million or the equivalent of 8,000 teachers. Here the problem is twofold: The increasing compensation claims consume a substantial share of public resources and reduce, in turn, the quality of the services – a downwards spiral.

IV. Public Inquiries and Negotiations

56 It is sometimes the case that civil proceedings are linked to either independent public inquiries commissioned by the Government often as a political response

[64] The World Economic Forum in Davos 2004, had a session devoted to this topic: "Is there a Multi-Billion Dollar Lawsuit in Your Future?".

[65] Furedi "Courting Mistrust" 1999, reported by the BBC 19 April 1999. According to Lord Levene (the Chairman of Lloyds of London this figure is £ 10 billion per annum and rising by 15% each year) 16 September 2003, talking in Los Angeles USA.

[66] Association of Personal Injury Lawyers (APIL), press release 26 March 2004, AP 244 and 5 April 2004 AP 246.

to public outrage.[67] Alternatively criminal proceedings may be commenced. In evidential terms, given the lower burden of proof required for civil proceedings (where the case must be proved on "the balance of probabilities" viz. more likely than not, rather than "beyond reasonable doubt" as in the case of criminal prosecutions), the existence of a damning public report or a criminal conviction can often serve to attenuate civil proceedings. The fact that someone (whether an individual or company) has already been convicted for the same event or set of circumstances can either make the probability of successful proceedings higher or may avoid them altogether, by the resulting claim being settled without recourse to a full trial. Current studies undertaken by the Department of Constitutional Affairs suggest that 8% of large cases are settled on the day of the trial.[68] The relation between these various viz. civil and criminal proceedings and public inquiries is usefully illustrated by the Sea Empress environmental disaster outlined below.

The grounding of the crude oil tanker known as the Sea Empress in February 57
of 1996 resulted in the discharge of approximately 72,000 tonnes of oil into the seas around the coast of South-West Wales. Various organizations and many individuals monitored the environmental effects of this pollution emergency. More than 100 km of outstanding coastline became seriously polluted by oil. Ecosystems of conservation, fishery and recreational importance were affected. A massive clean-up operation was launched, both at sea and onshore. A ban was imposed on commercial and recreational fishing in the region and there was concern that tourism, important to the local economy, would be badly affected by the heavily oiled beaches. Several thousand oiled birds washed ashore, leading to a major cleaning and rehabilitation operation.[69] The impacts were large and caused compensation claims against the port authority and the ship owner. Other organisations took part in the fact finding as well. They monitored the environmental effects of this pollution emergency. The Sea Empress Environmental Evaluation committee (SEEEC) was an independent committee established by Government in 1996 *inter alia*

> "... To co-ordinate monitoring work carried out by government departments and other public bodies to assess the environmental impact of the Sea Empress oil spill and the subsequent clean-up activities".

At the time of the initial report £ 2 million was allocated by the Government to fund the initial recommendations (half of this came from the Welsh Office), and £ 250,000 was awarded to the Countryside Council for Wales to research environmental effects. The accident itself and the resulting salvage operation

67 Similar observations also apply to the holding of coroners inquiries.

68 Source: *Further Findings a Continuing Evaluation of the Civil Justice Reforms*, August 2002, § 4.4.

69 Source: <http://www.archive.official-documents.co.uk/document/seeec/impact/seeec-1.htm>. SEEEC, the Environmental Impact of the Sea Empress Oil Spill – Sea Empress Environmental Evaluation Committee 17 February 1998 (source: <http://www.swan.ac.uk/biosci/empress/>). The parliament report can be found at <http://www.parliament.uk/post/pn075.pdf>.

were investigated by the Marine Accident Investigation Branch (MAIB) of the Department of the Environment, Transport and the Regions (DETR), which published its report in July 1997 and found the cause of the grounding to have been contributed to by pilot error. The Marine Pollution Control Unit (MPCU) produced a detailed account of the clean-up operation. The SEEEC Report notes that

> "environmental monitoring work to assess the initial impact started soon after the grounding of the tanker, and SEEEC supplemented this work with a programme of longer-term studies. It was clearly impossible to cover every aspect of the ecology of the region, but all the main types of onshore and marine environments were included in the programme, focusing on key species that were heavily impacted by the oil, indicative of the health of the environment, of conservation importance to the area, important in the marine food chain, or of economic value".[70]

Several compensation claims where made to cover the following costs:

- *Tourism*: An analysis of the impact on tourism throughout Pembrokeshire suggested a downturn of about £ 2 million in the commercial service sector in 1996 set against an estimated £ 160 million contributed by tourists to the economy in 1995. Despite satisfaction with the quality of the environment by those visiting the area, there was evidence from further questionnaires that for one in five who actually considered visiting Pembrokeshire in 1996, the Sea Empress spill was significant in leading to rejection. [SEEEC Report].
- *Environment*: The main environmental impacts of the spill included large numbers of marine organisms killed either as fresh oil came ashore or when raised levels of hydrocarbons in the water column affected bivalve molluscs and other sediment-dwelling species. Populations of amphipods (small crustaceans) disappeared from some areas and were severely depleted in others, both onshore and on the seabed near the site of the grounding. Several thousand birds were killed by oil. Studies showed that there was a significant impact on breeding guillemots in particular. A significant decrease in the population of the rare cushion starfish in the rock pools of West Angle Bay, close to the site of the grounding occurred, with numbers falling from more than 150 to 13.[71]
- *Clean-up*: The Department for Transport Summary Report of the incident estimated that at its peak 1,100 personnel were involved in the oil clean-up.[72] Ultimately, "in a major incident, such as the Sea Empress, the amounts

[70] The eventual programme of projects proposed by SEEEC was funded by the Government and its agencies with support from local authorities, the European Commission (EC), voluntary organisations and industry.

[71] Following the spill from the Sea Empress in mid-February 1996, 6,900 oiled birds of 28 species were collected up to 1 June that year, including approximately 3,495 that were dead or that subsequently died. Those included 1,818 dead common scoters and 1,416 dead auks, predominantly guillemots or razorbills.

[72] <http://www.dft.gov.uk/stellent/groups/dft_shipping/documents/page/dft_shipping_505 333.hcsp>.

can run into millions of pounds. These costs (so long as they are "reasonable") will eventually be reimbursed by the ship-owner's insurer and, when appropriate, the International Oil Pollution Compensation Fund 1992 ("1992 Fund"). However, in a complex case full reimbursement can take many years. During this time, the unexpected, and therefore unbudgeted, financial burden has to be borne by the local authorities".[73] Government gave increases in the Tourism Marketing budget (as funded by the Welsh tourist board and the insurer).[74] Fishing restrictions in the main continued (except oysters) until 1997.[75] The total cost of clean-up was estimated at £ 23 million.

- *Texaco's Sea Empress claim*: In February 2002 a claim was submitted by Texaco just before the final deadline for the loss of cargo. The Port Authority faces a £ 9.5 million claim for the disaster. Texaco stated that it has made its claim to protect its legal position in the aftermath of the disaster. It has issued proceedings against the Milford Haven Port Authority and Milford Haven Pilotage Limited.
- *The Environment Agency* took out a private prosecution against the Port Authority and the Harbourmaster some 17 months after the accident. The Agency used its statutory powers under the Water Resources Act 1991 to prosecute for the pollution of controlled waters in England and Wales. It commissioned a detailed study of the costs of the *Sea Empress* incident and it was estimated that the financial costs of the disaster were between £ 60 million and £ 114 million. The majority of these – between £ 49 million and £ 58 million – arose from the clean-up and salvage operations. Economic costs range between £ 75 million and £ 106 million, with a value of between £ 23 million and £ 35 million estimated for environmental impacts. The Port Authority was convicted and fined £ 4 million in January 1999, but this was later reduced on its appeal to the Court of Appeal to £ 750,000 in March 2000.
- *The International Oil Pollution Compensation Fund* is also seeking £ 34 million for the money it paid out to the victims of the disaster together with any further compensation it may have to pay in future. Texaco commenced proceedings to claim £ 9.5 million from the Port Authority carried by the Sea Empress. No final decision has been made yet. Although compensation claims are mainly dealt with by insurance coverage, it is important to notice how responsibility shifts between the courts or insurance and other specialist agencies and political committees. The latter's findings may be complementary, supporting each other or conflicting; disagreements about proof itself may cause compensation claims. International funds are established to protect victims – in that case mainly communities and industries (such as tourism) – against the long delays that can arise as a result of legal process.

[73] Observation of the Joint Committee on the draft Civil Contingencies Bill 11 November 2003 written evidence memorandum of the International Tanker Owners Pollution Federation Ltd.
[74] See Nick Ainger MP House of Commons 14 March 2001.
[75] House of Commons Written Answer 17 March 1997; Jonathan Evans.

Part XI. Concluding Remarks

58 We have been focusing on the two main pillars of the UK compensation regime and outlined some of the procedural issues to settle disputes in this regime. The main characteristic of the British system is its reliance on individual responsibility and therefore the focus on insurance solutions. The state is strongly involved in compensation issues; however, hardly any financial commitments that go beyond minimal contributions can be identified. Evaluating this individualistic approach, the main guideline must be the distinction between compensation and prevention. Given that compensation and prevention are mutually exclusive, the British compensation regime can be expected to be economically efficient. The social inequalities that are generated by such a market-based approach are hardly dealt with at the political level; this seems to be one of the fundamental differences between the British and the continental European approaches to compensation. Generally, prevention will therefore play a minor role in the UK system; compensation and litigation about the size of compensation will dominate in the UK and have an impact on the role of the legal system. Exceptions might occur when the regulatory framework is fundamentally altered as in the context of flood insurance. But the general tendency for individualised, compensation-oriented solution can be expected to prevail in the UK. The existence of a compensation culture is one strong indicator of this development. It remains to be seen which of these tendencies will prevail in the future; this has also implications for the dominance of the law vis-à-vis public inquiries and political negotiations.

List of References

Information by the Federal or Provincial Government or Other Authorities

ABI, *Inland Flooding Risk – Issues Facing the Insurance Industry*, London, 2000 (85, Research Report No. 10).

ABI, *Insurers Announce New Principles for Flood Insurance* press release of 26 September 2002.

Chartered Insurance Institute, *Climate change and insurance*, CII, London 2001 (Research report of).

Council Regulation 2012/2002 11 November 2002, instituting solidarity funding in the event of natural disasters (OJ L 311 14 November 2002).

DEFRA, *Flood and Coastal Defence. The Autumn 2000 Floods* (2002), 5 (<http://www.defra.gov.uk/environ/fcd/floodingincidents/floodinf.htm>).

DEFRA, *National appraisal of assets at risk from flooding and coastal erosion, including the potential impact of climate change* (2001). Final report July 2001, <http://www.defra.gov.uk/environ/fcd/default.htm>, 11.

Department of Constitutional Affairs, *Survey of Litigation Costs: Summary of Main Findings Annex III* (November 2003).

Department of Constitutional Affairs in its Report: *Further Findings a Continuing Evaluation of the Civil Justice Reforms*, August 2002.

Disaster Litigation, *Practice Guidelines for Solicitors* (October 2003), 1.

EA, *Environment Agency Response to the Independent Report on the Easter 1998 Floods* (1998).

General Secretariat Advisory Committee on Multi-disciplinary Issues, *Lessons Learned in Dealing with Large-Scale Disasters* SG/AU (2003)1 15 September 2003, <http://www.oecd.org/dataoecd/8/39/21121542.df>.

Home Office Consultation paper, *Compensation for Victims of Violent Crime: Possible Changes to the Criminal Injuries Compensation Scheme* (29 March 1999), § 11.

Interdepartmental Committee on Social Insurance and Allied Services (chaired by Sir William Beveridge), *Social Insurance and Allied Services*: A Report. Presented to Parliament by Command of His Majesty, November 1942–3 HMSO Cmd. 6404.

Judicial Statistics 2002 (HMSO).

Lord Chancellor's Department, *Access to Justice Final Report* (July 1996).

NAO, *Inland Flood Defence*, London, 2001 (Report by the controller and auditor general HC 299 Session 2000–2001: 15 March 2001).

OECD, *OECD Economic Outlook* (2002, no. 1), 71.

Sigma Report, *Natural Catastrophes and man-made disasters in 2000* (2/2001), 4.

SwissRe, *Floods – an insurable risk?* (1998).

SwissRe, *Opportunities and risks of climate change* (2002).

Swiss Re's Economic Research & Consulting Team, based in Zurich, New York and Hong Kong approximately eight times a year (<http://www.swissre.com/>).

The Law Society, *Disaster Litigation: Practice Guidelines for Solicitors* (October 2003).

Literature

M. Brewer/T. Clark/T. Wakefield, Social security in the UK under new labour: What did the third way mean for welfare reform?, [2002] *Fiscal Studies* 23(4), 505–37.

D. Crichton, UK and Global Insurance Responses to Flood Hazard, [2002] *Water International* 27 (1), 127.

D. Crichton, *Flood insurance in England and Wales: are there lessons to be learned from Scotland?* (2003) (Technical Papers 1, Benfield Greig Hazard Research Centre).

S. Elahi, *Easter Floods, UK*, Case Study Report of Project on the Uninsured Elements of Natural Catastrophic Losses (2000), 9.

P. Fenn/N. Rickman, *Costs of Low Value Employers' Liability Claims* (2003).

C.S. Fullerton/R.J. Ursano/A.E. Norwood/H.H. Holloway, Trauma, Terrorism and Disaster, in: C.S. Fullerton/R.J. Ursano/A.E. Norwood (eds.), *Terrorism and Disaster: individual and community health interventions* (2003).

J. Hadmer, *Flood insurance and relief in the US and in Britain* (1990), 21.

D. Harris/M. Maclean/H. Genn/S. Lloyd-Bostock/P. Fenn/P. Corfield/Y. Brittan, *Compensation and Support for Illness and Injury* (1984).

M. Huber, Institutional differences in the insurability of floods, [2004] *The Geneva Papers of Risk and Insurance* 28 (4).

M.A. Jones, *Textbook on Torts* (8th edn. 2002), 31.

B.S. Markesinis/S.F. Deakin, *Tort Law* (4th edn. 1999).

J.H. Merryman, *The Civil Law Tradition: An Introduction to the Legal Systems of Western Europe and Latin America* (2nd edn. 1985), 1.

D.J. Parker, The Institutional and Policy Context, in: J. Handmer (ed.), *Flood Hazard Management. British and international perspective* (1987), 36.

R. Salthouse, Lessons to be leaned from the autumn 2000 flood disaster in the UK [2002] *Insurance Research and Practices* 17 (1), 71.

UNITED STATES

Robert L. Rabin and Suzanne A. Bratis

Part I. Introduction

I. The Role of Tort: Responsible Party

On the evening of 20 February 2003, a rock band, Great White, staged a concert in an overcrowded nightclub, The Station, in West Warwick, Rhode Island, using pyrotechnics (also described as stage fireworks) as part of their act that ignited foam insulation on the walls of the club. The ensuing fire turned the club into a raging inferno and led to 100 deaths and more than 200 injuries, many of which were very serious burn cases. Early estimates of the total prospective claims in tort ranged in the area of one billion dollars.[1] 1

Prospective tort defendants were not hard to identify. The foam insulation appeared to be highly flammable, which suggested the possibility of suits against the owners of the nightclub, as well as the company that supplied the foam, and its manufacturer.[2] The foam had been in place for nearly three years, and yet the municipal fire inspector had certified the club as recently as two months before the fire – strongly suggesting viable claims against the municipality. The band itself, of course, and its manager, were certain defendants. And in the search for deep pockets, Clear Channel, the largest operator of radio stations in the country, which had promoted the concert on its local affiliate and whose disc jockey introduced the band, was named in early filings.[3] So too, were sponsors of the event, such as Anheuser-Busch Co., one of the largest breweries in the United States, and Shell Oil Co.[4]

[1] See Ch. Rowland/J. Salzman, Tragedy in Rhode Island; Suit Filed in Fire as R.I. Mulls Aid Fund Liability Claims Seen Topping $1B, [Mar. 5, 2003] *Boston Globe*, A 1.

[2] Apparently, the supplier's salesman was a neighbor of the owners. The salesman allegedly suggested the product when informed about noise complaints from other neighbors. J. Saltzman, Purchase of Foam at Club Is Traced, [Mar. 6, 2003] *Boston Globe*, B 5.

[3] See J. Saltzman, R.I. Fire Victims' Lawyers Eye Firm Suits Expected To Name Radio Station's Owner, [Mar. 8, 2003] *Boston Globe*, B 1.

[4] See *Passa v Derderian*, 308 *Federal Supplement* (F.Supp). 2d 43 (2004) (upholding the jurisdiction of the federal district court in Rhode Island to consolidate claims brought in other courts with the claims pending before it). The court's decision in *Passa* was reached under a newly passed Congressional Statute entitled the Multiparty, Multiforum Trial Jurisdiction Act of 2002, 28 *United States Code* (U.S.C.) § 1369 (2004).

2 One could anticipate the plaintiffs relying on a number of tort theories: In the claims against the band members and their manager, negligence in setting off incendiary devices in an enclosed structure with no forethought about the flammable nature of the surroundings; in the claims against the municipal officials, negligent failure to inspect adequately; in the claims against the nightclub owners, negligent failure to warn; and in the case of those responsible for sale and distribution of the insulation material, strict liability (or negligence) claims for supplying a defective product. In all of these cases, there would undoubtedly be claims not just of negligence but reckless disregard of safety as well, which could trigger punitive as well as compensatory damages under the United States tort system.

It is one thing, however, to *identify* defendants and establish viable tort theories, and another to *recover* damages in tort. In the West Warwick case, the prospect of insolvency casts a pall on tort litigation. The owners, band members, and those in the supply chain of the foam insulation materials all are likely to be marginally solvent defendants with limited insurance coverage.[5] The town's liability, even if established, is limited by state statute to $ 100,000 per plaintiff.[6] It seems unlikely that even by recourse to joinder of defendants, anywhere near the out-of-pocket loss will be recoverable against these most "immediate" defendants – let alone claims for intangible loss (consider, once again, the many serious burn cases, along with the prospect of 100 wrongful death claims, and trauma claims of those who managed to escape serious physical injury in the fire).[7]

Moreover, in the absence of settlement, a protracted litigation process will almost certainly ensue, during which the plaintiffs will be left to their own resources. Indeed, eighteen months after the fire, most of the cases had just recently been filed, and the claims were still simply at the jurisdictional stage.[8] Nor is there any real certainty that the defendants whose connection with the case is more attenuated, such as sponsors of the event like Anheuser-Busch and Shell Oil, will ultimately be found responsible. These major corporate defendants are joined principally because recourse to their substantial assets, if attainable, would assure full compensation in tort to the plaintiffs.

3 The Rhode Island nightclub fire serves as a useful introductory scenario for thinking about financial compensation in catastrophic loss cases in the United States, in situations where human responsibility for the disaster can arguably be established. As the following sections of this report will indicate, social welfare

[5] The insurance coverage might, in fact, be unavailable against those defendants whose criminal liability is established. The owners of the nightclub and the manager of the rock group have been indicted. See E. Mehren, 3 Indicted in R.I. Club Blaze; The Station's co-owners and band manager each face 200 involuntary manslaughter counts, [Dec. 10, 2003] *L.A. Times*, A 15.

[6] Ch. Rowland/J. Saltzman, [Mar. 5, 2003] *Boston Globe*.

[7] The federal district court in *Passa, supra* fn. 4, 46, reports that 412 people were inside the nightclub and, "[o]nly seventy-seven people are reported to have escaped the building without physical harm, yet, even for these lucky few who escaped bodily injury, the disaster continues to haunt their memories and affect their lives".

[8] Nearly 250 claims in addition to the five plaintiffs in *Passa, supra* fn. 4, were filed for deaths and injuries in mid-summer 2004. See Rhode Island: Survivors, Families Sue Over Nightclub Inferno, [July 23, 2004] *L.A. Times*, A 24.

legislation in the U.S. that would provide recovery for financial harm associated with catastrophic loss is relatively underdeveloped when compared to European social welfare systems. Private health, auto, homeowner's, and commercial property insurance coverage go part of the way towards filling the gap, but only part of the way.[9] For all of these reasons, when a potentially responsible third party can be identified, it is virtually always the case that recovery in tort is pursued.[10]

Moreover, the prominent role played by tort in the U.S. is not simply a function of its serving as a gap-filler under a system where large gaps exist in meeting the out-of-pocket losses, let alone the intangible costs, associated with unanticipated accidental harm. Just as significantly, the U.S. tort system is notably generous both in its body of substantive tort principles and remedial rules of damages – and this circumstance creates strong incentives to litigate in tort, even when first-party insurance coverage is present.

In particular, the expansive damages categories in tort create a substantial incentive to litigate whenever an arguably responsible defendant can be identified. The central precept underlying damage recovery in U.S. tort law is to restore an injury victim as closely as possible to an approximation of his/her pre-injury status. In addition to recognizing a right of recovery for all medical expenses, this underlying tenet of damage recovery entitles a victim, or a victim's survivors in a wrongful death action, to claim future wage loss (along with actual past wage loss) calculated to take account of the full expectation damages of the victim. Similarly, an individualized assessment of intangible loss – pain and suffering – is a standard heading of compensatory damages.[11] Hence, even in circumstances where private insurance coverage and/or a no-fault legislative compensation system provide benefits – circumstances to be discussed in detail in later sections of this report – tort provides damage awards (in particular, individualized, case-by-case assessment of wage loss and non-economic harm) that would not be recoverable under even the most generous insurance system. And, as another incentive to seek tort recovery, where a colourable case can be made out that the defendant's conduct was egregious in nature, punitive damages may be available.[12]

[9] In any event, recovery of private insurance benefits is generally ignored under the collateral source rule if an injury victim recovers in tort (i.e. "double-recovery" is allowed, although at times subject to subrogation rights of the insurer). Thus, private insurance coverage does not necessarily diminish the incentive to sue in tort.

[10] This is not to suggest that catastrophic loss cases are necessarily litigated to a jury verdict and through an exhaustive appeals process. To the contrary, most catastrophic loss cases – like most tort cases generally – are settled at some point prior to final judgment. In D.R. Hensler/M.A. Peterson, Understanding Mass Personal Injury Litigation: A Socio-legal Analysis, [1993] *Brooklyn Law Review* (Brook. L. Rev.) 59, 961, the authors offer brief case descriptions of the major personal injury mass disasters of the preceding decade and find that virtually every aggregation of cases was settled prior to final disposition in court.

[11] In a serious injury case, a derivative claim may also be entered by a spouse, or in some states a wider category of close relatives, for loss of companionship – technically referred to as "loss of consortium".

[12] While punitive damages are capped in some states and subject to due process limitations under recent U.S. Supreme Court rulings, see especially, *State Farm Mut. Auto. Ins. Co. v Campbell*, 538 *United States Supreme Court Reports* (U.S.) 408 (2003), juries retain very broad discretion to set an award that reflects considerations tailored to the particular case.

4 It is important to note, as well, that it has become common in recent mass tort litigation to find "secondary" categories of defendants, with far more attenuated relationships to mass tort claimants, named as defendants when the "primary" harm-imposers are either insolvent or impecunious.[13] This phenomenon corresponds to a broad judicial conception of the duty obligation in tort law that has emerged in the past thirty years.[14] In a like vein, courts have developed expansive approaches to causation, such as market share liability in a discrete category of joint responsibility situations, which reflect a commitment to distribute broadly the harm associated with toxic products, rather than allowing the loss to fall on injury victims.[15]

In sum, tort functions as a default financial recovery system in cases of catastrophic harm (and indeed in accident cases more generally) that is routinely invoked where a colourable claim can be made that a responsible party exists, irrespective of whether private and/or public insurance systems are available.[16]

II. Natural Disasters

5 But what of situations, so-called natural disasters, where no human agency can be charged with responsibility for catastrophic harm? In these cases there is no recourse to tort in most instances, and victims of catastrophic loss ordinarily must rely exclusively on private insurance coverage, or, when available, on public insurance systems.[17] The latter can be parsed into two separate categories: social welfare schemes (discussed in Part II of this report), such as government disability and unemployment insurance legislation, which are available to *all* claimants meeting general eligibility requirements – without reference to the source of the harm that has occurred. And, legislative no-fault or insurance schemes that have been established with designated types of catastrophic loss in mind. This second category of social welfare legislation will be discussed, along with a description of private insurance coverage, in Part IV – after exam-

[13] A particularly salient recent example is the asbestos litigation. See D. Hensler, As Time Goes By: Asbestos Litigation After Amchem and Ortiz, [2002] *Texas Law Review* (Tex. L. Rev.) 80, 1899.

[14] An especially influential case, which opened the floodgates of asbestos litigation, was *Borel v Fibreboard Paper Products Corp.*, 493 F.2d 1076 (5th Cir. 1973), *cert. denied*, 419 U.S. 869 (1974).

[15] See the leading case involving DES litigation, *Sindell v Abbott Labs.*, 607 P.2d 924 (Cal. 1980), *cert. denied* 449 U.S. 912 (1980).

[16] One qualification is necessary. Some legislative no-fault schemes require the claimant either to opt out of tort in order to claim benefits, or preclude resort to tort altogether by eligible claimants.

[17] Even in natural disaster situations, one qualification is necessary, reflecting the broad sweep of U.S. tort law. At times, in these cases – an earthquake, for example – if injury claimants can establish that greater foresight (perhaps on the part of a building construction contractor) might have anticipated the consequences that came to fruition through an "act of God", there may be resort, once again, to tort litigation. Thus, it is more accurate, as a general proposition, to think of tort in the context of U.S. catastrophe compensation as a *complementary* system of redress, rather than a default system, offering the prospect of damage recovery that takes full account of the injury victim's loss when its liability standards are satisfied.

ining the government agency whose work is devoted exclusively to disaster relief (in Part III on the Federal Emergency Management Agency).

Part V of the report will serve as a reprise on the somewhat patchwork design of the U.S. system by isolating for special consideration three case studies of particularly salient disaster events that illustrate the range of approaches discussed earlier: First, the terrorist acts of September 11, and, in particular, the legislative no-fault compensation scheme that was enacted to compensate the personal injury victims; second, Hurricane Andrew, which initiated a mixed private/public insurance scheme in Florida and recast FEMA's approach to disaster relief; and third, commercial airline crashes, as a category, which invoke tort as the principal source of disaster relief compensation.

In a concluding Part VI of the report, we will return to a more general overview of the system, offering a brief final commentary on fairness and efficacy considerations.

Part II. Social Welfare Legislation in the U.S.: General Disability Provisions

I. The U.S. Social Security System: Background

The social security system in the U.S. was originally created in response to the 6
widespread social hardships of the Great Depression. In the early 1930s, the number of unemployed workers skyrocketed. The nation's elderly was one cohort group facing serious danger. As family incomes and savings dropped, care of the elderly became a heavy burden on families and charity groups were unable to meet the demands for aid. President Franklin Delano Roosevelt submitted a social security program proposal to Congress in 1935.[18]

The original Social Security Act of 1935 emerged from Congress as a two-part social insurance program that included provisions for federal old-age insurance and for federal grants to state-run unemployment compensation programs.[19] The old-age insurance component created retirement benefits that were available to primary workers at the age of 65. From the outset, some argued for the inclusion of disability funding, as well. Many viewed disabled workers as a group greatly in need of federal support but left without care under the Social Security system. Finally, in 1954, Congress responded, introducing the first disability benefits program.

II. Disability Provisions: Eligibility Standards

The initial scope of disability benefits was limited. Disability was defined 7
conservatively as the

[18] Economic Security Bill, H.R. 4120, 74th Cong. (1935).

[19] At the time, legal scholars were uncertain whether Congress had the authority under the U.S. Constitution to enact such sweeping social welfare legislation. In 1937, the U.S. Supreme Court responded in the affirmative. See *Helvering v Davis*, 301 U.S. 619 (1937) (finding Social Security Act to be a valid exercise of Congress' constitutional authority and rejecting claim that the Act violated the Tenth Amendment); *Steward Machine Co. v Davis*, 301 U.S. 548 (1937) (finding Social Security Act does not violate the reserved powers of the states); *Carmichael v So. Coal & Coke Co.*, 301 U.S. 495 (1937).

> "inability to engage in any substantial gainful activity by reason of any medically determinable physical or mental impairment which can be expected to result in death or to be of long-continued and indefinite duration".

Benefits were only available for insured workers between the ages of 50 and 65.

Over time, however, Congress amended and expanded the disability provisions. It added coverage for dependents of disabled workers and disabled children of retired or deceased workers. The minimum age requirement was removed and the definition of "disability" was loosened to include impairments "expected to last for a continuous period of not less than 12 months". With these and other changes, the size of the program grew significantly as did the amount of funds being doled out annually.[20]

In its current form, the Social Security Administration manages two federal disability benefits programs: the Social Security disability insurance program (SSDI) (Title II of the Social Security Act) and the supplemental security income program (SSI) (Title XVI of the Act). While neither program was specifically designed as a catastrophe-mitigation scheme, disabilities caused by a catastrophic event are covered, provided they meet the general requirements of the Act.

Title II has several requirements that applicants must meet. First, SSDI benefits are only available for "insured" workers (and their dependents under certain conditions). To be "insured" for purposes of the Act, an individual must have contributed to the Social Security trust fund through the Social Security tax deducted from their employment earnings. Second, the individual must have accumulated a certain number of "work credits" at the point of filing for disability.[21]

Most critically, the applicant's impairment must meet the definition of "disability" set forth in the Act. A disability for Social Security purposes is

> "the inability to engage in any substantial gainful activity by reason of any medically determinable physical or mental impairment(s) which can be expected to result in death or which has lasted or can be expected to last for a continuous period of not less than 12 months".[22]

In essence, then, SSDI benefits are limited to prospective *permanent* and *total* disability. The program is circumscribed insofar as it does not pay benefits for partial or short-term disabilities. At the same time, its scope is broad in that it

[20] By 1960, the number of awards issued by the SSA to disabled beneficiaries and nondisabled dependants reached 388,861. In 1975, that number rose to 1,305,345. Social Security Admin., Annual Statistical Report on the Social Security Disability Insurance Program tbl. 30 (2002), available at <http://www.ssa.gov/policy/docs/statcomps/di_asr/2002/index.html>.

[21] Work credits are based on total yearly wages (or total income for self-employed workers). A worker can earn up to four work credits per year. Generally, SSDI requires a worker to have accumulated forty work credits, ten of which must be earned in the ten years immediately prior to the claimed disability.

[22] Social Security Act, 42 U.S.C. § 416(i)(1)(A) (2004).

defines disability in terms of capability of performing work functions and not general life activities.

The limits of the SSDI program may be seen as a reflection of its intended role in relation to other forms of economic support. Given the program's limits, a worker must rely on state workers' compensation programs, personal insurance and personal savings to weather short-term disability episodes.[23]

The second general disability program, Supplemental Security Income, differs in some ways from SSDI benefits. The purpose of the SSI program is to ensure that the basic needs of the aged, blind and disabled individuals in the *poorer* segment of the nation's society are provided for. To be eligible for SSI benefits, an individual must be over 65 years of age, blind, *or disabled.* In addition, the eligibility requirements set a maximum annual income and total resource level.[24] Essentially, an applicant's monthly income must not be greater than the federal benefit rate[25] and the value of the individual's personal property cannot exceed the amount dictated by the SSA.[26]

III. Benefit Levels, Treatment of Collateral Sources, and Funding

Benefit levels under SSDI and SSI differ. SSDI benefit rates are based on the 8
claimant's lifetime average earnings covered by Social Security. No form of social security is intended as a full replacement for earned wages. The benefits tend to fall below 50% of the claimant's average yearly salary. Claimants with higher salaries are generally eligible for a lower percentage of their wage in benefits than claimants with lower average yearly salaries.

Under the SSI program, a national maximum payment rate is established every year. For 2004, the highest federal SSI monthly payment was set at $ 564 for an individual and $ 846 for a couple.[27] The amount that an individual claimant will receive is generally based on the person's income for the two months prior to each monthly payment. States are free to supplement the na-

[23] In addition to meeting the definition of "disability", a worker must also show that his or her impairment is "severe". The Social Security Administration maintains a list of medical conditions that per se qualify as "severe". If an applicant's impairment is not listed, the Administrator assesses whether it is of equal severity to a listed impairment. If it is deemed not to be of equal severity, the Administrator determines if the condition nonetheless interferes with the applicant's ability to do the work previously undertaken or to adjust to other work. To determine if an applicant can adjust to new work, the claimant's age, education, work experience, and transferable skills are considered.

[24] Eligibility requirements for Supplemental Security Income benefits are set forth in Social Security Act, 42 U.S.C. § 1382(a) (2004).

[25] The federal benefit rate as of January 2003 is $ 552 for an individual and $ 829 for a couple. See Social Security Administration, *Social Security Handbook* (2003), § 2113.1. These amounts can be supplemented by State programs. 42 U.S.C. § 1382(e). States can enter into an agreement with the SSA to have SSA administer the State supplemental program and distribute those benefits along with the federal benefits. If such an agreement is entered into, SSA charges the state a fee for every supplementary payment issued. See Social Security Administration, *Social Security Handbook* (2003), § 2016.1.

[26] As of 2003, the limits were $ 2,000 for an individual and $ 3,000 for a couple. Social Security Administration (*supra* fn. 25), § 2113.2.

[27] Social Security Administration, *A Guide to Supplemental Security Income (SSI) for Groups and Organizations*, available at <http://www.ssa.gov/pubs/11015.html>.

tional SSI funds and may apply their own rules for establishing the rates of the supplements. Payments are generally made on a monthly basis, though provisions exist for requesting a lump sum payment.

9 The treatment of collateral sources raises an important question, because disabled workers claiming benefits under the SSDI program generally do have other sources of benefits available: Private health insurance, private pension plans, and state workers' compensation programs are some leading examples. When the government calculates SSDI benefits for which a person is eligible, it does not consider any money that person has collected from private insurance. In other words, disability benefits from private sources such as private pensions and insurance do not reduce SSDI benefits.[28] At the same time, disability benefits from *public* sources may reduce SSDI benefits. Workers' compensation, civil service disability benefits, military benefits, and state temporary benefits are all examples of public sources of compensation. The combined amount of benefits from public sources cannot exceed 80% of the claimant's pre-disability income. If the combined benefits do exceed that amount, the excess is subtracted from the SSDI contribution.[29]

Finally, with respect to funding, SSDI and SSI are financed by different sources, lending some insight into their differing objectives. The SSDI program is funded by wage-based tax payments made by workers, employers, and self-employed persons. By contrast, the SSI program is financed through general tax revenues.

IV. Administration

10 Applying for SSDI benefits is generally a non-adversarial, administrative process with responsibilities allocated between federal and state officials. Applications are submitted to the Social Security District Office, which is responsible for assisting applicants in filling out the necessary paperwork and gathering evidence needed to determine entitlement.[30] Once the District Office has completed its tasks, it forwards the application to a state disability determination unit. This state-level administration of the federal program is accomplished through a formal agreement between the state and federal governments.[31]

The state office determines whether the applicant qualifies as "disabled" under the Act.[32] Once a formal determination is reached, a written notice is

[28] However, when a private insurer calculates the amount that it will pay out, it may consider SSDI income and adjust its payout accordingly. National Organisation of Social Security Claimants' Representatives, *Social Security Practice Guide* (2003), § 7.03.

[29] Veterans Administration benefits and SSI payments are not included in the calculation of combined benefits.

[30] National Organisation of Social Security Claimants' Representatives (*supra* fn. 28), § 10.01.

[31] *Idem*, § 10.10.

[32] The determination is made by a team composed of a trained disability analyst and a medical consultant. The team makes its disability determination based on application forms, medical evidence, and other data. To be eligible for compensation under either the SSDI or SSI program, a claimant must have a "medically determinable impairment". The impairment must be

sent to the applicant.[33] If a claim is approved, disability benefits are dispersed on a monthly basis from the federal funds. Benefits under the SSDI program typically cannot begin until five months after the onset of the claimed disability. By contrast, under the SSI program, benefits can begin as early as the date that the applicant filed the claim. A "presumptive disability" advance can be made in certain cases to sustain the applicant for up to six months while the formal application review process takes place. There is no requirement that the monies be refunded if the application is ultimately denied.

If a claim is denied, the applicant can file an appeal. The first step in the appeals process is a request for reconsideration of the initial determination. If such a request is made, the primary examining office will re-examine the administrative record and the applicant is permitted to submit new evidence to support her eligibility. The applicant can appeal this second determination by requesting a hearing before an Administrative Law Judge (ALJ) of the federal Office of Hearings and Appeals. The next step is to request a review of the ALJ's decision by the Office of Hearings' Appeals Council. Finally, a dissatisfied applicant can enter the federal court system by filing a civil action against the Social Security Administrator in federal district court. The district court can affirm, modify, or reverse an SSA decision and can remand the application back to SSA for reconsideration or it can enter a final judgment on the case with remand.[34]

V. Health Care Benefits

Medicare is a federal health insurance program that was created in 1965 to en- 11
sure that retired and disabled Americans have access to basic health care.[35] Medicare is available to individuals who are 65 or older and individuals of any age who suffer from certain disabilities.[36] Medicare coverage can be obtained in two ways, directly from the government (Original Medicare Plan) or from participating private insurance companies (Medicare Advantage Plan).[37]

The Original Medicare Plan has two parts. Part A (Hospital Insurance) covers a portion of short-term, inpatient care in hospitals and critical access

established through medical evidence. A claimant's own statement of symptoms is insufficient to secure benefits. To prove a disability, the applicant must provide medical records of symptoms, diagnoses, and/or laboratory findings substantiating her claim. If an applicant fails to submit sufficient medical evidence herself, the disability examiner may request an additional examination be conducted by a state consulting physician. The reviewing team makes an independent determination of disability based on the medical records and other evidence filed and does not take the evaluations of consulting physicians to be dispositive. Social Security Administration (*supra* fn. 25), § 604.3.

33 20 *United States Code of Federal Regulations* (C.F.R.), § 404.1562 (2003).

34 See Social Security Administration (*supra* fn. 25), §§ 2000–2019.

35 Social Security Amendments of 1965, 42 U.S.C. §§ 1395 *et seq.* (2004).

36 Medicare's disability provision is tied to SSDI. Medicare is available to individuals under the age of 65 who have met the requirements of the SSDI benefits program for a period of at least 24 consecutive months. See 42 U.S.C. §§ 1395(c), 1395(o) (2004).

37 Private insurers that offer Medicare Advantage Plans can provide a wider range of coverage options than is available through the Original Medicare Plan (e.g. expanded prescription drug coverage) and can charge monthly premium rates for the added benefits.

facilities. Most working Americans pay for Part A coverage through a Medicare tax deducted from their pay checks during the term of their employment. If an individual is 65 or older, or disabled, but did not pay the Medicare tax while employed, she may be able to purchase Part A coverage from the government. Part B (Medical Insurance) helps to cover outpatient medical care, such as doctor's visits, outpatient hospital care, some types of physical therapy, and some medical supplies.

Part B requires a monthly premium payment. In 2004, the monthly cost was $ 66.60. For both Parts A and B, the insured must pay a deductible amount before federal funds are available. If medical costs exceed that deductible, then Medicare and the insured share the remaining costs according to the program cost schedule.

VI. Concluding Observations

12 By definition, the general governmental disability provisions in the U.S. were not enacted with special reference to providing compensation for catastrophic loss. As a consequence, the gaps in coverage, which are apparent even when the benefit schemes are assessed under ordinary circumstances of accidental harm, stand out when a mass disaster occurs.

More specifically, federal social welfare legislation provides only a limited safety net for injury victims along at least three critical dimensions. First, there is no governmental scheme of national health insurance in the U.S. The coverage afforded under the principal federal scheme, Medicare, is largely limited to the elderly. Second, there is only limited coverage of wage loss in the case of disabling injury: the federal SSDI scheme provides benefits only in the case of permanent total disability. While state disability schemes and unemployment compensation insurance offer supplemental assistance, they are limited in scope, and in any event, provide only limited wage replacement. Finally, property loss is not covered at all under governmental programs of general applicability. Here, the gap is filled in part by disaster relief programs discussed in sections Part III and Part IV, just as gaps in personal injury out-of-pocket loss are covered, if at all, through private insurance coverage, also discussed in section Part IV.

Part III. Disaster Relief: The Role of the Federal Emergency Management Agency

I. Introduction

13 The Federal Emergency Management Agency (FEMA) was created in 1979 as an attempt to unify the diverse federal disaster relief programs then in existence. FEMA, once an independent agency, is now part of the recently created Department of Homeland Security. The Agency is responsible for administering federal disaster relief funds, as well as managing the government's myriad preparedness and prevention programs. FEMA's jurisdiction covers the gamut of emergencies – both natural and man-made. Since its inception, FEMA has provided assistance in the aftermath of earthquakes, hurricanes, tornadoes, the

hazardous waste contamination of Love Canal, the accident at Three Mile Island nuclear power plant, the Cuban refugee crisis, and the terrorist attacks on September 11, 2001.[38]

Two types of assistance are administered by FEMA: individual and public. Individual assistance provides monies to individuals, families, and businesses in the form of low-interest loans, housing grants, tax refunds, unemployment benefits, and even free legal counseling. FEMA's Public Assistance Grant Program provides funding to state and local governments and certain types of private non-profit organizations to help in the rebuilding of communities harmed by a disaster event. In addition to serving as a source of funding, FEMA also coordinates post-disaster relief efforts, including support from other agencies of the federal government.

As discussed in greater detail below, state and local governments bear the initial responsibility for relief and recovery after catastrophes that take place in their region. The federal funds administered by FEMA are meant to support the efforts of state and local governments when relief requirements overwhelm their capabilities.

II. FEMA: Coordination with State and Local Entities

A. The Role of Local Government

Disaster assistance in the United States begins at the local level. Thousands of 14
emergencies occur nationwide every year and most of them are handled by local governments. Local elected officials (e.g. mayors, city councils, boards of commissioners) have primary responsibility for protecting their citizens. Upon learning of a potentially imminent emergency, local officials have a duty to warn their citizens and take whatever steps are warranted to minimize damage. Evacuation orders are most often issued at the local level.

If a disaster does occur, aid and protection are provided by local medical crews, rescue workers, fire fighters, and police. Private and public utility crews work to restore downed power, transportation, and communication systems. Private and non-profit aid organizations, such as the Red Cross, Salvation Army, and churches, offer food, housing and clothing to victims in coordination with the local government. Voluntary agencies lend assistance regardless of whether an official "state of emergency" has been declared by any level of government. They typically coordinate their efforts and work with government officials to determine the community's needs.

In the aftermath of a disaster, local governments must coordinate and provide both short-term and long-term recovery. Short-term recovery includes the restoration of essential community services, ensuring houses are habitable to allow families to return home from temporary housing, and repair of major

[38] More recently, FEMA has been actively engaged in providing disaster relief in the wake of a cluster of four hurricanes, beginning with Hurricane Charley, which caused enormous damage in the state of Florida in August-September 2004. For discussion, see A. Goodnough, In Florida, Officials are Hoping for One Final Storm Recovery, [Sept. 29, 2004] *New York Times*, A 21.

roads, water distribution services, and communication lines. Long-term recovery involves the extensive repair and rebuilding necessary to put the community as close to its pre-disaster conditions as possible. In addition, long-term recovery often includes implementing strategies to minimize the damage of similar events in the future.

Often, local communities enter mutual aid agreements with surrounding localities. These agreements allow local governments to rely on their neighbours for financial and service assistance in the case of an emergency. Such agreements may be inadequate, however, where a disaster hits an entire region. The greater the magnitude of a disaster, the more likely that state government will be involved.

B. *The Role of State Government*

15 If local resources are overwhelmed, the state government may be called upon to declare a state of emergency in the affected area. The local officials submit a request to the state governor (the chief executive official of the state), providing specific information about the emergency, its effects (deaths, injuries, level of property damage, etc.), and the type of aid needed from the state. Such requests are reviewed by the state emergency management office and a recommendation is issued to the governor.

All states have emergency and disaster response laws that set forth the state government's responsibilities in the event of an emergency and the governor's duties and powers, including the power to declare a state of emergency and decide when to end that declaration.[39] Nearly every state has some form of emergency management office.[40] Such agencies have the responsibility to prepare for emergencies and coordinate the activation and allocation of state resources as needed to help localities respond to and recover from disasters.

State-level personnel can engage in monitoring and information gathering even before a declaration of emergency by the governor. When an emergency is declared at the state level, it releases state funds, personnel and equipment for use in aiding local governments' response efforts. Additionally, state personnel may be called on to provide technical assistance and resources that would not ordinarily be available to local officials. Just as local governments can enter into mutual aid agreements, many states are part of the Emergency Management Assistance Compact or similar cooperative arrangements that allow participating states to draw on a common pool of personnel, equipment, and supplies in emergency situations. These agreements allow states to expand their own resource base without needing to ask for federal assistance.[41]

The state may provide a variety of services depending on the determined need of the affected community. The Department of Public Safety may deploy engineers and heavy equipment to conduct damage assessments of bridges and

[39] See e.g. California Code Regulations (Cal. Code Regs.) title 19, §§ 2400 *et seq.* (2002).

[40] See Homepage of California's Governor's Office of Emergency Service, available at <http://www.oes.ca.gov/Operational/OESHome.nsf/1?OpenForm>.

[41] See e.g. Michigan Emergency Management Assistance Compact (2002), available at <http://www.michigan.gov/documents/MEMACFINAL7-3-03_69499_7.pdf>.

other infrastructure and assist in reconstruction plans that will create greater resistance in future disasters. Safety personnel may assist with evacuation efforts, crowd control, search, and rescue. Public health units may also be used to monitor water and food supplies and manage efforts to control communicable diseases.

State social service agencies can be called upon to manage shelters and provide counselling services to individuals and families to help people cope with the trauma of a disaster. The governor may call the State National Guard into service in an affected area to provide civil control and supplemental law enforcement services. Public health agencies, the state department of agriculture, and natural resource agencies may also have a role to play depending on the type of disaster and relief efforts needed by the local community.

III. FEMA: Core Responsibilities

A. *Historical Overview*

If the resource capacities of both the state and local governments are exceeded 16
by a disaster event, the federal government is the next in line to provide aid. Prior to 1950, the federal government had no unified disaster relief law in place. Congress had to pass a new law every time it sought to release federal funds for disaster assistance. In 1950, Congress passed the Federal Disaster Relief Act[42] which created a mechanism for federal emergency relief. The Act set forth the principle that federal aid is to be a *supplement* to state and local resources, not a primary source of relief. It conditioned federal disaster aid on a presidential declaration of a "major disaster" and required state and local governments to commit a "reasonable amount of funds" before federal monies could be distributed.[43]

In 1979, President Carter consolidated federal emergency management and mitigation responsibilities into a single agency: the Federal Emergency Management Agency. The decision was motivated by a plea from state governors who found navigating their way through the disparate federal programs extremely difficult, especially during crisis times. It was also an attempt to increase efficiency and efficacy. The Robert T. Stafford Disaster Relief and Emergency Assistance Act,[44] which was passed in 1988, is the statute that currently gives the government the authority to dispense federal funds for response and recovery assistance.

The Federal Response Plan (FRP), coordinated by FEMA, provides guidance to federal emergency response efforts.[45] The FRP is a signed agreement between more than 20 departments and agencies of the federal government that describes how federal resources will be used to meet state and local response and recovery needs. It provides federal supplemental assistance in 12

[42] Public Law (Pub. L.) No. 81–875 (1950).

[43] *Idem.*

[44] 42 U.S.C. §§ 5121 *et seq.* (1988).

[45] Federal Emergency Management Agency, *Federal Response Plan* (2003), available at <http://www.fema.gov/rrr/frp/>.

critical areas. These "emergency support functions" are: 1) transportation; 2) communications; 3) public works and engineering; 4) fire fighting; 5) information and planning; 6) mass care; 7) resource support; 8) health and medical services; 9) urban search and rescue; 10) hazardous materials; 11) food; and 12) energy. FEMA assistance in these 12 areas takes various forms including direct, hands-on assistance through dispatch of federal personnel and immediate emergency funds, and longer-term assistance in the form of grants. For example, in the immediate aftermath of major hurricanes, FEMA frequently provides equipment, personnel, and financial assistance for debris removal, reestablishment of communication lines, reopening of main transportation routes, and immediate health, nutrition, and shelter needs. In addition, the Agency extends its relief and recovery efforts into the weeks and months following such disasters as it distributes financial grants to private citizens, area businesses, and community government to help with structural repairs and economic recovery efforts.

B. Obtaining Federal Assistance

17 As suggested above, federal funding for disaster relief is not automatically available when an emergency event occurs. The state governor must request a presidential declaration of major disaster and must support that request with a demonstration that the situation has surpassed state and local economic capabilities. The process is initiated by a Preliminary Damage Assessment (PDA), which is an analysis of the damage that has occurred as a result of an incident. The PDA is assembled through a coordinated effort between state and local officials and FEMA regional officials. The PDA allows the federal decisionmakers to assess the impact and magnitude of damage, the needs of individuals and businesses, and the capabilities of state and local emergency management funds. It also provides information on which to base estimates of the types and extent of federal assistance needed.

Once the PDA is compiled, the governor reviews the document and supporting evidence (photographs, surveys, etc.) and determines whether federal assistance is needed. Before the governor can submit a formal request for a presidential disaster declaration, the state must have implemented its own Emergency Operations Plan. If that action has been taken, the governor can submit a declaration request to the President, which includes specific information about the type and amount of state and local resources slotted for disaster-related efforts. Additionally, the request must guarantee that the Stafford Act's cost-sharing provisions will be met.

The FEMA Regional Director then evaluates the request and makes a recommendation to the national FEMA director, who, in turn, makes a recommendation to the President. In analyzing the request, FEMA officials consider a number of factors, including the amount and type of damage, the impact on citizens, businesses, and government entities, non-federal resources available to the community including insurance coverage, federal assistance available without a formal disaster declaration, threats to life and safety, and whether the state has suffered other recent disaster events.

Once the President decides to declare a major disaster, he appoints a Federal Coordinating Officer. The federal and state coordinating officers[46] work together to establish a disaster field office,[47] and an agreement is signed by FEMA and state officials. This FEMA-State Agreement sets the time parameters, types of assistance and eligible regions, cost-share arrangements, and other terms.

C. The Federal Response

In general, disaster relief under FEMA is available for both immediate needs for emergency support, discussed above, and longer-term restorative assistance to victims. On the latter score, FEMA provides loans and grants for property damage directly caused by a disaster event. Importantly, the intent of FEMA is to return a damaged region to a functional state. It is not to return the area to its pre-disaster condition. In this regard, it is strikingly more modest in design than tort law, discussed earlier. 18

Federal response comes in various forms. The following sub-sections give a more detailed discussion of the types of federal personnel and financial assistance available to victims of disaster.

1. Federal Personnel Available

When a major disaster occurs, federal personnel teams are coordinated by the FEMA Regional Director of the affected region and dispatched. Different types of personnel teams can be created. The Emergency Response Team is a federal interagency group that is activated only after a presidential declaration. It operates from a Disaster Field Office and coordinates the overall federal response and recovery efforts and assistance. It coordinates with state and local governments to ensure that the federal employees maintain their role as supplemental to, rather than supplanting, local efforts. In addition, an Emergency Support Team functions at FEMA headquarters to coordinate local efforts and serves as a point source for information. 19

In the case of predictable disasters, such as hurricanes and floods, when advance warning allows officials to make early estimates of the magnitude of impending damage, an advance team of federal personnel may be dispatched to an area even before a disaster is officially declared. This Advance Emergency Response Team will establish emergency communications systems in an area and work with state and local officials to help coordinate early response efforts and identify what assistance may be needed.

Once a major disaster occurs, the FEMA Regional Director of the affected region will coordinate the Regional Support Team and possibly an Emergency Support Team and the Emergency Response Team.

[46] The State Coordinating Officer (SCO) is the point of contact for the state and local officials and is the person charged with overseeing and coordinating the state and local response/recovery efforts.

[47] The Disaster Field Office is the on-site coordination center for disaster relief personnel. It is not a public reception center. Other spaces are designated for public outreach activities.

2. Types of Federal Assistance Provided for Individuals and Businesses

20 Immediate needs funding is a unique category of federal funding. The Public Assistance Program allows a completed Preliminary Damage Assessment, mentioned above, to trigger federal funding for emergency work in the most in-need areas even before a presidential declaration has been issued. Up to 50% of the total federal share estimated in the PDA can be used for emergency work. This provision is meant to allow funding to be available for the most basic necessities in the heart of the crisis so that administrative delays do not contribute to the human suffering in an emergency of disaster proportions.

Under the regular scheme, as distinguished from immediate needs funding, federal assistance is available for individuals and businesses. This assistance comes in many forms. The primary concern in the aftermath of a disaster is ensuring that victims' most basic needs are met. To that end, various efforts are made to provide food, temporary shelter, and longer-term restorative funds for housing and commercial redevelopment. In the accompanying footnote we offer a partial description of some of the principal forms of grants and loans, designed to provide a sense of the strategies used to get disaster victims off to a fresh start.[48]

[48] The U.S. Department of Agriculture (USDA) houses the Food and Nutrition Service, a federal agency that oversees the federal Disaster Food Stamp and Food Commodities Programs. The food stamp program provides food coupons to eligible individuals and families. Once USDA gives federal approval, the program is administered by state and/or local social service agencies and stamps are distributed through an application process. The food commodities program involves federal distribution of surplus commodities to applicants. The applicant pool typically consists of state or voluntary assistance organizations (e.g. the Red Cross) or individual households.

The Disaster Housing Program makes federal funds available for home restoration. The funding is only intended to restore homes to a "safe, sanitary, and functional condition". Funds from this program can also be used for rent payments if the applicants show that they lived in a house damaged by the disaster event. Finally, this program also provides assistance for rent or mortgage payments to homeowners or renters who can show that they suffered financial hardship related to the disaster.

The Individuals and Household Program has a Housing Assistance component. Housing Assistance makes federal funds available to homeowners and renters for rental assistance, repair and replacement expenses, and costs of building a permanent home; assistance can be direct or in the form of financial aid through grants.

In addition to addressing victims' most immediate needs, FEMA also coordinates more long-term recovery assistance for individuals and businesses. Such aid comes in the form of loans, unemployment compensation, tax aid, legal and mental health services, and other aid. Individuals may qualify for federal loans to help finance property repairs. Even absent a presidential disaster declaration, the Small Business Administration has the authority to make available low interest loans. The monies can be used for repair or replacement of homes and personal property. Small businesses may be eligible for a few different types of loans from the SBA. Physical loss loans provide money for repairing property damage including inventory. Economic injury loans can give small businesses and small agricultural cooperatives working capital to get them through the aftermath of the disaster.

3. Types of Federal Assistance Provided for Communities

Community assistance takes two predominant forms: hazard mitigation assistance and public assistance. 21

The purpose of hazard mitigation assistance is to reduce or eliminate an area's vulnerability to similar disasters in the future. As with many other features of FEMA, the purpose of this type of assistance is to bolster local self-sufficiency, reduce the need for federal relief funds, and avoid damage to property and loss of life wherever possible. Hazard mitigation[49] assistance is limited insofar as it becomes available only in cases where personal or public assistance has also been declared available. However, it is broad insofar as use of its funds is not limited to the areas included in the disaster declaration. Rather, it can be used throughout the state.

Public assistance initiatives seek to help restore damaged communities to a functional state. Upon a declaration of disaster by the President, FEMA becomes authorized to provide supplemental monetary assistance to the recovery efforts of the state and local governments and non-profit organizations that provide services of a "governmental nature" (e.g. medical and emergency facilities, utilities, custodial care and education facilities). Monies are available only for use in carrying out certain types of work. Emergency work includes things like removal of debris, search and rescue and other activities aimed at saving lives and protecting public and private property from damage. Permanent work is that which is needed to restore an affected community to its pre-disaster state. Rebuilding of transportation infrastructure and utilities are included in this category.[50]

IV. Funding of FEMA and Coordination with Collateral Sources

The funds distributed by FEMA under the Stafford Act are from general revenues of the U.S. government. This is consistent, of course, with the conception 22

[49] Hazard mitigation is a significant component of the federal emergency management program. "Hazard mitigation" is defined as "any action taken to reduce or eliminate the long-term risk to human life and property from natural hazards", 44 C.F.R. § 206.41 (2004). Grants issued under the Hazard Mitigation Grant Program can cover up to 75% of the costs of an eligible mitigation project. Once a project is approved by the program, the state becomes responsible for implementing the program and for providing the remaining 25% of needed funding (in cooperation with local sources).

[50] Federal Emergency Management Agency, *A Citizen's Guide to Disaster Assistance* (2003), 3–24. Public Assistance grants contain a cost-share requirement that mandates that some portion of the total grant be non-federal and that that portion be split between the state and the applicant. Additionally, insurance proceeds may be deducted from the total grant amount.
Other assistance programs also exist that are activated by a presidential declaration of disaster. Examples include Farm Service Agency loans for rural water system restorations and U.S. Department of Health and Human Services and Food and Drug Administration programs for sanitation system improvements. In addition, federal agencies can be ordered by the President to lend their expertise, personnel, and equipment in response to disasters. The Army Corps of Engineers has specialized flood response experience; the U.S. Forest Service may respond to a fire; and the U.S. Coast Guard can be of assistance for search and rescue operations. Generally, this type of assistance can only come after a specific request by the governor supported with information regarding state and local response capabilities. *Idem*, 3-24–3-26.

of FEMA as an agency that responds primarily to natural disasters for which there is no assignable source that might be deterred in the future by earmarked financial responsibility.[51]

As far as coordination of FEMA benefits with collateral sources is concerned, federal assistance provided through the Stafford Act is available only for those needs that cannot be met through private insurance coverage.[52] The Stafford Act provides,

> "with respect to any property to be replaced, restored, repaired, or constructed with such assistance, such types and extent of insurance will be obtained and maintained as may be reasonably available, adequate, and necessary, to protect against future loss to such property".

In determining what insurance is reasonably available, FEMA relies on the assessments of the State insurance commissioner.

V. Concluding Observations

23 FEMA's declared mission is to aid state and local governments in preparing for, mitigating the impacts of, responding to, and recovering from disaster events. FEMA faces a number of challenges in program operations and criticisms about its performance as an agency. As we have discussed above, FEMA was originally created as an attempt by the federal government to consolidate its disparate emergency response efforts. The goal was to facilitate the dispersal of federal aid to state and local disaster sites and provide strong, unified federal leadership during disaster events. Management and coordination are important elements of an effective federal emergency response program and form the focus of most criticism that has been levied against FEMA.[53]

The aspects of FEMA's operations that are most persistently identified as areas of needed improvement are adequacy of staff and efficacy of resource distribution. FEMA's budgetary resources have increased notably over time. At its creation in 1979, FEMA distributed approximately $ 1 billion from its disaster relief fund. In 2001, that number reached nearly $ 3.5 billion.[54] Between 1998 and 2002, the Agency's budgetary resources grew from $ 8 billion to $ 12 billion.[55] Yet in that same span, staff resources grew by only 400 FTEs.[56]

In the aftermath of an event, FEMA officials are responsible for assessing whether the damage reaches a "disaster level" and whether to recommend

51 Note, however, that FEMA funding does attempt to reduce the likelihood of similar catastrophic events in the future, even though there are no assignable risk-generating sources to deter.

52 42 U.S.C. § 5154 (2004).

53 See e.g. Governor's Disaster Planning and Response Rev. Committee, Final Report: *Hurricane Andrew* (1993); available at <http://floridadisaster.org/dem/files/lewisr.pdf>.

54 *Idem*, 18.

55 United States General Accounting Office (U.S. Gen. Acct. Office), *Major Management Challenges and Program Risks: Federal Emergency Management Agency* (GAO-03-113 2003).

56 *Idem*. FTE designates "full-time equivalency" and is generally used to represent a single full time employee.

that the President issue a disaster declaration. Further, the staff bears the burden of determining what projects qualify for federal relief funding, often an enormously important decision for those seeking aid. In 1999, FEMA proposed a credentialing program for evaluating the skills and knowledge of its staff as a means of improving program implementation and building greater public confidence in the agency. As of 2003, the program was not yet implemented.[57]

A second key area of criticism focuses on the evaluation criteria used by FEMA in assessing disaster events. Under the Stafford Act, federal assistance only becomes available when the President determines that emergency conditions have exceeded state and local government capabilities. Of course, the President's decision rests heavily on the recommendation and information provided by FEMA. Thus, the underlying criteria that FEMA employs in assessing the damage done by an event and the state/local financial capabilities are extremely important. FEMA has published regulations establishing the formal criteria that it uses for these assessments. The criteria include a number of qualitative factors, including the local impact of the event and the recent occurrence of other disasters in the state. The U.S. General Accounting Office has repeatedly recommended that FEMA develop more objective standards so as to better capture a state's true financial capacity. It suggests a focus on the state's total taxable resources or another comparable assessment of state-wide funding capabilities. Evaluating FEMA's current operations, the GAO has concluded that federal funds are being dispersed to some states that do not have a legitimate need, while leaving other states' needs unmet.[58] 24

Finally, the Agency's oversight of dispersed funds has been criticized for being weak. FEMA lacks an effective grants management system, a problem that allows grantees' non-compliance with regulations, outright fraud, and monetary waste to go undetected.[59] It also lacks mechanisms for recovering improper assistance payments even in cases where they are revealed.[60] 25

In addition to these ongoing institutional challenges, FEMA faces new hurdles in the wake of the September 11 terrorist acts. FEMA's fiscal response to September 11 surpassed the assistance monies it had distributed up to that

[57] *Idem*, 11–12. The General Accounting Office conducted a study of FEMA's performance in 2001 and found that FEMA's training budget had decreased between 1999 and 2001 by more than $ 1 million. U.S. Gen. Acct. Office, *Disaster Assistance: Improvement Needed in Disaster Declaration Criteria and Eligibility Assurance Procedures* (GAO-01-837 2001), 18. Further, it found that training in FEMA's disaster field offices was oftentimes either untimely, or not offered at all. *Idem*, 18–19.

[58] U.S. Gen. Acct. Office (*supra* fn. 55), 8.

[59] See Federal Emergency Management Agency, *Audit of FEMA's Debris Removal Program* (2001).

[60] FEMA's Inspector General uncovered an $ 8.5 million improper grant payment and brought it to the attention of FEMA management in February 2001. By September 2001, FEMA had still not recovered the funds. U.S. Gen. Acct. Office (*supra* fn. 55), 14.

point, both in absolute terms and in terms of percentage of need.[61] If such increased assistance levels are viewed as a precedent, the Agency's future costs could rise significantly. Of greater potential importance is the Bush Administration's formation of the Department of Homeland Security. FEMA, once an independent agency, is now subsumed under this new federal department. The Department of Homeland Security's primary objective is, obviously, maintaining domestic security. There is a notable risk that FEMA's natural disaster programs will receive inadequate attention and budgetary support in this new environment.[62]

Since FEMA's inception, the U.S. has experienced some of the most deadly and costly emergency events in its history. Hurricane Andrew, the Northridge Earthquake, and the terrorist attacks of September 11, 2001 rank as major catastrophic events, not only within the U.S., but also worldwide. FEMA doled out enormous sums of federal assistance to the victims of these disasters, providing food, shelter, and other basic needs to people whose lives had been devastated. In the complex landscape of victim compensation, FEMA clearly plays a prominent role. In an agency imbued with such responsibility and tasked with functioning in the chaos of emergencies, improvements to management and efficacy will always be possible.

[61] Under the Stafford Act, an area hit by disaster can petition for FEMA to provide 75 to 100% of the region's eligible recovery and response costs. Generally, FEMA limits its aid to the 75% level. By statute, the remaining portion of any allocation less than 100% must be matched by state and local officials; as a consequence, FEMA is reluctant to recommend a 100% share – viewing a lesser recommendation as a means of creating incentives for state and local officials to keep recovery costs down and closely evaluate projects. Nonetheless, FEMA provided 100% of eligible costs for New York's September 11 damage. See U.S. Gen. Acct. Office (*supra* fn. 55), 9. In total, FEMA spent $ 7.4 billion in public assistance-related funding in the New York City area. Activities funded include grants to state and local governments for emergency response, such as debris removal, and permanent work, such as the repair of disaster-damaged public facilities. FEMA also provided public assistance-related funding specifically directed by Congress that would not otherwise have been eligible for assistance (e.g. reimbursing costs of instructional time for students who lost school time after the terrorist attacks). The major uses for this funding were as follows:

- $ 1.7 billion for debris removal operations and insurance;
- $ 2.8 billion to repair and upgrade the transportation infrastructure of Lower Manhattan;
- $ 0.6 billion to the New York City Police and Fire Departments for such purposes as emergency efforts and replacing destroyed vehicles;
- $ 0.3 billion to miscellaneous city agencies for a wide range of activities (e.g., instructional time for students and building cleaning);
- $ 0.7 billion for non-New York City agencies for many purposes (e.g. office relocations and repair of damaged buildings);
- $ 1.2 billion available on June 30, 2003, for public assistance-related reimbursements to New York City and state (work to be decided).

U.S. Gen. Acct. Office, *Disaster Assistance: Information on FEMA's Post 9/11 Public Assistance to the New York City Area* (GAO-03-926 2003).

[62] *Idem*, 16.

Part IV. Insurance: The Intersecting Private/Public Sectors

I. Introduction

There are a variety of types of private insurance coverage that may come into play as a consequence of a catastrophic event. In the case of mass personal injuries, life, health, and private disability insurance coverage may be applicable. With regard to property damage, homeowners' insurance and commercial casualty insurance would be the policy coverages most likely to be triggered. As in the case of public welfare programs (Part II), these insurance provisions have broader applicability than mass disaster events. But they do provide baseline private coverage when such events occur. 26

In general, insurance policies are written so as to protect the insured against a specified loss regardless of the cause of that loss. For example, the standard homeowners' insurance policy provides coverage for damage to a home by fire, with little regard to the cause of the fire itself. But insurance policies fall into the realm of private contracts and insurers generally have the authority to determine the scope of the coverage that they are willing to offer. Nonetheless, typically, "disasters" have not been excluded from private insurance coverage – and no such general exclusion exists today. The standard residential homeowners' policy offered by private insurance carriers is an "all risk" policy, under which only those events that are specified are excluded from coverage – and specification remains unusual, although as we will see, floods and earthquakes now get special exclusionary treatment.[63]

As is true of nearly every aspect of the American landscape, the events of September 11 impacted the U.S. insurance industry. Before September 11, most insurance actuaries deemed it feasible for acts of terrorism to fall within standard personal coverage. Since the September 11 attacks and the ensuing "War on Terrorism," the threat of terrorism has become much harder to calculate and too significant a risk to simply fold into general coverage. Although not the subject of a general exclusion, federal legislation has changed the landscape of coverage for acts of terrorism. Similarly, more localized catastrophes, such as the Northridge earthquake in California, have triggered reluctance on the part of private insurers to continue coverage of certain risks.[64] Both the

[63] There are also "named risk" policies that are marketed, but banks will generally not accept them for lending purposes. It should be noted, however, that with respect to personal property coverage – as distinguished from real property coverage – specification of items covered is a common practice. The realm of commercial property coverage practices differs and is harder to capture in any general way; the policies tend to be less standardized, with named risks often tailored to the particular commercial structure.

[64] A "catastrophe" is defined within the property insurance industry in terms of the value of claims an event is expected to generate. Under the definition established by the insurance industry, a natural or man-made disaster becomes a catastrophe when the resultant claims are expected to reach $ 25 million. The definition has changed in recent years. In 1997, the threshold for expected claims was set at $ 5 million. Insurance Information Institute (Ins. Info. Inst.), *Catastrophes: Insurance Issues* (July 2004); available at <http://www.iii.org/media/hottopics/insurance/xxx>. The Institute simply uses the $ 25 million threshold for designating an event a "catastrophe" for internal purposes of categorizing events; it does not indicate that such a definition has any effect on insurance coverage such as refusing coverage when claims reach the threshold.

federal and state governments within the U.S. have demonstrated their willingness to step in and supplement and/or regulate private insurance to ensure needed guarantees for public catastrophe compensation.

This section will focus on the types of private insurance most often affected by disaster events and provide a general survey of the industry's involvement in different types of events that have occurred in the U.S. A disaster such as the Rhode Island nightclub fire, discussed in the introductory section, where tort liability plays a major role, is likely to activate private liability insurance coverage to injured third parties under a standard commercial policy, as well as casualty loss coverage for fire-related damage to the insured's property under the standard protection with regard to first-party losses. The section below will focus on the gaps in private insurance coverage and the government's response in those categories of protection that now get special treatment in the case of catastrophic loss.

27 It is possible to discern three distinct models that have emerged. First, governmental regulation provides a structure within which private insurers remain the principal guarantors against risk. The Price-Anderson Act, addressing potential commercial nuclear energy releases, discussed immediately below, offers an example of this approach. Second, government provides coverage above a baseline of risk that remains under the coverage of private insurers. The Federal Terrorism Risk Program, discussed in the succeeding sub-section, offers an illustration of this approach. And third, a governmental entity actually steps in and assumes the risks of a potentially hazardous event. Earthquake and flood insurance, discussed in following sub-sections, take this approach. While these are certainly not the only variants that might be adopted, they do constitute the major pathways that are being pursued at present in the U.S. in catastrophe scenarios.

II. Types of Insurance Coverage Triggered by Disaster Events

A. *Nuclear Reactor Accidents: Price-Anderson Act*

28 Congress passed the Price-Anderson Act[65] in 1957 with the express purpose of encouraging private development of nuclear energy in the United States. Though still long before the tragedy of Chernobyl or the scare at Three Mile Island, the threat of ruinous tort litigation was a barrier to private involvement in the nuclear energy industry. The Act created a mixed system of compulsory private insurance coverage and emergency compensation funding designed to lessen the financial impact of post-accident litigation on holders of nuclear power plant licenses, in order to create incentives to operate reactors. In addition, it placed a cap on the total amount of liability that each reactor operator faced in the event of a nuclear accident. In essence, the Act sets the ground rules for private contribution and responsibility, but that is the limit of government intervention.

Participation in the program created by the Price-Anderson Act is mandatory for all nuclear reactor operators. The statute requires operators to obtain

[65] 42 U.S.C. 2210 (1988 & Supp. 1992).

the maximum amount of private insurance coverage available. In 2003, that was $ 300 million per reactor per accident.[66] In addition to each reactor's primary insurance policy, the Act provides for the creation of a secondary insurance fund. This secondary fund is created in the event of an accident at any U.S. reactor that causes damages greater than the affected reactor's primary insurance coverage. Each U.S. reactor operator is compelled to contribute to the fund. Contributions are based on the damage caused by the accident. Damages in excess of the affected operator's $ 300 million of private insurance are prorated among the pool of U.S. operators up to a set cap. By 2003 figures, each licensed operator can be responsible for contributory payments up to $ 95.8 million. In 2003, there were 104 licensed operators within the U.S., so had an accident occurred in that year, the Act would have required a disaster relief fund with a ceiling of $ 8.6 billion dollars.

In the event that an accident exceeds the maximum amount available in the secondary fund, the Act requires Congress to assess the accident, but does not require the federal government to expend any funds to cover the excess liability. Thus, the burden of the fund's limits could fall on the accident victims if the government chooses not to intervene. Other federal funding, e.g. FEMA-administered disaster relief funds described in the previous section, may be available.

Under Price-Anderson, victims of nuclear accidents are free to pursue tort claims for property damage and personal injuries against the reactor operators or any other potentially responsible party in accordance with state tort law. The only limitation imposed by the Act on recovery in such suits is in the form of the total monetary cap on insurance funding, referred to above. In the event of an "extraordinary nuclear occurrence",[67] the Act requires all claims to be consolidated in federal court. The Act creates strict liability in tort for licensees involved in nuclear incidents and abrogates the defence of contributory negligence.[68] Each individual claimant still bears the burden of establishing causation and particularized proof of economic loss and intangible harm.[69]

B. Federal Terrorism Risk Insurance Act

The Terrorism Risk Insurance Act of 2002 (TRIA) exemplifies the federal 29
government assuming the role of excess liability insurer, in effect providing a cap on the losses for which the private insurance industry will be responsible in the event of a major act of terrorism.

In terms of insurance losses, the terrorist attacks on the World Trade Center and Pentagon on September 11, 2001, rank as the most costly catastrophe

[66] United States Nuclear Regulatory Commission (U.S. Nuclear Reg. Commission); Fact Sheet: *Nuclear Insurance and Disaster Relief Funds* (Sept. 2003), available at <http://www.nrc.gov/reading-rm/doc-collections/fact-sheets/funds.html>.

[67] "Extraordinary nuclear occurrence" is defined as "any event causing a discharge or dispersal of source, special nuclear, or byproduct material ... in amounts offsite, or causing radiation levels offsite", 42 U.S.C. § 2014(j) (2004).

[68] *Idem*, § 2210(n)(1).

[69] See 10 C.F.R. § 140.81 (2004).

in U.S. history.[70] This is without reference to the personal injury claims compensated under the Victim Compensation Fund, totalling nearly $ 7 billion, discussed in a separate section of this report.[71] By the middle of October 2003, private insurance companies had received 35,094 claims related to the September 11 attacks on the World Trade Center alone, representing a total of $ 19.07 billion, including massive numbers of personal property and business interruption claims (the latter including claims for lost income and expenses related to restarting or reinvigorating affected businesses).[72] Workers compensation claims paid by the industry came to 5,660. These aggregate costs far exceeded past terrorism-related damage claims in the U.S.[73]

In the aftermath of the attacks, even before massive numbers of claims began to be filed, the U.S. Congress was faced with widespread concern about the solvency of the American insurance industry. On November 26, 2002, President George W. Bush signed into law the Terrorism Risk Insurance Act of 2002.[74] TRIA was created to ensure the continuing availability of insurance for terrorism risk. Its goals encompassed both protecting the American public, by ensuring continued insurance coverage, and protecting the insurance industry as it rebuilt after the losses caused by September 11. The Act created a mechanism by which the federal government and private insurance providers would share the burden of property and casualty losses resulting from any future terrorist attacks.

30 Essentially, all commercial insurers doing business within the U.S. are required to participate in the program. Under the Act's provisions, insurers are required to make available coverage for insured losses resulting from acts of terrorism in all of their commercial property and casualty insurance policies. The coverage cannot differ materially from the terms, amounts, and other limitations of policies written to cover losses arising from non-terrorist causes.[75] In addition to the continued availability of coverage, insurers must inform policyholders of the premium charged for coverage and the federal share of compensation provided for under the Act.[76]

In return for such actions on the part of insurers, the federal government assumes a percentage of an insurer's losses from compensating claims arising from terrorist acts. Each insurer is responsible for a deductible amount.[77] But once that

[70] Ins. Info. Inst., Catastrophes (2004); available at <http://www.iii.org/media/facts/statsbyissue/catastrophes> (citing statistics from Swiss Re, *sigma*, No. 1/2004. *Insured Losses for Natural Catastrophes in the United States* (2004)).

[71] See section V(A), case study of September 11 Victim Compensation Fund.

[72] Ins. Info. Inst. (*supra* fn. 64).

[73] The Los Angeles riots of 1992 were the second most expensive for private insurers with a total of $ 775 million. Ins. Info. Inst. (*supra* fn. 64).

[74] 31 C.F.R. § 50.1 *et. seq.* (2004).

[75] The Act does not specify the premium rates that insurers are to charge.

[76] 31 C.F.R. § 50.10 (2004).

[77] The deductible amount increases each year of the program. In the first year of the program, an insured's deductible equals its direct earned premiums from the previous year multiplied by 7%. That amount is increased to 10% and 15%, respectively, for years two and three of the program. 31 C.F.R. § 50.10 (2004).

threshold is reached, federal funds are used to reimburse the insurer 90% of the insured losses in excess of the deductible.[78] Importantly, the Act imposes a $ 100 billion annual industry-aggregate limit on federal reimbursements.[79]

The program's reimbursement provision is triggered only by the occurrence of an "act of terrorism". To qualify, an event must meet a three-part definition, in addition to a threshold dollar amount of $ 5 million. The act must: 1) be "a violent act or an act that is dangerous to human life, property or infrastructure"; 2) result in damage within the U.S. (or outside of the U.S. in the case of air carriers, vessels, and U.S. missions), committed by one or more individuals, on behalf of foreign interests, in an "effort to coerce the civilian population of the United States or to influence the policy or affect the conduct of the United States Government by coercion"; and 3) be certified as an "act of terrorism" by the Secretary of the Treasury in concurrence with the Secretary of State and the Attorney General.[80] Reimbursement of the insured (including the federal contribution), and risk management administration, remains in the hands of the private insurer.

In addition to providing for reimbursement, the Act also contains provisions for managing litigation arising out of certified acts of terrorism. Once an act of terrorism is certified, the Act creates an exclusive federal cause of action and remedy for property damage, personal injury, or death arising out of or relating to the terrorist act. The federal cause of action preempts certain state law claims and provides for the consolidation of all civil claims. Additionally, the Act provides that punitive damages awarded in actions for property damage, personal injury, or death are not to be counted as "insured losses" and are not paid under the Program. Finally, the United States is provided the right of subrogation with respect to any payment made by the United States under the Program.[81]

The provisions of the Act make it clear that Congress did not intend the program to be a primary source of compensation. Compensation provided for by other federal programs cannot be duplicated by funds from the Program. For example, disaster relief provided under FEMA or benefit awards under the September 11th Victim Compensation Fund must be deducted from the total amount otherwise payable under TRIA.[82] Moreover, the TRIA Program is a stopgap measure. The Act expires in 2005 and the deductible amount attributed to the insurers increases annually until that point to reduce the total amount of losses subject to federal reimbursement.

C. California Earthquake Authority

The 1994 Northridge Earthquake in California caused more than $ 15 billion 31
in insured losses.[83] After that event, many private insurers in the state attempt-

[78] *Idem*, § 50.50.
[79] *Idem*, § 50.50(d).
[80] *Idem*, § 50.5(b).
[81] *Idem*, § 50.84.
[82] Social Security Disability Insurance benefits are not deducted, however. *Idem*, § 50.51.
[83] Insurance Information Network of California (Ins. Info. Network of Cal.), *Financial Aftershocks: 10 Years Later, Northridge Earthquake Prompts Physical, Fiscal Preparedness* (Jan. 2004), available at <http://www.iinc.org/news/home/Northridge_EQ2004.html>.

ed to terminate their earthquake coverage offerings. The state was challenged to find a solution that would keep its citizenry protected from future earthquake-related losses while also protecting the state's insurance industry. In 1996, California revamped its insurance laws related to earthquake coverage and created the California Earthquake Authority (CEA).[84]

Insurance providers that sell "residential property insurance"[85] in the state of California are permitted to exclude earthquake-related losses from their standard policy coverage, but are required by law to offer their customers earthquake insurance in some form.[86] An insurer must notify its customer that the primary residential property insurance policy issued by the insurer does not contain a provision for earthquake damage and must make an offer of an independent policy (or an addition to the primary policy) for such coverage. The insurer can meet its obligations in several ways. It can offer to underwrite the earthquake coverage itself or it can arrange for coverage by another affiliated (or unaffiliated) insurance provider.[87] Most residential property insurers – those comprising about 80% of the market, including the largest homeowners' insurers in the state – have chosen to opt out of providing coverage themselves, and instead simply administer policy coverage for the CEA, which assumes primary risk-bearing responsibility.

32 Homeowners and renters are not required by law to carry earthquake insurance. Thus, once the requisite offer of coverage is made by the insurance provider, the insured is free to accept or reject the offer.[88] If the insured does decide to purchase earthquake insurance, the insurance provider must provide coverage that complies with the applicable CEA regulations.[89] In its administrative capacity (for the CEA), an insurance provider is not required to abandon its usual underwriting standards in issuing earthquake insurance. Rather, it can use these standards to determine whether or not it is willing to provide

[84] Cal. Ins. Code § 10089.6 (2004).

[85] "Policy of residential property insurance" is defined as "a policy insuring individually owned residential structures of not more than four dwelling units, individually owned condominium units, or individually owned mobile homes, and their contents, located in this state and used exclusively for residential purposes or a tenant's policy insuring personal contents of a residential unit located in this state. 'Policy of residential property insurance,' as defined, shall not include insurance for real property or its contents used for any commercial, industrial or business purpose, except a structure of not more than four dwelling units rented for individual residential purposes. A policy that does not include any of the perils insured against in a standard fire policy shall not be included in the definition of 'policy of residential property insurance'". *Idem*, § 10087(a).

[86] *Idem*, § 10081.

[87] *Idem*, §§ 10081, 10084 (2004); see also V. Sidbury/B. Wiener/P.H. Cyril/S.M. Gordon/G.E. Sayre, *California Insurance Law and Practice* (2004), § 36.15 (citing Cal. Ins. Code § 10086 (2004)).

[88] If the insured does not accept the offer of coverage, the insurance provider is required to renew the offer every other year. Renewal must be "in connection with any continuation, renewal, or amendment of the policy, in connection with any reinstatement of the policy following any lapse, or with respect to any other policy that extends, changes, supersedes, or replaces the policy of residential property insurance". See V. Sidbury/B. Wiener/P.H. Cyril/S.M. Gordon/G.E. Sayre (*supra* fn. 87), § 36.15.

[89] Cal. Ins. Code § 10089 (2004) establishes the minimum coverage required.

an earthquake policy for each particular customer. However, if the insurer determines that a home does not meet its underwriting standards and decides not to issue earthquake insurance, the provider also becomes foreclosed from providing a primary residential property insurance policy for the home.[90] Nor can an insurance provider cancel a residential property insurance policy on the grounds that the customer accepted the offer for earthquake insurance.[91] But the critical point is that the CEA assumes the risk within the stated policy limits if an earthquake should occur – as mentioned, the private insurer plays an exclusively administrative role.

The Authority is a privately financed entity that provides earthquake insurance to California residents. It is composed of insurance companies licensed to do business in California and is governed by a three-member board of state officials including the Governor, the State Treasurer and the State Insurance Commissioner.[92] The Board has the authority to conduct certain oversight and financial duties,[93] but the issuance and management of earthquake policies is done by the private member companies. The Authority is charged with setting a rate for earthquake insurance[94] and writing a residential earthquake insurance policy that is in compliance with the insurance laws discussed above and approved by the Board. Insurance policies are available for homeowners, renters, mobile home owners and condominium owners. Coverage generally extends to costs of repair or replacement of property damaged by earthquake activity.

The Authority is funded by participating insurers, along with bond sales, reinsurance, and the premiums charged for policies sold.[95] Initial operating capital was provided through mandatory contributions by the participating insurers.[96] If the Board determines, at any time, that claims will exceed the working capital of the Authority and that no additional sources of funding (e.g. assessments, reinsurance, private capital market monies) will be available to the Authority to pay claims, the Board can present a plan for pro rata or instalment payments of claims for approval by the Insurance Commissioner. The Board is obligated to ensure the Authority has sufficient capital to main-

[90] *Williams v State Farm Fire & Cas. Co.*, 216 California Courts of Appeal (Cal. App.) 3d 1540, 1543 (1989).

[91] Cal. Ins. Code § 10086.5 (2004).

[92] *Idem*, § 10089.7.

[93] *Idem*, § 10089.7(c).

[94] *Idem*, § 10089.40. "Rates established by the authority shall be actuarially sound so as to not be excessive, inadequate, or unfairly discriminatory. Rates shall be established based on the best available scientific information for assessing the risk of earthquake frequency, severity, and loss …".

[95] *Idem*, §§ 10089.5(b), (f), (m), 10089.10, 10089.15, 10089.23, 10089.29, 10089.30.

[96] "Initial operating capital shall be contributed by insurance companies admitted to write residential property insurance in the state. Each insurer that elects to participate in the authority shall contribute as its share of operating capital an amount equal to one billion dollars ($ 1,000,000,000) multiplied by the percentage representing that insurer's residential earthquake insurance market share as of January 1, 1994, as determined by the board. A minimum of seven hundred *million* dollars ($ 700,000,000) in commitments shall be required before the authority may become operational". *Idem*, § 10089.15(a).

tain operation.[97] The State itself has no liability to pay claims in excess of the Authority's capability.[98]

Thus, by establishing a ceiling on the mandated contributions from private insurers, and pooling these risks, the CEA represents a model under which the state has relieved the private insurers of the uncertainty and potentially catastrophic losses associated with a major earthquake. Similar options are available for insurers of commercial property. In practice, however, major commercial insurance brokers have created pools of private insurers to offer coverage on large commercial properties.

D. National Flood Insurance Program

33 The National Flood Insurance Program (NFIP), administered by FEMA, is an example of the federal government assuming the role of primary insurer. NFIP can be regarded as a variant on the just-discussed California Earthquake Authority: Like the state of California, under the latter program, the federal government has stepped in and assumed the risk of financial loss associated with a disastrous flood under the flood insurance scheme.

NFIP was established by the National Flood Insurance Act of 1968.[99] The program was a response, in part, to private insurers' reluctance to sell flood coverage.[100] This reluctance was principally due to the character of flood risk. Because the chance of flooding is geographically limited, the pool of flood insurance purchasers consists only of those living in floodplain areas. Adverse selection is a significant barrier to private insurance companies providing flood insurance, since only those people with the less desirable risks and higher expected losses choose to insure. Relatedly, the small pool of interested buyers makes it very difficult for the insurance providers to spread the risk in a satisfactory fashion.[101] As a consequence, the dearth of private insurance placed a heavy burden on federal relief funds when flooding occurred.

Congress created NFIP to serve two main purposes. First, the Program was intended, over time, to make flood insurance available wherever needed through the cooperative efforts of the federal government and the private insurance industry.[102] Second, Congress sought to encourage disaster mitigation by giving state and local governments incentives to constrict development on flood-prone lands.[103]

[97] *Idem*, § 10089.35.

[98] *Idem*, § 10089.35(e).

[99] 2 U.S.C. §§ 4001 *et seq.* (2004).

[100] *Idem* (stating as one of the purposes for the Act's passage, "The Congress also finds that (1) many factors have made it uneconomic for the private insurance industry alone to make flood insurance available to those in need of such protection in reasonable terms and conditions; but (2) a program of flood insurance with large-scale participation of the Federal Government and carried out to the maximum extent practicable by the private insurance industry is feasible and can be initiated").

[101] See S.J. Singer, Flooding the Fifth Amendment: The National Flood Insurance Program and the "Takings" Clause, [1990] *Boston College Environmental Affairs Law Review* (B.C. Envtl. Aff.L.Rev.) 17, 332–33.

[102] 42 U.S.C. § 4001(d).

[103] *Idem*, § 4001(e).

The National Flood Insurance Program is voluntary. Communities located in areas identified by FEMA as posing a special flood hazard are eligible to participate in the Program. In order to participate, a community must implement land management ordinances and use practices that are in compliance with federal guidelines.[104] The land management practices are designed to limit development in regions threatened by potential flooding and to reduce future damage caused by flooding.[105] Importantly, eligibility for national flood insurance is limited to residents of participating communities.

In theory, eligible residents can choose whether or not to purchase flood insurance. However, the Flood Disaster Protection Act of 1973 mandated flood insurance coverage for certain properties. The Act prohibits regulated lending institutions from making, increasing, extending or renewing any loan secured by improved real estate located in areas identified as having special flood hazards and to which flood insurance has been made available under NFIP unless the property is covered by flood insurance for the length of the loan.[106] Additionally, federal agencies are prohibited from providing financial assistance for acquisition or construction in such areas.[107] Perhaps most noteworthy for the purposes of this report, federal agencies are also barred from providing flood-related disaster assistance loans or grants to property located within identified hazard areas unless the community is participating in the Program.[108]

FEMA works in conjunction with private insurance companies to administer 34
the program. NFIP policies are sold through state-licensed insurance agents and through private insurance companies. In 1983, FEMA started the "Write Your Own" program that allows private insurance companies to sell and service NFIP flood insurance.[109] WYO companies issue flood insurance policies in their own name and keep the premiums collected in a segregated account. The company is responsible for paying claims under the policy but can collect FEMA letters of credit for any claim amount that exceeds its available premium funds. WYO companies issue and service the insurance policies, but they are required to charge the premium rate set by FEMA and enforce the rates, coverage limitations and eligibility requirements of NFIP.[110] Premium rates are risk-based and reflect the flood hazards of the particular community. In 2002, FEMA determined that 95% of all NFIP policies were written through the WYO Program.[111]

[104] Communities must meet FEMA's criteria for zoning, subdivision, hazard mitigation plans, building requirements, flood control projects, warning systems and emergency preparedness planning. 44 C.F.R. §§ 60.2–60.7 (2004).

[105] 42 U.S.C. § 4102.

[106] *Idem*, § 4012a.

[107] *Idem*, § 4106.

[108] *Idem*, § 4106.

[109] 44 C.F.R § 61.13(f).

[110] *Idem*, § 61.13.

[111] Federal Emergency Management Agency, *National Flood Insurance Program: Program Description* (2002), available at <http://www.fema.gov/nfip/libfacts.shtm>.

It should be noted that the design of the NFIP program differs from a traditional reinsurance scheme. Under a reinsurance system, the private insurers would act as independent providers to the public, issuing flood insurance policies and assuming the risk of a flood event that exceeds their actuarial calculations. Private insurers could hedge their risk by purchasing reinsurance from a third party (e.g. the federal government). Under a reinsurance scheme the private insurer maintains two distinct contractual relationships, one with the insured and one with the reinsurer. The insured and reinsurer are not in privity. The private insurer retains the risk that a flood event will result in losses that exceed the premium that it charged the insured and the coverage that it secured from the reinsurer. By contrast, under the NFIP program, the private insurer is exposed to no financial risk at all. Rather, the private insurer acts as a sort of mouthpiece for the federal government. It administers the WYO policy, collects premiums, and settles all claims that can be covered by the premiums collected. However, if the losses stemming from a flood event exceed the premiums collected by the private insurer, the government steps in and compensates the insured party for all such excess covered losses.

The Standard Flood Insurance Policy specifies the terms established by NFIP. Those eligible to purchase national flood insurance policies include owners, renters, condominium associates, and builders in the process of construction. Insurance is available for residential, business, agricultural, state and local government properties and properties occupied by non-profit organizations located in eligible areas. The Policy provides coverage for direct physical losses to structures and their contents[112] caused by flood.[113] The Program sets maximum amounts of coverage. For example, under the regular program, a single family dwelling is eligible for up to $ 250,000 in building coverage and up to $ 100,000 in personal property coverage.[114] In 2002, the average amount of combined building and contents insurance coverage purchased under NFIP was $ 131,670.[115]

Since the Program was started in 1969, it has paid $ 11.9 billion in claims. In the absence of the Program, this cost would have been borne by the taxpayers through federal disaster assistance funding or by the victims individually. In addition, by requiring communities to comply with FEMA floodplain management standards as a condition of participation, FEMA estimates that the program saves $ 1 billion per year in avoided damages.[116]

III. Concluding Observations

35 Private insurance tends to provide the first layer of coverage for victims of catastrophic events in the U.S. Generally, the emergency benefit programs funded by the federal government are designed to supplement, not to replace private insurance. The National Flood Insurance Program, however, is an example of the

[112] 44 C.F.R. § 61.3.
[113] *Idem*, § 59.1 for definition of "flood" in the Act.
[114] *Idem*, § 61.6.
[115] Federal Emergency Management Agency (*supra* fn. 111), 25.
[116] *Idem*, 28.

federal government alleviating the private sector entirely of insurance responsibility. As indicated, California has taken similar action with respect to earthquake risks. The Price-Anderson Act and the new Federal Terrorism Insurance Act illustrate more limited models of federal involvement in the industry. Such involvement is more generally characterized by the government's attempt to further national policy goals by providing risk mitigation in the background of private industry.

Whatever the mode of intervention, the government has become a major player in the web of insurance coverage. In some instances, government intervention has been responsible for preventing the total withdrawal of private insurers from an area; for example, hurricane insurance for Florida residents after Hurricane Andrew (discussed in greater detail in Part V) and earthquake coverage for California residents after the Northridge quake. While some view the government's actions as necessary for public welfare, others argue that it actually causes more harm than good.

Hurricane Andrew provides an illustration of the contrasting viewpoints. Be- 36
fore Andrew, Hurricane Hugo of 1989 ranked as the largest tropical storm event in terms of insured losses. The insurance industry used the $ 4 billion of insured losses from Hugo as a basis for assessing their future risks. Hurricane Andrew's $ 17 billion insurance price tag invalidated the industry's forecasting models, bankrupted a number of smaller insurers, and mandated a reassessment of hurricane risk. Most insurers sought to pull out of the business of covering hurricane-related losses because of the uncertainties associated with calculation of risk and attendant premiums charges. Likewise, reinsurers sought to reduce their exposure to an uncertain risk by limiting available coverage and raising both premium and deductible rates.[117]

Under normal market forces, the private insurance industry would most likely have responded to Hurricane Andrew by reducing or eliminating its hurricane coverage or significantly increasing premium rates in an attempt to hedge the uncertainty of risk it faced in offering coverage at all. The result for individual consumers would have been either a complete inability to obtain coverage, and so a forced assumption of the full risk of future catastrophe-related loss, or soaring premiums. In the case of Hurricane Andrew, Florida's government imposed regulations that forced private insurers to continue offering hurricane coverage and maintained a lower-than-actuarially-optimal premium rate.[118] Proponents of government intervention laud this type of involvement, arguing that without it the public would be forced to assume too much expense and risk.[119] In addition, proponents assert that the government is in a better position than private insurers to bear catastrophic risk because of its

[117] See Congressional Budget Office, *Federal Reinsurance for Disasters* 12 (2002), available at <ttp://www.cbo.gov/showdoc.cfm?index=37878&sequence=0>. One insurer's reinsurance deductible for catastrophic loss coverage rose from $ 30 million to $ 100 million after Hurricane Andrew. A. Gron/A. Winton, Risk Overhang and Market Behavior, [Oct. 2001] 74 *Journal of Business* (J. Bus.) 4, 591–612 (Oct. 2001).

[118] See Congressional Budget Office (*supra* fn. 117), 5–7.

[119] *Idem*, 19–20.

broad resource base and borrowing capabilities. The government is able to withstand uncertainty and loss that would bankrupt private providers.[120]

On the other side of the issue, many argue that government intervention in the catastrophe insurance market has substantial detrimental effects. First, by regulating availability of coverage and premium levels, the government distorts the insurance market. Under such a system, insurance price and availability no longer reflect the risk level of the activity being insured (e.g. living in hurricane-prone coastal regions) and so eliminate a potentially powerful economic deterrent to risky behavior. Thus, government intervention forces the public at large to subsidize the risky lifestyle of a segment of society.[121]

Another argument raised is that government intervention actually propagates the gap in private insurance coverage that it is created to fill. In most examples, the government initially acts in order to protect the public from a coverage failure within the private insurance industry. However, by using regulations to force insurance coverage and premium rates that are out of step with the actuarial assessments of the private insurers, the government creates a market in which private insurers are unable to compete, even if they wanted to re-enter. Florida's Residential Property and Casualty Joint Underwriting Association is an example. The program was created as a stop-gap measure to fill the void in hurricane-related damage coverage that plagued the state after Hurricane Andrew in 1992. In 1996, FRPCJUA was the second-largest insurer in Florida. The state was forced to create incentives, such as cash payments and special assessment exemptions to private insurers, in order to decrease its role in the market.[122]

Whichever arguments prevail, there is little doubt that the role of government intervention in the catastrophe insurance market will remain an important issue within the United States. Higher overall population, greater clustering in the coastal zones, predictions of more intense climatic events, and the heightened risk of terrorism all force catastrophe compensation to the forefront of the American dialogue.

Part V. Three Case Studies of Compensation for Catastrophic Loss

37 We have selected for closer examination three distinct illustrations of approaches taken by the U.S. legal system to compensation for financial loss in particularly notable instances: 1) the personal injury and death toll stemming from the terrorist attacks on September 11, 2001; 2) the property damage suffered in the single most costly hurricane in recent U.S. history, Hurricane Andrew; and 3) the profile of recovery in the prototypical mass tort disaster, a commercial airline crash.

[120] *Idem.*
[121] *Idem*, 20–21.
[122] *Idem*, 36.

I. The September 11 Victim Compensation Fund

In the immediate aftermath of Sept. 11, a no-fault compensation plan was enacted that closely reflected the anxieties and emotions stirred up by the horrendous toll of deaths and injuries occurring on that fateful day.[123] The September 11 Victim Compensation Fund (the Fund), signed into law just eleven days after the terrorist attacks, addressed only personal injury and fatality claims. Losses related to property damage, as well as business losses or interruptions, remained compensable only in tort, if at all. Moreover the Fund was part of a broader legislative scheme, the Air Transportation Safety and System Stabilization Act, offering a package of loans and subsidies to the airlines to avoid a potential collapse of the U.S. commercial air transport system. 38

A. *The September 11 Victim Compensation Fund: Statutory Framework*

Within limits, the Fund was meant to create baseline assurance that victims of physical injury and their survivors would receive benefits.[124] More precisely, the Fund established eligibility for individuals "present at [any of the three crash sites] at the time, or in the immediate aftermath, of the terrorist-related aircraft crashes",[125] and who "suffered physical harm or death" as a result of the crashes.[126] For this circumscribed class, the Fund provided benefits for both economic and non-economic losses on a no-fault basis. 39

In spelling out those benefits, however, the Fund appeared to be far more generous than earlier-enacted no-fault systems in the U.S., virtually all of which follow the traditional model established in the early twentieth century for addressing the toll of industrial injuries: workers' compensation schemes. Under workers' compensation, eligible claimants recover medical expenses and a percentage of lost income (generally based on a schedule of awards in cases of permanent disabling conditions and in death benefit cases), subject to a statutory ceiling.[127]

[123] By mid-June 2004, when the no-fault program was closed, 4,430 personal injury claims had been filed, of which compensation was made in 2,675 cases, and 2,973 death cases were deemed eligible for benefits. D.W. Chen, After Weighing Cost of Lives, 9/11 Fund Completes Its Task, [June 16, 2004] *N.Y. Times*, A 1.

[124] The description of the Fund and regulations that follows draws in part on an earlier treatment, see R.L. Rabin, The Quest for Fairness in Compensating Victims of September 11, [1991] *Cleveland State Law Review* (Clev. St. L.Rev.) 49, 573.

[125] Air Transportation Safety and System Stabilization Act, Pub. L. No. 107-42, 405(b)(2), 115 Stat. 230, 238 (2001) (codified as amended at 49 U.S.C. § 40101 (2004)).

[126] *Idem*, § 405(c)(2)(A)(ii).

[127] Death benefits are typically calculated as a fixed percentage of the decedent's average weekly wage, which is capped at a level that varies from state to state, but generally approximates the average weekly wage in the state. See United States Department of Labor (U.S. Dept. of Labor), *State Workers' Compensation Laws* (2003), available at <http://www.dol.gov/esa/regs/statutes/owcp/stwclaw/tables-pdf/table-12.pdf>; see also The American Federation of Labor and Congress of Industrial Organizations (AFL-CIO), *Workers' Compensation Comparisons* (2001), available at <http://www.aflcio.org/yourjobeconomy/safety/wc/upload/comptable.pdf>. See generally L.K. Larson, *Larson's Workers' Compensation Law* (2000), § 93.01 ("The beginning point in calculating the amount of benefits is the 'average weekly wage'. This, when the fixed statutory percentage of roughly between one-half and two-thirds has been applied to it,

By contrast, under the Fund economic loss was defined to include not just medical expenses and loss of present earnings, but "loss of business or employment opportunities to the extent recovery for such loss is allowed under applicable state law"[128] – presumably, a reference to individual, case-by-case tort principles. And non-economic loss was broadly defined to include

> "losses for physical and emotional pain, suffering, inconvenience, physical impairment, mental anguish, disfigurement, loss of enjoyment of life, loss of society and companionship, loss of consortium (other than loss of domestic service), hedonic damages, injury to reputation, and all other nonpecuniary losses of any kind or nature".[129]

Interestingly, no parallel to the economic loss definition that referenced "[as] allowed under applicable state law" was included in this latter definition of non-economic loss. Nonetheless, the pervasive influence of the tort perspective of doing individualized justice – disparaged by critics of the tort system, trumpeted by its advocates – was apparent on the face of both provisions.

But there was one substantial qualification to this apparent generosity of spirit. Under traditional tort principles, there is recovery in tort of out-of-pocket expenses even if they have been reimbursed by "collateral" sources such as health and disability insurance. Under the Fund, there is no recovery for these items.[130] Indeed, the restriction on "double recovery," as tort critics would put it, was written in exceedingly broad terms to cover "all collateral sources, including life insurance, pension funds, death benefit programs, and payments by Federal, State, or local governments related to the terrorist-related aircraft crashes …".[131]

Thus, the Fund steered a somewhat uncertain course between collective principles that would emphasize timely compensation and filling the gaps of unmet need, on the one hand, and individualized recovery that would pull in the direction of the tort model, on the other. Before examining this tension in somewhat more detail, however, consider the escape hatch provided in the Act: the prospect of lodging a tort claim instead of proceeding under the Fund.

40 One can only speculate about why a statutory tort cause of action for claimants was established in the Fund legislation; perhaps in recognition of the fact

becomes the unit of benefit by which practically all compensation … is measured, subject to maximum and minimum limits"). In many states, including New York, the surviving spouse continues to receive the weekly benefit during the entire period of time that they remain a widow/widower (until the individual remarries or dies). Some states, however, impose limits on the duration (e.g., 500 weeks in Michigan) or the total dollar amount (e.g. $ 160,000 in California) of the death benefits. *Idem*, § 98.03[1]; 10 Larson Appendix B-16; New York Workers Compensation Law (N.Y. Workers' Comp). § 16 (McKinney 2002); California Labor Code (Cal. Lab. Code) § 4702 (West 2002) For the New York schedule of benefits for serious injuries (permanent partial disability), see N.Y. Workers' Comp. § 15 (1991).

[128] Air Transportation Safety Act (*supra* fn. 125), § 402(5).

[129] *Idem*, § 402(7).

[130] Nor is it possible to recover punitive damages under the Fund. *Idem*, § 405(b)(5).

[131] *Idem*, § 402(4). In treating life insurance and pension funds as "primary," the Fund departs from the parameters of other no-fault schemes.

that some victims with substantial collateral source recoveries – most notably, victims with major life insurance holdings, accrued pension benefits, or accidental death coverage – might well have anticipated no recoverable benefits under the Fund.[132] Or realistically, Congress may have simply recognized that substantial categories of September 11 victims – most clearly, those suffering property damage and psychological harm without accompanying physical injury – were simply not covered by the Fund.[133] Of course, tort, as the default system, would have been available for addressing these claims – how successfully is another matter – without the need for establishing a federal cause of action under the Act. But this would arguably have created the appearance of treating Fund beneficiaries as second-class citizens if they were offered no tort option.

Whatever the case, Congress's ambivalent embrace of tort is highlighted by the title of section 408, which created the federal cause of action: "*Limitation* on Air Carrier Liability".[134] If Congress was determined to leave tort as an option, it was equally determined to constrain tort along lines familiar to observers of late twentieth century U.S. tort reform. The Act established a ceiling on tort liability of the air carriers, providing that liability "shall not be in an amount greater than the limits of the liability coverage maintained by the air carrier."[135] In subsequent legislation, this protective cap on liability, linking it to the limits of insurance coverage, was carried over to aircraft manufacturers, property owners in the World Trade Center, airport owners, and governmental entities.[136]

Ceilings aside, exclusive jurisdiction to hear "all actions brought for any claim (including any claim for loss of property, personal injury, or death) resulting from or relating to the terrorist-related aircraft crashes" was located in the federal district court for the Southern District of New York.[137] But no federal common law was created; rather, the court was to apply the substantive law of the state in which the crash occurred.[138] Finally, just to leave no doubt

[132] Note, however, that the Special Master softened the offset provision in the Final Rule. See *infra* fn. 145–146 and accompanying text.

[133] See the statute's provision identifying a claimant as an individual who has "suffered physical harm or death." Air Transportation Safety Act (*supra* fn. 125, § 405(c)(2)(A)(ii). In addition, the Special Master's decisions were made final, with no recourse to judicial review. *Idem*, § 405(b)(3).

[134] *Idem*, § 408 (emphasis added).

[135] *Idem*, § 408(a). The amount of insurance coverage was reported to be $ 1.5 billion per plane. See J. VandeHei/M. Geyelin, Economic Impact: Bush Seeks to Limit Liability of Companies Sued as Result of Attacks, [Oct. 25, 2001] *Wall Street Journal*, A 6.

[136] See Title II – "Liability Limitation" of the subsequent compromise, Aviation and Transportation Security Act, Pub. L. No. 107-71, § 201(b)(2), 115 Stat. 597 (Nov. 19, 2001). It is noteworthy, however, that the same act refused to limit the liability of companies supplying airport security: "Nothing in this section shall in any way limit any liability of any person who is engaged in the business of providing air transportation security and who is not an airline or airport sponsor or director, officer, or employee of an airline or airport sponsor". *Idem*. This provision was in turn subsequently modified to limit the liability of some airport screening companies. See Homeland Security Act of 2002, Pub. L. No. 107–296, § 890, 116 Stat. 2135.

[137] Air Transportation Safety Act (*supra* fn. 125), § 408(b)(3).

[138] *Idem*, § 408(b)(2).

about it, section 408(b)(1) declared that the federal cause of action was to be "the exclusive remedy for damages arising out of the hijacking and subsequent crashes of such flights".[139]

Thus, claimants eligible under the Fund were put to a choice – they had either to elect a claim for benefits under the Fund or to waive their rights and pursue a tort claim.[140] At the same time, for those falling outside the eligibility limits of the Fund – such as those claiming solely economic loss – tort, as circumscribed in the Act, remained available. Interestingly, the tort option provided in the Fund legislation is not found in the traditional workers' compensation model, which precludes recourse to tort altogether (other later-enacted, no-fault schemes vary in this regard). Nonetheless, in its benefit provisions, as indicated, the Fund was far more generous than any other existing no-fault scheme in the U.S.

These singular aspects of the Fund were not lost on the Special Master, appointed under the Act, who faced the immediate task of developing a concrete program for determining benefit awards for victims of Sept. 11. His efforts offer an alternative vision of how one might design a no-fault model for future victims of terrorism, or catastrophic loss more broadly conceived.

B. The September 11 Victim Compensation Fund: Regulatory Guidelines

41 When the Special Master, Kenneth Feinberg, was appointed on November 26, 2001, his initial task was to promulgate regulations resolving the principal tensions in the Act and filling in some important blanks.[141] He issued a set of draft regulations ("Interim Final Rule") for commentary on December 21, 2001, and subsequently, on March 8, 2002, he issued final regulations ("Final Rule"), spelling out his interpretations of Fund provisions.[142]

Feinberg's reading of the main provisions of the Fund reveals an interesting effort to strike a balance between understanding the Act in traditional no-fault terms that would have emphasized meeting scheduled basic loss of victims, and interpreting the Act in an open-ended fashion that essentially would have offered tort-type, individualized compensation in a no-fault setting. His manner of resolving this tension is evident in the approach taken to the three key substantive benefit provisions already discussed: collateral source offset, economic loss, and non-economic loss.

[139] *Idem*, § 408(b)(1).

[140] *Idem*, § 405(c)(3)(B). In the Final Rule, the Special Master, appointed to promulgate rules and administer the Fund, included a provision offering claimants an opportunity to request a rough calculation of benefits under the Fund before deciding between options. Warily Circling the Sept. 11 Fund, [June 5, 2002] *N.Y. Times*, A 26.

[141] See D.B. Henriques/D. Barstow, A Nation Challenged: The Special Master; Mediator Named to Run Sept. 11 Fund, [Nov. 27, 2001] *N.Y. Times*, B 1.

[142] September 11th Victim Compensation Fund of 2001, 67 Federal Register (Fed. Reg.) 11233 (Mar. 13, 2002) (to be codified at 28 C.F.R. pt. 104) (hereinafter Final Rule).

1. Collateral Source Offset

As mentioned earlier, the Act explicitly called for the offset of life insurance and pension benefits. These provisions raised a firestorm of criticism from victims' families (in particular, the well-endowed), concerned that they were likely to receive nothing in Fund benefits because of the foresight of the deceased, who it was argued, had earned or set aside funds for just such a contingency as occurred.[143] These protests were sharpened to a fine point by prospective claimants observing that unconstrained tort – the absence of a Fund – would be a superior option, since life insurance and pension benefits traditionally are not offset under the tort system.[144] 42

The Special Master responded to these criticisms in the Final Rule, by interpreting the Act to allow reduction of the offset to the extent of victims' self-contributions.[145] More generally, Feinberg announced that it would be "very rare" for *any* eligible claimant to receive less than $ 250,000.[146] It should be noted that neither of these interpretive moves is grounded in the language of the Act.

Rather, the Special Master's actions reflected a fundamental philosophical difference buried in the esoteric legal language of collateral offset. On the one hand, a need-based approach to compensation would point to full offset of all collateral sources, as the Act appeared to require, since these outside benefits do contribute to meeting basic needs. On the other hand, under an individual claimant-focused, tort-type inquiry as to the "deserving" status of the victim, offsets arguably would be ignored entirely. In the end, the Special Master arrived at something of a compromise, liberalizing the statute from the victims' perspective by reducing the offset through recognition of victims' contributions and ignoring entirely outside private charity received by Fund-eligible claimants, as well as establishing a quite substantial presumptive minimum recovery.

2. Economic Loss

As indicated, in addressing economic loss the Act appears to be at cross-purposes with the literal terms of the collateral source offset provision, in referring to recovery of "loss of business or employment opportunities" as defined in state tort law.[147] On its face, this would seem to suggest an individualized inquiry in every case into the lifetime earnings prospects of each deceased victim, entirely at odds with the traditional no-fault approach of scheduled benefits.[148] 43

In the Final Rule, the Special Master again crafted a compromise. Although there is no mention of scheduling in the statute, Feinberg established a

[143] See D.B. Henriques, A Nation Challenged: The Federal Fund; Official Vows All Families of Victims Will Get Aid, [Dec. 28, 2001] *N.Y. Times*, B 7.

[144] This assumes, of course, that liability would have been possible to establish in tort.

[145] Final Rule (*supra* fn. 142), § 104.43.

[146] *Idem*, 67. Fed. Reg. at 11234 (Statement by the Special Master).

[147] Air Transportation Safety Act (*supra* fn. 125), § 402(5).

[148] See discussion in text, *supra* fn. 128).

grid applicable to the range of potential claimants – a "presumed economic loss" schedule – based on age, size of family, and recent past earnings, along with a presumptive cap applicable to the upper 2% of income earners.[149] In devising this strategy, he provided for awards that recognized very considerable future earnings disparities, an announced range of $ 250,000 to $ 3–4 million.[150] But at the same time, he rejected an approach that would have recognized entirely open-ended, case-by-case speculation about future earnings prospects.[151]

3. Non-economic Loss

44 Although there are exceptions, no-fault schemes typically do not provide for pain and suffering loss, apart from optional or supplemental recourse to tort.[152] In fact, tort law itself, as encapsulated in wrongful death statutes, did not traditionally provide any pain and suffering loss for survivors – that is, loss of companionship.[153] Indeed, many states still do not recognize non-pecuniary loss as compensable to survivors in tort, limiting recovery to economic loss.[154] And some other states, such as California, refuse to recognize pain and suffering of the deceased *victim* prior to death as recoverable in tort.[155]

Nonetheless, the Special Master provided for *scheduled* non-economic benefit awards under the Fund, for each victim and every surviving eligible family member. In the Interim Final Rule, $ 250,000 was to be awarded for each victim; a figure that remained unchanged in the Final Rule.[156] With respect to survivors, the Interim Final Rule provided $ 50,000 for the spouse and each dependent, a figure that was increased to $ 100,000 each in the Final Rule.[157] Thus, a surviving spouse with two children would receive benefits of $ 550,000 for non-economic loss in a claim under the Fund.

4. Resolving Tensions: A Hybrid Model

45 The implementation strategy that emerges from the Fund and its subsequent interpretation in the Final Rule can be seen as a hybrid model: one foot in no-fault precepts and the other in tort principles. Neither the Fund provisions nor

[149] Final Rule (*supra* fn. 142), § 104.43. In the case claiming that Feinberg had ventured beyond the framework created by the statute, *Schneider v Feinberg*, 345 F.3d 135 (2d Cir.2003), the Special Master's presumptive cap was the subject of special attack, but to no avail.

[150] The final rule indicates that awards less than $ 250,000 "will be very rare" and "awards in excess of $ 3 or $ 4 million will be rare". Final Rule (*supra* fn. 142), 67 Fed. Reg. at 11234 (Statement by the Special Master).

[151] See Putting a Value on Lives, [Jan. 24, 2002] *N.Y. Times*, A 26.

[152] See, e.g., L.K. Larson, *Larson's Workers' Compensation Law* (2000), § 1.03[4] ("There is no place in [workers'] compensation law for damages on account of pain or suffering, however dreadful they may be").

[153] See, e.g., *Liff v Schildkrout*, 404 N.E.2d 1288 (N.Y. 1980).

[154] See D.B. Dobbs, *The Law of Torts* (2001), § 297.

[155] See *Williamson v Plant Insulation Co.*, 28 *California Reporter* (Cal. Rptr.) 2d 751 (Cal. Ct. App. 1994); see also California Code of Civil Procedure (Cal. Code Civ. Proc.) § 377.34 (West 2003).

[156] Final Rule (*supra* fn. 142), § 104.44.

[157] *Idem.*

the implementing regulations can be read, however, apart from the long shadow cast by three related considerations: 1) the constraints on the tort action provided as an optional remedy; 2) the fundamental structure of common law tort rules; and 3) the September 11 events themselves.

Consider initially the constraints on the tort remedy enacted along with the Fund. As mentioned earlier, this statutory tort action, replacing common law tort rights (albeit adopting common law *substantive* tort principles), capped tort at insurance limits against virtually all potential defendants.[158] As a practical matter, this was taken to mean that recovery under the tort option, if it were exercised, might be severely limited after all the outside property damage claims (which of necessity would be brought in tort) were aggregated with personal injury claims: $ 1.5 billion per air carrier, it was thought, would soon be exceeded.[159] To the extent that this perception was accurate, it created pressure for a no-fault option sufficiently generous to avoid coercing claimants into substantially diminished recoveries in tort.

Related to this point, tort was by no means clearly an available option. The applicable common law rules required a considerable stretch to provide a remedy to victims in the buildings; and as far as passengers on the flights were concerned, negligence of the carriers and baggage inspectors – let alone more attenuated defendants – was not a foregone conclusion.

Finally, the event itself cast a long shadow. Public sentiments would almost certainly have been offended by the prospect of coercing the surviving families into a long, drawn-out pursuit of recovery in tort, given the special sympathy for their plight.

In view of these factors, the Special Master's strategy emerges and becomes apparent. He sought to closely enough approximate the range of tort compensation to make no-fault benefits under the Fund an offer that could not be refused by most eligible parties.[160] In this regard, he seems to have been highly successful: 97 percent of the 2,973 surviving families eligible for benefits applied, and only 70 opt-out lawsuits were filed against the airlines.[161]

Note, however, that the Special Master's strategy reflects a very different set of motivations than one ordinarily finds underlying no-fault systems. Workers' compensation, auto accident no-fault, black lung disease benefits for coal miners, and virtually every other system of no-fault in the U.S., unapologetically provide a form of social insurance against risk; they are not fraught with symbolic significance associated with heroism and patriotic feelings.

158 See *supra* fn. 135. Subsequent legislation also capped the liability of the airport screeners, for the most part. See *supra* fn. 136.

159 See L. Alvarez/S. Labaton, A Nation Challenged: The Bailout; An Airline Bailout, [Sept. 22, 2001] *N.Y. Times*, A 1; M. Jacoby, Lawyers Say Suits May Benefit Clients, [Nov. 15, 2001] *St. Petersburg Times*, 1 A; B. Van Voris, Lawyers Take Over Ground Zero, [Mar. 11, 2002] *National Law Journal* (Nat'l L.J.); D.W. Chen, Suits by 950 Families Allege Safety Lapses at the Towers, [Sept. 14, 2002] *N.Y. Times*, B 3.

160 See R.L. Rabin (*supra* fn. 124) for more detailed discussion.

161 Compensation in death cases averaged about $ 2.1 million, ranging from $ 250,000 to $ 7.1 million. The range of payments in injury cases was from $ 500 to $ 8.7 million. See D.W. Chen (*supra* fn. 123).

II. Compensating Hurricane Damage: Hurricane Andrew

46 On August 24, 1992, Hurricane Andrew made landfall in the United States. This Category 4 hurricane struck just east of Homestead Air Force Base in Florida, passed through the southern Florida peninsula and moved onto south-central Louisiana. When it hit Florida, the storm had sustained wind speeds of approximately 145 mph, with gusts of at least 175 mph,[162] and storm surges up to 16,9 feet.[163]

Natural events only become "disasters" because of the impact that they have on human settlements. And disaster events are typically ranked relative to one another based on the costs associated with the damage that they cause. When it struck, Hurricane Andrew became the costliest natural disaster in U.S. history, both in terms of the FEMA relief required[164] and total estimates of property damaged.[165] Total property damage was estimated to be more than $ 25 billion.[166] Florida witnessed 28,066 of its homes destroyed and another 107,380 damaged.[167] 180,000 people were left homeless, 82,000 businesses were destroyed or damaged, 1.4 million residents were left without power and 32,000 acres of farmland were damaged.[168] In addition, twenty-six deaths were found directly attributable to the hurricane's impact and another 39 lives were lost as an indirect result of the storm.[169]

A. *Role of Private Insurance*

1. Hurricane-related Losses Compensated by Insurance

47 Hurricane Andrew caused $ 17 billion in insured damage.[170] Homeowner policy holders in Florida submitted 280,000 claims and recovered over $ 11 billion or 65% of total insured losses resulting from Andrew.[171] The other types

[162] E. Rappaport, Nat'l Hurricane Center, Preliminary Report: *Hurricane Andrew* (1992, updated 1993).

[163] Governor's Disaster Planning & Response Review Committee, *Final Report 1* (1993).

[164] Federal Emergency Management Agency, *Top Ten Natural Disasters: Ranked by FEMA Relief Costs*, available at <http://www.fema.gov/library/df_8.shtm>. Hurricane Andrew has since been eclipsed by both the Northridge Earthquake of 1994 and Hurricane Georges of 1998.

[165] See D.R. Godschalk/T. Beatly/P. Berke/D.J. Brower/E.J. Kaiser, *Natural Hazard Mitigation: Recasting Disaster Policy and Planning* (1999).

[166] See R. Lyskowski/S. Rice (eds.), *The Big One: Hurricane Andrew* (1992), 10–12; see also E. Rappaport (*supra* fn. 162), tbl. 3a (estimating $ 26 billion combined losses between Bahamas, Florida, and Louisiana with Dade County losses alone totalling $ 25 billion).

[167] Governor's Disaster Planning & Response Rev. Comm. (*supra* fn. 163).

[168] *Idem.*

[169] E. Rappaport (*supra* fn. 162), at tbl. 3a.

[170] Congressional Budget Office (*supra* fn. 117). Estimates of the total insured losses vary. See The Florida Department of Insurance, *Hurricane Andrew's Impact on Insurance in the State of Florida* (1993) available at <http://www.fldfs.com/Consumers/Hurricane_Andrew/andrewimpactonins.pdf> (hereinafter Impact on insurance) (estimating $ 15.018 billion based on claims filed to date); see also National Association of Insurance Commissioners (Nat'l Ass'n of Ins. Commissioners), Most Costly Insured Catastrophes in the United States, available at <http://www.naic.org/research/Research_Division/Reports/perils.htm> (estimating $ 19,595,600,000).

[171] Congressional Budget Office (*supra* fn. 117), 10, tbl. 3.

of insurance coverage triggered by the event included commercial multiperil ($ 3.767 billion), commercial fire ($ 1.062 billion), automobile/physical damage ($ 365 million), mobile-home owners ($ 204 million), and farm owners ($ 16 million).[172]

The size of the disaster caught many insurance companies unprepared, which affected the efficiency of claims processing. First, insurers were, themselves, victims of the disaster. Many of the insurers' employees who lived in the south Florida area suffered property damage making it difficult for them to attend to their business duties and their own home crises.[173] Additionally, the storm damaged office buildings, communications services, and data storage facilities of the insurance companies. This damage created hurdles for efficient operation of business.[174]

There was also simply a dearth of claims adjusters in relation to the magnitude of claims filed. Florida's Department of Insurance streamlined its process of licensing claims adjusters in the days following the storm, enabling insurers to use emergency adjusters to deal with the volume of claims. Some insurers did not take advantage of this emergency provision and the shortage of adjusters introduced delays in the system. With so many policyholders left homeless or severely in need in the first few days after the storm, these delays resulted in many people having to wait for the temporary living expense funds they needed to pay for basic necessities like food, shelter, and clothing.[175]

2. Uncompensated Losses

While Hurricane Andrew may rank as one of the costliest disasters in the U.S. 48
in terms of insured losses, there was still a gap between the amount of compensation meted out by insurance companies and the total expectations of the insured. The loophole created by "Ordinance or Law" provisions in many property insurance contracts explains some of the discrepancy.

"Ordinance or Law" provisions are designed to prevent homeowners from gaining a windfall as a consequence of a natural disaster and from putting the burden of compliance with updated building codes on insurers. Thus, while most property insurance policies will compensate a homeowner insofar as it is necessary to return their home to its pre-disaster state, many policies exclude from coverage those costs associated with upgrading the home to a better condition than it was in previously. Specifically, such "ordinance or law" provisions exclude the costs of bringing a home into compliance with building regulations that the home was not in compliance with before the natural disaster event.[176]

[172] *Idem* (all in 1999 dollars).

[173] The Florida Department of Insurance (*supra* fn. 170), 4.

[174] *Idem.*

[175] *Idem*, 14.

[176] See H.L. Wood, Jr., The Insurance Fallout Following Hurricane Andrew: Whether Insurance Companies Are Legally Obligated to Pay for Building Code Upgrades Despite the "Ordinance or Law" Exclusion Contained in Most Homeowner Policies, [1994] *University of Miami Law Review* (U.Miami L.Rev.) 48, 949–950 (quoting Your State Farm Homeowners Policy, Special Form 3, at 10 (Dec. 1990)).

At the same time, as discussed in detail in the earlier chapters addressing FEMA and the National Flood Insurance Program, much of the federal government's disaster relief funding is conditioned upon community compliance with mitigation practices. For example, many communities are forced to pass new building codes with higher elevation requirements for homes located in flood plain areas to reduce the risk of flood damage. Additionally, these codes set forth requirements for construction materials and methods for the same purpose. If a new home in a flood plain area sustained damage and needed "substantial improvement",[177] it was then forced to comply with all of the codes' flood mitigation provisions.[178]

As a consequence, homeowners were caught in a bind. FEMA disaster relief and NFIP availability for the community was dependent on the local government's enforcement of proper mitigation practices, but home repairs that were dictated by the County's building codes fell squarely within the "Ordinance or Law" exception to homeowner coverage.

At least 3,000 south Dade County homeowners were caught in this bind. They could not obtain building permits to rebuild their damaged or destroyed homes unless they raised the foundations of their houses above federal flood levels. Raising the foundation of a two thousand square foot house by several feet could cost more than $ 30,000 in 1992.[179] Nor could they rebuild without complying with the upgraded requirements for building materials and methods. But because these rebuilding requirements were mandated by law, the costs were not covered by insurers.[180]

B. Impacts on the Insurance Industry

49 In 1992, property insurers in Florida collected $ 1.5 billion in premiums.[181] They paid out about 10 times that amount to victims of Hurricane Andrew. The costs of the hurricane were greater than any company expected and forced members of the Florida insurance industry to recalculate their risks. In the aftermath of Hurricane Andrew, the landscape of Florida's insurance industry changed dramatically. Before Andrew struck, nearly 300 insurers provided a variety of coverage options to Florida's citizenry.[182] As a result of the losses

[177] "Substantial improvement" is defined as: "any combination of repairs, reconstruction, alteration, or improvements to a structure, taking place during the life of a structure (a fifty-year period), in which the cumulative cost equals or exceeds fifty (50) percent of the market value of the structure. The market value of the structure shall be (1) the appraised value of the structure prior to the start of the initial repair or improvement, or (2) in the case of damage, the value of the structure prior to the damage occurring". Dade County, Florida Building Code 11C-2(ff) (1987).

[178] Homes already built were grandfathered in.

[179] See Don Fine Frock, Insurance Could Pay to Elevate Houses, [Nov. 18, 1992] *Miami Herald*, 1 A.

[180] The Miami Herald estimated that construction costs for Dade County residents resulting from Hurricane Andrew could costs as much as $90 million due to the building code upgrades. *Idem.*

[181] Florida House of Representatives Committee on Insurance (Fla. H.R. Comm. on Ins.), *Florida's Property Insurance Crisis 1* (1994) (on file with Comm.).

[182] The Florida Department of Insurance, *Recommendations on Improving Property Insurance Availability in Florida* 1 (1993).

caused by Andrew, seven small insurers became insolvent, 34 insurers informed Florida's Department of Insurance of their intent to withdraw from the market entirely, and 29 reduced their coverage options in the state.[183] Reinsurers also contributed to the situation. Primary insurers are restricted in the coverage that they can offer by the reinsurance available to them and many reinsurers became reluctant to provide coverage after the events of Hurricane Andrew.[184]

The Florida Legislature responded to the state's insurance crisis by creating the Residential Property and Casualty Joint Underwriting Association and the Florida Hurricane Catastrophe Fund, which are currently of major importance.

1. Residential Property and Casualty Joint Underwriting Association

In December 1992, during a special legislative session, the Legislature created 50
the Florida Residential Property and Casualty Joint Underwriting Association (RPCJUA).[185] The purpose of RPCJUA was to provide a state response to the post-Hurricane Andrew shortage of residential property insurers by serving as an insurer of "last resort" for the state's residents. The program was meant to provide residential property insurance coverage for those residents unable to obtain coverage from a private insurer.[186]

The new law required all insurers authorized to write property and casualty insurance policies in Florida to participate in the Association. Members of the association were required to apportion among themselves the coverage of eligible policyholders unable to secure coverage on the voluntary market. This was done through the imposition of regular and emergency assessments.[187] In other words, a risk-pool was established among property insurance companies, similar to the assigned risk pool in which auto liability insurers participate in many states, with the companies continuing to bear shared, primary risk responsibility through the new entity.

The RPCJUA was designed as a stopgap measure, but by 1998 it had become the second largest property insurer in the state based on the number of policies issued and value of property insured.[188] By September 1996, it had issued 937,000 policies. This represented $ 98 billion in exposure and 17.7% of the state's residential property insurance policies.[189] Despite a number of incentives created by the state to reduce the number of policyholders seeking

[183] *Idem.*

[184] *Idem*, 4.

[185] Florida Statute (Fla. Stat.) 627.351(6) (1993).

[186] Department of Financial Services (Dept. of Fin. Services), *Florida's Residual Insurance Market*, available at <http://www.oppaga.state.fl.us/profiles/4102/02/> (last updated 4/12/04).

[187] Fla. Stat. 627.351(6)(b)(3) (1997). The Association is administered by a Board, consisting of representatives of the insurance industry, consumer advocates, and the Department of Insurance. The Board was authorized to write residential property policies and set premiums. The premium rates charged by the RPCJUA could not be lower than the average rates of the highest commercial carrier among the state's twenty highest-volume carriers. See J. Gorrie, Property Insurance in Florida: The 1997 Legislative Reform Package, [1998] *Florida State University Law Review* (Fla. St. U. L. Rev.) 25, 351 and 352.

[188] *Idem*, 353.

[189] Dept. of Fin. Services (*supra* fn. 186).

coverage from RPCJUA, including incentives to the private insurance market, by 2000 the number of policies had dropped only to 66,004 which still represented $ 10.4 billion in exposure.[190]

2. Florida Hurricane Catastrophe Fund

The Florida Hurricane Catastrophe Fund is a state/private risk sharing program created by the Florida Legislature in 1993.[191] Essentially, the Fund acts as a reinsurer of the state's property insurance providers. Each insurer writing "covered policies"[192] in the state is required to enter into a reimbursement contract with the State Board of Administration (Board),[193] the body that administers the Fund. Under the terms of the contract, the insurer must pay the Board an annual "reimbursement premium".[194] In exchange for the annual reimbursement premium, the Board agrees to reimburse the insurer 45%, 75%, or 90% of its losses from each covered event, depending on what agreement the insurer elects.[195] The insurer's premium is adjusted depending on the level of coverage it elects. Reimbursement is available to cover the insurer's losses for "covered events", which are defined as any single storm declared by the National Hurricane Center to be a hurricane that causes insured losses in the state of Florida.[196]

51 In establishing the Fund, the Florida legislature noted the state's compelling interest in maintaining a viable private sector property insurance market but recognized that after the losses caused by Hurricane Andrew, private insurers felt the need to reduce their catastrophic exposures in order to maintain solvency.[197] Thus, the Legislature determined that it was the state's responsibility to protect the public from the private insurance industry's inability (or unwillingness) to provide sufficient property insurance to state residents. So it created the Florida Hurricane Catastrophe Fund to "provide a stable and ongoing source of reimbursement to insurers for a portion of their catastrophic hurricane losses."[198]

Reimbursement from the Fund is not reduced by reinsurance paid to the insurer from another source, but if the aggregate of reimbursement from the

[190] *Idem.*

[191] Fla. Stat. § 215.555 (2004).

[192] *Idem*, § 215.555(c) for definition of "covered policy".

[193] As of January 7, 2003, the Board's trustees are the Governor, the Chief Financial Officer, and the Attorney General. The Board is guided by a nine-member advisory panel consisting of an actuary, a meteorologist, an engineer, a representative of insurers, a representative of insurance agents, a representative of reinsurers, and three consumers representing affected industries. *Idem*, § 215.555(8).

[194] Fla. Stat. § 215.555(5) defines "reimbursement premiums".

[195] *Idem*, § 215.555(4)(b). Joint underwriting associations and risk apportionment plans must elect the 90% coverage option. *Idem*, § 215.555(4)(b)(2).

[196] *Idem*, § 215.555(2)(b). Eligible losses are those in excess of the insurer's retention plus adjustment expenses equaling 5% of total reimbursed losses. *Idem*, § 215.555(4)(b). "Retention" is calculated according to the provisions established in § 215.555(2)(e).

[197] *Idem*, § 215.555(1)(a)–(b).

[198] *Idem*, § 215.555 (1)(e).

Fund and other sources exceeds 100% of the insurer's losses, the excess is to be returned to the Fund.[199] Reimbursement from the Fund in any given year is not to exceed the actual claims-paying capacity of the Fund or $ 11 billion, whichever is lower.[200]

The Fund is financed through a combination of sources. The primary source 52
of funding is the premium payments made by participating insurers.[201] The Fund invests the premium revenues in short-term securities to increase its liquid assets.[202] In addition to premiums, the Fund received periodic appropriations from the Florida Legislature.[203] If a hurricane event occurs and the Board determines that the Fund has insufficient assets to meet its reimbursement contracts, the Fund is authorized to issue revenue bonds.[204] Finally, if bond issuance still proves insufficient, the Board has the authority to direct the Office of Insurance to levy an emergency assessment on all property and casualty insurers doing business in the state.[205]

As of December 31, 2003, the Fund disbursed $ 13,133,973 to participating property insurers in Florida. Hurricanes Erin and Opal, both in 1995, caused the greatest reimbursable damage under the Fund, prior to the current Hurricane Charley, discussed below.[206]

C. *Role of FEMA*

Hurricane Andrew is ranked third on FEMA's list of costliest natural disas- 53
ters.[207] In total, FEMA distributed $ 1.4 billion in relief.[208] The National Flood Insurance Program tallied $ 168 million in expenditures related to Hurricane Andrew. Total federal financial assistance was over $ 4 billion.[209]

FEMA was subjected to extreme scrutiny and widespread criticism after Hurricane Andrew. The disaster was one of the first major tests of the still rel-

[199] *Idem*, § 215.555(4)(b)(3).

[200] *Idem*, § 215.555(4)(c)(1) (providing an exception to the $ 11 billion annual cap in years where the fund has an estimated claims-paying capacity in excess of $ 22 billion).

[201] State Board of Administration of Florida (Board of Admin. of Fla.), *Florida Hurricane Catastrophe Fund* (2004), available at <http://www.oppaga.state.fl.us/profiles/4042 (last updated 3/23/04)>.

[202] *Idem*.

[203] *Idem*. As of December, 2003, the Legislature had appropriated a total of $ 99,052,090 to the Fund.

[204] Fla. Stat., § 215.555(6) (2004).

[205] *Idem*, § 215.555(6)(a)(3) (emergency assessment provision does not apply to insurers providing workers' compensation, accident, or health coverage).

[206] Board of Admin. of Fla. (*supra* fn. 201).

[207] Federal Emergency Management Agency (*supra* fn. 164).

[208] *Idem*. Under FEMA's relief programs, it distributed $ 823 million in public assistance grants, $ 128 million of temporary housing, $ 23 million in mitigation grants, $ 177 million in individual and family grants, and $ 83 million in other expenses.

[209] Congressional Budget Office (*supra* fn. 117), 16, tbl. 5. The Small Business Administration issued $ 177 million in loans to individuals and businesses and the Department of Agriculture spent over $ 1 billion in post-Andrew financial assistance. Other federal entities that contributed to the disaster relief included the Departments of Commerce, Defense, Education, Health and Human Services, Housing and Urban Development, and Transportation.

atively new agency and significant shortfalls in the agency's newly unveiled Federal Response Plan were uncovered.[210] At the time, federal funding under the Stafford Act was not released to a disaster area until a presidential disaster declaration had been made. In the case of Hurricane Andrew, this provision impacted Florida's ability to undertake short-term preparation measures to mitigate the oncoming damage in the time before Andrew hit land. For example, federal resources, including military personnel and equipment, were not available to Florida medical facilities as they attempted to airlift hospital patients out of the Florida Keys on the day before the storm.[211]

FEMA staff was present in Dade County in the days leading up to the hurricane's landfall, but none there had the authority or resources needed to initiate response operations or establish a commanding federal presence.[212] In fact, three days passed after Andrew hit south Dade County before federal assistance began.[213] FEMA was awaiting a presidential disaster declaration, the president was awaiting a formal request from the Florida governor, and the Florida governor felt the dramatic destruction within his state was an adequate plea for help.[214]

Even after it was mobilized, FEMA was criticized for its inefficiency in getting relief where it was most needed. One of the key shortcomings was a failure to adequately assess the needs of the community and the people. Under the general design of FEMA, local governments and states are tasked with taking the lead on response and recovery efforts. This system fell apart in the face of such large scale destruction. When Andrew hit, it decimated government offices as well as private homes, destroyed the region's communication systems, and made response leadership by the local government an implausible expectation. The local and state governments were unable to make an accurate assessment of the damage done and the immediate needs of its citizenry, yet FEMA failed to step in and perform a needs assessment on its own. Rather, it waited for aid requests from the local level, introducing significant delays into the process of relieving need.[215]

Indeed, failure among the various government emergency managers and activated response teams to coordinate and establish a clear line of command was a fault noted by nearly every commentator on the event.[216]

[210] The Federal Response Plan has been updated since 1992. This discussion refers to the FRP in its 1992 form.

[211] See Testimony of F. Koutnik, *Hearing Before the Subcommittee on Toxic Substances, Research and Development of the Committee on Environment and Public Works* (United States Senate 1993).

[212] Federal Emergency Management Agency, FEMA02: *Develop a More Anticipatory and Customer-Driven Response to Catastrophic Disasters* (2002), available at <http://govinfo.library.unt.edu/npr/library/reports/FEMA2.html>.

[213] E. Kleinberg, State, U.S. Learn From Andrew Mistakes Dealing with Storm's Aftermath Important Part of Preparedness, [June 1, 2001] *Palm Beach Post*, 8 A.

[214] *Idem.*

[215] See Opening Statement of Senator Bob Graham, Hearing Before the Subcommittee on Toxic Substances, *Research and Development of the Committee on Environment and Public Works* (United States Senate 1993).

[216] See Government Accountability Office (Gov't Acct. Off.), *Disaster Management: Improving the Nation's Response to Catastrophic Disasters* (1993).

D. Concluding Observations

The risk of hurricane events occurring in Florida is continuous. If anything, climate change studies indicate that the frequency and severity of such storms will increase in the future. And the potential damage that a storm of Andrew's calibre could inflict today far exceeds the destruction that occurred in 1992. One study estimated that if Hurricane Andrew hit with the same force in the same location today, it would cause close to $ 70 billion in damage, nearly twice the 1992 figure.[217] As coastal area populations continue to increase and infrastructure continues to grow denser, the potential impact of future hurricanes becomes more devastating. 54

The catastrophe-response infrastructure of both Florida and FEMA were heavily analyzed in the aftermath of the storm. Since 1992, FEMA has updated the Federal Response Plan twice, attempting to strengthen federal coordination, management, and leadership. Likewise, Florida's insurance industry underwent a major overhaul, along the lines discussed above.

The 2004 summer hurricane season put both the national and the state relief reforms to an unprecedented test. Beginning with Hurricane Charley, the southeast coastal states suffered through four significant hurricanes between August and October. As of late October, 2004, combined state and federal disaster aid for Florida alone reached more than $ 2 billion.[218]

This cluster of hurricanes will provide a test for Florida's insurance industry, as well as FEMA. Florida's government will be challenged both in its role as a primary catastrophe insurer, through the state's newly formed Citizens Property Insurance Corporation,[219] and as a reinsurer, through the Florida Hurricane Catastrophe Fund. These programs were created by the state in direct response to the lessons learned from Hurricane Andrew. As the state cleans up from Hurricane Charley and its three successors, and Florida's residents begin rebuilding their homes and their lives, onlookers will have the opportunity to assess whether Andrew's lessons were well-heeded.

[217] K. Kaye/R. Benedick, What if Hurricane Andrew hit South Florida today?, [Aug. 24, 2002] *Sun Sentinel*, available at <http://www.sun-sentinel.com/news/weather/hurricane/sfl-sandrew24aug24,0,1246678.story>.

[218] Federal Emergency Management Agency, *Florida Disaster Aid Tops $ 2 Billion* (Release No. 1539-238, Oct. 27, 2004), available at <http://fema.gov/news/newsrelease.fema?id=15024>).

[219] Citizens incorporates the Florida Residential Property and Casualty Joint Underwriting Association, discussed above, and the Florida Windstorm Underwriting Association, a similar state insurance entity offering coverage specifically for wind-related damage. The FRPCJUA and FWUA were combined to form Citizens in 2002. After the reformation, insured parties maintained the coverage that they had obtained from the individual associations with little change in policy terms, but they realized new benefits. For instance, in its new form, Citizens is eligible for federal tax exemptions that neither FRPCJUA nor FWUA could realize on their own. Fla. Dep't of Ins., *A handbook for consumers and agents on the combination of the Florida Residential Property and Casualty Joint Underwriting Association and the Florida Windstorm Underwriting Association resulting in the newly formed: Citizens Property Insurance Corporation* (2002), 5.

III. Catastrophic Loss in Tort: The Case of Commercial Airline Crashes

55 Commercial airline crashes are perhaps the prototypical instance of a catastrophic accident in which responsibility is assigned to human agency. When a commercial airliner crashes, there is typically mass loss of life and a number of potential defendants in the ensuing tort litigation. In the U.S., there is no legislative compensation scheme that specifically applies to airline crash victims. Hence, the tort system is the only available channel of recourse, other than private insurance coverage that the victims may have available and general welfare benefits.

We will begin with a brief discussion of the tort principles applicable in these cases, after which we will indicate the background social welfare and insurance systems that may contribute to overall compensation of victims and their survivors. Finally, we will summarize the findings of the major empirical study that was conducted of this litigation by the RAND Institute for Civil Justice.[220] Although the study was conducted in the mid-1980s, it is the best available examination of the system in action, and remains largely accurate today, in our view.

A. *Applicable Tort Principles*

56 When a commercial passenger airplane crashes, the most likely defendant is the airline itself – with the further possibility, which will not be discussed here, of claims against more collateral defendants such as the airplane manufacturer (products liability) and the Federal Aviation Agency (for negligence on the part of air traffic controllers). The basic elements in a negligence case of duty, proximate cause, and damages are generally easily established. The contestable issues, as might be expected, are breach of duty and cause in fact – that is, whether there was any causal negligence on the part of the pilot, crew, or maintenance personnel, including failure to detect a defect. On the breach of duty issue, assuming that there is no direct evidence of what happened (since there are generally no survivors among the passengers and crew), the surviving families, as plaintiffs, benefit particularly from the potential applicability of the doctrine of *res ipsa loquitur* (translated, causal negligence can be inferred from the accident itself).[221] In many jurisdictions, plaintiffs would get the added benefit of the common carrier doctrine, which provides that commercial airlines owe passengers "the highest duty of due care".

Once liability has been established, there are certain aspects of damage assessment that are specific to the airline context, but for the most part damages are governed by general rules of recovery in tort. Thus, in the majority of jurisdictions in the U.S., wrongful death statutes would award "pecuniary loss" to the survivors; in particular, the loss of financial contribution from the dece-

[220] See J.S. Kakalik/E.M. King/M. Traynor/P.A. Ebener/L. Picus, *Costs and Compensation Paid in Aviation Accident Litigation* (1988).

[221] On the tort principles applicable to airline litigation generally, see L.S. Kreindler, *Aviation Accident Law* (1994). A major factor in civil airline litigation is the investigation conducted by the Federal Aviation Administration, including information from the flight recorder tape. Often, however, this evidence is inconclusive.

dent that the survivors might have expected over the decedent's lost years of life. In this regard, many states would define pecuniary loss broadly to include loss of advice and counsel. A substantial minority of states would go even further and allow the survivors additional recovery for loss of companionship (i.e. intangible loss).

The more specifically airline-related item of damages is for recovery by the decedent's estate for pain and suffering during the brief period of remaining life from the moment when the victim became aware of impending death to the actual time of demise. Most state courts would allow recovery for this concededly imprecise figure.[222] Indeed, there are cases standing for the proposition that fear-of-death recovery is warranted in cases where a reasonable person would expect impending death, even if the pilot then avoids the accident through emergency actions.[223]

It can be inferred from this brief summary that airline crash cases would be ripe for class action disposition under American procedural provisions, since all of the victims are similarly situated and there is a common scenario of conduct on the part of the defendant(s). But just because the tort rules are so straightforward and liability is so likely to ensue, most of the mass airline crash cases in the U.S. are settled *en masse* rather than litigated, as discussed below in the RAND summary.[224] Thus, tort is the principal avenue of recovery in this prototypical category of catastrophic loss where blame can be assigned – as it would be in similar mass disaster events that bespeak negligent conduct, such as a sudden structural collapse or fire in a place of public accommodation.[225]

B. Background Social Welfare and Insurance Systems

It is unusual for there to be survivors of a commercial airline disaster. As a 57
consequence, the principal private insurance and social welfare programs that are called into play by an airline crash are those providing death benefits. In the case of privately held insurance, this would typically be life insurance, as well as death benefits associated with a workplace pension plan. Obviously, not all plane crash victims carry this coverage, but as the next section mentions, airplane crash victims are disproportionately from the higher end of the socioeconomic stratum, so the likelihood of such coverage is correspondingly greater than in the population at large.

As far as public social insurance coverage is concerned, the main source of compensation would be the survivor benefits under the Social Security program, when eligibility as a designated beneficiary can be established, as discussed in the earlier part on welfare programs. If in fact there were survivors of the crash,

[222] See e.g., *Shu-Tao Lin v McDonnell Douglas Corp.*, 742 F.2d 45 (2d Cir. 1984).

[223] See e.g., *Quill v Trans World Airlines, Inc.*, 361 N.W. 2d 438 (Minn. App. 1985).

[224] International airline crashes are subject to the rules embodied in the Warsaw Convention, but are beyond the scope of this discussion.

[225] Recall the Rhode Island night club fire, discussed at the outset of the introductory chapter. See also, D.R. Hensler/M.A. Peterson (*supra* fn. 10), for description of major hotel disasters of recent vintage.

SSDI benefits for permanent disability could be recovered, and Medicare-eligible victims could recover health benefits. In addition, workers' compensation would be available where the injuries were in the course of employment (say, on a business trip); so too, would state disability payments. And, private health insurance would cover at least some of any accident-related medical expenses. As suggested earlier, not all of these benefits would necessarily be cumulative. However, the critical point to keep in mind is that under the common law collateral source rule any *tort* recovery would *not* be reduced because of insurance coverage, no matter what the type of benefits involved.[226]

C. Empirical Analysis of the Compensation System

58 In 1985, the RAND Institute for Civil Justice (ICJ) completed a comprehensive study of cases arising from aviation accidents. ICJ looked at the records of every death case arising from a major aviation accident in the U.S. from 1970–1984.[227] Its study described the characteristics of the decedents in these cases and the litigation stemming from these accidental deaths. It also provided data on compensation paid and litigation costs, and compared these figures with each other and with similar figures for other types of tort cases.

The compensation figures do not represent current award levels, since they are based on awards twenty and more years ago. However, when viewed comparatively and in context, the findings remain interesting and relevant today, in our estimation. The average compensation in the death cases studied was $ 363,000 (in 1986 dollars),[228] aggregating to an average of $ 32 million per accident for the 25 accidents studied. No punitive damages were paid in any of these cases.

Actual compensation per victim varied widely: one-fourth of the claimants received less than $ 100,000; one-half received less than $ 179,000; about 8 percent received more than $ 1,000,000; and the maximum award was $ 5,000,000. This range of awards reflects the individualized approach to tort damages in the U.S., described earlier. Settled claims that did not involve lawsuits had an average compensation of $ 256,200. Claims that did involve lawsuits but settled before trial had an average compensation of $ 387,600. For cases that went to trial, average compensation was about $ 599,000.

An earlier ICJ study had found that a defendant in the average tort case paid about $ 37,300 (again in 1986 dollars), $ 18,700 of which was net compensation to plaintiffs and the remainder constituting litigation expenditures. By contrast, a defendant in the average airline accident case paid about $ 412,233 of which $ 291,170 was net compensation to the plaintiffs. In this latter regard, it is re-

[226] At the same time, however, some of these insurance sources, such as workers' compensation and private health insurers, might exercise a right of subrogation against a responsible defendant like the airline. But this is far less likely in the cases of death-related coverage such as life insurance and pension benefits.

[227] It defined "major" as accidents involving commercial aircraft with more than 60 passenger seats and more than five deaths. Twenty-five accidents fit ICJ's study criteria and involved 2,228 total deaths.

[228] This includes total outlays by all defendants, including economic and non-economic loss and legal fees and expenses.

vealing that these figures suggest that airline accident cases have a considerably lower ratio of transaction costs to total expenditures than general tort cases. Plaintiffs' lawyers take lower contingency fees percentage-wise in airline cases, reflecting an overall datum about the litigation: that the cases are disposed of in a more routine fashion because disputes over liability are less prevalent.

But while most cases settle – 85% of the lawsuits settled before trial according to ICJ – on average, a claimant was more likely to take a claim to trial rather than enter into a settlement agreement as the value of economic loss suffered increased. More generally, claims involving larger losses were more likely to result in lawsuits, to go to trial, and to take longer to settle: A one percent increase in loss to survivors increased the probability of a suit by four percentage points, the probability of a trial by 1.7 percentage points, and the length of time to resolve a case by almost nine percentage points.

Finally, with respect to the parties and their attorneys, the profile of the average airline accident victim was different than the profile of the average American. On average, the decedents in ICJ's study were predominantly male and middle-aged (almost certainly, this would be less true today with a dramatic increase of women in the white-collar workforce). Two-thirds were employed with an annual income twice the national average. As far as attorneys were concerned, ICJ looked at the trends in legal representation for both sides. On the defence side, ICJ found that the direct insurer of the involved airline coordinated the defence and led negotiations with the plaintiff. On the plaintiff side, ICJ found that almost one-third of the 2,258 cases examined were handled by only 14 law firms – indicating the degree of specialization in this discrete area of mass tort litigation.

Part VI. Critical Assessment of the System

In cases of catastrophic loss involving human error in the U.S., tort remains 59
the most prominent system for affording financial compensation to victims. Virtually without exception, injury victims suffering substantial loss assert tort claims even under circumstances where they have private insurance coverage and are entitled to baseline social welfare benefits. In part, this near-universal resort to tort is a function of the collateral source rule: Recovery in tort is not reduced for benefits received from private or public insurance sources (although in some circumstances the insurer may exercise a subrogation right against a third-party wrongdoer that would eliminate "double recovery"). An even more significant explanation for the resort to tort, however, is the continuing adherence in the U.S. to the common law principle of individualized recovery. An injury victim is entitled to compensation for loss of income (including future loss) measured by the prospects of his/her own individual earning power, and recovers pain and suffering loss (intangible loss) evaluated in terms of personal psychic harm – generally, as evaluated by a jury.[229]

[229] As indicated earlier, in wrongful death cases, the surviving beneficiaries similarly can establish their own and the decedent's economic circumstances – and in a minority of states their intangible loss of companionship, as well – in the damages phase of a tort case. It is also critical to note that all of these damages assessments are made, in most cases, by a jury in the U.S. system.

There are at least two important qualifications, however, to the breadth of tort law in catastrophic loss cases. First, under some circumstances, the sheer prospect of imposing mass tort liability on a defendant for a single instance of wrongful conduct leads courts to impose a limited duty rule. A leading example is the New York City power outage in 1977, in which the city was thrown into complete darkness for 25 hours due to gross negligence on the part of Consolidated Edison, the power supplier. The New York Court of Appeals denied the personal injury claim of a city resident who was not in contractual privity with the power supplier, holding that a duty would be recognized only to those in privity.[230] But a limitation of this sort on personal injury is fairly rare; consider the victims of airline crashes, or the nightclub fire victims discussed in the introductory section of this report – it would be inconceivable that a court would deny recovery in such cases on the basis of a potentially large number of claims.[231]

60 A second, more commonly invoked limitation on recovery is the so-called "economic loss" rule, under which tort plaintiffs whose claims are based exclusively on economic loss such as lost profits, without attendant personal injury or property damage, are denied a right of recovery – based on a concern over the administrative feasibility of drawing lines that would prevent virtually unlimited recovery against a defendant.[232] This latter limitation, it should be noted, is not invoked exclusively in catastrophic loss cases; it is a concern about excessive liability that courts express in tort claims across-the-board.

Whatever the doctrinal limitations, tort is frequently criticized from the broader perspectives of economic efficiency, distribution of risk, and fairness. Certainly from a compensation vantage point, the latter two concerns loom large. Tort only provides compensation: 1) when the *wrongdoing* of a defendant can be established, and 2) when the defendant is *solvent* (again, recall the discussion in the introductory section of this report). These limitations, along with the no-duty rules just discussed, mean that it is often the case that victims suffering similar injuries are not treated in a like fashion – and indeed that the disparities are sometimes glaring (ranging from no recovery to millions of dollars for similar accidental injuries or deaths). Thus, both in terms of risk distribution and fairness, it can be argued that tort leaves much to be desired.

Moreover, these limitations spill over into a critique from an economic, deterrence-oriented perspective, as well: No-duty rules, as well as insolvency, that insulate risk generators from bearing the cost of accidents for which they are responsible, translate into inadequate incentives on risk generators to provide safety precautions. In addition, the high administrative cost of shifting losses in tort is frequently invoked as an independent shortcoming of the sys-

[230] *Strauss v Belle Realty Co.*, 482 N.E.2d 34 (N.Y. 1985).

[231] There is also one category of potential catastrophic loss in which special legislative provision for tort recovery and pooled insurance has been enacted, nuclear reactor mishaps under the Price-Anderson Act, discussed earlier in Part IV.

[232] See e.g. 532 *Madison Ave. Gourmet Foods, Inc. v Finlandia Center, Inc.*, 750 N.E.2d 1097 (N.Y. 2001).

tem – undermining both its deterrence function and its efficacy from a risk-distribution and fairness perspective.[233]

As indicated in the section on insurance, the limitations of tort do not mean that those suffering personal injury loss as a consequence of catastrophic harm go entirely uncompensated.[234] About 85% of the U.S. population is covered to some extent by private health insurance, and Medicare offers public health insurance coverage to those over 65 years of age. The resulting gap in medical coverage – while still fairly substantial – is not as wide as the shortfall in coverage for wage loss. Private disability insurance coverage in the U.S. is quite uncommon, and while state disability and unemployment insurance benefits provide short-term partial relief, they do not fill the gap in cases of longer-term or very serious injuries. On this latter score, the federal SSDI insurance program, as indicated earlier, does offer scheduled benefits – although considerably short of full economic restoration – to those experiencing permanent total disability. In sum, the public welfare schemes in the U.S. leave quite large gaps in coverage for the economic consequences of personal injury, and private insurance sources fill only part of the gap, primarily for those carrying generous health insurance. 61

With regard to residential and commercial property and casualty loss, private insurance is the avenue of recourse. In the case of residential property, it is likely to be held by homeowners; much less likely to be held by renters. There are no general exclusions in the standard policies that would apply to catastrophic loss – just as there is none for third-party liability in the personal injury setting.

These non-tort private insurance sources of benefits would also be applicable in cases of catastrophic harm from *natural* disasters. Tort, in most instances, would not. But in the case of natural disasters, the federal and state governments have come to play a more proactive role in recent years. There is no single pattern, in part because the U.S. is a federal system in which much of the responsibility for public safety and welfare continues to reside in state governments – each of which takes an independent tack reflecting regional considerations – rather than in the national authority. In the case of disaster relief generally, however, the federal government has entered the field in a major way with the establishment of the Federal Emergency Management Agency, which as we have seen in Part III, provides frontline coordination and restorative grants and loans to get the victims of a disaster back to a semblance of normality. In the cases of hurricanes, earthquakes, and floods, states that tend to be most heavily affected have devised insurance schemes, discussed in Part IV, whereby they either provide excess liability insurance or in some instances, 62

[233] It is generally thought that injury victims in tort receive roughly 50% of total expenditures by tort defendants. See J.S. Kakalik/N. Pace, *Costs and Compensation Paid in Tort Litigation* (1985).

[234] Indeed, a 1991 study conducted by the Rand Institute for Civil Justice found that over all areas of personal injury, payments in tort comprised 11% of total benefits received by accident victims – although the percentage would almost certainly be higher for victims in catastrophic loss cases. D. Hensler *et al.*, *Compensation for Accidental Injuries in the United States* (1991).

such as the California Earthquake Authority, actually have taken over the role of primary risk-bearer.

For the most part, these publicly-initiated insurance schemes aimed at compensating for the personal injury toll of natural catastrophes – and even more frequently, for property damage and economic devastation – operate from a different set of assumptions than tort about the purposes of financial relief. Tort aims at individualized recovery that will as closely as possible restore victims to their life circumstances before the injury occurred. By contrast, the government schemes – whether they provide scheduled benefits for personal injury or grants and loans for property/economic loss – are more likely to operate from the perspective of restoring the victim to a baseline state of normalcy requisite to resumption of ordinary life.

In the case of relief from natural disasters, deterrence concerns are less of an issue than in the cases of human error and responsibility discussed above. But they are not entirely absent: As mentioned in Part IV, a community can only qualify for federal flood insurance coverage if it offers a plan incorporating provisions that take account of future regional vulnerability to flood damage. In addition, states and local communities have enacted specific legislative programs requiring community and individual action to safeguard against potential damage from catastrophes such as earthquakes, floods, and fires. But these latter legislative safety-promoting schemes ordinarily operate independently of social welfare programs providing compensatory relief – not surprisingly, perhaps, in view of the commonly shared norm that victims of natural disasters should be afforded relief by the state without blaming them for their plight (in the sense of imposing strings or sanctions on recovery).

63 In the final analysis, the U.S. has what might well be termed a patchwork system for providing financial compensation for catastrophic loss: partly tort, partly public social welfare benefit programs, and partly private insurance coverage (often mandated); in some instances federally-initiated and in some instances at the behest of state government. Inevitably, in such a multifaceted milieu, where the tendency has been to develop discrete schemes in response to particularized categories of disasters (or rely on general welfare schemes that were enacted without disaster relief in mind), there will be ongoing fine-tuning of the system and a continuing dialogue over the efficacy of the measures in place. While the description of the U.S. system may not point to a single best model for delivering financial compensation for catastrophic harm in all circumstances, its very complexity indicates the variety of pathways that might be taken.

List of References

Information by the Federal or Provincial Government or Other Authorities

The American Federation of Labor and Congress of Industrial Organizations (AFLCIO), *Workers' Compensation Comparisons* (2001), available at <http://www.aflcio.org/yourjobeconomy/safety/wc/upload/comptable.pdf>.

California's Governor's Office of Emergency Service, available at <http://www.oes.ca.gov/Operational/OESHome.nsf/1?OpenForm>.

Congressional Budget Office, *Federal Reinsurance for Disasters* 12 (2002), available at <ttp://www.cbo.gov/showdoc.cfm?index=37878&sequence=0>.

Department of Financial Services (Dept. of Fin. Services), *Florida's Residual Insurance Market*, available at <http://www.oppaga.state.fl.us/profiles/4102/02/> (last updated 4/12/04).

Federal Emergency Management Agency, *National Flood Insurance Program: Program Description* (2002), available at <http://www.fema.gov/nfip/libfacts.shtm>.

Federal Emergency Management Agency, FEMA02: *Develop a More Anticipatory and Customer-Driven Response to Catastrophic Disasters* (2002), available at <http://govinfo.library.unt.edu/npr/library/reports/FEMA2.html>.

Federal Emergency Management Agency, *Federal Response Plan* (2003), available at <http://www.fema.gov/rrr/frp/>.

Federal Emergency Management Agency, *Top Ten Natural Disasters: Ranked by FEMA Relief Costs*, available at <http://www.fema.gov/library/df_8.shtm>.

Federal Emergency Management Agency, *Florida Disaster Aid Tops $ 2 Billion* (Release No. 1539-238, Oct. 27, 2004), available at <http://fema.gov/news/newsrelease.fema?id=15024>.

Florida Department of Insurance (Fla. Dept. of Ins.), *Hurricane Andrew's Impact on Insurance in the State of Florida* (1993) available at <http://www.fldfs.com/Consumers/Hurricane_Andrew/andrewimpactonins.pdf>.

Governor's Disaster Planning and Response Rev. Committee, Final Report: *Hurricane Andrew* (1993), available at <http://floridadisaster.org/dem/files/lewisr.pdf>.

Insurance Information Institute (Ins. Info. Inst.), *Catastrophes: Insurance Issues* (July 2004); available at <http://www.iii.org/media/hottopics/insurance/xxx>.

Ins. Info. Inst., Catastrophes (2004), available at <http://www.iii.org/media/facts/statsbyissue/catastrophes>.

Insurance Information Network of California (Ins. Info. Network of Cal.), *Financial Aftershocks: 10 Years Later, Northridge Earthquake Prompts Physical, Fiscal Preparedness* (Jan. 2004), available at <http://www.iinc.org/news/home/Northridge_EQ2004.html>.

Michigan Emergency Management Assistance Compact (2002), available at <http://www.michigan.gov/documents/MEMACFINAL7-3-03_69499_7pdf>.

National Association of Insurance Commissioners (Nat'l Ass'n of Ins. Commissioners), Most Costly Insured Catastrophes in the United States, available at <http://www.naic.org/research/Research_Division/Reports/perils.htm>.

Social Security Administration, *A Guide to Supplemental Security Income (SSI) for Groups and Organizations*, available at <http://www.ssa.gov/pubs/11015.html>.

United States Nuclear Regulatory Commission (U.S. Nuclear Reg. Commission); Fact Sheet: *Nuclear Insurance and Disaster Relief Funds* (Sept. 2003), available at <http://www.nrc.gov/reading-rm/doc-collections/fact-sheets/funds.html>.

United States Department of Labor (U.S. Dept. of Labor), *State Workers' Compensation Laws* (2003), available at <http://www.dol.gov/esa/regs/statutes/owcp/stwclaw/tables-pdf/table-12.pdf>.

State Board of Administration of Florida (State Board of Admin. of Fla.), *Florida Hurricane Catastrophe Fund* (2004), available at <http://www.oppaga.state.fl.us/profiles/4042 (last updated 3/23/04)>.

Literature

L. Alvarez/S. Labaton, A Nation Challenged: The Bailout; An Airline Bailout, [Sept. 22, 2001] *N.Y. Times*, A 1.

D.W. Chen, Suits by 950 Families Allege Safety Lapses at the Towers, [Sept. 14, 2002] *N.Y. Times*, B 3.

D.W. Chen, After Weighing Cost of Lives, 9/11 Fund Completes Its Task, [June 16, 2004] *N.Y. Times*, A 1.

D.B. Dobbs, *The Law of Torts* (2001), § 297.

Don Fine Frock, Insurance Could Pay to Elevate Houses, [Nov. 18, 1992] *Miami Herald*, 1 A.

Federal Emergency Management Agency, *A Citizen's Guide to Disaster Assistance* (2003), 3–24.

Federal Emergency Management Agency, *Audit of FEMA's Debris Removal Program* (2001).

Florida House of Representatives Committee on Insurance (Fla. H.R. Comm. on Ins.), *Florida's Property Insurance Crisis* (1994).

Fla. Dept. of Ins., *Recommendations on Improving Property Insurance Availability in Florida* (1 1993).

D.R. Godschalk/T. Beatly/P. Berke/D.J. Brower/E.J. Kaiser, *Natural Hazard Mitigation: Recasting Disaster Policy and Planning* (1999), 104.

A. Goodnough, In Florida, Officials are Hoping for One Final Storm Recovery, [Sept. 29, 2004] *New York Times*, A 21.

J. Gorrie, Property Insurance in Florida: The 1997 Legislative Reform Package, [1998] *Florida State University Law Review* (Fla. St. U. L. Rev.) 25, 351, 352.

Government Accountability Office (Gov't Acct. Off.), *Disaster Management: Improving the Nation's Response to Catastrophic Disasters* (1993).

B. Graham, Hearing Before the Subcommittee on Toxic Substances, *Research and Development of the Committee on Environment and Public Works* (United States Senate 1993).

A. Gron/A. Winton, Risk Overhang and Market Behavior, [Oct. 2001] 74 *Journal of Business* (J. Bus.) 4, 591–612 (Oct. 2001).

D.B. Henriques, A Nation Challenged: The Federal Fund; Official Vows All Families of Victims Will Get Aid, [Dec. 28, 2001] *N.Y. Times*, B 7.

D.B. Henriques/D. Barstow, A Nation Challenged: The Special Master; Mediator Named to Run Sept. 11 Fund, [Nov. 27, 2001] *N.Y. Times*, B 1.

D. Hensler, As Time Goes By: Asbestos Litigation After Amchem and Ortiz, [2002] *Texas Law Review* (Tex.L.Rev.) 80, 1899.

D. Hensler *et al.*, *Compensation for Accidental Injuries in the United States* (1991).

D.R. Hensler/M.A. Peterson, Understanding Mass Personal Injury Litigation: A Sociolegal Analysis, [1993] *Brooklyn Law Review* (Brook. L. Rev.) 59, 961.

M. Jacoby, Lawyers Say Suits May Benefit Clients, [Nov. 15, 2001] *St. Petersburg Times*, 1 A.

J.S. Kakalik/N. Pace, *Costs and Compensation Paid in Tort Litigation* (1985).

J.S. Kakalik/E.M. King/M. Traynor/P.A. Ebener/L. Picus, *Costs and Compensation Paid in Aviation Accident Litigation* (1988).

K. Kaye/R. Benedick, What if Hurricane Andrew hit South Florida today?, [Aug. 24, 2002] *Sun Sentinel*, available at <http://www.sun-sentinel.com/news/weather/hurricane/sfl-sandrew24aug24,0,1246678.story>.

E. Kleinberg, State, U.S. Learn From Andrew Mistakes Dealing with Storm's Aftermath Important Part of Preparedness, [June 1, 2001] *Palm Beach Post*, 8 A.

F. Koutnik, *Hearing Before the Subcommittee on Toxic Substances, Research and Development of the Committee on Environment and Public Works* (United States Senate 1993).

L.S. Kreindler, *Aviation Accident Law* (1994).

L.K. Larson, *Larson's Workers' Compensation Law* (2000).

R. Lyskowski/S. Rice (eds.), *The Big One: Hurricane Andrew* (1992).

E. Mehren, 3 Indicted in R.I. Club Blaze; The Station's co-owners and band manager each face 200 involuntary manslaughter counts, [Dec. 10, 2003] *L.A. Times*, A 15.

National Organisation of Social Security Claimants' Representatives, *Social Security Practice Guide* (2003), § 7.03.

R.L. Rabin, The Quest for Fairness in Compensating Victims of September 11, [1991] *Cleveland State Law Review* (Clev. St. L. Rev.) 49, 573.

E. Rappaport, Nat'l Hurricane Center, Preliminary Report: *Hurricane Andrew* (1992, updated 1993).

Rhode Island: Survivors, Families Sue Over Nightclub Inferno, [July 23, 2004] *L.A. Times*, A 24.

Ch. Rowland/J. Salzman, Tragedy in Rhode Island; Suit Filed in Fire as R.I. Mulls Aid Fund Liability Claims Seen Topping $1B, [Mar. 5, 2003] *Boston Globe*, A 1.

J. Saltzman, Purchase of Foam at Club Is Traced, [Mar. 6, 2003] *Boston Globe*, B 5.

J. Saltzman, R.I. Fire Victims' Lawyers Eye Firm Suits Expected To Name Radio Station's Owner, [Mar. 8, 2003] *Boston Globe*, B 1.

V. Sidbury/B. Wiener/P.H. Cyril/S.M. Gordon/G.E. Sayre, *California Insurance Law and Practice* (2004), § 36.15.

S.J. Singer, Flooding the Fifth Amendment: The National Flood Insurance Program and the "Takings" Clause, [1990] *Boston College Environmental Affairs Law Review* (B.C. Envtl. Aff. L. Rev.) 17, 332–33.

Social Security Administration, *Social Security Handbook* (2003), § 2113.1 and § 2016.1.

J. Van de Hei/M. Geyelin, Economic Impact: Bush Seeks to Limit Liability of Companies Sued as Result of Attacks, [Oct. 25, 2001] *Wall Street Journal*, A 6.

B. van Voris, Lawyers Take Over Ground Zero, [Mar. 11, 2002] *National Law Journal* (Nat'l L. J.).

H.L. Wood, Jr., The Insurance Fallout Following Hurricane Andrew: Whether Insurance Companies Are Legally Obligated to Pay for Building Code Upgrades Despite the "Ordinance or Law" Exclusion Contained in Most Homeowner Policies, [1994] *University of Miami Law Review* (U. Miami L. Rev.) 48, 949–950.

Compulsory Catastrophe Extension of First Party Property Insurance from a Competition Policy Perspective

Roger Van den Bergh

Part I. Introduction

In many European countries, several laws have been enacted to grant specific relief to victims of catastrophes. Natural disasters (in particular floods) or industrial catastrophes (for example, great fires and exploding factories) may cause very substantial physical injury and property damage. The harm caused will only partly be covered by social security and tort claims. Specific disaster laws provide different schemes, according to which victims can claim additional compensation. Three different types of public intervention exist in Europe. Whereas the two first schemes are both examples of public law instruments, the third scheme leaves an important role to private market players.[1] 1

The first scheme awards compensation to victims on an *ad hoc* basis. Under this approach, after the occurrence of a disaster the government officially declares that this event is a "catastrophe" and specifies the conditions under which victims can obtain monetary relief. Such *ad hoc* solutions are applied in several countries, including the Netherlands, Germany and Sweden. In other countries a structural solution has been worked out in the form of a disaster fund. Under this second scheme, public action is taken ex ante rather than ex post. The legislator does not wait to intervene until after the occurrence of catastrophes, but creates a fund that will compensate victims of a disaster (for a limited amount of the harm suffered) according to a previously determined procedure. An example is the Belgian Disaster Fund Act of 1976. A completely different approach is a regulatory intervention in private insurance markets, which imposes a duty on persons who voluntarily subscribed a property insurance policy to purchase a catastrophe extension. The best known example is the French scheme, which takes the form of mandatory disaster coverage for potential victims who have already subscribed first party property insurance. Consequently, damage to houses and cars will also be covered if it is caused 2

[1] Below, only a short characterization of the different schemes is provided. A detailed description of the various legal systems can be found in the other contributions published in this book.

by a natural disaster. The French solution was introduced in Belgium in 2003, and currently other countries (including Germany and Italy) are equally considering the introduction of similar mandatory first party disaster coverage.

3 The different schemes raise several questions concerning the efficiency of the various compensation mechanisms. The fund solutions have been criticized in the Law and Economics literature because they dilute the incentives of potential victims to take preventive measures or to look for alternative relief. Besides the important issues relating to the prevention of catastrophes, the various schemes also differ as regards their effects on competition in the relevant insurance markets. The compulsory disaster insurance schemes (existing in France and proposed in other European countries) involve a tie-in agreement, whereby a potential buyer of one service (property insurance) is forced to purchase another service (insurance of catastrophic loss) to be able to acquire the first service. Tie-in arrangements limit competition, since free choices of consumers are excluded and separate markets for both services will not be able to develop. Consequently, a compulsory catastrophe extension of first party property insurance generates effects that competition law is trying to avoid. Art. 81 and 82 of the EC Treaty explicitly prohibit tying. Also, an analysis of the current EC group exemption for insurance contracts[2] makes clear that the main features of the existing compulsory insurance for catastrophic loss are at odds with the goal to achieve competitive insurance markets. For these reasons, the Italian Competition Authority has voiced a negative opinion on the proposal to introduce a compulsory catastrophe extension of fire insurance policies in Italy.[3]

4 It must be added that art. 81 and 82 of the EC Treaty are concerned solely with the conduct of undertakings and not with laws emanating from Member States. Nonetheless, the latter can be held liable for a violation of the EC Treaty if they introduce measures of a legislative nature, which may render ineffective the competition rules applicable to undertakings.[4] By forcing companies to make use of tying agreements, the state causes competitive distortions that would be prohibited if they had been entered into by private insurance companies. When restrictions of competition are imposed by legal requirements, difficult policy issues arise. Since companies may not be held liable for infringements of the competition laws that result from legal requirements, there is a risk that they may abuse this "state compulsion defense" by asking governments to impose welfare reducing restrictions of competition. If the state requires the conclusion of prohibited cartel agreements, it clearly violates its duties under the EC Treaty. A more delicate question is whether the state also infringes the EC Treaty by adopting measures that generate effects, which are exactly opposite to the goals of European competition law. The state will, in-

[2] Commission Regulation No. 358/2003 of 27 February 2003 on the application of art. 81 (3) of the Treaty to certain categories of agreements, decisions and concerted practices in the insurance sector, OJ L 53, 28 February 2003, 8 (hereafter: Regulation).

[3] Decision of the *Autorità Garante della Concorrenza e del Mercato* (Italian Antitrust Authority) *Atto Senato* (AS) 270 of 20 November 2003, Bulletin n. 47/2003.

[4] Advocate General Léger in his Opinion in Case C-35/99, Arduino, [2002] *European Court Reports* (ECR) I-01529, § 34.

deed, face a difficult dilemma when the restrictions of competition can be justified on other public interest grounds. The negative attitude of competition authorities points at a possible conflict between the goals of competition policy and central ambitions of the welfare state. How should the restrictions of competition be assessed when they are part of a regulatory system that implements the principle of national solidarity? This paper re-assesses the conformity of compulsory disaster insurance by way of a mandatory extension of first party property insurance contracts with the prohibitions of competition law, assuming that the goal of these rules is to achieve allocative efficiency. Such an analysis will make it possible to limit the conflict between competition policy and other ambitions of the state to its right proportions. It will also provide useful information for balancing the different goals, if and where policy makers cannot escape from welfare trade-offs.

The paper is structured as follows. After this introduction (Part I), mandatory 5
disaster insurance arrangements will be confronted with current rules of competition law (Part II). These schemes will be described in somewhat greater detail in order to find out whether they are at odds with the goal to achieve competitive insurance markets. If there is a violation of art. 81 and/or 82 of the EC Treaty, the next question to be addressed is whether the restraints on competition in compulsory disaster insurance schemes are in line with the conditions to be exempted from the ban of anti-competitive practices. Particular attention will be devoted to the potential liability of both the state and the insurance companies for infringement of the art. 81 and 82 of the EC Treaty. The focus of the second section will be on European competition law, in particular the group exemption for the insurance industry. There are good reasons for the limitation of the analysis to European competition law. Since 1 May 2004 national competition authorities (and judges) are also empowered to enforce the European competition rules in full (including the granting of exemptions). Moreover, the contents of the laws of the Member States (in particular Italy) are largely similar to the European rules. The next section of the paper will provide an assessment of the application of the principles of competition law to compulsory disaster insurance schemes (Part III). The central research question is whether the restrictions of competition, caused by a compulsory catastrophe extension of property insurance contracts can be justified on grounds of allocative efficiency. In this respect, the major argument is that compulsory insurance is a remedy to adverse selection in markets for insurance of catastrophic loss. Adverse selection occurs when only the less desirable and highest risks seek insurance coverage. If such a practice was allowed under the rules of competition law, insurance companies would force low risks to purchase insurance coverage in order to avoid adverse selection and make catastrophic loss insurable. If this argument cannot legitimize the restrictions of competition (tying) on grounds of allocative efficiency, it must be investigated whether they can be justified on other policy grounds. In particular, the wish to base compensation for victims of catastrophes on the principle of national solidarity may constitute a relevant trade-off and ultimately overcome concerns of competition policy. Finally, concluding remarks will be formulated (Part IV).

Part II. The Anti-Competitive Effects of a Compulsory Catastrophe Coverage Extension of First Party Property Insurance

I. The French Law and the Italian Proposal

6 The French scheme of mandatory disaster coverage is usually advanced as a point of reference by countries, which consider replacing or complementing forms of public intervention by private market solutions. The main features of the French system are the following.[5] Since 1982 all individuals who have purchased first party property insurance must pay a supplementary premium for a mandatory coverage of natural disasters. Hence, there is no generalized duty to insure catastrophic risks, but a compulsory coverage extension of voluntarily subscribed property insurance contracts. Property damage policies in France are widespread and, consequently, a large group of individuals are forced to pay an additional amount for the coverage of natural disasters. The supplementary coverage for catastrophic loss is financed through an additional premium of 12% on all property insurance contracts. The mandatory coverage is applied to all insured individuals, irrespective of whether they are particularly vulnerable to natural disasters and thus exposed to the risk. Reinsurance is provided through the "*Caisse centrale de réassurance*", which is fully controlled by the French state. After the explosion in Toulouse (in the AZF-factory) on 21 September 2001 a legislative change was effectuated in July 2003, as a result of which owners of property insurance now also possess coverage for damage caused by technological risks. Again, additional compulsory disaster coverage is linked with voluntarily subscribed first party property insurance. The latter extension is, however, debated in France. The point is made that it is not clear why in the case of man-made technological disasters, where a liable wrongdoer can be identified, a mandatory coverage for victims had to be introduced. Imposing solvency guarantees on the side of the wrongdoer, such as compulsory liability insurance, has been suggested as a preferable solution.[6]

7 The French scheme is becoming increasingly popular in Europe: compulsory insurance for catastrophic loss caused by natural disasters has been introduced in Belgium and other countries (such as Germany and Italy) are considering similar changes of their current systems of compensation. In May 2003, Belgium replaced the compensation fund solution by property insurance contracts. The new Belgian scheme looks like the French one, but a major difference is that the mandatory supplementary coverage of harm caused by floods applies only with respect to specifically designated risk areas. The rationale of the Belgian rules is that only those who are exposed to a particular risk should bear the costs of the additional premium. However, as a result of difficulties in designating the specific risk areas, the new Act has not yet entered into force. In Italy, the discussion to reform the disaster recovery system was initiated already in 1997. The latest Italian proposal, which was a part of the draft of the

[5] See for more information the contribution by O. Moréteau/M. Cannarsa/F. Lafay, published in this book.

[6] O. Moréteau/M. Cannarsa/F. Lafay (*supra* fn. 5), no. 51.

Budgetary Law for 2004,[7] provided for a compulsory coverage of natural catastrophic risk tied to voluntarily subscribed fire insurance policies. At a first stage, the compulsory extension would apply only to new insurance policies entered into by private businesses and individuals after the enactment of the new law, and later on it would be extended to all existing policies. Insurance premiums would be defined on the basis of different indexes reflecting the degree of risk in different areas of Italy. The draft also provided for rules relating to the contract terms, including franchises and modalities of compensation. In addition, the draft imposed the establishment of a co-reinsurance consortium, which would be responsible for the collection of premiums for natural catastrophic risk coverage. Finally, the draft provided for a yearly maximum indemnification cap, beyond which the Italian State would cover any residual compensation not paid by the consortium.[8] The Italian Antitrust Authority severely criticized the restrictions of competition contained in the proposal and, ultimately, the draft was not approved by the Italian parliament.

II. Competition Law: The Prohibition of Cartel Agreements and Abuses of a Dominant Position

For the purposes of this paper, it is not necessary to dwell at length on the very complex body of European competition law and the competition laws of the Member States. It seems sufficient to briefly sketch the framework under which the effects of compulsory disaster insurance schemes on competition may be assessed. The most relevant queries relate to the qualification of crucial provisions of these schemes as anti-competitive practices prohibited by art. 81 and 82 of the EC Treaty,[9] the conditions under which the restrictions of competition may be exempted from the ban on anti-competitive practices, and the issue of liability for the potential infringements of competition law. The latter question is particularly relevant, since the restraints of competition are laid down in legislation and do not result directly from anti-competitive practices of insurance companies. It is, of course, possible that insurance companies favour compulsory insurance and that they would consider introducing such schemes if they were not prohibited by rules of competition law. Forcing individuals who are not exposed to risk to buy insurance coverage may transform the insurance of high risks from a loss-making into a profitable business. If this goal is achieved by legislative intervention without any threat of liability under the rules of competition law, the insurance industry may expand its activities more easily into markets for risks that are difficult to insure. 8

Art. 81 (1) of the EC Treaty prohibits agreements between undertakings, decisions of associations of undertakings and concerted practices that restrict competition and have an impact on interstate trade. An undertaking is defined as every entity engaged in an economic activity, irrespective of the legal status of 9

[7] Article 40 of the proposed *Legge finanziaria* for 2004 (budgetary law 2004).

[8] See for more information on the various Italian proposals relating to catastrophic risk coverage, the contribution by A. Monti/F. Chiaves, published in this book, no. 9.

[9] The third set of competition rules, which pertain to merger control, are not relevant for the analysis of the insurance schemes discussed in this paper.

the entity and the way in which it is financed.[10] The impact on competition must be noticeable, so that the prohibition will usually not apply if the undertakings have very low market shares. The EC competition rules apply only when an impact on interstate trade can be shown. However, anti-competitive practices that have an impact only within the territory of a single Member State are prohibited by provisions of national competition laws, which are similar to their European counterparts. If certain conditions are met, anti-competitive agreements can be exempted from the ban on prohibited cartels. To qualify for an exemption, art. 81 (3) of the EC Treaty requires that four conditions are satisfied. The agreements must (1) contribute to improving the production or distribution of goods or to promoting technical or economic progress, (2) allow consumers a fair share of the resulting benefit, (3) not impose restrictions which are not indispensable to attain the mentioned objectives, and (4) not give undertakings the possibility of eliminating competition in respect of a substantial part of the products in question. The competition laws of the EC Member States all provide for the possibility of an exemption under the same conditions as art. 81 (3) of the Treaty.

10 Art. 82 of the EC Treaty prohibits abuse of a dominant position. The application of this prohibition requires that a dominant position on a relevant insurance market can be established. Dominance is defined as the possibility of a company to prevent effective competition by behaving independently of its competitors and customers.[11] In practice, it is determined by reference to the market share of the undertaking under investigation. A market share of 50% is indicative of a dominant position and a smaller share of 40 to 45% is equally sufficient, provided the company enjoys a number of competitive advantages compared to the other market players.[12] The list of abuses, mentioned in art. 8 2 (d) of the EC Treaty, includes tying clauses.

III. The Restrictions of Competition Resulting from a Compulsory Extension of First Party Property Insurance

11 Mandatory disaster insurance schemes generate anti-competitive effects that competition law wants to prevent. First, the extension of voluntarily subscribed first party insurance is achieved by a tying clause. Tying occurs if a supplier who is selling two products makes the sale of one of these products to a particular buyer dependent upon the purchase of the second product by the same buyer. Tying is mentioned explicitly in art. 81 (1, e) of the EC Treaty as an example of prohibited agreements. The cartel prohibition outlaws agreements that

> "make the conclusion of contracts subject to acceptance by the other parties of supplementary obligations which, by their nature or according to

[10] Case C-41/90, *Höfner and Elser v Macroton GmbH* [1991] ECR I-1979, § 21.

[11] Case 27/76, *United Brands v Commission*, [1978] ECR 207, § 65.

[12] Case C-62/86, *Akzo Chemie BV v Commission* [1991] ECR I-3359, § 60; Case T-228/97, *Irish Sugar plc v Commission* [1999] ECR II-2969, § 70; Case 27/76, *United Brands v Commission* [1978] ECR 207.

commercial usage, have no connection with the subject of such contracts".

The French law and the Italian proposal favour prohibited cartel agreements. The consequence of the legal duty to extend the coverage of property insurance to catastrophic loss is that all insurance companies will insert such extension clauses in their policies. Since insurers are not left free to offer property insurance without the extension for catastrophic loss, the effect of the legislative measures are similar to those of prohibited cartel agreements that impose tying clauses. Tying may also be prohibited as an abuse if the firm imposing tie-in contracts enjoys a dominant position. Art. 82 (d) of EC Treaty contains a list of examples of abuses of a dominant position and outlaws tying by using the same wording as art. 81 (1, e) of the EC Treaty. 12

The overwhelmingly negative attitude towards tying in competition law has its origin in the "leverage theory", which holds that a firm having a dominant position in the market for the tying product uses tying arrangements to extend its dominant position into the market for the tied product.[13] As a consequence, there are two deadweight losses and a dominant firm obtains a monopoly profit twice. This argument would be relevant when competition on property insurance markets was seriously limited and tying property insurance with disaster insurance could be qualified as an abuse of a dominant position (art. 82 of the EC Treaty). Even though the leverage argument may not hold in current property insurance markets, anti-competitive effects of tying cannot be excluded. In non-regulated markets, tying may be employed strategically to raise barriers to entry and so worsen the performance of the market for the tying good. If capital markets are imperfect, so that the entrant's investments will not be funded, tying may be used for strategic reasons. The effect of the compulsory catastrophe extension is that competing insurance companies will have to enter two markets at the same time. In sum, the mandatory disaster insurance schemes generate anti-competitive consequences that are similar to those of tying mechanisms used by private firms. 13

Second, the amount of the premium for the catastrophe extension is laid down in legislation. In France, it is expressed as a percentage of the premium for the original contract. On any first party property insurance a mandatory additional premium of 12% is added for the coverage of catastrophic loss. According to the Italian proposal, premiums would have been regulated on the basis of different indicators reflecting the degree of risk in different Italian areas. In both systems, insurers cannot compete on prices for disaster coverage. Competition authorities generally regard price agreements as the most serious infringement of art. 81 (1) of the EC Treaty. The effect of premium regulation is similar to compulsory membership of a price cartel. Fixed premiums carry the risk that insurance firms will have no incentives to increase productive efficiency and hurt the interests of individuals and businesses willing to buy insurance cover- 14

[13] The "leverage theory" was formulated by the American Supreme Court in *Northern Pacific Railway Company v United States*, 356 [1958] *United States Reports* (U.S.) 1.

age. These negative effects may occur both on the market for disaster insurance and the market for property insurance. Because of the tying clause, which requires that property insurance contracts are expanded by a cover for harm caused by disasters, the price regulation may also affect the terms and conditions of the original property insurance contract. From an insurance technical point of view, there is no connection between the premium for property insurance and the premium for natural disaster coverage. To calculate actuarially fair premiums, different data and criteria must be taken into consideration. Fixed premiums may ultimately also worsen the performance of the first market, for example if the insurers increase the franchise of the property insurance contract to circumvent the regulation of the premiums for the compulsory cover of catastrophic risk.[14]

15 Third, mandatory reinsurance is organized by the state (France) or insurers are forced to participate in a co-reinsurance consortium (Italy). Co-reinsurance can allow insurers to provide insurance for risks for which they might only offer insufficient cover in the absence of the pool. However, in a free market insurers should be free to choose whether they will join co-reinsurance groups, depending on their experience of risks and the working rules of the co-reinsurance groups. Compulsory reinsurance limits this freedom and is, therefore, also a violation of the ban on anti-competitive agreements.

IV. Compulsory Catastrophe Extension of First Party Property Insurance and the Group Exemption for the Insurance Industry

16 Restrictions of competition can be saved from the ban of art. 81 (1) of the EC Treaty by showing that the conditions for exemption are met. In contrast, there is no possibility for an exemption if the schemes infringe the prohibition of abuse of a dominant position, contained in art. 82 of the EC Treaty. To be exempted under art. 81 (3) of the EC Treaty, it must be shown that the restrictions of competition achieve efficiency savings (improvements of production or distribution, contributions to technical and economic progress), which benefit consumers and neither go further than necessary (requirement of proportionality) nor give the undertakings the possibility to exclude competition for a substantial part of the products involved. The assessment whether these conditions are satisfied lies within the competence of both the European Commission and the national competition authorities and judges. For certain categories of agreements, the conditions under which an exemption can be granted are specified in Regulations. Traditionally, group exemptions specified the restrictions that may, or may not, appear in the agreements. The modern Regulations have moved away from the approach of establishing white lists of exempted clauses and black lists of prohibited clauses. Instead, they define categories of agreements that are exempted up to a certain level of market power and specify the restrictions that are not to be contained in such agreements.

[14] See also the paper by A. Monti/F. Chiaves (*supra* fn. 8), no. 137.

For the insurance industry, the relevant rules are contained in Regulation No. 358/2003.[15] This group exemption does not entirely follow the new approach based on the size of the market shares in the relevant market, because of the specificity of the insurance sector. The reason is that exchange of information between insurers, including companies with high market shares, will promote competition by helping smaller insurers to make reliable calculations of risks. The main provisions of the group exemption for the insurance industry are described below. If the conditions of the group exemption are not satisfied, individual exemptions are still possible but very difficult to obtain. For reasons of clarity, it must be recalled that the analysis of the group exemption for the insurance industry only serves the purpose of illuminating the potential conflicts between competition policy and other goals of public interest, such as national solidarity. Insurance companies do not violate art. 81 of the EC Treaty if the restrictions of competition are the direct consequence of legal requirements (see for further analysis, Part II.V of this paper). 17

An analysis of Regulation 358/2003 shows that a compulsory catastrophe extension of first party insurance is at odds with principles of European competition policy. Fixed premiums, tying clauses and compulsory reinsurance are all in conflict with the goal of creating competitive insurance markets. First, the premium for the disaster coverage is fixed by state regulation. This has a direct impact on the amount of the commercial premiums, which should remain fully subject to the forces of competition. The group exemption extends to the establishment of common risk premium tariffs, common standard policy conditions, common coverage of certain types of risks and security devices. To illustrate the scope of the group exemption, the following examples are illustrative. Insurance companies may make use of joint calculations, tables and studies to improve their knowledge of risks and facilitate the rating of risks for individual companies. The collaboration between insurance undertakings may include the calculation of the average cost of covering a specified risk in the past or, for life insurance, tables of mortality rates or of the frequency of illness, accident and invalidity. The collaboration may also include joint studies on the probable impact of extraneous circumstances that may influence the frequency or scale of claims. However, the exemption does not cover agreements on commercial premiums. Indeed, commercial premiums may be lower than the amounts indicated by the results of the calculations, tables or studies, since insurers can use the revenues from their investments in order to reduce their premiums.[16] Also, the joint establishment of standard policy conditions is exempted provided that there is no indication of the level of commercial premiums and that their use is not in any way recommended (art. 5–6). 18

Second, mandatory disaster coverage is an example of tying, which is not covered by the group exemption either. Of particular importance for the analysis of a mandatory catastrophe extension of property insurance is the explicit ex- 19

[15] See *supra* fn. 2.
[16] Regulation, 9, recital no. 10.

clusion from the scope of the group exemption of clauses, which "impose comprehensive cover including risks to which a significant number of policyholders are not simultaneously exposed" (art. 6, 1 c). More generally, the group exemption also excludes clauses which require the policyholder to obtain cover from the same insurer for different risks (art. 6, 1 i). In the Commission's view, bundling of unrelated risks can be a disincentive for insurers to offer a separate and specific insurance cover.[17] The text of the Group Exemption seems to imply that, from a competition policy perspective, the French scheme is more problematic than the Belgian regulation. The French scheme forces all holders of property damage insurance to buy mandatory coverage for disasters, irrespective of whether they are particularly vulnerable to natural disasters. By contrast, the Belgian scheme extends only to people living in designated risk areas. The latter approach may avoid that a comprehensive cover is imposed upon individuals who are not exposed to catastrophic risks. The Belgian approach thus seems preferable to the French solution from a competition policy perspective.

20 Third, the role of the state as mandatory re-insurer (France) or the compulsory participation in a consortium of insurance undertakings for re-insurance purposes (Italy) is equally conflicting with the principles of Regulation 358/2003. On this point, the Group Exemption distinguishes between genuinely new risks and risks that are not new. A pooling arrangement for the co-insurance or co-reinsurance exclusively of new risks can be exempted for a period of three years (art. 7,1). New risks are defined as

> "risks which did not exist before, and for which insurance cover requires the development of an entirely new insurance product, not involving an extension, improvement or replacement of an existing insurance product" (art. 2, 7).

21 This definition excludes risks which existed but were not insured (for example, floods) or risks whose nature changed significantly (for example, terrorist attacks). Hence, for the disaster insurance schemes, discussed in this paper, different rules serve as a benchmark to assess their anti-competitive effects. In the case of risks that are not new, insurance companies must remain free to choose whether they will join the co-insurance or co-reinsurance groups. They should retain the power to withdraw a certain risk, in whole or in part, from the insurance pool. The agreement should also not allocate markets or customers. Finally, in the case of co-reinsurance the market share of the group should not exceed 25% of the relevant market (art. 8). Clearly, the legislation on reinsurance of mandatory disaster coverage reaches results that are opposite to the rules of the group exemption for the insurance industry.

22 In sum, the analysis in this section leads to the conclusion that mandatory insurance for harm caused by disasters by way of a compulsory extension of property insurance contracts is difficult to reconcile with the European compe-

[17] Regulation, 10, recital no. 17.

tition philosophy. Since the restrictions of competition are not the direct consequence of voluntary decisions by insurance undertakings, the latter may invoke the state compulsion defense. The scope of this defense will be further analyzed below. Excluding infringements of art. 81 and 82 of the EC Treaty by insurance companies raises the question who will ultimately bear liability for the anti-competitive effects. In no less than three ways, legislative measures jeopardize the goals of competition policy in insurance markets: by imposing tying clauses, fixing premiums and organizing mandatory co-reinsurance. Hence, the delicate question is whether EC Member States violate the Treaty if they introduce the mandatory disaster insurance schemes described above (see Part II.I).

V. The State Compulsion Defense

A particular feature of schemes of disaster coverage achieved by way of a 23
compulsory extension of voluntarily subscribed first party insurance is that the restrictions of competition (such as tying and fixed premiums) result from state legislation. If anti-competitive behaviour is imposed by state regulation, companies may escape from the ban on prohibited cartels by arguing that the illegal behaviour was imposed by the state, which has left no scope for competition to develop in the relevant market. In particular, the European Commission has made clear that insurance companies do not violate art. 81 (1) of the EC Treaty "where there is a legal requirement on insurers to include in policies cover for risks to which a significant number of policyholders are not simultaneously exposed".[18] In this section, the scope for a state compulsion defense in both European competition law and the competition laws of the Member States will be further investigated. It will equally be examined to what extent Member States can be held liable for the enactment of legislation that conflicts with the competition provisions of the EC Treaty.

According to the case law of the European Court of Justice, undertakings are 24
not liable under art. 81 of the EC Treaty where the state by measures of public authority requires them to engage in anti-competitive conduct.[19] In such a situation they cannot be held accountable for an infringement of the cartel prohibition. However, the state compulsion defense operates only where the state requires certain behaviour.[20] If a law of a Member State merely allows, encourages or makes it easier for undertakings to engage in autonomous anti-competitive conduct, the state compulsion defense cannot prevent the finding of an infringement of art. 81 of the EC Treaty. Even when the state requires the undertakings to engage in anti-competitive conduct, the undertakings can still be held liable if they remain at least partially capable to autonomously restrict competition. The latter hypothesis materializes when the state requires

[18] Regulation, 10, recital no. 17.

[19] Case C-13/77, *GB-Inno-BM* [1977] ECR 2115.

[20] Case C-198/01, *Consorzio Industrie Fiammiferi (CIF)*, [2003] ECR I-8055. In this judgment it was also decided that national competition authorities must not apply state measures that require or facilitate anti-competitive behaviour.

anti-competitive conduct but leaves a margin of discretion in the implementation of the national legislation to the undertakings.

25 In the most recent case law, the scope for a state compulsion defense seems to be declining. In addition, recent changes of competition law in the Member States have further limited the possibility of such a defense. In the recent *Fiammiferi* judgment, the Court of Justice has increased the effectiveness of the cartel prohibition by deciding that national competition authorities must not apply anti-competitive regulations.[21] Where undertakings engage in conduct contrary to art. 81 of the EC Treaty and where that conduct is required or facilitated by state legislation, national competition authorities have a duty to give effect to art. 81 of the EC Treaty. The consequence of this judgment is that (associations of) undertakings can no longer escape liability under art. 81 of the EC Treaty by invoking the state compulsion defense when a decision by a national competition authority to not apply the state measures has become definitive. The effect of the Fiammiferi judgment is reinforced by recent changes in the national competition laws. Whereas the defense is still available in the French competition law,[22] the provision that anti-competitive conduct required by legislative measures is exempted from the cartel prohibition has been deleted from the text of the Dutch competition law.

26 When state measures impose or favour practices that infringe the competition provisions of the EC Treaty, the Commission and other Member States can start infringement proceedings under art. 226 and 227 of the EC Treaty. Also persons negatively affected by the state measures can introduce an action for damages against the member state for breach of EC law. In the past, the European Court of Justice has consistently held that art. 3 (1)(g),10 (2) and 81 (1) of the EC Treaty are infringed when a Member State requires or favours the adoption of agreements, decisions or concerted practices, which violate the competition provisions of the Treaty, or reinforces their effects, or where it divests its own rules of the character of legislation by delegating to private economic operators responsibility for taking decisions affecting the economic sphere.[23] In the past, several cartel agreements facilitated by the state were considered as an infringement of those articles. In this way, competition law is able to prevent harmful anti-competitive practices even in cases where these have been approved or facilitated by state law. Where a state adopts measures that are contrary to the provisions of European competition law, national courts and national administrative bodies (including national competition authorities) have a duty to interpret state legislation in the light of those Community provisions and, if necessary, a duty to not apply the rules that are in conflict with the EC Treaty.

[21] Case C-198/01, *Consorzio Industrie Fiammiferi (CIF)* [2003] ECR I-8055, § 51.

[22] Ordonnance No. 86-1243 of 1 December 1986 "relative a la liberté des prix et de la concurrence".

[23] Advocate General Léger in his Opinion in Case C-35/99, *Arduino*, [2002] ECR I-01529, § 34–35.

In the light of the case law discussed above, difficult questions arise with respect to the liability of both insurance companies and the state for potential infringements of the rules of EC competition law. Who should bear the ultimate liability for the anti-competitive effects generated by a compulsory catastrophe extension of first party property insurance? The scope for autonomous infringements of art. 81 of the EC Treaty by insurance companies will depend on the more or less detailed contents of the state measures. If insurance companies remain free to decide about some of the contract terms of the disaster insurance policies (for example, deductibles and modalities of payment) they will remain subject to the ban of anti-competitive agreements. Art. 81 of the EC Treaty will also be violated if the insurers of catastrophic loss enter into agreements affecting the competition in the market for property insurance. Since the state regulation does not extend to the original contract, the cartel prohibition will unrestrictedly apply in the property insurance market. Moreover, as a consequence of the Fiammiferi judgment, legislative measures only shield insurers from all the consequences of an infringement of art. 81 and 82 of the EC Treaty until the moment at which the national competition authority establishes an infringement and the decision not to apply the national law becomes definitive. 27

With respect to the liability of the state, it must be investigated whether the state favours the adoption of practices prohibited by art. 81 and 82 of the EC Treaty. Clearly, the insurance industry may profit from a compulsory catastrophe extension of property insurance contracts. Insurers may be generally unwilling to cover damage caused by natural disasters, because they fear that only high risks would have a demand for disaster insurance. A compulsory catastrophe extension may be a solution to the adverse selection problem. Even though it is a less dramatic remedy than totally excluding the coverage of natural disasters, also tying causes anti-competitive effects. If French insurers generally favour compulsory coverage of catastrophic loss achieved through tying property insurance and disaster insurance[24] and if it can be shown that they have lobbied the state to make a catastrophe extension of first party property insurance compulsory, the French state may have violated its duties under the EC Treaty. Under such circumstances, the enactment of a law making the purchase of disaster coverage compulsory would come close to a "rubberstamp approval" of a prohibited cartel agreement. Such an arrangement makes insurance companies immune under the EC competition rules, but the liability for violation of the latter will shift to the state. If underlying anti-competitive practices of the French insurance industry can be proven, the argument can be made that the French state has favoured the adoption of practices prohibited by art. 81 and 82 of the EC Treaty. The effects of the state measures are similar to the anti-competitive effects that the competition rules are trying to prevent and 28

[24] In 1997 the Italian supervisory body for the insurance industry proposed a scheme, according to which it would not be mandatory but rather voluntary for citizens to stipulate a disaster insurance coverage when subscribing a fire insurance policy (see the contribution by A. Monti/ F. Chiaves (*supra* fn. 8), no. 128).

they render these rules ineffective. In sum, it may not be excluded that the French disaster insurance scheme and the similar schemes that have been introduced or are proposed in other European countries (Belgium, Italy) have features which trigger the liability of the state for infringements of EC competition law.

29 If the state compulsion defense is not able to save compulsory insurance disaster schemes entirely from the prohibition of art. 81 of the EC Treaty and states may violate their duties under the EC Treaty by enacting such legislative measures, only a re-assessment of the four conditions to grant an individual exemption can eliminate the objections based on EC competition law. Two alternative escape routes should be further investigated. Both approaches rely on the insight that the disadvantages resulting from anti-competitive restrictions can be made good by advantages in terms of other welfare goals. The first line of reasoning is that efficiency savings may outweigh the harm caused to competition. Competition authorities may examine whether the existing mandatory insurance schemes for catastrophic loss create efficiency benefits that outweigh the losses resulting from the anti-competitive effects. An efficiency analysis, which is broader than the approach in the group exemption, may provide new arguments to legalize the restrictions of competition. This exercise is not yet a complete policy assessment. From a global welfare perspective, rules restricting competition may be inspired also by goals of national solidarity. In a welfare state, citizens may agree that persons in serious difficulties have a right to financial assistance. In recent judgments relating to health services, the European Court of Justice has created a solidarity exception, which precludes the applicability of art. 81 and 82 of the EC Treaty. In the remainder of this paper, it will be investigated (1) whether compulsory disaster insurance schemes generate efficiency benefits that make good the anti-competitive effects, or (2) whether it is possible to apply a solidarity exception with the purpose of excluding the applicability of competition law on compulsory disaster insurance schemes. Both lines of reasoning may provide new insights to answer the question whether – and if yes, to what extent – the state and the insurers infringe rules of EC competition law when they make disaster coverage available by way of a compulsory catastrophe extension of first party property insurance contracts.

Part III. Compulsory Catastrophe Extension of First Party Property Insurance Re-assessed: Efficiency Defense or Solidarity Exception?

I. Coverage of Catastrophic Loss in a Competitive Insurance Market and the Problem of Adverse Selection

30 The previous section has shown that compulsory disaster coverage, as it exists in France and is proposed in Italy, is difficult to reconcile with principles of competition policy. The above analysis implicitly provides arguments in favour of forms of public intervention, such as *ad hoc* solutions, leaving it to the government to decide whether compensation will be awarded after the occurrence of a particular catastrophe, or the establishment of compensation funds, which pro-

vide relief in a structural way. Under the latter forms of government intervention, there are neither fixed insurance premiums nor tying clauses, imposing the duty upon holders of property insurance to buy disaster coverage as well. Insurers are also left free to decide whether they will join co-reinsurance groups. A clear decision in favour of public intervention thus avoids conflicts with basic principles of competition law. However, the alternative schemes for providing compensation to victims of catastrophes have been criticized in the Law and Economics literature because they dilute the incentives of victims to take preventive measures or to look for alternative relief. One author has qualified compensation funds as "catastrophic responses to catastrophic risks".[25] Endres, Ohl and Rundshagen have argued that compensation by the state dilutes any incentives to "self insure" by victims or to take preventive measures in the framework of an effective risk management. Those who can be certain that they will be compensated by public funds can keep the insurance premium in their pocket and hence free ride on the state.[26]

The disadvantages of compensation funds or *ad hoc* solutions invite a re-as- 31
sessment of the role private insurers may play in providing monetary relief to victims of catastrophes. Several authors have advocated a greater reliance on insurance markets to guarantee compensation to victims of catastrophes.[27] However, this suggestion implies that insurance markets for catastrophic risks may sufficiently develop without government intervention. Market solutions may not work because of lacking demand or restricted supply: either victims do not voluntarily seek to purchase disaster coverage or insurers systematically exclude the disaster risk from (property) insurance policies. Lacking demand may be caused by the fact that people systematically underestimate the risk of catastrophes ("it will not happen to me") or are unaware about the availability of insurance coverage. It may be assumed that citizens are averse to the risk of large (property) damage as a consequence of natural catastrophes and are willing to pay a premium to have that risk removed from them. However, there are a number of papers showing that there is a small demand for flood insurance[28] or for earthquake insurance.[29] If this low demand is caused by a lack of information, a compulsory catastrophe extension of first party insurance would be a disproportionate remedy. If citizens do not purchase insurance because they lack information on the probability and magnitude of the risk and/or on the availability of insurance, information remedies are the ap-

[25] R.A. Epstein, Catastrophic responses to catastrophic risks, [1996] *Journal of Risk and Uncertainty* (J. Risk Uncertainty) 12, 287–308.

[26] A. Endres/C. Ohl/B. Rundshagen, Land unter! Ein institutionenökonomischer Zwischenruf, [2003] *List Forum für Wirtschafts- und Finanzpolitik* 29, 284–294.

[27] G. Priest, The government, the market and the problem of catastrophic loss, [1996] J. Risk Uncertainty 12, 219–237.; H.C. Kunreuther *et al.* (eds.), *Disaster insurance protection: public policy lessons* (1978); H. Kunreuther/P. Freeman, Insurability, environmental risks and the law, in: A. Heyes (ed.), *The Law and Economics of the Environment* (2001), 304–305.

[28] H. Kunreuther, Mitigating disaster losses through insurance, [1996] J. Risk Uncertainty 12, 171–187; R. Zeckhauser, The economics of catastrophes, [1996] J. Risk Uncertainty 12, 113–140.

[29] H. Kunreuther/N. Doherty/A. Kleffner, Should society deal with the earthquake problem?, [1992] *Regulation – The Cato Review of Business and Government* 15(2).

propriate answer to cure these information deficiencies.[30] Restricted supply may be the consequence of reluctance on the side of the insurance industry to offer coverage for catastrophic loss. In several European countries, natural disasters have been traditionally considered as uninsurable by the insurance industry and governments have stepped in to provide compensation to victims (either *ad hoc* or through payments by a compensation fund). It is well known from an abundant literature on insurance economics that it is not the size of the loss in itself but rather the danger of adverse selection that makes certain risks uninsurable.[31] Adverse selection occurs when the less desirable risks and highest expected losses seek disaster coverage, whereas low risks do not subscribe such insurance contracts. Under these circumstances, the risk cannot be spread in a satisfactory fashion. If the problem of adverse selection cannot be overcome, private insurance markets will not offer insurance contracts to high risks or will decide to reduce the extent of the insurance cover. Even though a compulsory catastrophe extension is a disproportionate remedy to cure information deficiencies on the demand side, it should be further investigated whether it is an appropriate remedy to adverse selection in insurance markets for catastrophic risks.

II. The Need to Cope with Adverse Selection and the Conditions for an Exemption from the Cartel Prohibition

32 The important insight that adverse selection may lead to a breakdown of private insurance markets offers a useful start point to re-assess the conditions under which restrictions of competition may benefit from an exemption. At the outset, it must be stressed that competition is not a goal in itself. The dominant view in the current literature on the goals of competition law is that the prohibition of cartel agreements (or the abuse of a dominant position) is an instrument to achieve efficiency. This goal implies that production costs are minimized (productive efficiency), that consumers are offered their preferred set of goods and services at competitive prices (allocative efficiency), and that an optimal amount of innovative goods and services are offered on the market (dynamic efficiency).[32] Efficient outcomes are not only endangered by restrictions of competition but also by other forms of market failure, such as information asymmetries. Even though competition authorities often pay lip service to such an economic approach, in deciding real-life cases there is a tendency to find an infringement of the competition rules wherever and whenever some form of competition is possible, without a further analysis of whether competition is the best suited instrument to reach efficient outcomes. Stressing efficiency as the ultimate goal makes it possible to broaden the debate by addressing other potential sources of inefficiency in insurance markets. The analysis

[30] A. Schwartz/L. Wilde, Intervening in markets on the basis of imperfect information: a legal and economic analysis, [1979] *University of Pennsylvania Law Review* (U. Pa. L. Rev.), 630–682.

[31] See S.J. Chandler, Insurance Regulation, in: B. Bouckaert/G. De Geest (eds.), *Encyclopedia of Law and Economics* (vol. III, 2000), No. 5700.

[32] R. Van den Bergh/P. Camesasca, *European Competition Law and Economics. A Comparative Perspective* (2001), 1–7.

below offers a different perspective on the desirability of compulsory insurance for catastrophic loss by balancing the anti-competitive effects and the need to avoid adverse selection.

Even though the formulation of the group exemption seems too narrow to legalize the compulsory disaster insurance schemes discussed in this paper, a broader efficiency defense may create scope for a more tolerant view. An argument can be made in favour of an individual exemption by showing that (section Part III.II.A) compulsory insurance is needed to avoid adverse selection and thus improves production since insurance markets could otherwise not sufficiently develop, (section Part III.II. Part III.II.B) consumers benefit from the availability of disaster coverage, (section Part III.II.C) a tie-in clause is the most efficient way to implement the duty to insure and (section Part III.II.D) there remains sufficient scope for competition between insurance companies offering disaster coverage. It is not suggested here that these conditions can be easily satisfied and that the French model of compulsory disaster coverage does not cause antitrust concerns. However, the wording of the group exemption and the opinion delivered by the Italian antitrust authority do not offer a complete picture of the advantages and disadvantages of compulsory disaster coverage. The purpose of the analysis below is to broaden the debate and to offer more refined criteria for an individual assessment of different types of mandatory insurance for catastrophic loss. 33

A. *The First Condition: Improvement of Production or Distribution, or Technical or Economic Progress*

In this section of the paper, it will be investigated whether there are efficiency benefits that may justify the introduction of a duty to insure catastrophic loss. Since the compulsory disaster coverage is achieved through tying property insurance and disaster insurance, it will also be examined whether the tie-in is able to generate advantages that outweigh the disadvantages resulting from the restrictions of competition. If this analysis leads to the conclusion that a compulsory catastrophe extension of first party property insurance enables private insurance markets to expand the available insurance coverage and thus better satisfy the demand of potential insured, the tension between competition policy and the wish to provide adequate relief to victims of catastrophes may disappear. 34

A broadly interpreted efficiency defense opens the door for the argument that a duty to insure imposed on low risk individuals is needed to prevent adverse selection. The application of rules of competition law supposes that a market has already sufficiently developed. If this is not the case, private or public law remedies will be necessary to create the basic conditions of an efficient market. Adverse selection negatively affects allocative efficiency in two possible ways. If insurers are able to identify high risks, they will consider it unprofitable to offer insurance coverage to those risks, when there is no sufficient risk spreading in the insurance pool. If insurers cannot distinguish high risks and 35 low risks, they may decide to charge a higher (uniform) premium or reduce the scope of the insurance cover. Allocative efficiency implies that prospective buyers are able to purchase the goods and services they desire at an affordable price. In both cases, this goal is not achieved. If screening of risks is possible, high risks will not be able to subscribe insurance contracts, even though they would be willing and able to pay the actuarially fair premium. In the opposite case, either the insurance premium will be too high for low risk businesses and individuals or the insurance contract will not satisfy the full demand for insurance coverage.

36 When high risks can be identified, insurers may be reluctant to offer insurance policies to high risk businesses or individuals. Flood insurance offers a good illustration. The chance of flooding is geographically limited. Insurers are able to identify the risky areas and may consider it uneconomic to make flood insurance available to everybody living in such areas. Adverse selection occurs when only people with the less desirable risks and higher expected losses choose to insure. This small pool of interested buyers will make it very difficult for the insurers to spread the risk in a satisfactory fashion.[33] Theoretically, if screening of risks was possible at zero costs, all risks willing to pay the actuarially fair premium would get coverage. In reality, information deficiencies in insurance markets prevent an efficient outcome. High risks will have to pay a prohibitively high premium or are not offered any coverage; insurers will either select the best risks or withdraw from the market altogether. A duty to insure imposed upon low risk individuals enlarges the insurance pool, prevents adverse selection and makes natural disasters insurable.

37 Remarkably, the French Insurance Code defines loss resulting from natural catastrophes as "non insurable direct material damage whose determining cause was the abnormal intensity of a natural agent (…)".[34] Lawyers have criticized this definition since it seems confusing to call uninsurable a risk that the law makes insurable by compulsory coverage.[35] However, the paradox disappears if one realizes that compulsory insurance is a remedy to adverse selection, which may make natural disasters uninsurable. By imposing a duty to insure the law transforms an uninsurable risk into an insurable one. Compulsory insurance may enable the private insurance market to cover harm caused by natural disasters in geographically limited areas. Floods and earthquakes are clear examples, but the French compulsory disaster insurance coverage also extends to snowfalls, droughts, heavy tempests, terrorist attacks and technological catastrophes.[36] Compared to floods and earthquakes, the risks of snowfalls, droughts and tempests exist in larger geographical areas and, consequently, the risk of adverse selection will be lower. Also property insurance

[33] R.L. Rabin/S.A. Bratis, United States, in: M. Faure/T. Hartlief (eds.), *Financial Compensation for Victims of Catastrophes* (2005), at Part IV.II.D.

[34] Article L. 125-1 par 3; see the contribution by O. Moréteau/M. Cannarsa/F. Lafay (*supra* fn. 5), no. 19.

[35] O. Moréteau/M. Cannarsa/F. Lafay (*supra* fn. 5), no. 19 and 84.

[36] O. Moréteau/M. Cannarsa/F. Lafay (*supra* fn. 5), no. 19–25.

for terrorist attacks and technological disasters may be subscribed by a more diversified group of victims. If it is less easy to identify the locations where terrorist attacks can take place or technological disasters may happen, the argument that insurers will exclude high risks to avoid adverse selection loses strength. Hence, one should not too easily accept the argument that compulsory insurance is a response to adverse selection impeding the achievement of allocative efficiency in a competitive market. The merits of this reasoning must be decided on a case-by-case basis.

For the purposes of this paper, the logical next question is whether the risk of 38
adverse selection may form the basis of an efficiency defense under art. 81 (3) of the Treaty.[37] It may be argued that devices coping with problems of adverse selection improve production, since they make forms of insurance coverage that would not be offered in a purely competitive market available. So far, European competition law does not offer an easy escape route for agreements in the insurance industry that contribute to efficiency. The restrictive rules of the group exemption have already been discussed above: risks that previously existed but were not insured (floods) or risks whose nature changed significantly (terrorist attacks) are not considered to be "new risks". Competition authorities should realize that the mandatory disaster insurance schemes may create dynamic efficiencies by enabling a better development of an insurance market for catastrophic risks. On the one hand, according to the text of the Group Exemption for the insurance industry, the European Commission is of the opinion that bundling unrelated risks hampers rather than promotes innovation, since it is a disincentive for insurers to offer a separate and specific insurance cover.[38] On the other hand, according to the Guidelines of the European Commission on the interpretation of art. 81 (3) of the EC Treaty, both cost efficiencies and qualitative efficiencies can be advanced.[39] Cost efficiencies include synergies from an integration of assets, economies of scale and economies of scope, and better planning of production. Qualitative efficiencies generate benefits in the form of improved goods and services, which would not have been possible without the restrictive agreement or would have been possible only with substantial delay or at higher cost. It could thus be argued that a sufficient supply of certain insurance products can only be guaranteed if a duty to insure is imposed on low risk individuals and businesses. However, the examples given in the Guidelines are far remote from the argument of adverse selection, which is discussed here. The Commission mentions research and development agreements, license agreements and agreements with specialized distributors. In sum, the achievement of qualitative efficiencies in the form of a sufficient supply of catastrophic risk policies is a powerful argument to justi-

[37] The conditions for an exemption make clear that the goal of competition law is not total welfare. Losses to consumers cannot be made good by gains to producers, since the former must get a fair share of the resulting improvement of production. This does, however, not preclude an efficiency defence, provided that the argument is broadened by an analysis of distributive effects.

[38] Regulation, 10, no. 17.

[39] Communication on the application of art. 81 (3) of the Treaty, OJ C 101, 27.4.2004, 97.

fy a duty to insure, even though it may not be accepted easily by competition authorities.

39 The use of tying clauses may further reduce the chances to obtain an individual exemption. Even if the argument that compulsory disaster coverage schemes are needed to avoid adverse selection is accepted, the question remains why this goal is to be achieved by tying clauses. This raises the issue of the proportionality of the tying clauses, which is discussed below (see Part III.II.C). Here, the basic insights about the possible efficiency benefits of tying are summarized and applied to the compulsory disaster insurance schemes under investigation. It is well known from the Law and Economics literature that tying may have both negative and positive consequences for economic welfare. The foreclosure explanation of tying is challenged by other theories stressing that firms may have several reasonable business rationales for tying. The literature also deplores that the efficiency benefits are not sufficiently taken into account by competition authorities.[40] Hence, the question arises whether the most common efficiency justifications for tying hold in the case of mandatory disaster insurance. Tie-in sales are benign if they generate efficiencies. Many products are naturally and efficiently tied together or bundled. There is no reason for antitrust intervention when consumers desire assembled products.[41] Another reason to engage in tying is quality assurance and the related protection from opportunistic behaviour.[42] Generally, a firm may assure quality by forcing customers to buy another of its products or services and to not use substitutes. For example, a manufacturer of durable goods may decide to operate through a network of exclusive dealerships forcing customers to purchase servicing from the network. Similar efficiency justifications may apply in the case of mandatory disaster coverage. Many individuals, who have voluntarily subscribed property insurance, may be interested in purchasing an extended cover for harm caused by catastrophes from the same insurer. Also the quality of the insurance services (for example, economies of scope in the handling of claims) may increase if a single insurer offers both property damage and disaster damage coverage. Given the arguments supporting an efficiency defense of tying under the first condition of art. 81 (3) of the EC Treaty, it should be further investigated whether also the other conditions for an individual exemption can be satisfied.

B. Benefits to Consumers

40 To qualify for an exemption, it must be shown that consumers receive a fair share of the benefits resulting from the improvement of production. If compulsory insurance is able to cope with the adverse selection problem in insurance markets for catastrophic loss and thus creates qualitative efficiencies, the effects on global consumer welfare must still be investigated. In the Commission's view, the second condition of art. 81 (3) of the EC Treaty incorporates a

[40] R. Van den Bergh/P. Camesasca (*supra* fn. 32), 277–285.
[41] D.W. Carlton/J.M. Perloff, *Modern Industrial Organization* (1999), 303 and 642.
[42] R. Van den Bergh/P. Camesasca (*supra* fn. 32), 280.

sliding scale: "The greater the restriction of competition found under art. 81 (1) the greater must be the efficiencies and the pass-on to consumers".[43] Since the restrictions are indeed quite severe (mandatory coverage through tying and fixed prices), the savings will need to be high and the benefits to consumers large.

The impact of mandatory disaster insurance on consumer welfare is ambiguous: some individuals and businesses will profit but others will be hurt by a mandatory catastrophe extension of their property insurance policies. It is likely that the high risk groups will benefit from compulsory insurance, whereas the low risk groups will be harmed. As explained above, to cope with adverse selection in a competitive insurance market, insurers will selectively offer insurance coverage and exclude risks that do not allow for a sufficient risk spreading. When selection of risks is possible, insurers will not offer contracts to high risk businesses and individuals though they would pay the actuarially fair premium. Consequently, potential insured who can be identified as high risks, such as people living in floodplain areas, suffer a welfare loss. A duty to insure imposed upon low risks will enlarge the risk pool and allow insurers to offer coverage also to high risk groups. However, this solution will reduce the economic welfare of the low risk groups that are forced to buy insurance coverage against their will. The overall effects on consumer welfare will depend on the size of each of the affected groups. The requirement of art. 81 (3) of the EC Treaty that consumers should get a fair share of the benefit will be easily satisfied if the group of consumers who are forced to buy disaster insurance coverage against their will is relatively small. The potential negative effects on consumer welfare of compulsory insurance can be reduced if the duty to obtain coverage is limited to individuals actually exposed to the risk. The new Belgian Act of May 2003 restricts the applicability of the disaster insurance to individuals living in specified risk areas. This regulatory scheme avoids that persons are forced to purchase coverage for which they have no demand. Consequently, it can be more easily demonstrated that consumers get a fair share of the benefits, as required by art. 81 (3) of the EC Treaty. But even when there is a general duty to insure (not limited to specific risk groups) the argument can be made that the gains of victims who receive compensation are (substantially) larger than the losses of individuals who have to pay an additional insurance premium. Under these circumstances, there is a Kaldor-Hicks improvement and the second condition for an individual exemption seems satisfied. 41

C. *The Proportionality Requirement*

The argument that compulsory insurance is needed to avoid adverse selection in private insurance markets is not sufficient to save the compulsory catastrophe extension of first party insurance from the ban of cartel agreements. The reason is that there is no general duty to insure catastrophic risks, but only a 42

[43] Communication (*supra* fn. 39), no. 90.

compulsory extension of voluntarily subscribed property insurance contracts. Therefore, to qualify for an exemption, it must also be shown that tying property insurance and disaster insurance is the most efficient way to implement the duty to insure. By outlawing clauses that "impose comprehensive cover including risks to which a significant number of policyholders are not simultaneously exposed" (art. 6, 1 c), the group exemption is not hospitable to contracts which impose a mandatory catastrophe extension on holders of first party property insurance, who are not exposed to the same risk. Also, the requirement imposed on the policyholder to obtain cover from the same insurer for different risks is excluded from the scope of the group exemption (art. 6, 1 i). Hence, the only way to save the tying clause is by arguing that it is a proportional remedy to the problem of adverse selection and, therefore, merits an individual exemption.

43 An argument in favour of compulsory disaster insurance schemes is that the costs of enforcing the duty to insure would be prohibitively high if no use can be made of tying clauses. For some forms of compulsory (liability) insurance, such as the compulsory fire insurance for publicly accessible buildings in Belgium, the costs of controlling whether owners of buildings have purchased the required coverage may still be reasonable. Conversely, the costs of controlling whether every owner of a house or a car has purchased a separate disaster coverage would be prohibitively high. A compulsory disaster insurance imposed on all holders of property insurance contracts will save on such enforcement costs. A further argument in favour of mandatory disaster insurance of the French type is that the administrative costs of identifying groups of individuals exposed to specific risks are very high. The fact that the Belgian legislation has not yet entered into force shows that there are also substantial (political) costs in identifying the specific risk areas. Therefore, an argument favouring compulsory disaster insurance achieved through a compulsory extension of property insurance contracts is that tying clauses substantially save on the costs of identifying the groups that are specifically exposed to the risk. If these savings in administrative and enforcement costs are higher than the losses caused by the restrictions of competition, a generalized mandatory coverage of catastrophic loss (such as the one existing in France) may be warranted. A compulsory catastrophe extension of first party insurance policies will be efficient from a total welfare perspective if the savings resulting from a reduction in costs of implementation and enforcement exceed the losses of the individuals and businesses that have no demand for disaster coverage. In sum, the argument that tying is the most efficient way to implement a duty to insure catastrophic loss (and thus avoid adverse selection so that the risk becomes insurable) leaves the door for an individual exemption open.

D. A Sufficient Degree of Remaining Competition

44 To obtain an individual exemption, the last requirement to be satisfied is that the restrictions of competition may not allow undertakings to eliminate competition in respect of a substantial part of the products in question. The analy-

sis above has provided arguments to be used in an efficiency defense of a compulsory catastrophe extension of property insurance contracts. This analysis was subject to the caveat that competition authorities will not easily grant an individual exemption to tying clauses. Nevertheless the argument can be made that the risk of adverse selection may justify a duty to insure, that the overall impact of such a measure on consumer welfare may be beneficial and that tying property insurance and disaster insurance is a proportionate remedy to the problem of adverse selection. Even if one accepts that the three first conditions for an individual exemption are satisfied, the requirement that sufficient room should be left for competition causes further problems.

If price competition on the market for the disaster coverage is totally exclud- 45
ed, the fourth condition of art. 81 (3) of the EC Treaty will not be satisfied. Two features of the French model of compulsory disaster coverage cannot be saved by an efficiency defense: fixed premiums and compulsory re-insurance by the state. By fixing the additional premium for the disaster coverage, governments limit competition between insurers and make the competition rules of the EC Treaty ineffective. The effect of this type of state regulation is similar to compulsory membership of a price cartel. Clearly, fixed premiums leave no sufficient room for competition, as required by the fourth condition of art. 81 (3) of the EC Treaty. Also re-insurance by the state seriously distorts the market mechanism: insurance may be provided at a lower price than the market price and wrong signals are given as far as stimulating insurability is concerned. Contrary to the rules of the group exemption, private insurers are also not left free to decide whether they want to use the possibility of state reinsurance or not. Again, the French model of compulsory disaster coverage makes the European competition rules ineffective. As far as the French scheme of mandatory disaster coverage is based on underlying anti-competitive agreements of the insurance industry, the French state seems to have violated its duties under the EC Treaty. Since no efficiency justification can be offered for fixed premiums and mandatory re-insurance through the state, the question arises whether the latter restrictions could profit from a solidarity exception.

III. The Solidarity Exception

The thought experiment carried out in the previous section has led to the con- 46
clusion that the French model of compulsory disaster coverage does not satisfy all criteria for exemption in art. 81 (3) of the EC Treaty. Consequently, France may have infringed the EC Treaty if the scheme of compulsory disaster insurance cannot be considered as the result of sovereign state action, which blocks the applicability of the competition rules, but must be qualified rather as an act guided by cartel-like considerations of the insurance industry. This outcome raises the question whether there is a possibility to escape the applicability of the EC competition rules altogether, so that there is no need to prove that the requirements for an exemption are satisfied. In a number of rulings, the Court of Justice has decided that social health insurance funds, which fulfill an exclusively social function and carry out activities based on the princi-

ple of solidarity, cannot be qualified as "undertakings", so that the art. 81 and 82 of the EC Treaty do not apply.[44] In compulsory social security schemes, the principle of solidarity is implemented in several ways: benefits are identical for all those who receive them, the financial contributions are proportional to income, and both sick and healthy people are obliged to pay contributions. This case law raises the question whether rules aiming at guaranteeing compensation to victims of catastrophes should equally profit from a solidarity exception.

47 For policy makers, not only competition concerns are relevant. In a traditional vision of the welfare state, citizens are entitled to full restoration of damages caused by natural catastrophes as a manifestation of national solidarity. In this view, restrictions of competition may be presented as the price to pay for guaranteeing that victims of catastrophes are appropriately compensated. The main features of the French model of compulsory disaster coverage may all be justified on grounds of national solidarity. First, a general duty to purchase disaster coverage is disadvantageous for victims who do not run any risk. Consequently, in a competitive insurance market, individuals and businesses who are not exposed to the risk of natural catastrophes will not buy coverage. A generalized duty to insure causes a cross subsidization, whereby those who run no risk contribute to the insurance costs of those who may actually benefit. As it is the case with healthy people who are forced to pay the cost of care of sick people, a requirement on citizens living in areas not particularly subject to risks can be equally justified on grounds of national solidarity. By forcing the low risk groups (or even the groups who run no risk at all) to contribute to financing the actual insurance costs of high risk groups, insurance coverage will become available for the entire population. Second, when premiums are fixed in relation to the degree of risk, not everyone exposed to risk will be able to obtain and/or financially afford coverage in a competitive insurance market. A premium fixed by the state, which is the same for all of the insured, again reflects the solidarity principle. Third, the same reasoning applies to mandatory re-insurance organized by the state. From a perspective of national solidarity, it seems perfectly defensible that the state acts as an insurer of last resort. In this way, the state guarantees that citizens in serious difficulties receive financial assistance.

48 Obviously there are differences between solidarity based health insurance schemes and the French model of compulsory disaster coverage discussed in this paper. First, insurance companies providing coverage for catastrophic loss operate on a commercial basis and are, therefore, to be qualified as undertakings for the purposes of competition law. Second, there is no generalized duty to buy coverage for catastrophic risk but only a mandatory extension of voluntarily subscribed first party property insurance policies. By contrast, social

[44] Joined Cases C-159/91 and C-160/91, *Poucet and Pistre* [1993] ECR I-637, §§ 15 and 18; Joined Cases C-264/01, C-306/01, C-354/01 and C-355/01, *AOK Bundesverband and others* [2004] ECR I- not yet reported.

health insurance is based on compulsory affiliation. Third, in compulsory social security schemes benefits are identical for all those who obtain them and there is no equivalence between the financial contributions paid (which are proportionate to income or an average contribution) and the received payments. Conversely, the premium paid for disaster insurance may be linked to the degree of risk in different areas (Belgian law, Italian proposal). In sum, it cannot be concluded that a compulsory catastrophe extension of first party property insurance may escape from the ban of art. 81 and 82 of the EC Treaty. However, the solidarity exception for social security systems invites further thinking on the adaptations that would be necessary to make it possible for compulsory disaster insurance schemes to profit from the same immunity.

Part IV. Conclusions

In European countries, there are three different methods for providing compensation to victims of catastrophes: payments through compensation funds, *ad hoc* solutions decided by governments after a particular catastrophe, and disaster insurance schemes based on a compulsory extension of first party property insurance. Each of these schemes is laid down in legislation. There has been a broad debate on which solution is preferable from a social welfare perspective. Legal economists have criticized both compensation funds and *ad hoc* solutions, because they distort incentives of victims to take preventive measures and impede the development of market solutions. By contrast, insurance solutions have been favoured because they keep incentives for prevention intact and allow for an adequate risk differentiation. However, private market solutions may not work because of lack of demand or restricted supply. In particular, insurers may be unwilling to offer disaster coverage to high risks in order to avoid adverse selection. Making insurance compulsory overcomes the latter problem, but carries with it the disadvantage that a number of individuals who have no demand for disaster insurance are forced to buy such cover. A duty to buy insurance coverage imposed on low risk groups may nevertheless be justified on grounds of national solidarity. 49

This chapter has added an additional layer of complexity to this debate by focusing on the anti-competitive effects of compulsory disaster coverage. The most popular solution is the French model, which takes the form of a compulsory catastrophe extension of voluntarily subscribed first party property insurance contracts. This scheme generates anti-competitive effects that competition law is trying to prevent, in three different ways. First, tying clauses impede competition on the market for disaster insurance, limit consumer choices and may also negatively affect the competition on the market for property insurance. Second, fixed premiums are clearly at odds with the major goal of competition law to protect price competition. Third, compulsory re-insurance is not in conformity with the rules of the group exemption for the insurance industry, which require the possibility for each member of the insurance group to withdraw a risk from the insurance pool. Since the restrictions of competition are laid down in legislation, insurance companies may escape from the prohibitions laid down in art. 81 and 82 of the EC Treaty, provided that they have no 50 possibility to autonomously restrict competition (state compulsion defense). A more delicate question is whether states violate their duties under the EC Treaty when they enact legislative measures, which achieve results that are opposite to the effects European competition law wants to prevent. Ultimately, there may be a trade-off between the goals of competition policy and other ambitions of the welfare state, in particular the right to state assistance in case of catastrophes, which is based on the principle of national solidarity.

51 By offering a re-assessment of the anti-competitive effects and the efficiency gains of compulsory disaster coverage, the paper has been able to downsize the conflict between goals of competition policy and objectives of national solidarity and to limit the inescapable trade-off to its right proportions. If the compulsory catastrophe extension of first party property insurance can be justified both on grounds of allocative efficiency and grounds of national solidarity, the tension between competition policy and the wish to offer compensation to victims of disasters will disappear. The paper has shown that the approach in the group exemption for the insurance industry does not allow taking account of all possible efficiencies resulting from a mandatory coverage of catastrophic loss. Compulsory insurance can be justified as a method to overcome adverse selection and thus achieve allocative efficiency. If the risk cannot be spread in a satisfactory fashion, insurance markets for catastrophic loss will not sufficiently develop. Expanding insurance coverage to high risk businesses and individuals is an improvement both in terms of allocative efficiency and national solidarity. From a consumer welfare point of view, it must also be shown – as required by the second condition of art. 81 (3) of the EC Treaty – that the gains of the high risk groups are sufficiently large to compensate for the losses of the low risk groups. Again, if this condition is satisfied both allocative efficiency goals and national solidarity objectives are achieved. A further requirement is that tying is not a disproportionate remedy to the problem of adverse selection. Here, the argument can be made that tying property insurance and disaster insurance avoids the administrative costs of identifying individuals who are exposed to a particular catastrophic risk and that it substantially lowers the enforcement costs, compared to a general duty to insure catastrophic loss. If the savings in administrative and enforcement costs are larger than the losses of businesses and individuals who have no demand for disaster insurance, allocative efficiency will again be achieved (next to goals of national solidarity). Finally, the rules of competition law require that the restrictions of competition should not give the possibility to undertakings to eliminate competition for a substantial part of the products in question. Consequently, fixed premiums for disaster coverage and mandatory reinsurance organized by the state seem to be the major reasons why the French model of compulsory disaster coverage is not in conformity with principles of competition law. If insurers are left free to fix premiums, competition concerns will disappear but premiums may be too high for some risk groups, who cannot financially afford insurance coverage. Similarly, reinsurance by the state may lead to lower prices and provide a guarantee of last resort to all citizens. Hence, there is an unavoidable trade-off between competition policy goals and objectives of national solidarity. The creation of a

solidarity exception, similar to the one that already applies with respect to social security schemes, is the only remaining possibility to avoid a conflict with principles of competition policy.

This chapter does not attempt to give a definite answer to the question which 52
system for the coverage of catastrophic loss is optimal. Its contribution is more modest. It has been argued that any attempt to answer that question must take account of the anti-competitive effects of the proposed scheme. The inefficiencies resulting from the restrictions of competition weaken the case for adopting the French model of compulsory disaster coverage. Legislative action to provide monetary relief to victims of catastrophes can take several forms that are not plagued by inefficiencies resulting from restrictions of competition. The state may step in and alleviate the private sector entirely of insurance responsibility: compensation funds and *ad hoc* solutions are examples of such an approach. Alternatively, the state may opt for a public-private partnership and encourage the insurers to enlarge their offer by assuming responsibility to cover any residual compensation above an indemnification cap set by state regulation. The question which of these schemes is optimal from a social welfare point of view must be left to further research.

List of References

R. Van den Bergh/P. Camesasca, *European Competition Law and Economics. A Comparative Perspective* (2001), 1–7.

D.W. Carlton/J.M. Perloff, *Modern Industrial Organization* (1999), 303 and 642.

S.J. Chandler, Insurance Regulation, in: B. Bouckaert/G. De Geest (eds.), *Encyclopedia of Law and Economics* (vol. III, 2000), Nr. 5700.

A. Endres/C. Ohl/B. Rundshagen, Land unter! Ein institutionenökonomischer Zwischenruf, [2003] *List Forum für Wirtschafts- und Finanzpolitik* 29, 284–294.

R.A. Epstein, Catastrophic responses to catastrophic risks, [1996] *Journal of Risk and Uncertainty* (J. Risk Uncertainty) 12, 287–308.

H. Kunreuther, Mitigating disaster losses through insurance, [1996] J. Risk Uncertainty 12, 171–187.

H.C. Kunreuther *et al.* (eds.), *Disaster insurance protection: public policy lessons* (1978).

H. Kunreuther/N. Doherty/A. Kleffner, Should society deal with the earthquake problem?, [1992] *Regulation – The Cato Review of Business and Government* 15(2).

H. Kunreuther/P. Freeman, Insurability, environmental risks and the law, in: A. Heyes (ed.), *The Law and Economics of the Environment* (2001), 304–305.

O. Moréteau/M. Cannarsa/F. Lafay, France, in: M. Faure/T. Hartlief (eds.), *Financial Compensation for Victims of Catastrophes* (2005), 92–135.

A. Monti/F. Chiaves, published in this book, no. 9.

G. Priest, The government, the market and the problem of catastrophic loss, [1996] J. Risk Uncertainty 12, 219–237.

R.L. Rabin/S.A. Bratis, United States, in: M. Faure/T. Hartlief (eds.), *Financial Compensation for Victims of Catastrophes* (2005), 346–411.

A. Schwartz/L. Wilde, Intervening in markets on the basis of imperfect information: a legal and economic analysis, [1979] *University of Pennsylvania Law Review* (U. Pa. L. Rev.), 630–682.

R. Zeckhauser, The economics of catastrophes, [1996] J. Risk Uncertainty 12, 113–140

Comparative and Policy Conclusions

Michael Faure

Part I. Introduction

In this chapter we will make an attempt to compare the legal solutions offered for the compensation of victims of catastrophes in the various countries that were discussed in the country reports, being Austria, Belgium, France, Germany, Italy, the Netherlands, Sweden, the United Kingdom and the United States. Of course not every aspect that has been discussed in the country reports can be mentioned within this comparative analysis. Some aspects, such as e.g. differences in tort law, have already been addressed in an elaborate way in other reports drafted by ECTIL. Thus those issues will not be discussed here.[1] The goal of this comparative analysis is therefore rather to address in a problem oriented manner what kind of legal instruments are primarily used in the various countries to provide compensation to victims of catastrophes and what one may learn from these differences. 1

Of course it makes no sense to repeat the analysis of the country reporters within this comparative research. We will therefore largely refer to the country reports when discussing some particular solutions. In order to promote the reader friendliness of this comparative analysis we will refer to the marginal numbers provided for in the various reports. 2

A particular problem for this whole project and thus also for the comparative analysis is that in most of the countries (probably only with the exception of Austria, maybe Germany and Sweden) the financial compensation for victims after catastrophes seems to be in full evolution. For instance in Belgium a new Act was introduced in May 2003 (changing the compensation basically from a fund towards an insurance solution) but until today (September 2005) the Act has not entered into force yet since a debate still takes place concerning the implementing decrees. Moreover, recently a political deal was concluded which will lead to a change of the Act of May 2003 even before it enters into force. 3

[1] See in that respect *inter alia* C. Von Bar, *Gemeineuropäisches Deliktsrecht* (vol. I, 1996).; C. Von Bar, *The common European law of tort* (1999) and W. Van Gerven/J. Lever/P. Larouche, *Cases, materials and texts on national, supranational and international tort law* (2000) and see more particularly the various publications of the European Group on Tort Law (like for instance B.A. Koch/H. Koziol (eds.), *Unification of tort law: strict liability* (2002).

Also in Germany, Italy and the United Kingdom serious debates take place *inter alia* concerning the insurance situation. To some extent we will take into account these recent evolutions in this comparative analysis (in as far as they have been discussed by the country reporters). The reader should, however, be aware of the fact that this is a domain that apparently is in full evolution in many countries, so that further changes in the legal regimes cannot be excluded and may even be quite likely.

4 In this comparative analysis we will address various topics according to a scheme whereby mostly simply the alphabetical order of the countries will be followed (this is also the way in which the country reports have been included in this book). However, for every topic something of interest has not been reported on in every country and in other cases similar solutions in various countries will be discussed in an integrated manner.

5 After this introduction first a very brief insight in the general compensation system for each country will be provided, simply to indicate whether it is mainly e.g. insurance based or relies upon funds or other solutions (Part II). After that brief attention will be paid to the role played by social security systems (Part III), liability rules (Part IV), insurance solutions (Part V) and compensation funds (Part VI). Particular attention will be given to some procedural issues (Part VII), to the question who finances the compensation schemes (Part VIII), the amounts and heads of damages paid under the various systems (Part IX) and the rules concerning the cumulation of compensation from various sources (Part X). Finally attention will be paid to reform efforts in the various countries (Part XI) and a critical economic analysis of some evolutions in the country reports will be provided (Part XII).

6 The various case studies representing the empirical evidence with respect to specific catastrophes will of course not be repeated within this comparative analysis. The findings of these case studies will however be taken into account when discussing various other points. This comparative analysis therefore follows the order of the questionnaire which may increase the comparability.

Part II. General Compensation System

7 There seems to be in general quite a large variety as far as the rules concerning compensation are concerned. Of course almost all legal systems provide basic social security to compensate for personal injury and allow tort claims against those who have caused man-made disasters. In addition private insurance plays a role as well, more particularly in providing compensation for those heads of damage not compensated for by social security. That is for instance the case with respect to property damage caused as a result of flooding. However, with these generalities the similarity seems to stop, since there are of course many differences in the details. This concerns more particularly the question whether, in addition to these general starting points, the particular country has introduced additional specific regimes for the compensation of victims of catastrophes,

either on a structural or on an *ad hoc* basis. Structural solutions can then take the form of either insurance solutions (usually compulsory insurance) or of government financed compensation funds. Again, in these choices the legal systems seems to differ quite a bit.

I. Austria

8 Austria for instance, in addition to the general systems discussed above (tort and social security) created a statute on a fund for catastrophes in 1996. It is the provinces of Austria that will provide compensation according to this so-called *Katastrophenfondsgesetz*, but only for property damage due to natural catastrophes as defined by the statute. The fund, however, only compensates for a limited amount of the damage (on average between 30 and 50% of the property damage suffered) and only when the damage was not covered by insurance. Before 2002 damage caused by natural catastrophes such as flooding was not covered in an average building policy, but since the large flood in 2002 insurers now offer broader cover, also for such catastrophes. The Austrian fund therefore has rather a subsidiary character in the sense that it intervenes when insurance is not (sufficiently) available.

II. Belgium

9 The Belgian system is in a way comparable to the Austrian in that a large number of various solutions exist that victims of catastrophes can use. In addition to tort and social security victims in Belgium will largely use all kinds of first party insurances. Important is that in Belgium the risk of damage caused by storms is mandatorily included in the first party fire insurance. In addition Belgium has, as most other European countries, a large number of compulsory liability insurances. Of particular interest is an Act of 1979 introducing compulsory fire insurance for publicly accessible buildings. This means that e.g. the licensee of a disco has to show insurance to cover his liability towards third party victims.[2] Most important is that Belgium knows, just as Austria, an Act of 1976 concerning the introduction of a fund for catastrophes. There already was an Act of 1939 introducing a fund for mining damage, but particularly the catastrophes fund of 1976 is of importance for victims of natural disasters. With both funds the Belgian state will provide compensation based on the idea of solidarity with the victims.[3]

III. France

10 One of the probably most interesting countries, at least in the European context, is undoubtedly France. The reason is that the compensation system in France is based on the central idea that the French welfare state should protect its citizens in case of a disaster. Citizens hence expect the state to intervene

[2] Belgium, 8. The Belgian respondant, however, notices the fact that in practice only a limited amount will be available for the victims.

[3] Belgium, 10.

and provide assistance. The French population is apparently also willing and prepared to pay additional taxes to finance this state intervention. The basis for this expectation is again the idea of solidarity with the victims.[4] Tort law, according to the French reporters, plays only a minor role for the compensation of victims of catastrophes. In general victims in France can call on a large number of compulsory coverages[5] (additional coverage on voluntary first party insurances), of which the scope was recently enlarged as a result of a legislative change in July 2003.

11 The first party insurances (for natural disasters and technological risks) are basically voluntary. However, if potential victims purchase such an insurance, their damage caused by catastrophes will mandatorily be covered as well.

12 As far as catastrophes are concerned, the French reporters make a clear distinction (which also plays a role in many other countries) between personal injury on the one hand and property damage on the other hand. As far as personal injury is concerned most victims in France (but of course also in most other countries) will use the social security system to obtain coverage for lost income and medical expenses. Since this may not provide full compensation it can be supplemented by tort law. For example for providing coverage for pain and suffering. Moreover, since 2000 French insurers offer a particular first party insurance, referred to as the *garantie des accidents de la vie*. This provides coverage for only € 15 per month for the consequences of any accident, even if this were caused by catastrophes.

13 As far as property damage is concerned potential victims will usually voluntarily take first party insurances, such as a housing insurance. Damage as a result of disasters (and terrorism) is compulsorily covered under these voluntary insurances. If the government *ex post* declares a certain event to be a catastrophe[6] the private insurance companies have to provide cover.

14 In addition France has chosen a fund solution as far as terrorism is concerned and for all systems (disasters and terrorism) reinsurance is provided through the state.

15 France therefore has a rather complex but interesting model which largely relies on insurance, albeit that the coverage has been mandatorily extended to disasters as a result of a state intervention. Since the French model is today discussed in many other countries (like Belgium, Germany, Italy and the Netherlands) as an attractive model, it seems worthwhile to sketch the complicated French compensation mechanism in a scheme:

[4] The solidarity notion is even to be found in the French Constitution of 1958 (see France, 2).
[5] Although most of the time for these compulsory coverages only property damage and not personal injury will be taken into account.
[6] Although a draft has recently been introduced by Senator Claude Biwer (on 12 August 2004) to deprive the Government, in certain circumstances, of this power, more particularly when damage is caused by drought. Then, compensation would take place automatically when the statutory conditions are fulfilled.

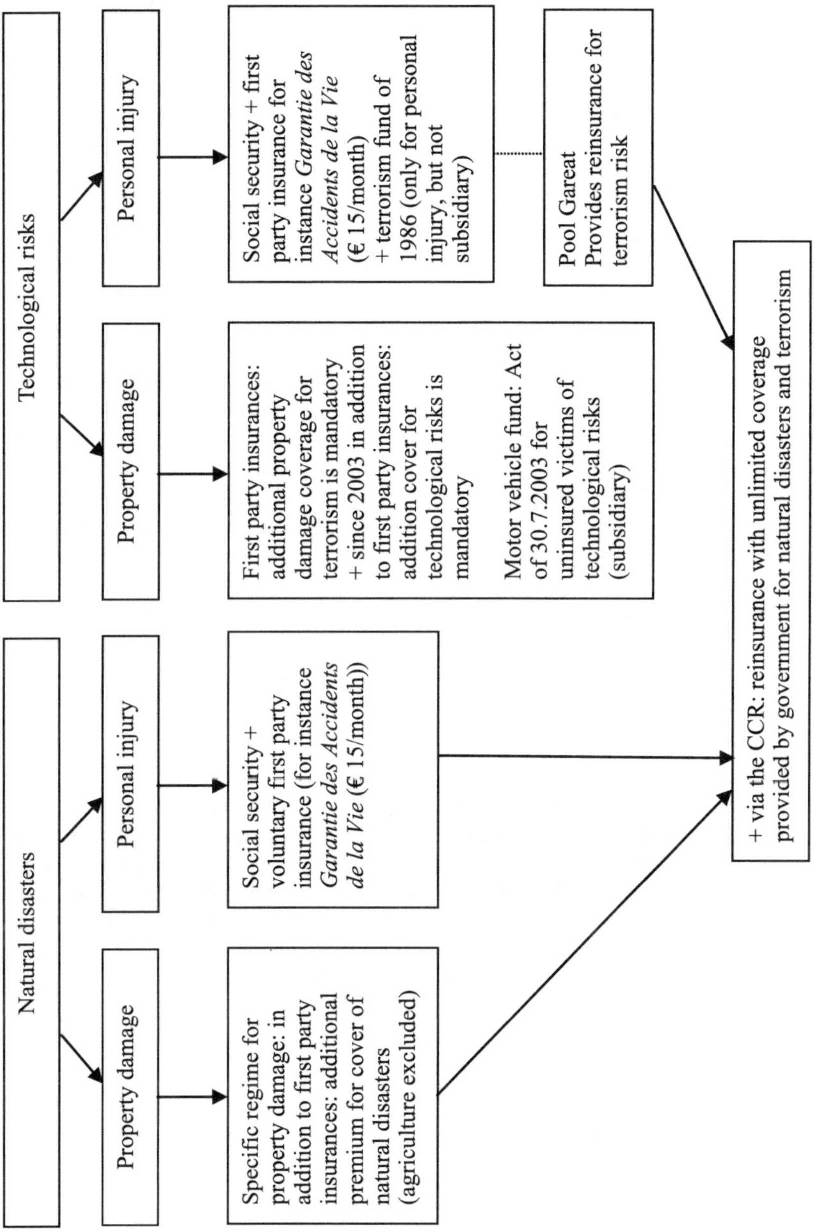
Natural disasters
Technological risks
Property damage
Personal injury
Property damage
Personal injury
Specific regime for property damage: in addition to first party insurances: additional premium for cover of natural disasters (agriculture excluded)
Social security + voluntary first party insurance (for instance Garantie des Accidents de la Vie (€ 15/month))
First party insurances: additional property damage coverage for terrorism is mandatory + since 2003 in addition to first party insurances: addition cover for technological risks is mandatory
Motor vehicle fund: Act of 30.7.2003 for uninsured victims of technological risks (subsidiary)
Social security + first party insurance for instance Garantie des Accidents de la Vie (€ 15/month) + terrorism fund of 1986 (only for personal injury, but not subsidiary)
Pool Gareat Provides reinsurance for terrorism risk
+ via the CCR: reinsurance with unlimited coverage provided by government for natural disasters and terrorism

IV. Germany

16 Germany is (as we will see below, like Sweden) an example of a country where on paper no particular structural arrangement has been made for the victims of catastrophes so that victims in principle have to rely on the "normal" mechanisms like social security, tort law (if available) and insurance. However, although there is no structural solution for victims of catastrophes the German government seems to intervene very generously on an *ad hoc* basis. For instance the Elbe flooding in 2002 (which caused more than 30 deaths and a total damage of € 8.1 billion) led to compensation only in the province of Sachsen of a total amount of more than € 6 billion from a special compensation fund.

17 The German respondent also opened his report with the interesting but painful remark that it may be curious to pay so much attention to the victims of so-called catastrophes, whereas in Germany 18 people are killed on a daily basis in traffic, a result which is apparently not qualified as "catastrophic". Thus the German respondent rightly asks the question why victims of so-called catastrophes would deserve a farther reaching protection than "normal" victims, simply because of the fact that they belong to a larger group of victims.[7]

18 In addition the German model is interesting since after 11 September Extremus Versicherung AG has been erected which provides cover against the terrorism risk up to € 3 billion. When the damage is higher there is a coverage as a result of a state intervention up to € 10 billion.[8]

V. Italy

19 Italy seems to belong largely to the German/Sweden camp where in addition to social security and the law of torts victims cannot structurally call on compensation through a e.g. government fund but where substantial government aid is provided on an *ad hoc* basis. The many disasters (man-made and natural) that Italy has been a victim of[9] led to substantial compensation via private funding, but also through government provided *ad hoc* compensation. In addition insurance can play a role as well, although the Italian respondents make clear that insurance coverage for natural catastrophes is infrequent and mostly only contracted by the industrial sector.[10] It is particularly as a result of the lacking insurance coverage today that many law reform bills have been presented to the Italian parliament, all of which propose (in different forms) the introduction of mandatory insurance cover for the consequences of disasters.[11] With this tendency towards mandatory coverage for (natural) disaster damage Italy seems to follow the French model.

[7] Germany, 1.
[8] Germany, 17.
[9] Italy, 91–115.
[10] Italy, 79.
[11] Italy, 131–144.

VI. The Netherlands

That may be the case for the Netherlands as well. As will be illustrated below the Netherlands had, as a result of a cartel agreement between insurers, no coverage for the consequences of natural disasters like flooding or earthquakes. Insurers considered those risks as uninsurable and thus made a cartel agreement prohibiting insurers from covering those risks. Although this agreement has (not surprisingly) been abandoned as a result of the pressure from the European cartel authorities first party coverage for the consequences of (natural) disasters is still not widely available in the Netherlands today. Since 1998 the Netherlands has an act concerning the compensation for victims of catastrophes, but its scope seems to be relatively limited. The act came into being because of the considered insurability of catastrophes by insurers, but it only applies if the government declares a certain event as a catastrophe. Since its implementation in 1998 this act has only been applied four times. Moreover, the Netherlands has recently suffered from important man-made disasters (a large explosion of a fireworks factory in Enschede, a fire on New Year's Eve in a disco in Volendam and a legionella infection in Bovenkarspel). On none of these important events was the Act of 1998 applied, mostly because the government considered the damage as insurable. However, although compensation was thus not provided through this Act of 1998 (given the strict conditions of application) the Dutch government largely provided additional public funding e.g. in the case of the fire in the disco in Volendam. This therefore leads to the paradoxical situation that the act which was created in 1998 to cover compensation of victims of catastrophes is apparently not adequate to deal with that issue, which is clearly shown by the fact that notwithstanding the existence of this act the government still intervenes to provide additional *ad hoc* compensation. Therefore a commission has been evaluating the functioning of this Act of 1998 and has proposed reforms. Remarkably, one of the alternatives which is examined by the commission that evaluates the act is once more the French model of additional mandatory coverage on voluntary first party insurances. 20

Finally it should be mentioned that in the Netherlands, like in France and Germany, there is a specific regime for the terrorism risk in that the government provides reinsurance through a national reinsurance pool. 21

VII. Sweden

As already mentioned before Sweden largely follows the German (and probably Italian) model, since no structural solutions exist for the victims of catastrophes, with the exception of *ad hoc* solutions. It is remarkable that the Swedish respondents therefore largely refer both to the need for victims to call on social security, but also on tort law to obtain compensation. In addition the respondents notice that the social security system is often supplemented with collective and private first party insurances, which often make a call on tort law unnecessary. In addition, for instance at the occasion of a large fire in a discotheque in Gothenburg additional *ad hoc* compensation was provided through public means.[12] 22

[12] Sweden, 1.

VIII. United Kingdom

23 The United Kingdom is definitely a highly interesting country within the context of this project since the starting point seems to be totally different from the French. The notion of solidarity also plays a role in the UK model, but only to cope with cases of individual hardship. The UK model seems to rely much more strongly on individual responsibilities, with the clear consequence that there is a strong tradition of the British state to distance itself from compensation payments.[13]

24 Perhaps as a consequence of this starting point of non-intervention insurance coverage to cope with the consequences of catastrophes seems to be largely available. The British system is therefore primarily based upon individual insurance agreements, both for property damage as well as for damage to life and personal injuries.[14] However, there seems to be an interesting cooperation between British insurers and the Government whereby the Government has acted in order to facilitate the provision of private insurance cover. This is based on a remarkable Gentlemen's Agreement whereby the insurance industry gave the guarantee to Government that for residential properties it would not refuse to offer flood insurance for any residential property no matter what the risk is. Flood insurability was therefore as a result of this agreement more or less unconditional. However, recently this seems to be changing in the sense that insurance cover now can be made conditional (and thus premium differentiation can be applied). Moreover, the idea has now been introduced that (more particularly for the increasing number of bad risk properties) the state would have to act as insurer of last resort.[15] As a result of these evolutions the UK model for the compensation of damage caused by flooding is still largely based on insurance, although there is a clear tendency towards a division of responsibility whereby the state also assumes part of the (residual) risk. The latter model, of the state taking responsibility as well, is even more clear in the case of the terrorism risk: as a result of the IRA-terrorism the state already took early action to act as an insurer of last resort (called Pool Re).[16]

IX. United States

25 The probably most interesting but at the same time complex model from a European perspective is undoubtedly the case of the US. The complexity has to do with the fact that for many of the specific risks (flooding, earthquakes, terrorism) different specific regimes have been worked out whereby, moreover, some of these specific regimes providing additional relief for victims of catastrophes have been developed at federal level, whereas others have come into being at state level. Moreover, today the US model seems (especially as a result of the reactions after 9/11) to represent a patchwork of different models,

[13] UK, 1.
[14] UK, 8.
[15] UK, 52–53.
[16] UK, 1.

using both tort, social security (to a limited extent), insurance and in some cases compensation funds.

Not surprisingly social security plays (at least compared to the European countries) a rather modest role in compensating victims of catastrophes. The basic social security schemes in fact only provide relief for the elderly and disabled for medical expenses and – under restrictive conditions – some basic needs. Tort law may, as is illustrated by the first case discussed in the US report, potentially play a large role, but this role is of course limited to the so-called man-made or technological disasters.[17] The most important federal initiative with respect to disasters is the Federal Disaster Relief Act of 1950 which created a mechanism for federal emergency relief.[18] If specific conditions apply, federal relief can supplement state and local resources if a presidential declaration of major disaster has been given and the state governor has requested specific federal assistance. In that case disaster relief can be provided through the competent Federal Emergency Management Agency (FEMA) both for immediate needs and for emergency support.[19] 26

As far as insurance for catastrophic losses is concerned interesting examples of state intervention can be found in those cases where there is reluctance on the part of private insurers to continue coverage of particular risks. Although there is no compulsory coverage (like in the French model) several examples are provided in the US report of cases where the federal government (in case of the Terrorism Risk Insurance Act of 2002) or the state (in case of the California Earthquake Authority) intervene in order to facilitate the provision of insurance by private insurers. Interestingly, in the terrorism case the federal government assumes a percentage of the insurers' losses that result from the particular risk; in the case of the California Earthquake Authority the state even assumed the entire risk. Although the victims still take voluntary insurance policies with the participating insurers the (federal or state) government has in fact relieved the private insurers of the uncertainty and potentially catastrophic losses associated with particular catastrophic risks.[20] 27

Yet another model is represented by the National Flood Insurance Programme (NFIP) which is administered by the already mentioned FEMA. In that case the federal government assumes the role of primary insurer. In that particular case the private insurers still administer the insurance, but the flood insurance coverage is provided through federal government. Hence, this NFIP-programme completely alleviates the private sector of insurance responsibility since they only administer the programme, but bear no financial risk at all.[21] 28

[17] See US, 1–4.
[18] See US, 16–21.
[19] US, 18.
[20] See US, 29–32.
[21] Thus the US reporters mention that this model is not comparable to a model whereby the state or federal government would only act as reinsurer, since in that particular case the primary commercial insurers would still run risks, whereas this is not the case under the national flood insurance programme, whereby the federal government assumes the role of primary insurer (US, 33–34).

29 Finally it should be mentioned that in some cases fund-like solutions apply. This is for instance the case for damage caused by hurricanes whereby the Florida Hurricane Catastrophe Fund as created in 1993 by the Florida legislator applies[22] and for the September 11 Victim Compensation Fund[23] which was meant to create baseline assurance that victims of physical injury and their survivors would receive benefits.

30 Finally it should be mentioned that, other than is the case in some European countries, in the US there are apparently no exclusions in standard insurance policies (e.g. those held by home-owners) that would apply to catastrophic losses. Only as a result of the threats by private insurers about the difficult-to-insure nature of some natural disasters the federal and state governments have intervened. But this proactive role of government in the US has only led to stimulating insurability by private insurers, although in some cases (like the one of the California Earthquake Authority) the government has actually taken over the role of primary risk bearer.[24]

X. Summary

31 In sum one can notice that we did indeed find a large variety of the different compensation models that were already sketched in the introduction. Although it is of course difficult to generalise, one can notice that some European systems largely rely on structural compensation funds, although they seem to be in the minority. This is indeed the case in Austria and in Belgium. However, one should stress that these compensation funds have a limited role in the sense that the Belgian fund for natural disasters was, in May 2003, reformed towards an insurance model and the Austrian fund only covers a limited part of the damage. Other systems do rely on state intervention as well, albeit not on a structural basis. Examples of those were Germany, Sweden, the Netherlands and Italy. In those countries compensation is usually provided by government on an *ad hoc* basis, although there is a tendency towards reform. The latter is more particularly the case in the Netherlands and in Italy, where insurance solutions are discussed. These are indeed best represented in the French model where compensation is largely provided through private insurance, but where the cover for natural catastrophes is mandatorily provided in addition to voluntary insurance policies. Strikingly France therefore has no compensation fund for natural disasters since the damage is covered through insurance. However, additional coverage is provided through the reinsurance via the state (through the CCR).

32 Yet a fourth model can indeed be found in the UK and in some US examples. It still relies largely on voluntary private insurance, but there is active state intervention to facilitate this private insurance. In the UK example this consists of the Gentlemen's Agreement whereby insurers promised to provide cover-

[22] US, 51–52, although this is in fact a reinsurance fund.
[23] US, 39.
[24] US, 61–62.

age for flooding. In some US examples it consists of (federal or state) government intervention to act as insurer of last resort or even as primary risk bearer. Remarkably the UK seems to present an example of a model where as a starting point there is no government intervention for the consequences of catastrophes, but where at the same time the insurance market (more particularly for the case of flooding) seems to be well developed.

Let us now address some of the particular compensation mechanisms in some countries in somewhat more detail, whereby of course social security and tort will only be touched upon briefly (Part III and Part IV), but more attention will be given to the insurance and fund solutions (Part V and Part VI). 33

Part III. Social Security

Many of the countries that were examined have an elaborate system of social security. It is of course not useful within the framework of this project addressing the financial compensation of victims after catastrophes to address these systems in detail since the differences (more particularly between the European systems) do not seem to be that large. Moreover, there are many comparative studies available in which the social security systems have been compared.[25] 34

For instance the Austrian reporters hold that 97.6% of all Austrians are covered by social security[26] and those numbers may well be similar for other countries as well. *Austria*, like other systems provides both benefits in kind (such as medical treatment and hospital care) as well as specific financial awards, for instance in case of the inability to work as a result of an illness. Usually for work-related accidents and specific occupational diseases there is a more generous social accident insurance system.[27] Notably, social security benefits are of course paid out irrespective of the cause of the illness or accidents and can therefore often provide primary relief, also to victims of catastrophes. 35

Belgium has an elaborate system of social security as well[28] and also has an interesting mandatory insurance of employers to the benefit of employees for work-related accidents. In the absence of insurance an employer will automatically join the fund for work-related accidents. However, the full damage is not compensated, but standardised payments for the material professional losses are provided. The Belgian regulation in case of illness provides on the one hand for compensation for medical expenses and also compensation for lost income (again based on standardised amounts) on the condition that the disability to work is at least 66%.[29] 36

[25] See for instance D. Pieters (ed.), *Introduction into the social security law of the member states of the European Community* (1993) and D. Pieters, *Introduction into the basic principles of social security* (1993).

[26] Austria, 15.

[27] Austria, 17.

[28] Belgium, 12–17.

[29] Belgium, 16.

37 Again *France* has an elaborate system of social security for all citizens and inhabitants of France. It was created in 1945 as a *régime général de la sécurité sociale* and provides general coverage for medical costs for victims who periodically paid contributions to the social security body. In addition there is *couverture maladie universelle*, which provides compensation for the less wealthy victim who does not pay contributions. This means that in France even the "have-nots" are entitled to compensation of medical costs. Of course this social security system can also be used by the victims of catastrophes.[30] For specific medical expenses there is a deductible[31] but one can again obtain insurance on a voluntary basis to cover this as well. For instance the *garantie des accidents de la vie*, discussed above[32] is an example of such a voluntary insurance which provides additional coverage for those issues not covered under social security.

38 As the other reporters mention as well, the *German* reporter indicates that social security can of course provide a certain kind of relief for victims of catastrophes, but never a guarantee of full indemnification.[33] Although more than 90% of all Germans are protected against the consequences of disability, accidents and illness via social security, this system can never provide the full compensation guarantee (as is in principle the case under tort law). Social security will therefore not provide compensation for non-pecuniary losses nor for property damage (except for a minimal exceptional compensation in case of need).

39 The Swedish social security system is managed through the National Social Insurance Board which, as in the other European countries, provides compensation for medical expenses and (to a limited extent) lost income. In principle all those who live in *Sweden* and generate an income are covered through the system.[34] Although the Swedish system is traditionally known for its generosity[35] there are important limitations and exceptions as well. For instance for pharmaceuticals the compensation is in principle limited to an amount of maximum € 200 per year; for additional compensation the victim in Sweden will thus also have to use voluntary first party insurances. The coverage for lost income is in Sweden also limited to 77.6% of the lost income.[36] Other rules apply in case of permanent disability, but again full compensation is of course not the rule. Moreover, the Social Services Act forces the communities in Sweden to guarantee every inhabitant a minimum standard of living. However, this concerns a minimum to provide for basic needs in case of necessity; similar rules apply in other European countries.

[30] France, 12.
[31] Referred to as ticket modérateur.
[32] France, 17.
[33] Germany, 18.
[34] Sweden, 6.
[35] For details see Sweden, 7–12.
[36] Sweden, 8.

Similar principles apply in the – also elaborate – *UK* social security system: treatment through the national health service (which provides *inter alia* hospital care) is given for free and financed through the tax system. Those not willing to rely on the national health service purchase coverage for private healthcare and pay for it through health insurance schemes. The principle of the British social welfare system, explained in detail in the British report[37] is that coverage is extensive, but that the benefits and services are delivered at a low level. Again, the principle in the UK is apparently that, following the characteristics of a liberal market economy, the state wishes to distance itself from very generous compensation payments.[38] 40

Not surprisingly the basic *US* model stands, as is well-known, in a rather sharp contrast with the European models. The US reporters argue that social welfare legislation that would provide recovery for financial harm associated with catastrophic loss is relatively underdeveloped in the US, at least when compared to European social welfare systems.[39] The US report makes clear that the social welfare legislation in the US basically only provides disability payment in response to hardship, unless one has first contributed through a particular compensation scheme.[40] For instance the social security disability insurance programme provides coverage in case of disability on the condition that an individual must have contributed to the social security trust fund and in essence the SSDI benefits are limited to prospective permanent and total disability.[41] Other instruments, aiming at the provision of basic needs e.g. for the aged, blind and disabled individuals seem also to be restricted to the contributors to the programme (wage earners).[42] Healthcare benefits are also relatively limited: medicare is basically only available to individuals who are 65 or older and individuals of any age that suffer from certain disabilities. It is therefore, so the reporters argue, only a limited safety net for injury victims.[43] 41

Summarizing, one can hold that the role of social security in compensating victims of catastrophes is (of course depending upon the scope of the particular programme) on the one hand large, but on the other hand limited as well. It is large in the sense that all victims (especially in Europe) who suffer personal injury losses as a result of catastrophes incur medical expenses and suffer disability to work will primarily rely upon the social security system. Social security in essence does not test the cause of the disability and hence it can serve victims of catastrophes as well as any other victims. In other words: the threshold for compensation under social security is relatively limited.[44] This low threshold 42

[37] UK, 10–12.
[38] UK, 11.
[39] US, 3.
[40] An exception constitutes the situation of those who are employed since they can receive benefits under the workmen's compensation scheme.
[41] US, 7.
[42] As mentioned by the reporters in US, 7.
[43] US, 12.
[44] This is, so it has been argued, one of the major differences with the tort system.

makes the system thus important in practice, but at the same time shows the limits. The price to be paid is, as all the examples showed, limited compensation. Social security will never provide a full compensation, even for the heads of damage it covers. In addition some particular heads of damage may not be covered at all, like non-pecuniary losses and (particularly important in case of e.g. flooding) property damage. Thus, although social security may, as all the respondents indicate, be the primary source of compensation for victims of catastrophes, it will in practice often have to be supplemented with other instruments like private insurance or (where available) tort. Those systems are then often used to recover that part of the damage (or those heads of damage) not covered under social security.

43 Moreover, the mere fact that social security does not address the source of the damage or payment does not mean it is completely indifferent in this respect. Indeed, although the primary beneficiaries will receive compensation irrespective of the source, the fact that e.g. payment needed to be made as a result of an accident may in some systems result in a recovery action of the social security carrier by way of subrogation, e.g. against an injurer in tort.

44 This shows that although social security may be considered the primary compensation system, its scope is limited to personal injury (and even in that respect limited in amount); thus other systems may be called upon to provide additional compensation.

Part IV. Tort

45 Differences between the tort law regimes of legal systems, also those discussed in the framework of this project have already been illuminated in many comparative projects.[45] Therefore we can suffice here with noting a few particularities.

46 Most legal systems, such as the one presented in the report on *Austria*, still have fault as the basic liability rule whereby tortfeasors are held to compensate the damage of the victim if the latter can prove a causal relationship between the act of the tortfeasor and the damage.[46] Specific statutes have introduced strict liability for instance for damage caused by motor vehicles and railways, airplanes and nuclear facilities.[47] Many of these strict liabilities are, moreover, the result of the implementation of international conventions, so that, not surprisingly, there are not that many differences between the legal systems, at least as far as these specific statutory strict liability rules are concerned. The Austrian reporters also indicate that unlimited strict liability seems to be the exception; usually in case of strict liability there are damage caps.[48] Interesting within the perspective of disasters is particularly the possibility of state liability. This is not only theoretically an issue, as after the flood in 2002 lawyers examined the possibilities to

[45] See *inter alia* the various publications of the European Group on Tort Law.
[46] See Austria, 4–5.
[47] Austria, 8.
[48] Austria, 11–12.

hold public legal entities liable for the damage which resulted from this catastrophe.[49]

Also the *Belgian* reporter discusses in detail the traditional conditions of fault liability on the basis of art. 1382 of the Civil Code (the same as in France). She also points in the direction of an increasing number of strict liabilities, but again in some of these statutory strict liabilities a damages cap applies. The Belgian respondent holds that this tendency towards strict liability is based on the phenomenon of mass tort.[50] 47

Remarkably the *French* reporters indicate that in case of a catastrophe in France the victim will usually not be necessitated to use tort law himself, unless in the exceptional case when there would be no insurance coverage available. Tort law in France is therefore only used by the subrogated insurer.[51] A particular feature of French tort law is that there is a traditional difference between tort liability in private law and liability in public law, which applies *inter alia* to liability of public authorities. As far as private law is concerned, French tort law has known a similar development as the earlier mentioned legal systems: basically the system is still fault liability, but there is a strong tendency, both in statute and in case law towards strict liability. As far as case law is concerned the French reporters indicate the large interpretation given by the *Cour de Cassation* to the liability of the guardian of a defective object based on art. 1384, al. 1 of the Civil Code.[52] Liability in public law is based on administrative law. In addition to a liability based on fault there is also an objective duty to compensate based on the *égalité devant les charges publiques*.[53] Again, there is discussion in France on the liability of the government for failure to guarantee safety in public places. Apparently the liability is, however, limited to the case of a *faute lourde* which is, according to the French reporters, difficult to prove.[54] The French reporters hold that the tendency is much more to introduce new compensation mechanisms instead of looking for the possibilities to enlarge liability of public authorities. However, subrogated insurers may seek recovery through state liability.[55] 48

The *German* reporter indicates that the applicability of tort law will seldom be the case with natural disasters. Like in the other countries Germany also notices the introduction of a large number of statutory strict liabilities, for instance in case of a catastrophe with a train.[56] However, the reporter also indicates that in most of these strict liability statutes liability is denied in case of *force majeure*. A terrorist attack would certainly be considered as *force majeure* and would 49

[49] A claim was, however, dismissed. For further details see Austria, 85–86.
[50] Belgium, 19.
[51] France, 30.
[52] For further detail see France, 34.
[53] France, 35.
[54] France, 36.
[55] The French reporters indicate that after a flooding of two fast flowing rivers with 23 casualties as a consequence, the liability of both the state and the local authority was accepted and the call on *force majeure* was denied (France, 37).
[56] Germany, 10.

hence exclude liability. Also in Germany the specific strict liability statutes include financial caps.[57]

50 Liability rules under tort are also discussed in much detail in the *Italian* report.[58] Again a distinction is made between the basic principle based on fault and specific strict liability in case of dangerous activities. The Italian reporters hold that this provision (art. 2050 of the Civil Code) may apply in case of man-made accidental disasters, but is generally excluded in case of natural disasters due to the fact that in that case the damage is often caused by *force majeure*.[59] Also in Italy the liability of public authorities is undisputed and has in specific catastrophic cases indeed played a role.[60]

51 In the *Netherlands* a lot of debate has taken place concerning the role of tort law, more particularly also in relation to catastrophes. The general fault liability of art. 6:162 of the Civil Code may of course play a role in case of man-made disasters, although in that particular case the specifically statutory strict liabilities (incorporated in art. 6:175 and following of the Civil Code) may play a role as well. Still the literature holds that even in the so-called strict liability cases a particular shortcoming on the side of the tortfeasor is required. It is equally stressed in the Dutch report that the possibilities of state liability come easily into the picture, for instance at the occasion of the catastrophes in Volendam and Enschede. Lacking control and supervision by government authorities raises the question in the Netherlands of whether they should be held liable for the damage. However, it was usually held in case law that a lack of adequate supervision could not lead to state liability since there was no formal duty of the government towards the enforcement of laws.

52 *Sweden* knows a specific tort liability act in which the basis is still fault liability. For specific dangering activities a strict liability rule applies. A specifically interesting strict liability case is the one that may apply in case of the breach of a dam. Since Sweden is for its energy largely dependant on hydro energy, chapter 11 of the Environmental Code introduced a specific strict liability for damage caused by a defect in a dam.[61]

53 Although the formal structure of tort law is different in the *UK* liability is again based on fault, most usually negligence. Still there may be important hurdles for the victim to surmount in order to recover damage resulting from a disaster based on tortious liability.[62] The UK reporters indicate that particularly in case of natural disasters (where no other tortfeasor may be sued) public bodies be-

[57] For a critical assessment see Germany, 14.
[58] Italy 10–24.
[59] Italy, 24.
[60] Italy, 16.
[61] The Swedish reporters indicate that in 1973 and 1985 Sweden was confronted with large damage resulting from a breach in a dam (Sweden, 26).
[62] See general UK, 8.

come an attractive target for liability on the basis of a breach of duty.[63] Nevertheless, although in principle there is nothing to prevent the liability of a public body or agency, to date the liability of public bodies has in the UK played a minimal role in compensating catastrophes.[64]

Of course many of the particular features of the *US* tort system are well-known to a European readership. The case discussed in the introduction to the US report also makes clear that in case of a catastrophic fire (like the one discussed in the introduction of the US report) the potential scope of tort law is large and victims may well have incentives to use the tort system now that social welfare legislation in the US is relatively underdeveloped.[65] Moreover, compensation awards in tort are generous and punitive damages may be available as well. The US reporters therefore hold that also in cases of natural disasters victims might look for recovery in tort and this irrespective of whether private and/or public insurance systems are available.[66] 54

Summarizing, this brief overview shows that there is, based on the information in the country reports, quite some scope for the application of tort law to disasters and many of the cases presented as empirical evidence show that tort claims are effectively brought by victims as well. Many reporters indicate that one can well understand why victims would use tort law: it is the system that provides the "luxury" of a full compensation, this in contrast to social security. Of course there may be differences as far as the heads of damage and amounts of compensation are concerned, but most reporters agree that it is the system that provides the most complete compensation to victims of catastrophes. 55

Not surprisingly most reporters argue that tort law will particularly be used in case of so-called man-made disasters, where an identifiable injurer can be found. The legal basis can, as the country reports showed, vary. If the victim cannot prove the fault of the tortfeasor in some cases strict liability rules apply, although there seem to be some differences as far as the scope of the strict liability rules is concerned. 56

There is probably less scope for the applicability of tort law in case of natural disasters. There it is often argued that these are caused by an "act of God". The only liability that comes in the picture in that case is the liability of the government e.g. for not taking adequate preventive measures or for inadequate warnings, e.g. in case of flooding. However, although all reporters point at the possibility of liability of public authorities on paper, they equally indicate that the scope of this type of liability in practice is still rather limited. In some country reports it is even explicitly mentioned that the tendency is rather to seek compensation through public compensation mechanisms rather than examining the possibilities of tort liability of public authorities. 57

[63] UK, 35.
[64] UK, 35.
[65] US, 3.
[66] For further detail US, 4 and the corresponding footnotes.

58 In sum, in case of so-called technological disasters the tort system may well be the primary system of recovery, based on the notion that these are "man-made".[67] For natural disasters, with the exception of the liability of public authorities, tort may play a less important role. For those cases other systems (first party insurance or public compensation fund) will thus have to provide relief to victims. But even in case of technological disasters, where an injurer can be identified, the mere possibility of a tort suit will of course not guarantee compensation to the victim, given the insolvency problem.[68] Thus one can understand that, within the context of insurance, many legal systems have introduced specific duties to seek financial coverage as well.

Part V. Insurance

I. General

59 As all of the country reporters indicate, various types of insurance may play a role in the coverage of the consequences of catastrophes. Potential injurers may seek to cover their potential liability through third party liability insurances, potential victims of disasters may seek coverage through first party insurances. These can take the form of either generalized accident insurance coverage (in case of personal injury) or they can cover specific property damage. In most European legal systems the general accident insurance coverage would provide specific compensation for costs that the victim would incur as a result of an accident. Depending upon the policy this can be for lost income, coverage of (additional) medical expenses and in some cases even for pain and suffering. These insurance policies, which focus on personal injury compensation, usually provide compensation in addition to the social security payments and of course more particularly for the damage not covered under the social security schemes.

60 Usually these policies do not make a distinction as to whether the source of the accident is a catastrophe or not. Hence, assuming that these policies are available, well-informed potential victims can purchase coverage according to their own demand for insurance, of course in the hypothesis that competitive insurance markets offer those policies. Apparently, as the country reports indicate, more difficulties arise as far as the coverage for property damage is concerned. Many of these policies contained, at least in some countries, exclusions for property damage caused as a result of natural disaster. In some cases insurers argue outright that the consequences of disasters like flooding or earthquakes cannot be covered. In other cases there seems to be either a lacking demand or a lacking supply of coverage as a result of which cover for the consequences of natural disasters (more particularly for property damage) is not occurring. In some countries this has led to specific legislative action by

[67] Even though, like in the French AZF case, often a tort case should not even be brought since cases are often settled.

[68] Even though some victims may be so "lucky" to find a solvent injurer (again like in the French AZF case).

the government in order to stimulate the availability of insurance. In some cases this goes as far as imposing mandatory coverage for the consequences of disasters; in other cases the government takes specific steps to cope with the difficult-to-insure nature of disasters, either by acting as primary insurer or by assisting in the provision of reinsurance.

II. Austria

The Austrian case already illustrates the main difficulties for victims in obtaining coverage for the consequences of a natural disaster like flooding. The report shows that a standard Austrian housing insurance policy would not have covered damage caused by flooding. Only since 1997 would flooding coverage at an additional premium have been made available. However, the reporters argue that serious caps apply on coverage (to € 7,500) and that not all harm caused by water is compensated. Moreover, after the flood of 2002 those living in risky areas would no longer be able to receive insurance coverage.[69] Also after the Galtür avalanche of 1999 it appeared that the traditional building insurance only covered a very small amount of the damage.[70] 61

III. France

France knows an elaborate system of first party insurances for property damage.[71] 85% of all inhabitants of France have such a first party insurance[72] and therewith also a right of compensation of property damage within the scope of the insurance policy. A typical example of such a policy is the so-called *multirisque habitation*, covering most risks with respect to real estate and the movables within a house. 62

Typical for the French system is that in addition to the voluntary first party insurance there is a mandatory additional cover for the consequences of natural disasters. The "Code des Assurances" offers a definition of what is considered as a natural disaster. Remarkably it is argued that it should concern an accident with damage that is normally not insurable, unusual and unavoidable.[73] The reason for the mandatory additional coverage is precisely the fact that this damage would normally be uninsurable.[74] Insurers are only held to compensate damage if the government declares a certain incident as a natural disaster. Agricultural damage is excluded. 63

[69] Austria, 77 and footnote 107.
[70] Austria, 57.
[71] At this instance we prefer to discuss the French case first, since the new Belgian model relies heavily on the French case.
[72] This can be deduced from the AZF case, where it was noticed that (only) 15% of the victims were uninsured.
[73] France, 19.
[74] France, 19 in fine.

64 The fire insurance in France equally covers damage as a result of storms, cyclones and tornados. Also here it concerns a mandatory additional coverage on a voluntary insurance policy.

65 In addition to these specific regimes for natural disasters France also has a regime for the man-made disaster, also referred to as technological risks. On the one hand there is in addition to certain voluntary first party policies an additional mandatory coverage for property damage caused as a result of terrorism; in addition victims can largely use their individual accident insurances, car insurance or the *garantie des accidents de la vie*. Uninsured victims can under strict conditions call on a fund for uninsured victims. In addition a new Act of 30 July 2003 has, at the occasion of the catastrophe in Toulouse on 21 September 2001 extended the mandatory coverage on voluntary policies by applying these as well to the case of technological accidents. Moreover, for the uninsured victims of those "technological disasters" since 2003, the motor vehicle fund can be used. The legislative change in 2003 thus has as a consequence that when damage emerges that, according to the definition in the "Code des Assurances" is considered a "technological disaster" additional coverage on the first party insurance is due. Again, the compensation by the insurer is only due if the government first declares the event as a catastrophe. This mandatory extension of voluntary insurance policies applies, however, only to property damage.[75] Victims of personal injury still have to call on social security, eventually supplemented with a first party insurance like the *garantie des accidents de la vie*.

IV. Belgium

66 It was already indicated that Belgium has a system comparable to France in the sense that in some cases there is compulsory coverage in addition to certain voluntary insurances. For instance damage caused by storm is mandatorily covered with the "voluntary" fire insurance. Moreover, the Belgian legislator on 21 May 2003 changed the act on natural disasters of 1976 in order to limit the role of the fund for natural disasters. The new regime should, according to the French model, provide a mandatory coverage for damage caused by flooding in the (voluntary) fire insurance.[76] However, a major difference with the French system is that the Belgian regime would only apply for persons within a certain risk area. The Belgian reporter indicates that the goal of this system is prevention: building in risk zones should thus be prevented. This new flooding insurance has, however, not entered into force yet. This will only be the case when the regions indicate the risk zones. Recent evolutions have shown that the indication of the risk zones has led to political difficulties as a consequence of which this new Belgian regime had in 2004 not entered into force yet and will very probably even be modified before its entry into force.

[75] France, 26.
[76] Belgium, 27.

V. Germany

According to the German reporter, private first party insurances could in practice be quite important in the compensation of catastrophic losses. Again the reporter stresses that (as one can notice in other countries as well) most first party insurances aiming at the compensation of personal injury (like accident or life insurances) do not have an exclusion for damage caused by disasters. Property insurances, however, often exclude catastrophic damage from coverage. Although (depending upon the provisions in the policy) coverage is thus available, the German reporter equally made clear that, e.g. at the occasion of the Elbe flooding in 2002, the number of insured persons was relatively limited. Hence, potential German victims do not always use the possibilities available on the market. 67

In addition Germany reacted to September 11 by introducing Extremus Versicherungs AG for the terrorism risk: it covers property damage and economic losses in case the damage is higher than € 25 million. In that case Extremus can cover up to an amount of € 3 billion; above that amount there is a state intervention up to € 10 billion.[77] 68

VI. Italy

In Italy authors have claimed that insurance is not an adequate instrument to deal with catastrophic losses.[78] The Italian reporters also hold that the generous *ad hoc* compensation by the Italian state is one of the reasons why private insurance covering natural disasters has never been fully developed in Italy.[79] Insurance coverage for the consequences of natural catastrophes would be fairly infrequent in Italy and mostly be limited to the industrial sector.[80] However, for the particular environmental pollution risks specific initiatives have been developed. For instance an environmental pool, Pool RC *Inquinamento* was established in 1979[81] and more particularly in the context of environmental insurance the Italian reporters stress the contribution of insurance to prevention and risk reduction.[82] As was mentioned in the introduction, there are, however, serious attempts in Italy to come to a mandatory insurance coverage for disasters, partially following the French model, but these initiatives have not led to concrete changes yet.[83] 69

VII. The Netherlands

As far as the Netherlands is concerned we already indicated that in the 1950s the Dutch insurers' association issued a so-called "binding decision" on all of 70

[77] Germany, 17.
[78] Italy, 52.
[79] Italy, 74.
[80] Italy, 79.
[81] Italy, 82.
[82] Italy, 85.
[83] Italy, 131–144.

its members, prohibiting them from insuring flood and earthquake risks (the latter being relatively small in the Netherlands with the exception of the area around Southern Limburg). Their argument was that these risks were technically not insurable and that therefore its members should all refrain from covering them. The arguments concerning the uninsurability seem highly doubtful, but they also clearly violate competition law. At the time a European Commission Regulation 3932/92 of 21 December 1992 exempted many cartel agreements in the insurance world from the prohibition under the old art. 85(3) of the EEC Treaty, provided that certain strict conditions were met.[84] This exemption was heavily criticised by law and economics scholars, who argued that competition policy should be fully applied to insurance markets as well.[85]

71 The binding decisions not to insure flood and earthquake risks not only clearly limits supply (it effectively excludes it as a result of a cartel agreement), but it also violates the conditions of Regulation 3932/92. Consideration 8 preceding the exemption states that standard policy conditions may in particular not contain any systematic exclusion of specific types of risk without providing for the express possibility of including that cover by agreement. This is repeated in art. 7(1)(a) of the exemption. The European Commission also issued a report to the European Parliament and to the Council on 12 May 1999 on the functioning of the exemption regulation number 3932/62.[86] In this report the Commission explicitly discusses these so-called binding decisions. The report states that, as a result of the questions asked by the Commission, the Dutch Association of Insurers decided to bring its binding decision into line with art. 7.1 sub-§ a by simply converting it into a non-binding recommendation, leaving each insurer free to extend cover to flood risks.[87] This Dutch example shows that a lacking supply of insurance coverage may well be the result of anti-competitive behaviour by insurers, who mutually agree not to cover particular catastrophic risks.[88] After the cartel agreement collapsed (as a result of European pressure) a debate emerged on the structure of flood insurance. Dutch insurers argued that disaster insurance entails a great risk of adverse selection, meaning that only bad risks will purchase insurance coverage. In order to make the risk insurable, so it was held, also good risks should be covered. This could only be reached if disaster insurance (in casu for flooding) were made compulsory. If good risks were also forced to purchase insurance coverage adverse selection could be avoided.

[84] *Official Journal* (OJ), L 398/7 of 31 December 1992. For a comment on this exemption regulation see Levie and Cousy (1994).

[85] M. Faure/R. van den Bergh, Restrictions of competition on insurance markets and the applicability of EC anti-trust law, [1995] *Kyklos*, 48, 65–85.

[86] COM(1999), 192 final.

[87] M. Faure/T. Hartlief, *Insurance and expanding systemic risks* (2003), 222–225.

[88] Now this issue is dealt with by Commission regulation no. 358/2003 of 27 February 2003 on the application of art. 81(3) of the treaty to certain categories of agreements, decisions and concerted practices in the insurance sector, OJ, L 53/8 of 28 February 2003.

As a result of these discussions a proposal was introduced to force every person who has a household insurance to mandatorily also purchase coverage against flooding.[89] The Dutch Council of State formulated serious criticism of this proposal, as a result of which the whole bill was withdrawn. Interestingly enough the Council of State *inter alia* argued that it would also be wrong to let people who run no risk at all pay for the additional coverage. 72

VIII. Sweden

Sweden provides relatively few specific features as far as insurance coverage for disasters is concerned. The Swedish reporters stress again that most damage caused by catastrophes will in Sweden be covered through the social security system. Only the part not covered through social security will be dealt with by private insurance. Strikingly the Swedish reporters indicate that first party insurances for personal injury do not only cover income losses, but also non-pecuniary losses.[90] Also for property damage a victim in Sweden will usually call on his own first party insurance.[91] However, specific insurance solutions (like in France) for catastrophes are not known in Sweden. Whether the specific damage is therefore covered will be dependant upon the scope of the insurance policy. 73

IX. United Kingdom

As already indicated in the introduction in the United Kingdom the basic system for compensating natural hazards relies on the assumption that property owners purchase private insurance cover. Although there is no formal compulsory insurance the British reporters point at the fact that insurance coverage against flooding will often be required by banks granting a mortgage as a result of which the system has become de facto compulsory.[92] Private insurance therefore nearly covers all damage and – remarkably – insurers concluded a Gentlemen's Agreement with the state in which they guaranteed to the government that they would not refuse to offer flood insurance for any residential property, no matter what the risk is.[93] However, insurers could decline coverage in exceptional cases. The reason for this Gentlemen's Agreement was apparently industry's fear of a formal regulation. However, the UK reporters criticized the system for providing too few incentives for risk reduction. On the one hand the state would have no incentive for appropriate flood protection, knowing that the consequences of flooding are covered and house owners would lack incentives as well as flood insurance is automatically included at no extra premiums.[94] Not surprisingly the system has therefore recently been under attack. Recently there would appear to be a trend towards more differentiated premiums and thus more accurate pricing.[95] As a result of recent changes the state 74

[89] This was based on the French example of the coverage against natural disasters.
[90] Sweden, 13.
[91] Sweden, 16.
[92] UK, 19.
[93] UK, 22.
[94] UK, 23.
[95] UK, 47.

now has to act as an insurer of last resort, since flood insurance is no longer unconditional.[96]

X. United States

75 As we already indicated in the introduction to this comparative analysis, the US report points at various innovative insurance solutions which are based on an interesting private-public partnership, based on the notion that without specific government intervention (to facilitate insurance) private insurance may not be sufficiently available. The US reaction seems – generalizing – different to e.g. the French regulatory solution to introduce mandatory insurance. Insurances remain largely voluntary, but government intervention aims at increasing the availability of insurance. Several schemes, already discussed in the introduction, illustrate the functioning of this model. Apparently various types of private insurances play an important role in case of catastrophic events. For property damage it would more particularly be the home owners insurance and commercial casualty insurances that would be triggered.[97] Although most of these policies are so-called "all risk" policies, some specific risks, such as floods, earthquakes and terrorism receive specific treatment. For instance for the case of terrorism as a result of the Terrorism Insurance Act of 2002 (TRIA) the federal government assumes the role of excess liability insurer. All commercial insurers are required to participate in the programme and insurers must provide coverage for insured losses also resulting from acts of terrorism.[98] In return for this the federal government assumes a percentage of the insurers' losses. Thus the victim brings a claim to his private insurer and it is this insurer that will provide coverage. A part of the damage (above a certain threshold) is then reimbursed by the federal government to the insurer.

76 A similarly interesting private-public partnership can be found in the model of the California Earthquake Authority (CEA). In that particular case the government intervention even goes further since it is the authority itself (CEA) which assumes primary risk bearing responsibility for the earthquake risk. The private insurer thus plays an exclusively administrative role and the risk is taken over by the CEA. As a consequence in this model the state has relieved private insurers of the uncertainty of major earthquakes, but still uses insurers to administer the system.

77 A similar model has been developed within the National Flood Insurance Programme (NFIP) administered by FEMA. In that case it is the federal government that assumes the role of primary insurer and thus the American reporters consider this a variant of the California Earthquake Authority.[99] Note again that both earthquake insurance and flooding insurance is voluntary. The state intervention thus only aims at alleviating the private sector entirely of insur-

[96] UK, 53.
[97] US, 26.
[98] US, 29–30.
[99] US, 33.

ance responsibility. The NFIP is, moreover, not a traditional reinsurance scheme since under reinsurance private insurers would still run a risk, which is not the case under NFIP. The role of insurers in that case is limited to administrating the system. Thus the American reporters indicate that the government has become a major player in the web of insurance coverage.[100] The argument in favour of this government intervention is that without intervention it might have been impossible for individuals to obtain insurance coverage; others argue that the flipside of this government intervention is that it distorts the normal functioning of the insurance market. The main argument in favour is that the government only temporarily intervenes to fill a gap that was created in private insurance coverage. Since in these particular cases governments do not provide coverage themselves but through the insurance companies a market is still created in which private insurers are able to compete.[101]

XI. Summary

One can notice various reactions of governments to increase insurability of the disaster risk, the main argument probably being that there is either a too low demand (like in the case of Germany) for e.g. flooding insurance or insufficient supply (like in the case of the Netherlands where lacking supply was caused by a cartel agreement not to provide coverage). Interestingly, the European legal system where the availability of (flooding) insurance does not seem to be problematic is exactly the country where as a matter of principle the government does not provide public funding in case of catastrophes, being the United Kingdom. It is more particularly the Italian reporters who argued that the lacking availability of insurance coverage for disasters in a country like Italy might precisely be due to the (too) generous *ad hoc* coverage by the government. 78

The model that is apparently followed in Europe to promote coverage is to introduce compulsory coverage. In this respect it is remarkable that the model where this was first introduced, being France, was precisely defended with the argument that disaster coverage needed to be made compulsory since otherwise it would be uninsurable. France, however, does not have a generalized duty to insure, but a compulsory complementary coverage on (voluntary) property damage contracts. All individuals who purchase such a policy have to pay for the additional coverage for natural disasters. The system is apparently accepted in France because the risk of cross subsidization may be small: France seems to be confronted with many types of natural disasters. Thus, if one is presumably (as inhabitant of an apartment on the 20th floor) not exposed to the risk of flooding, one may be exposed to other natural disasters, such as earthquakes or the risks caused by heavy storms.[102] The Belgian sys- 79

[100] US, 35 in fine.
[101] US, 36 in fine.
[102] Similar point is made by Schwarze and Wagner that, if previously distinct risks are sold (like flood, wind, storms and hale) individual exposure to some risk would almost be guaranteed (R. Schwarze/G. Wagner, In the aftermath of Dresden. New directions in German flood insurance, [2004] *Geneva Papers on Risk and Insurance Issues and Practice* (G.P.R.I.I.P.) 29(2), 154–168).

tem looked interesting in that respect since the mandatory supplementary coverage would only apply for specific risk areas. Thus the risks of cross subsidization could be limited since those who are not exposed to the risk are not forced to take out coverage.[103] In Italy and Germany legislative initiatives are proposed, equally aiming at some form of mandatory coverage against damage caused by disasters.

80 Note, moreover, that in France as a result of the explosion in Toulouse on 21 September 2001 a legislative change was effectuated in July 2003 as a result of which victims now also have additional compulsory coverage for damage caused by technological risks (such as the explosion in Toulouse). That latter solution is, however, debated (also in France). It is not so clear why in this case of technological disasters, where a liable wrongdoer can be identified a mandatory coverage for victims was introduced[104] rather than examining the introduction of solvency guarantees on the side of the wrongdoer, such as compulsory liability insurance.

81 In sum, there seems a clear tendency in many European legal systems towards some form of compulsory coverage of the consequences of disasters on a first party basis. This tendency could on the one hand be criticized from an economic perspective since it is not sure that there is in all cases an effective demand for such a coverage. However, this problem can at least be reduced (see the example of the legislative change in Belgium in May 2003) if the duty to obtain coverage is limited to those individuals actually exposed to the risk.[105] This enables on the one hand an adequate risk differentiation and avoids that persons are forced to purchase coverage for which they would have no demand. It can also avoid a negative redistribution. It may only in some cases be costly to identify what groups are especially exposed to the risk and to whom the mandatory coverage should thus apply. If the administrative costs of this differentiation are higher than the benefits, a generalized mandatory coverage (like in France) may be warranted.

82 However, the discussion of the American example made clear that there may well be an alternative model to the solutions chosen in Europe so far whereby the disadvantages of mandatory coverage may be reduced, being to have a government intervention to stimulate the availability of insurance in case commercial insurers would not provide sufficient coverage. The American and European approaches seem to differ in the sense that the Europeans apparently fear a lack of demand (probably as a result of a presumed lack of information of consumers) and thus react with the (paternalistic) measure of compulsory coverage, whereas the Americans recognize that the problem with disaster

[103] Unfortunately very recently (in November 2004) an agreement was concluded between the insurers and the Belgian Government, linking the flood coverage mandatorily to the fire insurance. As a result, the Act will probably be changed to eliminate the division in the risk zones.

[104] Again it concerns a mandatory supplementary coverage for damage caused by technological disasters on voluntary insurance contracts.

[105] But again it became clear recently that this idea will probably never be realised in Belgium.

coverage is more a lacking supply (as a result of fears by insurers concerning the uncertainties with e.g. earthquake risks). Thus the American regulatory solution aims at improving supply rather than at regulating demand through mandatory coverage.

Part VI. Compensation Funds

The comparison of the various insurance solutions made clear that in many countries (with the notable exception of the UK) some form of regulatory intervention takes place to stimulate insurability of damage caused by disasters. In some cases (like in the US) this can go as far as the government acting as primary insurer. An alternative may be to provide this regulatory support through a public compensation fund. The assumption would then probably be that regulatory solutions cannot fully correct the failure in insurance markets or insurances may not be able to provide sufficient coverage. One can indeed notice some role for compensation funds with respect to catastrophic losses, although their role seems to be (increasingly) limited. The general trend now seems to be that where insurance solutions can be worked out they seem to be preferred. Hence, it seems interesting to analyze for what particular kind of damage and situations the countries have introduced fund solutions. They are mainly presented as alternatives for the liability and insurance system. 83

Austria has a statute on a fund for catastrophes of 1996,[106] but it is the provinces which are in charge of making the actual payments to the citizens. The fund is financed from income and corporate taxes and only covers part of the property damage suffered by victims of a catastrophe. The specific conditions for compensation are thus provided in the directives issued by the provinces.[107] 84

Also *Belgium* has with the Act of 12 July 1976 chosen a fund solution. This act defines what constitutes a catastrophe and makes a distinction between general and agricultural catastrophes.[108] An incident, however, only leads to compensation from the fund if it is recognized as a catastrophe by a Royal Decree; the Royal Decree will then also determine the geographical scope of the "disaster area". At the occasion of the introduction of the disaster fund in Belgium a lot of attention was paid to the possibility of the liability of public authorities. The Belgian legislator has explicitly chosen to determine in the act itself that the compensation fund exists irrespective of any government liability. The compensation paid from the fund would only be reduced with the amounts that the victim would receive via tort law.[109] As weak points of this disaster fund are *inter alia* mentioned the fact that the procedure would take too long, that the fund would not compensate all damage and that many incidents which are also "catastrophic" are not officially recognized as a disaster within the scope of the disaster fund.[110] 85

[106] Austria, 20 *et seq.*
[107] Austria, 26 *et seq.*
[108] Belgium, 24.
[109] Belgium., 24.
[110] Belgium, 26.

86 We already mentioned that *France* knows several funds that could play a role in case of catastrophes. Like many other European countries France has traditionally a guarantee fund for motor vehicles (existing since 1951), which provides compensation for victims of traffic accidents in case the injurer is insolvent or not identified. The working of this fund has been enlarged by the Act of 30 July 2003 in order to include the damage suffered by uninsured victims of technological disasters as well.[111] Second, France also knows an agricultural fund since 1964 that compensates for uninsurable losses of an exceptional nature caused by a natural disaster. Third, France knows a fund for the victims of terrorism, financed through a levy on the premium for property insurance policies. However, this fund only compensates for personal injury damage and not for property damage;[112] it functions not as a supplementary, but as a primary fund. This means that compensation will be paid from this fund even if the terrorists are known and the victim could thus in theory use tort law. The basis for this specific compensation to victims of terrorism is the idea of solidarity. Note, however, that France does not have a compensation fund for damage caused by natural disasters. As mentioned above France relies as far as natural disasters are concerned entirely on insurance which apparently removes the necessity to have a fund for that type of damage.

87 It was mentioned earlier that *Germany* does not have a structural compensation fund (like Austria or Belgium), but rather relies on *ad hoc* solutions. An example constitutes the *Flutopferhilfesolidaritätsgesetz* of 2002 introduced at the occasion of the "Jahrhundertflut" of the river Elbe in 2002. The German reporter argues that this fund constitutes a model for how Germany reacts with financial compensation after catastrophes. The fund was introduced firstly to provide immediate aid to victims (*Soforthilfe*) and second to provide assistance with restoration (*Ausbauhilfe*). The basic idea is that companies and families receive assistance from the fund in as far as they had no insurance or compensation from other sources. The fund is therefore in theory supplementary. However, it was apparently not required that the victim should first exercise all possible claims before a call on the fund is possible. This *ad hoc* arrangement provided through the *Flutopferhilfesolidaritätsgesetz* was especially meant to provide a quick compensation for victims suffering property damage; most damage resulting from personal injury is in Germany covered through the social security scheme.

88 *Italy* had, as mentioned above, no specific compensation funds, but only *ad hoc* solutions. Nevertheless, the amounts paid by the Italian government (on average € 3.5–4 billion per year) to indemnify damage caused by catastrophic events[113] shows that the *ad hoc* solution is not necessarily cheaper than the structural fund. Thus, although the compensation is *ad hoc*, the Italian reporters indicate that a relevant share of the state's yearly budget is devoted to re-

[111] France, 27.
[112] Those who insure themselves for property damage thus pay a premium for personal injury resulting from terrorism.
[113] Italy, 71.

storing damage incurred as a result of catastrophes.[114] In addition, the Italian reporters also pay attention to the European Union solidarity fund established by EC Council Regulation number 2012/2002 of 11 November 2002 of which Italy has regularly been a beneficiary as well.[115]

The *Netherlands* has, as earlier mentioned, no structural fund, but an Act of 1998 concerning the compensation of victims of catastrophes on the basis of which the government can, on an *ad hoc* basis, decide how much to contribute to victims of a particular catastrophe. However, the conditions are that stringent that in practice this act is rarely applied. As a consequence victims still call on other *ad hoc* compensation funds which are government funded, for instance for the victims of the legionella epidemic in Bovenkarspel. 89

Sweden has, just as Germany, no structural fund solution and thus relies greatly on *ad hoc* solutions. An important example, largely discussed in the Swedish report is a fire in a disco in Gothenburg in 1998 whereby 63 people died and 200 were seriously injured. In that case both the local government (the community of Gothenburg) as well as the Swedish state provided for compensation. However, other than in Germany, no particular statutory basis was provided for this compensation and no formal fund was instituted. According to the Swedish model, it is the local communities that are responsible for providing the compensation. The state therefore provided additional means to the communities who in turn compensated the victims. 90

It will be no surprise to read that the *United Kingdom* formally has no compensation fund for catastrophic losses,[116] given the restricted role of Government in this respect. However, in case of flooding there is a so-called Bellwin scheme that can provide emergency financial assistance to local authorities.[117] These Bellwin grants are basically paid to local authorities and the amount of state intervention is still minimal compared to the total amount of damage caused by flood. In addition, as far as terrorism is concerned, there is no formal fund, but the state acts as an insurer of last resort, as was already mentioned earlier.[118] But in addition to that there are no general compensation funds providing relief for damage caused by disasters in the UK aside from the local discretionary powers exercisable by local authorities. 91

Although, as explained above, the regime in the *United States* is also primarily based on insurance, supported by government assistance, there are a few examples of funds as well. The Federal Emergency Management Agency (FEMA) distributes – *inter alia* to local governments – substantial amounts from its disaster relief fund.[119] However, most of this federal assistance through 92

[114] Italy, 74.
[115] Italy, 75–77.
[116] UK, 21.
[117] UK, 25.
[118] UK, 26–27.
[119] According to the US report in 2001 FEMA paid $ 3.5 billion from its disaster relief fund (US, 23).

FEMA is provided as emergency aid, hazard mitigation assistance or public assistance to communities. It is therefore not comparable with a compensation fund that directly pays compensation for damage to victims, as is the case e.g. in Austria or Belgium. The latter is the case with the September 11 Victim Compensation Fund.[120] This fund was meant to create baseline assurance that victims of physical injury and their survivors would receive benefits. By American standards this fund seems to be relatively generous since it covers both economic loss and (broadly defined) non-economic losses as well. The basis for compensation under this fund is, however, personal injury damage, so that property damage is in principle excluded.[121] The American report provides other examples of interesting funds, like the Florida Hurricane Catastrophe Fund, a state/private risk sharing programme, created by the Florida legislator in 1993.[122] This is not a classic fund (in the European sense) since this fund acts as a reinsurer of Florida's property insurance provider. The fund is basically financed through premium payments made by participating insurers as is the case with classic reinsurance.[123]

93 One can therefore notice a few funds, although in most cases their role is limited to providing supplementary compensation. Only in the case of Austria and Belgium does the compensation fund seem to play a primary role in the indemnification of victims of catastrophes. But in Austria the compensation provided through the fund is limited to 30–50% of the damage and in Belgium the nature of the compensation fund was dramatically changed in May 2003 since Belgium turned to the French solution of an additional mandatory coverage on voluntary insurance policies. It seems that in the other legal systems the fund has either an *ad hoc* nature (like in Germany) or only provides immediate disaster relief for specific cases of need (like the Bellwin grants in the UK). Only for understandable (political) reasons the September 11 Victim Compensation Fund seems to aim at creating a baseline assurance particularly for the victims of physical injury and their survivors. But that should of course also be seen in the context of the modest compensation under social security schemes in the US; note that property damage is excluded from coverage under that fund. It seems therefore fair to hold that in most (European) countries today the additional (supplementary to tort and social security) compensation scheme in case of catastrophes seems to be insurance. The few countries where a (structural) compensation fund for catastrophes existed in Western-Europe are either recently under revision or limited in scope. The latter of course does not exclude governments from providing *ad hoc* compensation (like in the Netherlands, Germany and Italy).

[120] US, 39 and following.
[121] For further detail see US, 39 and following.
[122] US, 51.
[123] US, 52.

Part VII. Procedural Aspects

Having discussed the most important features of the compensation mechanism in the various countries we will now turn to a few other aspects that have practical relevance as well, although we can discuss them more briefly. A first issue concerns the possibilities for victims to effectuate their claim either through legal aid or through other procedures facilitating to effectuate their claim. Many reporters have discussed in detail e.g. legal aid provisions, others have argued that when victims seek relief within the framework of tort law they can for instance claim a prepayment on the compensation due via a summary proceedings. In this respect we can refer to the details in the country reports. Here we will briefly examine whether the countries examined reported specific procedures in case the victims of a catastrophe were seeking compensation via any of the specific regimes (compulsory insurance or compensation funds). In that respect some interesting information has been presented. 94

As far as insurance is concerned many countries report that either based on insurance law or on the insurance contract the victim is forced to file a claim within a relatively short period of time. Especially in case of catastrophes this may constitute a problem. For instance in *Austria* in principle the incident and claim for damages have to be notified to the insurer within a deadline of 3 days after the incident, which may be quite hard in practice. However, the Austrian reporters indicate that in practice insurers do not always insist on this 3 day period. For instance after the catastrophic Kaprun ski train fire in 2000 the operator's insurance company announced that it would waive the applicable deadline.[124] Another interesting feature in Austria is that many insurance companies have apparently provided clauses for cumulative damages in case of massive damages. The insurer thus sets a maximum amount payable to all victims (e.g. of a flood), which has as a consequence that an individual victim may only receive a part of the compensation agreed upon in the insurance contract.[125] 95

The *Belgian* insurance act has no specific time limit within which the victim has to report the accident; the insurance policy will therefore be decisive in that respect. The Belgian reporter argues that it can often take a very long time before compensation on the basis of insurance takes place since the insurer will only pay the compensation after the criminal procedure (which often takes place at the occasion of a catastrophe) has been concluded. Thus for instance victims of an airline crash in Oostende did not receive any compensation even 5 years after the event.[126] For the case of fire insurance some guidelines for payment by the insurance company entered into force on 1 July 2004.[127] As far as the disaster fund is concerned, the Royal Decree that will declare a phenomenon as disaster will also determine the time limit within 96

[124] Austria, 99.
[125] Austria, 58, 76–77.
[126] Belgium, 31.
[127] Belgium 32

which victims have to file their claim. That may thus vary. Usually it can last 3 months. However, also here the Belgian reporter argues that it can take years before the victim receives any decision from the government (and thus compensation).[128]

97 In *France* legal claims are in principle avoided since most victims will simply call upon their first party insurer to seek compensation. Tort law (and thus procedures) are only used by subrogated (social) insurers or by victims for the amount not covered under first party insurance or social security. This would, however, be the exception.[129] Important is that in France the government first has to declare an incident a natural disaster before the insurer is bound to provide cover. This is an administrative act that hence also can give rise to an administrative appeal.[130] The declaration of the event as disaster will be published in the *Journal Officiel*. From the date of that publication the victim only has 10 days to file a claim with his insurer. The idea of this very short time limit is to exercise pressure on the victim to act carefully and to allow the experts of the insurer to establish the extent of the damage as soon as possible. The *Code des Assurances* further stipulates that the insurer has to make an offer within 3 months after the claim by the victim. Moreover, within a period of 2 months an advance payment needs to be made.[131] The fund for non-insured, suffering property damage in case of traffic accidents related to technological disasters (instituted by the Act of 30 July 2003), applies the same procedure. In case of personal injury suffered as a result of terrorism, the period to file a claim for the victim is, however, 10 years. Again the insurer needs to formulate an offer within 3 months after the victim filed the claim. If that offer is accepted this so-called "transaction" is valid as a contract and thus binding for both the victim and the fund.

98 The *German* report also discusses in detail the applicable rules in case of tort law and social security. The rules applicable in case of insurance will depend upon the insurance policy. However, in order to wish to preserve a client friendly image insurers would be striving for an unbureaucratic and quick settling of claims.[132] The German reporter especially pays attention to the procedure followed at the occasion of the compensation of the Elbe flooding in 2002 through the *Flutopferhilfesolidaritätsgesetz*. In that case the rules were not laid down in the formal act, but the province (in casu Sachsen) laid down the rules for dividing the compensation in an administrative procedure to be followed by the local authorities. The local authorities formulate a proposal for compensation to the victim and the case is settled, unless the victim holds that compensation would wrongly be denied.[133]

[128] Belgium, 33.
[129] France, 39.
[130] France, 40.
[131] France, 41.
[132] Germany, 23.
[133] For further details see Germany, 21.

A similar procedure seems to be followed in case of the *ad hoc* compensation by the state in *Italy*. The state of emergency is officially declared and this approval opens the way for government intervention and compensation.[134] 99

The reporters on *Sweden* especially discuss the procedures followed by victims at the occasion of the Gothenburg fire.[135] Various parties intervened in that particular case: the community of Gothenburg provided compensation in addition to the first party insurer of the victims and the three liability insurers of the four injurers. Standardized amounts of compensation were paid in order to avoid a legal procedure. The large media attention given to the case would have led insurers to be quite generous in providing the compensation. The Swedish reporters recalled that the insurers might have paid more than what would have been due under a strict application of liability rules, in order to avoid a loss of goodwill and to avoid a legal procedure. Some victims have in addition filed a law suit against the liability insurers of the injurers;[136] that procedure is still pending. Victims who did not have first party insurance sought compensation from the crime victim compensation and support authority. In November 2003, 5 years after the fire in Gothenburg, 19 persons were still waiting on a compensation from this crime victim compensation and support authority.[137] 100

The *United Kingdom* has, so the report shows, made serious efforts to improve access to justice and to avoid legislation where possible.[138] Also a protocol for personal injury claims aims at reaching settlements and avoiding litigation.[139] In case of insurance for natural hazards (like flooding) these are in principle contractual claims subject to the contractual conditions that establish the procedure to be followed by the claimant.[140] The UK also has a specific compensation regime for the compensation of criminal injuries; in that case the claim must be submitted within 2 years of the relevant incident.[141] 101

The *US* regime of course knows a variety of different procedures, depending upon the applicable regime. Noteworthy is that, as is the case in all legal systems that have a specific regime for disaster coverage, some administrative decision will have to be taken to declare a certain event a disaster. This is also the case *inter alia* to obtain the federal funding for disaster relief through the FEMA. In order to be eligible the state governor must request a presidential declaration of major disaster and must show that the situation surpassed the state and local economic capabilities.[142] Special mention deserves also the fact 102

[134] Italy, 73.
[135] Sweden, 36.
[136] This concerned victims who were not satisfied with the amount of non-pecuniary losses offered by the insurer.
[137] Sweden, 36.
[138] UK, 28–30.
[139] UK, 31.
[140] UK, 44.
[141] UK, 45.
[142] US, 17.

that the September 11 Victim Compensation Fund has been managed through a so-called Special Master. This Special Master apparently sets the regulations indicating the procedure and the heads and amounts of damages to be paid under the fund regime.[143] The Special Master also implemented the programme of benefit distribution. This was possible since the regulations allowed for a good deal of discretion.

103 This brief overview of procedural aspects shows that every legal system that instituted a specific regime for the victims of disasters unavoidably has to cope with the definition of a disaster or has to come up with an administrative system indicating that a specific incident will be considered as a disaster. In the literature these are referred to as the so-called sorting costs. Apparently some countries like France and Belgium provide a broad definition of (in those cases natural) disasters, but at the same time still require an administrative decision (by the government or by Royal Decree) indicating that a specific incident was a disaster. Thus, the act provides the broad framework and some guidance for the administrative decision in order to decide whether the specific incident qualifies as a disaster or not. The decision is of course of major importance for victims since only if the incident formally qualifies as a disaster will the additional compensation be provided.

104 We also noticed important differences as far as the time limits are concerned within which the victim has to file the claim, either with the insurer or with a compensation fund. France apparently opted for very stringent and short (10 days after the publication in the official gazette) periods to file the claim. But on the other hand they also force the insurer to make an offer of compensation within three months after the claim has been filed.[144] The other regimes seem to be less stringent than the French, but of course in both ways (for the victim and for the one who is obliged to pay the compensation).

105 Finally it was also striking that most reporters indicate that usually there is a lot of flexibility as far as the proof of damage is concerned. For instance in case of *ad hoc* compensation regimes (like the German *Flutopferhilfesolidaritätsgesetz*) it is not required to follow the formal rules of civil procedure, but evidence of damage is accepted in a rather flexible way. This may be due to the fact that the damage is usually not fully compensated and that a deductible will be applied with these regimes.

[143] For further detail US, 41–45.

[144] France follows apparently the model that has already been introduced for traffic accidents through the so-called Loi Badinter. For details on this regime see A. Tunc, Traffic liability and victim protection: lessons from 10 years of experience with the 'Loi Badinter', in: M. Faure/T. Hartlief (eds.), *Verkeersaansprakelijkheid in België en Nederland* (1998), 217–234 and A. Tunc, The '*Loi Badinter*', Ten Years of Experience, [1996] *Maastricht Journal of European and Comparative Law*, 3(4), 329–340.

Part VIII. Financing

I. General

An unavoidable question is of course who finances a specific compensation regime and for what amounts. In this respect it is of course not very exciting to examine how tort law is financed in the various countries since it is relatively clear that this is in principle done by the injurers, in some cases supplemented with (sometimes compulsory) liability insurance. Also a comparison of the financing of the social security systems in Europe is of course not feasible within the scope of this project. First party insurances are of course primarily paid through the private parties that seek insurance coverage, being the potential victims of disasters. In some cases some indication of the premium can be given, especially when these are laid down in regulation (like in France). As far as the additional specific regimes (funds) are concerned, the exciting question is of course who pays for the additional protection awarded to the victims? In that respect the question especially arises whether the money for the fund simply comes from the general budget (in which case the general taxpayer will intervene) or whether specific targeted groups have to provide the compensation. 106

II. Financing of Funds

In *Austria* the disaster fund is financed from revenues from income and corporate taxes. A certain percentage of this money is transferred on a monthly basis to the fund and is invested into it.[145] The same model is followed in *Belgium*: the disaster fund is financed through the general taxes. It is, however, remarkable that although the disaster fund in Belgium is a structural one, the financing takes place on an *ad hoc* basis. This simply means that the Belgian government only seeks the compensation that will be paid through the disaster fund after the incident has happened.[146] Also the *German Flutopferhilfesolidaritätsgesetz* 2002 instituted a fund which was financed through the general taxes: half of the amount came from the federal government and half from the provinces, as has been stipulated in the act itself. Similar financing models are followed in *Italy* and the *Netherlands*. The Italian reporters make clear that on average the Italian government spends € 3.5–4 billion to indemnify damage caused by catastrophic events.[147] Disaster recovery therefore lays every year a serious burden upon the state budget, which explains that there is a tendency to reform to get a larger involvement of the private insurance sector.[148] Also in the *Netherlands* in the (rare) cases in which compensation is paid through the act on the compensation of victims of catastrophes, the financing simply takes place out of the public budget. 107

[145] Austria, 23.
[146] Belgium, 25.
[147] Italy, 71.
[148] Italy, 72.

108 The various *US* models that were discussed are in that respect not different in the sense that the September 11 Victim Compensation Fund seems mainly to be financed also through general tax revenues.[149] That is, hence, not a surprising conclusion: if a public compensation fund is installed for the relief of victims of disasters apparently in all countries these funds (where they exist) are financed through the public budget. An exception only constitutes the specific case of compensation funds for victims of crime injuries, which are funded by the convicted perpetrators. However, these play less of a role in case of most disasters (with the exception of terrorism of course), so that these were not discussed here any further.

III. Financing of Insurance Solutions

109 It is especially interesting to examine how financing takes place in case the relief of disaster victims does not take place via a fund but through an insurance solution, like in *France*. The French reporters hold that the entire complex system is paid through contributions and premiums paid by the insured and through a reinsurance which is guaranteed by the state. Financing of the compensation funds which accompanied the system was, according to the French reporters, possible at relatively low costs.[150] The additional premium for the (mandatory) supplementary coverage of natural disasters has in France been fixed by law. Of course the amount that is finally paid by the insured depends upon the premium that will have to be paid on the particular first party insurance policy. The percentages for the additional (natural disaster) coverage are:[151]

- On property damage contracts the additional contribution originally was 5.5% (when the regime was introduced in 1982). The next year the percentage was already increased to 9% and in 2000 to 12%, which is the current percentage.
- On motor vehicle insurance contracts: 6% of the premium for theft and fire insurance and 0.5% of the premium for a property damage insurance.

110 For the also (mandatory) supplementary coverage for technological risks (introduced by the Act of 30 July 2003) an additional premium of € 5 per year was asked from 1 January 2004. This supplementary coverage applies to approximately 50 million existing (voluntary) insurance policies and thus already leads to a coverage of € 250 million for this risk. The latter way of financing is, however, debated according to the French reporters. In this case it is indeed the potential victims that pay for additional protection and not the injurers. The reporters therefore rightly indicate that a compulsory liability insurance might have been more appropriate.

[149] US, 39 and following.
[150] France, 50.
[151] See France, 51.

Reinsurance in France is offered through the *Caisse Centrale de Réassurance* (CCR), which is completely owned by the state. Half of all the premiums for the coverage of natural disasters are paid to this CCR. As a consequence this CCR will always cover half of the insured natural disaster and consequently pay.[152] Moreover, via this CCR the French government additionally provides unlimited coverage for natural disasters and for the terrorism risk. According to the French reporters the financial results of this CCR would be quite beneficial.[153] 111

As far as the other funds are concerned the yearly contributions to the fund are determined through an administrative decision.[154] We also already mentioned that the terrorism fund is financed through a mandatory contribution of € 3 on property damage contracts (in 2003). Here we find hence an exception to the rule that funds are usually financed through the public means. In this case it is not all taxpayers, but only those who have (voluntary) property damage contracts that finance the fund. 112

Finally it was also mentioned that the traditional guarantee fund for motor vehicles was enlarged in 2003 to cover also the uninsured victims of technological risks. Financing again takes place through various ways (laid down in regulation): 113

- insurance companies contribute to 12% of the total expenses of the fund;
- uninsured injurers contribute 10% to the fund in addition to the compensation they are due to victims;
- 2% of all premiums paid by insured go to the fund;
- 50% of the fine imposed on those who do not comply with the statutory duty to insure is also paid to the fund;
- finally the fund is also financed through the exercise of the subrogation rights by the fund against liable third parties.

Here again one finds an example of a fund which is not simply financed through the general taxpayers, but where there seems to be a more correct distribution in the sense that those who contribute to the risk (like uninsured injurers or those who do not comply with the statutory obligation to insure) have to contribute to the fund. 114

IV. Public-Private Partnerships

The *UK* had a remarkable arrangement in that the insurers agreed in the Gentlemen's Agreement concerning flood insurance that the additional premium for the flood coverage would not exceed 0.5% of the sum insured and this (originally) "no matter what the risk".[155] This amount seems relatively low, 115

[152] France, 52.
[153] France, 52 in fine.
[154] France, 54.
[155] UK, 22.

compared to the French model where the additional disaster coverage today costs 12% of the premium. However, the flood insurance in the UK seems to be under revision and premium differentiation is one aspect of the reform.[156]

116 In the *American* models where the state intervenes to facilitate insurability one can notice that, since in those cases the government acts as primary insurer, they primarily finance the system. The coverage is, however, based on a private-public partnership, so that insurers engage in the financing of the system (partially) as well. For instance with the Terrorism Risk Insurance Act of 2002 the federal government assumes a percentage of each insurer's losses for compensating claims arising from terrorist acts, but the commercial insurers who are required to participate in the programme of course finance the system as well.[157] The same seems to be the case with the California Earthquake Authority. Although this CEA represents a model whereby the state has relieved the private insurers of uncertainty, it would not be correct to state that the system is completely state funded. Indeed, the US report makes clear that the CEA itself is funded by participating insurers, along with bond sales, reinsurance and the premiums charged for policies sold. The initial operating capital was provided through mandatory contributions by the participating insurers.[158] The system is hence still primarily funded through premium payments (and that is the case with flood insurance as well). Hence, this seems like an interesting model whereby on the one hand insurers do engage actively in the financing of a system like the CEA, but where in turn the CEA intervention relieves private insurers of the uncertainty associated with a major earthquake, thus enabling them to continue the earthquake coverage. In these systems, governments take over responsibility for potentially catastrophic losses, but private insurers still primarily fund the system.

V. Summary

117 This shows that different models exist as far as the financing of additional coverage is concerned. In case of *ad hoc* financing usually only the general public budget is used to finance the *ad hoc* compensation, so that losses are redistributed from the victims of disasters to the general taxpayers. Even in case of a structural fund like the Belgian disaster fund only *ad hoc* financing through the general budget takes place. In some cases, more particularly in France, some other allocation mechanism has been developed whereby also those who might be considered liable to the creation of the risk (like uninsured drivers or those otherwise violating the duty to insure) contribute to a fund.

118 As far as the insurance solutions are concerned, the French model is striking in the sense that it apparently relies heavily on regulation, therefore leaving little scope for competition, which was precisely criticized from a competition law perspective.[159] Moreover, the percentages of the contribution for mandatory nat-

[156] UK, 51.
[157] US, 30.
[158] US, 32 especially footnote 96.
[159] See the contribution of Roger Van den Bergh to this volume.

ural disaster coverage in France seem to be higher than for flooding coverage in the UK. The US model moreover shows that there may be alternatives whereby not all the financing takes place via either the insured or the government, but is rather based on a risk sharing. The American model, whereby the state in fact only relieves the insurers from some of the additional risks (but imposes no mandatory insurance), may be less interventionistic and have less restrictive effects on competition.

Part IX. Damages

As far as the damages paid through the various systems are concerned, it seems interesting to briefly address whether specific regimes are installed for either personal injury or property damage or for both. In addition the question arises whether the specific regimes can, just as in tort law, provide a guarantee of complete compensation or whether certain thresholds or limits are applied. Again, within the framework of this comparative overview we will not compare the amounts paid through tort law or social security, since that has been done in earlier studies. The differences between those regimes are, moreover, well-known: social security has a low threshold, but a low compensation regime, whereas tort law has higher thresholds, but in principle a guarantee of full compensation. One can expect that the specific compensation regimes for victims of catastrophes may, especially when thresholds are low, not provide the full compensation as guaranteed through tort law. 119

Austria clearly shows that the disaster fund provides only limited compensation. It only intervenes for property damage due to natural catastrophes,[160] applies a deductible of more than € 1,000 and only pays a basic compensation up to 20% of the damage to buildings and furniture with a maximum of 50% in cases of particular hardship.[161] Originally the fund only covered direct damages. As a result of the avalanche of Galtür also losses of earnings and costs of rescue operations could be compensated.[162] 120

The same applies to the disaster fund in *Belgium*: only direct material damage to private property can be compensated through the fund.[163] Also a deductible applies (of € 250) and a strict causal link is required between the disaster and the damage.[164] The amounts awarded for damaged buildings and property are standardized. One can notice a similar stringency in other countries that apply a fund solution. For instance at the occasion of the Elbe flooding in 2002 in *Germany* the fund only compensated for property damage and was focused on the restoration of damage to buildings and properties. Lost income or pure 121

[160] Austria, 26.

[161] Austria, 29, 36.

[162] Austria, 55.

[163] Belgium, 25.

[164] The Belgian reporter gives the example of a case of the Court de Cassation where it was decided that the costs for painting a wall higher than the level where the water came was not considered direct damage, but a luxury expense (Belgium, 25 footnote 110).

economic loss was not compensated through the fund, nor was personal injury damage.[165] The same seems to apply for the many schemes of disaster relief that have been introduced in the *US*. For instance under FEMA disaster relief is available primarily for property damage directly caused by a disaster event.[166] Also the national flood insurance programme (NFIP) is primarily aimed at real estate and thus at property damage.[167] The September 11 Victim Compensation Fund seemed more broad and generous by compensating both economic and non-economic loss.[168] By contrast, property damage was not covered under the September 11 Victim Compensation Fund.

122 *France* takes, as usual, a specific position. The scheme presented earlier makes clear that a difference is made between property damage on the one hand and personal injury on the other. The mandatory additional coverage for natural disasters only applies for property damage; victims suffering personal injury in principle need to use social security, supplemented with first party insurances like the *garantie des accidents de la vie* or specific compensation funds (for terrorism or uninsured victims of technological risks). For natural disasters there is a deductible which, since 1 January 2002, is € 380 for private households. Interestingly, in communities that did not provide a *plan de prévention de risques* the deductible will be higher. The goal is thus to provide an incentive to the local citizens to force their community to introduce such a prevention plan or to relocate to safer areas. This focus on prevention can also be found in the insurance for technological risks. Insurance coverage is excluded in specific areas that are, according to a prevention plan for technological risks, specifically dangerous for human health. The idea is again to provide an incentive not to build in specific risk zones.[169]

123 This brief overview shows that many systems make a distinction between property damage on the one hand and personal injury on the other. That can be understood since in most countries (of course with differences) social security will provide a minimum compensation for medical expenses, healthcare costs and lost income. The need for a specific regime was therefore especially felt for property damage, like the damage caused to houses as a result of flooding. There usually no social security scheme applies. Most legal systems that have a collective arrangement still limit the compensation in various ways. First one usually sees a standardization of the amounts (also to reduce transaction costs) and second they usually apply a deductible (to control moral hazard). Some (also collective) systems try to introduce some type of risk differentiation in the sense that either a higher deductible applies if no specific prevention plan is established (like in France) or compensation is denied altogether from the collective sources if specific preventive measures have not been taken. Although most collective arrangements like compensation funds provide

[165] Germany, 27.
[166] US, 18.
[167] US, 33 and following.
[168] US, 39.
[169] France, 68.

lump sump payments to victims without any differentiation some examples show that also in applying collective mechanisms it seems possible to introduce insurance-like types of risk differentiation. The goal of these is of course to serve prevention of disasters in the first place. Also a limitation on the amount of compensation, standardization of the compensation and a deductible may on the one hand reduce transaction costs (through standardization) and at the same time remedy moral hazard.

Part X. Cumulation

The country reports make clear that usually social security and tort law provide for the basic compensation, eventually supplemented with (first party or liability) insurance. Most countries that have specific collective arrangements for the compensation of victims will make sure that these have a subsidiary or supplementary character, meaning that other mechanisms have to be used first and a collective arrangement is used in a last resort. Moreover, traditionally legal systems have arrangements to allow (first party or social) insurance carriers to exercise a right of redress against the liable injurer or his insurer, being subrogated in the rights of the victim. Nevertheless there are some notable particularities and distinctions between the systems. Without discussing the important issues of cumulation and redress in any detail a few peculiarities with respect to the collective arrangements can be noticed. 124

For instance in *Austria* it is clearly stated that the disaster fund will not intervene if private insurance or any other third party covers the loss. On the other hand, compensation out of the funds may not be considered by private insurers and must thus not reduce the victim's claim against the insurer.[170] A similar rule applies in *Belgium*: compensation by the disaster fund does not prevent the victim from using tort law (even against public authorities). However, if compensation is obtained via tort law this will reduce the amount paid through the disaster fund.[171] 125

In *France* the basic model remains simple, especially as far as personal injury is concerned: the victim first needs to use social security and in addition the private insurances that would be at his disposition (like the *garantie des accidents de la vie*). In addition a fund could be used if available (as for victims of terrorism) and in fact the victim will only exceptionally use tort law. As far as the compensation funds are concerned, a distinction is made between funds that have a clear supplementary character (like the motor vehicle fund) and funds that do not. The motor vehicle fund will only intervene when no third party can be identified and held liable to pay the compensation due. Such a fund clearly does have a supplementary character. The fund for the victims of terrorism is, on the contrary, a primary source of compensation. Victims of terrorism can claim compensation from this fund even before any liability 126

[170] Austria, 37.
[171] Belgium, 34.

claim has been filed against the injurer. Of course the fund will then be subrogated in the rights of the victim against the liable terrorist.[172]

127 *Germany* has, as many other countries, as a general rule that a victim can in principle not cumulate compensation from various sources for a similar damage.[173] The *Flutopferhilfesolidaritätsgesetz* concerning the Elbe flooding of 2002 in principle has a subsidiary character. The Act itself clearly stipulates that the fund only intervenes as far as no compensation can be obtained from third parties, especially from insurers. The compensation to be paid by the fund will also be reduced with payments made by third parties. However, if a successful claim against the third party cannot be realized in the short term, the victim is entitled to compensation from the fund, but is held to transfer his rights against the third party to the fund.[174]

128 The *Netherlands* has, in general, similar rules. More particularly concerning the debated act on the compensation of victims of catastrophes (WTS 1998) it was clearly stated during the parliamentary proceedings that this Act would only intervene for damage that is considered uninsurable. Thus it should have a supplementary character, although there is some debate on this issue in the literature.

129 Remarkably the rules concerning cumulation in *Sweden* seem to diverge pretty much from those in other systems. The general rule apparently is that insurance monies the victim has received are taken into account when assessing the compensation due by the injurer, without the insurer receiving a right of redress. As a consequence, the fact that the victim was compensated through (private or social) insurance thus reduces the duty of the injurer to compensate. Only in exceptional cases, as with marine insurance, does the insurer get a right of redress. In some cases victims can even cumulate compensation from different sources. That is for instance the case when the victim received compensation from a first party insurance for which the victim paid the premium himself.

130 The *United Kingdom* has, as most other systems, strict rules to avoid cumulative effects between various compensation systems, more particularly concerning social security benefits and insurance.[175] This corresponds with the general principle of tort law that damages are recoverable once only.[176] However, the UK reporters indicate that the rules concerning the recovery of cumulative benefits are complex and extensive.[177] As a general rule payments made by insurance companies or voluntary donations are not deducted from any

[172] France, 76.
[173] Germany, 25.
[174] Germany, 96.
[175] UK, 14 in fine.
[176] UK, 40.
[177] UK, 42.

award. This especially applies in case of payments that have to be made by the tortfeasor.

In the *US*, interestingly, recovery of private benefits is generally ignored under the collateral source rule if an injury victim recovers in tort. In other words: US law allows double recovery, only sometimes leading to subrogation rights of the insurer.[178] Some specific rules apply in case specific compensation mechanisms have intervened or compensated losses. In those cases subrogation rights are awarded. This is for instance the case with the federal Terrorism Risk Insurance Act (TRIA) which grants a right of subrogation to the United States with respect of any payment made under the programme.[179] 131

This brief overview of the approach towards cumulation of compensation shows that although there may be important differences between the countries, these differences are not specifically related to the financial compensation of victims after catastrophes. Although most countries have as a general rule that victims may not benefit in the sense that they could be better off after an accident (by cumulating compensation from various sources), this does not seem to be the rule in all countries, more particularly not in the US. Some countries also strongly rely on full exposure of the tortfeasor to the full damage he has caused (probably relying on the preventive effects of such an exposure), although others (like Sweden) seem to let the tortfeasor benefit from the fact that others have compensated the victim. 132

In general specific compensation mechanisms for disaster victims (like compensation funds) seem to have a supplementary character, in the sense that victims must either first use other available compensation mechanisms (tort or insurance) or the amounts received under those other mechanisms are taken into account when the compensation due by the fund is established. However, it is not always strictly required from the victim to fully exercise all procedural rights e.g. against a tortfeasor before payment from the fund can be expected. If it is apparently not held reasonable to expect the victim to exercise a claim in tort (perhaps because this is too costly or would take too long) in some cases. The fund nevertheless intervenes, but is then subrogated in the rights of the victim. In most legal systems one can indeed notice that funds are subrogated in the victims' rights against possible liable third parties, although it is doubtful whether these subrogation rights are often used in practice. In other cases funds do not have a supplementary, but rather a primary character (although that seems to be the exception). In that case (for instance with the victims of terrorism fund in France) victims are not required first to use tort law and can directly obtain compensation from the fund. Of course also in that case subrogation of the fund in the rights of the victim takes place. 133

[178] US, 3, specially footnote 9. And see equally – with respect to the September 11 Victim Compensation Regime US, 42 and US, 57 in fine.
[179] US, 30.

Part XI. Reforms and Criticisms

134 As was already indicated before, the systems of compensating victims of catastrophes are in full evolution in many of the countries. Moreover, even in those legal systems where there are no official reform plans, criticisms are formulated in the literature which are worth examining.

135 Interestingly enough *Austria* seems to be one of the only countries where there is no such call for reform. The Austrian reporters hold that the current multilayer system of compensation (tort, social security, private insurance and the disaster fund) is considered to be workable to a large extent.[180] The only point which seems to be an issue for reform is the amount of non-pecuniary losses awarded to victims, more particularly after the train catastrophe in Kaprun.

136 The report on *Belgium* is more critical, precisely on the point that victims have to receive compensation from various sources, meaning that victims will sometimes have to go to these various sources (social security, insurance, liability) to be fully compensated. Also the fact that victims sometimes have to wait many years before they are effectively compensated is considered as a disadvantage.[181] Note also that the Belgian system was recently reformed in May 2003 to change from a fund solution towards the (French model of) compulsory insurance for flooding. The new system has, however, not entered into force yet.

137 In *France* the public and legal doctrine seems generally to be rather satisfied with the current system, arguing that it has shown itself able to provide in an adequate way compensation to victims of catastrophes and to do so at reasonable costs. However, the disadvantage is, as was shown above, that the compensation system is highly complex, consisting of a large variety of different approaches. The link between compensation and prevention is also qualified as positive. In sum the reporters qualify the French system as effective but complex. Their main call for reform seems to be towards simplification of the system.[182] Note also that France has been subject of many statutory reforms, the most recent one being of July 2003 (extending the mandatory coverage to technological risks). One specific reform plan is under discussion at this moment: On 12 August 2004 Senator Claude Biwer proposed a draft following the difficulties faced by agricultural workers after the 2003 summer drought. The substance of this legislative draft is to deprive the Government of the power to issue a public declaration of "disaster" after which the insurance monies would become due. As a result of the draft the compensation would be awarded whatever the intensity of the drought and the consequential soil movements might be.

[180] Austria, 114.
[181] Belgium, 43.
[182] France, 84.

In *Germany* there is criticism of an important and principle nature, being the fact that with the current *ad hoc* approach the German authorities spend, e.g. at the occasion of the *Jahrhundertflut* in Sachsen billions of Euro in public money for the victims, whereas the government would do nothing at all at the occasion of smaller incidents. The German reporter also criticizes the fact that when insufficient means are available to cover the damage *de facto* a priority rule is applied (this problem also arises when the damage is capped). This means that who comes first is first served, meaning that the "last" victims could be uncompensated. The German reporter pleads to replace the priority rule by a proportionality principle. Specific plans for reform were introduced at the occasion of a meeting of the *Deutsche Juristentag* in 1998 which was devoted to the phenomenon of mass torts. In 2002 German tort law was substantially reformed, *inter alia* leading to the admittance of non-pecuniary losses as well in case of strict liability.[183] Also the limits regarding the various statutory strict liabilities were increased and harmonized.[184] Note in addition that in the literature some have proposed the introduction of mandatory flooding insurance according to the French model.[185] These proposals have, however, not yet reached the legislative level. 138

Also in *Italy* the disaster recovery system is in full evolution. The Italian reporters indicate that various proposals have been introduced since 1993, which are all in favour of the French model of compulsory disaster coverage.[186] The Italian reporters highly criticize the current *ad hoc* system, since it also imposes very heavy burdens on the public budget; they propose a shift towards an increased use of insurance, such as in the French model. The Italian reporters present various proposals that have been introduced since 1993 and which should lead to mandatory insurance for disasters. The problem is that in most of these proposals there would be – *inter alia* – a fixing of premiums (for the disaster coverage) by the government, which would collide with European competition rules. It is, however, in the opinion of the Italian reporters likely that in the near future Italy will set aside the traditional indemnificatory position of the state and replace it with a system where there is a larger role for the private insurance sector, eventually complemented with state intervention.[187] 139

Remarkably the *Netherlands* may be going in a similar direction, although the outcome of the current reform process is less certain. There is serious criticism of the fact that currently there is a large uncoordinated variety of various 140

[183] See in that respect *inter alia* C. Huber, *Das neue Schadensersatzrecht* (2003) and V. Heutger, Hervorming van het schadevergoedingsrecht in Duitsland, [2002] AV&S, 19–21.

[184] Germany, 29.

[185] See particularly the publications by Schwarze and Wagner (R. Schwarze/G. Wagner, Hochwasser-Katastrophe in Deutschland: über Soforthilfe hinaus denken, [2002] DIW Wochenbericht 35 (<http://www.diw.de>); R. Schwarze/G. Wagner, [2004], G.P.R.I.I.P. 29(2), 154–168) and the criticisms on these proposals by A. Endres/C. Ohl/B. Rundshagen, Land unter! Ein institutionenökonomischer Zwischenruf, [2003] *List Forum für Wirtschafts- und Finanzpolitik* 29, 284–294.

[186] Italy, 116–144.

[187] Italy, 147.

mechanisms that could be used by victims of catastrophes, supplemented with a largely *ad hoc* approach. Especially the fact that the Act of 1998 which came into being to compensate victims of catastrophes is almost never applied and still supplemented with *ad hoc* solutions is subject of criticism. The *ad hoc* solutions as such are also criticized because they would violate the equality principle: victims of catastrophes are in that sense apparently better off than other victims since they may be receiving additional funding. The Dutch reporters therefore argue that it would (as in Italy) be wiser to focus on an increased use of insurance possibilities instead of continuing the current *ad hoc* approach. As far as insurability is concerned, the Dutch reporters on the one hand mention the promotion of first party insurances, which are now slowly developing since the prohibited cartel has been abrogated; on the other hand it is also mentioned that additional duties should be imposed upon potential injurers to seek sufficient financial coverage, e.g. in case of fires in discos or in case of exploding fireworks factories. It is not entirely clear in what direction the revisions will go. A commission is currently evaluating the functioning of the Act of 1998 and formulating new legislative proposals. The French model of mandatory disaster coverage has played a role in that respect, although it is at this stage (November 2004) unclear in what directions the revisions will go. But that the current Dutch system will be subject to reform seems rather straightforward.

141 For *Sweden* it is reported that there seems to be great satisfaction with the current model since social security and private insurance seem quite well able to provide adequate compensation. As a result victims in Sweden would rarely feel the need to use tort law. However, the cases of the fire in the disco in Gothenburg showed that also in Sweden victims of such a catastrophe will try to seek compensation via tort law of those components not covered via social security, more particularly of non-pecuniary losses.

142 In the *United Kingdom* also interesting new developments and criticisms are reported.[188] In 2002 a new agreement between the state and the insurance industry was signed with respect to flood insurance, as a result of which coverage is no longer unconditional and premium differentiation can be introduced. Since insurers can now exclude bad risks from coverage the state can be expected to act as insurer of last resort.[189] Therefore, one can notice also in the UK a move towards a stronger private-public partnership. Generally the British reporters hold the current system as efficient since a clear distinction is made between compensation and prevention. In the case of flood insurance the tendency is now to focus more on prevention.[190] At the same time the authors also warn that there is a growing idea of the existence of a "compensation culture", leading to higher damages amounts.[191]

[188] UK, 49 and following.
[189] UK, 53.
[190] UK, 58.
[191] UK, 55.

In the *US* especially the so-called collateral source role is the subject of criticism: this means that recovery in tort is not reduced with benefits received from private or public insurance sources. That may, according to the American reporters, explain a too large reliance on the tort system.[192] In addition the American tort system is, according to the reporters, also criticized from equality perspectives: victims suffering similar injuries are not treated in a like fashion and moreover the system fails to provide adequate incentives to risk generators to provide safety precautions.[193] For natural disasters, however, private insurance sources are far more important than tort and the US reporters seem to be largely satisfied with the private-public partnership whereby the government has in some cases taken over the role of primary risk bearer in order to promote insurability of risks.[194] The US report does not indicate any specific revisions with respect to the financial compensation for victims of catastrophes. This can be understood since for many specific disasters (earthquakes, flooding, hurricanes) elaborate systems are already in place (usually at the state level) and for other risks (more particularly terrorism) either elaborate systems were already in place (at the federal level) or have recently been changed in the aftermath of September 11. 143

Part XII. Critical Economic Analysis

We will now shift the approach by addressing some of the rich economic literature with respect to the financial compensation for victims of catastrophes.[195] It seems useful, within the framework of this comparative and policy analysis to also briefly address the main lessons from this economic literature and to confront these with some of the findings in the comparative results. 144

I. Liability and Liability Insurance

A. Importance

In this respect we can be brief: when a liable tortfeasor can be identified, economists hold that tort law should be used to provide him with adequate incentives for prevention. This is the standard result of the economic analysis of tort law.[196] Some have therefore qualified tort law as the primary reaction to catastrophic personal injuries.[197] If the tortfeasor can be held to compensate the damage he caused by the disaster, the goal of prevention will be reached 145

[192] US, 59.
[193] US, 60.
[194] US, 62.
[195] See generally on the economic analysis of law *inter alia* the recent book by S. Shavell, *Foundations of Economic Analysis of Law* (2004) and specifically for the economics of catastrophes, R. Posner, *Catastrophe. Risk and response* (2004).
[196] See e.g. S. Shavell, Strict Liability versus Negligence, [1980] *Journal of Legal Studies* (JLS) 9, 1–25.
[197] W.M Landes/R.A. Posner, Tort law as a regulatory regime for catastrophic personal injuries, [1984] JLS 13, 417–434.

and corrective justice is achieved since the costs are related to the one who created the risk.

146 Of course a debate could be held on the question whether in case of disasters tort law can be used at all and whether a negligence or a strict liability rule should be applied. The availability of tort law will largely depend upon the cause of the catastrophe. Natural disasters are often caused by an "act of God". The only liability that comes in the picture in that respect is, as the country reports showed, a liability of the government e.g. for not taking adequate preventive measures or for inadequate warnings, e.g. in case of flooding. But in addition to this government responsibility the scope of liability law will be very limited in case of natural disasters. That is different in case of technological disasters, which are usually "man-made".[198]

147 Several arguments have been formulated in the economic literature that a strict liability rule would be appropriate in case of ultra-hazardous activities (like running a nuclear power plant or a petrochemical company) which could exactly be the source of technological disasters.[199] However, the literature equally indicates that strict liability is efficient only if the insolvency problem can be cured, otherwise it may lead to underdeterrence.[200] Hence, from an economic perspective, strict liability should be introduced only if solvency can be guaranteed. This follows from the economic literature on the so-called "judgment-proof" problem, which indicates that insolvency of the tortfeasor will lead to underterrence.[201] Therefore it has been held that compulsory liability insurance should be introduced in cases where the potential loss caused by the disaster may exceed the injurer's assets.[202] There is hence a pretty strong economic argument in favour of a duty to purchase financial coverage since the magnitude of the damage caused as a result of a disaster can of course largely outweigh the assets of the individual tortfeasor.

[198] Of course to some extent catastrophes are produced jointly by nature and humans: R. Zeckhauser, The economics of catastrophes, [1996] *Journal of Risk and Uncertainty* 12, 113–140.

[199] See on the choice between negligence and strict liability for technological risks among others H-B. Schäfer/A. Schönenberger, Strict liability versus negligence, in: B. Bouckaert/G. De Geest (eds.), *Encyclopaedia of law and economics, II, Civil law and economics* (2000), 597–624; A. Endres/B. Staiger, Ökonomische Aspekte des Umwelthaftungsrechts, in: M. Ahrens/J. Simon (eds.), *Umwelthaftung, Risikosteuerung und Versicherung* (1996), 79–93; A. Monti, Environmental risk: a comparative law and economics approach to liability and insurance, [2001] *European Review of Private Law* (E.R.P.L.) 9, 51–79 and B. Pozzo, The liability problem in modern environmental statutes, [1996] E.R.P.L. 4, 112–129.

[200] W.M. Landes/R.A. Posner, [1984] JLS 13, 417–434 and M. Faure/D. Grimeaud, Financial assurances issues of environmental liability, in: M. Faure (ed.), *Deterrence, insurability and compensation in environmental liability. Future developments in the European Union* (2003).

[201] S. Shavell, The judgment-proof problem, [1986] *International Review of Law and Economics* (Int'l. Rev. Law & Econ.), 43–58.

[202] H. Kunreuther/P. Freeman, Insurability, environmental risks and the law, in: A. Heyes (ed.), *The Law and Economics of the Environment* (2001), 304–305.

B. Tort Law as Deterrent

The country reports showed that, when victims suffer harm as a result of a catastrophe, most of the personal injury damage will in the European legal systems be covered (although not completely) through social security.[203] Victims will therefore only use tort law for the part of personal injury damage that has not been compensated through social security (usually pain and suffering and the top of the income loss which is not covered under social security). Also property damage is usually not covered under social security, but victims may have purchased first party insurance. In Europe tort law is therefore often used by subrogated (social) insurers who have first provided compensation to the victim. To the extent that these social security carriers effectively use tort law against injurers adequate incentives can still be provided. Nevertheless, given the high costs of these subrogative actions there is a tendency in some countries (e.g. in Sweden) by (social) insurers not to use these rights of redress against injurers. That may lead to underdeterrence. 148

The extent to which tort law can effectively be used by accident victims (or their insurers) seems to play (at least implicitly) an important role in many legal systems, at least when one envisages the general structure of the law concerning financial compensation after catastrophes. Most legal systems make a clear distinction between on the one hand natural disasters and on the other hand technological catastrophes.[204] Given the different role of tort law in both cases this may well make a lot of sense. Indeed, as indicated, in case of natural disasters tort law will (with the exception of government liability) usually play a very limited role, which explains that in those cases other solutions are developed. In case of "technological" disasters liability law may well be the primary system, given that these are usually "man-made". Nevertheless one has to realize that with catastrophes the deterrent role of tort may in practice be limited. The reason is that for industry often stringent regulatory constraints are in place that alter irrespective of tort law. Moreover, large incidents may lead to huge reputational losses, e.g. for the airline industry or for the nuclear sector. Hence, incentives towards prevention certainly come through other ways than merely through tort. 149

As far as the contents of tort law are concerned, one can also – notwithstanding clear differences – notice a tendency in many European legal systems to introduce strict liability for technological risks.[205] This seems to comply with the economic model. Nevertheless, there are still important differences as well.[206] 150

[203] U. Magnus (ed.), *The impact of social security law on tort law* (2003).

[204] This is more particularly the case in France where different regulatory structures are in place for the compensation after natural disasters than after technological catastrophes.

[205] For an overview see the contributions in B.A. Koch/H. Koziol (*supra* fn. 1).

[206] For instance the French/Belgian systems go quite far in that respect by accepting a strict liability for damage caused by defective "things" (on the basis of art. 1384, al. 1 of the Code Civil), whereas e.g. English law is far more restrictive in that respect. See C. Von Bar (*supra* fn. 1), 333–398.

C. Compulsory Insurance

151 In addition the country reports also indicate an increasing tendency to impose obligations to seek financial coverage upon potential injurers, although also in that respect important differences apply. For instance compulsory environmental liability insurance exists effectively only in Germany and Sweden.[207] Compulsory liability insurance for e.g. the risk of fires in public places like nightclubs and restaurants does exist in Belgium, but not in the Netherlands. This led a Belgian author to the conclusion that if the dramatic fire in a disco in Volendam (the Netherlands) on New Year's Eve in 2000 had occurred in Belgium victims would have been largely compensated through the compulsory liability regime.[208]

152 In sum, these mandatory solvency guarantees could be used at a much greater level to guarantee that the potential tortfeasor who causes the technological disaster can also meet his financial obligations.[209] For instance in the Netherlands after the explosion of a fireworks factory in Enschede causing 19 deaths and 150 injuries on 13 May 2000 the question was asked whether the licensee of such a factory should not be under the obligation to purchase some form of financial coverage, which was not the case when the explosion occurred.[210]

II. First Party Insurance

A. Market Failure?

153 The blessings of various first party insurance schemes have been well described in economic literature. It has more particularly been argued that first party insurance schemes have the advantage that they allow a much better adaptation of the premium and policy condition to the risk and thus a better risk differentiation than liability insurance. This point has especially been advanced by Priest.[211] Many other law and economics scholars have pointed at the advantages of first party insurance as well.[212] One can now in various areas

[207] For an overview of the German system see *inter alia* B.J. Richardson, Financial institutions for sustainability, [2000] *Environmental Liability* (Env. Liability), 61–62 and for a description of the Swedish system see M. Faure/D. Grimeaud (*supra* fn. 194), 189–192.

[208] C. Van Schoubroeck, Objectieve aansprakelijkheid en verzekeringsplicht bij schade door rampen. Een Belgische case-studie, in: A. Akkermans/E. Brans (eds.), *Aansprakelijkheid en schadeverhaal bij rampen* (2002), 145–171.

[209] See also M. Faure/T. Hartlief (*supra* fn. 81), 211–219.

[210] T. Hartlief, De meerwaarde van het aansprakelijkheidsrecht, in: T. Hartlief/S. Klosse (eds.), *Einde van het aansprakelijkheidsrecht?* (2003), 58–59.

[211] G. Priest, The current insurance crisis and modern tort law, [1987] *Yale Law Journal* (Yale L.J.), 1521–1590, but also criticized by V. Kip Viscusi, The dimension of the product liability crisis, [1991] JLS 20, 147–177.

[212] W. Bishop, The Contract-tort Boundary and the Economics of Insurance, [1983] JLS 12, 241–266; R.A. Epstein, Product Liability as an Insurance Market, [1985] JLS 14, 645–669 and R.A. Epstein, *Simple rules for a complex world* (1995).

see an increasing tendency to move away from third party liability insurance towards first party or direct insurance schemes.[213]

It is therefore no surprise that also many potential victims of disasters seek coverage through first party insurances. These can take the form of either generalized accident insurance coverage (in case of personal injury) or they can cover specific property damage. In most European legal systems the general accident insurance coverage provides coverage for specific costs that a victim would incur as a result of an accident. Depending upon the policy this can be lost income, coverage of (additional) medical expenses and in some cases even pain and suffering.[214] These policies which focus on personal injury compensation usually do not make a distinction as to whether the source of the accident is a catastrophe or not. Hence, well-informed potential victims can purchase coverage according to their own degree of risk aversion and corresponding demand for insurance, of course assuming that competitive insurance markets offer those policies. Since property damage is, as the comparative report also indicated, usually not covered under social security, one would expect a large demand for coverage against property damage, especially if this was caused by a catastrophe. 154

The differences between the legal systems discussed seem in that respect, strikingly, to be quite large. In some countries, such as e.g. in Germany, it was established as the result of a recent flooding of the Elbe in 2002 that only a very small percentage of victims had insurance coverage. This corresponds to the finding in the literature that there is generally no adequate demand for these flooding insurances[215] or for earthquake insurance.[216] The lack of adequate insurance coverage for damage caused by flooding is, so it is held, not a problem of a lacking supply but of a lacking demand.[217] Endres/Ohl/Rundshagen (2003) have recently held that the lack of adequate insurance coverage may be the result of a lacking demand, because there would be no aversion against these flooding risks.[218] They refer to psychological experiments that show that people may *ex ante* prefer uncertain losses than the certain loss by paying the premium.[219] Kunreuther showed 155

213 See for the area of environmental insurance M. Faure, Environmental Damage Insurance in Theory and Practice, in: T. Swanson (ed.), *An introduction to the law and economics of environmental policy: issues in institutional design* (2002), 283–328.

214 This is more particularly the case in the French policy referred to as "Garantie contre les accidents de la vie". This new insurance policy provides broad (first party) compensation against accidents and compensates as if tort law were applicable, therefore including compensation for pain and suffering.

215 H. Kunreuther, Mitigating disaster losses through insurance, [1996] *Journal of Risk and Uncertainty* 12, 171–187 and R. Zeckhauser [1996] *Journal of Risk and Uncertainty* 12, 135.

216 H. Kunreuther/N. Doherty/A. Kleffner (eds.), Should society deal with the earthquake problem?, [1992] *Regulation – The Cato Review of Business and Government* 15(2).

217 M. Nell, Gesellschaftliches Risikomanagement für Hochwasserschäden. Beitrag zum Zeitgespräch: Brauchen wir eine Zwangsversicherung gegen Elementarschäden?, [2002] *Wirtschaftsdienst* 82, 10, 582–585.

218 A. Endres/C. Ohl/B. Rundshagen, [2003] *List Forum für Wirtschafts- und Finanzpolitik* 29, 284–294.

219 D. Kahnemann/A. Tversky, Prospect theory: an analysis of decision under risk, [1979] *Econometrica* 47, 263–291 and P. Slovic *et al.*, Preferences for Insuring against Probable Small Losses: Insurance Implications, [1977] J.R. & I. 44, 237–258.

this more particularly also concerning the decision to purchase insurance against the risk of flooding.[220]

156 The problem according to this literature is that *ex ante* the potential victim (like a house owner) is confronted with the certain loss of a premium, whereby the expected damage in case of flooding can only be estimated and therefore constitutes an uncertain loss. Moreover, individuals tend to take an "it will not happen to me attitude".[221] Endres/Ohl/Rundshagen rightly indicate that whether there is risk aversion against disasters such as e.g. flooding should of course be the subject of further empirical research.[222] Anyway they stress the point that it is too easily accepted (at the policy level) that there is risk aversion, whereby this may not always be the case. In the latter case, the lacking demand could simply explain the lacking existence of flood insurances e.g. on the German market. Other literature, however, indicates that a low demand for disaster coverage should not come as a surprise since victims count on *ex post* government relief.[223] This regulation makes it harder for markets to function and market failure becomes a self-fulfilling prophecy as a result of misguided regulation.[224] This was confirmed in the Italian report and the UK success story (large insurance coverage for flooding) may well be due to the principle attitude of the UK government not to provide any government relief for disaster victims.

B. Compulsory Insurance?

157 Assuming that citizens are averse against the risk of damage caused by certain catastrophes and hence have a demand for adequate coverage against a fair premium on a competitive insurance market, the question arises what regulatory intervention should be taken if insurance coverage nevertheless fails. The classic economic rationale behind compulsory (liability) insurance was the externality argument: in the absence of adequate insurance injurers could (through their insolvency) externalize risk. That may be an argument in favour of compulsory liability insurance. However, that argument is not very convincing in the case of first party insurance. One could still make the argument that victims who were not adequately insured for personal injury would then extensively call on the healthcare system and thus "externalize" that risk. But given the

[220] H.C. Kunreuther *et al.* (eds.), *Disaster insurance protection: public policy lessons* (1978) and P.J.H. Schoemaker/H.C. Kunreuther, An experimental study of insurance decisions, [1979] J.R. & I. 46(4), 603–618.

[221] H. Kunreuther, [1996] *Journal of Risk and Uncertainty* 12, 171–187; R.A. Epstein, Catastrophic Responses to Catastrophic Risks, [1996] *Journal of Risk and Uncertainty* 12, 287–308; R. Schwarze/G. Wagner, [2002] *DIW Wochenbericht* 35 (<http://www.diw.de>) and R. Zeckhauser [1996] *Journal of Risk and Uncertainty* 12, 115.

[222] A. Endres/C. Ohl/B. Rundshagen, [2003] *List Forum für Wirtschafts- und Finanzpolitik* 29, 284–294.

[223] R.A. Epstein, [1996] *Journal of Risk and Uncertainty* 12, 287–308 and S.E. Harrington, Rethinking disaster policy, [2000] *Regulation – The Cato Review of Business and Government*, 23(1), 40–46.

[224] So R.A. Epstein, [1996] *Journal of Risk and Uncertainty* 12, 305.

fact that most European legal systems provide (through social security) wide coverage for healthcare (precisely through mandatory healthcare insurances) one cannot see why that should be supplemented with an additional compulsory accident insurance. The same is true for the property damage that victims may suffer as a result of a (natural) disaster. Of course the absence of insurance may lead to additional calls from those victims on government relief (and as a result of political pressure caused through the large number involved they may succeed), but there is as such no direct issue of externalization of their harm.

The second traditional economic argument in favour of compulsory insurance 158
would be information problems. This would assume that citizens are averse against the risk of large damage as a consequence of catastrophes and would be willing to pay a premium to have that risk removed from them, but simply do not purchase insurance because they lack information e.g. on the probability and magnitude of the risk and/or on the availability of insurance. Regulation would then be the classic remedy to cure an information deficiency.[225]

This could constitute an argument in favour of compulsory (first party) insur- 159
ance e.g. for property damage caused as a result of natural disasters if empirical evidence showed that victims would greatly underestimate these risks and would, being well informed, definitely have a demand for insurance. If these conditions were not met, a regulatory intervention forcing potential victims to take out insurance coverage would amount to mere paternalism.

There are, however, various drawbacks to such a duty: *first*, a lack of informa- 160
tion should primarily be remedied through regulation aiming at the provision of information. Only when the information asymmetry continues, notwithstanding the (mandatory) provision of information can there be a reason for a duty to insure. *Second*, if a general duty to purchase "disaster coverage" were to be introduced for all victims that may be disadvantageous for those victims who do not run any risk. Take the example of flood insurance: one can imagine that a person living in a house close to a river might have a demand for flood insurance, but the same is probably not true for someone living in an apartment in a city on the 20th floor. A generalized duty to purchase disaster insurance coverage (like in France) would therefore force all individuals to take insurance coverage, even those that run no risk at all and therefore have no demand for insurance. This could thus create inefficiencies and lead to a cross subsidization whereby those who run no risk would have to contribute to the premium of those who may actually benefit from the insurance coverage. A more efficient solution may therefore be the one whereby the compulsory coverage (e.g. for flood risks) is limited to those individuals who actually are exposed to the particular risk.

[225] See generally A. Schwartz/L. Wilde, Intervening in markets on the basis of imperfect information: a legal and economic analysis, [1979] *University of Pennsylvania Law Review* (U. Pa. L. Rev.), 630–682.

161 *Third*, economists always warned that introducing a duty to insure may be efficient only if sufficient competition on the particular insurance market exists. Otherwise the introduction of a duty to insure creates a dependence upon the insurance market whereby the (concentrated) insurance market can *de facto* decide at which conditions to sell its product. Obviously, in a monopolistic market compulsory insurance will create inefficiencies.[226] The potential anti-competitive effects of mandatory disaster coverage have been well explained in the contribution of Van den Bergh to his volume.[227]

162 *Fourth,* some particular catastrophic risks may be so "new" that insurance markets may not yet have developed to cover them. If a differentiated offer of insurance policies is limited, one could again question whether it makes sense to introduce mandatory insurance if such coverage could only be found to a limited extent (or without sufficient competition) on private insurance markets.

163 *Fifth,* even if mandatory coverage is introduced, sufficient room should be left for competition, as pointed out by Van den Bergh. Hence the additional premium for the disaster coverage should not be fixed by law (like in France) but should be the result of competition in this respect between insurers.

164 Above it was questioned whether there is an adequate demand for disaster insurance. But even if there is such a demand, it is not always guaranteed that insurance cover will automatically be available. If initially too few actors have a demand for insurance, adverse selection may arise and optimal risk spreading may not be possible. Hence, at the policy level, it should be clear that competitive insurance markets are willing to offer the particular disaster insurance products before a duty to provide coverage should be introduced. Moreover, the UK and US examples make clear that insurance solutions may work adequately as well without the need to make it compulsory.

C. Outlook

165 As the comparative overview showed, there is a clear tendency in many of the (European) legal systems discussed towards some form of compulsory coverage of the consequences of disasters on a first party basis. This French model was recently followed in Belgium in May 2003, but is discussed as well in Italy, Germany and the Netherlands.

[226] It has, for instance, in relation to environmental insurance, also been indicated that if one makes the availability of insurance coverage a prerequisite for the operation of an enterprise, insurance undertakings become the *de facto* licensors of the industry. This may especially be problematic from a policy perspective if this happens on concentrated insurance markets. See A. Monti, [2001] E.R.P.L. 9, 65.

[227] See R. van den Bergh, Compulsory Catastrophe Extension of First Party Property Insurance from a Competition Policy Perspective, contained in this volume.

Even though these regulatory interventions can be questioned from an economic perspective one should realize that politicians will (given the high number of voters involved) always have the tendency to provide some form of compensation after a large number of victims is affected by a disaster. In that respect the solution of some form of mandatory coverage for those who actually run the risk seems – as will be indicated below – superior to *ad hoc* or structural fund solutions whereby public means are randomly used to compensate victims.[228] The first best solution consists of course of the UK/US approach to abstain from making coverage mandatory and simply stimulate the working of the insurance market. But if the regulator judged that a regulatory intervention is necessary, an insurance solution would seem to be superior to government relief. First party insurance at least guarantees that victims themselves pay for the protection they will afterwards obtain. Moreover, through an adequate risk differentiation, first party insurance may have some preventive effects.[229] Thus the mandatory coverage for disaster risks whereby the government relies on the insurance market to provide coverage seems at least a superior regulatory solution to government relief. Government relief programmes have been insufficiently able to provide incentives for prevention[230] as risk differentiation under insurance does. All of this, however, assumes that coverage can be made available via competitive insurance markets. If that condition is not met, making insurance compulsory would be a bad policy option. 166

In this respect Van den Bergh indicates that a problem arises with the French/ Belgian solution from the angle of competition law: in that case insured who voluntarily purchased property damage contracts are also forced to take the mandatory coverage for disaster insurance. This so-called tie-in agreement, forcing a consumer to buy a specific service/product together with another product may well violate the conditions of the exemption agreement concerning the application of competition law to insurance markets.[231] On the other hand an outright duty to purchase disaster insurance for all citizens may be hard to enforce. This is hence an issue that definitely merits further research. Also the regulatory fixing of the additional premiums for the disaster coverage (as is the case in France) may seriously restrict compensation. 167

If such a system of mandatory coverage for disaster losses is in place, this may provide adequate compensation. However, that may not always be the case 168

[228] Compare: G. Priest, The government, the market and the problem of catastrophic loss, [1996] *Journal of Risk and Uncertainty* 12, 219–237 and L. Kaplow, Incentives and government relief for risk, [1991] *Journal of Risk and Uncertainty* 4, 167–175.

[229] In the sphere of flood insurance one can think of risk differentiation whereby good risks would take adequate preventive measures and are rewarded with lower premiums or bad risks (those who chose to construct a house near to a river) are punished with a higher premium. See also R. Schwarze/G. Wagner [2004] G.P.R.I.I.P 29(2).

[230] G. Priest, [1996] *Journal of Risk and Uncertainty* 12, 219–237 and R. Epstein, [1996] *Journal of Risk and Uncertainty* 12, 297.

[231] That was precisely one of the objections of the Italian competition authority against an Italian draft that provided for compulsory supplementary disaster coverage on the (voluntary) fire insurance. See *supra* Italy, 137.

when extremely large losses occur. The amount of the damage caused can sometimes be that high that it outweighs the possibilities of an individual insurer or of the national insurance market altogether. The question then arises whether additional public intervention is indicated.

III. Public Intervention

A. Government as (Re-)Insurer or Santa Claus?

169 The government intervention in case of financial compensation after catastrophes can take different forms. The most modest form is, in addition to providing regulation for the prevention of disasters, to impose – as indicated – where warranted a duty to purchase (third party or first party) insurance coverage. The intervention could go much further where the government provides e.g. via a fund – direct compensation to the victims of catastrophes. Another alternative would be to let the government act as reinsurer for the larger risks.[232]

170 There is no clear unanimity in the economic literature on which of these last two is the better solution.[233] Chicago law and economics scholars Gron and Sykes are relatively critical as far as a role for government as reinsurer is concerned.[234] They argue that it would be unjust for the government to provide (re)insurance at a lower price than the market price. This would also give a wrong signal to the market as far as stimulating insurability is concerned. They are – remarkably – in favour of *ad hoc* solutions whereby compensation is provided to accident victims on an *ex post* basis. This at least avoids that market participants are suggested that the government will anyway guarantee a compensation. Also Dutch lawyers Ammerlaan and Van Boom have, at the occasion of the decision of the Dutch government to participate in a reinsurance against terrorism, formulated serious criticism: they argue that the premium that would be demanded would not be the correct market premium. Moreover, they argue that it should not be the task of the state to provide private insurance. Damage caused as a result of terrorism, so they hold, should be financed through the public purse.[235]

[232] A. Gron, Insurer demand for catastrophe reinsurance, in: K.A. Froot (ed.), *The financing of catastrophe risk* (1999), 23–44 and D.M. Cutler/R.J. Zeckhauser, Reinsurance for catastrophes and cataclysms, in: K.A. Froot (ed.), *The financing of catastrophe risk* (1999), 233–269 as well as other contributions in K.A. Froot (ed.), *The financing of catastrophe risk* (1999).

[233] Assuming of course that any government intervention is warranted at all; from an economic perspective victim compensation is as such not a goal of accident law. However, given the political needs and pressure it can be examined what the most effective role for government may be, given the desire to provide some form of compensation.

[234] A. Gron/A.O. Sykes, Should the government provide terrorism insurance over the short or long term? A role for government?, [2002–2003] *Regulation*, 44–51.

[235] K. Ammerlaan/W. van Boom, De Nederlandse herverzekeringsmaatschappij voor terrorismeschaden en de rol van de overheid bij het vergoeden van terreurschade, [2003] *Nederlands Juristenblad* (NJB), 2335–2336.

Notwithstanding these criticisms there are many examples where states act as reinsurer or at least provide some guarantee of a last resort. That phenomenon is of course not new. Already in the nuclear liability conventions of the 1960s a compensation system consisting of various layers was introduced whereby a part of the damage is paid by the liable licensee of the nuclear power plant, a second layer by the state and a third layer by all contracting parties.[236] After 11 September 2001, when airline risks became more difficult to insure the US federal government also guaranteed insurance coverage.[237] The US report makes clear that this federal or state intervention occurs in many cases (earthquakes, hurricanes, flooding) in order to make catastrophic risks better insurable. Similarly in Germany a reinsurance company called Extremus was erected to cover the terrorism risk with a state guarantee for amounts above € 3 billion and until € 10 billion. A similar model was recently also introduced in the Netherlands where a reinsurance company for terrorism damage was erected, being the Dutch reaction to 11 September 2001.[238] This Dutch reinsurer relies heavily on intervention by the state through reinsurance. Also France knew already for a longer time the *Caisse Centrale Réassurance* (CCR), that provides reinsurance via the state and even provides for unlimited coverage (in reinsurance) for natural disasters and technological risks.[239] And a similar construction exists in the UK with PoolRe which provides reinsurance for the terrorism risk. 171

The critical attitude of economists and some lawyers does hence not correspond with legal reality. The question indeed arises whether a model of reinsurance guaranteed by the state is as bad as suggested. When the capacity on private insurance market is falling behind (which may indeed be the case when the amount of the damage resulting from a catastrophe is large) reinsurance by the state seems an adequate method to facilitate the insurability.[240] In that case the government supplements the market where insurance capacity fails. On the condition that the government charges an actuarially fair premium for its intervention there seems to be hardly any objection against this. Such an intervention seems moreover to be preferred above collective solutions like funds, sponsored through the public purse. When the government acts as reinsurer this at least has the advantage that a premium can be paid by those who actually cause or run the risk. This type of government intervention thus, as the many US examples clearly show, facilitates market solutions and avoids a negative redistribution. The argument by Gron/Sykes that *ad hoc* 172

[236] For further details see M. Faure, Economic Models of Compensation for Damage caused by Nuclear Accidents: some Lessons for the Revision of the Paris and Vienna Conventions, [1995] *European Journal of Law and Economics*, 21–43 and M. Trebilcock/R. Winter, The Economics of Nuclear Accident Law, [1997] Int'l. Rev. Law & Econ., 215–243.

[237] K.S. Abraham, United States of America. Liability for acts of terrorism under US law, in: B.A. Koch (ed.), *Terrorism, tort law and insurance. A comparative survey* (2004), 176–188.

[238] Nederlandse Herverzekeringsmaatschappij voor Terrorismeschade.

[239] For further information on this CCR see <http:\\www.ccr.fr>.

[240] This point of view is equally supported by H. Kunreuther, Mitigating disaster losses through insurance, [1996] *Journal of Risk and Uncertainty* 12, 171–187; S.E. Harrington, [2000] *Regulation – The Cato Review of Business and Government* 23(1), 40–46, R. Schwarze/G. Wagner, [2002] DIW, Wochenbericht 35 (<http://www.diw.de>).

funds would be preferable to reinsurance is also hardly convincing: it is particularly these *ad hoc* solutions on which victims will always count that may provide the wrong signal to market participants.[241] Of course such a state intervention as reinsurer should still leave freedom with the individual insurer to use the possibility of this state-reinsurance or not. A duty to call on the state provided reinsurance might again endanger competition on insurance markets as was again shown in the contribution by Van den Bergh to this volume.[242]

B. Fund or Ad Hoc?

173 When the government does not act as reinsurer but (as suggested by Gron/Sykes) should provide compensation through the public purse, the question arises whether a structural arrangement should be put in place or whether *ad hoc* solutions should be preferred whereby the government decides, depending upon the size of the catastrophe, whether public funds will be made available or not. Here again the economic and legal approach seem to differ. Gron/Sykes' argument about providing a wrong signal definitely applies to a structural fund. If market participants are aware that in case of a catastrophe the financial consequences would be covered through government intervention, this will provide them little incentive to develop financial solutions themselves. Also Endres/Ohl/Rundshagen indicate that a compensation by the state dilutes any incentive to "self insure" by the victim or to take preventive measures in the framework of an effective risk management. Those who can be certain that they will be compensated by the state can keep the insurance premium in their pocket and hence free ride on the state, so they hold.[243] If the state simply provides full compensation *ex post* this will dilute any *ex ante* preventive effect that one would normally expect with differentiated insurance premiums.[244] Of course here, once more one has to be realistic: incentives to take preventative actions do not merely come from the failure of government to recompense, other incentives may play a role as well.

174 Lawyers on the other hand, as some of the country reports also indicate, stress that the *ad hoc* solutions create legal uncertainty. For one catastrophe an *ad hoc* solution may be introduced, but for another not.[245] The German reporter

[241] See equally R. Epstein [1996] *Journal of Risk and Uncertainty* 12, 287–308; L. Kaplow, [1991] *Journal of Risk and Uncertainty* 4, 167–175 and R. Schwarze/G. Wagner, [2004] G.P.R.I.I.P. 29(2).

[242] That was another objection of the Italian competition authority against a bill that introduced compulsory disaster coverage with compulsory reinsurance, see Italy.

[243] A. Endres/C. Ohl/B. Rundshagen, [2003] *List Forum für Wirtschafts- und Finanzpolitik* 29, 290. A similar point has also been made often, being that the incentives to insure against disaster losses will be diluted in case of government relief R. Epstein, [1996] *Journal of Risk and Uncertainty* 12, 287–308 and by R. Schwarze/G. Wagner, [2004] G.P.R.I.I.P. 29(2).

[244] H. Kunreuther [1996] *Journal of Risk and Uncertainty* 12, 177, however, points out that there is no empirical evidence that victims refuse insurance coverage because they would count on *ex post* government relief. He therefore points at other reasons for a lacking demand for disaster coverage.

[245] E.H. Huls, Schadefondsen bij rampen, in: A. Akkermans/E. Brans (eds.), *Aansprakelijkheid en schadeverhaal bij rampen* (2002), 209–210.

for instance holds that the German legislator provided very generous compensation for the victims of flooding through the so-called *Flutopferhilfesolidaritätsgesetz* after the 2002 Elbe-flooding (up to € 6 billion!), but that this on the other hand creates a great inequality vis-à-vis other victims of catastrophes (or other accidents!) where this *ad hoc* generosity does not apply.[246] The disadvantage is not only the possible violation of the equality principle in applying *ad hoc* solutions,[247] but also that the procedures, amounts of compensation etc. will be different for every *ad hoc* case.[248] Lawyers therefore plead, in the interest of victims, for a uniform and structural arrangement, so that victims know whether they can be entitled to compensation after a catastrophe.[249] And it is of course precisely that certainty that economists would like to avoid, since it dilutes any incentive to develop adequate market solutions. Schwarze and Wagner indicate that here one discovers the crucial difference between the economic and the European legal approach: law and economics would suggest to deny all help to individuals living in risky areas to provide them incentives to develop insurance solution themselves,[250] whereas this strategy would probably be incompatible with the concept of the welfare state as this applies to most EU Member States.[251]

This difficulty indicates once more that it might be more warranted to first look for (mandatory) coverage of disasters through insurance, eventually supplied with reinsurance through the state. If that functions adequately, *ad hoc* or other structural solutions (with all of their difficulties) could be avoided. The UK success story of flooding insurance supports the thesis that, with a well functioning insurance market, fund solutions become superfluous. Indeed, the law and economics literature is generally not very enthusiastic concerning the use of compensation funds. Although the literature is rather scarce in this respect,[252] it is usually indicated that there are not many reasons why, if both in- 175

246 Compare R. Zeckhauser, [1996] *Journal of Risk and Uncertainty* 12, 113–140.

247 An argument also made in the Netherlands by: A.R. Bloembergen, Een schadefonds geweldmisdrijven?, in: A.R. Bloembergen (ed.), *Bloembergen's werk* (1992), 167–178.

248 Also the US case provides examples of the unequal treatment of victims: victims of a mass terrorist attack at a federal building in Oklahoma City received nothing; victims of the earlier incident of terrorism at the World Trade Centre got nothing. Asbestos victims get nothing in the way of fund-based recovery. Only the September 11 victims receive very large government awards.

249 See for instance also K. Ammerlaan/W. Van Boom, [2003] NJB, 2336 and R. Schwarze/G. Wagner, [2004] G.P.R.I.I.P. 29(2). They argue that the concept of the welfare state essentially demands that anyone in serious difficulties be provided government assistance. That point may well justify social security systems (covering lost income and health care expenses), but it is highly questionable whether that also justifies public interventions for property damage.

250 So equally R. Epstein, [1996] *Journal of Risk and Uncertainty* 12, 287–308.

251 R. Schwarze/G. Wagner, [2004] G.P.R.I.I.P. 29(2), 154–168.

252 An exception constitutes a few papers by G. Skogh, Public insurance and accident prevention, [1982], Int'l. Rev. Law & Econ., 67–80; G. Skogh, The combination of private and public regulation of safety, in: M. Faure/R. van den Bergh (eds.), *Essays in law and economics. Corporations, accident prevention and compensation for losses* (1989), 87–101 and the American (critical) law and economics studies concerning superfund (see e.g. R. Revesz/R. Stewart (eds.), *Analysing superfund, economics, science and the law* (1995)).

surance and funds were in theory available, a compensation fund would provide better protection against insolvency than private insurance markets. Insurance, so it is generally held,[253] better enables an adequate risk differentiation and risk spreading; if insurance markets are competitive, insurers can be assumed to be better able to deal with classic insurance problems such as moral hazard and adverse selection than the administrators of a compensation fund.[254] A compensation fund therefore only comes into the picture if insurance may not be able to provide coverage for certain risks. But as indicated earlier, the preferred solution would be first to examine whether the functioning of insurance markets could be facilitated.

IV. Policy Conclusions

176 In this part of the comparative conclusions we tried to show that the law and economics methodology can be used in a meaningful way to structure the actual policy debate in many countries on the reform of compensation mechanisms for victims of catastrophes. From an economic perspective victim compensation is as such not a goal of accident law, but still economics can show what the most effective instruments to guarantee such a compensation might be and what negative effects could be connected with other mechanisms. As rightly mentioned by Priest, however generous governments may be, they all face serious budget constraints. Applying insurance principles may thus serve to maximize government coverage to best achieve its humanitarian ends.[255]

177 European politicians seem to have understood Priest's lessons: if compensation of disaster victims is politically wanted, the trend which one can now see in many European countries is towards an increasing use of (mandatory) disaster coverage on first party insurances, backed up with reinsurance by the state. The insurance model clearly has advantages compared to the mere application of fund solutions, which would only invite potential accident victims to free ride on the public purse.[256] Hence, also in Europe the legislators seem increasingly to follow the lesson of the literature to adopt insurance solutions as a means to avoid "catastrophic reactions to catastrophic risks".[257]

178 Still several questions remain and need further research. One of those is whether potential victims actually have a clear demand for disaster coverage and whether the potential underestimation of the risk warrants mandatory coverage. Comparing the UK with the French solution shows that insurance could be demanded and provided on a large scale even without making disaster cov-

[253] See especially G. Priest, [1996] *Journal of Risk and Uncertainty* 12, 219–237 and L. Kaplow, [1991] *Journal of Risk and Uncertainty* 4, 167–175.

[254] See, with an application to environmental insurance M. Faure/T. Hartlief, Compensation Funds versus Liability and Insurance for Remedying Environmental Damage, [1996] *Review of European Community and International Environmental Law* (RECIEL), 321–326 and with respect to disaster insurance R. Schwarze/G. Wagner, [2004] G.P.R.I.I.P. 29(2), 154–168.

[255] G. Priest, [1996] *Journal of Risk and Uncertainty* 12, 219–237.

[256] L. Kaplow, [1991] *Journal of Risk and Uncertainty* 4, 167–175.

[257] R. Epstein, [1996] *Journal of Risk and Uncertainty* 12, 287–308.

erage formally mandatory.[258] Also the compatibility of the mandatory coverage with competition law needs, as Van den Bergh showed, further examination. For instance the tie-in character of the mandatory coverage and the mandatory fixing of the premium for the disaster coverage (as in France) seem debatable from a competition perspective. An insurance solution which (as a result of mandatory regulation) seriously restricts competition might well be inferior to *ad hoc* solutions.

The question also arises whether it is possible to limit the duty to obtain mandatory coverage to risky areas (as was originally the plan in Belgium in 2003) or whether this differentiation leads to substantial administrative costs that may not outweigh the advantages. 179

Although there are, in sum, also in the law and economics literature, still various questions that remain to be answered and issues that are still debated, this is of course no argument against the use of these arguments in the policy debate. The aim of this part of the conclusions was – *inter alia* – to show that the rich law and economics literature with respect to disaster (insurance) can clearly enable the rationalization of the discussion on various policy alternatives and thus enrich the policy debate on disaster relief. 180

List of References

K.S. Abraham, United States of America. Liability for acts of terrorism under US law, in: B.A. Koch (ed.), *Terrorism, tort law and insurance. A comparative survey* (2004), 176–188.

K. Ammerlaan/W. van Boom, De Nederlandse herverzekeringsmaatschappij voor terrorismeschaden en de rol van de overheid bij het vergoeden van terreurschade, [2003] *Nederlands Juristenblad* (NJB), 2335–2336.

C. von Bar, *Gemeineuropäisches Deliktsrecht* (vol. I, 1996).

C. von Bar, *The common European law of tort* (1999).

R. van den Bergh, Compulsory Catastrophe Extension of First Party Property Insurance from a Competition Policy Perspective, in: M. Faure/T. Hartlief (eds.), *Financial Compensation for Victims of Catastrophes. A Comparative Legal Approach* (2005), 409–438.

W. Bishop, The Contract-tort Boundary and the Economics of Insurance, [1983] *Journal of Legal Studies* (JLS) 12, 241–266.

A.R. Bloembergen, Een schadefonds geweldmisdrijven?, in: A.R. Bloembergen (ed.), *Bloembergen's werk* (1992), 167–178.

D.M. Cutler/R.J. Zeckhauser, Reinsurance for catastrophes and cataclysms, in: K.A. Froot (ed.), *The financing of catastrophe risk* (1999), 233–269.

A. Endres/C. Ohl/B. Rundshagen, [2003] *List Forum für Wirtschafts- und Finanzpolitik* 29, 284–294.

A. Endres/B. Staiger, Ökonomische Aspekte des Umwelthaftungsrechts, in: M. Ahrens/J. Simon (eds.), *Umwelthaftung, Risikosteuerung und Versicherung* (1996), 79–93.

[258] Although in practice, also in the UK, many will be forced to purchase this coverage, e.g. if one wishes to obtain a mortgage on a house.

R.A. Epstein, Product Liability as an Insurance Market, [1985] JLS 14, 645–669.
R.A. Epstein, *Simple rules for a complex world* (1995).
R.A. Epstein, Catastrophic Responses to Catastrophic Risks, [1996] *Journal of Risk and Uncertainty* 12, 287–308.
M. Faure, Economic Models of Compensation for Damage caused by Nuclear Accidents: some Lessons for the Revision of the Paris and Vienna Conventions, [1995] *European Journal of Law and Economics*, 21–43.
M. Faure, Environmental Damage Insurance in Theory and Practice, in: T. Swanson (ed.), *An introduction to the law and economics of environmental policy: issues in institutional design* (2002), 283–328.
M. Faure/R. van den Bergh, Restrictions of competition on insurance markets and the applicability of EC anti-trust law, [1995] *Kyklos* 48, 65–85.
M. Faure/D. Grimeaud, Financial assurances issues of environmental liability, in: M. Faure (ed.), *Deterrence, insurability and compensation in environmental liability. Future developments in the European Union* (2003).
M. Faure/T. Hartlief, Compensation Funds versus Liability and Insurance for Remedying Environmental Damage, [1996] *Review of European Community and International Environmental Law* (RECIEL), 321–326.
M. Faure/T. Hartlief, *Insurance and expanding systemic risks* (2003), 222–225.
K.A. Froot (ed.), *Financing of catastrophe risk* (1999).
W. van Gerven/J. Lever/P. Larouche, *Cases, materials and texts on national, supranational and international tort law* (2000).
A. Gron, Insurer demand for catastrophe reinsurance, in: K.A. Froot (ed.), *The financing of catastrophe risk* (1999), 23–44.
A. Gron/A.O. Sykes, Should the government provide terrorism insurance over the short or long term? A role for government?, [2002–2003] *Regulation*, 44–51.
S.E. Harrington, Rethinking disaster policy, [2000] *Regulation – The Cato Review of Business and Government*, 23(1), 40–46.
T. Hartlief, De meerwaarde van het aansprakelijkheidsrecht, in: T. Hartlief/S. Klosse (eds.), *Einde van het aansprakelijkheidsrecht?* (2003), 58–59.
V. Heutger, Hervorming van het schadevergoedingsrecht in Duitsland, [2002] *Aansprakelijkheid Verzekering en Schade* (AV&S), 19–21.
B. Huber, *Das neue Schadensersatzrecht* (2003).
E.H. Huls, Schadefondsen bij rampen, in: A. Akkermans/E. Brans (eds.), *Aansprakelijkheid en schadeverhaal bij rampen* (2002), 209–210.
D. Kahnemann/A. Tversky, Prospect theory: an analysis of decision under risk, [1979] *Econometrica* 47, 263–291.
L. Kaplow, Incentives and government relief for risk, [1991] *Journal of Risk and Uncertainty* 4, 167–175.
B.A. Koch/H. Koziol (eds.), *Unification of tort law: strict liability* (2002).
H. Kunreuther, Mitigating disaster losses through insurance, [1996] *Journal of Risk and Uncertainty* 12, 171–187.
H.C. Kunreuther *et al.* (eds.), *Disaster insurance protection: public policy lessons* (1978).
H. Kunreuther/N. Doherty/A. Kleffner (eds.), Should society deal with the earthquake problem?, [1992] *Regulation – The Cato Review of Business and Government* 15 (2).
H. Kunreuther/P. Freeman, Insurability, environmental risks and the law, in: A. Heyes (ed.), *The Law and Economics of the Environment* (2001), 304–305.
W.M. Landes/R.A. Posner, Tort law as a regulatory regime for catastrophic personal injuries, [1984] JLS 13, 417–434.
U. Magnus (ed.), *The impact of social security law on tort law* (2003).

A. Monti, Environmental risk: a comparative law and economics approach to liability and insurance, [2001] *European Review of Private Law* (E.R.P.L.) 9, 51–79.

M. Nell, Gesellschaftliches Risikomanagement für Hochwasserschäden. Beitrag zum Zeitgespräch: Brauchen wir eine Zwangsversicherung gegen Elementarschäden?, [2002] *Wirtschaftsdienst* 82 (10), 582–585.

D. Pieters (ed.), *Introduction into the social security law of the member states of the European Community* (1993).

D. Pieters, *Introduction into the basic principles of social security* (1993).

R. Posner, *Catastrophe. Risk and response* (2004).

B. Pozzo, The liability problem in modern environmental statutes, [1996] E.R.P.L. 4, 112–129.

G. Priest, The current insurance crisis and modern tort law, [1987] *Yale Law Journal* (Yale L. J.), 1521–1590.

G. Priest, The government, the market and the problem of catastrophic loss, [1996] *Journal of Risk and Uncertainty* 12, 219–237.

R. Revesz/R. Stewart (eds.), *Analysing superfund, economics, science and the law* (1995).

B.J. Richardson, Financial institutions for sustainability, [2000] *Environmental Liability* (Env. Liability), 61–62.

H-B. Schäfer/A. Schönenberger, Strict liability versus negligence, in: B. Bouckaert/G. De Geest (eds.), *Encyclopaedia of law and economics, II, Civil law and economics* (2000), 597–624.

P.J.H. Schoemaker/H.C. Kunreuther, An experimental study of insurance decisions, [1979] J.R. & I. 46(4), 603–618.

C. Van Schoubroeck, Objectieve aansprakelijkheid en verzekeringsplicht bij schade door rampen, in: A. Akkermans/E. Brans (eds.), *Aansprakelijkheid en schadeverhaal bij rampen* (2002), 145–171.

A. Schwartz/L. Wilde, Intervening in markets on the basis of imperfect information: a legal and economic analysis, [1979] *University of Pennsylvania Law Review* (U. Pa. L. Rev.), 630–682.

R. Schwarze/G. Wagner, In the aftermath of Dresden. New directions in German flood insurance, [2004] *Geneva Papers on Risk and Insurance Issues and Practice* (G.P.R.I.I.P.) 29(2), 154–168.

R. Schwarze/G. Wagner, Hochwasser-Katastrophe in Deutschland: Über Soforthilfe hinaus denken, [2002] DIW, Wochenbericht 35 (<http://www.diw.de>).

S. Shavell, Strict Liability versus Negligence, [1980] *Journal of Legal Studies* (JLS) 9, 1–25.

S. Shavell, The judgment-proof problem, [1986] *International Review of Law and Economics* (Int'l. Rev. Law & Econ.), 43–58.

S. Shavell, *Foundations of Economic Analysis of Law* (2004).

G. Skogh, Public insurance and accident prevention, [1982], Int'l. Rev. Law & Econ., 67–80.

G. Skogh, The combination of private and public regulation of safety, in: M. Faure/R. Van den Bergh (eds.), *Essays in law and economics. Corporations, accident prevention and compensation for losses* (1989), 87–101.

P. Slovic *et al.*, Preferences for Insuring against Probable Small Losses: Insurance Implications, [1977] J.R. & I. 44, 237–258.

M. Trebilcock/R. Winter, The Economics of Nuclear Accident Law, [1997] Int'l. Rev. Law & Econ., 215–243.

A. Tunc, The '*Loi Badinter*', Ten Years of Experience, [1996] *Maastricht Journal of European and Comparative Law*, 3 (4), 329–340.

A. Tunc, Traffic liability and victim protection: lessons from 10 years of experience with the 'Loi Badinter', in: M. Faure/T. Hartlief (eds.), *Verkeersaansprakelijkheid in België en Nederland* (1998), 217–234.
V.K. Viscusi, The dimension of the product liability crisis, [1991] JLS 20, 147–177.
R. Zeckhauser, The economics of catastrophes, [1996] *Journal of Risk and Uncertainty* 12, 113–140.

Annnex: Questionnaire

Michael Faure and Ton Hartlief

Part I. Introduction

In recent years citizens in many European countries have increasingly become victims of catastrophes of various kinds. In some cases human faults (or intentional acts) lay at the origin, like with huge fires and explosions. In other cases disasters have a natural cause. The typical example in that respect for Belgium, the Netherlands and France is the damage caused as a result of heavy rains or floods.

In all of these cases where catastrophes hit a large number of victims at the same time the question arises whether they can use the legal system to receive compensation for their damage. In some cases, where an injurer can be identified tort law can be used, if the conditions therefore are fulfilled. However, injurers are not always identifiable and if they are, they are sometimes insolvent or the amount of the damage caused by the catastrophe is larger than the liability insurance covers. In other cases no liable injurer can be found at all (typically with the disasters that have a natural cause) and the question in that particular case arises how victims can receive compensation. Some damage will be covered under social security systems, sometimes victims have purchased first party insurance and in some countries specific regimes have been installed to provide victims with compensation e.g. through a publicly funded compensation fund. In some cases these funds are clearly institutionalised and seem to have a rather permanent character; in other cases they are more incidental and do not always carry the name of a fund.

In the Netherlands currently a debate is going on concerning the optimal way of providing compensation to these victims of catastrophes via different techniques. Therefore this comparative research has been started to identify precisely how the victim of a catastrophe in your particular country receives compensation of his damage. One of the reasons for this project lies in the fact that increasingly the Dutch government noticed that it had to intervene on an "ad hoc" basis to provide compensation after catastrophes. In this respect one has the impression that (Dutch) citizens nowadays primarily address themselves to the government and expect to be fully compensated. In those cases the "ad hoc" solution becomes the basis for compensation instead of a subsidiary solution (after other solutions – tort, insurance – failed). We wonder whether a similar tendency can be found in your country as well.

Part II. Method

The goal of the project is to obtain as precise as possible information on the compensation system in your country, but also on the interdependencies between various systems (tort law, insurance, public compensation mechanisms). We would like to know what the precise reasons were for the legislator to choose a particular compensation regime and how it functions in practice (what heads of damage are paid, according to what procedure and conditions and what is the precise amount of compensation under the various systems). In addition we would like you to make a critical assessment of the current system in all of its aspects. That means that we would like to know how the system is considered (e.g. by politicians, the public at large or legal scholars) on the one hand from an efficiency aspect (the influence of the system on the incentives on prevention, the cost of the system etc.) and on the other hand under distributional aspects (who pays for the compensation system – tortfeasors or the government – do victims obtain speedy and full compensation etc.?).

In the next questions we have compiled a questionnaire that we would like you to follow as much as possible in your report, since it makes the comparison for us easier. However, we fully understand that in some countries where e.g. a compensation fund exists (but the application of tort law is excluded) it may be more important to provide detailed information on that compensation system than on tort law. Obviously you have the freedom to elaborate especially on those aspects that are crucial for the situation in your particular country.

Part III. General Scope of the Compensation System

Please explain in general terms whether victims of a catastrophe have to rely primarily on tort, eventually supported with (first or third party) insurance schemes and social security or whether there is a specific compensation mechanism that applies in case a large number of victims are hit by a catastrophe. Again: do not just focus on a "formal" fund, but on any arrangement (support, subsidy) whether permanent or incidental that victims can use to receive compensation.

Do not go into the details yet, but provide at this stage a general overview of the way the various systems play their role in compensating victims of catastrophes.

If your country has particular features different from other legal systems (e.g. the *Assurance pour les accidents de la vie* in France) describe especially those.

Part IV. More Detailed Information

After having sketched generally the role of the various systems we would like you to provide more detailed information *inter alia* on the conditions under which catastrophe victims can use the tort system and whether it is actually applied. Do victims effectively sue e.g. the licensee of a fireworks enterprise that explodes and what would be the limits in a particular procedure like that?

Please pay particular attention to the possibilities of state liability. For instance in the case of a flood in some countries it has been argued that some of the damage may be due to inadequate measure taken by public authorities. Would that lead to state liability in your country? If so, is the state liability subsidiary in relation to the liability of the tortfeasor or is a combination of both possible?

Address also the existence of first party or third party liability schemes and what role they effectively play in compensating victims of catastrophes. Is there compulsory insurance and to what amounts are victims or tortfeasors insured? If there is compulsory insurance, is the liability also limited to the insured amount? Is there, in other words, a cap on liability?

Please provide a very general sketch of the social insurance system in your country. Of course this should not be detailed, but we should have some impression of whether particular heads of damage are largely covered by social security in your legal system, hence removing the need for victims to use alternative financing mechanism.

If your country would have a particular compensation mechanism for catastrophes (e.g. a compensation fund) please provide a detailed description of the legal history, reasons for setting up this compensation fund, the way it is financed and the scope of application. Does it then really cover all victims of catastrophes or are specific conditions to be met? Please also indicate whether the fund was set up because of precedents in various "ad hoc" solutions. The question also arises whether the goal of the compensation by the fund is real indemnification of damage suffered or more a "recognition that wrong has been done" to the victim.

Part V. Procedure

Please describe what type of procedure a victim of a catastrophe will have to follow to obtain compensation of his damage. Describe briefly how the procedure works under tort law and insurance schemes (does the victim have to go to court or are most cases settled out of court or are alternative dispute settlement mechanisms in place?). Please provide some indication of the timing of this procedure. How quickly would on average a victim receive compensation after the catastrophe occurred and on what does this depend?

If your legal system has a particular compensation mechanism for catastrophes (e.g. a compensation fund) please describe in detail the procedure victims have to use to receive compensation under this fund. What are the criteria on the basis of which the authority (please describe who this is) will decide upon the compensation and is an appeal possible?

Please describe also the elements of proof, which the victim must submit as evidence of his damage. Can for instance oral testimony on the value of lost or damaged property be used as evidence? Please describe whether the procedure is very formal or rather informal and whether e.g. the victim needs legal aid during the procedure. Please describe as well whether the victim can during the time necessary to make a final decision ask for a prepayment. One can think of victims who could have lost all their belongings as a result of a catastrophe and can hence not wait until a final decision on their entitlement is made.

Part VI. Cumulation

Please describe how the various financing techniques (tort, first and third party insurance, social security and specific compensation mechanism) cumulate or not. Is there a specific priority order? In other words: if an identifiable tortfeasor can be found should the victim then first use tort law before he can address himself e.g. to social security or specific compensation mechanisms? Please indicate clearly the relationship between the various systems: which has priority and which is the subsidiary system?

Can all the compensations from various sources be cumulated? Would it hence be possible that a victim calls on social security, his (first party) insurance, a specific compensation fund and uses tort law as well or are there specific rules to exclude such a cumulation?

Are there specific rules concerning recourse or redress? If e.g. a first party injurer or a public compensation fund has provided compensation can these afterwards exercise recourse against the tortfeasor and his liability injurer?

Please answer these cumulation issues not only from a theoretical perspective but try to give an indication as well as to whether this actually happens in practice. Please indicate especially whether victims in practice first address the fund or only when other solutions (tort, insurance) where not available, inapplicable or insufficient.

Part VII. Financing

Please describe how the compensation provided to victims of catastrophes under the various mechanisms (tort, first party or third party insurance, social security, specific compensation mechanisms) is financed. In this respect particularly the specific compensation mechanisms are interesting. Are these totally government funded or are there other sources as well? Is the amount paid to the victims dependent on the availability of money in e.g. a fund or does e.g. the fund have unlimited possibilities to call on additional money if needed?

Part VIII. Heads and Amounts of Damages

Please describe briefly (you can refer here of course to answers to earlier questions) what heads of damage are paid under the various systems (tort, first and third party insurance, social security and specific compensation mechanisms). Specifically if within your country a specific compensation mechanism exists for catastrophes we would be interested to know whether all types of damage are indeed covered. Please address specifically:

- Lost profit
- property damage
- pure economic loss
- lost income
- compensation in case of personal injury

- medical expenses
- disability payments
- pain and suffering
- lost income (in addition to payments made by social security)

Please also provide detailed information on the amounts paid (are there specific limitations or is there a standardization of the payments?) under these various heads of damages. Is, moreover, the assessment of damages concrete and specific for the particular victim or is it standardised and limited?

Could you please also explain how the compensation is paid under the various systems. Does the victim receive one single payment or are there periodic payments? Again: does the fact that the victim may have received compensation under other financing mechanisms (e.g. insurance) affect the decision to continue the compensation?

Part IX. Empirics

Please provide as far as possible some data on the practice of the financing of catastrophes in your country. It would be interesting if you could provide e.g. a few recent examples of catastrophes and describe the number of victims, amounts paid under the various financing mechanisms, total amounts paid for the catastrophe under the various financing mechanisms etc.

More particularly if a specific compensation mechanism for catastrophes exists we would be interested to know how often this is used on average and what role it effectively plays compared to the traditional compensation mechanisms (tort, first and third party insurance, social security).

Part X. Reforms/Criticism

Please provide, as some kind of final analysis, some insight on whether according to legal scholarship or public opinion in your country (or yourself!) the current system of financing the consequences of catastrophes is satisfactory from the angle of on the one hand efficiency (providing incentives for accident prevention, cost reduction and adequate financing) and distribution (providing speedy and adequate compensation to victims at relatively low cost).

We thank you very much for your kind cooperation in this project and are very much looking forward to your report.

Please keep in mind that it is absolutely crucial that your report reaches us electronically by Monday 1 December, since we are bound to very strict time limits to the Dutch government.

Maastricht, 7 October 2003

Index

The numbers in the following refer to the marginal notes of the respective reports, which are indicated by the following letters: A stands for Austria, B for Belgium, CPC for the Comparative and Policy Conclusions, CPP for the report on "Compulsory Catastrophe Extension of First Party Property Insurance from a Competition Policy Perspective", D for Germany, F for France, I for Italy, NL for the Netherlands, S for Sweden, UK for the United Kingdom, and US for the United States.

Publications

Principles of European Tort Law

Volume 1: *The Limits of Liability: Keeping the Floodgates Shut.*
Edited by Jaap Spier.
Kluwer Law International, The Hague. Hardbound.
ISBN 90-411-0169-1. 1996, 162 pp.

Volume 2: *The Limits of Expanding Liability. Eight Fundamental Cases in a Comparative Perspective.*
Edited by Jaap Spier.
Kluwer Law International, The Hague. Hardbound.
ISBN 90-411-0581-6. 1998, 244 pp.

Volumc 3: *Unification of Tort Law: Wrongfulness.*
Edited by Helmut Koziol.
Kluwer Law International, The Hague. Hardbound.
ISBN 90-411-1019-4. 1998, 144 pp.

Volume 4: *Unification of Tort Law: Causation.*
Edited by Jaap Spier.
Kluwer Law International, The Hague. Hardbound.
ISBN 90-411-1325-8. 2000, 161 pp.

Volume 5: *Unification of Tort Law: Damages.*
Edited by Ulrich Magnus.
Kluwer Law International, The Hague. Hardbound.
ISBN 90-411-1481-5. 2001, 255 pp.

Volume 6: *Unification of Tort Law: Strict Liability.*
Edited by Bernhard A. Koch and Helmut Koziol.
Kluwer Law International, The Hague. Hardbound.
ISBN 90-411-1705-9. 2002, 444 pp.

Volume 7: *Unification of Tort Law: Liability for Damage caused by Others*
Edited by Jaap Spier.
Kluwer Law International, The Hague. Hardbound.
ISBN 90-411-2185-4. 2003, 335 pp.

Volume 8: *Unification of Tort Law: Contributory Negligence.*
Edited by Ulrich Magnus and Miquel Martín-Casals.
Kluwer Law International, The Hague. Hardbound.
ISBN 90-411-2220-6. 2004, 300 pp.

Volume 9: *Unification of Tort Law: Multiple Tortfeasors.*
Edited by W.V. Horton Rogers
Kluwer Law International, The Hague. Hardbound.
ISBN 90-411-2319-9. 2004, 313 pp.

Volume 10: *Unification of Tort Law: Fault.*
Edited by Pierre Widmer.
Kluwer Law International, The Hague. Hardbound.
ISBN 90-411-2098-X. 2005, 393 pp.

Tort and Insurance Law

Volume 1: *Cases on Medical Malpractice in a Comparative Perspective.*
Edited by Michael Faure and Helmut Koziol.
Springer, Vienna/New York.
Softcover. ISBN 3-211-83595-4. 2001, 331 pp.

Volume 2: *Damages for Non-Pecuniary Loss in a Comparative Perspective.*
Edited by W.V. Horton Rogers.
Springer, Vienna/New York.
Softcover. ISBN 3-211-83602-0. 2001, 318 pp.

Volume 3: *The Impact of Social Security on Tort Law.*
Edited by Ulrich Magnus.
Springer, Vienna/New York.
Softcover. ISBN 3-211-83795-7. 2003, 312 pp.

Volume 4: *Compensation for Personal Injury in a Comparative perspective.*
Edited by Bernhard A. Koch and Helmut Koziol.
Springer, Vienna/New York.
Softcover. ISBN 3-211-83791-4. 2003, 501 pp.

Volume 5: *Deterrence, Insurability and Compensation in Environmental Liability. Future Developments in the European Union.*
Edited by Michael Faure.
Springer, Vienna/New York.
Softcover. ISBN 3-211-83863-5. 2003, 405 pp.

Volume 6: *Der Ersatz frustrierter Aufwendungen. Vermögens- und Nichtvermögensschaden im österreichischen und deutschen Recht.*
By Thomas Schobel.
Springer, Vienna/New York.
Softcover. ISBN 3-211-83877-5. 2003, 342 pp.

Volume 7: *Liability for and Insurability of Biomedical Research with Human Subjects in a Comparative Perspective.*
Edited by Jos Dute, Michael G. Faure and Helmut Koziol.
Springer, Vienna/New York.
Softcover. ISBN 3-211-20098-3. 2004, 445 pp.

Volume 8: *No Fault Compensation System in the Health Care Sector.*
Edited by Jos Dute, Michael G. Faure, Helmut Koziol.
Springer, Vienna/New York.
Softcover. ISBN 3-211-20799-6. 2004, 492 pp.

Volume 9: *Pure Economic Loss.*
Edited by Willem H. van Boom, Helmut Koziol and Christian A. Witting.
Springer, Vienna/New York.
Softcover. ISBN 3-211-00514-5.
2003, 214 pp.

Volume 10: *Liber Amicorum Pierre Widmer.*
Edited by Helmut Koziol and Jaap Spier.
Springer, Vienna/New York.
Softcover. ISBN 3-211-00522-6.
2003, 376 pp.

Volume 11: *Terrorism, Tort Law and Insurance. A Comparative Survey.*
Edited by Bernhard A. Koch.
Springer, Vienna/New York.
Softcover. ISBN 3-211-01867-0.
2004, 313 pp.

Volume 12: *Abschlussprüfer. Haftung und Versicherung.*
Edited by Helmut Koziol and Walter Doralt.
Springer, Vienna/New York.
Softcover. ISBN 3-211-20800-3.
2004, 180 pp.

Volume 13: *Persönlichkeitsschutz gegenüber Massenmedien/The Protection of Personality Rights against Invasions by Mass Media.*
Edited by Helmut Koziol and Alexander Warzilek.
Springer, Vienna/New York.
Softcover. ISBN 3-211-23835-2.
2005, 713 pp.

Volume 14: *Financial Compensation for Victims of Catastrophes.*
Edited by Michael Faure and Ton Hartlief.
Springer, Vienna/New York.
Softcover. ISBN 3-211-24481-6.
2006, 464 pp.

Volume 15: *Entwurf eines neuen österreichischen Schadenersatzrechts.*
Edited by Irmgard Griss, Georg Kathrein and Helmut Koziol.
Springer, Vienna/New York.
Softcover. ISBN 3-211-30827-X.
2006, 146 pp.

Volume 16: *Tort Law and Liability Insurance.*
Edited by Gerhard Wagner.
Springer, Vienna/New York.
Softcover. ISBN 3-211-24482-4.
2005, 361 pp.

Volume 17: *Children in Tort Law. Part I: Children as Tortfeasors.*
Edited by Miquel Martín-Casals.
Springer, Vienna/New York.
Softcover. ISBN 3-211-24480-8.
2006, 476 pp.

European Tort Law Yearbook

European Tort Law 2001.
Edited by Helmut Koziol and
Barbara C. Steininger.
Springer, Vienna/New York.
Softcover. ISBN 3-211-83824-4.
2002, 571 pp.

European Tort Law 2002.
Edited by Helmut Koziol and
Barbara C. Steininger.
Springer, Vienna/New York.
Softcover. ISBN 3-211-00486-6.
2003, 596 pp.

European Tort Law 2003.
Edited by Helmut Koziol and
Barbara C. Steininger.
Springer, Vienna/New York.
Softcover. ISBN 3-211-21033-4.
2004, 493 pp.

European Tort Law 2004.
Edited by Helmut Koziol and
Barbara C. Steininger.
Springer, Vienna/New York.
Softcover. ISBN 3-211-24479-4.
2005, 674 pp.

Principles of European Tort Law

Text and Commentary.
By European Group on Tort Law.
Springer, Vienna/New York.
Softcover. ISBN 3-211-23084-X.
2005, 282 pp.

Springer and the Environment